The Essential Reference of Domestic Brewers and Their Bottled Brands

3rd
Edition
2007

ISBN: 0-9774800-1-1

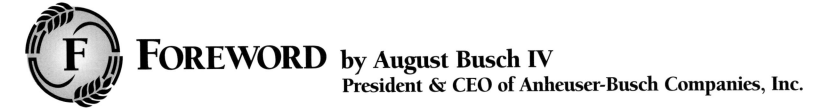

FOREWORD by August Busch IV
President & CEO of Anheuser-Busch Companies, Inc.

For more than 150 years, our company has strived to brew a variety of beers to appeal to beer lovers around the world. *The Essential Reference of Domestic Brewers and Their Bottled Brands* (DBBB)™ is a one-of-a-kind resource that goes a long way toward expanding an appreciation for the diversity of beer available in the United States.

Michael's 2nd Edition contained a wealth of information for those looking to sample specific brands or styles of beer. With this 3rd Edition, DBBB readers have at their fingertips detailed descriptions of what different beers look and taste like, plus their availability in specific bottle sizes, in cans or on draught.

We believe it's important for all brewers to keep our consumers focused on what makes beer great; its variety, its refreshment, and its historical legacy in our culture. Much like the "Here's To Beer" industry campaign we've spearheaded since 2005, the book and its online companion provide anyone who loves beer a terrific tool for appreciating the greatness of American beer.

Michael, we raise our glasses to you for a job well done.

August A. Busch IV

Acknowledgements

2006 was the year that *The Essential Reference of Domestic Brewers and Their Bottled Brands* (DBBB)™ went from a concept to a reality. This launch year was devoted to creating awareness for the book, and we finished the year with a fantastic write-up in *USA Today* that promoted both the book and the terrific brewers inside and with a recommendation from *STUFF Magazine* that touted the *DBBB* as a <u>Must Have</u> gift for the 2006 holiday season.

Not too bad for an idea hatched following a New Jersey Beer Fest! The idea for the DBBB began after attending a beer festival at Waterloo Village in New Jersey, where my wife Cathy and I watched passionate brewers fill countless foam-topped glasses and where we tasted any number of fantastic beers. Later we attempted, with limited success, to find some of these bottled brands at our local retailers.

In some cases, we remembered the style of beer but not the brewery; in other cases, we knew the brewery but were not too sure about the exact brand. What was certain, however, was that neither retailers nor I had a quick, easy way to satisfy my thirst for these new brands or to end my ongoing quest. This experience began a new journey to create and provide one nationally recognized reference, published annually, for all domestic breweries and their bottled brands.

Although many things about developing the DBBB have been rewarding, perhaps the most satisfying has been the enthusiasm we've encountered during our market research and while producing the 1st, 2nd , and now 3rd Editions of this book. This year we have visited the Craft Brewers Association Meeting, countless Brewer's Fests, been interviewed by a number of beer writers, had appearances on any number of radio shows, and gained recognition from the National Beer Wholesaler Association, the Beer Institute, the American Beverage Licensees, and the National Bartenders Association, just to name a few. The interest in the book and the excitement around beer has been outstanding.

I would like to thank my wife and incredible partner Catherine Ann, my daughters Melissa Ann and Rebecca Grace, and my family and friends, specifically my brothers David and William Kuderka and brother-in-law Bill Sahlin, for pitching in at the conventions and beer fests, and for all of their help, advice and encouragement. I would also like to thank my dear uncle, Fred Sisser III, for his incredible attention to detail in editing. Additionally, I would also like to recognize Chuck Bishop and Mike Pish, for their remarkable dedication to this project and the graphic design of this book. Likewise, I would also like to thank Colleen Colpek and Tom Kelley for their outstanding work on the publicity of our book both with the consumer and the professional societies. Finally, I would like to thank all of our advisors whose candid feedback shaped our content and solidified my commitment to producing this essential reference.

Michael S. Kuderka
MC Basset, LLC

INTRODUCTION

Our goal in developing this unique resource is to publish an annual reference of all breweries in the United States and their bottled brands. Our vision is to be *the* industry-recognized resource for information on all domestic beer brands and their producers so that all stakeholders in the three tier beer distribution system will embrace and utilize the *DBBB*™ as a means of enabling market demand by building better appreciation, education and awareness of beer.

The Essential Reference of Domestic Brewers and their Bottled Brands™ is the first annually published beer reference to offer brewery and brand listings broken down alphabetically, by beer style, by geographic location, by how brands are supplied, and by individual brewery portfolios. The "Brewery Portfolios" section is designed to offer brewers the opportunity to provide a more detailed description of their breweries and their marketed brands. These individual brand portfolios function well as shelf-talkers, and the *DBBB* itself is a great resource for retailers and consumers to discover new beer brands. With the purchase of the *DBBB* you also have access to the "Online Companion" *DBBB* database (updated monthly) and the printable brewery portfolios. Once you have registered on line, you will also begin receiving the monthly *Show Your Style* and *Style Trends* communications. Additionally, you will also receive *DBBB Alerts* to give you real-time information about new brewery brands and individual brewery events.

The DBBB and the book's "Online Companion" indexes, and details all domestic beer brewers and their bottled brands for beer retailers, beer wholesalers, convenience stores, supermarkets, restaurants and beer enthusiasts.

MC Basset, LLC collects, formats, indexes and distributes this information through the *DBBB*. Brand information in this resource is provided, edited, and approved by the individual brewing companies or derived from individual brewery web sites. We do not evaluate, rank, rate, or guarantee any of the brands or specifically recommend the breweries listed in the *DBBB*.

We are not responsible for providing brand information for breweries that have not chosen to participate in the compilation of this book or for those breweries not known to us before this edition went to press. Because brand information was provided by the manufacturer, we cannot accept responsibility for inaccuracies in the information provided directly to us or posted on the brewery web sites. The best source for specific brand information is the brewer.

Each edition is created through the investment of a considerable amount of time, effort and resources, and we hope it becomes a prized asset.

Michael S. Kuderka and Catherine A. Ench-Kuderka

How to Use This Book

First, *thank you* for purchasing *The Essential Reference of Domestic Brewers and Their Bottled Brands* (DBBB).™ If you have not purchased the book but have received this book as a new resource from your company or as a gift, congratulations! In either case, you have a great new tool and we would like to offer some suggestions for putting this resource to work.

The book is set up in seven sections:

Section I is an alphabetic listing of brewers in the United States. If you know exactly which brewery you are looking for, this is the best way to start.

Section II, the "Color And Bitterness Comparison Charts" (in color), can be an even better way to begin when you are considering expanding your beer selection, or when you are assisting a consumer in looking for something new.

There are a wide range of beers available in the US market, but seeing the similarities in the appearance and in the flavor between styles can encourage you or your customer to go beyond their current beer selection. These charts can help expand the variety of brands you currently offer or help the consumer expand the types of beer styles they presently enjoy.

Many of the brewers have supplied the SRM and IBU numbers for their individual brands, so after looking up a specific brand you can plot these numbers on the "Color And Bitterness Charts" and get a good idea of what this beer will look and taste like. If the SRM isn't listed, use the SRM range that goes with that beer's style listed, and plot the individual brand IBU.

Once a style has been selected, **Section III** opens with detailed descriptions of most of the styles from the "Color And Bitterness Charts," and then moves into the Beer Style Index. This Index allows you to see which breweries actually offer the beer style that you have selected.

In **Section IV** the "Availability by State" charts lets you quickly see if the brewer you've selected distributes their brands in your state. In **Section V** the book provides a "Geographic Brewer Index" so you get a better understanding of who is brewing in your area; this also can be a great travel guide to breweries when you are on the road or vacation. Many a beer quest has begun with this book!

Next in **Section VI** the "How Supplied" charts lets you see in what size bottles, cans and kegs a brewer's bottled brands are made available to the market.

Section VII, "Brewery Portfolio" section, is what we feel is the most exciting part of the book and one of the best reasons to register for the Online Companion (don't worry, this is all part of the cover price).

During our market research, retailers told us that they see the "Brewery Portfolio" section is a great source of beer brand shelf-talkers. The section is printable from our website www.mcbasset.com: simply place these on your beer case and they alert your customers, with the description and the color label, about one of your featured brands. Also, if you're into beer labels, this is a great section for you as well.

MC Basset actually sells a great suction cup portfolio holder to display individual portfolios on your beer case. Just e-mail us at mkuderka@mcbasset.com and we can get these out to you at a small cost.

TABLE OF CONTENTS

I. Brewery Index: An Alphabetical Brewery Listing 9
   Commentary – Are We There Yet? 102

II. Color & Bitterness Comparison Charts 103

III. Beer Style Index: Beer Brands by Style Listing 107

IV. Availability by State Charts 207

V. Geographic Brewery Index: A Brewery Listing by State 221
   Commentary – Hopping Around the Country 334

VI. How Supplied Charts 337

VII. Brewery Portfolios: Full Brewery Brands Portfolio Listing 447

Getting Access to Your DBBB Online

With your purchase of *The Essential Reference of Domestic Brewers and Their Bottled Brands* (DBBB)™ you also receive access to the book's Online Companion. This site is designed to let you view our database (updated monthly), an on-line copy of the reference, and the printable "Brewery Portfolio" section.

Your Online companion is provided as a bonus to your purchase of *The Essential Reference of Domestic Brewers and Their Bottled Brands* (DBBB)™ and access to this site is only granted for one year.

With the constant changes that occur in the U.S. Beer market, our database's monthly updates are included with your purchase to help you keep pace with these changes. Also, having the "Brewery Portfolio" section in a printable format allows you to utilize these individual brand listings as powerful shelf-talkers and forego cutting up your copy of the book.

How do I get access?

All you need to do is grab your copy of *The Essential Reference of Domestic Brewers and Their Bottled Brands* (DBBB)™ (MUST HAVE to get ACCESS), take out your green (3x5) access ticket, log in at http://www.essentialbeerreference.com, and register with your unique access code.

BREWERY INDEX

This section lists alphabetically, the breweries indexed in *The Essential Reference of Domestic Brewers and Their Bottled Brands* (DBBB).

Each brewery listing provides the brewery's name, address, phone number, company web site (if available), and a listing of the brewer's currently offered brands. The brewery and the brand listing are followed by the page number on which the brand appears as a full brewery portfolio listing.

BREWER INDEX (Alphabetical)

21st Amendment
563 2nd Street
San Francisco, CA 94107
415-369-0900
www.21st-amendment.com

BRANDS:
21st Amendment Brewery IPA (75 IBU)
21st Amendment Brewery Watermelon Wheat (17 IBU)

States Available: Contact Brewery

Abbey Beverage Company
Our Lady of Guadalupe Abbey, P.O. Box 1080
Pecos, NM 87552
505-757-6415

BRANDS:
Monk's Ale

States Available: NM

Abita Brewing Company
P.O. Box 1510
Abita Springs, LA 70420
985-898-3544
www.abita.com

BRANDS:
Abita Bock
Abita Brewing 20th Anniversary Pilsner
Abita Brewing Amber
Abita Brewing Christmas Ale
Abita Brewing Golden
Abita Brewing Purple Haze
Abita Brewing Red Ale
Abita Brewing Restoration Ale
Abita Brewing Turbodog
Abita Brewing Wheat
Abita Fall Fest
Abita Light

States Available: AL, AR, AZ, CA, CT, DC, FL, GA, IL, IN, KS, KY, LA, MA, MD, MI, MO, MS, NC, NJ, NV, NY, OH, OK, PA, SC, TN, TX, VA, WI

Alaskan Brewing Company – *page 448*
5429 Shaune Drive
Juneau, AK 99801
907-780-5866
www.alaskanbeer.com

BRANDS:
Alaskan Amber (22 SRM, 18 IBU) – *page 448*
Alaskan Big Nugget Barley Wine
Alaskan ESB (26 SRM, 35 IBU)
Alaskan IPA (12 SRM, 55 IBU)
Alaskan Pale (8.5 SRM, 24 IBU)
Alaskan Smoked Porter (92 SRM, 45 IBU)
Alaskan Stout (11 SRM, 28 IBU)
Alaskan Summer Ale (8 SRM, 18 IBU)
Alaskan Winter Ale (17 SRM, 27 IBU)

States Available: AK, AZ, CA, ID, MT, NV, OR, OR, WA, WY

Alesmith Brewing Company
9368 Cabot Drive
San Diego, CA 92126
858-549-9888
www.alesmith.com

BRANDS:
Alesmith Brewing Horny Devil
Alesmith Brewing IPA
Alesmith Brewing Old Numbskull
Alesmith Brewing Special Bitter
Alesmith Brewing Speedway Stout
Alesmith Brewing Wee Heavy
Alesmith Brewing X-Extra Pale Ale
Alesmith Brewing YuleSmith Holiday Ale

States Available: Contact Brewery

Allagash Brewing Company

100 Industrial Way
Portland, ME 04103
207-878-5385
www.allagash.com

BRANDS:
Allagash Brewing 11th Anniversary
Allagash Brewing Curieux
Allagash Brewing Dubbel (27 IBU)
Allagash Brewing Four (37 IBU)
Allagash Brewing Interlude
Allagash Brewing Musette
Allagash Brewing Odyssey
Allagash Brewing Tripel (30 IBU)
Allagash Brewing Victoria Ale
Allagash Brewing White Beer (18 IBU)
Allagash Grand Cru (30 IBU)

States Available: CA, CO, CT, FL, IN, MA, MD, ME, ME, NC, NJ, NY, OH, OR, PA, RI, TX, VA, VT

Alltech's Lexington Brewing Company

401 Cross Street
Lexington, KY 40508
859-887-3406
www.kentuckylight.com

BRANDS:
Lexington Brewing Kentucky Ale
Lexington Brewing Kentucky Bourbon Barrel Aged Ale
Lexington Brewing Kentucky Light

States Available: KY, NE, SD

Alpine Beer Company – *page 449*

2351 Alpine Boulevard
Alpine, CA 91901
619-445-2337
www.alpinebeerco.com

BRANDS:
Alpine Ale (38 IBU)
Alpine Beer Mchenney's Irish Red (10.7 IBU)
Alpine Beer Pure Hoppiness – *page 449*
Alpine Mandarin Nectar (4.1 IBU)

States Available: CA

Anchor Brewing Company – *page 450*

1705 Mariposa Street
San Francisco, CA 94107-2334
415-863-8350
www.anchorbrewing.com

BRANDS:
Anchor Brewing Bock Beer
Anchor Brewing Christmas Ale
Anchor Brewing Liberty Ale
Anchor Brewing Old Foghorn Barleywine Style Ale
Anchor Brewing Porter
Anchor Brewing Small Beer
Anchor Brewing Steam – *page 450*
Anchor Brewing Summer Ale

States Available: All 50 States

Anderson Valley Brewing Company – *page 451*

17700 Highway 253
Boonville, CA 95415
707-895-2337
www.avbc.com

BRANDS:
Anderson Valley Barney Flats Oatmeal Stout (13 IBU) – *page 452*
Anderson Valley Boont ESB Ale – *page 453*
Anderson Valley Boont Amber Ale (15 IBU) – *page 451*
Anderson Valley Brother David's Abbey Style Double (28 IBU)
Anderson Valley Brother David's Abbey Style Triple (26 IBU)
Anderson Valley Deependers Porter (17 IBU)
Anderson Valley High Rollers Wheat Beer (5 IBU)
Anderson Valley Hop Ottin' IPA (82 IBU) – *page 452*
Anderson Valley Poleeko Gold Pale Ale (34 IBU)
Anderson Valley Summer Solstice Cerveza Crema (4 IBU)
Anderson Valley Winter Solstice (5 IBU)

States Available: AZ, CO, CT, DE, ID, IL, IN, MA, MD, MI, NC, NJ, NM, NY, OH, OR, PA, RI, UT, VA, WA

Andrews Brewing Company

353 High Street
Lincolnville, ME 04846
207-763-3305
www.drinkmainebeer.com

BRANDS:
Andrews English Pale Ale
Andrews Northern Brown Ale
Andrews St. Nick Porter
Andrews Summer Golden Ale

States Available: CA, CO, CT, FL, IL, IN, MA, MD, ME, NC, NJ, NY, OH, OR, PA, RI, TX, VA, VT

Angel City Brewing – *page 454*

833 W. Torrance Blvd., Suite #105
Torrance, CA 90502
310-329-8881
www.angelcitybrewing.com

BRANDS:
Angel City Abbey (18 SRM, 30 IBU)
Angel City Ale (12 SRM, 30 IBU) – *page 454*
Angel City Dunkel (24 SRM, 20 IBU)
Angel City IPA (5.5 SRM, 45 IBU)
Angel City Lager (3.5 SRM, 20 IBU)
Angel City Pilz (3.5 SRM, 22 IBU)
Angel City Vitzen (5 SRM,15 IBU)

States Available: CA

Angry Minnow Brewing

10440 Florida Avenue
Hayward, WI 54843
715-934-3055
www.angryminnow.com

BRANDS:
Angry Minnow Honey Wheat Pale Ale

States Available: MI, MN, WI

Anheuser-Busch, Inc. – *page 455*

One Busch Place
St. Louis, MO 63118
314-577-2000
www.anheuser-busch.com

BRANDS:
Anheuser World Lager
Beach Bum Blonde Ale – *page 459*
Brew Masters' Private Reserve – *page 461*
Bud Dry
Bud Extra
Bud Ice
Bud Ice Light
Bud Light
Budweiser
Budweiser NA
Budweiser Select
Busch
Busch Ice
Busch Light
Busch NA
Chelada Bud
Chelada Bud Light
Hurricane High Gravity (HG)
Hurricane Ice
Hurricane Malt Liquor
Jack's Pumpkin Spice Ale – *page 457*
King Cobra
Land Shark Lager
Michelob – *page 459*
Michelob AmberBock – *page 460*
Michelob Bavarian-Style Wheat
Michelob Celebrate Chocolate – *page 461*
Michelob Celebrate Vanilla
Michelob Golden Draft
Michelob Golden Draft Light
Michelob Honey Lager – *page 460*
Michelob Light
Michelob Marzen
Michelob Pale Ale
Michelob Porter
Michelob Ultra
Michelob ULTRA Amber
Michelob ULTRA Lime
Michelob ULTRA Orange

BREWER INDEX (Alphabetical)

Michelob ULTRA Pomegranate
Natty Up
Natural Ice
Natural Light
O'Doul's
O'Doul's Amber
Redbridge Lager – *page 456*
Rock Green Light
Rolling Rock Extra Pale
Spring Heat Spiced Wheat – *page 458*
Stone Mill Pale Ale – *page 456*
Tequiza
Wild Blue
Wild Hop Lager – *page 457*
Wild Hop Organic Lager
Winter's Bourbon Cask Ale – *page 458*
ZeigenBock

States Available: All 50 States

Appalachian Brewing Company

50 North Cameron Street
Harrisburg, PA 17101
717-221-1080
www.abcbrew.com

BRANDS:
Appalachian Brewing Hoppy Trail IPA
Appalachian Brewing Jolly Scot Scottish Ale
Appalachian Brewing Kipona Fest Lager
Appalachian Brewing Mountain Lager
Appalachian Brewing Peregrine Pilsner
Appalachian Brewing Purist Pale Ale
Appalachian Brewing Susquehanna Stout
Appalachian Brewing Water Gap Wheat

States Available: PA

Arbor Brewing Company

720 Norris Street
Ypsilanti, MI 49198
734-480-2739
www.cornerbrewery.com

BRANDS::
Arbor Brewing Bavarian Bliss Hefeweizen
Arbor Brewing Brasserie Blonde Belgian
Arbor Brewing Olde Number 23 Alt Bier
Arbor Brewing Red Snapper Special Bitter
Arbor Brewing Sacred Cow IPA

States Available: MI

Arcadia Brewing Company – *page 462*

103 West Michigan Avenue
Battle Creek, MI 49017
269-963-9690
www.arcadiabrewingcompany.com

BRANDS:
Arcadia Brewing Ales Amber Ale (34 IBU)
Arcadia Brewing Ales Angler's Ale (34 IBU)
Arcadia Brewing Ales Battle Creek Special Reserve (23 IBU)
Arcadia Brewing Ales HopMouth (76 IBU)
Arcadia Brewing Ales Imperial Stout (59 IBU)
Arcadia Brewing Ales India Pale Ale (41 IBU) – *page 462*
Arcadia Brewing Ales London Porter (42 IBU)
Arcadia Brewing Ales Nut Brown Ale (26 IBU)
Arcadia Brewing Ales Scotch Ale (28 IBU)
Arcadia Brewing Ales Starboard Stout (29 IBU)
Arcadia Brewing Ales Whitsun (17 IBU)

States Available: IL, KY, MI, MN, MO, NJ, OH, PA, NY, VA

BREWER INDEX (Alphabetical)

Atlanta Brewing Company – *page 463*

2323 Defoor Hills Rd. NW
Atlanta, GA 30318
(404) 881-0300
www.atlantabrewing.com

BRANDS:
Atlanta Brewing PeachTree Pale Ale
Atlanta Brewing Red Brick Ale – *page 463*
Atlanta Brewing Red Brick Blonde
Atlanta Brewing Red Brick Summer Brew – Hefeweizen
Atlanta Brewing Red Brink Winter Brew – Double-Chocolate Oatmeal Porter

States Available: GA

Atlantic Brewing Company

15 Knox Road
Bar Harbor, ME 04609-7720
207-288-2337
www.atlanticbrewing.com

BRANDS:
Atlantic Brewing Bar Harbor Blueberry Ale
Atlantic Brewing Bar Harbor Real Ale
Atlantic Brewing Brother Adam's Honey Bragget
Atlantic Brewing Coal Porter
Atlantic Brewing Mount Desert Island Ginger
Atlantic Brewing Special Old Bitter Ale

States Available: ME

Atwater Block Brewery

237 Jos Campau Street
Detroit, MI 48207
313-877-9205
www.atwaterbeer.com

BRANDS:
Atwater Bloktoberfest
Atwater Dunkel Dark Lager
Atwater Hefeweizen
Atwater Hell Pale Lager
Atwater Mai Bock
Atwater Pilsner
Atwater Rost
Atwater Salvation IPA
Atwater Shaman's Porter
Atwater Vanilla Java Porter
Atwater Voodoo Vator Dopplebock
Atwater Winter Bock

States Available: CO, IL, IN, MI, OH, PA, WI

August Schell Brewing Company

1860 Schell Road
New Ulm, MN 56073-0128
507-354-5528
www.schellsbrewery.com

BRANDS:
August Schell Brewing Caramel Bock (30.8 SRM, 17 IBU)
August Schell Brewing Dark (23 SRM, 8 IBU)
August Schell Brewing FireBrick (15.2 SRM, 23 IBU)
August Schell Brewing Hefeweizen (3.4 SRM, 12 IBU)
August Schell Brewing Light (2.2 SRM, 8 IBU)
August Schell Brewing Maifest (8.3 SRM, 25 IBU)
August Schell Brewing Octoberfest (14 SRM, 20 IBU)
August Schell Brewing Original (2.8 SRM, 12.5 IBU)
August Schell Brewing Pale Ale (14 SRM, 35 IBU)
August Schell Brewing Pilsner (3.1 SRM, 27 IBU)
August Schell Brewing Schmaltz's Alt (49 SRM, 21 IBU)
August Schell Brewing Snowstorm
August Schell Brewing Zommerfest (4 SRM, 25 IBU)

States Available: IA, MI, MN, ND, PA, SD, WI

BREWER INDEX (Alphabetical)

Avery Brewing Company – *page 464*

5763 Arapahoe Avenue, Unit E
Boulder, CO 80303
303-440-4324
www.averybrewing.com

small brewery - BIG BEERS

BRANDS:
Avery Brewing 14'er ESB (37 IBU)
Avery Brewing Ellie's Brown (17 IBU)
Avery Brewing Hog Heaven Barley Wine (104 IBU)
Avery Brewing IPA (69 IBU) – *page 464*
Avery Brewing Karma Belgian Ale (10 IBU)
Avery Brewing Mephistopheles' Stout (107 IBU)
Avery Brewing New World Porter (45 IBU)
Avery Brewing Old Jubilation (30 IBU)
Avery Brewing Out of Bounds Stout (51 IBU)
Avery Brewing Red Point Amber Ale (22 IBU)
Avery Brewing Salvation (25 IBU)
Avery Brewing Samael's Oak Aged Ale (41 IBU)
Avery Brewing The Beast Belgian Grand Cru (68 IBU)
Avery Brewing The Czar Russian Imperial Stout (60 IBU)
Avery Brewing The Kaiser Imperial Oktoberfest (24 IBU)
Avery Brewing The Maharaja Imperial IPA (102 IBU)
Avery Brewing The Reverend Belgian Quadupel (10 IBU)
Avery Brewing Thirteen
Avery Brewing Twelve
Avery Brewing White Rascal Belgian-Style White Ale (10 IBU)

States Available: AZ, CA, CO, CT, DC, FL, GA, IL, IN, KS, KY, MA, MD, MI,
MN, NC, NJ, NM, OH, OR, PA, TN, TX, VA, WA, WI, WY

B.W. Beer Works USA

P.O. Box 9829
Baltimore, MD 21284-9829
410-321-1892
www.ravenbeer.com

BRANDS:
The Raven Christmas Lager
The Raven Special Lager

States Available: DC, IL, MA, MD, PA, SC, VA

Back Road Brewery

1315 Michigan Avenue
La Porte, IN 46350
219-362-7623
www.backroadbrewery.com

Take a Back Road home!

BRANDS:
Back Road Brewery American Pale Ale
  (8 SRM, 30 IBU)
Back Road Brewery Autumn Ale
Back Road Brewery Aviator Dopplebock (26 SRM, 15 IBU)
Back Road Brewery Back Road Ale (14 SRM, 13 IBU)
Back Road Brewery Belgian-Style Wit (2 SRM, 7 IBU)
Back Road Brewery Belle Gunness Stout (40 SRM, 45 IBU)
Back Road Brewery Blueberry Ale (14 SRM, 13 IBU)
Back Road Brewery Christmas Ale
Back Road Brewery Koza Brada Bock (17 SRM, 15 IBU)
Back Road Brewery Maple Gold City (17 SRM, 23 IBU)
Back Road Brewery Midwest IPA (12 SRM, 70 IBU)
Back Road Brewery Millennium Lager (4 SRM, 9 IBU)
Back Road Brewery No. 9 Barley-Style Ale (25 SRM, 83 IBU)
Back Road Brewery Pecker Head Red (19 SRM, 37 IBU)

States Available: IN

Backcountry Brewery

710 Main Street
Frisco, CO 080443
970-668-2337
www.backcountrybrewery.com

BRANDS:
Backcountry Brewery Peak One Porter (70.6 SRM, 35 IBU)
Backcountry Brewery Ptarmigan Pilsner (3.1 SRM, 42 IBU)
Backcountry Brewery Switchback Amber (16 SRM, 28 IBU)
Backcountry Brewery Telemark IPA (10.8 SRM, 60 IBU)
Backcountry Brewery Wheeler Wheat (3.6 SRM, 18 IBU)

States Available: CO

BREWER INDEX (Alphabetical)

Ballast Point Brewing Company – *page 465*

Ballast Point
Brewing Company.
San Diego, CA

10051 Old Grove Road, Suite B
San Diego, CA 92131-1654
619-298-2337
www.ballastpoint.com

BRANDS:
Ballast Point Big Eye IPA
Ballast Point Black Marlin Porter
Ballast Point Calico Amber Ale
Ballast Point Wahoo Wheat Beer
Ballast Point Yellowtail Pale Ale (22 - 28 IBU) – *page 465*

States Available: CA (San Diego, Orange, L.A.)

Bar Harbor Brewing Company

135 Otter Creek Drive
Bar Harbor, ME 04609
207-288-4592
www.barharborbrewing.com

BRANDS:
Bar Harbor Brewing Bar Harbor Peach
Bar Harbor Brewing Cadillac Mountain Stout
Bar Harbor Brewing Ginger Mild Brew
Bar Harbor Brewing Harbor Lighthouse Ale
Bar Harbor Brewing Thunder Hole Ale

States Available: ME

Bard's Tale Beer Company – *page 466*

211 NW Ward Road
Lee's Summit, MO 64063
203-831-8899
www.bardsbeer.com

BRANDS:
Bard's Tale Dragon's Gold Sorghum Lager (4 SRM, 35 IBU) – *page 466*

States Available: CA, CO, CT, DE, IA, IL, IN, KS, KY, MA, MN, MO, NC, NE, NH, NJ, NV, NY, OH, OR, PA, RI, SC, TX, UT, VA, VT

Barley Creek Brewing Company

Sullivan Trail and Camelback Road
Tannerville, PA 18372
570-629-9399
www.barleycreek.com

BRANDS:
Barley Creek Angler Black Widow Lager
Barley Creek Antler Brown Ale
Barley Creek Atlas Ale
Barley Creek Harvest Moon Oktoberfest
Barley Creek Light
Barley Creek Navigator Gold
Barley Creek Old '99 Barley Wine
Barley Creek Renovator Stout
Barley Creek Rescue India Pale Ale

States Available: NJ, PA

Barley Island Brewing Company

639 Conner Street (Hwy 32)
Nobelesville, IN 46062
317-770-5280
www.barleyisland.com

BRANDS:
Barley Island Brewing Bar Fly India Pale Ale (7.8 SRM, 60 IBU)
Barley Island Brewing Black Majic Java Stout
Barley Island Brewing Blind Tiger Pale Ale (7.1 SRM, 32.6 IBU)
Barley Island Brewing Bourbon Barrel-Aged Oatmeal Stout
Barley Island Brewing Brass Knuckles Oatmeal Stout (52.4 SRM, 24.4 IBU)
Barley Island Brewing Dirty Helen Brown Ale (17.8 SRM, 24.5 IBU)
Barley Island Brewing Sheet Metal Blonde

States Available: Contact Brewery

BREWER INDEX (Alphabetical)

Baron Brewing

1605 South 93rd Street, Bldg E Unit L
Seattle, WA 98108
206-764-1213
www.baronbeer.com

BRANDS:
Baron Bavarian Weizen
Baron Berliner-Weisse
Baron Bock
Baron Dampf Bier
Baron Doppelbock
Baron Dunkel-Weisse
Baron Dusseldof Altbier
Baron Hefe-Weisse (SRM 5, IBU 15)
Baron Helles Bock
Baron Liberator Doppelbock (SRM 25, IBU 20)
Baron Munich Helles Lager
Baron Oktoberfest (SRM 13, IBU 15)
Baron Pils (SRM 2.5, IBU 35)
Baron Rauchbier
Baron Roggen
Baron Schwarzbier (SRM 25, IBU 13)
Baron Uber-Weisse

States Available: WA

Barrel House Brewing Company

544-B West Liberty Street
Cincinnati, OH 45214
513-421-2337
www.barrelhouse.malz.com

BRANDS::
Barrel House Belgian Style Winter Ale
Barrel House Boss Cox Double Dark IPA
Barrel House Cumberland Pale Ale
Barrel House Duveneck's Dortmunder Style Lager
Barrel House Hocking Hills HefeWeizen
Barrel House Red Leg Ale

States Available: Contact Brewery

Bayern Brewing

1507 Montana Street
Missoula, MT 59801
406-721-1482
www.bayernbrewery.com

BRANDS:
Bayern Brewing Amber
Bayern Brewing Doppelbock
Bayern Brewing Flathead Lake Monster Lager
Bayern Brewing Hefeweizen
Bayern Brewing Killarney
Bayern Brewing Maibock
Bayern Brewing Oktoberfest
Bayern Brewing Pilsner
Bayern Brewing Schwarzbier
Bayern Brewing Trout Slayer

States Available: ID, MT, OR

Bayhawk Ales, Inc.

2000 Main St Suite A
Irvine, CA 92614-7202
949-442-7565
www.bayhawkales.com

BRANDS:
Bayhawk Ales Amber Ale (23 IBU)
Bayhawk Ales Beach Blonde (9.5 IBU)
Bayhawk Ales California Pale Ale (CPA) (49 IBU)
Bayhawk Ales Chocolate Porter (35 IBU)
Bayhawk Ales Hefe Weizen (13 IBU)
Bayhawk Ales Honey Blonde (9 IBU)
Bayhawk Ales IPA (64 IBU)
Bayhawk Ales O.C. Lager (14 IBU)
Bayhawk Ales Stout (30 IBU)

States Available: AZ, CA, HI, NV, TX

17

Brewer Index (Alphabetical)

Bear Republic Brewing Company

345 Healdsburg Avenue
Healdsburg, CA 95448
707-431-7258
www.bearrepublic.com

BRANDS:
Bear Republic Brewing Big Bear Stout Ale (68 IBU)
Bear Republic Brewing Hop Rod Rye (90+ IBU)
Bear Republic Brewing Pete Brown's Tribute Ale
Bear Republic Brewing Racer 5 (69 IBU)
Bear Republic Brewing Red Rocket Ale (65+ IBU)
Bear Republic Brewing Special XP Pale Ale (55 IBU)

States Available: AZ, CA, CO, DE, IL, KY, MA, MD, MI, NC, NY, OR, VA, WA, WI

Beautiful Brews, Inc.

1200 Holland Drive
Boca Raton, FL 33432
561-241-7373

BRANDS:
Beautiful Brews Honey Amber Rose

States Available: Contact Brewery

Beermann's Beerwerks

8284 Industrial Avenue
Roseville, CA 95678
916-781-2337
www.beermanns.com

BRANDS:
Beermann's Hefe Weizen
Beermann's Honey Brew
Beermann's India Pale Ale
Beermann's Lincoln Lager – Helles Lager
Beermann's Rip Roarin' Red – Red Ale

States Available: CA

Bell's Brewery, Inc.

8939 Krum Avenue
Galesburg, MI 49053
269-382-2338
www.bellsbeer.com

BRANDS:
(Non-participating Brewery – Please consult brewery)

States Available: IL, IN, KY, MI, MN, MO, ND, OH, WI

Berkshire Brewing Company – *page 467*

P.O. Box 251
South Deerfield, MA 01373
413-665-6600
www.berkshirebrewingcompany.com

BRANDS:
Berkshire Brewing Berkshire Traditional Pale Ale
Berkshire Brewing Cabin Fever Ale
Berkshire Brewing Coffeehouse Porter
Berkshire Brewing Drayman's Porter
Berkshire Brewing Gold Spike Ale
Berkshire Brewing Hefeweizen
Berkshire Brewing Holidale
Berkshire Brewing Imperial Stout
Berkshire Brewing Lost Sailor India Pale Ale
Berkshire Brewing Maibock Lager
Berkshire Brewing Ocktoberfest Lager
Berkshire Brewing Raspberry Strong Ale
Berkshire Brewing River Ale
Berkshire Brewing "Shabadoo" Black & Tan Ale
Berkshire Brewing Steel Rail Extra Pale Ale – *page 467*

States Available: CT, MA, RI, VT

Big Easy Brewing Company

5200 Taravella Road
Marreor, LA 70072
504-347-8200
www.bigeasybeer.com

BRANDS:
Bourbon Street Bock
Mojo Red Ale
Tiger Town Beer

States Available: LA

18

BREWER INDEX (Alphabetical)

Big Horn Brewing (CB Potts)

1427 West Elizabeth Street
Ft. Collins, CO 80521
970-221-5954
www.cbpotts.com

BRANDS:
Big Horn Blonde (5 SRM, 20 IBU)
Big Horn Hefeweizen (7 SRM, 12 IBU)
Big Red AIPA (15 SRM, 60 IBU)
Buttface Amber Ale (22 SRM, 22 IBU)
Total Disorder Porter (60 SRM, 22 IBU)

States Available: CO, WY

Big Sky Brewing Company – *page 468*

5417 Trumpeter Way
Missoula, MT 59808-7170
406-549-2777
www.bigskybrew.com

BRANDS:
Big Sky Brewing Crystal Ale – *page 468*
Big Sky Brewing IPA
Big Sky Brewing Moose Drool Brown Ale
Big Sky Brewing Powder Hound Winter Ale
Big Sky Brewing Scape Goat Pale Ale
Big Sky Brewing Summer Honey Seasonal Ale

States Available: AK, CA, CO, ID, MN, MT, ND, NV, OR, SD, WA, WI, WY

Bison Brewing

2598 Telegraph Avenue
Berkeley, CA 94704
510-697-1537
www.bisonbrew.com

BRANDS:
Bison Brewing Organic Barleywine (30 SRM, 87 IBU)
Bison Brewing Organic Belgain Ale (30 SRM, 87 IBU)
Bison Brewing Organic Chocolate Stout (45 SRM, 30 IBU)
Bison Brewing Organic Farmhouse (7 SRM, 24 IBU)
Bison Brewing Organic Gingerbread Ale (35 SRM, 25 IBU)
Bison Brewing Organic Honey-Basil (6 SRM, 24 IBU)
Bison Brewing Organic IPA (12 SRM, 59 IBU)
Bison Brewing Organic Red Ale (16 SRM, 25 IBU)
Bison Brewing Organic Winter (32 SRM, 27 IBU)

States Available: CA, FL, GA, IN, NC, OH, OR, VA, WA

Bitter Root Brewing

101 Marcus Street
Hamilton, MT 59840
406-363-7468
www.bitterrootbrewing.com

BRANDS:
Bitter Root Brewing Amber
Bitter Root Brewing India Pale Ale (7.5 SRM, 50 IBU)
Bitter Root Brewing Nut Brown (20 SRM, 25 IBU)
Bitter Root Brewing Pale Ale (10 SRM, 35 IBU)
Bitter Root Brewing Porter (30 SRM, 35 IBU)
Bitter Root Brewing Sawtooth Ale (5 SRM, 20 IBU)
Bitter Root Brewing Winter Ale

States Available: ID, MT

BREWER INDEX (Alphabetical)

BluCreek Brewing – *page 470*

2310 Daniels Street, Suite 148
Madison, WI 53718
608-204-0868
www.blucreek.com

BRANDS:
BluCreek (Honey) Herbal Ale (9.3 SRM, 20 IBU)
BluCreek Altbier (12 SRM, 30 IBU)
BluCreek Blueberry Ale (9 SRM, 25 IBU)
BluCreek Zen IPA (7.2 SRM, 41.5 IBU) – *page 470*

States Available: FL, IL, MN, OH, WI

Blue & Gray Brewing Company, Inc.

3321A Dill Smith Drive
Fredricksburg, VA 22408
540-538-2379
www.blueandgraybrewingco.com

BRANDS:
Blue & Gray Classic Lager
Falmouth American Pale Ale
Fred Red Ale
Spiced Winter Ale (Nov. - Jan.)
Stonewall Stout
Von Steuben Oktoberfest (Sept. - Oct)

States Available: VA

Blue Point Brewing – *page 471*

2310 Daniels Street, Suite 148
161 River Avenue
Patchogue, NY 11772
631-475-6944
www.bluepointbrewing.com

BRANDS:
Blue Point Brewing Blueberry Ale (14 IBU)
Blue Point Brewing Cherry Imperial Stout (67 IBU)
Blue Point Brewing ESB (35 IBU)
Blue Point Brewing Golden Ale (16 IBU)
Blue Point Brewing Hefeweizen (15 IBU)
Blue Point Brewing Hoptical Illusion (60 IBU)
Blue Point Brewing Oatmeal Stout (30 IBU)
Blue Point Brewing Octoberfest (28 IBU)
Blue Point Brewing Old Howling Bastard (78 IBU)
Blue Point Brewing Pale Ale (36 IBU)
Blue Point Brewing Porter (26 IBU)
Blue Point Brewing Summer Ale (16 IBU)
Blue Point Brewing Toasted Lager (28 IBU) – *page 471*
Blue Point Brewing Winter Ale (16 IBU)

States Available: MA, MD, NJ, NY, PA, RI

Bluegrass Brewing Company – *page 472*

636 E. Main Street
Louisville, KY 40202
502-584-2739
www.bbcbrew.com

BRANDS:
BBC Altbier (14 SRM, 30 IBU)
BBC American Pale Ale (14 SRM, 52 IBU) – *page 472*
BBC Bearded Pat's Barleywine (18 SRM, 100+ IBU)
BBC Bluegrass Gold (3 SRM, 10 IBU)
BBC Dark Star Porter (35 SRM, 35 IBU)
BBC Hell For Certain (16 SRM, 25 IBU)
BBC Jefferson's Reserve Bourbon Barrel Stout (40+ SRM, 15 IBU)
BBC Nut Brown Ale (22SRM, 28 IBU)
BBC White Wedding Ale (4 SRM, 10 IBU)

States Available: CT, IN, KY, OH, TN, VA

BREWER INDEX (Alphabetical)

Bootie Beer Company
620 North Demming Drive #100
Winter Park, FL 32789
407-319-1999
www.bootiebeer.com

BRANDS:
Bootie Beer
Bootie Light

States Available: FL

Bonnema Brewing Company
6900 El Camino Real
Atascadero, CA 93423
805-462-3660

BRANDS:
Bonnema Brewing Marzen
Bonnema Brewing Mudhole Porter
Bonnema Brewing Pozo Pale Ale
Bonnema Brewing Raspberry Wheat
Bonnema Brewing Red Kroeker Ale
Bonnema Brewing Whalerock Wheat
Bonnema Brewing White Christmas
Gold Hill Gold Trail Pale Ale

States Available: Contact Brewery

The Boston Beer Company – page 473
30 Germania Street
Boston, MA 02130
617-368-5000
www.samueladams.com

SAMUEL ADAMS

BRANDS:
Sam Adams 1790 Root Beer Brew
Sam Adams George Washington Porter
Sam Adams James Madison Dark Wheat Ale
Sam Adams Light (11 SRM, 10 IBU) – page 474
Sam Adams Traditional Ginger Honey Ale
Samuel Adams 375 Colonial Ale
Samuel Adams Black Lager (50 SRM, 19 IBU)
Samuel Adams Boston Ale (14 SRM, 32 IBU)
Samuel Adams Boston Lager (11 SRM, 30 IBU) – page 473
Samuel Adams Brown Ale (26 SRM, 18 IBU)
Samuel Adams Cherry Wheat (8 SRM, 23 IBU)
Samuel Adams Chocolate Bock (75 SRM, 16 IBU)
Samuel Adams Cranberry Lambic (13.5 SRM, 22 IBU)
Samuel Adams Cream Stout (80 SRM, 28 IBU)
Samuel Adams Double Bock (38 SRM, 25 IBU)
Samuel Adams Hefeweizen (7 SRM, 14 IBU)
Samuel Adams Holiday Porter (55 SRM, 40 IBU)
Samuel Adams Honey Porter
Samuel Adams Imperial Pilsner (20 SRM, 110 IBU)
Samuel Adams Millennium (30 SRM, 27 IBU)
Samuel Adams Octoberfest (20 SRM, 17 IBU) – page 474
Samuel Adams Old Fezziwig Ale (37.5 SRM, 25 IBU)
Samuel Adams Pale Ale (8 SRM, 23 IBU)
Samuel Adams Scotch Ale (28.5 SRM, 35 IBU)
Samuel Adams Summer Ale (7.5 SRM, 10 IBU) – page 475
Samuel Adams Triple Bock (200 SRM, 31 IBU)
Samuel Adams Utopias (34 SRM, 25 IBU)
Samuel Adams White Ale (8 SRM, 12 IBU) – page 475
Samuel Adams Winter Lager (25 SRM, 22 IBU)– page 476

States Available: All 50 States

BREWER INDEX (Alphabetical)

Boulder Beer Company – *page 477*

2880 Wilderness Place
Boulder, CO 80301-2258
303-444-8448
www.boulderbeer.com

BRANDS:
Boulder Beer Buffalo Gold Golden Ale
 (10.3 SRM, 22 IBU)
Boulder Beer Hazed & Infused Dry-Hopped Ale (19.7 SRM, 38 IBU) – *page 477*
Boulder Beer Killer Penguin Barleywine (34.5 SRM, 42 IBU)
Boulder Beer Mojo India Pale Ale (12 SRM, 63 IBU)
Boulder Beer Mojo Risin' Double IPA (12 SRM, 80 IBU)
Boulder Beer Never Summer Ale (36.9 SRM, 45 IBU)
Boulder Beer Pass Time Pale Ale (13.8 SRM, 23 IBU)
Boulder Beer Planet Porter (45 SRM, 26 IBU)
Boulder Beer Singletrack Copper Ale (13.3 SRM, 30 IBU)
Boulder Beer Sundance Amber (19.6 SRM, 29 IBU)
Boulder Beer Sweaty Betty Blonde Wheat Beer (4 SRM, 12 IBU)

States Available: AZ, CO, CT, FL, IL, IN, KS, KY, MA, MN, ND, NE, NJ, NM,
    NY, OH, OR, PA, RI, SD, UT, WA, WY

Boulevard Brewing Company – *page 478*

2501 Southwest Boulevard
Kansas City, MO 64108
816-474-7095
www.boulevard.com

BRANDS:
Boulevard Brewing Bob's '47 (27 IBU)
Boulevard Brewing Bully! Porter (47 IBU)
Boulevard Brewing Dry Stout (28 IBU)
Boulevard Brewing Irish Ale (28 IBU)
Boulevard Brewing Lunar Ale – *page 478*
Boulevard Brewing Nutcracker Ale (31 IBU)
Boulevard Brewing Pale Ale (31 IBU) – *page 479*
Boulevard Brewing Unfiltered Wheat Beer (13 IBU) – *page 479*
Boulevard Brewing ZÔN (12 IBU)

States Available: AR, IA, IL, KS, MN, MO, ND, NE, OK, SD, WY

Boundary Bay Brewing Company

1107 Railroad Avenue
Bellingham, WA 98225
360-647-5593
www.bbaybrewery.com

BRANDS:
Boundary Bay Best Bitter
Boundary Bay Cabin Fever
Boundary Bay Inside Passage Ale
Boundary Bay Scotch
Boundary BayBarley Wine

States Available: WA

Breckenridge Brewery

471 Kalamath Street
Denver, CO 80204
303-623-BREW
www.breckenridgebrewery.com

BRANDS:
Breckenridge Autumn Ale (21 IBU)
Breckenridge Avalanche Ale (19 IBU)
Breckenridge Christmas Ale (22 IBU)
Breckenridge Hefe Proper (9 IBU)
Breckenridge Oatmeal Stout (31 IBU)
Breckenridge Summerbright Ale (15 IBU)
Breckenridge Vanilla Porter (16 IBU)
Trademark Pale Ale (40 IBU)
471 IPA (70 IBU)

States Available: AR, CO, IA, IL, IN, KS, KY, MI, MN, MO, ND, NE, NM, OH,
    OK, TX, VA, WI, WY

BREWER INDEX (Alphabetical)

Brewery Ommegang – *page 480*

656 County Highway 33
Cooperstown, NY 13326
607-544-1800
www.ommegang.com

BRANDS:
Hennepin Farmhouse Saison Ale
Ommegang Abbey Ale Dubbel
Ommegang Witte Ale
Rare Vos Amber Ale
Three Philosophers Quadrupel Ale – *page 480*

States Available: AK, AZ, CA, CO, CT, DC, DE, FL, GA, ID, IL, IN, KY, LA,
MA, MD, ME, MI, MO, NC, NE, NH, NJ, NV, NY, OH, OR,
PA, RI, TX, VA, VT, WA, WI

BridgePort Brewing Company (Gambrinus)

1313 NorthWest Marshall
Portland, OR 97209
503-241-7179
www.bridgeportbrew.com

BRANDS:
Beer Town Brown (20 IBU)
BridgePort Black Strap Stout (30 IBU)
BridgePort Blue Heron Pale Ale (25 IBU)
BridgePort Ebenezer Ale (40 IBU)
BridgePort ESB (30 IBU)
BridgePort IPA (60 IBU)
BridgePort Old Knucklehead (60 IBU)
BridgePort Ropewalker (18 IBU)

States Available: AK, AL, AZ, CA, CO, GA, ID, KS, MI, MN, MO, MT, NC,
NM, OK, OR, TN, TX, WA

Bristol Brewing Company

1647 South Tejon
Colorado Springs, CO 80906
719-633-2555
www.bristolbrewing.com

BRANDS:
Bristol Brewing Beehive Honey Wheat (16 IBU)
Bristol Brewing Edge City Octoberfest (24 IBU)
Bristol Brewing Edge City Pale Bock (31 IBU)
Bristol Brewing Edge City Wit Bier (18 IBU)
Bristol Brewing Laughing Lab Scottish Ale (19 IBU)
Bristol Brewing Mass Transit Ale (21 IBU)
Bristol Brewing Old No. 23 Barley Wine (67 IBU)
Bristol Brewing Red Rocket Pale Ale (28 IBU)
Bristol Brewing Winter Warlock Oatmeal Stout (44 IBU)

States Available: CO

Brooklyn Brewery

79 North Eleventh Street
Brooklyn, NY 11211
718-486-7422
www.brooklynbrewery.com

BRANDS:
Brooklyn Black Chocolate Stout (70 IBU)
Brooklyn Brown Ale (30 IBU)
Brooklyn East India Pale Ale (40 IBU)
Brooklyn Lager (28-30 IBU)
Brooklyn Monster Ale (70 IBU)
Brooklyn Oktoberfest (20 IBU)
Brooklyn Pennant Ale (26 IBU)
Brooklyn Pilsner (30 IBU)
Brooklyn Weisse (13 IBU)
Post Road Pumpkin Ale (24 IBU)

States Available: CT, DC, DE, GA, MA, MD, MI, NC, NJ, NY, OH, PA, RI, SC,
VA

BREWER INDEX (Alphabetical)

Buckeye Brewing

25200 Miles Road
Bedford Heights, OH 44128
216-292-2739
www.buckeyebrewing.com

BRANDS:
Buckeye Brewing Cleveland Lager
Buckeye Brewing Czech Pilsner
Buckeye Brewing Hippie I.P.A
Buckeye Brewing Ho Ho Ho Magical Dubbel
Buckeye Brewing Martian Marzen Lager
Buckeye Brewing Seventy-Six
Buckeye Brewing Vanilla Bean Porter
Buckeye Brewing Wheat Cloud

States Available: Contact Brewery

Buffalo Bill's Brewery

1082 B Street
Hayward, CA 94541
510-886-9823
www.buffalobillsbrewery.com

BRANDS:
Buffalo Bill's Brewery Orange Blossom Cream Ale
Buffalo Bill's Brewery Pumpkin Ale

States Available: Contact Brewery

Butte Creek Brewing

945 West Second Street
Chico, CA 95928
530-894-7906
www.buttecreek.com

BRANDS:
Butte Creek Christmas Cranberry Ale
Butte Creek Creekside Wheat
Butte Creek Gold Ale
Butte Creek Mt. Shasta Extra Pale Ale
Butte Creek Organic Ale
Butte Creek Organic India Pale Ale
Butte Creek Organic Pilsner
Butte Creek Organic Porter
Butte Creek Roland's Red
Butte Creek Spring Ale
Butte Creek Summer Pilsner
Butte Creek Winter Ale

States Available: CA

Butternuts Beer & Ale – *page 481*

4021 State Highway 51
Garrattsville, NY 13342
607-263-5070
www.butternutsbeerandale.com

BRANDS:
Heinnieweisse Weissbier (11 IBU)
Moo Thunder Stout (25 IBU)
Porkslap Pale Ale (24 IBU) – *page 481*
Snapperhead IPA (40 IBU)

States Available: NJ, NY

BREWER INDEX (Alphabetical)

Buzzards Bay Brewing Company

98 Horseneck Road
Westport, MA 02790
508-636-2288
www.buzzardsbrew.com

BRANDS:
Buzzards Bay Brewing Hefe-Weizen (40 IBU)
Buzzards Bay Brewing Lager (35 IBU)
Buzzards Bay Brewing Octoberfest
Buzzards Bay Brewing Pale Ale (47 IBU)
Buzzards Bay Brewing Weizen Dopplebock (17 IBU)

States Available: CT, MA, ME, RI, VT

Caldera Brewing Company – *page 482*

540 Clover Lane
Ashland, OR 97520
541-482-4677
www.calderabrewing.com

BRANDS:
Caldera Brewing Pale Ale – *page 482*

States Available: OR

Cape Ann Brewing

27 Commercial Street
Glouchester, MA 01930
978-282-0772
www.capeannbrewing.com

BRANDS:
Cape Ann Brewing Fisherman's Brew (30 IBU)
Cape Ann Brewing Fisherman's IPA (64 IBU)

States Available: MA, ME, NY

Capital Brewery Company, Inc. – *page 483*

7734 Terrace Avenue
Middleton, WI 53562
608-836-7100
www.capital-brewery.com

BRANDS:
Capital Brewery Autumnal Fire
Capital Brewery Bavarian Lager (22 IBU)
Capital Brewery Blonde Dopplelbock
Capital Brewery Brown Ale (25 IBU)
Capital Brewery Fest Beer
Capital Brewery Island Wheat – *page 483*
Capital Brewery Maibock (25 IBU)
Capital Brewery Munich Dark (28 IBU)
Capital Brewery Oktoberfest (23 IBU)
Capital Brewery Special Pilsner (32 IBU)
Capital Brewery Winter Skal (25 IBU)
Capital Brewery Wisconsin Amber (25 IBU)

States Available: IA, IL, MN, WI

Carolina Beer & Beverage Company – *page 484*

110 Barley Park Lane
Mooresville, NC 28115-1183
888-601-2739
www.carolinablonde.com

BRANDS:
Carolina Beer Carolina Blonde – *page 484*
Carolina Beer Carolina Light
Carolina Beer Cottonwood Almond Stout
Carolina Beer Cottonwood American Wheat
Carolina Beer Cottonwood Endo IPA
Carolina Beer Cottonwood Frostbite Ale
Carolina Beer Cottonwood Irish Style Red Ale
Carolina Beer Cottonwood Lift your Kilt Scottish Ale
Carolina Beer Cottonwood Low Down Brown
Carolina Beer Cottonwood Pumpkin Spiced Ale

States Available: GA, NC, SC, TN, VA

BREWER INDEX (Alphabetical)

Carolina Brewing

140 Thomas Mill Road
Mooresville, NC 28115-1183
Holly Springs, NC 27540-9372
919-557-2337
www.carolinabrew.com

BRANDS:
Carolina Brewing IPA
Carolina Brewing Nut Brown Ale
Carolina Brewing Oktoberfest Lager
Carolina Brewing Pale Ale
Carolina Brewing Spring Bock
Carolina Brewing Summer Ale
Carolina Brewing Winter Stout

States Available: NC

Cascade Lakes Brewing Company

2141 South West First Street
Redmond, OR 97756
541-923-3110
www.cascadelakes.com

BRANDS:
Cascade Lakes 20" Brown (35 IBU)
Cascade Lakes Angus MacDougal's Amber (30 IBU)
Cascade Lakes Blonde Bombshell (26 IBU)
Cascade Lakes IPA (65 IBU)
Cascade Lakes Monkey Face Porter (34 IBU)
Cascade Lakes Pine Marten Pale Ale (38 IBU)
Cascade Lakes Rooster Tail Ale (20 IBU)

States Available: Contact Brewery

Catawba Valley Brewing

212 S. Gree Street
Morganton, NC 28655
828-584-9400
www.cvbc.homestead.com/about.html

BRANDS:
Catawba Valley Brewing Buffalo Nickel Ale
Catawba Valley Brown Bear Ale
Catawba Valley Firewater IPA
Catawba Valley Honust Injun Stout
Catawba Valley Indian Head Red
Catawba Valley King Coconut Porter
Catawba Valley King Don's Original Pumpkin Ale
Catawba Valley King Karma Ale

States Available: NC, SC, TN

Central Coast Brewing

1422 Monterey Street
San Luis Obispo, CA 93401
805-783-2739
www.centralcoastbrewing.com

BRANDS:
Central Coast Brewing Cream Ale
Central Coast Brewing Golden Glow Ale
Central Coast Brewing Honey Wheat Ale
Central Coast Brewing Old Mission Ale
Central Coast Brewing Stenner Stout Ale
Central Coast Brewing Topless Blonde Ale

States Available: CA

BREWER INDEX (Alphabetical)

Central Waters Brewing Company
701 Main Street
Junction City, WI 54443
715-457-3322

BRANDS:
Central Waters Happy Heron Pale Ale
Central Waters Junc Town Brown Ale
Central Waters Kosmyk Charlie Y2K Catastrophe Ale
Central Waters Lac Du Bay IPA
Central Waters Mud Puppy Porter
Central Waters Ouisconsing Red Ale
Central Waters Reserve Bourbon Barrel Stout
Central Waters Reserve Irish Dry Stout
Central Waters Reserve Irish Red Ale
Central Waters Reserve Oktoberfest
Central Waters Satin Solstice Imperial Stout
Central Waters White Water Weizen

States Available: WI

Charleston Brewing Company
557 East Bay Street, Suite #21482
Charleston, SC 29403
843-200-0070
www.charlestonbrewing.com

BRANDS:
Charleston Brewing East Bay IPA
Charleston Brewing Half Moon Hefeweizen

States Available: GA, NC, SC

Charleville Brewing Company
1693 Boyd Road
Ste. Geneviev, MO 63670
573-756-4537
www.charlevillevineyard.com

BRANDS:
Charleville Brewing Amber Ale
Charleville Brewing Belgium Wheat
Charleville Brewing Lager

States Available: MO

Christian Moerlein Brewing Company
3400 Yankee Road
Cincinnati, OH 45200
513-771-0690
www.christianmoerlein.com

BRANDS:
Christian Moerlein Doppelbock
Christian Moerlein Hefeweisen
Christian Moerlein Oktoberfest
Christian Moerlein Select Dunkel
Christian Moerlein Select Lager
Christian Moerlein Select Light

States Available: Contact Brewer

Cisco Brewers, Inc.
5 Bartlett Farm Road
Nantucket, MA 02554
508-325-5929
www.ciscobrewers.com

BRANDS:
Cisco Brewers Baggywrinkle Barleywine
Cisco Brewers Bailey's Ale
Cisco Brewers Captain Swain's Extra Stout
Cisco Brewers Celebration Libation
Cisco Brewers Moor Porter
Cisco Brewers Sankaty Light
Cisco Brewers Summer of Lager
Cisco Brewers Whale's Tale Pale Ale

States Available: CT, DC, DE, MA, MD, NJ, NY, RI

City Brewery

925 South Third Street
La Crosse, WI 54601
608-785-4200
www.citybrewery.com

BRANDS:
City Brewery Golden Leaf Unfiltered Wheat
City Cream Ale
City Festbier
City Lager
City Light
City Pale Ale
City Slicker Malt Liquor
City Winter Porter
KUL
KUL Lite
LaCrosse Lager
LaCrosse Light

States Available: IA, IL, MN, OH, PA, WI

Clay Pipe Brewing Company

1203 New Windsor Road
Westminster, MD 21157
410-871-9333
www.cpbrewing.com

BRANDS:
Clay Pipe Brewing Blackfin Pale Ale (8.0 SRM)
Clay Pipe Brewing Blue Tractor Ale (28 IBU)
Clay Pipe Brewing Pursuit of Happiness Winter Warmer (12 SRM, 46 IBU)
Hop-ocalypse India Pale Ale (50 IBU)

States Available: MD

Climax Brewing Company – *page 485*

540 Clover Lane
112 Valley Road
Roselle Park, NJ 07204-1402
908-620-9585
www.climaxbrewing.com

BRANDS:
Climax Brewing Cream Ale
Climax Brewing Extra Special Bitter Ale
Climax Brewing India Pale Ale
Climax Brewing Nut Brown Ale
Climax Hoffmann Bavarian Dark
Hoffmann Doppel Bock – *page 485*
Climax Hoffmann Helles
Climax Hoffmann Oktoberfest

States Available: NJ, NY, PA

Clipper City Brewing Company – *page 486*

4615 Hollins Ferry Road, Suite B
Baltimore, MD 21227
410-247-7822
www.clippercitybeer.com

BRANDS:
Clipper City BaltoMärzHon
Clipper City Brewing Gold Ale
Clipper City Brewing Pale Ale
Clipper City McHenry Old Baltimore Style Beer
Heavy Seas Brewing Below Decks
Heavy Seas Brewing "Holy Sheet"
Heavy Seas Brewing Loose Cannon Hop[3] Ale – *page 486*
Heavy Seas Brewing Peg Leg Stout
Heavy Seas Brewing Red Sky at Night Saison Ale
Heavy Seas Brewing Small Craft Warning Über Pils
Heavy Seas Brewing Winter Storm "Category 5" Ale
Oxford Hefeweizen
Oxford Raspberry

States Available: CT, DC, DE, FL, GA, IL, IN, KY, MA, ME, MD, NC, NY, OH, OH, PA, RI, VA

Brewer Index (Alphabetical)

Coastal Extreme Brewing Company, LLC

P.O. Box 628
Newport, RI 02840-0006
401-849-5232
www.newportstorm.com/index.asp

BRANDS:
Newport Storm Annual Limited Release
Newport Storm Blizzard Porter (49 SRM, 30 IBU)
Newport Storm Cyclone Series - Derek Stout
Newport Storm Hurricane Amber Ale (16 SRM, 24 IBU)
Newport Storm Maelstrom IPA (13 SRM, 48 IBU)
Newport Storm Regenschauer Oktoberfest (14 SRM, 17 IBU)
Newport Storm Rhode Island Blueberry (9 SRM, 11 IBU)
Newport Storm Thunderhead Irish Red (32 SRM, 31 IBU)

States Available: CT, MA, RI, VA

Coeur d'Alene Brewing Company

209 Lakeside Avenue
Coeur d'Alene, ID 83814
208-664-2739
www.cdabrewing.com

BRANDS:
Coeur d'Alene Brewing Centennial Pale Ale
Coeur d'Alene Brewing Honeymoon Wheat
Coeur d'Alene Brewing Huckleberry Ale
Coeur d'Alene Brewing Lake Side British Ale

States Available: ID

Coffaro Beer Company

5769 N Andrews Way
Fort Lauderdale, FL 33309-2364
732- 261-4888
www.coffarobeer.com

BRANDS:
Coffaro Italian Style Beer

States Available: NJ, NY, PA

Columbus Brewing Company

535 Short Street
Columbus, OH 43215-5614
614-224-3626
www.columbusbrewing.com

BRANDS:
Columbus Brewing 90 Schilling Ale
Columbus Brewing Apricot Ale
Columbus Brewing Ohio Honey Wheat
Columbus Brewing Pale Ale

States Available: Contact Brewery

Concord Brewery, Inc.

199 Cabot Street
Lowell, MA 01854
978-937-1200
www.concordbrew.com

BRANDS:
Concord Grape Ale (16 IBU)
Concord IPA (38 IBU)
Concord North Woods Ale (38 IBU)
Concord Pale Ale (26 IBU)
Concord Porter (32 IBU)
Rapscallion Blessing (36 IBU)
Rapscallion Creation (18 IBU)
Rapscallion Premier (26 IBU)

States Available: MA, RI

Cooper's Cave Ale Company, LTD. – *page 487*

2 Sagamore Street
Glens Falls, NY 12801
518-792-0007
www.cooperscaveale.com

BRANDS:
Cooper's Cave Ale Company Bumppo's Brown Ale
  (35 IBU)
Cooper's Cave Ale Company Pale Ale (55 IBU)
Cooper's Cave Ale Company Pathfinder's Porter (53 IBU)
Cooper's Cave Ale Company Radeau Red Ale (35 IBU) – *page 487*
Cooper's Cave Ale Company Sagamore Stout (30 IBU)
Cooper's Cave Ale Company Tavern Ale (30 IBU)

States Available: NY

BREWER INDEX (Alphabetical)

Cooperstown Brewing Company

110 River Street, P.O. Box 276
Milford, NY 13807
607-286-9330
www.cooperstownbrewing.com

BRANDS:
Cooperstown Brewing Back Yard India Pale Ale
Cooperstown Brewing Benchwarmer Porter
Cooperstown Brewing Nine Man Ale
Cooperstown Brewing Old Slugger Pale Ale
Cooperstown Brewing Pride Of Milford Special Ale
Cooperstown Brewing Strike Out Stout

States Available: CT, MA, NJ, NY, PA, RI

Cottrell Brewing Company

100 Mechanic Street
Pawcatuck, CT 06379
860-599-8213
www.cottrellbrewing.com

BRANDS:
Cottrell Brewing Old Yankee Ale

States Available: CT, RI

Crabtree Brewing Company

625 3rd Street (#D)
Greely, CO 80634
970-356-0516
www.crabtreebrewing.com

BRANDS:
Crabtree Brewing Downtown Nut Brown
Crabtree Brewing Twisted Creek Wheat

States Available: Contact Brewery

Crested Butte Brewery

1600 West Evans Avenue, Suite L
Englewood, CO 80110
720-884-1023
www.cbbrewery.com

BRANDS:
Crested Butte Brewery Paradise Crisp Golden Ale
Crested Butte Brewery Red Lady Ale
Crested Butte Brewery White Buffalo Peace Ale

States Available: CO, WA

Cricket Hill Brewing Company, Inc. – *page 488*

24 Kulick Road
Fairfield, NJ 07004
973-276-9415
www.crickethillbrewery.com

BRANDS:
Cricket Hill Brewing American Ale
Cricket Hill Brewing East Coast Lager – *page 488*
Cricket Hill Brewing Colonel Blides Altbier
Cricket Hill Brewing Hopnotic IPA

States Available: NJ, NY, PA

D.G. Yuengling & Son, Inc. – *page 489*

540 Clover Lane
5TH & Mahantongo Streets
Pottsville, PA 17901
570-622-4141
www.yuengling.com

BRANDS:
Yuengling Black and Tan
Yuengling Dark Brewed Porter
Yuengling Light Beer
Yuengling Light Lager
Yuengling Lord Chesterfield Ale
Yuengling Premium Beer
Yuengling Traditional Lager – *page 489*

States Available: AL, DC, DE, FL, MD, NC, NJ, NY, PA, SC, VA

BREWER INDEX (Alphabetical)

D L Geary Brewing Company

38 Evergreen Drive
Portland, ME 04103-1066
207-878-2337
www.gearybrewing.com

BRANDS:
Geary's Autumn Ale
Geary's Hampshire Special Ale
Geary's London Porter
Geary's Pale Ale
Geary's Summer Ale
Geary's Winter

States Available: CT, MA, MD, ME, MI, NC, NH, NJ, NY, OH, PA, RI, SC, VA, VT

Dark Horse Brewing Company

511 South Kalamazoo Street
Marshall, MI 49068
269-781-9940
www.darkhorsebrewery.com

BRANDS:
Dark Horse 750 ml Imperial Stout
Dark Horse Belgian Amber Ale
Dark Horse Crooked Tree IPA
Dark Horse Double Crooked Tree IPA
Dark Horse Fore Smoked Stout
Dark Horse One Oatmeal Stout Ale
Dark Horse Raspberry Ale
Dark Horse Sapient Trip Ale
Dark Horse Scotty Karate Scotch Ale
Dark Horse Special Reserve Black Bier Ale
Dark Horse Too Cream Stout
Dark Horse Tres Blueberry Stout

States Available: IN, MI

Deschutes Brewery – *page 490*

901 SW Simpson Avenue
Bend, OR 97702
541-385-8606
www.deschutesbrewery.com

BRANDS:
Deschutes Bachelor ESB (50 IBU)
Deschutes Black Butte Porter (30 IBU) – *page 490*
Deschutes Bond Street Brown
Deschutes Broken Top Bock
Deschutes Buzzsaw Brown (30 IBU)
Deschutes Cascade Ale (28 IBU)
Deschutes Cinder Cone Red Ale (55 IBU)
Deschutes Hop Henge India Pale Ale (85 IBU)
Deschutes Hop Trip Pale Ale (35 IBU)
Deschutes Inversion IPA (75 IBU)
Deschutes Jubelale (60 IBU)
Deschutes Mirror Pond Pale Ale (40 IBU)
Deschutes Obsidian Stout (50 IBU)
Deschutes Quail Springs IPA
Deschutes The Abyss
Deschutes Twilight Ale (35 IBU)

States Available: AK, AZ, CA (Northern), CO, HI, ID, MT, NM, NV (Western), OR, WA, WY

Diamond Bear Brewing Company

323C Cross Street
Little Rock, AR 72201
501-708-2739
www.diamondbear.com

BRANDS:
Diamond Bear Honey Weiss (21 IBU)
Diamond Bear Irish Red Ale (31 IBU)
Diamond Bear Pale Ale (33 IBU)
Diamond Bear Party Porter (38 IBU)
Diamond Bear Presidential IPA (57 IBU)
Diamond Bear Rocktoberfest (32 IBU)
Diamond Bear Southern Blonde (28 IBU)
Diamond Bear Ultra Blonde (18 IBU)

States Available: AR, MO

Dick's Brewing Company – *page 491*

540 Clover Lane
5945 Prather Road
Centralla, WA 98531
800-586-7760
www.dicksbeer.com

BRANDS:
Bottleworks India Pale Ale
Dick's Barley Wine Ale
Dick's Belgian Double
Dick's Belgian Tripel
Dick's Best Bitter
Dick's Cream Stout
Dick's Danger Ale – *page 491*
Dick's Double Diamond Winter Ale
Dick's Grand Cru
Dick's Harvest Ale
Dick's Imperial Stout
Dick's India Pale Ale
Dick's Irish Ale
Dick's Lave Rock Porter
Dick's Mountain Ale
Dick's Pale Ale
Dick's Rye Ale
Dick's Silk Lady
Dick's Smoked Porter
Dick's Working Man's Brown Ale

States Available: OR, WA

Dillion DAM Brewery

100 Little Dam Street
Dillon, CO 80435
866-326-6196

BRANDS:
DAM DAM Straight Lager
Dillion DAM Extra Pale Ale
Dillion DAM Olde Forster's Scotch Ale
Dillion DAM Winter Warmer
Sweet George's Brown Ale

States Available: CO

Dixie Brewing Company

2401 Tulane Avenue
New Orleans, LA 70119-7444
504-822-8711

BRANDS:
Dixie Brewing Blackened Voodoo Lager
Dixie Brewing Crimson Voodoo Ale
Dixie Brewing Dixie Beer
Dixie Brewing Jazz Amber Light

States Available: Contact Brewery

Dogfish Head Craft Brewery – *page 492*

6 Cannery Village Center
Milton, DE 19968-1327
888-836-4347
www.dogfish.com

BRANDS:
Dogfish Head 60 Minute IPA (60 IBU) – *page 492*
Dogfish Head 90 Minute Imperial IPA (90 IBU)
Dogfish Head 120 Minute Imperial IPA (120 IBU)
Dogfish Head Aprihop (55 IBU)
Dogfish Head Au Courant
Dogfish Head Black & Blue
Dogfish Head Burton Baton
Dogfish Head Chicory Stout (22 IBU)
Dogfish Head Fort
Dogfish Head Golden Shower Imperial Pilsner (80 IBU)
Dogfish Head Immort Ale (40 IBU)
Dogfish Head Indian Brown Ale (50 IBU)
Dogfish Head Midas Touch Golden Elixir (12 IBU)
Dogfish Head Old School Barleywine
Dogfish Head Punkin Ale (24 IBU)
Dogfish Head Raison D'Etre (25 IBU)
Dogfish Head Red & White
Dogfish Head Shelter Pale Ale (25 IBU)
Dogfish Head Snowblown Ale (33 IBU)
Dogfish Head World Wide Stout (80 IBU)

States Available: AK, AZ, CO, CT, DC, DE, FL, GA, IL, IN, KY, MA, MD, ME, NC, NJ, NY, OH, OR, PA, RI, TN, TX, VA, VT, WA, WI

BREWER INDEX (Alphabetical)

Downtown Brewing Company
1119 Garden Street
San Luis Obispo, CA 93401
805-543-1843
www.slobrews.com

BRANDS:
SLO Brewing Amber Ale
SLO Brewing Blueberry Ale
SLO Brewing Cole Porter
SLO Brewing Extra Pale Ale
SLO Olde Highland Ale

States Available: CA

Dragonmead Microbrewery
14600 East Eleven Mile Road
Warren, MI 48089
586-776-9428
www.dragonmead.com

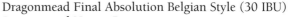

BRANDS:
Dragonmead 90 Shilling
Dragonmead Andromeda Heather Ale
Dragonmead Armageddon Grand Cru
Dragonmead Big Larry's Pale Ale
Dragonmead Bill's Witbier
Dragonmead Bishop Bob's Holy Smoke
Dragonmead Bock Tubock
Dragonmead Breath Of The Dragon English Bitter
Dragonmead Broken Paddle India Pale Ale
Dragonmead Bronze Griffin Belgian Style
Dragonmead Castlebrite Apricot Ale
Dragonmead Copper Shield Bitter Harvest
Dragonmead Corktown Red
Dragonmead Crooked Door Amber Ale
Dragonmead Crown Jewels IPA (57 IBU)
Dragonmead Crusader Dark Mild Ale
Dragonmead Dead Monk Abbey Ale
Dragonmead Dragon Daze Hemp Ale
Dragonmead Dragon Slayer Altbier Style
Dragonmead Drei Kronen 1308
Dragonmead Dubbel Dragon Ale
Dragonmead Earl's Spit Stout
Dragonmead Erik the Red Irish Style Amber Ale (20.5 IBU)
Dragonmead Excalibur Barley Wine

Dragonmead Final Absolution Belgian Style (30 IBU)
Dragonmead Honey Porter
Dragonmead Imperial Stout
Dragonmead Inquisition Pale Ale
Dragonmead Jul 01
Dragonmead Kaiser's Kölsch
Dragonmead Lady Guinevere's Golden Belgian Style
Dragonmead Lancelot's Cream Ale
Dragonmead Larry's Lionheart Pale
Dragonmead Lil's Grumpkin Pumpkin Ale
Dragonmead London Brown Ale
Dragonmead Mariann's Honey Brown
Dragonmead Nagelweiss Wheat
Dragonmead Oktoberfest Marzen
Dragonmead Redwing Raspberry Wheat Beer
Dragonmead Reverend Fred's Oatmeal
Dragonmead Sir William's Extra Special Bitter (43 IBU)
Dragonmead Squire Pilsen
Dragonmead Tafelbeir Lager
Dragonmead Tayken Abock
Dragonmead Tuhelles Enbock
Dragonmead Under The Kilt Wee Heavy (30 IBU)
Dragonmead Wench Water Belgian Pale Ale
Dragonmead Willy's Oompa-Loompa
Dragonmead Woody's Perfect Porter

States Available: MI

Drake's Brewing Company
1933 Davis St Suite 177
San Leandro, CA 94577-1256
510-562-0866
www.drinkdrakes.com

BRANDS:
Drake's Amber Ale
Drake's Blonde Ale
Drake's Hefe-Weizen
Drake's IPA

States Available: CA

Duck-Rabbit Craft Brewery
4519 West Pine Street
Farmville, NC 27828
252-753-7745
www.duckrabbitbrewery.com

BRANDS:
Duck-Rabbit Amber Ale
Duck-Rabbit Baltic Porter (in NC only)
Duck-Rabbit Barleywine Ale (in NC only)
Duck-Rabbit Brown Ale
Duck-Rabbit Milk Stout
Duck-Rabbit Porter
Duck-Rabbit Russian Imperial Stout (in NC only)
Duck-Rabbit Wee Heavy Scotch Style Ale (in NC Only)

States Available: NC, SC, TN

Dunedin Brewery – *page 493*
937 Douglas Avenue
Dunedin, FL 34698
727-736-0606
www.dunedinbrewery.com

BRANDS:
Dunedin Brewery Beach Tale Brown Ale
  (21 SRM, 41 IBU) – *page 493*
Dunedin Brewery Celtic Gold Ale (5 SRM, 25 IBU)
Dunedin Brewery Christmas Farm Ale (11 SRM, 37 IBU)
Dunedin Brewery Drop Kick Monday's Erin Red Ale
Dunedin Brewery Highland Games Ale (20 SRM, 39 IBU)
Dunedin Brewery Leonard Croon's Old Mean Stout
Dunedin Brewery Lowland Wheat Ale (5 SRM, 11.5 IBU)
Dunedin Brewery Oktoberfest Ale (10 SRM, 15 IBU)
Dunedin Brewery Piper's Pale Ale (7 SRM, 37 IBU)
Dunedin Brewery Razzbeery Wheat Ale (7 SRM, 12 IBU)
Dunedin Brewery Redhead Red Ale (11 SRM, 30 IBU)
Dunedin Brewery Summer Apricot Wheat Ale (5 SRM, 11 IBU)
Dunedin Brewery Summer Buzz

States Available: FL

Durango Brewing Company
3000 Main Street
Durango, CO 81301
970-247-3396
www.durangobrewing.com

BRANDS:
Durango Brewing Amber Ale (20 IBU)
Durango Brewing Dark Lager (17 IBU)
Durango Brewing Derail Ale
Durango Brewing Ian's Pale Ale (57 IBU)
Durango Brewing Wheat Beer (10 IBU)

States Available: CO

E.J. Phair Brewing
975-E Detroit Avenue
Concord, CA 94518
925-680-4523
www.ejphair.com

BRANDS:
E.J. Phair India Pale Ale
E.J. Phair Marzen
E.J. Phair Pale Ale
E.J. Phair Pilsner

States Available: CA

Edenton Brewing Company
1249-A Wicker Drive
Raleigh, NC 27604
919-834-0045
www.edentonbrewing.com

BRANDS:
Edenton Brewing Helles Angel
Edenton Brewing Horniblow's Tavern
Edenton Brewing Joseph Hewes
Edenton Brewing King David's Red
Edenton Brewing Uncle Nut's

States Available: NC, PA, VA

BREWER INDEX (Alphabetical)

Eel River Brewing Company

1777 Alamar Way
Fortuna, CA 95540
707-725-2739
www.climaxbeer.com

BRANDS:
Eel River Brewing California Blonde Ale
Eel River Brewing Climax California Classic
Eel River Brewing Organic Amber Ale
Eel River Brewing Organic Extra Pale Ale
Eel River Brewing Organic India Pale Ale
Eel River Brewing Organic Porter
Eel River Brewing Ravensbrau India Pale Ale
Eel River Brewing Ravensbrau Porter

States Available: AL, AZ, CA, FL, ID, MT, NV, OR, WA, WY

El Toro Brewing

17370 Hill Road
Morgan Hill, CA 95037
408-778-2739

BRANDS:
El Toro Bravo
El Toro Deuce Imperial IPA
El Toro IPA
El Toro Keller Bier
El Toro Negro Oatmeal Stout
El Toro Oro Golden Ale
El Toro Peach Ale
El Toro Poppy Jasper Amber Ale
El Toro William Jones Wheat
El Toro "Yo" Winter Brew
Gena's Honey Blonde Ale

States Available: CA, WI

Electric Beer Company

1326 Highway 92 #8, P.O. Box 354
Bisbee, AZ 85603
520-432-5465
www.electricbrewing.com

BRANDS:
Dave's Electric Beer
OK Ale

States Available: Contact Brewery

Ellicottville Brewing Company – *page 494*

28A Monroe Street
Ellicottville, New York 14731
716-699-2537
www.ellicottvillebrewing.com

BRANDS:
Ellicottville Brewing Black Jack Oatmeal Stout
Ellicottville Brewing Blueberry Wheat – *page 494*
Ellicottville Brewing German Red
Ellicottville Brewing Nut Brown
Ellicottville Brewing American Pale Ale
Ellicottville Brewing Toasted Lager

States Available: Contact Brewery

Elmwood Brewing Company

118 East Main Street
Elmwood, IL 61529
309-742-4200
www.elmwoodbrewing.com

BRANDS:
Elmwood Brewing Amber Ale
Elmwood Brewing Dopple Bock
Elmwood Brewing Dry Stout
Elmwood Brewing Dunkle Weizen
Elmwood Brewing Lawnmower
Elmwood Brewing Nut Brown
Elmwood Brewing Oktoberfest
Elmwood Brewing Pale Ale

States Available: Contact Brewery

BREWER INDEX (Alphabetical)

Elysian Brewing Company

1221 East Pike Street
Seattle, WA 98122
206-860-1920
www.elysianbrewing.com

BRANDS:
Ambrosia Maibock
Avatar Jasmine IPA
Bete Blanche Belgian-Style Tripel (31 IBU)
Bifrost Winter Ale (42 IBU)
Dragonstooth Stout (36 IBU)
Elysian Fields Pale Ale (36 IBU)
Immortal India Pale Ale (42 IBU)
Loki Lager
Night Owl Pumpkin Ale
Pandora's Bock
Perseus Porter (25 IBU)
Saison Elysee
The Wise Extra Special Bitter (39 IBU)
Zephyrus Pilsner (38 IBU)

States Available: AK, ID, OR, WA

Empyrean Brewing – *page 495*

729 Q Street
Lincoln, NE 68508
402-434-5959
www.empyreanbrewingco.com

BRANDS:
Empyrean Ales Burning Skye Scottish Ale
  (7 SRM, 13 IBU)
Empyrean Ales Chaco Canyon Honey Gold (5 SRM, 23 IBU)
Empyrean Ales Dark Side Vanilla Porter (75 SRM, 19 IBU)
Empyrean Ales Luna Sea ESB (10 SRM, 31 IBU) – *page 495*
Empyrean Ales Third Stone Brown (18 SRM, 13 IBU)

States Available: NE

English Ales Brewery

223-A Reindollar Avenue
Marina, CA 93933
831-883-3000
www.englishalesbrewery.com

BRANDS:
English Ales Black Hound Stout
English Ales Black Prince Porter
English Ales Brew 66
English Ales Dragon Slayer India Pale Ale
English Ales Edinburgh Winter Ale
English Ales English Pale Ale
English Ales Jubilee Golden Ale
English Ales Monk's Brown Ale
English Ales Monterey Bay Wheat
English Ales Ramsey's Fat Lip Ale
English Ales Triple B (Borthwick's Best Bitter)
English Ales Victory ESB

States Available: CA

Erie Brewing

1213 Veshecco Drive
Erie, PA 16501
814-459-7741
www.eriebrewingco.com

BRANDS:
Erie Brewing Drake's Crude Oatmeal Stout (19 IBU)
Erie Brewing Fallenbock (18 IBU)
Erie Brewing German Wheat (16 IBU)
Erie Brewing Golden Fleece Maibock Lager (21 IBU)
Erie Brewing Heritage Alt (15 IBU)
Erie Brewing Mad Anthony's Ale (13 IBU)
Erie Brewing Presque Isle Pilsner (18 IBU)
Erie Brewing RailBender Ale (26 IBU)
Erie Brewing Red Ryder Big Beer (35 IBU)
Erie Brewing Sunshine Wit (17 IBU)

States Available: NY (Western), OH (Eastern), PA

BREWER INDEX (Alphabetical)

Estes Park Brewery
470 Prospect Drive, P.O. Box 2136
Estes Park, CO 80517
970-586-5421
www.epbrewery.net

BRANDS:
Estes Park Gold
Estes Park Porter
Estes Park Raspberry Wheat
Estes Park Renegade
Estes Park Samson Stout
Estes Park Staggering Elk
Estes Park Stinger Wild Honey Wheat
Estes Park Trail Ridge Red

States Available: CO, KS, SD, WI

Etna Brewing Company
131 Callahan Street
Etna, CA 96027
530-467-5277
www.etnabrew.com

BRANDS:
Etna Classic Gold
Etna Old Grind Porter
Etna Phoenix Red

States Available: Contact Brewery

Falls Brewing Company
782 N. Main Street, P.O. Box 10
Oconte Falls, WI 54154
920-846-4844
www.fallsbrewing.com

BRANDS:
Falls Brewing Falls Dirty Blonde Ale
Falls Brewing Falls Hot Tail Ale
Falls Brewing Falls Nut Brown Ale
Falls Brewing Falls Porter

States Available: WI

Far West Brewing Company
7289 West Lake Sammamish Parkway NE
Redmond, WA 98052
425-883-2432
www.farwestbrewing.com

BRANDS:
Hedgerow Red
Ranger IPA
Three Threads Porter

States Available: WA

Farmhouse Brewing Company
7050 Monterey Street
Gilroy, CA 95020
408-842-1000
www.farmhousebrewing.com

BRANDS:
Farmhouse Hayloft Pils
Farmhouse Kölsch Bier
Farmhouse Oasthouse IPA
Farmhouse Saison 7
Farmhouse Stone Fence Porter
Farmhouse Two Tractor Pale Ale

States Available: Contact Brewery

Firestone Walker Brewing Company
1400 Ramada Drive
Paso Robles, CA 93446
805-238-2556
www.firestonewalker.com

BRANDS:
Firestone Walker Double Barrel Ale (16 SRM, 32 IBU)
Firestone Walker Lager (4 SRM, 24 IBU)
Firestone Walker Pale Ale (7 SRM, 38 IBU)
Firestone Walker Walker's Reserve (75 SRM, 45 IBU)

States Available: CA, NV

BREWER INDEX (Alphabetical)

Fish Brewing Company – *page 496*

515 Jefferson Street SE
Olympia, WA 98501
360-943-3650
www.fishbrewing.com

BRANDS:
Fish Tale Blonde Ale (15 IBU)
Fish Tale Detonator Doppelbock Lager (44 IBU)
Fish Tale Leviathan Barleywine (62 IBU)
Fish Tale Monkfish Belgian-style Triple Ale (32 IBU)
Fish Tale Mudshark Porter (24 IBU)
Fish Tale Old Woody English Old Ale
Fish Tale Organic Amber Ale (22 IBU)
Fish Tale Organic India Pale Ale (53 IBU) – *page 496*
Fish Tale Poseidon's Imperial Stout (79 IBU)
Fish Tale Thornton Creek Ale (45 IBU)
Fish Tale Trout Stout (31 IBU)
Fish Tale Wild Salmon Organic Pale Ale (32 IBU)
Fish Tale Winterfish Ale (70 IBU)
Leavenworth Beers Blind Pig Dunkle Weizen Ale (25 IBU)
Leavenworth Beers Friesian Pilsner (40 IBU)
Leavenworth Beers Hodgson's India Pale Ale (80 IBU)
Leavenworth Beers Ingall's Extra Special Bitter (64IBU)
Leavenworth Beers Nosferatu Red Ale (55 IBU)
Leavenworth Beers Oktoberfest Bier (23 IBU)
Leavenworth Beers Snowblind Winter Warmer
Leavenworth Beers Spring Bock Lager
Leavenworth Beers Whistling Pig Hefeweizen (22 IBU)

States Available: WA

Fletcher Street Brewing Company

124 West Fletcher Street
Alpena, MI 40707
800-848-3221
www.fletcherstreetbrewing.com

BRANDS:
Alpena Wheat Ale
Lumber Lager Red
Paper Maker Light
Paper Maker Pilsner
Pewabic Pale Ale
Sanctuary Stout
Thunder Bay Bock

States Available: MI

Florida Beer Company – *page 497*

725 Silver Palm Avenue
Melbourne, FL 32901
321-728-3412
www.floridabeer.com

BRANDS:
Beachside American Lager
Beachside Porter
Beachside Sun Light
Hurricane Reef Caribbean Pilsner
Hurricane Reef Lager
Hurricane Reef Pale Ale
Hurricane Reef Raspberry Wheat
Key West Golden Lager
Key West Pilsner Light
Key West Sunset Ale – *page 497*
La Tropical
Ybor Gold Amber Lager
Ybor Gold Brown Ale
Ybor Gold Gaspar's Porter
Ybor Gold Light
Ybor Gold Wheat Ale

States Available: AL, FL, GA, NC, NY, VA

BREWER INDEX (Alphabetical)

Flying Bison Brewing Company
491 Ontario Street
Buffalo, NY 14207-1641
716-837-1557
www.flyingbisonbrewing.com

BRANDS:
Flying Bison Brewing Aviator Red
Flying Bison Brewing Barnstormer Pale Ale
Flying Bison Brewing Blackbird Oatmeal Stout
Flying Bison Brewing Buffalo Lager
Flying Bison Brewing Dawn Patrol Gold

States Available: NY (Western)

Flying Dog Brewery, LLC – *page 498*
2401 Blake Street
Denver, CO 80205-2199
303-292-5027
www.flyingdogales.com

BRANDS:
Doggie Style Pale Ale
  (19 SRM, 36 IBU) – *page 498*
Dogtoberfest (20 SRM, 30 IBU)
Heller Hound Mai Bock (9 SRM, 26 IBU)
Horn Dog Barley Wine Style Ale (95 SRM, 45 IBU)
In Heat Wheat (5 SRM, 13 IBU)
K9 Winter Cruiser (35 SRM, 30 IBU)
Old Scratch Amber (21 SRM, 20 IBU)
Road Scottish Porter (38 SRM, 26 IBU)
Snake Dog IPA (11 SRM, 60 IBU)
Tire Bite Golden Ale (4 SRM, 17.5 IBU)
Gonzo Imperial Porter (135 SRM, 80 IBU)
Wild Dog Colorado Saison (8 SRM, 20 IBU)
Wild Dog Weizenbock Ale (25 SRM, 30 IBU)

States Available: AK, AL, AR, AZ, CA, CO, CT, DC, DE, FL, GA, HI, IA, IL, IN,
          KS, KY, LA, MA, MD, ME, MI, MN, MS, NC, ND, NE, NH,
          NJ, NM, NV, NY, OH, OK, OR, PA, SC, TN, TX, VT

Flying Fish Brewing – *page 499*
1940 Olney Avenue
Cherry Hill, NJ 08003
856-489-0061
www.flyingfish.com

BRANDS:
Flying Fish Brewing Belgian Abbey Dubbel
  (21.2 SRM, 38.7 IBU) – *page 499*
Flying Fish Brewing ESB Ale (12.2 SRM, 25.3 IBU)
Flying Fish Brewing Extra Pale Ale (12.2 SRM, 14.4 IBU)
Flying Fish Brewing Farmhouse Summer Ale
Flying Fish Brewing Grand Cru Winter Reserve
Flying Fish Brewing Hopfish (21.2 SRM, 18.8 IBU)
Flying Fish Brewing Imperial Espresso Porter
Flying Fish Brewing Oktoberfish
Flying Fish Brewing Porter

States Available: DC, DE, MD, NJ, PA

Fordham Brewing Company
1284 Mcd Drive
Dover, DE 19901-4639
302-678-4810
www.fordhambrewing.com

BRANDS:
Fordham Brewing C126 Light
Fordham Brewing Copperhead Ale
Fordham Brewing Fordham Lager
Fordham Brewing Oyster Stout
Fordham Brewing Tavern Ale

States Available: DE, MD, NC, NJ, PA, VA

BREWER INDEX (Alphabetical)

Founders Brewing Company

648 Monroe NW
Grand Rapids, MI 49503
616 776-1195
www.foundersbrewing.com

BRANDS:
Founders Brewing Bad Habit Belgium Quad
Founders Brewing Black Rye (64 IBU)
Founders Brewing Blushing Monk
Founders Brewing Breakfast Stout (25 IBU)
Founders Brewing Centennial IPA (46 IBU)
Founders Brewing Curmudgeon Old Ale (50 IBU)
Founders Brewing Devil Dancer Triple IPA (24 IBU)
Founders Brewing Dirty Bastard (50 IBU)
Founders Brewing Imperial Stout (25 IBU)
Founders Brewing Kentucky Breakfast (25 IBU)
Founders Brewing Pale Ale (32 IBU)
Founders Brewing Porter (40 IBU)
Founders Brewing Red's Rye (68 IBU)
Founders Brewing Rubaeus (24 IBU)

States Available: Contact Brewery

Four Peaks Brewing Company – *page 501*

1340 East 8th Street #104
Tempe, AZ 85281
480-303-9967
www.fourpeaks.com

BRANDS:
Four Peaks Arizona Peach
Four Peaks Hefeweizen
Four Peaks Kölsch
Four Peaks Oatmeal Stout
Hopknot IPA
Kiltlifter Scottish-Style Ale – *page 501*
The Raj India Pal Ale
8th Street Ale

States Available: AZ

Four Plus Brewing Company

1722 South Fremont Drive (2375 West)
Salt Lake City, UT 84104
801-467-0909

BRANDS:
Four Plus DUNK'L Amber Wheat (15 SRM, 24 IBU)
Four Plus Monkshine Belgian Style Pale Ale (9 SRM, 19 IBU)
Four Plus PUNK'N Pumpkin Harvest Ale (13 SRM, 118 IBU)
Four Plus WILDFIRE Extra Pale Ale (8 SRM, 41 IBU)

States Available: CA, ID, NV, UT, VA

Franconia Notch Brewing Company

686 Main Street
Bethlehem, NH 03574
603-444-6258
www.4front.com/brewery

BRANDS:
Franconia Notch Brewing Grail Pale Ale
Franconia Notch Brewing River Driver Ale

States Available: MA, NH, RI

Frankenmuth Brewery

425 South Main Street
Frankenmuth, MI 48734
989-652-6183
www.frankenmuthbrewery.com

BRANDS:
Frankenmuth German Style Pilsner
Frankenmuth Hefeweizen
Frankenmuth Irish Dry Stout
Frankenmuth Mel-O-Dry Light Lager
Frankenmuth Mitternacht Munchner Dark Lager
Frankenmuth Oktoberfest
Frankenmuth Old Detroit Amber Ale
Frankenmuth Original Geyer's American Cream Ale
Frankenmuth Pioneer Pale Ale
Frankenmuth Winter Bock

States Available: Contact Brewery

BREWER INDEX (Alphabetical)

Freeport Brewing Company

46 Durham Road
Freeport, ME 04032
207-767-2577

BRANDS:
Brown Hound Brown Ale

States Available: ME

Full Sail Brewing Company – *page 502*

506 Columbia Street
Hood River, OR 97031-2000
541- 386-2247
www.fullsailbrewing.com

BRANDS:
Full Sail Brewing Amber – *page 502*
Full Sail Brewing Holiday Wassail Ale
Full Sail Brewing IPA
Full Sail Brewing Pale Ale
Full Sail Brewing Rip Curl
Full Sail Brewing Session Premium Lager

States Available: AK, AZ, CA, CO, HI, ID, MN, MT, NM, NV, OK, OR, TX, UT, WA, WY

Glacier Brewing – *page 503*

6 Tenth Avenue East
Polson, MT 59860
406-883-2595
www.glacierbrewing.com

BRANDS:
Glacier Brewing Flathead Cherry Ale (3.8 SRM, 12 IBU)
Glacier Brewing Golden Grizzly Ale (5.8 SRM, 14.6 IBU)
Glacier Brewing Northfork Amber Ale (14 SRM, IBU 22.3)
Glacier Brewing Port Polson Pilsner (3.5 SRM, 13.1 IBU)
Glacier Brewing Select Dunkel Hefeweizen (13.4 SRM, 14.3 IBU)
Glacier Brewing Select Oktoberfest (16.2 SRM, 4.4 IBU) – *page 503*
Glacier Brewing Slurry Bomber Stout (44 SRM, 36.6 IBU)
Glacier Brewing St. Arnold's Autumn Ale (19.4 SRM, 47.3 IBU)

States Available: MT (Western)

Gold Hill Brewery

5660 Vineyard Lane
Placerville, CA 95667
530-626-6522
www.goldhillvineyard.com

BRANDS:
Gold Hill 49'er Red
Gold Hill Axe Pic n Stout
Gold Hill Gold Strike Light
Gold Hill Hank's Porter
Gold Hill Old Miners Scotch Ale

States Available: CA

Gluek Brewing Company – *page 504*

219 N Red River Avenue, P.O. Box 476
Cold Spring, MN 56320-0476
320-685-8686
www.gluek.com

BRANDS:
Gluek Brewing Honey Bock
Gluek Brewing Red Bock
Gluek Golden Light
Gluek Ice
Gluek Northern Golden Lager
Gluek Northern Reserve Ice Lager
Gluek Northern Reserve Low Carb Light
Gluek Stite Amber Red Reserve
Gluek Stite Black and Tan
Gluek Stite Golden Lager
Gluek Stite Golden Pilsner – *page 504*
Gluek Stite Light Lager

States Available: MN, WI

BREWER INDEX (Alphabetical)

Golden City Brewery

920 12th Street
Golden, CO 80401-1181
303-279-8092

BRANDS:
Golden City Centurion Barley Wine Ale
Golden City IPA
Golden City Mad Molly Brown Ale
Golden City Oatmeal Stout
Golden City Pale Ale
Golden City Red Ale

States Available: CO

Golden Valley Brewery

980 North East 4th Street
McMinnville, OR 97128
503-472-2739
www.goldenvalleybrewery.com

BRANDS:
Golden Valley American Pale Ale (38 IBU)
Golden Valley Black Panther Imperial Stout (48 IBU)
Golden Valley Chehalem Moutain IPA (55 IBU)
Golden Valley Dundee Porter (26 IBU)
Golden Valley Geist Bock (35 IBU)
Golden Valley Red Hills Pilsner (38 IBU)
Golden Valley Red Thistle Ale (40 IBU)
Golden Valley Tannen Bomb (50 IBU)

States Available: Contact Brewery

Goose Island Beer Company

1800 West Fulton Street
Chicago, IL 60612
312-226-1119
www.gooseisland.com

BRANDS:
Bourbon County Stout (100 SRM, 60 IBU)
Demolition (5 SRM, 55 IBU)
Goose Island 312 Urban Wheat Ale (4 SRM, 15 IBU)
Goose Island Christmas Ale (30 SRM, 55 IBU)
Goose Island Honker's Ale (15 SRM, 32 IBU)
Goose Island India Pale Ale (10 SRM, 58 IBU)
Goose Island Kilgubbin Red Ale (20 SRM, 25 IBU)
Goose Island Nut Brown Ale (50 SRM, 29 IBU)
Goose Island Oatmeal Stout (80 SRM, 30 IBU)
Goose Island Oktoberfest (15 SRM, 25 IBU)
Goose Island Summertime (4 SRM, 25 IBU)
Imperial IPA (12 SRM, 90 IBU)
Matilda (13 SRM, 32 IBU)
Pere Jacques (32 SRM, 26 IBU)

States Available: Contact Brewery

Gordon Biersch Brewery

41 Hugus Alley At One Colorada
Pasadena, CA 91103
626-449-0052
www.gordonbiersch.com

BRANDS:
Gordon Biersch Blonde Bock (23 IBU)
Gordon Biersch Festbier (Restaurants Only)
Gordon Biersch Hefeweizen (12 IBU)
Gordon Biersch Maibock - Lager (Restaurants Only)
Gordon Biersch Marzen (18 IBU)
Gordon Biersch Pilsner (28 IBU)
Gordon Biersch Winter Bock (24 IBU)

States Available: AZ, CA, HI, NV, OH

BREWER INDEX (Alphabetical)

Grand Teton Brewing Company

430 Old Jackson Hole Highway
Victor, ID 83455
888-899-1656
www.grandtetonbrewing.com

BRANDS:
Black Cauldron Imperial Stout
Grand Teton Bitch Creek ESB (51 IBU)
Grand Teton Double IPA
Grand Teton Old Faithful Ale (23 IBU)
Grand Teton Paradise Pilsner
Grand Teton Sweetgrass IPA (58 IBU)
Grand Teton Teton Ale (24 IBU)
Grand Teton Workhorse Wheat (10.4 IBU)

States Available: CA, ID, MT, UT, WY

Gray Brewing

2424 West Court Street
Janesville, WI 53545
608-752-3552
www.graybrewing.com

BRANDS:
Gray's Brewing Black & Tan
Gray's Brewing Honey Ale
Gray's Brewing Oatmeal Stout
Gray's Brewing Pale Ale

States Available: IL, WI

Great Beer Company

21119 Superior Street
Chatsworth, CA 91311-4309
818-718-2739
www.greatbeerco.com
BRANDS:
Great Beer Hollywood Blonde

States Available: CA

Great Divide Brewing Company

2201 Arapahoe Street
Denver, CO 80205
303-296-9460
www.greatdivide.com

BRANDS:
Great Divide Brewing Denver Pale Ale (40 IBU)
Great Divide Brewing Fresh Hop Pale Ale (55 IBU)
Great Divide Brewing Hercules Double IPA (85 IBU)
Great Divide Brewing Hibernation Ale (37 IBU)
Great Divide Brewing HotShot ESB (32 IBU)
Great Divide Brewing Oak Aged Yeti Imperial Stout (75 IBU)
Great Divide Brewing Old Ruffian Barley Wine
Great Divide Brewing Ridgeline Amber (27 IBU)
Great Divide Brewing Saint Bridget's Porter (27.5 IBU)
Great Divide Brewing Samurai
Great Divide Brewing Titan IPA (65 IBU)
Great Divide Brewing Wild Raspberry Ale (21 IBU)
Great Divide Brewing Yeti Imperial Stout (75 IBU)

States Available: AZ, CO, FL, GA, IA, IL, IN, KS, KY, MA, MD, MI, MN, NC, NJ, NY, OH, OK, OR, PA, RI, TN, TX, VA, WA, WI

Great Lakes Brewing Company – *page 505*

2516 Market Avenue
Cleveland, OH 44113
216-771-4404
www.greatlakesbrewing.com
BRANDS:
Great Lakes Brewing Burning River Pale Ale (45 IBU)
Great Lakes Brewing Christmas Ale (40 IBU)
Great Lakes Brewing Commodore Perry India Pale Ale (80 IBU)
Great Lakes Brewing Conway's Irish Ale (25 IBU)
Great Lakes Brewing Dortmunder Golden Lager (30 IBU) – *page 505*
Great Lakes Brewing Edmund Fitzgerald Porter (37 IBU)
Great Lakes Brewing Eliot Ness Amber Lager (35 IBU)
Great Lakes Brewing Holy Moses White Ale (30 IBU)
Great Lakes Brewing Moondog Ale (25 IBU)
Great Lakes Brewing Nosferatu (75 IBU)

States Available: IL, KY, MI, NY, OH, PA, WI, WV

43

BREWER INDEX (Alphabetical)

Great Northern Brewing Company
2 Central Avenue
Whitefish, MT 59937
406-863-1000
www.greatnorthernbrewing.com
BRANDS:
Great Northern Brewing Bear Naked Amber (43 IBU)
Great Northern Brewing Big Fog Amber Lager (43 IBU)
Great Northern Brewing Buckin' Horse Pilsner (32 IBU)
Great Northern Brewing Fred's Black Lager (23 IBU)
Great Northern Brewing Going To The Sun Pale Ale (33 IBU)
Great Northern Brewing Hellroaring Amber Lager (18 IBU)
Great Northern Brewing Snow Ghost (16 IBU)
Great Northern Brewing Snow Ghost Winter Lager (15 IBU)
Great Northern Brewing Wheatfish Hefeweizen (12 IBU)
Great Northern Brewing Wild Huckleberry Wheat Lager (12 IBU)
States Available: ID, MT, WA

Great Sex Brewing, Inc. – *page 506*
12763 Encanto Way
Redding, CA 96003
530-275-2705
www.greatsexbrewing.com
BRANDS:
Great Sex Brewing Adam and Eve Ale – *page 506*
States Available: CA, CO, NV

Green Bay Brewing Company
313 Dousman
Green Bay, WI 54303
920-438-8050
www.hinterlandbeer.com
BRANDS:
Hinterland Pale Ale
States Available: WI

Green Flash Brewing Company
1430 Vantage Court #104a
Vista, CA 92083
760-597-9012
www.greenflashbrew.com
BRANDS:
Green Flash Barleywine
Green Flash Belgian Style Trippel
Green Flash Extra Pale Ale
Green Flash Imperial IPA
Green Flash Nut Brown Ale
Green Flash Ruby Red Ale
Green Flash West Coast IPA
States Available: Contact Brewery

Gritty McDuff's Brewing Company, LLC – *page 507*
396 Fore Street
Portland, ME 04101
207-772-2739
www.grittys.com
BRANDS:
Gritty McDuff's Best Bitter (25 IBU)
Gritty McDuff's Best Brown Ale (16 IBU)
Gritty McDuff's Black Fly Stout (16 IBU)
Gritty McDuff's Christmas Ale (28.5 IBU)
Gritty McDuff's Halloween Ale
Gritty McDuff's Original Pub Style Ale (20 IBU) – *page 507*
Gritty McDuff's Scottish Ale (25 IBU)
Gritty McDuff's Vacationland Summer Ale (22 IBU)
States Available: MA, ME, NH, NJ, NY, VT

BREWER INDEX (Alphabetical)

Hair of the Dog Brewing Company

4509 SE 23rd Avenue
Portland, OR 97202-4771
503-232-6585
www.hairofthedog.com

BRANDS:
Hair of the Dog Brewing Adam (50 IBU)
Hair of the Dog Brewing Doggie Claws (70 IBU)
Hair of the Dog Brewing Fred (65 IBU)
Hair of the Dog Brewing Rose (17 IBU)
Hair of the Dog Brewing Ruth

States Available: CA, NY, OR, WA

Hale's Ales

4301 Leary Way NW
Seattle, WA 98107
206-706-1544
www.halesales.com

BRANDS:
Hale's Cream Ale
Hale's Cream H.S.B.
Hale's Cream Stout
Hale's Drawbridge Blonde
Hale's Irish Style Nut Brown Ale
Hale's Mongoose IPA
Hale's O'Brien's Harvest Ale
Hale's Pale American Ale
Hale's Red Menance Big Amber
Hale's Troll Porter
Hale's Wee Heavy Winter Ale

States Available: Contact Brewery

Happy Valley Brewing Company

6452 Happy Valley Road
Somerset, CA 95684
530-644-4733
www.happyvalleybrewing.com

BRANDS:
Happy Valley Brewing Mission Ale Double
Happy Valley Brewing Mission Ale Wit

States Available: CA

Harbor City Brewing, Inc.

535 W Grand Avenue
Port Washington, WI 53074-2102
262-284-3118

BRANDS:
Harbor City Brewing Full Tilt IPA
Harbor City Brewing Harvest Wheat
Harbor City Brewing Main Street Brown Ale
Harbor City Brewing Mile Rock Amber Ale
Harbor City Brewing Raspberry Brown Ale

States Available: Contact Brewery

Harlem Brewing Company

360 West 125th Street
New York, NY 10027
888-559-6735
www.harlembrewingcompany.com

BRANDS:
Sugar Hill Golden Ale

States Available: Contact Brewery

Harpoon Brewery – *page 508*

306 Northern Avenue
Boston, MA 02210
617-574-9551
www.harpoonbrewery.com

BRANDS:
Harpoon 100 BBL Series
Harpoon Ale (24 IBU)
Harpoon Brown Ale
Harpoon Hibernian Ale (25 IBU)
Harpoon IPA (42 IBU) – *page 508*
Harpoon Munich Dark (35 IBU)
Harpoon Octoberfest (30 IBU)
Harpoon Summer (28 IBU)
Harpoon UFO Hefeweizen (19 IBU)
Harpoon UFO Raspberry Hefeweizen (12 IBU)
Harpoon Winter Warmer (22 IBU)

States Available: CT, DC, DE, FL, GA, IN, KY, MA, MD, ME, MI, NC, NH, NJ, NY, OH, PA, RI, SC, TN, VA, VT, WV

BREWER INDEX (Alphabetical)

Healthy Brew
6435 Nine Mile Bridge Road
Fort Worth, TX 76135
817-238-1334
www.healthybrew.com

BRANDS:
Healthy Brew 1-Day IPA
Healthy Brew Easy Amber
Healthy Brew Snowman's Revenge
Healthy Brew Strong Stout
Healthy Brew Wheat Serenity

States Available: Contact Brewery

Heiner Brau
P.O. 4238, 226 East Lockwood Street
Covington, LA 70434-4238
985-893-2884
www.heinerbrau.net

BRANDS:
Heiner Brau Hefe Weisse
Heiner Brau Kellerbier
Heiner Brau Kölsch
Heiner Brau Maerzen
Heiner Brau Maibock
Heiner Brau Mardi Gras Festbier
Heiner Brau Octoberfest Bier
Heiner Weihnachtsbock

States Available: Contact Brewery

Heinzelmannchen Brewery (Kegs/Growlers)
545 Mill Street, P.O. Box 2075
Sylva, NC 28779
828-631-4466
www.yourgnometownbrewery.com

BRANDS:
Heinzelmannchen Ancient Days Honey
Blonde Ale
Heinzelmannchen Black Forest Stout
Heinzelmannchen Gopher Ale
Heinzelmannchen Kilted Gnome Scottish Ale
Heinzelmannchen Middleworld Brown Ale
Heinzelmannchen Oktoberfest
Heinzelmannchen Weise Gnome Hefeweizen Style Ale

States Available: NC

Helmar Brewing Company
87 Oakdale Boulevard
Pleasant Ridge, MI 48069
248-882-0834
www.helmarbrewing.com

BRANDS:
Helmar Big League Brew

States Available: Contact Brewery

High & Mighty Brewing Company
108 Cabot Street
Holyoke, MA 01040
www.highandmigtybrewing.com

BRANDS:
High & Mighty Brewing Beer of the Gods
High & Mighty Brewing Two-Headed Beast
High & Mighty Brewing XPA

States Available: Contact Brewery

BREWER INDEX (Alphabetical)

High Falls Brewing

445 St. Paul Street
Rochester, NY 14605
585-263-9446
www.highfalls.com

BRANDS:
Genesee Beer
Genesee Cream Ale
Genesee Ice
Genesee NA
Genesee Red Lager
Genny Light
JW DunDee's American Amber Lager
JW DunDee's American Pale Ale
JW DunDee's Honey Brown Lager
Michael Shea's Irish Amber
Steinlager

States Available: AL, AR, AZ, CO, CT, DE, FL, GA, IL, IN, KS, KY, LA, MA, MD, ME, MI, MN, MO, NC, NE, NH, NJ, NM, NV, NY, OH, OK, OR, PA, RI, SC, TN, TX, VA, VT, WA, WI

High Point Wheat Beer Company

22 Park Place
Butler, NJ 07405
973-838-7400
www.ramsteinbeer.com

BRANDS:
Ramstein Blonde Wheat (8 SRM, 12.5 IBU)
Ramstein Classic Wheat Beer (60 SRM, 12.5 IBU)
Ramstein Golden Lager (6 SRM, 22 IBU)
Ramstein Maibock Lager Beer (37 IBU)
Ramstein Munich Amber Lager
Ramstein Winter Wheat ((70 SRM, 20 IBU)

States Available: NJ, NY, PA

Highland Brewing

42 Biltmore Avenue, P.O. Box 2351
Asheville, NC 28802
828-255-8240
www.highlandbrewing.com

BRANDS:
Highland Brewing Black Mocha Stout (25 IBU)
Highland Brewing Cold Mountain Winter Ale
Highland Brewing Gaelic Ale (32 IBU)
Highland Brewing Kashmir IPA (60 IBU)
Highland Brewing Oatmeal Porter (32 IBU)
Highland Brewing St. Terese's Pale Ale (24 IBU)
Highland Brewing Tasgall Ale (27 IBU)

States Available: GA, NC, SC, TN

Hood Canal Brewing

26499 Bond Road North East
Kingston, WA 98346
360-267-8316
www.hoodcanalbrewery.com

BRANDS:
Hood Canal Brewing Agate Pass Amber
Hood Canal Brewing Big Beef Oatmeal Stout
Hood Canal Brewing Dabob Bay India Pale Ale
Hood Canal Brewing Dosewallipps Special Ale
Hood Canal Brewing Southpoint Porter

States Available: Contact brewery

Hoppy Brewing Company

6300 Folsom Boulevard
Sacramento, CA 95819
916-451-6328
www.hoppy.com

BRANDS:
Hoppy Claus Holiday Ale
Hoppy Face Amber Ale
Liquid Sunshine Blonde Ale
Stony Face Red Ale
Total Eclipse Black Ale

States Available: CA

BREWER INDEX (Alphabetical)

Hoptown Brewery

3015 Hopyard Road, Suite D
Pleasanton, CA 94588-5253
925-426-5665
www.hoptownbrewing.com

BRANDS:

Hoptown Brown Nose Ale
Hoptown DUIPA Imperial Ale
Hoptown ESB
Hoptown Golden Ale
Hoptown IPA
Hoptown Old Yeltsin
Hoptown Paint the Town Red (25 IBU)
Hoptown Paleface Pale Ale
Hoptown Wheathopper Red Wheat Ale

States Available: CA

Hornpout Brewing

1713 Industrial Parkway #106
Lyndonville, VT 05851
802-748-2198

BRANDS:

Hornpout No Limit Amber Ale
Hornpout Pale Ale

States Available: Contact Brewery

Huebert Brewing

421 SW 26th Street
Oklahoma City, OK 73109
405-634-6528
http://groups.msn.com/HuebertBrewingCompany

BRANDS:

Huebert Brewing Huebert's Old Tyme Lager

States Available: OK

Ice Harbor Brewing Company

206 North Benton Street
Kennewick, WA 99336-3665
509-582-5340
www.iceharbor.com

BRANDS:

Ice Harbor Brewing Barley Wine Style Ale (84 IBU)
Ice Harbor Brewing Columbia Kölsch
Ice Harbor Brewing Harvest Pale Ale (40 IBU)
Ice Harbor Brewing Runaway Red Ale (25 IBU)
Ice Harbor Brewing Sternwheeler Stout (30 IBU)

States Available: OR, WA

Independence Brewing

3913 Todd Lane #607
Austin, TX 78744
512-797-7879
www.independencebrewing.com

BRANDS:

Independence Brewing Bootlegger Brown Ale (14 IBU)
Independence Brewing Freestyle Wheat Beer (15 IBU)
Independence Brewing Jasperilla Old Ale (29 IBU)
Independence Brewing Pale Ale (39 IBU)

States Available: TX

BREWER INDEX (Alphabetical)

Indian Wells Brewing

2565 North Highway 14
Inyokern, CA 93527
760-377-5989
www.mojave-red.com

BRANDS:
Indian Wells Desert Pale Ale
Indian Wells Eastern Sierra Lager
Indian Wells Irish Green Ale
Indian Wells Lobotomy Bock
Indian Wells Mojave Gold
Indian Wells Mojave Red
Indian Wells Mojave Silver
Indian Wells Oktoberfest
Indian Wells Orange Blossom Amber
Indian Wells Piute Stout
Indian Wells Raspberry Ale
Indian Wells Sidewinder Missile Ale
Indian Wells Springfest Lager
Indian Wells Vette's Honey Ale

States Available: Contact Brewery

Iron Horse Brewery

1000 Prospect Street, Suite 4
Ellensburg, WA 98926
509-933-3134
www.iron-horse-brewery.com

BRANDS:
Iron Horse Brown Ale
Iron Horse India Pale Ale
Iron Horse Loco-Motive Ale
Iron Horse Rodeo Extra Pale Ale

States Available: WA

Island Brewing Company

5049 Sixth Street
Carpinteria, CA 93013
805-745-8272
www.islandbrewingcompany.com

BRANDS:
Island Brewing Avocado Ale
Island Brewing Blonde (25 IBU)
Island Brewing Island Pale Ale (60 IBU)
Island Brewing Jubilee Ale (30 IBU)
Island Brewing London Porter (35 IBU)
Island Brewing Nut Brown Ale (25 IBU)
Island Brewing Paradise Pale Ale (35 IBU)
Island Brewing Starry Night Stout (50 IBU)
Island Brewing Tropical Lager
Island Brewing Weiss (15 IBU)

States Available: CA

Ithaca Beer Company, Inc.

600 Elmira Road
Ithaca, NY 14850-8745
607-273-0766
www.ithacabeer.com

BRANDS:
Ithaca Beer Company Apricot Wheat
Ithaca Beer Company CascaZilla
Ithaca Beer Company Double IPA
Ithaca Beer Company Finger Lakes Stout
Ithaca Beer Company Flower Power India Pale Ale
Ithaca Beer Company Nut Brown
Ithaca Beer Company Pale Ale
Ithaca Beer Company Partly Sunny
Ithaca Beer Company Winterizer
Ithaca Beer Gorges Smoked Porter

States Available: NY

BREWER INDEX (Alphabetical)

Jack Russell Brewing

2380 Larson Drive
Camino, CA 95709
530-644-4722
www.jackrussellbrewing.com

BRANDS:
Captain Boomer's IPA
Jack Russell's All American Premium Lager
Jack Russell's Harvest Apple Ale
Jack's Best Bitter Ale
Jack's Blackberry Abbey Ale
Jack's Blueberry Beer
Jack's Brown Ale
Jack's Farmhouse Ale
Jack's Huntsmans Lager
Jack's Irish Red Ale
Jack's London Porter
Jack's Olde Ale
Jack's Raspberry Imperial Stout
Jack's Scottish Ale
Jack's Whitewater Pale Ale

States Available: CA

Jacob Leinenkugel Brewing Company

124 East Elm Street, P O Box 337
Chippewa Falls, WI 54729-0337
888-534-6437
www.leinie.com

BRANDS:
Leinenkugel's Apple Spice
Leinenkugel's Berry Weiss
Leinenkugel's Big Butt Doppelbock
Leinenkugel's Creamy Dark
Leinenkugel's Honey Weiss
Leinenkugel's Light
Leinenkugel's Oktoberfest
Leinenkugel's Original
Leinenkugel's Red Lager
Leinenkugel's Sunset Wheat

States Available: CO, IA, IL, IN, KS, KY, MI, MN, MO, ND, NE, OH, OK, SD, WI, WV

JACOB LEINENKUGEL BREWING COMPANY

James Page Brewing Company, LLC

2617 Water Street
Stevens Point, WI 54481
715-344-9310
www.pagebrewing.com

BRANDS:
James Page Brewing Burly Brown Ale
James Page Brewing Iron Ranger Amber Lager
James Page Brewing Voyageur Extra Pale Ale

States Available: IL, MN, WI

Jolly Pumpkin Artisan Ales

3115 Broad Street
Dexter, MI 48130
734-426-4962
www.jollypumpkin.com

BRANDS:
Jolly Pumpkin Bam Biere
Jolly Pumpkin Biere de Mars
Jolly Pumpkin Calabaza Blanca
Jolly Pumpkin Fuego del Otono "Autumn Fire"
Jolly Pumpkin La Roja
Jolly Pumpkin Luciernaga "The Firefly"
Jolly Pumpkin Madrugada Obscura "Dark Dawn"
Jolly Pumpkin Maracaibo Especial
Jolly Pumpkin Oro de Calabaza

States Available: AK, CA, FL, GA, IL, IN, ME, MI, NY, OH, WI

BREWER INDEX (Alphabetical)

Jones Brewing Company

254 Second Street, P.O. Box 746
Smithton, PA 15479
724-872-6626
www.stoneysbeer.com

BRANDS:
Esquire Extra Premium
Stoney's Beer
Stoney's Black And Tan
Stoney's Harvest Gold
Stoney's Light

States Available: Contact Brewery

Joseph Huber Brewing Company, Inc.

1208 14th Avenue
Monroe, WI 53566-0277
608-325-3191
www.huberbrewery.com

BRANDS:
Berghoff Classic Pilsner (10 IBU)
Berghoff Famous Bock Beer (24 IBU)
Berghoff Famous Red Ale (21 IBU)
Berghoff Genuine Dark Beer (21 IBU)
Berghoff Hazelnut Winterfest Ale (20 IBU)
Berghoff Hefe-Weizen (14 IBU)
Berghoff Oktoberfest Beer (21 IBU)
Berghoff Original Lager Beer (20 IBU)
Berghoff Pale Ale (43 IBU)
Berghoff Solstice Wit Beer (11 IBU)

States Available: WI

Karl Strauss Breweries – *page 509*

1044 Wall Street
La Jolla, CA 92037
858-551-2739
www.karlstrauss.com

BRANDS:
Karl Strauss Brewing Amber Lager
 (15 SRM, 15 IBU) – *page 509*
Karl Strauss Brewing Endless Summer Light (6 SRM, 15 IBU)
Karl Strauss Brewing Oktoberfest (9 SRM, 27 IBU)
Karl Strauss Brewing Red Trolley Ale (30 SRM, 17 IBU)
Karl Strauss Brewing Stargazer IPA (14 SRM, 40 IBU)
Karl Strauss Brewing Woodie Gold (5 SRM, 18 IBU)

States Available: Southern CA

Keegan Ales

20 Saint James Street
Kingston, NY 12401
845-331-BREW
www.keeganales.com

BRANDS:
Keegan Ales Hurricane Kitty (8.9 SRM, 69.9 IBU)
Keegan Ales Mother's Milk (29.7 SRM, 25.4 IBU)
Keegan Ales Old Capital (3.5 SRM, 11.1 INU)

States Available: NY

Kelley Brothers Brewing Company

112 East Yosemite Avenue
Manteca, CA 95336
209-825-1727
www.kelleybrewing.com

BRANDS:
Kelley Brothers Four Towers IPA
Kelley Brothers Inferno Red

States Available: CA

BREWER INDEX (Alphabetical)

Keoki Brewing Company
2976 Aukele Street, B-7
Linhue, HI 96766
808-245-8884
www.keokibrewing.com
BRANDS:
Keoki Gold
Keoki Sunset

States Available: HI

Kettle House Brewing Company
602 Myrtle Street
Missoula, MT 59801
406-728-1660
www.kettlehouse.com
BRANDS:
Double Haul IPA

States Available: MT

Keweenaw Brewing Company
408 Shelden Avenue
Houghton, MI 49931
906-482-5596
www.keweenawbrewing.com
BRANDS:
Keweenaw Brewing Coal Porter
Keweenaw Brewing Empress Hefeweizen
Keweenaw Brewing Hilde's Brown Ale
Keweenaw Brewing Magnum Pale Ale
Keweenaw Brewing Pickaxe Blonde Ale
Keweenaw Brewing R.A.M. Stout
Keweenaw Brewing Red Jacket Amber Ale

States Available: MI

King Brewing Company
985 Oakland Avenue
Pontiac, MI 48340
248-745-5900
www.kingbrewing.com
BRANDS:
King Annihilater Doppel Bock
King Big Red
King Cherry Ale
King Continental Lager
King Crown Brown Ale
King Festbier
King Hefeweizen
King IPA
King Irish Red Ale
King King's Gold
King Loranger Lager
King Mocha Java Stout
King Pale Ale
King Pontiac Porter
King Red Ox Amber Ale
King Royal Amber
King Two Fisted Old Ale

States Available: Contact Brewery

Kodiak Island Brewing Company (Kegs/Growlers)
338 Shelikof
Kodiak, AK 99615
907-486-2537
www.kodiakbrewery.com
BRANDS:
Kodiak Island Cloud Peak Hefeweizen
Kodiak Island Island Fog Barley Wine
Kodiak Island Liquid Sunshine
Kodiak Island Night Watch Porter
Kodiak Island North Pacific Ale
Kodiak Island Sweet Georgia Brown

States Available: AK

BREWER INDEX (Alphabetical)

Kona Brewing LLC

75-5629 Kuakini Highway
Kailua-Kona, HI 96740
808-334-1133
www.konabrewingco.com

BRANDS:
Kona Brewing Big Wave Golden Ale
 (8 SRM, 20 IBU)
Kona Brewing Fire Rock Pale Ale (14 SRM, 36 IBU)
Kona Brewing Longboard Island Lager (6 SRM, 25 IBU)
Kona Brewing Pipeline Porter (85 SRM, 30 IBU)

States Available: AK, AZ, CA, FL, HI (Big Wave HI Only), ID, KY, MT, NJ,
        NM, NY, OR, UT, WA, WY

LaConner Brewing Company

117 South First Street
LaConner, WA 98257
360-466-1415

BRANDS:
Skagit Sculler's IPA

States Available: Contact Brewery

Lagunitas Brewing

1280 North McDowell Boulevard
Petaluma, CA 94954
707-769-4495
www.lagunitas.com

BRANDS:
Lagunitas Brewing Brown Shugga
Lagunitas Brewing Cappuccino Stout
Lagunitas Brewing Czech Style Pilsner
Lagunitas Brewing Dogtown Pale Ale
Lagunitas Brewing Imperial Red Ale
Lagunitas Brewing Imperial Stout
Lagunitas Brewing India Pale Ale
Lagunitas Brewing IPA Maximus
Lagunitas Brewing Number 10 Ale
Lagunitas Brewing Olde GnarlyWine
Lagunitas Brewing The Censored Rich Copper Ale

States Available: AZ, CA, CO, DC, ID, MA, NV, NY, OR, TX, VA, WA

Lake Louie Brewing, LLC

7556 Pine Road
Arena, WI 53503
608-753-2675
www.lakelouie.com

BRANDS:
Lake Louie Brewing Arena Premium
Lake Louie Brewing Brother Tim Tripel
Lake Louie Brewing Coon Rock Cream Ale
Lake Louie Brewing Dino's Dark
Lake Louie Brewing Milk Stout
Lake Louie Brewing Prairie Moon Belgian Style Farmhouse Ale
Lake Louie Brewing Tommy's Porter
Lake Louie Brewing Warped Speed Scotch Ale

States Available: WI

Lake Placid Craft Brewing

1472 Military Turnpike
Plattsburgh, NY 12901
518-563-3340
www.ubuale.com

BRANDS:
Lake Placid Craft Brewing 46'er India Pale Ale
Lake Placid Craft Brewing Barkeater Amber Ale
Lake Placid Craft Brewing Moose Island Ale
Lake Placid Craft Brewing Ubu Ale

States Available: MA, NJ, NY, PA, RI, VT

BREWER INDEX (Alphabetical)

Lake Superior Brewing Company

2711 West Superior Street
Duluth, MN 55806
218-723-4000
www.lakesuperiorbrewing.com

BRANDS:
Lake Superior Brewing 7 Bridges Brown
Lake Superior Brewing Kayak Kölsch
Lake Superior Brewing Mesabi Red
Lake Superior Brewing Oktoberfest
Lake Superior Brewing Old Man Winter Warmer
Lake Superior Brewing Sir Duluth Oatmeal Stout
Lake Superior Brewing Special Ale
Lake Superior Brewing Split Rock Bock
Lake Superior Brewing St. Louis Bay IPA
Lake Superior Brewing Windward Wheat

States Available: MN, WI

Lakefront Brewery, Inc.

1872 N Commerce Street
Milwaukee, WI 53212-3701
414-372-8800
www.lakefrontbrewery.com

BRANDS:
Lakefront Big Easy Beer (6 SRM, 24 IBU)
Lakefront Bock Beer (18 SRM, 24 IBU)
Lakefront Cattail Ale (5 SRM, 15 IBU)
Lakefront Cherry Lager (10 SRM, 12 IBU)
Lakefront Cream City Pale Ale (14 SRM, 40 IBU)
Lakefront Eastside Dark (22 SRM, 15 IBU)
Lakefront Fuel Café Stout (45 SRM, 20 IBU)
Lakefront Holiday Spice Lager Beer (12 SRM, 14 IBU)
Lakefront Klisch Pilsner (4 SRM, 32 IBU)
Lakefront New Grist (2 SRM, 8 IBU)
Lakefront Oktoberfest (10 SRM, 24 IBU)
Lakefront Organic ESB (12 SRM, 36 IBU)
Lakefront Pumpkin Lager (12 SRM, 12 IBU)
Lakefront Riverwest Stein (15 SRM, 36 IBU)
Lakefront Snake Chaser Stout (55 SRM, 26 IBU)
Lakefront White Beer (3 SRM, 15 IBU)

States Available: CA, CO, CT, FL, IL, IN, MD, MI, MN, NC, NV, NY, OH, RI, TN, VA, WA, WI

Lancaster Brewing Company

302-304 North Plum Street
Lancaster, PA 17602
717-391-6258
www.lancasterbrewing.com

BRANDS:
Lancaster Brewing Amish Four Grain Pale Ale (28 IBU)
Lancaster Brewing Doppel Bock
Lancaster Brewing Franklinfest Lager 17 IBU)
Lancaster Brewing Gold Star Pilsner (33 IBU)
Lancaster Brewing Hop Hog IPA (55 IBU)
Lancaster Brewing Milk Stout (22 IBU)
Lancaster Brewing Oktoberfest
Lancaster Brewing Spring Bock
Lancaster Brewing Strawberry Wheat (16 IBU)
Lancaster Brewing Winter Warmer

States Available: MD, NJ, PA, VA

BREWER INDEX (Alphabetical)

Landmark Beer Company – *page 510*

3650 James Street, Room 105
Syracuse, NY 13206
315-720-2013
www.landmarkbrewing.com

BRANDS:
Landmark Colonel Hops Red Ale
Landmark India Pale Ale
Landmark Vanilla Bean Brown Ale – *page 510*

States Available: NY

Lang Creek Brewery – *page 511*

655 Lang Creek Road
Marion, MT 59925
406-858-2200
www.langcreekbrewery.com

BRANDS:
Lang Creek Huckleberry N' Honey (8 IBU)
Lang Creek Taildragger Honey Wheat (8 IBU)
Lang Creek Tri-Motor Amber (26 IBU) – *page 511*
Lang Creek Windsock Pale Ale (27 IBU)

States Available: ID, MT, OR, WA

LANG CREEK BREWERY
MARION, MONTANA
AMERICA'S MOST REMOTE BREWERY

Latrobe Brewing

119 Jefferson St
Latrobe, PA 15650-1474
724-539-3394
www.rollingrock.com

BRANDS:
Latrobe Pilsner
Old German

States Available: Contact Brewery

Left Coast Brewing

1245 Puerta Del Sol
San Clemente, CA 92673
949-481-0731
www.leftcoastbrewing.com

BRANDS:
Left Coast Gold
Left Coast Hefeweizen
Left Coast India Pale Ale
Left Coast Pale Ale

States Available: Southern CA

Left Hand Brewing Company – *page 512*

1265 Boston Avenue
Longmont, CO 80501
303-772-0258
www.lefthandbrewing.com

BRANDS:
Left Hand Brewing Black Jack Porter (27 IBU)
Left Hand Brewing Chainsaw Ale (55 IBU)
Left Hand Brewing Deep Cover Brown (20 IBU)
Left Hand Brewing Goosinator (27 IBU)
Left Hand Brewing Haystack Wheat (14 IB)
Left Hand Brewing Imperial Stout (65 IBU)
Left Hand Brewing Jackman's Pale Ale (42 IBU)
Left Hand Brewing JuJu Ginger Ale (17 IBU)
Left Hand Brewing Milk Stout (22 IBU) – *page 512*
Left Hand Brewing Polestar Pilsner (33 IBU)
Left Hand Brewing Ryebock Lager (17 IBU)
Left Hand Brewing Sawtooth Ale (27 IBU)
Left Hand Brewing Smokejumper Imperial Porter (67 IBU)
Left Hand Brewing Snowbound Ale (16 IBU)
Left Hand Brewing St. Vrain Ale (20 IBU)
Left Hand Brewing Twin Sisters (87 IBU)
Left Hand Brewing Warrior IPA (60 IBU)
Left Hand Brewing Widdershins Barleywine (70 IBU)

States Available: AL, AZ, CO, FL, GA, IA, IL, IN, KY, MA, MN, NC, NJ, NM, OH, OK, PA, TN, TX, VA, WI

BREWER INDEX (Alphabetical)

Legacy Brewing Company

545 Canal Street
Reading, PA 19602
610-376-9996

BRANDS:
Legacy Brewing Hedonism Red Ale (110 IBU)
Legacy Brewing Midnight Wit Ale (17 IBU)

States Available: NJ, PA

Legend Brewing Company

321 W Seventh Street
Richmond, VA 23224-2307
804-232-8871
www.legendbrewing.com

BRANDS:
Legend Brewing Brown Ale
Legend Brewing Golden IPA (35 IBU)
Legend Brewing Lager
Legend Brewing Legend Oktoberfest (25 IBU)
Legend Brewing Legend Pale Ale
Legend Brewing Pilsner (40 IBU)
Legend Brewing Porter

States Available: VA

Lewis & Clark Brewing

939 Getchell Street
Helena, MT 59601
406-442-5960
www.lewisandclarkbrewing.com

BRANDS:
Lewis & Clark Back Country Scottish Ale
Lewis & Clark Lager
Lewis & Clark Miner's Gold Hefe-Weizen
Lewis & Clark Tumbleweed IPA
Yellowstone Beer

States Available: MT

The Lion Brewery, Inc. – *page 561*

700 North Pennsylvania Avenue
Wilkes Barre, PA 18705
570-823-8662
www.lionbrewery.com

BRANDS:
Lion Brewing Pocono Black & Tan
Lion Brewing Pocono Caramel Porter
Lion Brewing Pocono Lager
Lion Brewing Pocono Light
Lion Brewing Pocono Pale Ale
Lion Brewing Pocono Summer Wheat
Lionshead
Lionshead Malt Liquor
Stegmaier 1857 American Lager
Stegmaier Brewhouse Bock – *page 561*
Stegmaier Gold Medal
Stegmaier Oktoberfest
Stegmaier Porter

States Available: CT, DE, NJ, NY, PA

The Long Trail Brewing Company – *page 513*

Jct. Route 4 & 100A, P.O. Box 168
Bridgewater Corners, VT 05035-0168
802-672-5011
www.longtrail.com

BRANDS:
Blackberry Wheat (8 IBU) – *page 514*
Brewmasters Limited Edition Series – Unfiltered IPA
  (56 IBU) – *page 514*
Double Bag (25 IBU)
Harvest (24 IBU) – *page 515*
Hefeweizen (14 IBU) – *page 515*
Hibernator (25 IBU) – *page 516*
Hit the Trail (25 IBU)
Long Trail Ale (30 IBU) – *page 513*
Traditional IPA (56 IBU) – *page 516*

States Available: CT, MA, ME, NH, NJ, NY, RI, VT

BREWER INDEX (Alphabetical)

Lost Coast Brewery & Café – *page 517*

617 4th Street
Eureka, CA 95501-1013
707-445-4480
www.lostcoast.com

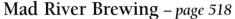

BRANDS:
Lost Coast 8 Ball Stout (48 IBU)
Lost Coast Alleycat Amber (35 IBU)
Lost Coast Downtown Brown (33 IBU)
Lost Coast Great White (27 IBU) – *page 517*
Lost Coast Indica IPA (62 IBU)
Lost Coast Raspberry Brown
Lost Coast Winterbraun (45 IBU)

States Available: AZ, CA, FL, IA, ID, IN, KS, NC, NM, NV, NY, OR, PA, TN, VA, WA, WI

MacTarnahan's Brewing Company

2730 NW 31st Avenue
Portland, OR 97210
503-226-7623
www.macsbeer.com

BRANDS:
MacTarnahan's Brewing Blackwatch Cream Porter
MacTarnahan's Brewing Mac's Amber Ale (30 IBU)
MacTarnahan's Oregon Honey Beer (16 IBU)

States Available: AK, AK, AR, CA, CO, DC, HI, IA, ID, IL, IN, KS, MI, MN, MO, MT, NE, NJ, NV, OH, OR, OR, PA, SC, SC, TN, TX, VA, VT, WA, WI

Mad Anthony Brewing Company

2002 Broadway
Ft. Wayne, IN 46802
219-426-2537
www.madbrew.com

BRANDS:
Mad Anthony Auburn Lager
Mad Anthony Gabby Blonde Lager
Mad Anthony Old Fort Porter
Mad Anthony Pale Ale

States Available: IN

Mad River Brewing – *page 518*

P.O. Box 767, 193 Taylor Way
Blue Lake, CA 95525
707-668-4151
www.madriverbrewing.com

BRANDS:
Mad River Jamaica Red (42 IBU)
Mad River Jamaica Sunset West Indies Pale Ale (65 IBU)
Mad River John Barleycorn Barleywine Style Ale (96 IBU)
Mad River Steelhead Extra Pale Ale (24.6 IBU) – *page 518*
Mad River Steelhead Extra Stout (32.7 IBU)
Mad River Steelhead Scotch Porter (39.1 IBU)

States Available: AZ, CA, CO, FL, ID, NC, NV, OR, PA, VA, WI

Madison River Brewing Company

20900 Frontage Road, Building B
Belgrade, MT 59714
406-388-0322
www.madisonriverbrewing.com

BRANDS:
Copper John Scotch Ale
Irresistible E.S.B.
Salmon Fly Honey Rye
Hopper Pale Ale

States Available: Contact Brewery

Brewer Index (Alphabetical)

Magic Hat Brewing Company

5 Bartlett Bay Road
South Burlington, VT 05403-7727
802-658-2739
www.magichat.net

BRANDS:
Magic Hat Brewing #9 (9 SRM, 18 IBU)
Magic Hat Brewing Blind Faith (12.5 SRM, 40 IBU)
Magic Hat Brewing Circus Boy (5 SRM, 18 IBU)
Magic Hat Brewing Fat Angel (9.2 SRM, 29 IBU)
Magic Hat Brewing HI.P.A. (6.8 SRM, 45 IBU)
Magic Hat Brewing Hocus Pocus(4.5 SRM, 13 IBU)
Magic Hat Brewing Jinx (22 SRM, 20 IBU)
Magic Hat Brewing Mother Lager (3.2 SRM, 17 IBU)
Magic Hat Brewing Participation Ale (54 SRM, 28 IBU)
Magic Hat Brewing Ravell (63.6 SRM, 22 IBU)
Magic Hat Brewing Roxy Rolles

States Available: CT, DE, MA, MD, ME, NH, NJ, NY, PA, RI, VA, VT

Maine Coast Brewing

102 Eden Street
Bar Harbor, ME 04609
207-288-4914
http://www.bhmaine.com/MCBCPrimary.html

BRANDS:
Jack's Best Brown
Maine Coast Brewing Black Irish Style Stout
Maine Coast Brewing Eden Porter
Maine Coast Brewing Wild Blueberry Ale

States Available: ME

Mammoth Brewing Company

P.O. Box 611
Mammoth Lakes, CA 93546
760-934-2337
www.mammothbrewingco.com

BRANDS:
Mammoth Brewing Company Amber
Mammoth Brewing Company Double Nut Brown
Mammoth Brewing Company Gold
Mammoth Brewing Company India Pale Ale
Mammoth Brewing Company Pale Ale

States Available: CA

Mantorville Brewing Company, LLC

501 North Main Street
Mantorville, MN 55955
651-387-0708
www.mantorvillebeer.com

BRANDS:
Mantorville Brewing Stagecoach Amber Ale
Mantorville Brewing Stagecoach Double Barrel Porter
Mantorville Brewing Stagecoach Smoked Porter

States Available: Contact Brewery

BREWER INDEX (Alphabetical)

Marin Brewing Company

1809 Larkspur Landing Circle
Larkspur, CA 94939-1801
415-461-4677
www.marinbrewing.com

BRANDS:
Marin Brewing Albion Amber Ale
Marin Brewing Blueberry Ale
Marin Brewing Hefe Doppel Weizen
Marin Brewing Hefe Weiss
Marin Brewing Hoppy Holidaze Flavored Ale
Marin Brewing India Pale Ale
Marin Brewing Mt. Tam Pale Ale
Marin Brewing "Old Dipsea" Barleywine Style Ale
Marin Brewing Point Reyes Porter
Marin Brewing Raspberry Trail Ale
Marin Brewing San Quentin's Breakout Stout
Marin Brewing Star Brew
Marin Brewing Stinson Beach Peach
Marin Brewing Tripel Dipsea
Marin Brewing White Knuckle Ale

States Available: CA, OR

Maritime Pacific Brewing Company

1514 North West Leary Way
Seattle, WA 98107
206-782-6181
www.maritimebrewery.citysearch.com

BRANDS:
Maritime Pacific Flagship Red Ale
Maritime Pacific Imperial Pale
Maritime Pacific Islander Pale
Maritime Pacific Nightwatch Dark

States Available: WA

Mehana Brewing Company, Inc.

275 E Kawili Street
Hilo, HI 96720-5074
808-934-8211
www.mehana.com

BRANDS:
Mehana Brewing Hawaii Lager
Mehana Brewing Humpback Blue Beer
Mehana Brewing Mauna Kea Pale Ale
Mehana Brewing Roy's Private Reserve
Mehana Brewing Volcano Red Ale

States Available: CA (Southern), CO, HI

Mendocino Brewing Company

1601 Airport Road
Ukiah, CA 94582
707-463-6610
www.mendobrew.com

BRANDS:
Mendocino Brewing Black Hawk Stout
Mendocino Brewing Blue Heron Pale Ale
Mendocino Brewing Eye of the Hawk
Mendocino Brewing Peregrine Golden Ale
Mendocino Brewing Red Tail Ale
Mendocino Brewing Red Tail Lager
Mendocino Brewing White Hawk Select IPA

States Available: Contact Brewery (in 38 States)

BREWER INDEX (Alphabetical)

Mercury Brewing Company – *page 519*

23 Hayward Street
Ipswich, MA 01938
978-356-3329
www.mercurybrewing.com

BRANDS:
Farmington River Blonde Ale
Farmington River Mahogany Ale
Mercury Brewing Dog Pound Porter
Mercury Brewing Eagle Brook Saloon's Blueberry Ale (14 IBU)
Mercury Brewing Ipswich Dark Ale (40 IBU)
Mercury Brewing Ipswich Harvest Ale (40 IBU)
Mercury Brewing Ipswich IPA (60 IBU)
Mercury Brewing Ipswich Nut Brown (25 IBU)
Mercury Brewing Ipswich Oatmeal Stout (69 IBU)
Mercury Brewing Ipswich Original Ale (30 IBU) – *page 519*
Mercury Brewing Ipswich Porter (48 IBU)
Mercury Brewing Ipswich Summer Ale (23 IBU)
Mercury Brewing Ipswich Winter Ale (35 IBU)
Mercury Brewing Stone Cat Ale
Mercury Brewing Stone Cat Barley Wine
Mercury Brewing Stone Cat Blonde (25 IBU)
Mercury Brewing Stone Cat Blueberry
Mercury Brewing Stone Cat ESB (35 IBU)
Mercury Brewing Stone Cat IPA (55 IBU)
Mercury Brewing Stone Cat Octoberfest (24 IBU)
Mercury Brewing Stone Cat Pumpkin Porter (25 IBU)
Mercury Brewing Stone Cat Scotch Ale (18 IBU)
Mercury Brewing Stone Cat Wheat Beer
Mercury Brewing Stone Cat Winter Lager (35 IBU)

States Available: CT, Stone Cat - MA / Ipswich Ale - MA, NJ, RI

Michigan Brewing Company, Inc.

1093 Highview Drive
Webberville, MI 48892
517-521-3600
www.michiganbrewing.com

BRANDS:
Michigan Brewing Celis Grand Cru
Michigan Brewing Celis Pale Bock
Michigan Brewing Celis Raspberry
Michigan Brewing Celis White
Michigan Brewing Golden Ale
Michigan Brewing High Seas IPA
Michigan Brewing Mackinac Pale Ale
Michigan Brewing Nut Brown Ale
Michigan Brewing Peninsula Porter
Michigan Brewing Petoskey Pilsner
Michigan Brewing Sunset Amber Lager
Michigan Brewing Superior Stout
Michigan Brewing Wheatland Wheat Beer

States Available: IL, MA, MI, NY, OH, OR, PA, TX, VA

BREWER INDEX (Alphabetical)

Middle Ages Brewing Company
120 Wilkinson Street, Suite 3, P.O. Box 1164
Syracuse, NY 13204-2490
315-476-4250
www.middleagesbrewing.com

BRANDS:
Middle Ages Apricot Ale
Middle Ages Beast Bitter
Middle Ages Black Heart Stout
Middle Ages Dragonslayer Imperial Stout
Middle Ages Druid Fluid Barley Wine
Middle Ages Grail Ale
Middle Ages Highlander Scotch Ale
Middle Ages Impaled Ale
Middle Ages Kilt Tilter Scotch Style Ale
Middle Ages Old Marcus Ale
Middle Ages Raspberry Ale
Middle Ages Swallow Wheat
Middle Ages Syracuse Pale Ale
Middle Ages The Duke of Winship Scottish Style Ale
Middle Ages Tripel Crown
Middle Ages Wailing Wench
Middle Ages Winter Wheat
Middle Ages Wizard's Winter Ale

States Available: Contact Brewery

Midnight Sun Brewing Company – *page 520*
7329 Arctic Boulevard, Suite #A
Anchorage, AK 99518
907-344-1179
www.midnightsunbrewing.com

BRANDS:

Midnight Sun Arctic Devil Barley Wine
Midnight Sun Arctic Rhino Coffee Porter (20 IBU)
Midnight Sun Co Ho Ho Imperial IPA (85 IBU)
Midnight Sun Epluche-Culotte (20 IBU)
Midnight Sun Kodiak Brown Ale (24 IBU)
Midnight Sun La Miatresse du Moine (40 IBU)
Midnight Sun Saison of the Sun (27 IBU)
Midnight Sun Sockeye Red IPA (70 IBU) – *page 520*

States Available: AK, OR

Millstream Brewing Company
835 48th Avenue, P.O. Box 284
Amana, IA 52203-0284
319-622-3672
www.millstreambrewing.com

BRANDS:
Millstream Brewing Colony Oatmeal Stout
Millstream Brewing German Pilsner
Millstream Brewing John's Generations White Ale
Millstream Brewing Maifest
Millstream Brewing Oktoberfest
Millstream Brewing Schild Brau Amber
Millstream Brewing Schokolade Bock
Millstream Brewing Warsh Pail Ale
Millstream Brewing Wheat

States Available: IA, IL, WI

Minhas Craft Brewery
1208 14th Avenue
Monroe, WI 53566-0277
608-325-3191
www.minhasbrewery.com

BRANDS:
Extreme Rockhead Malt Liquor
Hi Test Malt Liquor
Huber Bock Beer (23 IBU)
Huber Light Beer (7 IBU)
Huber Premium Beer (14 IBU)
Mountain Creek Classic Lager
Rhinelander (13 IBU)
Wisconsin Club

States Available: WI

BREWER INDEX (Alphabetical)

Mishawaka Brewing Company

3703 North Main Street
Mishawaka, IN 46545
574-256-9993
www.mishawakabrewingcompany.com

BRANDS:
Founders Classic Dry Stout
Four Horsemen Irish Ale
Hop Head Ale
INDIAna Pale Ale
Lake Effect Pale Ale
Mishawaka Kölsch
Raspberry Wheat Ale
Seven Mules Kick-Ass Ale
Wall Street Wheat Ale

States Available: IN

Mississippi Brewing Company

Utica, NY 13502-4092

BRANDS:
Mississippi Mud Black & Tan
Mississippi Mud Lager

States Available: Contact Brewery

Moab Brewery

685 South Main Street
Moab, UT 84532
435-259-6333
www.themoabbrewery.com

BRANDS:
Dead Horse Amber Ale
Scorpion Pale Ale

States Available: UT

Molson Coors Brewing Company

P.O. Box 4030, MS#N8470
Golden, CO 80401-0030
303-279-6565
www.coors.com

BRANDS:
Blue Moon Belgian White
Blue Moon Pumpkin Ale
Coors
Coors Extra Gold
Coors Light
Coors Non-Alcoholic
George Killian's Irish Red Lager
Keystone
Keystone Ice
Keystone Light
Winterfest

States Available: All 50 States

Mount Hood Brewing Company

P.O. Box 56
Government Camp, OR 97028
503-622-0768
www.mthoodbrewing.com

BRANDS:
Mount Hood Brewing Cascadian Pale Ale
Mount Hood Brewing Cloudcap Amber Ale
Mount Hood Brewing Double T Porter
Mount Hood Brewing Highland Meadow Blonde Ale
Mount Hood Brewing Hogsback
Mount Hood Brewing Ice Axe IPA
Mount Hood Brewing Imperial Ice Axxe
Mount Hood Brewing Multorporter

States Available: OR

BREWER INDEX (Alphabetical)

Moylan's Brewing Company

15 Rowland Way
Novato, CA 94945
415- 898-4677
www.moylans.com

BRANDS:
Moylan's Celts Golden Ale
Moylan's Hopsickle Imperial Triple Hoppy Ale
Moylan's India Pale Ale
Moylan's Kilt Lifter Scotch Ale
Moylan's Old Blarney Barleywine Style Ale
Moylan's Paddy's Irish Style Red Ale
Moylan's Ryan O'Sullivan's Imperial Stout
Moylan's Tipperary Pale Ale
Moylan's Wheat Berry Ale
Moylander Double IPA

States Available: AZ, CA, MA, NY, OH, OR, RI

Mt. Shasta Brewing Company

360 College Avenue
Weed, CA 96094
530-938-2394
www.mtshastabrewingcompany.com

BRANDS:
Abner Weed Amber Ale
Brewers Creek Pale Ale
Mountain High IPA
Shastafarian Porter
Weed Golden Ale

States Available: Contact Brewery

Mudshark Brewing Company

210 Swanson Avenue
Lake Havasu City, AZ 86403
928-453-2981
www.mudsharkbrewingco.com

BRANDS:
Mudshark Brewery Full Moon Belgian White Ale
Mudshark Brewery Dry Heat Hefeweizen (3.6 SRM, 18 IBU)

States Available: AZ

Nashoba Valley Brewery

100 Wattaquadoc Hill Road
Bolton, MA 01740
978-779-5521
www.nashobawinery.com

BRANDS:
Nashoba Valley Brewery Barleywine Ale (72 IBU)
Nashoba Valley Brewery Belgian Double
Nashoba Valley Brewery Belgian Pale Ale (26 IBU)
Nashoba Valley Brewery Blackberry Ale
Nashoba Valley Brewery Bolt 117 Lager (25 IBU)
Nashoba Valley Brewery Heron Ale (30 IBU)
Nashoba Valley Brewery Imperial Stout
Nashoba Valley Brewery IPA (50 IBU)
Nashoba Valley Brewery Peach Lambic (15 IBU)

States Available: Contact Brewery

Nectar Ales

620 McMurray Road
Buellton, CA 93427
805-686-1557
www.nectarales.com

BRANDS:
Nectar Ales IPA Nectar
Nectar Ales Pale Nectar
Nectar Ales Red Nectar

States Available: CA, NV

BREWER INDEX (Alphabetical)

New Belgium Brewing Company – *page 521*

500 Linden Street
Fort Collins, CO 80524-2457
970-221-0524
www.newbelgium.com

BRANDS:
New Belgium 2 Below (14.7 SRM, 28 IBU)
New Belgium 1554 Brussels Style Black Ale (45.7 SRM, 21 IBU)
New Belgium Abbey Belgian Style Ale (27.9 SRM, 20 IBU)
New Belgium Blue Paddle Pilsner (4.8 SRM, 32.5 IBU)
New Belgium Fat Tire Amber Ale (12.9 SRM, 18.5 IBU) – *page 521*
New Belgium Saison Harvest Ale
New Belgium Skinny Dip
New Belgium Springboard
New Belgium Sunshine Wheat (3.3 SRM, 14.5 IBU)
New Belgium Trippel Belgian Style Ale (7.9 SRM, 25 IBU)
States Available: AR, AZ, CA, CO, ID, KS, MO, MT, NE, NM, NV, OR, TX, WA, WY

New Century Brewing Company – *page 522*

P.O. Box 1498
Boston, MA 02117
781-963-4007
www.edisonbeer.com

BRANDS:
Moonshot
Edison The Independent Light Beer – *page 522*
States Available: IL, IN, MA, MI, NJ, OH, VA

New England Brewing Company

7 Selden Street
Woodbridge, CT 06525
203-387-2222
www.newenglandbrewing.com

BRANDS:
New England Brewing Atlantic Amber
New England Brewing Elm City Lager
New England Brewing Sea Hag IPA

States Available: CT

New Glarus Brewing

119 Elmer Road
New Glarus, WI 53574
608-527-5850
www.newglarusbrewing.com

BRANDS:
New Glarus Brewing Belgian Red
New Glarus Brewing Copper Kettle Weiss
New Glarus Brewing Enigma
New Glarus Brewing Fat Squirrel
New Glarus Brewing Hop Hearty Ale
New Glarus Brewing Raspberry Tart
New Glarus Brewing Road Slush Oatmeal Stout
New Glarus Brewing Spotted Cow
New Glarus Brewing Totally Naked
New Glarus Brewing Uff-da Bock
New Glarus Brewing Yokel

States Available: WI

New Holland Brewing Company

66 East 8th Street
Holland, MI 49423
616-355-6422
www.newhollandbrew.com

BRANDS:
New Holland Black Tulip
New Holland Blue Goat Doppelbock
New Holland Dragon's Milk
New Holland Ichabod
New Holland Mad Hatter
New Holland Pilgrim's Dole
New Holland Red Tulip
New Holland Sundog
New Holland The Poet
New Holland Zoomer Wheat Ale

States Available: IL, IN, MI, OH, PA

BREWER INDEX (Alphabetical)

New Knoxville Brewing Company
708 E Depot Avenue
Knoxville, TN 37917-7611
865-522-0029
www.newknoxvillebrewery.com
BRANDS:
New Knoxville Brewing Honey Wheat
New Knoxville Brewing India Pale Ale
New Knoxville Brewing Porter
New Knoxville Brewing Traditional Pale Ale
New Knoxville Brewing XX Pale Ale
States Available: Contact Brewery

New River Brewing Company
2015 Afond Court
Atlanta, GA 30341
770-841-2953
www.newriverbrewing.com
BRANDS:
New River Pale Ale (6.5 SRM, 35 IBU)
States Available: NC, VA, WV

New South Brewing Company (Kegs/Growlers)
851 Campbell Street
Myrtle Beach, SC 29577
843-916-2337
www.newsouthbrewing.com
BRANDS:
New South India Pale Ale
New South Lager
New South Nut Brown Ale
New South Oktoberfest
New South White Ale
States Available: NC, SC

Nicolet Brewing
3578 Brewery Lane, P.O. Box 650
Florence, WI 54121-0650
715-528-5244
BRANDS:
Nicolet Brewing Blonde
Nicolet Brewing Classic Pilsner
Nicolet Brewing Prostrator Doppelbock
Nicolet Brewing Winter Fest Beer
Nicolet Brewing Oktoberfest
Nicolet Brewing Dark Pilsner
States Available: Contact Brewery

Nimbus Brewing Company – *page 523*
3850 E. 44th Street
Tucson, AZ 85713
520-745-9175
www.nimbusbeer.com
BRANDS:
Nimbus Blonde Ale (4 SRM, 12 IBU) – *page 523*
Nimbus Brown Ale (21 SRM, 26 IBU) – *page 525*
Nimbus Oatmeal Stout (36 SRM, 45 IBU) – *page 525*
Nimbus "Old Monkeyhine" English Strong
 (16 SRM, 35 IBU) – *page 526*
Nimbus Pale Ale (8 SRM, 40 IBU) – *page 524*
Nimbus Red Ale (14 SRM, 29 IBU) – *page 524*
States Available: AZ, CA

Nine G Brewing Company, Inc.
1115 West Sample Street
South Bend, IN 46619
574-282-2337
www.ninegbrewing.com
BRANDS:
Bitchin' Betty Citrus Wheat Beer
Blacksnake Porter
Infidel Imperial India Pale Ale
Wingman Amber Ale
States Available: IN

BREWER INDEX (Alphabetical)

North Coast Brewing Company

455 N Main Street
Fort Bragg, CA 95437-3215
707-964-2739
www.northcoastbrewing.com

BRANDS:
North Coast ACME California Pale Ale (21 IBU)
North Coast ACME IPA (52 IBU)
North Coast Blue Star Great American Wheat Beer (17 IBU)
North Coast Brewing Brother Thelonious
North Coast Old No. 38 Stout (46 IBU)
North Coast Old Rasputin Russian Imperial Stout (75 IBU)
North Coast Old Stock Ale (36 IBU)
North Coast Pranqster Belgian Style Golden Ale (20 IBU)
North Coast Ruedrich's Red Seal Ale (45 IBU)
North Coast Scrimshaw Pilsner Style Beer (22 IBU)

States Available: AZ, CA, CO, CT, FL, GA, HI, IA, ID, IL, KY, LA, MA, MN, MO, MT, NC, NJ, NM, NV, NY, OH, OK, OR, PA, SC, TN, TX, VA, WA, WI

O'Fallon Brewery

26 West Industrial Drive
O' Fallon, MO 63366
636-474-2337
www.ofallonbrewery.com

BRANDS:
O'Fallon 5-Day IPA (in MO only)
O'Fallon Blackberry Scottish Ale
O'Fallon Cherry Chocolate Beer
O'Fallon Gold (in MO only)
O'Fallon Light
O'Fallon Pumpkin Ale
O'Fallon Smoked Porter
O'Fallon Summer Brew (in MO only)
O'Fallon Wheach
O'Fallon Wheat

States Available: CO, IA, IL, IN, KS, KY, MI, MN, MO, WI

Oak Creek Brewing Company

450 Jordan Road, Suite 7
Sedona, AZ 86336-4100
520-204-1300
www.oakcreekbrew.com

BRANDS:
Oak Creek Amber Ale
Oak Creek Golden Lager
Oak Creek Hefeweizen
Oak Creek Nut Brown Ale
Oak Creek Pale Ale

States Available: AZ

Oak Pond Brewery

101 Oak Pond Road
Skowhegan, ME 04976
207-474-3233
www.oakpondbrewery.com

BRANDS:
Oak Pond Brewing Dooryard Ale
Oak Pond Brewing Laughing Loon Lager
Oak Pond Brewing Nut Brown Ale
Oak Pond Brewing Oktoberfest
Oak Pond Brewing Storyteller Doppelbock
Oak Pond Brewing White Fox Ale

States Available: ME

Oaken Barrel Brewing Company

50 North Airport Parkway, Suite L
Greenwood, IN 46143-1438
317-887-2287
www.oakenbarrel.com

BRANDS:
Oaken Barrel Brewing Alabaster
Oaken Barrel Brewing Gnaw Bone Pale Ale
Oaken Barrel Brewing Indiana Amber Ale
Oaken Barrel Brewing Razz-Wheat
Oaken Barrel Brewing Snake Pit Porter

States Available: IN

BREWER INDEX (Alphabetical)

Oceanside Ale Works

3800 Oceanic Drive, #105
Oceanside, CA 92056
760-758-2064
www.oceansidealeworks.com

BRANDS:
Oceanside Ale Works Pier View Pale Ale
Oceanside Ale Works San Luis Rey Red

States Available: Contact Brewery

Odell Brewing Company

800 E Lincoln Avenue
Fort Collins, CO 80524
970-489-9070
www.odellbrewing.com

BRANDS:
Odell Brewing 5 Barrel Pale Ale
Odell Brewing 90 Shilling
Odell Brewing Curmudgeons NIP
Odell Brewing Cutthroat Porter
Odell Brewing Double Pilsner
Odell Brewing Easy Street Wheat
Odell Brewing Isolation Ale
Odell Brewing Levity Amber

States Available: CO, KS, MO, NE, NM, SD, WY

Old Dominion Brewing Company

44633 Guiliford Drive
Ashburn, VA 20147
703-742-9100
www.olddominion.com

BRANDS:
Dominion Ale
Dominion Lager
Dominion Millennium
Dominion Oak Barrel Stout
Dominion Octoberfest
Dominion Pale Ale
Dominion Spring Brew
Dominion Summer Wheat
Dominion Winter Brew
New River Pale Ale
Tuppers' Hop Pocket Ale
Tuppers' Hop Pocket Pils

States Available: DC, GA, MD, NC, OH, – Tuppers' and New River Only, PA, VA, WV

Olde Saratoga Brewing Company

131 Excelsior Avenue
Saratoga Springs, NY 12866
518-581-0492
www.oldesaratogabrew.com

BRANDS:
Olde Saratoga Brewing Saratoga Lager

States Available: NY

Olde Towne Brewing

214 Holmes Avenue
Huntsville, AL 35801
256-564-7404
www.oldetownebrewery.com

BRANDS:
Olde Towne Amber
Olde Towne Pale Ale

States Available: Contact Brewery

BREWER INDEX (Alphabetical)

Oregon Trail Brewery

341 SW Second Street
Corvallis, OR 97333
541-758-3527
www.oregontrailbrewery.com

BRANDS:
Oregon Trail Beaver Tail
Oregon Trail Brown Ale
Oregon Trail Ginseng Porter
Oregon Trail IPA
Oregon Trail Wit

States Available: Contact Brewery

Orlando Brewing Partners, Inc. (Kegs/Growlers)

1301 Atlanta Avenue
Orlando, FL 32806
407-872-1117
www.orlandobrewing.com

BRANDS:
Orlando Brewing Blackwater Ale
Orlando Brewing Blonde Ale (2.9 SRM, 10.2 IBU)
Orlando Brewing Mild Ale
Orlando Brewing Olde Pelican Ale
Orlando Brewing Pale Ale (7.6 SRM, 28.3 IBU)

States Available: Contact Brewery

Oskar Blues Grill & Brew

303 Main Street
Lyons, CO 80540
303-823-6685
www.oskarblues.com

BRANDS:
Oskar Blues Grill & Brew Dale's Pale Ale (65 IBU)
Oskar Blues Grill & Brew Gordon (35 IBU)
Oskar Blues Grill & Brew Leroy (90 IBU)
Oskar Blues Grill & Brew Old Chub (30 IBU)

States Available: AZ, CO, GA, ID, MA, NC, NJ, NM, NY, PA, VA, WA, WI

Otter Creek Brewing Company – *page 527*

793 Exchange Street
Middlebury, VT 05753
800-473-0727
www.ottercreekbrewing.com

BRANDS:
Otter Creek Brewing Alpine Ale (36 IBU)
Otter Creek Brewing Anniversary IPA
Otter Creek Brewing Copper Ale
 (21 IBU) – *page 527*
Otter Creek Brewing ESB
Otter Creek Brewing Oktoberfest (19 IBU)
Otter Creek Brewing Otter Summer Ale
Otter Creek Brewing Pale Ale (23 IBU)
Otter Creek Brewing Stovepipe Porter (30 IBU)
Otter Creek Brewing Vermont Lager (26 IBU)
Wolaver's Organic Brown Ale (21 IBU) – *page 573*
Wolaver's Organic India Pale Ale (55 IBU)
Wolaver's Organic Oatmeal Stout (40 IBU)
Wolaver's Organic Pale Ale (34 IBU)
Wolaver's Organic Wit Bier

States Available: CA, CT, IL, MA, MO, NC, NH, NJ, NY, OH, OR, PA, RI, VA, VT, WA, WI

BREWER INDEX (Alphabetical)

Pabst Brewing Company

P.O. Box 792627
San Antonio, TX 78279
210-226-0231
www.pabst.com

BRANDS:
Ballantine Ale
Blatz
Carling Black Label
Colt 45
Country Club Malt Liquor
Haffenreffer's Private Stock
Lone Star
Lone Star Light
McSorley's Black & Tan
McSorley's Irish Ale
National Bohemian
Old Milwaukee
Old Milwaukee Ice
Old Milwaukee Light
Old Milwaukee Non-Alcoholic
Old Style
Old Style Light
Olympia
Pabst Blue Ribbon
Pabst Blue Ribbon Light
Pabst Blue Ribbon Non-Alcoholic
Pearl
Piels
Piels Light
Rainer
Rainer Ale
Rainer Light
Schaefer
Schlitz
Schlitz Bull Ice
Schlitz Malt Liquor
Schlitz Red Bull
Schmidt's
Schmidt's Ice
Schmidt's Light
Special Export
Special Export Light
St.Ides
Stag

Stroh's
Stroh's Light
States Available: All 50 States

Palmetto Brewing Company, Inc.

289 Huger Street
Charleston, SC 29403-4522
803-937-0903

BRANDS:
Palmetto Brewing Amber Lager
Palmetto Brewing Lager
Palmetto Brewing Pale Ale
Palmetto Brewing Porter

States Available: SC

Paper City Brewery Company

108 Cabot Street
Holyoke, MA 01040
413-535-1588
www.papercity.com

BRANDS:
Paper City Brewing 1 Eared Monkey
Paper City Brewing Banchee Extra Pale Ale
Paper City Brewing Blonde Hop Monster
Paper City Brewing Cabot Street Summer Wheat
Paper City Brewing Denogginator
Paper City Brewing Dorado
Paper City Brewing Goats Peak Bock (20 IBU)
Paper City Brewing Golden Lager
Paper City Brewing Holyoke Dam Ale
Paper City Brewing India's Pale Ale
Paper City Brewing Ireland Parish Golden Ale
Paper City Brewing Nut Brown
Paper City Brewing P.C. Blue
Paper City Brewing Red Hat Razzberry
Paper City Brewing Riley's Stout
Paper City Brewing Summer Brew
Paper City Brewing Summer Time Pale Ale
Paper City Brewing Summit House Oktoberfest (23 IBU)
Paper City Brewing Winter Lager
Paper City Brewing Winter Palace Wee Heavy

States Available: CT, MA, RI

69

BREWER INDEX (Alphabetical)

Peak Organic Brewing Company

3 Little's Brook Ct #55
Burlington, MA 01803
520-360-8412
www.peakbrewing.com

BRANDS:
Peak Organic Amber Ale
Peak Organic Nut Brown Ale
Peak Organic Pale Ale

States Available: Contact Brewery

Pelican Pub & Brewery

P.O. Box 189, 33180 Cape Kiwanda Drive
Pacific City, OR 97135
503-965-7007
www.pelicanbrewery.com

BRANDS:
India Pelican Ale (85 IBU)

States Available: Contact Brewery

Penn Brewery (Pennsylvania Brewing) – *page 528*

800 Vinial Street
Pittsburgh, PA 15212-5128
412-237-9400
www.pennbrew.com

BRANDS:
Penn Crew Lager
Penn Dark Lager
Penn Gold
Penn Kaiser Pils
Penn Maibock
Penn Marzen
Penn Oktoberfest
Penn Pilsner – *page 528*
Penn St. Nikolaus Bock Bier
Penn Weizen

States Available: CA, DE, FL, MD, NY, PA

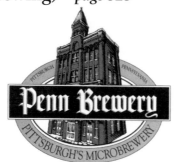

Pennichuck Brewing Company

127 Elm Street, Unit C
Milford, NH 03055
603-672-2750
www.pennichuckbrewing.com

BRANDS:
Pennichuck Brewing 2-6-0 Mogul
Pennichuck Brewing Engine Number 5
Pennichuck Brewing Pozharnik Espresso Russian Imperial Stout
Pennichuck Brewing The Big O

States Available: NH, RI. MA

Pete's Brewing (Gambrinus)

14800 San Pedro Avenue, Third Floor
San Antonio, TX 78232
210-490-9128
www.peteswicked.com

BRANDS:
Pete's Wicked Ale (18 IBU)
Pete's Wicked Strawberry Blonde(19 IBU)
Pete's Wicked Wanderlust Cream Ale (18 IBU)
Pete's Wicked Rally Cap Ale (22 IBU)

States Available: All 50 States

Pig's Eye Brewing Company

10107 Bridgewater Parkway
St. Paul, MN 55129
651-734-1661
www.pigseyebeer.com

BRANDS:
Pig's Eye Lean
Pig's Eye Pilsner
Pig's Eye Pitt Bull

States Available: AZ, CO, IA, IN, MN, ND, OK, PA, SD, WI

BREWER INDEX (Alphabetical)

Pike Brewing Company

1415 First Avenue
Seattle, WA 98101
206-622-6044
www.pikebrewing.com

BRANDS:
Pike Brewing Company India Pale Ale
Pike Brewing Company Kilt Lifter Scotch Ale
Pike Brewing Company Monk's Uncle
Pike Brewing Company Naughty Nellie Ale
Pike Brewing Company Old Bawdy Barley Wine
Pike Brewing Company Pale Ale
Pike Brewing Company Tandem
Pike Brewing Company XXXXX Stout

States Available: AK, ID, MT, OR, UT, WA

Pioneer Brewing Company

199 Arnold Road
Sturbridge, MA 01566
508-347-7500
www.hylandbrew.com

BRANDS:
Hyland's Sturbridge Amber Ale
Hyland's Sturbridge American Pale Ale
Hyland's Sturbridge Farmhand Ale
Hyland's Sturbridge Stout

States Available: MA

Pisgah Brewing Company

150 Eastside Business Park
Black Mountain, NC 28711
828-582-2175
www.pisgahbrewing.com

BRANDS:
Pisgah Equinox (47.5 IBU)
Pisgah Pale Ale (31.8 IBU)
Pisgah Porter
Pisgah Solstice
Pisgah Stout
Vortex I (133 IBU)

States Available: NC

Pittsburgh Brewing Company

3340 Liberty Avenue
Pittsburgh, PA 15201
412-692-1136
www.pittsburghbrewingco.com

BRANDS:
Pittsburgh Brewing American
Pittsburgh Brewing American Ice
Pittsburgh Brewing American Light
Pittsburgh Brewing Augustiner Amber Lager
Pittsburgh Brewing Augustiner Dark
Pittsburgh Brewing IC Light
Pittsburgh Brewing Iron City Beer Premium Lager
Pittsburgh Brewing Old German

States Available: AK, AZ, CO, CT, DC, FL, GA, IA, IN, KS, KY, MA, MD, MI, MN, MO, MS, NC, ND, NJ, NM, OH, OK, OR, PA, SC, TN, TX, VA, WI, WV

Pony Express Brewing Company

311 N Burch Street
Olathe, KS 66061-3649
913-764-7669
www.ponygold.com

BRANDS:
Pony Express Gold Beer
Pony Express Original Wheat
Pony Express Rattlesnake Pale Ale
Pony Express Tornado Red Ale

States Available: IA, KS, MI, NE, WI

BREWER INDEX (Alphabetical)

Port Brewing Company

155 Mata Way
San Marcos, CA 92069
760-891-0272
www.lostabbey.com

BRANDS:
High Tide Fresh Hop IPA
Old Viscosity Ale
Santa's Little Helper Imperial Stout
Sharkbite Red Ale
The Lost Abbey Avant Garde (24 IBU)
The Lost Abbey Cuvee de Tomme
The Lost Abbey Judgment Day
The Lost Abbey Lost & Found Abbey Ale (19 IBU)
The Lost Abbey Red Barn Ale
The Lost Abbey The Angel's Share
Wipeout IPA

States Available: AZ, CA, MA

Port Townsend Brewing Company

330 10th Street
Port Townsend, WA 98368
360-385-9967
www.porttownsendbrewing.com

BRANDS:
Port Townsend Dry-Hopped IPA
Port Townsend Reel Amber

States Available: WA

Pyramid Brewery – *page 529*

91 South Royal Brougham Way
Seattle, WA 98134
206-682-8322
www.pyramidbrew.com

BRANDS:
Pyramid Brewery Amber Weizen
  (17 IBU) – *page 530*
Pyramid Brewery Apricot Weizen
  (11 IBU) – *page 530*
Pyramid Brewery Curve Ball Kölsch (18 IBU) – *page 531*
Pyramid Brewery Hefe Weizen (18 IBU) – *page 529*
Pyramid Brewery Snow Cap Ale (47 IBU) – *page 532*
Pyramid Brewery ThunderHead IPA (67 IBU) – *page 531*

States Available: AK, AR, AZ, CA, CO, HI, IA, ID, IL, IN, KS, KY, MD, MI,
                MN, MO, MT, NC, NE, NM, NV, OH, OK, OR, PA, TN, TX,
                UT, VA, WA, WY

R.J. Rockers Brewing Company

113D Belton Drive
Spartanburg, SC 29302
864-587-1435
www.rjrockers.com

BRANDS:
R.J. Rockers Bald Eagle Brown (18 SRM, 25 IBU)
R.J. Rockers Buckwheat (4 SRM, 18 IBU)
R.J. Rockers First Snow Ale (8 SRM, 30 IBU)
R.J. Rockers Liberty Light (4 SRM, 25 IBU)
R.J. Rockers Patriot Pale Ale (6 SRM, 40 IBU)
R.J. Rockers Star Spangled Stout (60 SRM, 25 IBU)

States Available: NC, SC

Rahr & Sons Brewing Company

701 Galveston Avenue
Fort Worth, TX 76104
817-810-9266
www.rahrbrewing.com

BRANDS:
Rahr Brewing Blonde Lager (3 SRM, 19 IBU)
Rahr Brewing Bucking Bock – Miabock (10 SRM, 30 IBU)
Rahr Brewing Buffalo Batt Beer (20 SRM, 24 IBU)
Rahr Brewing Pecker Wrecker Imperial Pilsner (8 SRM, 62 IBU)
Rahr Brewing Rahr's Red (17 SRM, 22 IBU)
Rahr Brewing Summer Time Wheat (4 SRM, 18 IBU)
Rahr Brewing Ugly Pug (30 SRM, 24 IBU)

States Available: TX

Ramapo Valley Brewery

P.O. Box 1031, 143 Route 59, Building 6
Hilburn, NY 10931
845-369-7827
www.ramapovalleybrewery.com

BRANDS:
Ramapo Valley Brewery Copper Ale
Ramapo Valley Brewery Honey Lager
Ramapo Valley Brewery India Pale Ale
Ramapo Valley Brewery Octoberfest
Ramapo Valley Brewery Ramapo Razz Ale
Ramapo Valley Brewery Skull Crusher
Ramapo Valley Brewery Suffern Station Porter
Ramapo Valley Brewery Christmas Ale

States Available: CA, FL, IA, IL, MA, NJ, NY, PA, VT

Real Ale Brewing Company

405 Third Street
Blanco, TX 78606
830-833-2534
www.realalebrewing.com

BRANDS:
Real Ale Brewing Brewhouse Brown Ale
Real Ale Brewing Fireman's #4 Blonde Ale
Real Ale Brewing Full Moon Pale Rye Ale
Real Ale Brewing Rio Blanco Pale Ale
Real Ale Brewing Shade Grown Coffee Porter
Real Ale Brewing Sisyphus Barleywine Ale

States Available: Contact Brewery

ReaperAle, Inc.

26741 Portola Parkway, 1E #476
Foothill Ranch, CA 92610
949-223-0122
www.reaperale.com

BRANDS:
ReaperAle Deathly Pale Ale (45 IBU)
ReaperAle Inevitable Ale (22 IBU)
ReaperAle Mortality Stout (30 IBU)
ReaperAle Redemption Red Ale (35 IBU)
ReaperAle Ritual Dark Ale (50 IBU)
ReaperAle Sleighor Double IPA (105 IBU)

States Available: AZ, CA, DE, NJ, PA, VA

Red Bell Brewery & Pub

4421 Main Street
Philadelphia, PA 19127
215-482-9494
www.redbell.com

BRANDS:
Red Bell Brewing Philadelphia Original Light Lager

States Available: DE, NJ, PA

BREWER INDEX (Alphabetical)

Red Lodge Ales Brewing Company

417 North Broadway
Red Lodge, MT 59068
406-446-4607

BRANDS:
Red Lodge Ales Glacier Ale
Red Lodge Ales Hefeweizen

States Available: MT

Redhook Ale Brewery, Inc. – *page 533*

14300 NE 145th Street
Woodinville, WA 98072
425-483-3232
www.redhook.com

BRANDS:
Redhook Ale Brewery Blackhook Porter
 (51 SRM, 40 IBU)
Redhook Ale Brewery Blonde Ale (8.1 SRM, 18.3 IBU)
Redhook Ale Brewery Copperhook Spring Ale (11SRM, 20 IBU)
Redhook Ale Brewery ESB (13.2 SRM, 28 IBU) – *page 533*
Redhook Ale Brewery IPA (8.4 SRM, 38.5 IBU)
Redhook Ale Brewery Late Harvest Autumn Ale (21 SRM, 32 IBU)
Redhook Ale Brewery Sunrye Summer Ale (4.6 SRM, 16 IBU)
Redhook Ale Brewery Winter Hook Winter Ale (21.7 SRM, 27.6 IBU)

States Available: 48 States (NOT UT, OK)

Rheingold Brewing Company

372 Danbury Road, Suite 163
Wilton, CT 06897
212-481-1018
www.rheingoldbeer.com

BRANDS:
Rheingold Beer

States Available: Contact Brewery

Rio Grande Brewing Company

3760 Hawkins NE
Albuquerque, NM 87109
505-343-0903
www.riograndebrewing.com

BRANDS:
Rio Grande Brewing Bock Holiday (30 IBU)
Rio Grande Brewing Desert Pils (24 IBU)
Rio Grande Brewing Elfego Bock (26 IBU)
Rio Grande Brewing IPA (76 IBU)
Rio Grande Brewing Outlaw Lager (35 IBU)
Rio Grande Brewing Pancho Verde Chile Cerveza (12 IBU)
Rio Grande Brewing Stout (42 IBU)
Rio Grande Brewing Sunchaser Ale (32 IBU)

States Available: NM

River Horse Brewing Company – *page 534*

80 Lambert Lane
Lambertville, NJ 08530
609-397-7776
www.riverhorse.com

BRANDS:
River Horse Belgian Frostbite Winter Ale
River Horse Hop Hazard Pale Ale
River Horse Lager
River Horse Special Ale
River Horse Summer Blonde – *page 534*
River Horse Tripel Horse

States Available: CT, DE, MA, MD, NJ, NY (NYC, Long Island), OH, PA

Rock Art Brewery, LLC – *page 535*

254 Wilkens Street
Morrisville, VT 05661
802-888-9400
www.rockartbrewery.com

BRANDS:
Rock Art Brewery American Red Ale (14 IBU)
Rock Art Brewery Brown Bear Ale (11 IBU)
Rock Art Brewery Hell's Bock (75 IBU)
Rock Art Brewery India Pale Ale (22 IBU)
Rock Art Brewery Infusco (25 IBU)
Rock Art Brewery Magnumus ete Tomahawkus (80 IBU) – *page 535*
Rock Art Brewery Midnight Madness Smoked Porter (27 IBU)
Rock Art Brewery Ridge Runner Mild Barleywine (23 IBU)
Rock Art Brewery River Runner Summer Ale (12 IBU)
Rock Art Brewery Stock Ale (18 IBU)
Rock Art Brewery Stump Jumper Stout (40 IBU)
Rock Art Brewery Sunny and 75 (10 IBU)
Rock Art Brewery The Riddler (32 IBU)
Rock Art Brewery The Vermonster (100 IBU)
Rock Art Brewery Trail Cutter Dark Lager (12 IBU)
Rock Art Brewery Vermont Maple Wheat (8 IBU)
Rock Art Brewery Whitetail Ale (28 IBU)

States Available: Central NJ, VT

Rocky Bay Brewing Company

230 Park Street
Rockland, ME 04841
207-596-0300
www.rockybaybrewing.com

BRANDS:
Rocky Bay Brewing Foghorn Ale
Rocky Bay Brewing Seasider Oktoberfest
Rocky Bay Brewing Whitecap Ale
Rocky Bay Black Castle Ale
Rocky Bay Brewing Nor' Easter Stout
Rocky Bay Brewing Schooner Point Lager
Rocky Bay Brewing Katie's Celtic Red Ale

States Available: ME

Rocky Coulee Brewing Company – *page 536*

205 North First Street
Odessa, WA 99159
509-345-2216
www.rockycouleebrewingco.com

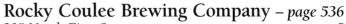

BRANDS:
Fireweed Honey Blonde – *page 536*

States Available: WA

Rogue Ales – *page 537*

2320 OSU Drive
Newport, OR 97365
541-867-3660
www.rogue.com

BRANDS:
Morimoto Black Obi Soba (30 IBU)
Rogue American Amber Ale (53 IBU)
Rogue Brutal Bitter (59 IBU)
Rogue Chamomellow Ale (34 IBU)
Rogue Chipotle Ale (35 IBU)
Rogue Chocolate Stout (69 IBU)
Rogue Dad's Little Helper Malt Liquor (25 IBU)
Rogue Dead Guy Ale (40 IBU) – *page 537*
Rogue Half-E-Weizen (34 IBU)
Rogue Hazelnut Brown Nectar (33 IBU)
Rogue 12PA Imperial India Pale Ale (74 IBU)
Rogue Imperial Stout (88 IBU)
Rogue Juniper Pale Ale (34 IBU)
Rogue Kells Irish Lager (28 IBU)
Rogue Mocha Porter (54 IBU)
Rogue Monk Madness Ale (108 IBU)
Rogue Morimoto Imperial Pilsner (74 IBU)
Rogue Morimoto Soba Ale (30 IBU)
Rogue Old Crustacean Barleywine (110 IBU)
Rogue Oregon Golden Ale (35 IBU)
Rogue Santa's Private Reserve (44 IBU)
Rogue Shakespeare Stout (69 IBU)
Rogue Smoke Ale (48 IBU)
Rogue St.Rogue Red (44 IBU)
Rogue Uberfest Pilsner (35 IBU)
Rogue Younger's Special Bitter (35 IBU)

States Available: All 50 States

Roslyn Brewing Company

208 Pennsylvania Avenue, P.O. Box 24
Roslyn, WA 98941
509-649-2232
www.roslynbrewery.com

BRANDS:
Roslyn Brewing Brookside Pale Lager
Roslyn Brewing Roslyn Dark Lager Beer

States Available: WA

Ruby Mountain Brewing Company

HC-60 Route 100
Clover Valley, NV 89835-0100
775-752-2337
www.rubymountainbrewing.com

BRANDS:
Ruby Mountain Brewing Angel Creek Amber Ale
Ruby Mountain Brewing Bristlecone Brown Porter
Ruby Mountain Brewing Vienna Style Lager
Ruby Mountain Brewing Wild West Hefeweizen

States Available: ID, NV

Rush River Brewing (Kegs)

W 4001 120th Avenue
Maiden Rock, WI 54750
715-448-2035
www.rushriverbeer.com

BRANDS:
Rush River Brewing BubbleJack IPA
Rush River Brewing Lost Arrow Porter
Rush River Brewing Small Axe Golden Ale
Rush River Brewing The Unforgiven Amber Ale

States Available: MN, WI

Russian River Brewing Company

725 4th Street
Santa Rosa, CA 95404
707-545-BEER
www.russianriverbrewing.com

BRANDS:
Russian River Brewing Beatification
Russian River Brewing Damnation (25 IBU)
Russian River Brewing Depuration (27 IBU)
Russian River Brewing Redemption (23 IBU)
Russian River Brewing Salvation (22 IBU)
Russian River Brewing Sanctification (27 IBU)
Russian River Brewing Supplication (27 IBU)
Russian River Brewing Temptation (27 IBU)

States Available: CA, DC, PA

BREWER INDEX (Alphabetical)

SAB Miller Corporation
3939 W Highland Boulevard
Milwaukee, WI 53208-2816
312-577-1754
www.sabmiller.com

BRANDS:
Hamm's
Hamm's Special Light
Henry Weinhard's Blue Boar Pale Ale
Henry Weinhard's Classic Dark
Henry Weinhard's Hefeweizen
Henry Weinhard's Northwest Trail Blonde Lager
Henry Weinhard's Private Reserve
Henry Weinhard's Summer Wheat
Icehouse
Icehouse 5.0
Icehouse Light
Magnum Malt Liquor
Mickey's Ice
Mickey's Malt Liquor
Miller Geniune Draft
Miller Geniune Draft Light
Miller High Life
Miller High Life Light
Miller Lite
Milwaukee's Best
Milwaukee's Best Ice
Milwaukee's Best Light
Old English 800 Malt Liquor
Olde English HG800
Olde English HG800 7.5
Peroni Nastro Azzurro
Pilsner Urquell
Red Dog
Sharp's
Southpaw Light
Sparks
Sparks Light
Sparks Plus 6%
Sparks Plus 7%
Steel Reserve High Gravity
Steel Reserve Triple

States Available: All 50 States

Sacramento Brewing Company Inc.
2713 El Paseo Lane
Sacramento, CA 95821
916-485-4677
www.sacbrew.com

BRANDS:
Sacramento Brewing Hefeweizen
Sacramento Brewing India Pale Ale
Sacramento Brewing Red Horse Ale
Sacramento Brewing River Otter Ale
Sacramento Brewing Russian Imperial Stout
Sacramento Brewing Sacsquatch Ale

States Available: CA

Saint Arnold Brewing Company – *page 538*
2522 Fairway Park Drive
Houston, TX 77092-7607
713-686-9494
www.saintarnold.com

BRANDS:
Saint Arnold Brewing Abbey American Quadruppel
Saint Arnold Brewing Amber Ale (31 IBU) – *page 538*
Saint Arnold Brewing Barleywine
Saint Arnold Brewing Brown Ale (24 IBU)
Saint Arnold Brewing Christmas Ale (35 IBU)
Saint Arnold Brewing Double IPA
Saint Arnold Brewing Elissa IPA (60 IBU)
Saint Arnold Brewing Fancy Lawnmower Beer (20 IBU)
Saint Arnold Brewing Oktoberfest (24 IBU)
Saint Arnold Brewing Spring Bock (24 IBU)
Saint Arnold Brewing Summer Pils (41 IBU)
Saint Arnold Brewing Texas Wheat (18 IBU)
Saint Arnold Brewing Winter Stout (36 IBU)

States Available: TX

BREWER INDEX (Alphabetical)

Sand Creek Brewing Company, LLC – *page 539*

320 South Pierce Street, P.O. Box 187
Black River Falls, WI 54615
715-284-7553
www.sandcreekbrewing.com

BRANDS:
Badger Porter (62 SRM, 21 IBU)
Cranberry Special Ale
Pioneer Black River Red (23 SRM, 25 IBU)
Pioneer Lager (12 SRM, 15 IBU)
Pioneer Oderbolz Bock (12.9 SRM, 25 IBU)
Sand Creek Brewing English Style Special Ale (13.4 SRM, 25 IBU)
Sand Creek Brewing Golden Ale (5.8 SRM, 11 IBU)
Sand Creek Brewing Groovy Brew (6 SRM, 6.5 IBU)
Sand Creek Brewing Oscar's Chocolate Oatmeal Stout
 (107 SRM, 30 IBU) – *page 539*
Sand Creek Brewing Wild Ride IPA (8.2 SRM, 64 IBU)
Sand Creek Brewing Woody's Wheat (12 SRM, 6 IBU)

States Available: IL, MN, WI

Santa Cruz Mountain Brewing – *page 540*

402 Ingallis Street, Suite 27
Santa Cruz, CA 95060
831-425-4900
www.santacruzmountainbrewing.com

BRANDS:
Santa Cruz Mountain Brewing India Pale Ale
Santa Cruz Mountain Brewing Nicky 666
Santa Cruz Mountain Brewing Organic Amber Ale
 – *page 541*
Santa Cruz Mountain Brewing Organic Devout Stout – *page 540*
Santa Cruz Mountain Brewing Organic Dread Brown Ale – *page 541*
Santa Cruz Mountain Brewing Pale Ale
Santa Cruz Mountain Brewing Wilder Wheat

States Available: CA, HI, OR, WA

Santa Fe Brewing Company

35 Fire Place
Santa Fe, NM 87508
505-424-3333
www.santafebrewing.com

BRANDS:
Santa Fe Brewing Santa Fe Chicken Killer Barley Wine (29 SRM, 86 IBU)
Santa Fe Brewing Santa Fe Nut Brown Ale (33 SRM, 18 IBU)
Santa Fe Brewing Santa Fe Pale Ale (13 SRM, 48 IBU)
Santa Fe Brewing Santa Fe State Pen Porter (77 SRM, 55 IBU)
Santa Fe Brewing Santa Fe Wheat (3.5 SRM, 23 IBU)

States Available: AZ, CA, CO, NM, NV, OK, TX, UT

Scuttlebutt Brewing Company

1524 W. Marine View Drive
Everett, WA 98201
425-257-9316
www.scuttlebuttbrewing.com

BRANDS:
Scuttlebutt 10 Below (22 IBU)
Scuttlebutt Amber Ale (23 IBU)
Scuttlebutt Gale Force IPA (96 IBU)
Scuttlebutt Homeport Blonde (17 IBU)
Scuttlebutt Porter (20 IBU)
Scuttlebutt Weizenbock (23 IBU)

States Available: WA

Seabright Brewery

519 Seabright Avenue
Santa Cruz, CA 95060
831-426-2793
www.seabrightbrewery.com

BRANDS:
Seabright Brewery Blur IPA
Seabright Brewery Oatmeal Stout
Seabright Brewery Resolution Red

States Available: CA

BREWER INDEX (Alphabetical)

Sebago Brewing Company – *page 543*

48 Sanford Drive
Gorham, ME 04038
207-856-2537
www.sebagobrewing.com

BRANDS:
Sebago Brewing Bass Ackwards Berryblue Ale
  (13.3 SRM, 16.1 IBU)
Sebago Brewing Boathouse Brown Ale
  (49.5 SRM, 24.4 IBU)
Sebago Brewing Frye's Leap India Pale Ale (11.5 SRM, 54.4 IBU) – *page 543*
Sebago Brewing Hefe-Weizen (4.6 SRM, 19.8 IBU)
Sebago Brewing Lake Trout Stout (171.5 SRM, 31.4 IBU)
Sebago Brewing Midnight Porter (98.0 SRM, 35.7 IBU)
Sebago Brewing Northern Light Ale
Sebago Brewing Runabout Red Ale (26.24 SRM, 37.3 IBU)
Sebago Brewing Slick Nick Winter Ale (21.1 SRM, 38.7 IBU)

States Available: MA, ME

Schlafly Beer

2100 Locust Street
St. Louis, MO 63103
314-241-2337
www.schlafly.com

BRANDS:
Schlafly American Pale Ale (50 IBU)
Schlafly Christmas Ale
Schlafly Coffee Stout (40 IBU)
Schlafly Hefeweizen
Schlafly IPA
Schlafly Irish Extra Stout (45 IU)
Schlafly No. 15 (15 IBU)
Schlafly Oatmeal Stout (40 IBU)
Schlafly Oktoberfest (25 IBU)
Schlafly Pale Ale (27 IBU)
Schlafly Pilsner (35 IBU) (Pilsner)
Schlafly Pumpkin Ale (16 IBU)
Schlafly Raspberry Hefeweizen
Schlafly Saison (22 IBU)
Schlafly Scotch Ale (25 IBU)
Schlafly Summer Kölsch (25 IBU)
Schlafly Winter ESB (45 IBU) (ESB)

States Available: IL, IN, KY, MI, MO

Sheepscot Valley Brewing Company

74 Hollywood Boulevard
Whitefield, ME 04353
207-549-5530
www.photo-ne.com/sheepscot/sheepscot4.html

BRANDS:
Sheepscot Valley Brewing Boothbay Special Bitter
Sheepscot Valley Brewing Damariscotta Double Brown
Sheepscot Valley Brewing Monhegan Wheat
Sheepscot Valley Brewing Pemaquid Ale

States Available: ME

Shenandoah Brewing Company

652 S Pickett Street
Alexandria, VA 22034
703-823-9508
www.shenandoahbrewing.com

BRANDS:
Shenandoah Brewing Big Meadow Pale Ale
Shenandoah Brewing Black and Tan Beer
Shenandoah Brewing Old Rag Mountain Ale
Shenandoah Brewing Skyland Red Ale
Shenandoah Brewing Stony Man Stout
Shenandoah Brewing White Water Wheat

States Available: DC, VA

Sherwood Forest Brewers

655 Farm Road
Marlborough, MA 01752
877-272-4376
www.sherwoodbrewers.com

BRANDS:
Sherwood Forest Archer's Ale

States Available: MA

The Shipyard Brewing Company – *page 544*

86 Newbury Street
Portland, ME 04103
207-761-0807
www.shipyard.com

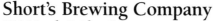

BRANDS:
Shipyard Brewing Bluefin Stout (110 SRM, 42 IBU)
Shipyard Brewing Brown (19 SRM, 28 IBU)
Shipyard Brewing Chamberland Pale Ale (7.5 SRM, 35 IBU)
Shipyard Brewing Export Ale (8.5 SRM, 29 IBU) – *page 544*
Shipyard Brewing IPA (11 SRM, 50 IBU)
Shipyard Brewing Light (3.5 SRM, 46 IBU)
Shipyard Brewing Longfellow (47 SRM, 40 IBU)
Shipyard Brewing Old Thumper Extra Special Ale (12 SRM, 34 IBU)
Shipyard Brewing Prelude Special Ale (29 SRM, 46 IBU)
Shipyard Brewing Pumpkinhead Ale (6 SRM, 14 IBU)
Shipyard Brewing Summer (6.5 SRM, 27 IBU)

States Available: All 50 States

Shmaltz Brewing Company – *page 545*

912 Cole Street, #338
San Francisco, CA 94117
415-339-7462
www.shmaltz.com

BRANDS:
Shmaltz Brewing Bittersweet Lenny's
R.I.P.A.
Shmaltz Brewing Genesis 10:10
Shmaltz Brewing Genesis Ale – *page 545*
Shmaltz Brewing Jewbelation
Shmaltz Brewing Messiah Bold

States Available: AZ, CA, CO, CT, DC, DE, FL, GA, ID, IL, IN, KY, MA, MD, MI, MO, NC, NJ, NY, OH, PA, SC, TN, VA, WI

Short's Brewing Company

121 North Bridge Street
Bellaire, MI 49615
231-533-6622
www.shortsbrewing.com

BRANDS:
Short's Brew Mystery Stout
Short's Brew The Curl (50 IBU)

States Available: MI

Sierra Blanca Brewing Company

503 12th Street, P.O. Box 308
Carrizozo, NM 88301
505-648-6606
www.sierrablancabrewery.com

BRANDS:
Sierra Blanca Brewing Alien Amber Ale
Sierra Blanca Brewing Nut Brown
Sierra Blanca Brewing Pale Ale
Sierra Blanca Brewing Pilsner

States Available: NM

Sierra Nevada Brewing Company

1075 E 20th Street
Chico, CA 95928-6722
530-893-3520
www.sierranevada.com

BRANDS:
Sierra Nevada Bigfoot Ale (38 SRM, 100 IBU)
Sierra Nevada Celebration Ale 21 SRM, 70 IBU)
Sierra Nevada Pale Ale (12 SRM, 38 IBU)
Sierra Nevada Porter (50 SRM, 39 IBU)
Sierra Nevada Stout (70 SRM, 53 IBU)
Sierra Nevada Summerfest (6 SRM, 30 IBU)
Sierra Nevada Wheat Beer (5 SRM, 26 IBU)

States Available: All 50 States

Brewer Index (Alphabetical)

Siletz Brewing Company, Inc.

P.O. Box 116
Siletz, OR 97380
541-444-7012
www.siletzbrewing.com

BRANDS:
Siletz Brewing Company Amber Ale (24.3 SRM, 53.5 IBU)
Siletz Brewing Company Black Diamond Imperial Porter (76.1 SRM, 45 IBU)
Siletz Brewing Company Chocolate Porter (86.9 SRM, 41.7 IBU)
Siletz Brewing Company Lovin Lager (11.6 SRM, 34.3 IBU)
Siletz Brewing Company Noggin Knocker (83.6 SRM, 67.9 IBU)
Siletz Brewing Company Oatmeal Cream Stout (87.2 SRM, 64.1 IBU)
Siletz Brewing Company Paddle Me IPA (12 SRM, 76.8 IBU)
Siletz Brewing Company Red Ale (19.1 SRM, 42.3 IBU)
Siletz Brewing Company Spruce Ale (25.7 SRM, 35.2 IBU)
Siletz Brewing Company Winter Warmer (38.5 SRM, 53.8 IBU)
Siletz Brewing Company Wooly Bully (16.8 SRM, 38.2 IBU)

States Available: OH, OR

Silver Gulch Brewing & Bottling

P.O. Box 82125
Fairbanks, AK 99708-2125
907-452-2739
www.silvergulch.com

BRANDS:
Silver Gulch Coldfoot Pilsner Lager (22 IBU)
Silver Gulch Copper Creek Amber Ale (24 IBU)
Silver Gulch Fairbanks Lager (21 IBU)
Silver Gulch Old 55 Pale Ale
Silver Gulch Pick Axe Porter (29 IBU)

States Available: AK

Ska Brewing Company – *page 546*

545 Turner Drive
Durango, CO 81301
970-247-5792
www.skabrewing.com

BRANDS:
Ska Brewing Buster Nut Brown Ale (19 SRM, 30 IBU) – *page 548*
Ska Brewing Decadent Imperial I.P.A. (14 SRM, 100 IBU) – *page 546*
Ska Brewing Mexican Logger
Ska Brewing Nefarious Ten Pin Imperial Porter (37 SRM, 77 IBU) – *page 547*
Ska Brewing Pinstripe Red Ale (10 SRM, 42 IBU) – *page 547*
Ska Brewing Special ESB (in cans) (8 SRM, 58 IBU) – *page 549*
Ska Brewing Steel Toe Stout (41 SRM, 29 IBU) – *page 549*
Ska Brewing Ten Pin Porter
Ska Brewing True Blonde Ale (4 SRM, 40 IBU) – *page 548*
Ska Brewing True Blonde Dubbel

States Available: CO, NC, NM

Skagit River Brewery

404 South 3rd Street
Mount Vernon, WA 98273
360-336-2884
www.skagitbrew.com

BRANDS:
Skagit River Brewing Sculler's IPA
Skagit River Yellow Jacket Pale Ale

States Available: Contact Brewery

BREWER INDEX (Alphabetical)

Slab City Brewing

West 3590 Pit Lane
Bonduel, WI 54107
715-758-2337
www.slabcitybeer.com

BRANDS:
Slab City Brewing Esker Alt
Slab City Brewing Milkhouse Stout
Slab City Brewing Old 47 Pale Ale
Slab City Brewing Shawano Gold
Slab City Brewing W.C. Bitter
Slab City Brewing Xenabock

States Available: WI

Sly Fox Brewing Company

519 Kimberton Road
Phoenixville, PA 19460
610-935-4540
www.slyfoxbeer.com

BRANDS:
Sly Fox Black Raspberry Reserve (16 IBU)
Sly Fox Christmas Ale (16 IBU)
Sly Fox Dunkel Lager (21 IBU)
Sly Fox Gang Aft Angley (20 IBU)
Sly Fox Ichor (20 IBU)
Sly Fox Incubus (39 IBU)
Sly Fox Instigator Doppelbock (20 IBU)
Sly Fox Odyssey (90 IBU)
Sly Fox Oktoberfest (25 IBU)
Sly Fox Phoenix Pale Ale (40 IBU)
Sly Fox Pikeland Pils (44 IBU)
Sly Fox Route 113 India Pale Ale (113 IBU)
Sly Fox Royal Weisse (11 IBU)
Sly Fox Saison VOS (32 IBU)

States Available: PA

Smuttynose Brewing Company

225 Heritage Avenue
Portsmouth, NH 03801-5610
603-436-4026
www.smuttynose.com

BRANDS:
Smuttynose Brewing Baltic Porter
Smuttynose Brewing Barleywine Style Ale
Smuttynose Brewing Big A IPA
Smuttynose Brewing Farmhouse Ale
Smuttynose Brewing Imperial Stout
Smuttynose Brewing Imperial IPA
Smuttynose Brewing IPA (65 IBU)
Smuttynose Brewing Maibock
Smuttynose Brewing Octoberfest
Smuttynose Brewing Old Brown Dog Ale (15 IBU)
Smuttynose Brewing Portsmouth Lager (15 IBU)
Smuttynose Brewing Pumpkin Ale
Smuttynose Brewing Really Old Brown Dog Old Ale
Smuttynose Brewing Robust Porter (15 IBU)
Smuttynose Brewing S'muttonator Doppelbock
Smuttynose Brewing Scotch Style Ale
Smuttynose Brewing Shoals Pale Ale (30 IBU)
Smuttynose Brewing Summer Weizen
Smuttynose Brewing Weizenheimer
Smuttynose Brewing Wheat Wine Ale
Smuttynose Brewing Winter Ale

States Available: CT, DE, MA, MD, ME, NC, NH, NJ, NY, PA, RI, VA, VT, WI

Snake River Brewing Company – *page 550*

P.O. Box 3317, 265 South Millward
Jackson Hole, WY 83001
307-739-2337
www.snakeriverbrewing.com

BRANDS:
Snake River Lager (18 IBU)
Snake River OB-1 Organic Ale (22 IBU) – *page 550*
Snake River Pale Ale (32 IBU)
Snake River Zonker Stout (36 IBU)

States Available: CO, ID, MT, OH, UT, WI, WY

BREWER INDEX (Alphabetical)

Snipes Mountain Brewing Company

905 Yakima Valley Highway, P.O. Box 274
Sunnyside, WA 98944
509-837-2739
www.snipesmountain.com

BRANDS:
Snipes Mountain Brewing Coyote Moon
Snipes Mountain Brewing Crazy Ivan's Imperial Stout
Snipes Mountain Brewing Extra Blonde Ale
Snipes Mountain Brewing Harvest Ale
Snipes Mountain Brewing Hefeweizen
Snipes Mountain Brewing India Pale Ale
Snipes Mountain Brewing Porter
Snipes Mountain Brewing Red Sky Ale
Snipes Mountain Brewing Roza Reserve
Snipes Mountain Brewing Sunnyside Pale Ale

States Available: ID, OR, WA

Snoqualmie Falls Brewing Company

8032 Falls Avenue South East, P.O. Box 924
Snoqualmie, WA 98065
425-831-2357
www.fallsbrew.com

BRANDS:
Avalanche Winter Ale (48 IBU)
Copperhead Pale Ale (32 IBU)
Harvest Moon Festbier (24 IBU)
PGA (Perfectly Great Amber) (23 IBU)
Spring Fever (32 IBU)
Steam Train Porter (28 IBU)
Summer Beer (28 IBU)
Wildcat IPA (75 IBU)

States Available: WA

Snowshoe Brewing Company

2050 Highway 4
Arnold, CA 95223
209-795-2272
www.snowshoebrewing.com

BRANDS:
Snowshoe Brewing Grizzly Brown Ale
Snowshoe Brewing Snoweizen Wheat Ale
Snowshoe Brewing Thompson Pale Ale

States Available: Contact Brewery

Sonoran Brewing Company (Kegs/Growlers)

10426 East Jomax Road
Scottsdale, AZ 85255
602-484-7775
www.sonorabrew.com

BRANDS:
Sonora Brewing Burning Bird Pale Ale
Sonora Brewing C.I.A. - Citrus Infused Ale
Sonora Brewing Desert Amber
Sonora Brewing India Pale Ale
Sonora Brewing Mandarin Orange Hefeweizen
Sonora Brewing Old Saguaro Barley Wine
Sonora Brewing Top Down Red Ale

States Available: Contact Brewery

South Shore Brewery

808 West Main Street
Ashland, WI 54806
715-682-4200
www.southshorebrewery.com

BRANDS:
South Shore Brewery Herbal Cream Ale
South Shore Brewery Honey Pils
South Shore Brewery Nut Brown
South Shore Brewery Rhodes' Scholar Stout

States Available: MI, MN, WI

BREWER INDEX (Alphabetical)

Southampton Publick House – *page 551*

SOUTH**S**AMPTON
Ales & Lagers

40 Bowden Square
Southampton, NY 11968
631-283-2800
www.publick.com

BRANDS:
Southampton 10th Anniversary Old Ale
Southampton Abbot 12
Southampton Biere de Garde
Southampton Double White Ale – *page 551*
Southampton Grand Cru
Southampton Imperial Porter
Southampton IPA
Southampton May Bock
Southampton Pumpkin Ale
Southampton Saison
Southampton Secret Ale
Southampton Triple

States Available: CT, MA, NJ, NY, PA, RI

Southern Tier Brewing Company – *page 552*

2051A Stoneman Circle
Lakewood, NY 14750-0166
716-763-5479
www.southerntierbrewing.com

BRANDS:
Southern Tier Brewing Belgian Tripel Ale
Southern Tier Brewing Big Red Imperial Red
Southern Tier Brewing Black Water Series Imperial Stout
Southern Tier Brewing Harvest Ale
Southern Tier Brewing Heavy Weizen
Southern Tier Brewing Hop Sun Summer Ale
Southern Tier Brewing Imperial IPA – *page 552*
Southern Tier Brewing Old Man Winter Warmer
Southern Tier Brewing Phin & Matt's
Southern Tier Brewing Porter

States Available: CT, DC, IN, IL, MA, MD, MI, NY, OH, PA, RI, WI, VA

Spanish Peaks Brewing Company/ United States Beverage

700 Canal Street
Stamford, CT 06902
203-961-8215
www.blackdogales.com

BRANDS:
Black Dog Ale (36 IBU)
Black Dog American Pale Ale (50 IBU)
Black Dog Honey Raspberry Ale (12 IBU)
Black Dog Summer White Ale

States Available: All 50 States

Speakeasy Ales & Lagers, Inc.

1195 Evans Avenue, Suite A
San Francisco, CA 94124
415-642-3371
www.goodbeer.com

BRANDS:
Speakeasy Big Daddy IPA
Speakeasy Double Daddy Imperial IPA
Speakeasy Prohibition Ale
Speakeasy Untouchable Pale Ale

States Available: AZ, CA, DC, IL, MI, NJ, NV, NY, OH, OR, PA, VA

Spilker Ales

300 W 4th Street
Cortland, NE 68331
402-798-7445
www.spilkerales.com

BRANDS:
Spilker Ales Hopluia Ale

States Available: NE

Sprecher Brewing

701 West Glendale Avenue
Glendale, WI 53209
414-964-7837
www.sprecherbrewery.com

BRANDS:
Sprecher Brewing Abbey Triple (13 IBU)
Sprecher Brewing Barley Wine (46 IBU)
Sprecher Brewing Black Bavarian (32 IBU)
Sprecher Brewing Bourbon Barrel Barley Wine (46 IBU)
Sprecher Brewing Bourbon Barrel Scotch Ale (21 IBU)
Sprecher Brewing Dopple Bock (31 IBU)
Sprecher Brewing Generation Porter (26 IBU)
Sprecher Brewing Hefe' Weiss (11 IBU)
Sprecher Brewing Imperial Stout (32 IBU)
Sprecher Brewing India Pale Ale (88 IBU)
Sprecher Brewing Irish Stout (26 IBU)
Sprecher Brewing Mai Bock (24 IBU)
Sprecher Brewing Mbege Ale (10 IBU)
Sprecher Brewing Micro-Light Ale (6 IBU)
Sprecher Brewing Oktoberfest (15 IBU)
Sprecher Brewing Piper's Scotch Ale (21 IBU)
Sprecher Brewing Pub Ale (17 IBU)
Sprecher Brewing Shakparo Ale (9 IBU)
Sprecher Brewing Special Amber (22 IBU)
Sprecher Brewing Winter Brew (0 IBU)

States Available: AL, AR, AZ, CA, IA, IL, IN, KS, KY, MA, MD, MI, MN, MO, OH, VA, WA, WI

Springfield Brewing Company

305 South Market
Springfield, MO 65806
417-832-8277
www.springfieldbrewingco.com

BRANDS:
Springfield Brewing Munich Lager (23 IBU)
Springfield Brewing Pale Ale (25 IBU)
Springfield Brewing Porter (30 IBU)
Springfield Brewing Unfiltered Wheat (15 IBU)

States Available: MO

St. Croix Beer Company

P.O. Box 16545
St. Paul, MN 55116
651-387-0708
www.stcroixbeer.com

BRANDS:
St. Croix Cream
St. Croix Maple Ale
St. Croix Serrano Pepper Ale

States Available: MN, WI

St. George Brewing Company – *page 553*

204 Challenger Way
Hampton, VA 23666
757-865-7781
www.stgeorgebrewingco.com

BRANDS:
St. George Brewing Company Golden Ale
  (6.9 SRM, 33 IBU)
St. George Brewing Company IPA
  (9 SRM, 50 IBU) – *page 553*
St. George Brewing Company Pale Ale
St. George Brewing Company Porter (81.1 SRM, 32 IBU)
St. George Brewing Company Vienna Lager (22 IBU)
St. George Brewing Fall Bock (28 IBU)

States Available: NC, SC, VA

Stampede Brewing Company

100 Highland Park Village #200
Dallas, TX 75205
214-295-3255
www.stampedebeer.com

BRANDS:
Stampede Light

States Available: Contact Brewery

Starr Hill Brewery

5391 Three Notched Road
Crozet, VA 22932
434-823-5671
www.starrhillbeer.com

BRANDS:
Starr Hill Amber Ale
Starr Hill Dark Starr Stout
Starr Hill Jomo Lager
Starr Hill Pale Ale

States Available: Contact Brewery

Steamworks Brewing Company

801 East Second Avenue
Durango, CO 81301
970-259-9200
www.steamworksbrewing.com

BRANDS:
Backside Stout (28.5 SRM, 42.1 IBU)
Colorado Kölsch (3.9 SRM, 18.8 IBU)
Conductor (11 SRM, 96 IBU)
Engineer Light Lager (4 SRM, 21.5 IBU)
Lizard Head Red (12.4 SRM, 27.8 IBU)
Spruce Goose (16.1 SRM, 21 IBU)
Steam Engine Lager (12.3 SRM, 21.9 IBU)
Third Eye Pale Ale (8.8 SRM, 59 IBU)

States Available: Contact Brewery

Stevens Point Brewery

2617 Water Street
Stevens Point, WI 54481
715-344-9310
www.pointbeer.com

BRANDS:
Point Cascade Pale Ale
Point Classic Amber
Point Honey Light
Point Premier Light
Point Special Lager
Point Spring Bock
Point White Bière

States Available: GA, IA, IL, IN, KS, MN, MO, ND, SD, WI

Stone Brewing Company – *page 554*

1999 Citracado Parkway
Escondido, CA 92029
760-471-4999 Ext. 1561
www.stonebrew.com

BRANDS:
Arrogant Bastard Ale
Double Bastard Ale (100+ IBU)
Stone Anniversary Ale
Stone Imperial Russian Stout (90 IBU)
Stone IPA (77 IBU)
Stone Levitation Ale (45 IBU)
Stone Old Guardian Barley Wine (95 IBU)
Stone Pale Ale (41 IBU)
Stone Ruination IPA (100+ IBU) – *page 554*
Stone Smoked Porter (53 IBU)
Stone Vertical Epic Ale

States Available: AK, AZ, CA, CO, DC, ID, IN, KY, MA, NJ, NM, NV, NY, OH, OR, PA, TN, TX, VA, WA

Stone Coast Brewing Company

23 Rice Street
Portland, ME 04103
207-347-5729
www.stonecoast.com

BRANDS:
Black Bear Porter
Jackson's Winter Ale
Knuckleball Bock
Stone Coast 420 India Pale Ale
Sunday River Alt
Sunday River Lager
Sunday River Sunsplash Golden Ale

States Available: CT, IL, MA, ME, NH, NY, RI, VT

Stoudt's Brewing Company

2800 North Reading Road, Route 272
Adamstown, PA 19501
717-484-4386
www.stoudtsbeer.com

BRANDS:
Stoudt's Abbey Triple (37 IBU)
Stoudt's American Pale Ale (40 IBU)
Stoudt's Blonde Double Maibock (35 IBU)
Stoudt's Double India Pale Ale (90 IBU)
Stoudt's Fat Dog Stout (55 IBU)
Stoudt's Gold Lager (25 IBU)
Stoudt's Oktoberfest (24 IBU)
Stoudt's Pils (40 IBU)
Stoudt's Scarlet Lady Ale (32 IBU)
Stoudt's Weizen (12 IBU)
Stoudt's Winter Ale

States Available: CA, DC, FL, GA, MA, MD, MI, NJ, NY, OH, PA, VA

Straub Brewing

303 Sorg Street
St. Mary's, PA 15857
814-834-2875
www.straubbeer.com

BRANDS:
Straub
Straub Light

States Available: OH, PA

Streich's Brewing Company, LLC

53 Richard Street Route 68
West Hartford, CT 06119
860-233-4545

BRANDS:
Streich's Brewing Naughty Fish Pale Ale

States Available: Contact Brewery

Sudwerk

2001 Second Street
Davis, CA 95616
530-756-2739
www.sudwerk.com

BRANDS:
Sudwerk Doppelbock
Sudwerk Hefe-Weizen
Sudwerk Lager
Sudwerk Leatherneck
Sudwerk Marzen
Sudwerk Pilsner

States Available: Contact Brewery

BREWER INDEX (Alphabetical)

Summit Brewing Company – *page 555*

910 Montreal Circle
St. Paul, MN 55102
651-265-7800
www.summitbrewing.com

BRANDS:
Summit ESB (26 SRM, 50 IBU) – *page 557*
Summit Extra Pale Ale
  (13 SRM, 42 IBU) – *page 555*
Summit Grand Pilsner
  (5 SRM, 25 IBU) – *page 558*
Summit Great Northern Porter
  (63 SRM, 50 IBU) – *page 556*
Summit Hefe Weizen (5 SRM, 18 IBU)
Summit India Pale Ale (25 SRM, 60 IBU) – *page 556*
Summit Maibock (10 SRM, 30 IBU)
Summit Oktoberfest (14 SRM, 25 IBU)
Summit Scandia Ale (5.5 SRM, 17 IBU) – *page 558*
Summit Winter Ale (45 SRM, 35 IBU) – *page 557*

States Available: CO, IA, IL, IN, KY, MI, MN, MT, ND, NE, OH, PA, SD, WI

Surly Brewing Company

4811 Dusharme Drive
Brooklyn Center, MN 55429
763-535-3330
www.surlybrewing.com

BRANDS:
Surly Brewing Bender
Surly Brewing Furious

States Available: MN

Sweetwater Brewing Company – *page 559*

195 Ottley Drive
Atlanta, GA 30324
404-691-2537
www.sweetwaterbrew.com

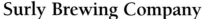

BRANDS:
Sweetwater Brewing 420 Extra Pale Ale – *page 559*
Sweetwater Brewing IPA
Sweetwater Brewing Sweet Georgia Brown
Sweetwater Brewing Sweetwater Blue
Sweetwater Brewing Sweetwater Festive Ale

States Available: AL, FL, GA, NC, SC, TN

Telegraph Brewing Company

416 North Salsipuedes Street
Santa Barbara, CA 93103
805-963-5018
www.telegraphbrewing.com
BRANDS:
Telegraph Brewing California Ale
Telegraph Brewing Golden Wheat Ale
Telegraph Brewing Stock Porter

States Available: CA

Terminal Gravity Brewing

803 South East School Street
Enterprise, OR 97828
541-426-0518
www.terminalgravitybrewing.com
BRANDS:
States Available: Contact Brewery

BREWER INDEX (Alphabetical)

Terrapin Beer Company – *page 560*

196 Alps Road #2-237
Athens, GA 30606
706-202-4467
www.terrapinbeer.com

BRANDS:
Terrapin All American Imperial Pilsner (75 IBU)
Terrapin Big Hoppy Monster (75 IBU)
Terrapin Golden Ale (21 IBU)
Terrapin Rye Pale Ale (45 IBU) – *page 560*
Terrapin Rye Squared (80 IBU)
Terrapin Wake-N-Bake Coffee Oatmeal Imperial Stout (75 IBU)

States Available: AL, GA, NC, SC, TN

Terre Haute Brewing Company

401-02 South 9th Street, P.O. Box 2027
Terre Haute, IN 47807
812-234-2800
www.cvbeer.com

BRANDS:
Terre Haute Brewing Champagne Velvet Amber
Terre Haute Brewing Champagne Velvet Bock
Terre Haute Brewing Champagne Velvet Pilsner

States Available: IN

The Academy of Fine Beers, LLC

435 Fernleaf
Corona Del Mar, CA 92625
949-862-5808
www.bierbitzch.com

BRANDS:
Josef Bierbitzch Golden Pilsner

States Available: AZ, CA, GA, IL, MI, NE, NV

The Bethlehem Brew Works

569 Main Street
Bethlehem, PA 18018
610-882-1300
www.thebrewworks.com

BRANDS:
Bethlehem Brew Works Pumpkin Ale
Bethlehem Brew Works Rude Elf's Reserve

States Available: Contact Brewery

The Black Mountain/Chili Beer Brewing Company – *page 469*

6245 E.Cave Creek Road
Cave Creek, AZ 85331-9046
602-488-4742
www.chilibeer.com

BRANDS:
Black Mountain Cave Creek Chili Beer – *page 469*
Black Mountain Frog Light
Black Mountain Gold
Black Mountain Juanderful Wheat
Black Mountain Ocotillo Amber
Black Mountain South of the Border Porter

States Available: AL, AZ, CA, CO, FL, GA, IA, IL, IN, KS, KY, MA, MN, MO, ND, NE, NJ, NY, OH, TN, TX, VA, WA, WI

The Church Brew Works

3525 Liberty Avenue
Pittsburgh, PA 15201
412-688-8200
www.churchbrew.com

BRANDS:
Church Brew Works Blast Furnace Stout (30 IBU)
Church Brew Works Celestial Gold (18 IBU)
Church Brew Works Millenium Trippel Ale
Church Brew Works Pious Monk Dunkel (20 IBU)
Church Brew Works Pipe Organ Pale Ale (30 IBU)
Church Brew Works Quadzilla

States Available: PA

BREWER INDEX (Alphabetical)

The Defiant Brewing Company

6 East Dexter Plaza
Pearl River, NY 10965
845-920-8602
www.Defiantbrewing.com

BRANDS:
Defiant Brewing 3
Defiant Brewing Big Thumper Ale
Defiant Brewing Christmas Ale
Defiant Brewing ESB
Defiant Brewing Inspiration Ale
Defiant Brewing Little Thumper Ale
Defiant Brewing Pearl River Lager
Defiant Brewing Pilsner
Defiant Brewing Porter
Defiant Brewing Stephano's Stout
Defiant Brewing The Horseman's Ale

States Available: Contact Brewery

The Dock Street Brewery Company

P.O. Box 301
Gladwyne, PA 19035
www.dockstreetbeer.com

BRANDS:
Dock Street Amber (16 SRM, 28 IBU)
Illuminator Dock Street Bock (27 SRM, 28 IBU)

States Available: DE, NJ, PA

The Fort Collins Brewery – *page 500*

196 Alps Road #2-237
1900 E. Lincoln Avenue, #B
Fort Collins, CO 80524
970-472-1499
www.fortcollinsbrewery.com

BRANDS:
Fort Collins Chocolate Stout
Fort Collins Edgar Lager
Fort Collins Major Tom's Pomegranate Wheat – *page 500*
Fort Collins Retro Red
Fort Collins The Kidd Lager
Fort Collins Z Lager

States Available: CO, IA, IN, MD, NC, NM, SC, VA, WI, WY

The Matt Brewing – *page 562*

811 Edward Street
Utica, NY 13502-4092
315-624-2400
www.saranac.com/products

BRANDS:
Saranac 12 Beers of Summer
Saranac 12 Beers of Winter
Saranac Adirondack Lager
Saranac Black & Tan
Saranac Black Forest
Saranac Caramel Porter
Saranac India Pale Ale
Saranac Lager
Saranac Octoberfest
Saranac Pale Ale – *page 562*
Saranac Season's Best
Saranac Trail Mix

States Available: CT, DC, DE, GA, IA, IN, KS, MA, NH, NJ, NY, OH, PA, RI, SC, VA, VT, WV

BREWER INDEX (Alphabetical)

The Narragansett Brewing Company

60 Ship Street
Providence, RI 02903
401-437-8970
www.narragansettbeer.com

BRANDS:
Narragansett Beer

States Available: MA, RI

The Northern Lights Brewing Company

1003 East Trent Avenue
Spokane, WA 99202
509-244-4909
www.nwbrewpage.com

BRANDS:
Northern Lights Blueberry Creme Ale
Northern Lights Chocolate Dunkel
Northern Lights Creme Ale
Northern Lights Crystal Bitter
Northern Lights Pale Ale
Northern Lights Winter Ale

States Available: ID, WA

The Palisade Brewery

P.O. Box 1535
Palisade, CO 81526
970-464-7257
www.palisadebrewery.com

BRANDS:
The Palisade Brewery Farmer's Friend
The Palisade Brewery Orchard Amber Ale
The Palisade Brewery PAL Beer
The Palisade Brewery Red Truck IPA

States Available: Contact Brewery

The Sea Dog Brewing Company – *page 542*

26 Front Street
Bangor, ME 04401
207-947-8009
www.seadogbrewing.com

BRANDS:
Sea Dog Apricot Wheat Beer (6 SRM, 8 IBU)
Sea Dog Old East India Pale Ale (18 SRM, 44 IBU)
Sea Dog Pumpkin Ale (6 SRM, 14 IBU)
Sea Dog Raspberry Wheat (6.4 SRM, 8.2 IBU)
Sea Dog Riverdriver Hazelnut Porter (54 SRM, 35 IBU)
Sea Dog Summer Ale (6 SRM, 14 IBU)
Sea Dog Wild Blueberry Wheat Ale – *page 542*
Sea Dog Winter Ale (23 SRM, 39 IBU)

States Available: All 50 States

The Spoetzl Brewing (Gambrinus)

603 East Brewery Street
Shiner, TX 77984
361-594-3383
www.shiner.com

BRANDS:
Shiner 96 Marzen Style Ale
Shiner Blonde
Shiner Bock
Shiner Dunkelweizen
Shiner Hefeweizen
Shiner Kölsch
Shiner Light

States Available: AK, AL, AR, AZ, CA, CO, FL, GA, IA, ID, KS, KY, LA, MD, MN, MO, MS, MT, NC, NE, NM, NV, OH, OK, OR, SC, TN, TX, UT, VA, WA, WY

The Weeping Radish Brewery – *page 570*

Highway 64, P.O. Box 471
Manteo, NC 27954
252-491-5205
www.weepingradish.com

WEEPING RADISH
FARM•BREWERY

BRANDS:
Weeping Radish Altier (12.2 SRM, 47.2 IBU)
Weeping Radish Black Radish
 (22.6 SRM, 27 IBU) – *page 570*
Weeping Radish Christmas Bier (21.2 SRM, 33.7 IBU)
Weeping Radish Corolla Gold (4.6 SRM, 15.2 IBU)
Weeping Radish Corolla Light (2.7 SRM, 11.8 IBU)
Weeping Radish Fest (11.2 SRM, 24 IBU)
Weeping Radish Kölsch (5 SRM, 23.8 IBU)
Weeping Radish Maibock (9.4 SRM, 31.5 IBU)
Weeping Radish Marzen (11.2 SRM, 28.4 IBU)
Weeping Radish Weizen (3.3 SRM, 15.2 IBU)

States Available: DC, MD, NC, PA, VA

Thirsty Dog Brewing Company

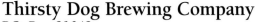

P.O. Box 31043
Independence, OH 44131
216-447-9336
www.thirstydog.com

BRANDS:
Thirsty Dog Balto Heroic Lager (17 IBU)
Thirsty Dog Hoppus Maximus (43 IBU)
Thirsty Dog Old Leghumper (24 IBU)
Thirsty Dog Siberian Night (58 IBU)

States Available: IN, KY, MD, OH, PA

Thomas Creek Brewery – *page 563*

2054 Piedmont Highway
Greenville, SC 29605-4840
864-605-1166
www.thomascreekbeer.com

BRANDS:
Thomas Creek Amber Ale (19.7 IBU)
Thomas Creek Dopplebock (20.7 IBU)
Thomas Creek IPA (45.8 IBU)
Thomas Creek Jingle Bell Bock (38.1 IBU)
Thomas Creek Multi Grain Ale (19.4 IBU)
Thomas Creek Octoberfest (18.9 IBU)
Thomas Creek Pilsner (18.2 IBU)
Thomas Creek Porter (40 IBU)
Thomas Creek Red Ale (14 IBU) – *page 563*
Thomas Creek Vanilla Cream Ale (15.8 IBU)

States Available: GA, NC, SC, TN

Thomas Hooker Brewing Company

P.O. Box 271062
West Hartford, CT 06127-1062
860-951-2739
www.troutbrookbeer.com

BRANDS:
Thomas Hooker American Pale Ale (7.6 SRM, 31 IBU)
Thomas Hooker Blonde Ale (1.93 SRM, 11 IBU)
Thomas Hooker Hop Meadow IPA (10.5 SRM, 73 IBU)
Thomas Hooker Imperial Porter (30 SRM, 61 IBU)
Thomas Hooker Irish Red (17.7 SRM, 22 IBU)
Thomas Hooker Liberator Doppelbock (20.4 SRM, 27 IBU)
Thomas Hooker Munich Golden Lager (3 SRM, 15 IBU)
Thomas Hooker Octoberfest (10 SRM, 11 IBU)
Thomas Hooker Old Marley Barley Wine (16 SRM, 74 IBU)

States Available: CT, GA, MA, NY, PA, RI

BREWER INDEX (Alphabetical)

Three Floyds Brewing Company

9750 Indiana Parkway
Munster, IN 46321
219-922-3565
www.threefloyds.com

BRANDS:
Three Floyds Brewing Alpha King (66 IBU)
Three Floyds Brewing Behemoth Barleywine
Three Floyds Brewing Black Sun Stout
Three Floyds Brewing Brian Boru
Three Floyds Brewing Christmas Porter
Three Floyds Brewing Dreadnaught IPA (100 IBU)
Three Floyds Brewing Gumballhead
Three Floyds Brewing Pride & Joy Mild Ale (21 IBU)
Three Floyds Brewing Rabbid Rabbit Saison
Three Floyds Brewing Robert the Bruce Scottish Ale (35 IBU)

States Available: DC, IA, IL, IN, NJ, OH, PA, RI, VA, WI

Tommyknocker Brewery

1401 Miner Street
Idaho Springs, CO 80452
303-567-4419
www.tommyknocker.com

BRANDS:
Tommyknocker Alpine Glacier Lager
Tommyknocker Butt Head Bock
Tommyknocker Imperial Nut Brown Ale
Tommyknocker Jack Whacker Wheat Ale
Tommyknocker Maple Nut Brown Ale
Tommyknocker Ornery Amber Lager
Tommyknocker Pick Axe Pale Ale
Tommyknocker Tundrabeary Ale

States Available: CO, IL, IN, KY, MN, ND, NE, OH, TX, VA, WI, WY

Tractor Brewing Company – *page 564*

120 Nelson Lane
Los Lunas, NM 87031-8299
505-866-0477
www.getplowed.com

BRANDS:
Tractor Brewing Double Plow Oatmeal Stout
Tractor Brewing Farmer's Tan – Red Ale – *page 564*
Tractor Brewing Haymaker – Honey Wheat Ale
Tractor Brewing Sod Buster Pale Ale

States Available: NM, NY

Trailhead Brewing Company

921 South Riverside Drive
St. Charles, MO 63302
636-946-2739
www.trailheadbrewing.com

BRANDS:
Missouri Brown Dark Ale
Old Courthouse Stout
Riverboat Raspberry Fruit Beer
Trailblazer Blonde Ale
Trailhead Red Amber Ale
Trailhead Spiced Pumpkin Ale

States Available: MO

Traverse Brewing Company

11550 US 31 South
Williamsburg, MI 49690
231-264-9343

BRANDS:
Traverse Brewing Batch 500 IPA
Traverse Brewing Manitou Amber Ale
Traverse Brewing Old Mission Lighthouse Ale
Traverse Brewing Power Island Porter
Traverse Brewing Sleeping Bear Brown Ale
Traverse Brewing Stout
Traverse Brewing Torch Lake Light Ale
Traverse Brewing Voss Wend Wheat

States Available: MI

BREWER INDEX (Alphabetical)

Tremont Brewery/Atlantic Coast Brewing Company – *page 565*

P.O. Box 52328
Boston, MA 02205
800-347-1150
www.tremontale.com

BRANDS:
Tremont Brewing Tremont Ale
  (14 SRM, 40 IBU) – *page 565*
Tremont Brewing Tremont IPA
  11.8 SRM, 50 IBU)
Tremont Brewing Tremont Summer
  (7 SRM, 22 IBU)
Tremont Brewing Tremont Winter (23 SRM, 39 IBU)

States Available: All 50 States

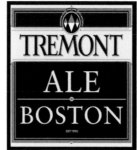

Tröegs Brewing Company – *page 566*

800 Paxton Street
Harrisburg, PA 17104
717-232-1297
www.troegs.com

BRANDS:
Tröegs Brewing Dreamweaver Wheat (15 IBU)
Tröegs Brewing Hopback Amber (55 IBU)
Tröegs Brewing Mad Elf (15 IBU)
Tröegs Brewing Nugget Nectar (93 IBU)
Tröegs Brewing Oatmeal Stout (60 IBU)
Tröegs Brewing Pale Ale (45 IBU)
Tröegs Brewing Rugged Trail Ale (28 IBU)
Tröegs Brewing Sunshine Pils (45 IBU)
Tröegs Brewing Troegenater Double Bock (25 IBU) – *page 566*

States Available: DE, MD, NJ, PA, VA

Trout River Brewing Company

P.O. Box 165
Lyndonville, VT 05851
802-626-9396
www.troutriverbrewing.com

BRANDS:
Trout River Brewing Chocolate Oatmeal Stout
Trout River Brewing Hoppin' Mad Trout
Trout River Brewing Rainbow Red Ale
Trout River Brewing Scottish Ale

States Available: NH, OR, VT

Tuckerman Brewing

64 Hobbs Street
Conway, NH 03818-1058
603-447-5400
www.tuckermanbrewing.com

BRANDS:
Tuckerman Brewing Headwall Alt
Tuckerman Brewing Pale Ale

States Available: MA, NH

Tuscan Brewing Company

25009 Kauffman Avenue
Red Bluff, CA 96080
530-529-9318
www.tuscanbrewery.com

BRANDS:
Tuscan Paradise Pale Ale
Tuscan Sundown Brown

States Available: CA

BREWER INDEX (Alphabetical)

Twisted Pine Brewing Company

3201 Walnut Street
Boulder, CO 80301
303-786-9270
www.isidb.com/twisted

BRANDS:
Big Daddy Espresso Stout
Billy's Chilies Beer
Twisted Pine American Amber Ale
Twisted Pine Blond Ale
Twisted Pine Honey Brown Ale
Twisted Pine Hoppy Boy
Twisted Pine Raspberry Wheat Ale
Twisted Pine Red Mountain Ale
Twisted Pine Twisted Stout

States Available: Contact Brewery

Two Brothers Brewing Company – *page 567*

30W 114 Butterfield Road
Warrenville, IL 60555
630-393-4800
www.twobrosbrew.com

BRANDS:
Two Brothers Bare Tree Weiss Wine (December)
Two Brothers Brown Project OPUS
Two Brothers Cane and Ebel (Limited Release)
Two Brothers Dog Days Dortmunder Style Lager
  (May-August)
Two Brothers Domaine Dupage French Country Ale (24 IBU) – *page 567*
Two Brothers Ebel's Weiss Beer (15 IBU)
Two Brothers Heavy Handed India Pale Ale (September-December)
Two Brothers Hop Juice Double India Pale Ale (100.1 IBU) (Limited Release)
Two Brothers Monarch White (March)
Two Brothers Northwind Imperial Stout (Winter)
Two Brothers Prairie Path Golden Ale (29 IBU)
Two Brothers The Bitter End Pale Ale (36 IBU)

States Available: IL, IN, MA, MI, OH, WI

Tyranena Brewing Company

1025 Owen Street, P.O. Box 736
Lake Mills, WI 53551
920-648-8699
www.tyranena.com

BRANDS:
Bitter Women IPA (9 SRM, 68 IBU)
Brewers Gone Wild! Bitter Women From Hell Extra IPA
Brewers Gone Wild! Hop Whore Imperial IPA
Brewers Gone Wild! Spank Me Baby Barley Wine
Brewers Gone Wild! Who's Your Daddy? Imperial Porter
Chief Black Hawk Porter (59 SRM, 35 IBU)
Fargo Brothers Hefeweizen (8 SRM, 12 IBU)
Fighting Finches Mai Bock (10 SRM, 25 IBU)
Gemuetlichkeit Oktoberfest (13 SRM, 22 IBU)
Headless Man Amber Alt (14 SRM, 25 IBU)
Rocky's Revenge (26 SRM, 30 IBU)
Shantytown Doppelbock (28 SRM, 23 IBU)
Stone Tepee Pale Ale (6 SRM, 32 IBU)
Three Beaches Honey Blonde (9 SRM, 68 IBU)

States Available: WI

Uinta Brewing Company – *page 568*

1722 South Fremont Drive (2375 West)
Salt Lake City, UT 84104
801-467-0909
www.uintabrewing.com

BRANDS:
Uinta Brewing Anglers Pale Ale (10 SRM, 39 IBU)
Uinta Brewing Anniversary Barley Wine (18 SRM, 72 IBU)
Uinta Brewing Blue Sky Pilsner (4 SRM, 20 IBU)
Uinta Brewing Bristlecone Brown Ale
Uinta Brewing Cutthroat Pale Ale (14 SRM, 22 IBU)
Uinta Brewing Gelande Amber Lager (15 SRM, 22 IBU)
Uinta Brewing Golden Spike Hefeweizen (8 SRM, 18 IBU)
Uinta Brewing King's Peak Porter (32 SRM, 25 IBU)
Uinta Brewing Solstice Kölsch (5 SRM, 25 IBU) – *page 568*
Uinta Brewing Trader IPA (10 SRM, 42 IBU)

States Available: CA, ID, NV, UT, VA

Upland Brewing Company

350 West 11th Street
Bloomington, IN 12411
812-336-BEER
www.uplandbeer.com

BRANDS:
Upland Brewing Company Amber (28 IBU)
Upland Brewing Company Bad Elmer's Porter (24 IBU)
Upland Brewing Company Dragonfly India Pale Ale (40 IBU)
Upland Brewing Company Maibock
Upland Brewing Company Pale Ale (19 IBU)
Upland Brewing Company Valley Weizen (9.8 IBU)
Upland Brewing Company Wheat Ale (11 IBU)

States Available: Contact Brewery

Utah Brewers Cooperative/Wasatch

1763 South 300 West
Salt Lake City, UT 84115
801-466-8855
www.utahbeers.com

BRANDS:
Chasing Tail Golden Ale
Squatters Captain Bastard's Oatmeal Stout
Squatters Full Suspension Pale Ale
Squatters Hefeweizen
Squatters India Pale Ale
Squatters Provo Girl Pilsner
Wasatch 1st Amendment Lager
Wasatch Apricot Hefe-Weizen
Wasatch Bobsled Brown Ale
Wasatch Evolution Amber Ale
Wasatch Polygamy Porter
Wasatch Pumpkin Ale
Wasatch Raspberry Wheat Beer
Wasatch Special Reserve Pale Ale

States Available: UT

Victory Brewing Company – *page 569*

420 Acorn Lane
Downingtown, PA 19335
610-873-0881
www.victorybeer.com

BRANDS:
Victory Festbier (15-20 IBU)
Victory Golden Monkey (20-25 IBU)
Victory HopDevil Ale (50-60 IBU) – *page 569*
Victory 'Hop' Wallop (70+ IBU)
Victory Lager (17-22 IBU)
Victory Moonglow Weizenbock (18-23 IBU)
Victory Old Horizontal Ale (60+ IBU)
Victory Prima Pils (40-50 IBU)
Victory St. Boisterous (20-25 IBU)
Victory St. Victorious (20-25 IBU)
Victory Storm King (70+ IBU)
Victory Sunrise Weissbier (13-18 IBU)
Victory Throwback Lager
Victory V Saison (25-30 IBU)
Victory V Twelve (25-30 IBU)
Victory Victorious Doppelbock
Victory Whirlwind Witbier (13-18 IBU)

States Available: CA, CT, DE, IL, MA, MD, MN, NC, NJ, NY, OH, OR, PA, TX, VA

Viking Brewing

234 Dallas Street West
Dallas, WI 54733
715-837-1824
www.vikingbrewing.com

BRANDS:
Viking Brewing Abby Normal
Viking Brewing Berserk
Viking Brewing Big Swede
Viking Brewing Blonde
Viking Brewing Copperhead
Viking Brewing Dim Whit
Viking Brewing Honey Pale Ale
Viking Brewing Honey Moon
Viking Brewing Hot Chocolate
Viking Brewing Invader
Viking Brewing J.S. Bock
Viking Brewing JuleOL
Viking Brewing Lime Twist
Viking Brewing Mj0d
Viking Brewing Morketid
Viking Brewing Queen Victoria's Secret
Viking Brewing Rauch
Viking Brewing Sylvan Springs
Viking Brewing Vienna Woods
Viking Brewing Weathertop Wheat
Viking Brewing Whole Stein

States Available: MN, WI

Wachusett Brewing Company

175 State Road East, Route 2A
Westminster, MA 01473-1208
978-874-9965
www.wachusettbrew.com

BRANDS:
Wachusett Black Shack Porter
Wachusett Blueberry
Wachusett Country Ale
Wachusett Green Monsta
Wachusett IPA
Wachusett Nut Brown Ale
Wachusett Octoberfest
Wachusett Quinn's Amber Ale
Wachusett Summer Breeze
Wachusett Winter Ale

States Available: MA, NY (Blueberry only)

Wagner Valley Brewing Company

9322 Route 414
Lodi, NY 14860
607-582-6450
www.wagnervineyards.com

BRANDS:
Wagner Valley Brewing Caywood Oatmeal Stout
Wagner Valley Brewing Dockside Amber Lager
Wagner Valley Brewing Grace House Wheat
Wagner Valley Brewing Indian Pale Ale
Wagner Valley Brewing Mill Street Pilsner
Wagner Valley Brewing Sled Dog Dopplebock
Wagner Valley Brewing Tripellbock Reserve

States Available: NY, RI

BREWER INDEX (Alphabetical)

Waimea Brewing Company

9400 Kaumualii Highway, P.O. Box 667
Waimea, HI 96796
425-443-3255
www.waimeabrewing.com

BRANDS:
Waimea Brewing Captain Cook's Original IPA (55 IBU)
Waimea Brewing Luau Lager (20 IBU)
Waimea Brewing Na Pali Pale Ale (26 IBU)
Waimea Brewing Pakala Porter (22 IBU)
Waimea Brewing Wai'ale'ale Ale (18 IBU)
Waimea Brewing Waimea Bay Pale Ale (40 IBU)

States Available: CA, HI

Warbird Brewing Company

10510 Majic Port Lane
Fort Wayne, IN 46819
260-459-2400
www.warbirdbrewing.com

BRANDS:
Warbird Brewing P47 Warbird Wheat (6 SRM, 18 IBU)
Warbird Brewing T-6 Red Ale (14.5 SRM, 15 IBU)

States Available: Contact Brewery

Weyerbacher Brewing Company

905g Line Street
Easton, PA 18042-7379
610-559-5561
www.weyerbacher.com

BRANDS:
Weyerbacher Brewing Autumn Fest
Weyerbacher Brewing Black Hole
Weyerbacher Brewing Blanche
Weyerbacher Brewing Blithering Idiot
Weyerbacher Brewing Decadence
Weyerbacher Brewing Double Simcoe
Weyerbacher Brewing Eleven
Weyerbacher Brewing ESB Ale
Weyerbacher Brewing HefeWeizen
Weyerbacher Brewing Heresy Imperial Stout
Weyerbacher Brewing Hops Infusion India Pale Ale
Weyerbacher Brewing Imperial Pumpkin Ale
Weyerbacher Brewing Insanity
Weyerbacher Brewing Merry Monk's Ale
Weyerbacher Brewing Old Heathen
Weyerbacher Brewing Prophecy
Weyerbacher Brewing QUAD
Weyerbacher Brewing Raspberry Imperial Stout
Weyerbacher Brewing Scotch Ale
Weyerbacher Brewing Winter Ale

States Available: DC, MA, MD, NJ, NY, OH, PA, RI, VA

BREWER INDEX (Alphabetical)

Whitstran Brewing Company

2800 Lee Road, Ste B
Prosser, WA 99350
509-786-3883

BRANDS:
11th Hour Pale Ale (46 IBU)
Friar Lawrence Belgium-Style Ale (18 IBU)
Friar's Decadence Chocolate Chocolate Imperial Stout (55 IBU)
Friar's Penance Barley Wine (96 IBU)
Highlander Scottish Style Ale (16 IBU)
Horse Heaven Hefe Bavarian Style Hefeweizen (14 IBU)
O2O Heavy Water Stout (63 IBU)
Over-The-Edge Dry-Hopped Pale Ale (46 IBU)
Steamy Cream California Common Ale (14 IBU)

States Available: WA

Widmer Brothers Brewing Company – *page 571*

929 N Russell Street
Portland, OR 97227-1733
503-281-2438
www.widmer.com

BRANDS:
Broken Halo IPA (10 SRM, 52 IBU)
Drop Top Amber Ale (14 SRM, 20 IBU)
OKTO (22 SRM, 25 IBU)
Snowplow Milk Stout (80 SRM, 26 IBU)
Summit Pale Ale (17 SRM, 34 IBU)
W '06 N.W. Red Ale (50 IBU)
Widmer Hefeweizen (7 SRM, 32 IBU) – *page 571*

States Available: AR, LA, ND, OK, TX, Not in UT

Wiedenmayer Brewing Company

P.O. Box 67
Bedminster, NJ 07921
908-470-4000
www.wiedenmayerbrewing.com

BRANDS:
Wiedenmayer Jersey Lager

States Available: Contact Brewery

Wild Goose Brewery, LLC – *page 572*

4607 Wedgewood Boulevard
Frederick, MD 21703-7120
301-694-7899
www.wildgoosebrewery.com

BRANDS:
Blue Ridge Amber Lager
Blue Ridge ESB Red Ale
Blue Ridge Golden Ale
Blue Ridge HopFest
Blue Ridge Porter
Blue Ridge Snowball's Chance
Blue Ridge Steeple Stout
Blue Ridge Subliminator Dopplebock
Crooked River ESB
Crooked River Irish Red Ale
Crooked River Kölsch Ale
Crooked River Pumpkin Harvest Ale
Crooked River Robust Porter
Crooked River Select Lager
Crooked River Yuletide
Hudepohl 14 – K
Little Kings Cream Ale
Wild Goose Amber (20 SRM, 25 IBU)
Wild Goose India Pale Ale (10 SRM, 50 IBU) – *page 572*
Wild Goose Nut Brown Ale (35 SRM, 20 IBU)
Wild Goose Oatmeal Stout (50 SRM, 45 IBU)
Wild Goose Porter (40 SRM, 55 IBU)
Wild Goose Pumpkin Patch (16 SRM, 28 IBU)
Wild Goose Snow Goose (16 SRM, 28 IBU)

States Available: Wild Goose/Blue Ridge: MD, AZ, CANADA, DC, IL, IN, IN, KS, KY, KY, MI, NC, OH, OH, OK, PA, PA, SC Crooked River: Ohio Only Little Kings: MD, VA, WV, WY

Williamsburg AleWerks

189-B Ewell Road
Williamsburg, VA 23188
757-220-3670
www.williamsburgalewerks.com

BRANDS:
Williamsburg AleWerks Brown Ale
Williamsburg AleWerks Chesapeake Pale Ale
Williamsburg AleWerks Colonial Wheat Ale
Williamsburg AleWerks Drake Tail India Pale Ale
Williamsburg AleWerks Washington's Porter
Williamsburg AleWerks Winter Barleywine

States Available: Contact Brewery

Woodstock Beer

1951 Canton Road NE, Suite 250
Marietta, GA 30066
770-795-1432
www.woodstockbrands.com

BRANDS:
Woodstock India Pale Ale (11 SRM, 77.6 IBU)
Woodstock Pilsner (2.4 SRM, 18.2 IBU)

States Available: Contact Brewery

Woodstock Inn Brewery

135 Main Street, P.O. Box 118
North Woodstock, NH 03262
603-745-3951
www.woodstockinnnh.com

BRANDS:
Woodstock Inn Brewery Pig's Ear Brown Ale
Woodstock Inn Brewery Red Rack Ale

States Available: NH

Yards Brewing – *page 574*

2439 Amber Street
Philadelphia, PA 19125
215-634-2600
www.yardsbrewing.com

BRANDS:
Yards Brewing Extra Special Ale – *page 574*
Yards Brewing General Washington Tavern Porter
Yards Brewing India Pale Ale
Yards Brewing Love Stout
Yards Brewing Philadelphia Pale Ale
Yards Brewing Poor Richard's Tavern Spruce
Yards Brewing Saison
Yards Brewing Thomas Jefferson Tavern Ale

States Available: CT, DC, DE, MD, NJ, PA, VA

Yazoo Brewing

1200 Clinton Street, #110
Nashville, TN 37203
615-320-0290
www.yazoobrew.com

BRANDS:
Yazoo Brewing Amarillo Pale Ale
Yazoo Brewing Dos Perros
Yazoo Brewing Hefeweizen
Yazoo Brewing Onward Stout
Yazoo Brewing Sly Rye Porter
Yazoo Brewing Yazoo ESB

States Available: IN

BREWER INDEX (Alphabetical)

Yellowstone Valley Brewing

2132-B First Avenue N
Billings, MT 59101
406-245-0918
www.yellowstonevalleybrew.com

BRANDS:
Yellowstone Valley Black Widow Oatmeal Stout
Yellowstone Valley Grizzly Wulff Wheat
Yellowstone Valley Renegade Red ESB
Yellowstone Valley Wild Fly Ale

States Available: CO, MN, MT, ND, OK, SD, WI, WY

Zuma Brewing Company

900 Wendell Court
Atlanta, GA 30336
404-691-6535
www.zumaimporting.com

BRANDS:
Cancun
Morena

States Available: GA, TN

101

It's not "just beer"
Commentary by Michael Kuderka

Are We There Yet? – Getting to Beer's Ultimate Destination...

My wife and I had recently gone out to dinner with friends. Arriving at the restaurant I was a little surprised to find that they didn't serve alcohol. In fact, instead of incurring the costs of acquiring a liquor license or of keeping a well stocked bar, the restaurant actually encouraged patrons to BYO (bring your own). My own, had I known, would have likely been the Belgian Wit that sat back home cooling in the refrigerator.

This became a non-issue however, when the hostess let us know that there was a package store just a few doors down the street. Always being one who is up for exploring a new liquor store (with the hope of happening upon an ale or lager that I haven't tried), I volunteered to secure the BOO (bring our own) and headed down the street with requests for a bottle of a chardonnay, a white zinfandel, and for my sake "some beer."

Stereotypically, "are we there yet" is that question that comes drifting forward from young passengers in the back seat while one is driving to the next family destination. Similarly, for me "are we there yet" is the personal assessment that comes drifting in while I am out in various retail stores searching for that next great bottle of beer.

When I first took an interest in craft beers, and subsequently home brewing, many of the breweries were supplying their brands in the larger 22 oz. bottles. The good news was that I could try a great variety of brands and styles without being stuck with a six-pack to recycle. Plus, these single bottles took up less room in the fridge and I could use them to bottle my own brews; the bad news was because the stores usually carried limited inventories of these beers they were often out of stock when I return in search of a second bottle of one of my new favorites.

In the liquor store down the street, it was evident that the 22 oz. or "dinner bottle" had made its comeback. Both larger and smaller brewers are again utilizing this bottle size and true to its name and my mission, the dinner bottle was perfect for bringing back and sharing during our meal. This 22 oz. bottle is great size and it fit perfectly in the chiller by our table. Due to the size, dinner bottles are not usually found by the branded six or four packs. It is best to hunt for these either near the chilling wines and Belgian beers or look for them warm on separate taller shelves. The dinner bottle also offers a great opportunity for beer education. After a little beer tasting session at the table, I am very sure I was able to foster a new-found appreciation for wheat beer.

In my experience with this question if you are even asking the question, you know full well that "you're not there". So, I admit the question to begin with was rhetorical. As a consumer, the destination I would like to see the beer industry get to is one that makes one orchestrated commitment to broadening the basic appreciation for the variety and diversity that US brewing has to offer.

From what I have witnessed over the years, most US consumers can tell you if they would prefer "the white or the red" wine with dinner? But how great would it be to be asked if you would prefer "the ale or the lager" with your meal?

Most people in this country can go beyond ordering a red or a white or in the dinner experience I shared above, request a specific style of wine with a fairly good understanding of what they should expect when the bottle arrives at the table. Aside from when visiting a brewpub or a brewery, it is a rare occasion when I have heard anyone request say a nice Pilsner or Hefeweizen.

When we began creating the data base that is behind *The Essential Reference of Domestic Brewers and Their Bottled Brands* (DBBB) and the Online Companion to the book, I couldn't believe that there were over 70 different brands of Blonde/ Golden Ale, over 100 different brands of Amber Ale, some 60 brands of ESBs, and well over 180 brands of India Pale Ale brewed and bottled here in the United States (Yes, I am sure, I just finished recounting them). In our database we follow over 350 US breweries that bottle brands and we have broken these brands out across over 65 different styles of beer.

Keeping this in mind, it surprises me to walk into a liquor store and find wines displayed by style (Merlot, Riesling, etc) or by origin (Napa Valley) or in larger stores by both style and origin and yet beer (very often) with all it has to offer, sits loosely alphabetized, stacked up like a commodity item or jammed into the beer case. And it isn't much different when one peruses the basic restaurant menu, with numerous wine categories and beer broken down simply into imported and domestic.

Appreciation for beer comes with education about beer. One look at our book's Color and Bitterness Charts, and most people are ready for trying a different style of beer. Prompting the consumer to seek education isn't about increased General Awareness; it is about changing how beer is being sold and challenging the consumer to expand their knowledge. Walking past the Saison beer rack a few times, could certainly prompt ones curiosity.

From Anheuser-Busch in St. Louis down to Cooper's Cave Ale Company in Upstate New York, the US offers the most diverse and exciting selection of beer styles anywhere and yet we still have people like myself being sent to the store to pick-up a chardonnay, a white zinfandel, and "some beer."

So, are we there yet? Unfortunately, I think we still have a considerable distance to go.

II COMPARISON CHARTS

Looking at beer styles by their color and range of bitterness provides an easy visual method for discovering new beer styles. There are a wide range of beers available in the US market, but seeing the similarities in the appearance and in the flavor between styles can encourage consumers to go beyond their current selection of beer or expand the variety of brands they currently enjoy.

The "Color & Bitterness Section" of the book can also give you some great insight into how an individual beer will look and taste. Simply find the brand name of a specific beer in which you are interested, check to see if this brand's listing is followed by numbers and the letters SRM (Standard Reference Method) or IBU (International Bitterness Units), and then return to the Color & Bitterness Charts. Plot these numbers on the Color & Bitterness Chart and you will have a better idea of what to expect from this beer's color and flavor. When the listing only has the IBU number available use the beer's stated style for the SRM range and plot the individual IBU.

Keep in mind that although many of the brewers were able to supply either their SRM or IBU information, some breweries consider this data to be proprietary and they are not always willing to share these numbers. For some of the smaller breweries, gathering this data is on their list of things to do and they may not have the numbers to supply as yet.

So what does it all mean? SRM or "Standard Reference Method" is how brewers measure and report beer color. You may also see some brewers using (degL or Degrees Lovibond). These numbers are about the same between the two scales. So, remember, the higher the number the darker the beer.

As for IBU or "International Bitterness Units," this is how brewers measure and report the hop bitterness of the finished beer. In this case, the higher the number, the more bitter the beer.

COMPARISON CHARTS

Standard Reference Method (SRM) Color Range

	Range Color (SRM)	Range Bitterness (IBU)	Bitterness (IBU)
Light Lager	(1.5-4)	(5-15)	
Wheat Ale	(2-10)	(10-35)	
Belgian White	(2-4)	(10-17)	
Lager	(2-4)	(5-14)	
Ice Lager	(2-5)	(10-22)	
Malt Liquor	(2-5)	(12-23)	
Weizen Beer	(2-9)	(3-15)	
Oktoberfest/Marzen	(2-15)	(7-25)	
Pilsner	(3-6)	(20-40)	
Blonde/Golden Ale	(3-7)	(15-25)	
Belgian-style Triple Ale	(3.5-7)	(20-25)	
Belgian-style Ale – Pale Strong	(3.5-7)	(20-50)	
Hefeweizen	(3-10)	(10-35)	
Kölsch	(4-7)	(18-25)	
Helles Bock/Maibock Pale Lager	(4-10)	(20-38)	
Cream Ale	(4-15)	(18-25)	
English Pale Ale	(5-14)	(20-40)	
Fruit or Vegetable Beer	(5-50)	(5-70)	
Herb & Spice Beer	(5-50)	(5-70)	
American Pale Ale	(6-14)	(28-40)	
India Pale Ale (AM or Eng)	(6-14)	(35-65)	
Amber Lager	(6-14)	(18-30)	
Lambic	(6-25)	(11-23)	
Doppelbock	(6-25)	(16-30)	

Bitterness scale: 0 - | - 5 - | -10- | -15- | -20- | -25- | -30- | -35- | -40- | -45- | -50- | -55- | -60- | -65- | -70- | -75- | -80

SRM Color scale: 1.5 (SRM), 2.5, 3.5, 4.5, 5.5, 6.5, 7.5

Order *The Essential Reference of Domestic Brewers and Their Bottled Brands* (DBBB)™ at www.thebeerbible.com or call (908) 537-6410

Based on the BJCP Beer Style Guidelines and the World Beer Cup Competition Style Descriptions and Specifications.

MC Basset, LLC

COMPARISON CHARTS

Bitterness scale: 0 - | - 5 - | -10- | -15- | -20- | -25- | -30- | -35- | -40- | -45- | -50- | -55- | -60- | -65- | -70- | -75- | -80

SRM color scale (left axis): 7.5 (SRM), 10, 12.5, 15, 17.5, 20, 22.5, 25, 27.5, 30, 32.5, 35, 37.5+

Standard Reference Method (SRM) Color Range

Beer Style	Range Color (SRM)	Range Bitterness (IBU)
Vienna-style Lager	(8-12)	(22-28)
ESB (Extra Special Bitter)	(8-14)	(30-55)
Scottish Ale	(8-17)	(9-20)
English Mild Ale	(8-17)	(10-24)
English/Scottish Strong Ale	(8-21)	(30-65)
Dark Lager	(8-30)	(22-30)
Dunkelweizen	(10-19)	(10-15)
Scotch Ale	(10-25)	(25-35)
Amber/Red Ale	(11-18)	(30-40)
Irish Ale	(11-18)	(20-28)
Dusseldorf-style Altbeir	(11-19)	(25-48)
Barleywine	(11-22)	(40-100)
California Common Beer	(12-17)	(35-45)
Old Ale	(12-30)	(30-65)
Belgian-style Dubbel Ale	(14-18)	(18-25)
Munich Dunkel	(14-28)	(18-28)
Brown Ale	(15-22)	(15-45)
Bock	(20-30)	(20-30)
Porter	(20-35)	(20-40)
Oatmeal Stout	(20+)	(20-40)
Imperial Stout	(20+)	(50-80)
Stout	(40+)	(30-60)
Irish Dry Stout	(40+)	(30-40)
Milk Stout	(40+)	(15-25)

Order *The Essential Reference of Domestic Brewers and Their Bottled Brands* (DBBB)™ at www.thebeerbible.com or call (908) 537-6410

Based on the BJCP Beer Style Guidelines and the World Beer Cup Competition Style Descriptions and Specifications.

Ales and Lagers – What is the Difference?

Like most things in life the difference starts at the beginning, for ales life begins with a top-fermenting yeast that tends to ferment more quickly compared to that of a lager. Ales offer a full range of flavors being described as anything from sweet, to fruity, to hoppy, to tart and usually command higher alcohol content when compared to those of lagers.

Lagers on the other hand begin with bottom-fermenting yeasts. They are commonly light and golden in color and tend to possess higher levels of carbonation. Lagers offer a very distinctive flavor and are often described as fresh, clean, bold, bitter or sweet in taste.

 # BEER STYLE INDEX

This section provides detailed information about the many different styles of beer, followed by a listing of the brewery's brands under their style category. Each brand name includes the name of the breweries indexed in *The Essential Reference of Domestic Brewers and Their Bottled Brands (DBBB)*.

In most cases breweries have selected the style category in which their brands are listed. Note that the Brewers Association recognizes some 35 styles of Ale, 15 styles of Lager, and 9 Special Styles. The DBBB's style categories are not as specialized as those published by the Brewers Association or those utilized in brewing competitions; however they do represent the broad style differences between brands.

The brand listing also includes the page number where the brand appears as a full brewery portfolio listing (Section VII).

Style Descriptions

Ales

Abbey Ales (Dubbel, Trippel, Singel) Monastic, or abbey, ales are an ancient tradition in Belgium, in much the same manner as wine production was once closely associated with monastic life in ancient France. Currently very few working monasteries brew beer within the order, but many have licensed the production of beers bearing their abbey name to large commercial brewers. These "abbey ales" can vary enormously in specific character, but most are quite strong in alcohol content, ranging from 6 percent alcohol by volume (ABV) to as high as 10 percent. Generally, abbey ales are labeled as either "dubbel" or "trippel," though this is not a convention that is slavishly adhered to. The former typically denotes a relatively less alcoholic and often darker beer, while the latter can often be lighter or blond in color and have a syrupy, alcoholic mouthfeel that invites sipping, not rapid drinking, The lowest gravity abbey ale in a Belgian brewer's range is usually referred to as a "singel," though it is rarely labeled as such.

Alt Put simply, an altbier has the smoothness of a classic lager with the flavors of ale. A more rigorous definition must take history into account. Ale brewing in Germany predates the now predominant lager production. As the lager process spread from Bohemia, some brewers retained the top-fermenting ale process but adopted the cold maturation associated with lager hence the name "old beer" (alt means old in German). Altbier is associated with Dusseldorf, Munster and Hanover. This style of ale is light compared to traditional English ale. In the United States, some amber ales are actually in the alt style.

Amber Ales Many North American brewers are now producing ales that are identified by the term "Amber Ale." This is a more modern, non-traditional style, and many of these beers borrow heavily from the characteristics associated with more classical styles such as "Pale Ales" or "Bitters." Amber ales are light to medium bodied and can be anywhere from light copper to light brown in hue. Flavorwise, they can vary from generic and quaffable to serious craft brewed styles with extravagant hoppy aromas and full malt character. Typically, amber ales are quite malty but not heavily caramelized in flavor. For our purposes, amber ales will also include ales commonly identified as "Red Ales," and "American Ales".

American Pale Ale These brews are golden to light copper in color with a more subtle overall character and lighter body than typical Pale Ales. English ale fruitiness will probably not be observed. However, the most important qualification is that they are brewed domestically and will have less body, malt and hop character than a pale ale from the same brewery.

Belgian-style Amber Ale This is not a classic style, but nonetheless encapsulates various beers of a similar Belgian theme that does not fit into the more classic mold. Expect amber hued, fruity and moderately strong ales (6 percent ABV) with a yeasty character.

Belgian-style Blonde Ale This is not a classic style of Belgian ale, but covers the more commercially minded Belgian ales that are lighter in color and moderate in body and alcoholic strength. Fruity Belgian yeast character and mild hopping should be expected.

Belgian-style Golden Ale Belgian golden ales are pale to golden in color with the lightest possible body for their deceptively alcoholic punch, as much as 9 percent alcohol by volume. Typically, such brews undergo three fermentations, the final one being in the bottle, resulting in fine champagne-like carbonation, and a huge rocky white head when they are poured. Often such beers can be cellared for six months to a year to gain roundness. These beers are probably best served chilled to minimize the alcoholic mouthfeel.

STYLE DESCRIPTIONS

BELGIAN-STYLE RED ALE These are also known as "soured beers," their defining character classically coming from having been aged for some years in well-used large wooden tuns, to allow bacterial action in the beer and thus impart the sharp "sour" character. Hops do not play much role in the flavor profile of these beers, but whole cherries can be macerated with the young beer to produce a cherry flavored Belgian Red Ale. These styles are almost exclusively linked to one producer in northern Belgium, Rodenbach. These ales are among the most distinctive and refreshing to be found anywhere.

BELGIAN-STYLE STRONG ALE Beers listed in this category will generally pack a considerably alcoholic punch and should be approached much like one would a barleywine. Indeed, some of them could be considered Belgian-style barleywines, such as those from Brasserie Dubuisson. Expect a fruity Belgian yeast character and a degree of sweetness coupled with a viscous mouthfeel.

BIERE DE GARDE Biere de garde is a Flemish and northern French specialty ale generally packaged distinctively in 750-mL bottles with a cork. Historically, the style was brewed as a farmhouse specialty in February and March, to be consumed in the summer months when the warmer weather didn't permit brewing. Typically produced with a malt accent, this is a strong (often over 6 percent), yet delicate bottle-conditioned beer. These brews tend to be profoundly aromatic and are an excellent companion to hearty foods.

BROWN ALE The precise definition of English Brown Ale would depend on where you are in England. It is nowadays much more closely associated with Northern England, specifically Tadcaster and Newcastle, home to Newcastle Brown Ale. These medium-bodied reddish-brown beers are malt accented with a nutty character, a gentle fruitiness, and low bitterness. Alcohol is moderate, a maximum of 5% ABV. The much less prevalent Southern English style, not seen abroad, is much darker in color, sweeter on the palate, and made in a lighter style. English style brown ales of the former type have become very popular with US brewers, no doubt for the same reason as they took hold in England, namely their great drinkability.

DUNKEL/DARK WEIZEN These dark wheat beers derive their character from the use of darker malts in the non-wheat ingredients, so that a richer, darker-colored beer can be achieved, along with fuller malt flavors. Dunkel weizens still display the floral, estery qualities of a pale wiezen. Dark weizens can be produced with or without a secondary fermentation in the bottle, with the corollary that these styles can be yeast sedimented or unsedimented depending upon the preference of the brewer.

ESB. Bitter is an English specialty, and very much an English term, generally denoting the standard ale — the "session" beer — in an English brewer's range. They are characterized by a fruity, light to medium body and an accent on hop aromas more than hop bitters. Colors range from golden to copper. Despite the name they are not particularly bitter. Indeed, British brewed "bitters" will often be less bitter than US craft brewed amber ales. A fuller-bodied bitter is labeled as "Extra Special Bitter" (ESB). These weightier versions of bitter often stand up better to the rigors of travel overseas than the lower gravity standard versions. An important element of faithful bitters are English yeast cultures used in fermentation. These impart a fruity, mild estery character that should be noted in examples of the style. Bitters are now widely emulated in North America, sometimes with domestically grown hops imparting a slightly more assertive character than seen in traditional English bitters.

FLAVORED PORTER Flavoring traditional beer styles is a particular feature of the ever creative US craft brewing scene. Flavorings used in porters are typically dark berry fruits and coffee, and when skillfully done the effect can be greater than the sum of its parts.

FLAVORED STOUT Flavored stouts are still stouts, be they sweeter or drier. Dark fruits, coffee and chocolate are particularly popular, and the marriage of flavors should at best be greater than the sum of its parts.

109

STYLE DESCRIPTIONS

FLEMISH STYLE BROWN ALE These are complex dark beers, most closely associated with the town of Oudenaarde in Flanders. The most authentic examples are medium to full-bodied beers that are influenced by a number of factors: high bicarbonate in the brewing water to give a frothy texture; a complex mix of yeasts and malts; blending of aged beers; and aging in bottles before release. In the best examples, the flavor profile is reminiscent of olives, raisins, and brown spices and could be described as "sweet and sour." These beers are not hop-accented and are of low bitterness.

HEFEWEIZEN Weizen bier is a top fermenting beer style that originates from southern Germany, particularly Bavaria, and is brewed with at least 50% wheat in the mash. Hefeweizens are refreshing, highly carbonated beers ideal for quenching summer thirsts. They undergo secondary fermentation, often in the bottle, and the yeast strains used for this purpose impart a spicy, clove-like flavor. Hefe (the German word for Yeast) denotes that the bottle contains yeast sediment. Alcohol content is typically 5-5.5% ABV, giving these beers a medium to medium-full body. Hop flavors, however, play a very insignificant role in the flavor profile.

IMPERIAL STOUT Imperial stout is an extra strong version of stout, which was originally brewed by the British to withstand the rigors of export to Russia and the Baltic states. This style is dense, opaque black and strong in alcohol (6-7%), with a note of sweetness. Burnt cocoa and dried fruit flavors are typical. Russian Imperial stouts originate from recipes that British brewers tailored to the tastes of the Imperial Russian court. The style has now been embraced by US craft brewers as a winter specialty.

INDIA PALE ALE (IPA) India Pale Ales are deep gold to amber in color, and are usually characterized by floral hop aromas and a distinctive hop bitterness on the finish. India Pale Ales were originally brewed by British brewers in the 19th Century, when British troops and colonizers depended on supplies of beer shipped from England. Standard ales did not survive the journey, hence brewers developed high gravity, highly hopped ales that survived shipment in casks to their largest market, India. This style, probably not anywhere near as bitter as it was when destined for India, continues to be brewed in a toned down manner in the UK and is currently undergoing a mini-revival. However, US craft brewers have claimed the style as their own, and often brew them with assertive Pacific Northwestern hop varieties with a hugely aromatic hop accent.

IRISH ALE Irish ales are characterized by their reddish color, malt accents, slightly sweet palate, and low hopping. They are not generally bitter, if true to style, reflecting the historical fact that the Irish have never taken to using huge amounts of hops in their traditional beers. Back home, Irish ales have long played second fiddle to stouts, and prior to that, porters. Lacking a truly indigenous character, many versions being revived in the USA owe more to Celtic marketing than to a distinct character, although the color and high drinkability are the usual reference point.

IRISH DRY STOUT Dry stout is closely associated with Ireland in general. These brews tend to be rich and dark with a definitive bitter note and a drying palate feel. They are classically paired with oysters, although any Irish Stout drinker will tell you that a pint it is a meal in itself. Draught (draft) Irish Stout is nitrogen-flushed to give it that tell-tale white creamy head. This process is also effected in cans and bottles with a nitrogen "widget".

STYLE DESCRIPTIONS

KÖLSCH Kölsch is an ale emanating from Cologne, Germany. In Germany (and the European Community), the term is strictly legally limited to the beers from within the city environs of Cologne. Simply put, Kölsch has the color of a pilsner with some of the fruity character of an ale. This is achieved with the use of top fermenting yeasts and pale pilsner malts. The hops are accented on the finish, which is classically dry and herbal. It is a medium to light-bodied beer and delicate in style.

KRISTALL WEIZEN A kristall weizen is a nonhazy weizen ale. "Kristall" on the label of a weizen specifically denotes that a weizen has been filtered prior to bottling, to remove the protein haze and yeast often suspended in such beers. Kristall weizens lack the yeasty and spicy complexity often associated with hefeweizen beers, and have a cleaner and more delicate flavor. Floral, fruity aromas are often noted in classic examples of this style, though healthy alcohol content of 5-5.5% will give a medium-full bodied character.

LAMBICS Geueze, Fruit Lambic, Faro. Lambic beers are perhaps the most individualistic style of beer in the world. Lambics are produced in tiny quantities immediately south of the Belgian capital of Brussels. Lambic brewers use native wild yeasts in the open-air fermentation process to produce these specialties. This unusual method, in conjunction with extended aging in ancient oak barrels, imparts a unique vinous character with a refreshing sourness and astonishing complexity. Lambics labeled as Geueze are a blend of young and old beers. Such blending results in a sharp, champagne-like effervescence and tart, toasty flavors. Those labeled as Faro have had sugar, caramel, or molasses added in order to impart a note of sweetness. Lambic beers, however, are more often seen in the US when they have been flavored with fruits. Kriek (cherry) and Framboise (raspberry) are the most popular and traditional fruits employed. Other exotic fruits are widely used in juice form in the more commercial examples of lambic beer, much to the consternation of purist connoisseurs.

MILD ALE Mild ale is a traditional style of English ale that is characterized by darker colors, sweetish malt flavors, and subtle hopping levels, all within a lower alcohol frame (typically 3.5%). Their purpose is to allow the drinker to get a full quotient of flavor in a "session" beer – a trick to which English ale brewing lends itself readily. In the 1940's, Mild was more popular than bitter in English pubs, though it is less common now. US craft brewers occasionally pay homage to this style.

OATMEAL STOUT This brew is a variation of sweet stout, with a small proportion of oats used in place of roasted malt, which has the effect of enhancing body and mouthfeel. They were originally brewed by the British in the earlier part of this century, when stouts were thought of as a nutritious part of an everyday diet. They tend to be highly flavorful with a velvety texture and sometimes a hint of sweetness. Oatmeal stouts are now a very popular staple of the US craft brewing scene.

PALE ALE Pale ales tend to be fuller-bodied, with a more assertive character on the palate. They're the standard bitter in an English brewer's portfolio. In England, it is generally bottled, as opposed to being sold on draft. Despite the name, pale ales are not pale but, in fact, more of an amber hue. The original designation was in reference to this style of beer being paler than the brown and black beers which were more popular at the time of the style's inception. In the US, pale ale styles have become one of the benchmarks by which craft brewers are judged. The US version of pale ale is crisper and generally much more hoppy. Indeed, this style is well suited to assertive domestic Pacific Northwestern hop varieties that give the US examples inimitable character. A good US example should be available on tap in any bar worth frequenting for its beer selection.

STYLE DESCRIPTIONS

PORTER Porters are reddish-brown to black in color, medium to medium-full bodied, and characterized by a flavor profile that can vary from a very subtle dark malt to a fully roasted, smoky flavor. Being a centuries-old style, there are differences of opinion with regard to what a true porter was actually like and there can be wide variations from one brewer's interpretation to the next. Roasted malt should provide the flavoring character, rather than roasted barley as is used with stouts. Stronger, darker versions and lighter more delicate versions are equally valid manifestations of the style. The influence of hops can often be notable in the richer craft brewed examples of the style. Although porter was the drink of the masses in 1700s London, it is not a significant factor in the British market today, despite the production of a few outstanding English examples. In the United States, it is enjoying newfound popularity among US craft brewers and many fine US examples are produced.

SAISON Saison beers are distinctive specialty beers from the Belgian province of Hainaut. These beers were originally brewed in the early spring for summer consumption, though contemporary Belgian saisons are brewed all year round with pale malts and well dosed with English and Belgian hop varieties. Lively carbonation ensues from a secondary fermentation in the bottle. The color is classically golden orange and the flavors are refreshing with citrus and fruity hop notes. Sadly, these beers are under appreciated in their home country and their production is limited to a small number of artisanal producers who keep this style alive. With a typically hoppy character, Saisons are an extremely esoteric style of beer that should appeal to any devotees of US craft beers, if you can track them down.

SCOTTISH ALE Scottish ales are typically full-bodied and malty, with some of the classic examples being dark brown in color. They are more lowly hopped than the English counterparts and often have a slightly viscous and sweet caramel malt character due to incomplete fermentation. Scottish style ales can be found in far flung corners of the world where faithful versions are brewed, this being a legacy of its popularity in the British Empire. In the US, many craft brewers produce a Scottish style ale. The "export" versions produced by Scottish brewers, the type mostly encountered in the US, are considerably stronger and more malty than the standard versions made available to Scottish beer drinkers.

STRONG ALE Strong Ales are sometimes referred to as old ales, stock ales or winter warmers. These beers are higher alcohol versions (typically between 5.5-7% ABV) of pale ales, though not as robust or alcoholic as barley wines. Usually a deep amber color, these brews generally have a sweet malty palate and a degree of fruitiness. If "bottle conditioned," strong ales can improve for some years, in some cases eventually obtaining Sherry-like notes.

SWEET STOUT Sweet stouts are largely a British specialty. These stouts have a distinctive sweetness to the palate and often show chocolate and caramel flavors. They are sometimes known as milk or cream stouts. These beers obtain their characters by using chocolate malts and lactic (milk) sugars in the brewing process.

TRAPPIST ALE According to EC law, trappist ale may only come from six abbeys of the trappist order that still brew beer on their premises. Five are in Belgium and one, La Trappe, comes from Holland. Although the styles may differ widely between them, they all share a common trait of being top fermented, strong, bottle conditioned, complex, and fully flavored brews. At most, each abbey produces three different varieties of increasing gravity. These can often improve with some years of cellaring. In all, there are 15 different trappist beers from the six monasteries. Trappist ales are among the most complex and old fashioned of beers that one can find – little wonder that many connoisseurs treat them as the holy grail of beer drinking.

STYLE DESCRIPTIONS

WEIZEN BOCK Weizen bocks are essentially winter wheat beers, originally brewed in Bavaria. The color can be pale gold to brown. They are of higher alcoholic strength, as high as 7% ABV, showing a warming personality, though they should still have a significant "rocky" head when poured. These beers combine the character of hefeweizens and dopplebocks and as such are rich and malty with estery, yeasty qualities and show a note of wheaty crispness through the finish.

WHEAT ALE As the name would suggest, these are ales that use a proportion of wheat in the mash to add a protein haze. Wheat ales, inspired by the German weizen tradition, were popular before Prohibition in the United States and are enjoying resurgence in popularity. This generic category encapsulates the diverse interpretation of the classic German weizen styles brewed in America and elsewhere. A host of variables, ranging from the wheat/malt ration hopping and filtration/nonfiltration, all contribute to wide variations on the theme. Generally, US examples feature a more marked hop accent than classic German weizen styles and are often dryer.

WHITE/WIT BEER Wit beer is a style of flavored wheat. It is distinctly Belgian in origin and is still very closely associated with their lowland country. Wits employ a proportion of unmalted wheat in the mash but also have flavor added in the form of Curacao orange peel and coriander, among other ingredients. Their appearance is marked by a hazy white precipitate and these beers generally have some sedimentation. Typically these are very refreshing summer thirst quenchers. They are not widely produced in the United States, but some notable examples can be found.

WINTER ALES Spiced winter ales are popular hybrids among US craft brewers. Typically they are strong ales that have had some spice added during the brewing process. True to their name, they make ideal sipping beers with which to ward off winter's chill and get a dose of seasonal spices. This style is usually brewed before Christmas and brewers frequently make annual adjustments to their often secret recipes in an effort to obtain that perfect symbiosis between spices, hops and malt.

LAGERS

AMBER LAGERS Amber lagers are a vaguely defined style of lager much favored by US lager brewers. They are darker in color, anywhere from amber to copper hued, and generally more fully flavored than a standard pale lager. Caramel malt flavors are typical and hopping levels vary considerably from one brewery to the next, though they are frequently hoppier than the true vienna lager styles on which they are loosely based. Alcohol levels are generally a maximum of 5% ABV.

BLACK/SCHWARZ BEER Originally brewed in Thuringia, a state in eastern Germany, these lager style brews were known to be darker in color than their Munich counterparts. Often relatively full-bodied, and rarely under 5% ABV, these beers classically feature a bitter chocolate, and/or roasted malt note and a rounded character. Hop accents are generally low. This obscure style was picked up by Japanese brewers and is made in small quantities by all of Japan's major brewers. Schwarz beers are not often attempted by US craft brewers.

BOCK Bocks are a type of strong lager historically associated with Germany and specifically the town of Einbeck. These beers range in color from pale to deep amber tones, and feature a decided sweetness on the palate. Bock styles are an exposition of malty sweetness that is classically associated with the character and flavor of Bavarian malt. Alcohol levels are quite potent, typically 5-6% ABV. Hop aromas are generally low though hop bitterness can serve as a balancing factor against the malt sweetness. Many of these beers' names or labels feature some reference to a goat. This is a play on words in that the word "bock" also refers to a male goat in the German language. Many brewers choose to craft these beers for consumption in the spring (often called Maibock) or winter, when their warmth can be fully appreciated.

STYLE DESCRIPTIONS

DOPPELBOCK This is a sub-category of the bock style. Doppelbocks are extra strong, rich and weighty lagers characterized by an intense malty sweetness with a note of hop bitterness for balance. Color can vary from full amber to dark brown and alcohol levels are potently high, typically 7-8% ABV. Doppelbocks were first brewed by the Paulaner monks in Munich. At the time, it was intended to be consumed as "liquid bread" during Lent. Most Bavarian examples end in the suffix -ator, in deference to the first commercial example which was named Salvator (savior) by the Paulaner brewers.

EISBOCK This is the strongest type of bock. It is made by chilling a doppelbock until ice is formed. At this point, the ice is removed, leaving behind a brew with a higher concentration of alcohol. This also serves to concentrate the flavors, and the resultant beer is rich and powerful, with a pronounced malt sweetness and a warm alcoholic finish. Alcohol levels run to at least 8% ABV.

GERMAN DARK LAGER/DUNKEL Dunkel is the original style of lager, serving as the forerunner to the pale lagers of today. They originated in and around Bavaria, and are widely brewed both there and around the world. This is often what the average consumer is referring to when they think of dark beer. At their best, these beers combine the dryish chocolate or licorice notes associated with the use of dark roasted malts and the roundness and crisp character of a lager. Examples brewed in and around Munich tend to be slightly fuller-bodied and sometimes have a hint of bready sweetness to the palate, a characteristic of the typical Bavarian malts used.

"LIGHT" AND REDUCED CALORIE LAGERS. These are the recently popular brews which are popular in a figure-conscious society. Essentially, these are pale lager styled beers with fewer calories. Like all other "diet products," the objective is to maintain flavor while minimizing calories. This is achieved quite successfully by some brands, despite the implausibility of the proposition.

MAIBOCK/PALE BOCK Maibocks are medium to full-bodied lagers whose alcohol content can vary widely, though is typically between 5-6% ABV. The color of pale bocks can vary from light bronze to deep amber and they are characterized by a sweet malty palate and subtle hop character. As its name would suggest, this is a bock style that traditionally makes a spring appearance in May as a celebration of a new brewing season. In a Germanic brewers portfolio, it should conventionally have a less assertive character than other bock offerings later in the year.

MUNICH HELLES Originating from Munich, this style of lager is very soft and round on the palate, and usually comes in a pale to golden hue. These beers traditionally tend to be malt accented with subtle hop character. They are generally weightier than standard pale lagers though less substantial than Dortmunder Export styles. All the finest examples still come from the brewing center of Munich and are relatively easy to find in major US markets.

PALE LAGERS Pale lagers are the standard international beer style. This style is the generic spin-off of the pilsner style. Pale lagers are generally light to medium-bodied, with a light to medium hop impression and a clean, crisp malt character. Quality, from a flavor point of view, is very variable within this style and many cheaper examples use a proportion of non-malt additives such as rice or corn to reduce the production costs. Alcohol content is typically between 3.5-5% ABV, with the upper end of the range being preferable if one is to get a true lager mouthfeel.

PILSNER Pilsner styles of beer originate from Bohemia in the Czech Republic. They are medium to medium-full bodied and are characterized by high carbonation and tangy Czech varieties of hops that impart floral aromas and a crisp, bitter finish. The hallmark of a fresh pilsner is the dense, white head. The alcohol levels must be such as to give a rounded mouthfeel, typically around 5% ABV. Classic pilsners are thoroughly refreshing, but they are delicate and must be fresh to show their best. Few beers are as disappointing to the beer lover as a stale pilsner. German pilsner styles are similar, though often slightly lighter in body and color. Great pilsners are technically difficult to make and relatively expensive to produce.

STYLE DESCRIPTIONS

RAUCHBIER The origins of Rauchbier lies with breweries in the region of Franconia in northern Bavaria which traditionally dried the barley over fires fueled by beech trees from local forests. The resulting pungent malt imparted an assertively smoky aroma and flavor to the beer from which it was made. These smoked lagers generally feature a very malty framework on which the intensely smoky character will not become overbearing. Rauchbiers are still brewed in the traditional manner by many of the breweries centered around the town of Bamberg, though enterprising brewers in other parts of the world have begun to make similarly styled beers.

VIENNA STYLE LAGERS AND MARZEN/FEST BEERS The classic amber to red lager which was originally brewed in Austria in the 19th century has come to be known as the Vienna style. These are reddish-amber with a very malty toasted character and a hint of sweetness. This style of beer was adapted by the Munich brewers and in their hands has a noted malty sweetness, as well as a toasted flavor with a touch more richness. The use of the term Marzen, which is German for March, implies that the beer was brewed in March and lagered for many months. On a label, the words "fest marzen," or "Oktoberfest," generally imply the Vienna style. Oktoberfest beers have become popular as September seasonal brews among US craft brewers, though they are not always classic examples of the German or Austrian style.

DORTMUNDER EXPORT Well balanced, smooth, and refreshing, Dortmunders tend to be stronger and fuller than other pale lagers or Munich Helles styles. They may also be a shade darker and a touch hoppier. The style originates from the city of Dortmund in northern Germany. Dortmunder Export came about during the industrial revolution, when Dortmund was the center of the coal and steel industries, and the swelling population needed a hearty and sustaining brew. The "export" appendage refers to the fact that Dortmunder beers were "exported" to surrounding regions. Today the term Dortmunder now widely refers to stronger lagers brewed for export, though not necessarily from Dortmund.

MIXED/HYBRID

BARLEY WINE "Barley wine" is the evocative name coined by British brewers to describe an extremely potent ale that can range from golden copper to dark brown in color. They are characterized by extravagant caramel malt flavors and bittering hops that prevent the malt sweetness from cloying. Rich and viscous, they can have in their most complex manifestations winey flavor profiles, with a hint of sweetness. Some examples are vintage dated and can improve with extended bottle age. These powerful brews are classically sold in small "nip" bottles and can be consumed after dinner or with dessert. The style has become popular among US craft brewers who often produce them as winter specialties.

BLACK & TAN Black & Tan was originally conceived as a British pub concoction of Stout and IPA mixed in a pint pot. Variations are still blended in some English pubs, but in the US the term is used by a small number of brands to loosely refer to a dark amber to brown colored beer with a malt accent, relatively light in alcohol and low in hop character.

CREAM ALE Cream Ale is a North American specialty that is somewhat of a hybrid in style. Despite the name, many brewers use both ale and lager yeasts for fermentation, or more often just lager yeasts. This style of beer is fermented like an ale at warm temperatures, but then stored at cold temperatures for a period of time, much as a lager would be. The resultant brew has the unchallenging crisp characteristics of a light pale lager, but is endowed with a hint of the aromatic complexities that ales provide. Pale in color, they are generally more heavily carbonated and more heavily hopped than light lagers.

STYLE DESCRIPTIONS

HERB-SPICED AND FRUIT BEERS These are lagers or ales to which herbs, fruits, or spices have been added in order to impart flavor or color. Depending on whether or not the seasonings have been used in the fermentation or as an addition of juice or extract, the beer will have more or less of the desired character. These beers are highly individualistic, and allow the brewers great creativity in their formulations. They will range from mild aromatic overtones to intense and pungently flavored concoctions.

MALT LIQUOR This category is BATF-mandated insofar as any lager stronger than 5% alcohol by volume cannot call itself a lager beer. There are a number commercial brands that have been created to fill this category, many of which do not have great merit from the connoisseur's perspective. Some strong European lagers adopt this labeling moniker for the US market.

BEER STYLES INDEX – TABLE OF CONTENTS

ALES

Abbey Style Ale .118
Altbier 118
Amber 118
American Pale Ale 122
Belgian Style Ale 127
Belgian White 130
Blonde/Golden Ale 131
Brown Ale 133
Dark Ale 136
Dubbel/Trippel/Quad Ale 136
English Mild Ale 138
English Pale Ale 138
English/Scottish Strong Ale 139
ESB (English Special Bitter) 140
Grand Cru 142
Hefeweizen 142
Imperial Stout 144
India Pale Ale (AM or Eng) 145
Irish Ale 152
Irish Dry Stout .153
Kölsch 154
Lambic 154
Light Ale 155
Milk Stout 155
Oatmeal Stout 155
Old Ale 156
Other Stout 157
Porter 158
Rauchbier 162
Red Ale 163
Scottish Ale 164
Seasonally Produced 165
Special Ale 166
Stout 167
Summer 168
Weizen Beer 169
Wheat Ale 170
Winter 172

LAGER

Amber Lager 175
Bock 175
Dark Lager 177
Doppelbock/Triplebock/Quadrupel . . .178
Dry Lager 179
Dunkelweizen 179
Dusseldorf-Style Altbeir 179
Helles Bock/Maibock Pale Lager 179
Ice Lager 180
Lager 181
Light Lager 186
Munich Dunkel .188
Oktoberfest/Marzen 188
Pilsner 190
Pilsner Light 193
Specialty Beer 193
Vienna-Style Lager 193

MIXED/HYBRID

Barleywine 195
Black & Tan 197
Caffeinated Beer 197
California Common Beer/Steam Ale . . .197
Cream Ale 197
Fruit or Vegetable Beer 198
Gluten Free 201
Herb & Spice Beer 201
Malt Liquor 202
No Applicable Style Category 202
Non-Alcohol Malt Beverage 202
Other Ale 203
Scotch Ale 204

BEER STYLES INDEX

Abbey Style Ale

Clipper City Heavy Seas Brewing "Holy Sheet"
(Clipper City Brewing Company)

Dragonmead Bronze Griffin Belgian Style
(Dragonmead Microbrewery)

Dragonmead Dead Monk Abbey Ale
(Dragonmead Microbrewery)

Dunedin Brewery Summer Buzz
(Dunedin Brewery)

English Ales Ramsey's Fat Lip Ale
(English Ales Brewery)

Happy Valley Brewing Mission Ale Double
(Happy Valley Brewing Company)

Jack's Blackberry Abbey Ale
(Jack Russell Brewing)

North Coast Brewing Brother Thelonious
(North Coast Brewing Company)

Ommegang Abbey Ale Dubbel
(Brewery Ommegang)

Sly Fox Ichor (20 IBU)
(Sly Fox Brewing Company)

Southampton Abbot 12
(Southampton Publick House)

Sprecher Brewing Abbey Triple (13 IBU)
(Sprecher Brewing)

The Lost Abbey Lost & Found Abbey Ale (19 IBU)
(Port Brewing Company)

Viking Brewing Abby Normal
(Viking Brewing)

Altbier

Alaskan Amber (22 SRM, 18 IBU) – *page 448*
(Alaskan Brewing Company)

Baron Dusseldof Altbier
(Baron Brewing)

BBC Altbier (14 SRM, 30 IBU)
(Bluegrass Brewing Company)

BluCreek Altbier (12 SRM, 30 IBU)
(BluCreek Brewing)

Cricket Hill Brewing Colonel Blides Altbier
(Cricket Hill Brewing Company)

Erie Brewing Heritage Alt (15 IBU)
(Erie Brewing)

Glacier Brewing Northfork Amber Ale (14 SRM, IBU 22.3)
(Glacier Brewing)

Otter Creek Brewing Copper Ale (21 IBU) – *page 527*
(Otter Creek Brewing Company)

Red Lodge Ales Glacier Ale
(Red Lodge Ales Brewing Company)

Slab City Brewing Esker Alt
(Slab City Brewing)

Tuckerman Brewing Headwall Alt
(Tuckerman Brewing)

Victory Throwback Lager
(Victory Brewing Company)

Weeping Radish Altier (12.2 SRM, 47.2 IBU)
(The Weeping Radish Brewery)

Yazoo Brewing Dos Perros
(Yazoo Brewing)

Amber

Abner Weed Amber Ale
(Mt.Shasta Brewing Company)

Anderson Valley Boont Amber Ale (15 IBU) – *page 451*
(Anderson Valley Brewing Company)

Angel City Ale (12 SRM, 30 IBU) – *page 454*
(Angel City Brewing)

Arcadia Brewing Ales Amber Ale (34 IBU)
(Arcadia Brewing Company)

BEER STYLES INDEX

Atlantic Brewing Bar Harbor Real Ale
(Atlantic Brewing Company)

Avery Brewing Red Point Amber Ale (22 IBU)
(Avery Brewing Company)

Backcountry Brewery Switchback Amber (16 SRM, 28 IBU)
(Backcountry Brewery)

Ballast Point Calico Amber Ale
(Ballast Point Brewing Company)

Bayhawk Ales Amber Ale (23 IBU)
(Bayhawk Ales, Inc.)

Beautiful Brews Honey Amber Rose
(Beautiful Brews, Inc.)

Beermann's Rip Roarin' Red - Red Ale
(Beermann's Beerwerks)

Black Dog Ale (36 IBU)
Spanish Peaks Brewing Company/United States Beverage

Black Mountain Ocotillo Amber
(The Black Mountain/Chili Beer Brewing Company)

Boulder Beer Singletrack Copper Ale (13.3 SRM, 30 IBU)
(Boulder Beer Company)

Boulder Beer Sundance Amber (19.6 SRM, 29 IBU)
(Boulder Beer Company)

Breckenridge Avalanche Ale (19 IBU)
(Breckenridge Brewery)

BridgePort Ropewalker (18 IBU)
(BridgePort Brewing Company (Gambrinus))

Bristol Brewing Mass Transit Ale (21 IBU)
(Bristol Brewing Company)

Butte Creek Organic Ale
(Butte Creek Brewing)

Buttface Amber Ale (22 SRM, 22 IBU)
(Big Horn Brewing (CB Potts))

Capital Brewery Wisconsin Amber
(Capital Brewery Company, Inc.)

Cascade Lakes Angus MacDougal's Amber (30 IBU)
(Cascade Lakes Brewing Company)

Concord Grape Ale (16 IBU)
(Concord Brewery, Inc.)

Cottrell Brewing Old Yankee Ale
(Cottrell Brewing Company)

Dark Horse Belgian Amber Ale
(Dark Horse Brewing Company)

Dead Horse Amber Ale
(Moab Brewery)

Deschutes Cinder Cone Red Ale (55 IBU)
(Deschutes Brewery)

Dick's Mountain Ale
(Dick's Brewing Company)

Dock Street Amber (16 SRM, 28 IBU)
(The Dock Street Brewery Company)

Dragonmead Crooked Door Amber Ale
(Dragonmead Microbrewery)

Duck-Rabbit Amber Ale
(Duck-Rabbit Craft Brewery)

Dunedin Brewery Oktoberfest Ale (10 SRM, 15 IBU)
(Dunedin Brewery)

Dunedin Brewery Redhead Red Ale (11 SRM, 30 IBU)
(Dunedin Brewery)

Durango Brewing Amber Ale (20 IBU)
(Durango Brewing Company)

Edenton Brewing Horniblow's Tavern
(Edenton Brewing Company)

Eel River Brewing Organic Amber Ale
(Eel River Brewing Company)

Elmwood Brewing Amber Ale
(Elmwood Brewing Company)

Estes Park Gold
(Estes Park Brewery)

Fish Tale Organic Amber Ale
(Fish Brewing Company)

Flying Bison Brewing Aviator Red
(Flying Bison Brewing Company)

119

BEER STYLES INDEX Amber (continued)

Flying Dog Old Scratch Amber (21 SRM, 20 IBU)
(Flying Dog Brewery, LLC)

Flying Fish Brewing ESB Ale (12.2 SRM, 25.3 IBU)
(Flying Fish Brewing)

Franconia Notch Brewing River Driver Ale
(Franconia Notch Brewing Company)

Full Sail Brewing Amber – *page 502*
(Full Sail Brewing Company)

Grand Teton Teton Ale (24 IBU)
(Grand Teton Brewing Company)

Great Sex Brewing Adam and Eve Ale – *page 506*
(Great Sex Brewing, Inc.)

Green Flash Ruby Red Ale
(Green Flash Brewing)

Hale's Red Menance Big Amber
(Hale's Ales)

Harbor City Brewing Mile Rock Amber Ale
(Harbor City Brewing, Inc.)

Healthy Brew Easy Amber
(Healthy Brew)

Highland Brewing Gaelic Ale (32 IBU)
(Highland Brewing)

Hood Canal Brewing Agate Pass Amber
(Hood Canal Brewing)

Hornpout No Limit Amber Ale
(Hornpout Brewing)

Hyland's Sturbridge Amber Ale
(Pioneer Brewing Company)

Jolly Pumpkin Fuego del Otono "Autumn Fire"
(Jolly Pumpkin Artisan Ales)

Keegan Ales Hurricane Kitty (8.9 SRM, 69.9 IBU)
(Keegan Ales)

Keoki Sunset
(Keoki Brewing Company)

Keweenaw Brewing Red Jacket Amber Ale
(Keweenaw Brewing Company)

Key West Sunset Ale – *page 497*
(Florida Beer Company)

King Red Ox Amber Ale
(King Brewing Company)

King Royal Amber
(King Brewing Company)

Lagunitas Brewing The Censored Rich Copper Ale
(Lagunitas Brewing)

Lake Placid Craft Brewing Barkeater Amber Ale
(Lake Placid Craft Brewing)

Lake Superior Brewing Mesabi Red
(Lake Superior Brewing Company)

Lost Coast Alleycat Amber (35 IBU)
(Lost Coast Brewery & Café)

MacTarnahan's Brewing Mac's Amber Ale (30 IBU)
(MacTarnahan's Brewing Company)

Mammoth Brewing Company Amber
(Mammoth Brewing Company)

Marin Brewing Albion Amber Ale
(Marin Brewing Company)

Mehana Brewing Volcano Red Ale
(Mehana Brewing Company, Inc.)

Mendocino Brewing Eye of the Hawk
(Mendocino Brewing Company)

Michael Shea's Irish Amber
(High Falls Brewing)

Middle Ages Grail Ale
(Middle Ages Brewing Company)

Mojo Red Ale
(Big Easy Brewing Company)

Mount Hood Brewing Cloudcap Amber Ale
(Mount Hood Brewing Company)

New Belgium Fat Tire Amber Ale (12.9 SRM, 18.5 IBU) – *page 521*
(New Belgium Brewing Company)

New England Brewing Atlantic Amber
(New England Brewing Company)

New Holland Sundog
(New Holland Brewing Company)

Newport Storm Hurricane Amber Ale (16 SRM, 24 IBU)
(Coastal Extreme Brewing Company, LLC)

Oak Creek Amber Ale
(Oak Creek Brewing Company)

Oaken Barrel Brewing Indiana Amber Ale
(Oaken Barrel Brewing Company)

Oceanside Ale Works San Luis Rey Red
(Oceanside Ale Works)

Odell Brewing Levity Amber
(Odell Brewing Company)

Olde Towne Amber
(Olde Towne Brewing)

Otter Creek Brewing Alpine Ale (36 IBU)
(Otter Creek Brewing Company)

Paper City Brewing Holyoke Dam Ale
(Paper City Brewery Company)

Peak Organic Amber Ale
(Peak Organic Brewing Company)

PGA (Perfectly Great Amber) (23 IBU)
(Snoqualmie Falls Brewing Company)

Port Townsend Reel Amber
(Port Townsend Brewing Company)

Rare Vos Amber Ale
(Brewery Ommegang)

Redhook Ale Brewery Copperhook Spring Ale (11SRM, 20 IBU)
(Redhook Ale Brewery)

Rogue American Amber Ale (53 IBU)
(Rogue Ales)

Ruby Mountain Brewing Angel Creek Amber Ale
(Ruby Mountain Brewing Company)

Rush River Brewing The Unforgiven Amber Ale
(Rush River Brewing (Kegs))

Samuel Adams Boston Ale (14 SRM, 32 IBU)
(The Boston Beer Company)

Santa Cruz Mountain Brewing Organic Amber Ale – *page 544*
(Santa Cruz Mountain Brewing)

Scuttlebutt Amber Ale (23 IBU)
(Scuttlebutt Brewing Company)

Sherwood Forest Archer's Ale
(Sherwood Forest Brewers)

Shipyard Brewing Export Ale – *page 544*
(Shipyard Brewing Company)

Sierra Blanca Brewing Alien Amber Ale
(Sierra Blanca Brewing Company)

Siletz Brewing Company Amber Ale (24.3 SRM, 53.5 IBU)
(Siletz Brewing Company, Inc.)

Silver Gulch Copper Creek Amber Ale (24 IBU)
(Silver Gulch Brewing & Bottling)

SLO Brewing Amber Ale
(Downtown Brewing Company)

Sly Fox Christmas Ale (16 IBU)
(Sly Fox Brewing Company)

Sonora Brewing Desert Amber
(Sonoran Brewing Company (Kegs/ Growlers))

Southern Tier Brewing Big Red Imperial Red
(Southern Tier Brewing Company)

Speakeasy Prohibition Ale
(Speakeasy Ales & Lagers, Inc.)

Sprecher Brewing Special Amber (22 IBU)
(Sprecher Brewing)

Starr Hill Amber Ale
(Starr Hill Brewery)

Stone Levitation Ale (45 IBU)
(Stone Brewing Company)

Thomas Creek Amber Ale (19.7 IBU)
(Thomas Creek Brewery)

Trailhead Red Amber Ale
(Trailhead Brewing Company)

Traverse Brewing Manitou Amber Ale
(Traverse Brewing Company)

Tröegs Brewing Hopback Amber (55 IBU)
(Tröegs Brewing Company)

Tröegs Brewing Nugget Nectar (93 IBU)
(Tröegs Brewing Company)

Two Brothers Domaine Dupage French Country Ale (24 IBU) – *page 567*
(Two Brothers Brewing Company)

Upland Brewing Company Amber (28 IBU)
(Upland Brewing Company)

Wachusett Quinn's Amber Ale
(Wachusett Brewing Company)

Wasatch Evolution Amber Ale
(Utah Brewers Cooperative/ Wasatch)

Widmer Brothers Brewing Company Drop Top Amber Ale
(14 SRM, 20 IBU)
(Widmer Brothers Brewing Company)

Wild Goose Amber (20 SRM, 25 IBU)
(Wild Goose Brewery, LLC)

Wingman Amber Ale
(Nine G Brewing Company, Inc.)

Yellowstone Beer
(Lewis & Clark Brewing)

Yellowstone Valley Wild Fly Ale
(Yellowstone Valley Brewing)

American Pale Ale

Anderson Valley Poleeko Gold Pale Ale (34 IBU)
(Anderson Valley Brewing Company)

Angry Minnow Honey Wheat Pale Ale
(Angry Minnow Brewing)

Atlanta Brewing PeachTree Pale Ale
(Atlanta Brewing Company)

August Schell Brewing Pale Ale (14 SRM, 35 IBU)
(August Schell Brewing Company)

Back Road Brewery American Pale Ale
(Back Road Brewery)

Ballantine Ale
(Pabst Brewing Company)

Barley Island Brewing Blind Tiger Pale Ale (7.1 SRM, 32.6 IBU)
(Barley Island Brewing Company)

Bayhawk Ales California Pale Ale (CPA) (49 IBU)
(Bayhawk Ales, Inc.)

BBC American Pale Ale (14 SRM, 52 IBU) – *page 472*
(Bluegrass Brewing Company)

Bear Republic Brewing Special XP Pale Ale (55 IBU)
(Bear Republic Brewing Company)

Berghoff Pale Ale (43 IBU)
(Joseph Huber Brewing Company, Inc.)

Berkshire Brewing Steel Rail Extra Pale Ale – *page 467*
(Berkshire Brewing Company)

Black Dog American Pale Ale (50 IBU)
Spanish Peaks Brewing Company/United States Beverage

Blue Point Brewing Pale Ale (36 IBU)
(Blue Point Brewing)

Boulder Beer Hazed & Infused Dry-Hopped Ale (19.7 SRM, 38 IBU)
 – *page 477*
(Boulder Beer Company)

Boulevard Brewing Pale Ale (31 IBU) – *page 479*
(Boulevard Brewing Company)

Brewers Creek Pale Ale
(Mt.Shasta Brewing Company)

BridgePort Blue Heron Pale Ale (25 IBU)
(BridgePort Brewing Company (Gambrinus))

Bristol Brewing Red Rocket Pale Ale (28 IBU)
(Bristol Brewing Company)

Butte Creek Mt. Shasta Extra Pale Ale
(Butte Creek Brewing)

Caldera Brewing Pale Ale – *page 482*
(Caldera Brewing Company)

BEER STYLES INDEX

Carolina Brewing Pale Ale
(Carolina Brewing)

Cascade Lakes Pine Marten Pale Ale (38 IBU)
(Cascade Lakes Brewing Company)

Catawba Valley Brewing Buffalo Nickel Ale
(Catawba Valley Brewing)

Central Coast Brewing Golden Glow Ale
(Central Coast Brewing)

Central Waters Happy Heron Pale Ale
(Central Waters Brewing Company)

Cisco Brewers Whale's Tale Pale Ale
(Cisco Brewers, Inc.)

City Pale Ale
(City Brewery)

Clay Pipe Brewing Blackfin Pale Ale (8.0 SRM)
(Clay Pipe Brewing Company)

Clipper City Brewing Pale Ale
(Clipper City Brewing Company)

Coeur d'Alene Brewing Centennial Pale Ale
(Coeur D'Alene Brewing Company)

Columbus Brewing Pale Ale
(Columbus Brewing Company)

Copperhead Pale Ale (32 IBU)
(Snoqualmie Falls Brewing Company)

Crested Butte Brewery White Buffalo Peace Ale
(Crested Butte Brewery)

Deschutes Hop Trip Pale Ale (35 IBU)
(Deschutes Brewery)

Deschutes Mirror Pond Pale Ale (40 IBU)
(Deschutes Brewery)

Dick's Pale Ale
(Dick's Brewing Company)

Dillion DAM Extra Pale Ale
(Dillion DAM Brewery)

Dogfish Head Shelter Pale Ale (25 IBU)
(Dogfish Head Craft Brewery)

Dunedin Brewery Piper's Pale Ale (7 SRM, 37 IBU)
(Dunedin Brewery)

Durango Brewing Derail Ale
(Durango Brewing Company)

E.J. Phair Pale Ale
(E.J. Phair Brewing)

Ellicottville Brewing American Pale Ale
(Ellicottville Brewing Company)

Elmwood Brewing Pale Ale
(Elmwood Brewing Company)

Elysian Fields Pale Ale (36 IBU)
(Elysian Brewing Company)

Falls Brewing Falls Hot Tail Ale
(Falls Brewing Company)

Falmouth American Pale Ale
(Blue & Gray Brewing Company, Inc.)

Farmhouse Two Tractor Pale Ale
(Farmhouse Brewing Company)

Firestone Walker Pale Ale (7 SRM, 38 IBU)
(Firestone Walker Brewing Company)

Fish Tale Wild Salmon Organic Pale Ale
(Fish Brewing Company)

Flying Bison Brewing Barnstormer Pale Ale
(Flying Bison Brewing Company)

Flying Fish Brewing Extra Pale Ale (12.2 SRM, 14.4 IBU)
(Flying Fish Brewing)

Fordham Brewing Tavern Ale
(Fordham Brewing Company)

Founders Brewing Pale Ale (32 IBU)
(Founders Brewing Company)

Four Plus WILDFIRE Extra Pale Ale (8 SRM, 41 IBU)
(Four Plus Brewing Company)

Franconia Notch Brewing Grail Pale Ale
(Franconia Notch Brewing Company)

Frankenmuth Pioneer Pale Ale
(Frankenmuth Brewery)

Full Sail Brewing Pale Ale
(Full Sail Brewing Company)

Golden City Pale Ale
(Golden City Brewery)

Golden Valley American Pale Ale (38 IBU)
(Golden Valley Brewery)

Goose Island Honker's Ale (15 SRM, 32 IBU)
(Goose Island Beer Company)

Gray's Brewing Pale Ale
(Gray Brewing)

Great Lakes Brewing Burning River Pale Ale (45 IBU)
(Great Lakes Brewing Company)

Great Northern Brewing Going To The Sun Pale Ale (33 IBU)
(Great Northern Brewing Company)

Great Northern Brewing Going To The Sun Pale Ale (33 IBU)
(Great Northern Brewing Company)

Hair of the Dog Brewing Ruth
(Hair of the Dog Brewing Company)

Hale's Pale American Ale
(Hale's Ales)

Harpoon Ale (24 IBU)
(Harpoon Brewery)

Henry Weinhard's Blue Boar Pale Ale
(SAB Miller Corporation)

High & Mighty Brewing XPA
(High & Mighty Brewing Company)

Highland Brewing St. Terese's Pale Ale (24 IBU)
(Highland Brewing)

Hinterland Pale Ale
(Green Bay Brewing Company)

Hopper Pale Ale
(Madison River Brewing Company)

Hoptown Paleface Pale Ale
(Hoptown Brewery)

Hornpout Pale Ale
(Hornpout Brewing)

Hurricane Reef Pale Ale
(Florida Beer Company)

Hyland's Sturbridge American Pale Ale
(Pioneer Brewing Company)

Ice Harbor Brewing Harvest Pale Ale (40 IBU)
(Ice Harbor Brewing Company)

Independence Brewing Pale Ale (39 IBU)
(Independence Brewing)

Indian Wells Desert Pale Ale
(Indian Wells Brewing)

Iron Horse Rodeo Extra Pale Ale
(Iron Horse Brewery)

Island Brewing Paradise Pale Ale (35 IBU)
(Island Brewing Company)

Ithaca Beer Company Pale Ale
(Ithaca Beer Company, Inc.)

James Page Brewing Voyageur Extra Pale Ale
(James Page Brewing Company, LLC)

JW DunDee's American Pale Ale
(High Falls Brewing)

Keweenaw Brewing Magnum Pale Ale
(Keweenaw Brewing Company)

King Pale Ale
(King Brewing Company)

Kodiak Island Liquid Sunshine
(Kodiak Island Brewing Company (Kegs/ Growlers))

Kona Brewing Fire Rock Pale Ale (14 SRM, 36 IBU)
(Kona Brewing LLC)

Lagunitas Brewing Dogtown Pale Ale
(Lagunitas Brewing)

Lake Effect Pale Ale
(Mishawaka Brewing Company)

Lake Louie Brewing Arena Premium
(Lake Louie Brewing, LLC)

Lakefront Cream City Pale Ale (14 SRM, 40 IBU)
(Lakefront Brewery, Inc.)

Lancaster Brewing Amish Four Grain Pale Ale (28 IBU)
(Lancaster Brewing Company)

Left Coast Pale Ale
(Left Coast Brewing)

Left Hand Brewing Jackman's Pale Ale (42 IBU)
(Left Hand Brewing Company)

Legend Brewing Legend Pale Ale
(Legend Brewing Company)

Lion Brewing Pocono Pale Ale
(Lion Brewery)

Mad Anthony Pale Ale
(Mad Anthony Brewing Company)

Mad River Steelhead Extra Pale Ale (24.6 IBU) – *page 518*
(Mad River Brewing)

Magic Hat Brewing Fat Angel (9.2 SRM, 29 IBU)
(Magic Hat Brewing Company)

Mammoth Brewing Company Pale Ale
(Mammoth Brewing Company)

Marin Brewing MT. Tam Pale Ale
(Marin Brewing Company)

Maritime Pacific Islander Pale
(Maritime Pacific Brewing Company)

Mehana Brewing Mauna Kea Pale Ale
(Mehana Brewing Company, Inc.)

Mendocino Brewing Blue Heron Pale Ale
(Mendocino Brewing Company)

Mercury Brewing Ipswich Harvest Ale (40 IBU)
(Mercury Brewing Company)

Michigan Brewing Mackinac Pale Ale
(Michigan Brewing Company, Inc.)

Middle Ages Syracuse Pale Ale
(Middle Ages Brewing Company)

Mount Hood Brewing Cascadian Pale Ale
(Mount Hood Brewing Company)

Moylan's Tipperary Pale Ale
(Moylan's Brewing Company)

Nashoba Valley Brewery Heron Ale (30 IBU)
(Nashoba Valley Brewery)

Nectar Ales Pale Nectar
(Nectar Ales)

New Knoxville Brewing Traditional Pale Ale
(New Knoxville Brewing Company)

New Knoxville Brewing XX Pale Ale
(New Knoxville Brewing Company)

New River Pale Ale (6.5 SRM, 35 IBU)
(New River Brewing Company)

Nimbus Pale Ale (8 SRM, 40 IBU) – *page 524*
(Nimbus Brewing Company)

North Coast Ruedrich's Red Seal Ale (45 IBU)
(North Coast Brewing Company)

Northern Lights Pale Ale
(The Northern Lights Brewing Company)

Oak Creek Pale Ale
(Oak Creek Brewing Company)

Oak Pond Brewing Dooryard Ale
(Oak Pond Brewery)

Oaken Barrel Brewing Gnaw Bone Pale Ale
(Oaken Barrel Brewing Company)

Oceanside Ale Works Pier View Pale Ale
(Oceanside Ale Works)

Odell Brewing 5 Barrel Pale Ale
(Odell Brewing Company)

Olde Towne Pale Ale
(Olde Towne Brewing)

Orlando Brewing Pale Ale 7.6 SRM, 28.3 IBU
(Orlando Brewing Partners, Inc. (Kegs/ Growlers))

Oskar Blues Grill & Brew Dale's Pale Ale (65 IBU)
(Oskar Blues Grill & Brew)

Otter Creek Brewing Pale Ale (23 IBU)
(Otter Creek Brewing Company)

Palmetto Brewing Pale Ale
(Palmetto Brewing Company, Inc.)

Paper City Brewing Banchee Extra Pale Ale
(Paper City Brewery Company)

Paper City Brewing Ireland Parish Golden Ale
(Paper City Brewery Company)

Paper City Brewing Summer Time Pale Ale
(Paper City Brewery Company)

Peak Organic Pale Ale
(Peak Organic Brewing Company)

Point Cascade Pale Ale
(Stevens Point Brewery)

Pony Express Rattlesnake Pale Ale
(Pony Express Brewing Company)

Porkslap Pale Ale (24 IBU) – *page 481*
(Butternuts Beer & Ale)

R.J. Rockers Patriot Pale Ale (6 SRM, 40 IBU)
(R.J. Rockers Brewing Company)

Real Ale Brewing Rio Blanco Pale Ale
(Real Ale Brewing Company)

ReaperAle Deathly Pale Ale (45 IBU)
(ReaperAle, Inc.)

Rio Grande Brewing Sunchaser Ale (32 IBU)
(Rio Grande Brewing Company)

River Horse Hop Hazard Pale Ale
(River Horse Brewing Company)

Rogue Juniper Pale Ale (34 IBU)
(Rogue Ales)

Saint Arnold Brewing Amber Ale (31 IBU) – *page 538*
(Saint Arnold Brewing Company)

Samuel Adams Pale Ale (8 SRM, 23 IBU)
(The Boston Beer Company)

Santa Cruz Mountain Brewing Pale Ale
(Santa Cruz Mountain Brewing)

Scorpion Pale Ale
(Moab Brewery)

Shenandoah Brewing Big Meadow Pale Ale
(Shenandoah Brewing Company)

Shipyard Brewing Chamberland Pale Ale
(Shipyard Brewing Company)

Shmaltz Brewing Genesis 10:10
(Shmaltz Brewing Company)

Shmaltz Brewing Genesis Ale – *page 545*
(Shmaltz Brewing Company)

Sierra Nevada Pale Ale (12 SRM, 38 IBU)
(Sierra Nevada Brewing Company)

Silver Gulch Old 55 Pale Ale
(Silver Gulch Brewing & Bottling)

Skagit River Yellow Jacket Pale Ale
(Skagit River Brewery)

Slab City Brewing Old 47 Pale Ale
(Slab City Brewing)

SLO Brewing Extra Pale Ale
(Downtown Brewing Company)

Sly Fox Phoenix Pale Ale (40 IBU)
(Sly Fox Brewing Company)

Smuttynose Brewing Shoals Pale Ale (30 IBU)
(Smuttynose Brewing Company)

Snake River Pale Ale (32 IBU)
(Snake River Brewing Company)

Southern Tier Brewing Phin & Matt's
(Southern Tier Brewing Company)

Speakeasy Untouchable Pale Ale
(Speakeasy Ales & Lagers, Inc.)

Springfield Brewing Pale Ale (25 IBU)
(Springfield Brewing Company)

Squatters Full Suspension Pale Ale
(Utah Brewers Cooperative/ Wasatch)

St. George Brewing Company Pale Ale
(St.George Brewing Company)

Starr Hill Pale Ale
(Starr Hill Brewery)

Stone Mill Pale Ale – *page 456*
(Anheuser-Busch, Inc.)

Stone Pale Ale (41 IBU)
(Stone Brewing Company)

Stoudt's American Pale Ale (40 IBU)
(Stoudt's Brewing Company)

Streich's Brewing Naughty Fish Pale Ale
(Streich's Brewing Company, LLC)

Sweetwater Brewing 420 Extra Pale Ale – *page 559*
(Sweetwater Brewing)

Terrapin Rye Pale Ale (45 IBU) – *page 560*
(Terrapin Beer Company)

Third Eye Pale Ale (8.8 SRM, 59 IBU)
(Steamworks Brewing Company)

Thomas Hooker American Pale Ale (7.6 SRM, 31 IBU)
(Thomas Hooker Brewing Company)

Three Floyds Brewing Alpha King (66 IBU)
(Three Floyds Brewing Company)

Tommyknocker Pick Axe Pale Ale
(Tommyknocker Brewery)

Tractor Brewing Sod Buster Pale Ale
(Tractor Brewing Company)

Traverse Brewing Old Mission Lighthouse Ale
(Traverse Brewing Company)

Tröegs Brewing Pale Ale (45 IBU)
(Tröegs Brewing Company)

Tuckerman Brewing Pale Ale
(Tuckerman Brewing)

Tuscan Paradise Pale Ale
(Tuscan Brewery)

Two Brothers The Bitter End Pale Ale (36 IBU)
(Two Brothers Brewing Company)

Tyranena Brewing Company Stone Tepee Pale Ale (6 SRM, 32 IBU)
(Tyranena Brewing Company)

Uinta Brewing Cutthroat Pale Ale
(Uinta Brewing Company)

Upland Brewing Company Pale Ale (19 IBU)
(Upland Brewing Company)

Wachusett Country Ale
(Wachusett Brewing Company)

Waimea Brewing Na Pali Pale Ale (26 IBU)
(Waimea Brewing Company)

Waimea Brewing Waimea Bay Pale Ale (40 IBU)
(Waimea Brewing Company)

Wasatch Special Reserve Pale Ale
(Utah Brewers Cooperative/ Wasatch)

Whitstran Brewing Over-The-Edge Dry-Hopped Pale Ale (46 IBU)
(Whitstran Brewing Company)

Widmer Brothers Brewing Company Summit Pale Ale (17 SRM, 34 IBU)
(Widmer Brothers Brewing Company)

Wild Goose India Pale Ale (10 SRM, 50 IBU) – *page 572*
(Wild Goose Brewery, LLC)

Williamsburg AleWerks Chesapeake Pale Ale
(Williamsburg AleWerks)

Wolaver's Organic Pale Ale (34 IBU)
(Otter Creek Brewing Company)

Yards Brewing Philadelphia Pale Ale
(Yards Brewing)

Yazoo Brewing Amarillo Pale Ale
(Yazoo Brewing)

Yuengling Lord Chesterfield Ale
(D.G. Yuengling & Son, Inc.)

Belgian Style Ale

Alesmith Brewing Horny Devil
(Alesmith Brewing Company)

Allagash Brewing Victoria Ale
(Allagash Brewing Company)

Allagash Grand Cru (30 IBU)
(Allagash Brewing Company)

Anderson Valley Brother David's Abbey Style Double (28 IBU)
(Anderson Valley Brewing Company)

Anderson Valley Brother David's Abbey Style Triple (26 IBU)
(Anderson Valley Brewing Company)

Angel City Abbey (18 SRM, 30 IBU)
(Angel City Brewing)

Avery Brewing Karma Belgian Ale (10 IBU)
(Avery Brewing Company)

Avery Brewing Twelve
(Avery Brewing Company)

BBC Hell For Certain (16 SRM, 25 IBU)
(Bluegrass Brewing Company)

Bethlehem Brew Works Rude Elf's Reserve
(The Bethlehem Brew Works)

Bison Brewing Organic Belgain Ale (30 SRM, 87 IBU)
(Bison Brewing)

Bison Brewing Organic Farmhouse (7 SRM, 24 IBU)
(Bison Brewing)

Bison Brewing Organic Winter (32 SRM, 27 IBU)
(Bison Brewing)

Black Dog Summer White Ale
Spanish Peaks Brewing Company/United States Beverage

Dark Horse Sapient Trip Ale
(Dark Horse Brewing Company)

Defiant Brewing Christmas Ale
(The Defiant Brewing Company)

Dick's Silk Lady
(Dick's Brewing Company)

Dogfish Head Au Courant
(Dogfish Head Craft Brewery)

Dogfish Head Black & Blue
(Dogfish Head Craft Brewery)

Dragonmead Wench Water Belgian Pale Ale
(Dragonmead Microbrewery)

Farmhouse Saison 7
(Farmhouse Brewing Company)

Flying Fish Brewing Belgian Abbey Dubbel (21.2 SRM, 38.7 IBU)
 – page 499
(Flying Fish Brewing)

Flying Fish Brewing Grand Cru Winter Reserve
(Flying Fish Brewing)

Founders Brewing Blushing Monk
(Founders Brewing Company)

Four Plus Monkshine Belgian Style Pale Ale
(Four Plus Brewing Company)

Heavy Seas Brewing Red Sky at Night Saison Ale
(Clipper City Brewing Company)

Hennepin Farmhouse Saison Ale
(Brewery Ommegang)

Ithaca Beer Company Partly Sunny
(Ithaca Beer Company, Inc.)

Jack's Farmhouse Ale
(Jack Russell Brewing)

Jolly Pumpkin Bam Biere
(Jolly Pumpkin Artisan Ales)

Jolly Pumpkin Biere de Mars
(Jolly Pumpkin Artisan Ales)

Jolly Pumpkin La Roja
(Jolly Pumpkin Artisan Ales)

Jolly Pumpkin Oro de Calabaza
(Jolly Pumpkin Artisan Ales)

Left Hand Brewing St. Vrain Ale (20 IBU)
(Left Hand Brewing Company)

Midnight Sun La Miatresse du Moine (40 IBU)
(Midnight Sun Brewing Company)

Midnight Sun Saison of the Sun (27 IBU)
(Midnight Sun Brewing Company)

Monk's Ale
(Abbey Beverage Company)

Nashoba Valley Brewery Belgian Pale Ale (26 IBU)
(Nashoba Valley Brewery)

Beer Styles Index

Nashoba Valley Brewery Peach Lambic (15 IBU)
(Nashoba Valley Brewery)

New Belgium Abbey Belgian Style Ale (27.9 SRM, 20 IBU)
(New Belgium Brewing Company)

New Belgium Saison Harvest Ale
(New Belgium Brewing Company)

New Belgium Trippel Belgian Style Ale (7.9 SRM, 25 IBU)
(New Belgium Brewing Company)

North Coast Pranqster Belgian Style Golden Ale (20 IBU)
(North Coast Brewing Company)

Pere Jacques (32 SRM, 26 IBU)
(Goose Island Beer Company)

Point White Bière
(Stevens Point Brewery)

Rapscallion Blessing (36 IBU)
(Concord Brewery, Inc.)

Rapscallion Creation (18 IBU)
(Concord Brewery, Inc.)

Rapscallion Premier (26 IBU)
(Concord Brewery, Inc.)

River Horse Belgian Frostbite Winter Ale
(River Horse Brewing Company)

River Horse Tripel Horse
(River Horse Brewing Company)

Rogue Monk Madness Ale (108 IBU)
(Rogue Ales)

Russian River Brewing Damnation (25 IBU)
(Russian River Brewing Company)

Russian River Brewing Redemption (23 IBU)
(Russian River Brewing Company)

Russian River Brewing Salvation (22 IBU)
(Russian River Brewing Company)

Russian River Brewing Temptation (27 IBU)
(Russian River Brewing Company)

Saison Elysee
(Elysian Brewing Company)

Sly Fox Saison VOS (32 IBU)
(Sly Fox Brewing Company)

Smuttynose Brewing Farmhouse Ale
(Smuttynose Brewing Company)

Southampton Biere de Garde
(Southampton Publick House)

Southampton Saison
(Southampton Publick House)

Spring Fever (32 IBU)
(Snoqualmie Falls Brewing Company)

Stone Vertical Epic Ale
(Stone Brewing Company)

The Lost Abbey Avant Garde (24 IBU)
(Port Brewing Company)

The Lost Abbey Cuvee de Tomme
(Port Brewing Company)

The Lost Abbey Judgment Day
(Port Brewing Company)

The Lost Abbey Red Barn Ale
(Port Brewing Company)

The Lost Abbey The Angel's Share
(Port Brewing Company)

Three Floyds Brewing Rabbid Rabbit Saison
(Three Floyds Brewing Company)

Three Philosophers Quadrupel Ale – *page 480*
(Brewery Ommegang)

Victory V Saison (25-30 IBU)
(Victory Brewing Company)

Victory V Twelve (25-30 IBU)
(Victory Brewing Company)

Whitstran Brewing Friar Lawrence Belgium-Style Ale (18 IBU)
(Whitstran Brewing Company)

Wild Dog Colorado Saison (8 SRM, 20 IBU)
(Flying Dog Brewery, LLC)

Yards Brewing Saison
(Yards Brewing)

Zephyrus Pilsner (38 IBU)
(Elysian Brewing Company)

BEER STYLES INDEX

Belgian White

Allagash Brewing 11th Anniversary
(Allagash Brewing Company)

Avery Brewing White Rascal Belgian-Style White Ale (10 IBU)
(Avery Brewing Company)

Back Road Brewery Belgian-Style Wit
(Back Road Brewery)

Ballast Point Wahoo Wheat Beer
(Ballast Point Brewing Company)

BBC White Wedding Ale (4 SRM, 10 IBU)
(Bluegrass Brewing Company)

Big Sky Brewing Summer Honey Seasonal Ale
(Big Sky Brewing Company)

Blue Moon Belgian White
(Molson Coors Brewing Company)

Boulevard Brewing ZÔN (12 IBU)
(Boulevard Brewing Company)

Erie Brewing Sunshine Wit (17 IBU)
(Erie Brewing)

Full Moon Belgian White Ale
(Mudshark Brewing Company)

Great Lakes Brewing Holy Moses White Ale (30 IBU)
(Great Lakes Brewing Company)

Happy Valley Brewing Mission Ale Wit
(Happy Valley Brewing Company)

Jolly Pumpkin Calabaza Blanca
(Jolly Pumpkin Artisan Ales)

Lake Louie Brewing Prairie Moon Belgian Style Farmhouse Ale
(Lake Louie Brewing, LLC)

Lakefront White Beer (3 SRM, 15 IBU)
(Lakefront Brewery, Inc.)

Legacy Brewing Midnight Wit Ale (17 IBU)
(Legacy Brewing Company)

Lost Coast Great White (27 IBU) – *page 517*
(Lost Coast Brewery & Café)

Michigan Brewing Celis White
(Michigan Brewing Company, Inc.)

Middle Ages Swallow Wheat
(Middle Ages Brewing Company)

Millstream Brewing John's Generations White Ale
(Millstream Brewing Company)

Oaken Barrel Brewing Alabaster
(Oaken Barrel Brewing Company)

Ommegang Witte Ale
(Brewery Ommegang)

Oregon Trail Wit
(Oregon Trail Brewery)

Penn Weizen
(Penn Brewery (Pennsylvania Brewing))

Rogue Half-E-Weizen (34 IBU)
(Rogue Ales)

Samuel Adams White Ale (8 SRM, 12 IBU) – *page 475*
(The Boston Beer Company)

Southampton Double White Ale – *page 551*
(Southampton Publick House)

Summit Scandia Ale (5.5 SRM, 17 IBU) – *page 558*
(Summit Brewing Company)

Two Brothers Monarch White
(Two Brothers Brewing Company)

Victory Whirlwind Witbier (13-18 IBU)
(Victory Brewing Company)

Viking Brewing Dim Whit
(Viking Brewing)

Weyerbacher Brewing Blanche
(Weyerbacher Brewing Company)

Wolaver's Organic Wit Bier
(Otter Creek Brewing Company)

Blonde/Golden Ale

Alaskan Pale (8.5 SRM, 24 IBU)
(Alaskan Brewing Company)

Andrews Summer Golden Ale
(Andrews Brewing Company)

Atlanta Brewing Red Brick Blonde
(Atlanta Brewing Company)

Barley Creek Navigator Gold
(Barley Creek Brewing Company)

Barley Island Brewing Sheet Metal Blonde
(Barley Island Brewing Company)

BBC Bluegrass Gold (3 SRM, 10 IBU)
(Bluegrass Brewing Company)

Beach Bum Blonde Ale – *page 459*
(Anheuser-Busch, Inc.)

Big Horn Blonde (5 SRM, 20 IBU)
(Big Horn Brewing (CB Potts))

Bitter Root Brewing Sawtooth Ale (5 SRM, 20 IBU)
(Bitter Root Brewing)

Blue Point Brewing Golden Ale (16 IBU)
(Blue Point Brewing)

Blue Ridge Golden Ale
(Wild Goose Brewery, LLC)

Boulder Beer Buffalo Gold Golden Ale (10.3 SRM, 22 IBU)
(Boulder Beer Company)

Butte Creek Gold Ale
(Butte Creek Brewing)

Carolina Beer Carolina Blonde – *page 484*
(Carolina Beer & Beverage Company)

Cascade Lakes Blonde Bombshell (26 IBU)
(Cascade Lakes Brewing Company)

Cascade Lakes Rooster Tail Ale (20 IBU)
(Cascade Lakes Brewing Company)

Central Coast Brewing Topless Blonde Ale
(Central Coast Brewing)

Chasing Tail Golden Ale
(Utah Brewers Cooperative/ Wasatch)

Church Brew Works Celestial Gold (18 IBU)
(The Church Brew Works)

Clay Pipe Brewing Blue Tractor Ale (28 IBU)
(Clay Pipe Brewing Company)

Clipper City Brewing Gold Ale
(Clipper City Brewing Company)

Columbus Brewing 90 Schilling Ale
(Columbus Brewing Company)

Cooperstown Brewing Nine Man Ale
(Cooperstown Brewing Company)

Crested Butte Brewery Paradise Crisp Golden Ale
(Crested Butte Brewery)

Dogfish Head Snowblown Ale (33 IBU)
(Dogfish Head Craft Brewery)

Dunedin Brewery Celtic Gold Ale (5 SRM, 25 IBU)
(Dunedin Brewery)

Edenton Brewing Joseph Hewes
(Edenton Brewing Company)

Empyrean Ales Chaco Canyon Honey Gold (5 SRM, 23 IBU)
(Empyrean Brewing)

English Ales Jubilee Golden Ale
(English Ales Brewery)

Etna Classic Gold
(Etna Brewing Company)

Falls Brewing Falls Dirty Blonde Ale
(Falls Brewing Company)

Farmington River Blonde Ale
(Mercury Brewing Company)

Fireweed Honey Blonde – *page 536*
(Rocky Coulee Brewing Company)

Fish Tale Blonde Ale
(Fish Brewing Company)

Flying Bison Brewing Dawn Patrol Gold
(Flying Bison Brewing Company)

Grand Teton Old Faithful Ale (23 IBU)
(Grand Teton Brewing Company)

Hale's Drawbridge Blonde
(Hale's Ales)

Heinzelmannchen Ancient Days Honey Blonde Ale
(Heinzelmannchen Brewery (Kegs/ Growlers))

Hoptown Golden Ale
(Hoptown Brewery)

Jack's Best Bitter Ale
(Jack Russell Brewing)

Keegan Ales Old Capital (3.5 SRM, 11.1 INU)
(Keegan Ales)

Keoki Gold
(Keoki Brewing Company)

Keweenaw Brewing Pickaxe Blonde Ale
(Keweenaw Brewing Company)

King King's Gold
(King Brewing Company)

Kona Brewing Big Wave Golden Ale (8 SRM, 20 IBU)
(Kona Brewing LLC)

Lakefront Cattail Ale (5 SRM, 15 IBU)
(Lakefront Brewery, Inc.)

Left Coast Gold
(Left Coast Brewing)

Liquid Sunshine Blonde Ale
(Hoppy Brewing Company)

Mantorville Brewing Stagecoach Ale
(Mantorville Brewing Company, LLC)

Mendocino Brewing Peregrine Golden Ale
(Mendocino Brewing Company)

Mercury Brewing Stone Cat Blonde (25 IBU)
(Mercury Brewing Company)

Mount Hood Brewing Highland Meadow Blonde Ale
(Mount Hood Brewing Company)

Moylan's Celts Golden Ale
(Moylan's Brewing Company)

Nimbus Blonde Ale (4 SRM, 12 IBU) – *page 523*
(Nimbus Brewing Company)

O'Fallon Gold (in MO only)
(O'Fallon Brewery)

O'Fallon Light
(O'Fallon Brewery)

O'Fallon Summer Brew (in MO only)
(O'Fallon Brewery)

Orlando Brewing Blonde Ale (2.9 SRM, 10.2 IBU)
(Orlando Brewing Partners, Inc. (Kegs/ Growlers))

Real Ale Brewing Fireman's #4 Blonde Ale
(Real Ale Brewing Company)

ReaperAle Inevitable Ale (22 IBU)
(ReaperAle, Inc.)

Redhook Ale Brewery Blonde Ale (8.1 SRM, 18.3 IBU)
(Redhook Ale Brewery)

Rock Art Brewery Whitetail Ale (28 IBU)
(Rock Art Brewery, LLC)

Rogue Oregon Golden Ale (35 IBU)
(Rogue Ales)

Rush River Brewing Small Axe Golden Ale
(Rush River Brewing (Kegs))

Russian River Brewing Depuration (27 IBU)
(Russian River Brewing Company)

Sand Creek Brewing Golden Ale (5.8 SRM, 11 IBU)
(Sand Creek Brewing Company, LLC)

Scuttlebutt Homeport Blonde (17 IBU)
(Scuttlebutt Brewing Company)

Shiner Blonde
(The Spoetzl Brewing (Gambrinus))

Ska Brewing True Blonde Ale – *page 548*
(Ska Brewing Company)

Snipes Mountain Brewing Extra Blonde Ale
(Snipes Mountain Brewing Company)

St. George Brewing Company Golden Ale (6.9 SRM, 33 IBU)
(St.George Brewing Company)

Sugar Hill Golden Ale
(Harlem Brewing Company)

Sunday River Sunsplash Golden Ale
(Stone Coast Brewing Company)

Terrapin Golden Ale (21 IBU)
(Terrapin Beer Company)

The Palisade Brewery PAL Beer
(The Palisade Brewery)

Thomas Hooker Blonde Ale (1.93 SRM, 11 IBU)
(Thomas Hooker Brewing Company)

Trailblazer Blonde Ale
(Trailhead Brewing Company)

Two Brothers Prairie Path Golden Ale (29 IBU)
(Two Brothers Brewing Company)

Tyranena Brewing Company Three Beaches Honey Blonde (9 SRM,68 IBU)
(Tyranena Brewing Company)

Waimea Brewing Wai' ale' ale Ale (18 IBU)
(Waimea Brewing Company)

Weed Golden Ale
(Mt.Shasta Brewing Company)

Brown Ale

Abita Brewing Turbodog
(Abita Brewing Company)

Andrews Northern Brown Ale
(Andrews Brewing Company)

Arcadia Brewing Ales Nut Brown Ale (26 IBU)
(Arcadia Brewing Company)

Avery Brewing Ellie's Brown (17 IBU)
(Avery Brewing Company)

Bar Harbor Brewing Thunder Hole Ale
(Bar Harbor Brewing Company)

Barley Creek Antler Brown Ale
(Barley Creek Brewing Company)

Barley Island Brewing Dirty Helen Brown Ale (17.8 SRM, 24.5 IBU)
(Barley Island Brewing Company)

BBC Nut Brown Ale (22 SRM, 28 IBU)
(Bluegrass Brewing Company)

Bear Republic Brewing Pete Brown's Tribute Ale
(Bear Republic Brewing Company)

Beer Town Brown (20 IBU)
(BridgePort Brewing Company (Gambrinus))

Big Sky Brewing Moose Drool Brown Ale
(Big Sky Brewing Company)

Bitter Root Brewing Nut Brown (20 SRM, 25 IBU)
(Bitter Root Brewing)

Boulevard Brewing Lunar Ale – page 478
(Boulevard Brewing Company)

Brooklyn Brown Ale (30 IBU)
(Brooklyn Brewery)

Capital Brewery Brown Ale
(Capital Brewery Company, Inc.)

Carolina Brewing Nut Brown Ale
(Carolina Brewing)

Cascade Lakes 20" Brown (35 IBU)
(Cascade Lakes Brewing Company)

Catawba Valley Brown Bear Ale
(Catawba Valley Brewing)

Central Waters Junc Town Brown Ale
(Central Waters Brewing Company)

Climax Brewing Nut Brown Ale
(Climax Brewing Company)

Coeur d'Alene Brewing Lake Side British Ale
(Coeur D'Alene Brewing Company)

Concord North Woods Ale (38 IBU)
(Concord Brewery, Inc.)

Crabtree Brewing Downtown Nut Brown
(Crabtree Brewing Company)

Deschutes Bond Street Brown
(Deschutes Brewery)

Deschutes Buzzsaw Brown (30 IBU)
(Deschutes Brewery)

Dick's Working Man's Brown Ale
(Dick's Brewing Company)

Dragonmead London Brown Ale
(Dragonmead Microbrewery)

Dragonmead Mariann's Honey Brown
(Dragonmead Microbrewery)

Duck-Rabbit Brown Ale
(Duck-Rabbit Craft Brewery)

Dunedin Brewery Beach Tale Brown Ale (21 SRM, 41 IBU) – *page 493*
(Dunedin Brewery)

Edenton Brewing Uncle Nut's
(Edenton Brewing Company)

El Toro Poppy Jasper Amber Ale
(El Toro Brewing)

Elmwood Brewing Nut Brown
(Elmwood Brewing Company)

Empyrean Ales Third Stone Brown (18 SRM, 13 IBU)
(Empyrean Brewing)

English Ales Monk's Brown Ale
(English Ales Brewery)

Falls Brewing Falls Nut Brown Ale
(Falls Brewing Company)

Geary's Autumn Ale
(D L Geary Brewing Company)

Golden City Mad Molly Brown Ale
(Golden City Brewery)

Goose Island Nut Brown Ale (50 SRM, 29 IBU)
(Goose Island Beer Company)

Green Flash Nut Brown Ale
(Green Flash Brewing)

Gritty McDuff's Best Brown Ale (16 IBU)
(Gritty McDuff's Brewing Company, LLC)

Hale's Irish Style Nut Brown Ale
(Hale's Ales)

Harbor City Brewing Main Street Brown Ale
(Harbor City Brewing, Inc.)

Harpoon Brown Ale
(Harpoon Brewery)

Heinzelmannchen Middleworld Brown Ale
(Heinzelmannchen Brewery (Kegs/ Growlers))

Hit the Trail (25 IBU)
(The Long Trail Brewing Company)

Hoptown Brown Nose Ale
(Hoptown Brewery)

Independence Brewing Bootlegger Brown Ale (14 IBU)
(Independence Brewing)

Iron Horse Brown Ale
(Iron Horse Brewery)

Island Brewing Nut Brown Ale (25 IBU)
(Island Brewing Company)

Ithaca Beer Company Nut Brown
(Ithaca Beer Company, Inc.)

Jack's Best Brown
(Maine Coast Brewing)

Jack's Brown Ale
(Jack Russell Brewing)

James Page Brewing Burly Brown Ale
(James Page Brewing Company, LLC)

Keweenaw Brewing Hilde's Brown Ale
(Keweenaw Brewing Company)

King Crown Brown Ale
(King Brewing Company)

Kodiak Island Sweet Georgia Brown
(Kodiak Island Brewing Company (Kegs/ Growlers))

Lagunitas Brewing Brown Shugga
(Lagunitas Brewing)

Lake Superior Brewing 7 Bridges Brown
(Lake Superior Brewing Company)

Beer Styles Index

Ales

Landmark Vanilla Bean Brown Ale – *page 510*
(Landmark Beer Company)

Landmark Vanilla Bean Brown Ale
(Landmark Beer Company)

Left Hand Brewing Deep Cover Brown (20 IBU)
(Left Hand Brewing Company)

Legend Brewing Brown Ale
(Legend Brewing Company)

Lost Coast Downtown Brown (33 IBU)
(Lost Coast Brewery & Café)

Lost Coast Raspberry Brown
(Lost Coast Brewery & Café)

Magic Hat Brewing Participation Ale (54 SRM, 28 IBU)
(Magic Hat Brewing Company)

Mammoth Brewing Company Double Nut Brown
(Mammoth Brewing Company)

Mercury Brewing Ipswich Dark Ale (40 IBU)
(Mercury Brewing Company)

Mercury Brewing Ipswich Nut Brown (25 IBU)
(Mercury Brewing Company)

Michigan Brewing Nut Brown Ale
(Michigan Brewing Company, Inc.)

Midnight Sun Kodiak Brown Ale (24 IBU)
(Midnight Sun Brewing Company)

Nashoba Valley Brewery Belgian Double
(Nashoba Valley Brewery)

New Glarus Brewing Enigma
(New Glarus Brewing)

New Glarus Brewing Fat Squirrel
(New Glarus Brewing)

New South Nut Brown Ale
(New South Brewing Company (Kegs/ Growlers))

Nimbus Brown Ale (21 SRM, 26 IBU) – *page 525*
(Nimbus Brewing Company)

Oak Creek Nut Brown Ale
(Oak Creek Brewing Company)

Oak Pond Brewing Nut Brown Ale
(Oak Pond Brewery)

Odell Brewing 90 Shilling
(Odell Brewing Company)

Oregon Trail Brown Ale
(Oregon Trail Brewery)

Oskar Blues Grill & Brew Leroy (90 IBU)
(Oskar Blues Grill & Brew)

Paper City Brewing Nut Brown
(Paper City Brewery Company)

Peak Organic Nut Brown Ale
(Peak Organic Brewing Company)

Pete's Wicked Ale (18 IBU)
(Pete's Brewing (Gambrinus))

Pike Brewing Company Tandem
(Pike Brewing Company)

Real Ale Brewing Brewhouse Brown Ale
(Real Ale Brewing Company)

Rock Art Brewery Brown Bear Ale (11 IBU)
(Rock Art Brewery, LLC)

Rocky Bay Brewing Foghorn Ale
(Rocky Bay Brewing Company)

Rogue Hazelnut Brown Nectar (33 IBU)
(Rogue Ales)

Russian River Brewing Supplication (27 IBU)
(Russian River Brewing Company)

Saint Arnold Brewing Brown Ale (24 IBU)
(Saint Arnold Brewing Company)

Samuel Adams Brown Ale (26 SRM, 18 IBU)
(The Boston Beer Company)

Santa Cruz Mountain Brewing Organic Dread Brown Ale – *page 541*
(Santa Cruz Mountain Brewing)

Santa Fe Brewing Santa Fe Nut Brown Ale (33 SRM, 18 IBU)
(Santa Fe Brewing Company)

Sebago Brewing Boathouse Brown Ale (49.5 SRM, 24.4 IBU)
(Sebago Brewing Company)

Sheepscot Valley Brewing Damariscotta Double Brown
(Sheepscot Valley Brewing Company)

Shipyard Brewing Brown
(Shipyard Brewing Company)

Shmaltz Brewing Messiah Bold
(Shmaltz Brewing Company)

Sierra Blanca Brewing Nut Brown
(Sierra Blanca Brewing Company)

Ska Brewing Buster Nut Brown Ale – *page 548*
(Ska Brewing Company)

Smuttynose Brewing Old Brown Dog Ale (15 IBU)
(Smuttynose Brewing Company)

Snake River OB-1 Organic Ale (22 IBU) – *page 550*
(Snake River Brewing Company)

Snipes Mountain Brewing Coyote Moon
(Snipes Mountain Brewing Company)

Snowshoe Brewing Grizzly Brown Ale
(Snowshoe Brewing Company)

South Shore Brewery Nut Brown
(South Shore Brewery)

Sprecher Brewing Pub Ale (17 IBU)
(Sprecher Brewing)

Sweet George's Brown Ale
(Dillion DAM Brewery)

Sweetwater Brewing Sweet Georgia Brown
(Sweetwater Brewing)

Tommyknocker Imperial Nut Brown Ale
(Tommyknocker Brewery)

Tommyknocker Maple Nut Brown Ale
(Tommyknocker Brewery)

Traverse Brewing Sleeping Bear Brown Ale
(Traverse Brewing Company)

Tröegs Brewing Rugged Trail Ale (28 IBU)
(Tröegs Brewing Company)

Tuscan Sundown Brown
(Tuscan Brewery)

Twisted Pine Honey Brown Ale
(Twisted Pine Brewing Company)

Tyranena Brewing Company Rocky's Revenge (26 SRM, 30 IBU)
(Tyranena Brewing Company)

Uinta Brewing Bristlecone Brown Ale
(Uinta Brewing Company)

Wachusett Nut Brown Ale
(Wachusett Brewing Company)

Wasatch Bobsled Brown Ale
(Utah Brewers Cooperative/ Wasatch)

Wild Goose Nut Brown Ale (35 SRM, 20 IBU)
(Wild Goose Brewery, LLC)

Williamsburg AleWerks Brown Ale
(Williamsburg AleWerks)

Wolaver's Organic Brown Ale (21 IBU)
(Otter Creek Brewing Company)

Woodstock Inn Brewery Pig's Ear Brown Ale
(Woodstock Inn Brewery)

Ybor Gold Brown Ale
(Florida Beer Company)

Dark Ale

Missouri Brown Dark Ale
(Trailhead Brewing Company)

New Belgium 1554 Brussels Style Black Ale (45.7 SRM, 21 IBU)
(New Belgium Brewing Company)

Dubbel/Trippel/Quad Ale

Allagash Brewing Dubbel (27 IBU)
(Allagash Brewing Company)

Allagash Brewing Four (37 IBU)
(Allagash Brewing Company)

Allagash Brewing Tripel (30 IBU)
(Allagash Brewing Company)

BEER STYLES INDEX

Avery Brewing Salvation (25 IBU)
(Avery Brewing Company)

Avery Brewing The Beast Belgian Grand Cru (68 IBU)
(Avery Brewing Company)

Avery Brewing The Reverend Belgian Quadupel (10 IBU)
(Avery Brewing Company)

Bete Blanche Belgian-Style Tripel (31 IBU)
(Elysian Brewing Company)

Buckeye Brewing Ho Ho Ho Magical Dubbel
(Buckeye Brewing)

Church Brew Works Millenium Trippel Ale
(The Church Brew Works)

Church Brew Works Quadzilla
(The Church Brew Works)

Defiant Brewing 3
(The Defiant Brewing Company)

Defiant Brewing Inspiration Ale
(The Defiant Brewing Company)

Dick's Belgian Double
(Dick's Brewing Company)

Dick's Belgian Tripel
(Dick's Brewing Company)

Dragonmead Dubbel Dragon Ale
(Dragonmead Microbrewery)

Dragonmead Final Absolution Belgian Style (30 IBU)
(Dragonmead Microbrewery)

Founders Brewing Bad Habit Belgium Quad
(Founders Brewing Company)

Green Flash Belgian Style Trippel
(Green Flash Brewing)

Hair of the Dog Brewing Fred (65 IBU)
(Hair of the Dog Brewing Company)

Hair of the Dog Brewing Rose (17 IBU)
(Hair of the Dog Brewing Company)

Lake Louie Brewing Brother Tim Tripel
(Lake Louie Brewing, LLC)

Marin Brewing Tripel Dipsea
(Marin Brewing Company)

Michigan Brewing Celis Grand Cru
(Michigan Brewing Company, Inc.)

Middle Ages Tripel Crown
(Middle Ages Brewing Company)

Midnight Sun Epluche-Culotte (20 IBU)
(Midnight Sun Brewing Company)

New Holland Black Tulip
(New Holland Brewing Company)

Pike Brewing Company Monk's Uncle
(Pike Brewing Company)

Saint Arnold Brewing Abbey American Quadruppel
(Saint Arnold Brewing Company)

Ska Brewing True Blonde Dubbel
(Ska Brewing Company)

Sly Fox Incubus (39 IBU)
(Sly Fox Brewing Company)

Smuttynose Brewing S'muttonator Doppelbock
(Smuttynose Brewing Company)

Southampton Triple
(Southampton Publick House)

Southern Tier Brewing Belgian Triple Ale
(Southern Tier Brewing Company)

Stoudt's Abbey Triple (37 IBU)
(Stoudt's Brewing Company)

Victory Golden Monkey (20-25 IBU)
(Victory Brewing Company)

Wagner Valley Brewing Tripellbock Reserve
(Wagner Valley Brewing Company)

Weyerbacher Brewing Merry Monk's Ale
(Weyerbacher Brewing Company)

Weyerbacher Brewing Prophecy
(Weyerbacher Brewing Company)

Weyerbacher Brewing QUAD
(Weyerbacher Brewing Company)

137

BEER STYLES INDEX

English Mild Ale

Arcadia Brewing Ales Battle Creek Special Reserve (23 IBU)
(Arcadia Brewing Company)

Bar Harbor Brewing Harbor Lighthouse Ale
(Bar Harbor Brewing Company)

Cooper's Cave Ale Company Bumppo's Brown Ale (35 IBU)
(Cooper's Cave Ale Company, LTD.)

Dragonmead Crusader Dark Mild Ale
(Dragonmead Microbrewery)

Erie Brewing Mad Anthony's Ale (13 IBU)
(Erie Brewing)

Gritty McDuff's Vacationland Summer Ale (22 IBU)
(Gritty McDuff's Brewing Company, LLC)

Three Floyds Brewing Pride & Joy Mild Ale (21 IBU)
(Three Floyds Brewing Company)

English Pale Ale

8th Street Ale
(Four Peaks Brewing Company)

Andrews English Pale Ale
(Andrews Brewing Company)

Appalachian Brewing Purist Pale Ale
(Appalachian Brewing Company)

Arcadia Brewing Ales Angler's Ale (34 IBU)
(Arcadia Brewing Company)

Back Road Brewery Back Road Ale
(Back Road Brewery)

Berkshire Brewing Berkshire Traditional Pale Ale
(Berkshire Brewing Company)

Big Sky Brewing Scape Goat Pale Ale
(Big Sky Brewing Company)

Bitter Root Brewing Pale Ale (10 SRM, 35 IBU)
(Bitter Root Brewing)

Boulder Beer Pass Time Pale Ale (13.8 SRM, 23 IBU)
(Boulder Beer Company)

Brooklyn Pennant Ale (26 IBU)
(Brooklyn Brewery)

Buckeye Brewing Seventy-Six
(Buckeye Brewing)

Buzzards Bay Brewing Pale Ale (47 IBU)
(Buzzards Bay Brewing Company)

Church Brew Works Pipe Organ Pale Ale (30 IBU)
(The Church Brew Works)

Concord Pale Ale (26 IBU)
(Concord Brewery, Inc.)

Cooper's Cave Ale Company Pale Ale (55 IBU)
(Cooper's Cave Ale Company, LTD.)

Cooperstown Brewing Old Slugger Pale Ale
(Cooperstown Brewing Company)

Defiant Brewing Little Thumper Ale
(The Defiant Brewing Company)

Deschutes Cascade Ale (28 IBU)
(Deschutes Brewery)

Diamond Bear Pale Ale (33 IBU)
(Diamond Bear Brewing Company)

Dragonmead Big Larry's Pale Ale
(Dragonmead Microbrewery)

Dragonmead Inquisition Pale Ale
(Dragonmead Microbrewery)

Dragonmead Larry's Lionheart Pale
(Dragonmead Microbrewery)

El Toro Oro Golden Ale
(El Toro Brewing)

English Ales English Pale Ale
(English Ales Brewery)

Flying Dog Doggie Style Pale Ale (19 SRM, 36 IBU) – *page 498*
(Flying Dog Brewery, LLC)

Full Sail Brewing Rip Curl
(Full Sail Brewing Company)

Geary's Pale Ale
(D L Geary Brewing Company)

Great Divide Brewing Denver Pale Ale (40 IBU)
(Great Divide Brewing Company)

Gritty McDuff's Best Bitter (25 IBU)
(Gritty McDuff's Brewing Company, LLC)

Gritty McDuff's Original Pub Style Ale (20 IBU) – *page 507*
(Gritty McDuff's Brewing Company, LLC)

Jack's Whitewater Pale Ale
(Jack Russell Brewing)

Lakefront Organic ESB (12 SRM, 36 IBU)
(Lakefront Brewery, Inc.)

Lang Creek Windsock Pale Ale (27 IBU)
(Lang Creek Brewery)

Lexington Brewing Kentucky Ale
(Alltech's Lexington Brewing Company)

Mercury Brewing Ipswich Original Ale (30 IBU) – *page 519*
(Mercury Brewing Company)

Michelob Pale Ale – *page 459*
(Anheuser-Busch, Inc.)

North Coast ACME California Pale Ale (21 IBU)
(North Coast Brewing Company)

Orlando Brewing Olde Pelican Ale
(Orlando Brewing Partners, Inc. (Kegs/ Growlers))

Pike Brewing Company Pale Ale
(Pike Brewing Company)

Santa Fe Brewing Santa Fe Pale Ale (13 SRM, 48 IBU)
(Santa Fe Brewing Company)

Saranac Pale Ale – *page 562*
(The Matt Brewing)

Sierra Blanca Brewing Pale Ale
(Sierra Blanca Brewing Company)

Snipes Mountain Brewing Sunnyside Pale Ale
(Snipes Mountain Brewing Company)

Sonora Brewing Burning Bird Pale Ale
(Sonoran Brewing Company (Kegs/ Growlers))

Summit Extra Pale Ale (13 SRM, 42 IBU) – *page 555*
(Summit Brewing Company)

Trademark Pale Ale (40 IBU)
(Breckenridge Brewery)

Tremont Brewing Tremont Ale – *page 565*
(Tremont Brewery/Atlantic Coast Brewing Company)

Trout River Brewing Hoppin' Mad Trout
(Trout River Brewing Company)

Uinta Brewing Anglers Pale Ale
(Uinta Brewing Company)

Viking Brewing Honey Pale Ale
(Viking Brewing)

Whitstran Brewing 11th Hour Pale Ale (46 IBU)
(Whitstran Brewing Company)

English/Scottish Strong Ale

Allagash Brewing Musette
(Allagash Brewing Company)

Avery Brewing Old Jubilation (30 IBU)
(Avery Brewing Company)

Barley Creek Atlas Ale
(Barley Creek Brewing Company)

Breckenridge Autumn Ale (21 IBU)
(Breckenridge Brewery)

Breckenridge Christmas Ale (22 IBU)
(Breckenridge Brewery)

Dogfish Head Burton Baton
(Dogfish Head Craft Brewery)

Dragonmead Under The Kilt Wee Heavy (30 IBU)
(Dragonmead Microbrewery)

Founders Brewing Dirty Bastard (50 IBU)
(Founders Brewing Company)

Heavy Seas Brewing Winter Storm "Category 5" Ale
(Clipper City Brewing Company)

Ithaca Beer Company Winterizer
(Ithaca Beer Company, Inc.)

Jack's Scottish Ale
(Jack Russell Brewing)

Lake Placid Craft Brewing Ubu Ale
(Lake Placid Craft Brewing)

Left Hand Brewing Chainsaw Ale (55 IBU)
(Left Hand Brewing Company)

Left Hand Brewing Snowbound Ale (16 IBU)
(Left Hand Brewing Company)

Middle Ages Wailing Wench
(Middle Ages Brewing Company)

Middle Ages Wizard's Winter Ale
(Middle Ages Brewing Company)

New Holland Dragon's Milk
(New Holland Brewing Company)

Nimbus "Old Monkeyshine" English Strong (16 SRM, 35 IBU) – *page 526*
(Nimbus Brewing Company)

Oskar Blues Grill & Brew Old Chub (30 IBU)
(Oskar Blues Grill & Brew)

Pyramid Brewery Snow Cap Ale (47 IBU) – *page 532*
(Pyramid Brewery)

Seven Mules Kick-Ass Ale
(Mishawaka Brewing Company)

Snipes Mountain Brewing Roza Reserve
(Snipes Mountain Brewing Company)

Wachusett Green Monsta
(Wachusett Brewing Company)

Yards Brewing Thomas Jefferson Tavern Ale
(Yards Brewing)

ESB (English Special Bitter)

Alaskan ESB (26 SRM, 35 IBU)
(Alaskan Brewing Company)

Alesmith Brewing Special Bitter
(Alesmith Brewing Company)

Anderson Valley ESB Ale – *page 453*
(Anderson Valley Brewing Company)

Atlantic Brewing Special Old Bitter Ale
(Atlantic Brewing Company)

Avery Brewing 14'er ESB (37 IBU)
(Avery Brewing Company)

Blue Point Brewing ESB (35 IBU)
(Blue Point Brewing)

Blue Ridge ESB Red Ale
(Wild Goose Brewery, LLC)

Boundary Bay Best Bitter
(Boundary Bay Brewing Company)

BridgePort ESB (30 IBU)
(BridgePort Brewing Company (Gambrinus))

Climax Brewing Extra Special Bitter Ale
(Climax Brewing Company)

Cooper's Cave Ale Company Tavern Ale (30 IBU)
(Cooper's Cave Ale Company, LTD.)

Cricket Hill Brewing American Ale
(Cricket Hill Brewing Company)

Crooked River ESB
(Wild Goose Brewery, LLC)

Defiant Brewing Big Thumper Ale
(The Defiant Brewing Company)

Defiant Brewing ESB
(The Defiant Brewing Company)

Deschutes Bachelor ESB (50 IBU)
(Deschutes Brewery)

Dick's Best Bitter
(Dick's Brewing Company)

Dragonmead Breath Of The Dragon English Bitter
(Dragonmead Microbrewery)

Dragonmead Sir William's Extra Special Bitter (43 IBU)
(Dragonmead Microbrewery)

Drake's Amber Ale
(Drake's Brewing Company)

Empyrean Ales LunaSea ESB (10 SRM, 31 IBU) – *page 495*
(Empyrean Brewing)

English Ales Triple B (Borthwick's Best Bitter)
(English Ales Brewery)

English Ales Victory ESB
(English Ales Brewery)

Estes Park Trail Ridge Red
(Estes Park Brewery)

Farmington River Mahogany Ale
(Mercury Brewing Company)

Firestone Walker Double Barrel Ale (16 SRM, 32 IBU)
(Firestone Walker Brewing Company)

Grand Teton Bitch Creek ESB (51 IBU)
(Grand Teton Brewing Company)

Great Divide Brewing HotShot ESB (32 IBU)
(Great Divide Brewing Company)

Great Lakes Brewing Moondog Ale (25 IBU)
(Great Lakes Brewing Company)

Gritty McDuff's Christmas Ale (28.5 IBU)
(Gritty McDuff's Brewing Company, LLC)

Gritty McDuff's Halloween Ale
(Gritty McDuff's Brewing Company, LLC)

Hoptown ESB
(Hoptown Brewery)

Irresistible E.S.B.
(Madison River Brewing Company)

Lake Superior Brewing Special Ale
(Lake Superior Brewing Company)

Lang Creek Tri-Motor Amber (26 IBU) – *page 511*
(Lang Creek Brewery)

Leavenworth Beers Ingall's Extra Special Bitter (40 IBU)
(Fish Brewing Company)

Left Hand Brewing Sawtooth Ale (27 IBU)
(Left Hand Brewing Company)

Mercury Brewing Stone Cat ESB (35 IBU)
(Mercury Brewing Company)

Middle Ages Beast Bitter
(Middle Ages Brewing Company)

Otter Creek Brewing ESB
(Otter Creek Brewing Company)

Redhook Ale Brewery ESB (13.2 SRM, 28 IBU) – *page 533*
(Redhook Ale Brewery)

River Horse Special Ale
(River Horse Brewing Company)

Rock Art Brewery Magnumus ete Tomahawkus (80 IBU) – *page 535*
(Rock Art Brewery, LLC)

Rogue Brutal Bitter (59 IBU)
(Rogue Ales)

Rogue Younger's Special Bitter (35 IBU)
(Rogue Ales)

Sacramento Brewing River Otter Ale
(Sacramento Brewing Company Inc)

Sand Creek Brewing English Style Special Ale (13.4 SRM, 25 IBU)
(Sand Creek Brewing Company, LLC)

Sheepscot Valley Brewing Boothbay Special Bitter
(Sheepscot Valley Brewing Company)

Shipyard Brewing Old Thumper Extra Special Ale
(Shipyard Brewing Company)

Ska Brewing Special ESB (in cans) – *page 549*
(Ska Brewing Company)

Slab City Brewing W.C. Bitter
(Slab City Brewing)

Snipes Mountain Brewing Red Sky Ale
(Snipes Mountain Brewing Company)

Stoudt's Scarlet Lady Ale (32 IBU)
(Stoudt's Brewing Company)

Summit ESB (26 SRM, 50 IBU) – *page 557*
(Summit Brewing Company)

The Wise Extra Special Bitter (39 IBU)
(Elysian Brewing Company)

Weyerbacher Brewing ESB Ale
(Weyerbacher Brewing Company)

Yazoo Brewing Yazoo ESB
(Yazoo Brewing)

Yellowstone Valley Renegade Red ESB
(Yellowstone Valley Brewing)

Grand Cru

Dick's Grand Cru
(Dick's Brewing Company)

Dragonmead Armageddon Grand Cru
(Dragonmead Microbrewery)

Jolly Pumpkin Luciernaga "The Firefly"
(Jolly Pumpkin Artisan Ales)

Southampton Grand Cru
(Southampton Publick House)

Hefeweizen

Atlanta Brewing Red Brick Summer Brew - Hefeweizen
(Atlanta Brewing Company)

August Schell Brewing Hefeweizen (3.4 SRM, 12 IBU)
(August Schell Brewing Company)

Baron Bavarian Weizen
(Baron Brewing)

Baron Hefe-Weisse (SRM 5, IBU 15)
(Baron Brewing)

Bayern Brewing Hefeweizen
(Bayern Brewing)

Bayhawk Ales Hefe Weizen (13 IBU)
(Bayhawk Ales, Inc.)

Beermann's Hefe Weizen
(Beermann's Beerwerks)

Berghoff Hefe-Weizen (14 IBU)
(Joseph Huber Brewing Company, Inc.)

Berkshire Brewing Hefeweizen
(Berkshire Brewing Company)

Big Horn Hefeweizen (7 SRM, 12 IBU)
(Big Horn Brewing (CB Potts))

Blue Point Brewing Hefeweizen (15 IBU)
(Blue Point Brewing)

Boulder Beer Sweaty Betty Blonde Wheat Beer (4 SRM, 12 IBU)
(Boulder Beer Company)

Breckenridge Hefe Proper (9 IBU)
(Breckenridge Brewery)

Brooklyn Weisse (13 IBU)
(Brooklyn Brewery)

Buckeye Brewing Wheat Cloud
(Buckeye Brewing)

Buzzards Bay Brewing Hefe-Weizen (40 IBU)
(Buzzards Bay Brewing Company)

Central Waters White Water Weizen
(Central Waters Brewing Company)

Charleston Brewing Half Moon Hefeweizen
(Charleston Brewing Company)

Christian Moerlein Hefeweisen
(Christian Moerlein Brewing Company)

Dragonmead Nagelweiss Wheat
(Dragonmead Microbrewery)

Drake's Hefe-Weizen
(Drake's Brewing Company)

Erie Brewing German Wheat (16 IBU)
(Erie Brewing)

Firestone Walker Walker's Reserve (75 SRM, 45 IBU)
(Firestone Walker Brewing Company)

Flying Dog In Heat Wheat (5 SRM, 13 IBU)
(Flying Dog Brewery, LLC)

Four Peaks Hefeweizen
(Four Peaks Brewing Company)

Frankenmuth Hefeweizen
(Frankenmuth Brewery)

Frankenmuth Old Detroit Amber Ale
(Frankenmuth Brewery)

Beer Styles Index

Glacier Brewing Select Dunkel Hefeweizen (13.4 SRM, 14.3 IBU)
(Glacier Brewing)

Gordon Biersch Hefeweizen (12 IBU)
(Gordon Biersch Brewery)

Great Northern Brewing Wheatfish Hefeweizen (12 IBU)
(Great Northern Brewing Company)

Great Northern Brewing Wheatfish Hefeweizen (12 IBU)
(Great Northern Brewing Company)

Harpoon UFO Hefeweizen (19 IBU)
(Harpoon Brewery)

Hefeweizen (14 IBU) – *page 515*
(The Long Trail Brewing Company)

Heiner Brau Hefe Weisse
(Heiner Brau)

Heinzelmannchen Weise Gnome Hefeweizen Style Ale
(Heinzelmannchen Brewery (Kegs/ Growlers))

Henry Weinhard's Hefeweizen
(SAB Miller Corporation)

Hood Canal Brewing Dosewallipps Special Ale
(Hood Canal Brewing)

Island Brewing Weiss (15 IBU)
(Island Brewing Company)

Keweenaw Brewing Empress Hefeweizen
(Keweenaw Brewing Company)

King Hefeweizen
(King Brewing Company)

Kodiak Island Cloud Peak Hefeweizen
(Kodiak Island Brewing Company (Kegs/ Growlers))

Lake Superior Brewing Windward Wheat
(Lake Superior Brewing Company)

Lang Creek Huckleberry N' Honey (8 IBU)
(Lang Creek Brewery)

Leavenworth Beers Whistling Pig Wheat Ale (22 IBU)
(Fish Brewing Company)

Left Coast Hefeweizen
(Left Coast Brewing)

Lewis & Clark Miner's Gold Hefe-Weizen
(Lewis & Clark Brewing)

Magic Hat Brewing Circus Boy (5 SRM, 18 IBU)
(Magic Hat Brewing Company)

Michelob Bavarian-Style Wheat
(Anheuser-Busch, Inc.)

Mudshark Brewery Dry Heat Hefeweizen (3.6 SRM, 18 IBU)
(Mudshark Brewing Company)

New Glarus Brewing Copper Kettle Weiss
(New Glarus Brewing)

New Glarus Brewing Spotted Cow
(New Glarus Brewing)

Oak Creek Hefeweizen
(Oak Creek Brewing Company)

Oxford Hefeweizen
(Clipper City Brewing Company)

Paper City Brewing Cabot Street Summer Wheat
(Paper City Brewery Company)

Pyramid Brewery Hefe Weizen (18 IBU) – *page 529*
(Pyramid Brewery)

R.J. Rockers Buckwheat (4 SRM, 18 IBU)
(R.J. Rockers Brewing Company)

Ramstein Blonde Wheat (8 SRM, 12.5 IBU)
(High Point Wheat Beer Company)

Red Lodge Ales Hefeweizen
(Red Lodge Ales Brewing Company)

Ruby Mountain Brewing Wild West Hefeweizen
(Ruby Mountain Brewing Company)

Sacramento Brewing Hefeweizen
(Sacramento Brewing Company Inc)

Samuel Adams Hefeweizen (7 SRM, 14 IBU)
(The Boston Beer Company)

Santa Cruz Mountain Brewing Wilder Wheat
(Santa Cruz Mountain Brewing)

Sebago Brewing Hefe-Weizen (4.6 SRM, 19.8 IBU)
(Sebago Brewing Company)

Shiner Hefeweizen
(The Spoetzl Brewing (Gambrinus))

Snipes Mountain Brewing Hefeweizen
(Snipes Mountain Brewing Company)

Snowshoe Brewing Snoweizen Wheat Ale
(Snowshoe Brewing Company)

Sonora Brewing Mandarin Orange Hefeweizen
(Sonoran Brewing Company (Kegs/ Growlers))

Sprecher Brewing Hefe' Weiss (11 IBU)
(Sprecher Brewing)

Squatters Hefeweizen
(Utah Brewers Cooperative/ Wasatch)

Sudwerk Hefe-Weizen
(Sudwerk)

Tröegs Brewing Dreamweaver Wheat (15 IBU)
(Tröegs Brewing Company)

Two Brothers Ebel's Weiss Beer (15 IBU)
(Two Brothers Brewing Company)

Tyranena Brewing Company Fargo Brothers Hefeweizen (8 SRM, 12 IBU)
(Tyranena Brewing Company)

Uinta Brewing Golden Spike Hefeweizen
(Uinta Brewing Company)

Warbird Brewing P47 Warbird Wheat (6 SRM, 18 IBU)
(Warbird Brewing Company)

Wasatch Apricot Hefe-Weizen
(Utah Brewers Cooperative/ Wasatch)

Whitstran Brewing Horse Heaven Hefe Bavarian Style
Hefeweizen (14 IBU)
(Whitstran Brewing Company)

Widmer Brothers Brewing Company Widmer Hefeweizen (7 SRM, 32 IBU)
 – *page 571*
(Widmer Brothers Brewing Company)

Yazoo Brewing Hefeweizen
(Yazoo Brewing)

Imperial Stout

Arcadia Brewing Ales Imperial Stout (59 IBU)
(Arcadia Brewing Company)

Avery Brewing The Czar Russian Imperial Stout (60 IBU)
(Avery Brewing Company)

Bear Republic Brewing Big Bear Stout Ale (68 IBU)
(Bear Republic Brewing Company)

Berkshire Brewing Imperial Stout
(Berkshire Brewing Company)

Black Cauldron Imperial Stout
(Grand Teton Brewing Company)

Blue Point Brewing Cherry Imperial Stout (67 IBU)
(Blue Point Brewing)

Central Waters Reserve Bourbon Barrel Stout
(Central Waters Brewing Company)

Central Waters Satin Solstice Imperial Stout
(Central Waters Brewing Company)

Dark Horse 750 ml Imperial Stout
(Dark Horse Brewing Company)

Deschutes The Abyss
(Deschutes Brewery)

Dick's Imperial Stout
(Dick's Brewing Company)

Dogfish Head World Wide Stout (80 IBU)
(Dogfish Head Craft Brewery)

Dragonmead Imperial Stout
(Dragonmead Microbrewery)

Duck-Rabbit Russian Imperial Stout (in NC only)
(Duck-Rabbit Craft Brewery)

Fish Tale Poseidon's Imperial Stout
(Fish Brewing Company)

Founders Brewing Imperial Stout (25 IBU)
(Founders Brewing Company)

Golden Valley Black Panther Imperial Stout (48 IBU)
(Golden Valley Brewery)

Great Divide Brewing Oak Aged Yeti Imperial Stout (75 IBU)
(Great Divide Brewing Company)

Great Divide Brewing Yeti Imperial Stout (75 IBU)
(Great Divide Brewing Company)

Heavy Seas Brewing Peg Leg Stout
(Clipper City Brewing Company)

Hoptown Old Yeltsin
(Hoptown Brewery)

Jack's Raspberry Imperial Stout
(Jack Russell Brewing)

Lagunitas Brewing Imperial Stout
(Lagunitas Brewing)

Left Hand Brewing Imperial Stout (65 IBU)
(Left Hand Brewing Company)

Middle Ages Dragonslayer Imperial Stout
(Middle Ages Brewing Company)

Moylan's Ryan O'Sullivan's Imperial Stout
(Moylan's Brewing Company)

Nashoba Valley Brewery Imperial Stout
(Nashoba Valley Brewery)

North Coast Old Rasputin Russian Imperial Stout (75 IBU)
(North Coast Brewing Company)

Rogue Imperial Stout (88 IBU)
(Rogue Ales)

Santa's Little Helper Imperial Stout
(Port Brewing Company)

Smuttynose Brewing Imerial Stout
(Smuttynose Brewing Company)

Southern Tier Brewing Black Water Series Imperial Stout
(Southern Tier Brewing Company)

Sprecher Brewing Imperial Stout (32 IBU)
(Sprecher Brewing)

Stone Imperial Russian Stout (90 IBU)
(Stone Brewing Company)

Stoudt's Fat Dog Stout (55 IBU)
(Stoudt's Brewing Company)

Thirsty Dog Siberian Night (58 IBU)
(Thirsty Dog Brewing Company)

Two Brothers Northwind Imperial Stout Winter)
(Two Brothers Brewing Company)

Victory Storm King (70+ IBU)
(Victory Brewing Company)

Viking Brewing Big Swede
(Viking Brewing)

Weyerbacher Brewing Heresy Imperial Stout
(Weyerbacher Brewing Company)

Weyerbacher Brewing Old Heathen
(Weyerbacher Brewing Company)

Weyerbacher Brewing Raspberry Imperial Stout
(Weyerbacher Brewing Company)

Whitstran Brewing Friar's Decadence Chocolate Chocolate
Imperial Stout (55 IBU)
(Whitstran Brewing Company)

India Pale Ale (AM or Eng)

21st Amendment Brewery IPA (75 IBU)
(21st Amendment)

471 IPA (70 IBU)
(Breckenridge Brewery)

Alesmith Brewing IPA
(Alesmith Brewing Company)

Alesmith Brewing X -Extra Pale Ale
(Alesmith Brewing Company)

Alpine Ale (38 IBU)
(Alpine Beer Company)

Alpine Beer Pure Hoppiness – *page 449*
(Alpine Beer Company)

Anderson Valley Hop Ottin' IPA (82 IBU) – *page 452*
(Anderson Valley Brewing Company)

Angel City IPA (5.5 SRM, 45 IBU)
(Angel City Brewing)

Appalachian Brewing Hoppy Trail IPA
(Appalachian Brewing Company)

Arcadia Brewing Ales HopMouth (76 IBU)
(Arcadia Brewing Company)

Arcadia Brewing Ales India Pale Ale (41 IBU) – *page 462*
(Arcadia Brewing Company)

Atwater Salvation IPA
(Atwater Block Brewery)

Avatar Jasmine IPA
(Elysian Brewing Company)

Avery Brewing IPA (69 IBU) – *page 464*
(Avery Brewing Company)

Avery Brewing The Maharaja Imperial IPA (102 IBU)
(Avery Brewing Company)

Back Road Brewery Midwest IPA
(Back Road Brewery)

Backcountry Brewery Telemark IPA (10.8 SRM, 60 IBU)
(Backcountry Brewery)

Ballast Point Big Eye IPA
(Ballast Point Brewing Company)

Barley Creek Rescue India Pale Ale
(Barley Creek Brewing Company)

Barley Island Brewing Bar Fly India Pale Ale (7.8 SRM, 60 IBU)
(Barley Island Brewing Company)

Bayhawk Ales IPA (64 IBU)
(Bayhawk Ales, Inc.)

Bear Republic Brewing Racer 5 (69 IBU)
(Bear Republic Brewing Company)

Beermann's India Pale Ale
(Beermann's Beerwerks)

Berkshire Brewing Lost Sailor India Pale Ale
(Berkshire Brewing Company)

Big Red AIPA (15 SRM, 60 IBU)
(Big Horn Brewing (CB Potts))

Big Sky Brewing IPA
(Big Sky Brewing Company)

Bison Brewing Organic IPA (12 SRM, 59 IBU)
(Bison Brewing)

Bitter Root Brewing India Pale Ale (7.5 SRM, 50 IBU)
(Bitter Root Brewing)

BluCreek Zen IPA (7.2 SRM, 41.5 IBU) – *page 470*
(BluCreek Brewing)

Blue Point Brewing Hoptical Illusion (60 IBU)
(Blue Point Brewing)

Bottleworks India Pale Ale
(Dick's Brewing Company)

Boulder Beer Mojo India Pale Ale (12 SRM, 63 IBU)
(Boulder Beer Company)

Boulder Beer Mojo Risin' Double IPA (12 SRM, 80 IBU)
(Boulder Beer Company)

Boundary Bay Inside Passage Ale
(Boundary Bay Brewing Company)

BridgePort IPA (60 IBU)
(BridgePort Brewing Company (Gambrinus))

Brooklyn East India Pale Ale (40 IBU)
(Brooklyn Brewery)

Buckeye Brewing Hippie IPA
(Buckeye Brewing)

Butte Creek Organic India Pale Ale
(Butte Creek Brewing)

Cape Ann Brewing Fisherman's IPA (64 IBU)
(Cape Ann Brewing)

Captain Boomer's IPA
(Jack Russell Brewing)

Carolina Beer Cottonwood Endo IPA
(Carolina Beer & Beverage Company)

Carolina Brewing IPA
(Carolina Brewing)

Cascade Lakes IPA (65 IBU)
(Cascade Lakes Brewing Company)

Catawba Valley Firewater IPA
(Catawba Valley Brewing)

BEER STYLES INDEX

Central Waters Lac Du Bay IPA
(Central Waters Brewing Company)

Charleston Brewing East Bay IPA
(Charleston Brewing Company)

Climax Brewing India Pale Ale
(Climax Brewing Company)

Concord IPA (38 IBU)
(Concord Brewery, Inc.)

Cooperstown Brewing Back Yard India Pale Ale
(Cooperstown Brewing Company)

Cricket Hill Brewing Hopnotic IPA
(Cricket Hill Brewing Company)

Dark Horse Crooked Tree IPA
(Dark Horse Brewing Company)

Dark Horse Double Crooked Tree IPA
(Dark Horse Brewing Company)

Deschutes Hop Hennch India Pale Ale (85 IBU)
(Deschutes Brewery)

Deschutes Inversion IPA (75 IBU)
(Deschutes Brewery)

Deschutes Quail Springs IPA
(Deschutes Brewery)

Diamond Bear Presidential IPA (57 IBU)
(Diamond Bear Brewing Company)

Dick's India Pale Ale
(Dick's Brewing Company)

Dogfish Head 120 Minute Imperial IPA (120 IBU)
(Dogfish Head Craft Brewery)

Dogfish Head 60 Minute IPA (60 IBU) – *page 492*
(Dogfish Head Craft Brewery)

Dogfish Head 90 Minute Imperial IPA (90 IBU)
(Dogfish Head Craft Brewery)

Dominion Ale
(Old Dominion Brewing Company)

Dominion Pale Ale
(Old Dominion Brewing Company)

Dragonmead Broken Paddle India Pale Ale
(Dragonmead Microbrewery)

Dragonmead Crown Jewels IPA (57 IBU)
(Dragonmead Microbrewery)

Dragonmead Inquisition Pale Ale
(Dragonmead Microbrewery)

Drake's IPA
(Drake's Brewing Company)

Durango Brewing Ian's Pale Ale (57 IBU)
(Durango Brewing Company)

E.J. Phair India Pale Ale
(E.J. Phair Brewing)

Eel River Brewing Organic India Pal Ale
(Eel River Brewing Company)

Eel River Brewing Ravensbrau India Pale Ale
(Eel River Brewing Company)

El Toro Deuce Imperial IPA
(El Toro Brewing)

El Toro IPA
(El Toro Brewing)

English Ales Dragon Slayer India Pale Ale
(English Ales Brewery)

Estes Park Renegade
(Estes Park Brewery)

Farmhouse Oasthouse IPA
(Farmhouse Brewing Company)

Fish Tale Organic India Pale Ale – *page 496*
(Fish Brewing Company)

Fish Tale Winterfish Ale (70 IBU)
(Fish Brewing Company)

Flying Dog Snake Dog IPA (11 SRM, 60 IBU)
(Flying Dog Brewery, LLC)

Flying Fish Brewing Hopfish (21.2 SRM, 18.8 IBU)
(Flying Fish Brewing)

Founders Brewing Centennial IPA (46 IBU)
(Founders Brewing Company)

147

Founders Brewing Devil Dancer Triple IPA (24 IBU)
(Founders Brewing Company)

Full Sail Brewing IPA
(Full Sail Brewing Company)

Golden City IPA
(Golden City Brewery)

Golden Valley Chehalem Moutain IPA (55 IBU)
(Golden Valley Brewery)

Goose Island India Pale Ale (10 SRM, 58 IBU)
(Goose Island Beer Company)

Grand Teton Double IPA
(Grand Teton Brewing Company)

Grand Teton Sweetgrass IPA (58 IBU)
(Grand Teton Brewing Company)

Great Divide Brewing Hercules Double IPA (85 IBU)
(Great Divide Brewing Company)

Great Divide Brewing Titan IPA (65 IBU)
(Great Divide Brewing Company)

Great Lakes Brewing Commodore Perry India Pale Ale (80 IBU)
(Great Lakes Brewing Company)

Green Flash Extra Pale Ale
(Green Flash Brewing)

Green Flash Imperial IPA
(Green Flash Brewing)

Green Flash West Coast IPA
(Green Flash Brewing)

Hale's Mongoose IPA
(Hale's Ales)

Harbor City Brewing Full Tilt IPA
(Harbor City Brewing, Inc.)

Harpoon IPA (42 IBU) – *page 508*
(Harpoon Brewery)

Healthy Brew 1-Day IPA
(Healthy Brew)

Loose Cannon Hop3 Ale – *page 486*
(Clipper City Brewing Company, LP)

High Tide Fresh Hop IPA
(Port Brewing Company)

Highland Brewing Kashmir IPA (60 IBU)
(Highland Brewing)

Hood Canal Brewing Dabob Bay India Pale Ale
(Hood Canal Brewing)

Hop Head Ale
(Mishawaka Brewing Company)

Hopknot IPA
(Four Peaks Brewing Company)

Hop-ocalypse India Pale Ale (50 IBU)
(Clay Pipe Brewing Company)

Hoppy Face Amber Ale
(Hoppy Brewing Company)

Hoptown DUIPA Imperial Ale
(Hoptown Brewery)

Hoptown IPA
(Hoptown Brewery)

Immortal India Pale Ale (42 IBU)
(Elysian Brewing Company)

Imperial IPA (12 SRM, 90 IBU)
(Goose Island Beer Company)

India Pelican Ale (85 IBU)
(Pelican Pub & Brewery)

INDIAna Pale Ale
(Mishawaka Brewing Company)

Infidel Imperial India Pale Ale
(Nine G Brewing Company, Inc.)

Iron Horse India Pale Ale
(Iron Horse Brewery)

Island Brewing Island Pale Ale (60 IBU)
(Island Brewing Company)

Ithaca Beer Company Double IPA
(Ithaca Beer Company, Inc.)

Beer Styles Index

Ithaca Beer Company Flower Power India Pale Ale
(Ithaca Beer Company, Inc.)

Karl Strauss Brewing Stargazer IPA (14 SRM, 40 IBU)
(Karl Strauss Breweries)

Kelley Brothers Four Towers IPA
(Kelley Brothers Brewing Company)

King IPA
(King Brewing Company)

Lagunitas Brewing India Pale Ale
(Lagunitas Brewing)

Lake Placid Craft Brewing 46'er India Pale Ale
(Lake Placid Craft Brewing)

Lake Superior Brewing St. Louis Bay IPA
(Lake Superior Brewing Company)

Lancaster Brewing Hop Hog IPA (55 IBU)
(Lancaster Brewing Company)

Landmark India Pale Ale
(Landmark Beer Company)

Leavenworth Beers Hodgson's India Pale Ale (70 IBU)
(Fish Brewing Company)

Left Coast India Pale Ale
(Left Coast Brewing)

Left Hand Brewing Warrior IPA (60 IBU)
(Left Hand Brewing Company)

Legend Brewing Golden IPA (35 IBU)
(Legend Brewing Company)

Lewis & Clark Tumbleweed IPA
(Lewis & Clark Brewing)

Lost Coast Indica IPA (62 IBU)
(Lost Coast Brewery & Café)

Mad River Jamaica Sunset West Indies Pale Ale (65 IBU)
(Mad River Brewing)

Magic Hat Brewing Blind Faith (12.5 SRM, 40 IBU)
(Magic Hat Brewing Company

Magic Hat Brewing H.I.P.A. (6.8 SRM, 45 IBU)
(Magic Hat Brewing Company)

Mammoth Brewing Company India Pale Ale
(Mammoth Brewing Company)

Marin Brewing India Pale Ale
(Marin Brewing Company)

Marin Brewing White Knuckle Ale
(Marin Brewing Company)

Maritime Pacific Imperial Pale
(Maritime Pacific Brewing Company)

Mendocino Brewing White Hawk Select IPA
(Mendocino Brewing Company)

Mercury Brewing Ipswich IPA (60 IBU)
(Mercury Brewing Company)

Mercury Brewing Stone Cat IPA (55 IBU)
(Mercury Brewing Company)

Michigan Brewing High Seas IPA
(Michigan Brewing Company, Inc.)

Middle Ages Impaled Ale
(Middle Ages Brewing Company)

Midnight Sun Sockeye Red IPA (70 IBU) – *page 520*
(Midnight Sun Brewing Company)

Millstream Brewing Warsh Pail Ale
(Millstream Brewing Company)

Mount Hood Brewing Ice Axe IPA
(Mount Hood Brewing Company)

Mount Hood Brewing Imperial Ice Axxe
(Mount Hood Brewing Company)

Mountain High IPA
(Mt.Shasta Brewing Company)

Moylan's India Pale Ale
(Moylan's Brewing Company)

Nashoba Valley Brewery IPA (50 IBU)
(Nashoba Valley Brewery)

Nectar Ales IPA Nectar
(Nectar Ales)

New England Brewing Sea Hag IPA
(New England Brewing Company)

New Glarus Brewing Hop Hearty Ale
(New Glarus Brewing)

New Holland Mad Hatter
(New Holland Brewing Company)

New Knoxville Brewing India Pale Ale
(New Knoxville Brewing Company)

New River Pale Ale
(Old Dominion Brewing Company)

New South India Pale Ale
(New South Brewing Company (Kegs/ Growlers))

Newport Storm Maelstrom IPA (13 SRM, 48 IBU)
(Coastal Extreme Brewing Company, LLC)

North Coast ACME IPA (52 IBU)
(North Coast Brewing Company)

Oak Pond Brewing White Fox Ale
(Oak Pond Brewery)

O'Fallon 5-Day IPA (in MO only)
(O'Fallon Brewery)

Oregon Trail IPA
(Oregon Trail Brewery)

Oskar Blues Grill & Brew Gordon (35 IBU)
(Oskar Blues Grill & Brew)

Otter Creek Brewing Anniversary IPA
(Otter Creek Brewing Company)

Paper City Brewing Blonde Hop Monster
(Paper City Brewery Company)

Paper City Brewing India's Pale Ale
(Paper City Brewery Company)

Pike Brewing Company India Pale Ale
(Pike Brewing Company)

Port Townsend Dry-Hopped IPA
(Port Townsend Brewing Company)

Pyramid Brewery ThunderHead IPA (67 IBU) – *page 531*
(Pyramid Brewery)

Ramapo Valley Brewery India Pale Ale
(Ramapo Valley Brewery)

Ranger IPA
(Far West Brewing Company)

ReaperAle Sleighor Double IPA (105 IBU)
(ReaperAle, Inc.)

Redhook Ale Brewery IPA (8.4 SRM, 38.5 IBU)
(Redhook Ale Brewery)

Rio Grande Brewing IPA (76 IBU)
(Rio Grande Brewing Company)

Rock Art Brewery India Pale Ale (22 IBU)
(Rock Art Brewery, LLC)

Rocky Bay Brewing Whitecap Ale
(Rocky Bay Brewing Company)

Rogue I2PA Imperial India Pale Ale (74 IBU)
(Rogue Ales)

Rush River Brewing BubbleJack IPA
(Rush River Brewing (Kegs))

Sacramento Brewing India Pale Ale
(Sacramento Brewing Company Inc)

Saint Arnold Brewing Double IPA
(Saint Arnold Brewing Company)

Saint Arnold Brewing Elissa IPA (60 IBU)
(Saint Arnold Brewing Company)

Sand Creek Brewing Wild Ride IPA (8.2 SRM, 64 IBU)
(Sand Creek Brewing Company, LLC)

Santa Cruz Mountain Brewing India Pale Ale
(Santa Cruz Mountain Brewing)

Saranac India Pale Ale
(The Matt Brewing)

Scuttlebutt Gale Force IPA (96 IBU)
(Scuttlebutt Brewing Company)

Sea Dog Old East India Pale Ale
(The Sea Dog Brewing Company)

Seabright Brewery Blur IPA
(Seabright Brewery)

Beer Styles Index

Sebago Brewing Frye's Leap India Pale Ale (11.5 SRM, 54.4 IBU) – *page 543*
(Sebago Brewing Company)

Shipyard Brewing IPA
(Shipyard Brewing Company)

Shmaltz Brewing Bittersweet Lenny's R.I.P.A.
(Shmaltz Brewing Company)

Sierra Nevada Celebration Ale 21 SRM, 70 IBU)
(Sierra Nevada Brewing Company)

Siletz Brewing Company Paddle Me IPA (12 SRM, 76.8 IBU)
(Siletz Brewing Company, Inc.)

Ska Brewing Decadent Imperial IPA – *page 546*
(Ska Brewing Company)

Skagit River Brewing Sculler's IPA
(Skagit River Brewery)

Skagit Sculler's IPA
(LaConner Brewing Company)

Sly Fox Odyssey (90 IBU)
(Sly Fox Brewing Company)

Sly Fox Route 113 India Pale Ale (113 IBU)
(Sly Fox Brewing Company)

Smuttynose Brewing Big A IPA
(Smuttynose Brewing Company)

Smuttynose Brewing Imperial IPA
(Smuttynose Brewing Company)

Smuttynose Brewing IPA (65 IBU)
(Smuttynose Brewing Company)

Snapperhead IPA (40 IBU)
(Butternuts Beer & Ale)

Snipes Mountain Brewing Harvest Ale
(Snipes Mountain Brewing Company)

Snipes Mountain Brewing India Pale Ale
(Snipes Mountain Brewing Company)

Snowshoe Brewing Thompson Pale Ale
(Snowshoe Brewing Company)

Sonora Brewing India Pale Ale
(Sonoran Brewing Company (Kegs/ Growlers))

Southampton IPA
(Southampton Publick House)

Southern Tier Brewing Imperial IPA – *page 552*
(Southern Tier Brewing Company)

Speakeasy Big Daddy IPA
(Speakeasy Ales & Lagers, Inc.)

Speakeasy Double Daddy Imperial IPA
(Speakeasy Ales & Lagers, Inc.)

Sprecher Brewing India Pale Ale (88 IBU)
(Sprecher Brewing)

Squatters India Pale Ale
(Utah Brewers Cooperative/ Wasatch)

St. George Brewing Company IPA (9 SRM, 50 IBU) – *page 553*
(St.George Brewing Company)

Stone Coast 420 India Pale Ale
(Stone Coast Brewing Company)

Stone IPA (77 IBU)
(Stone Brewing Company)

Stone Ruination IPA (100+ IBU) – *page 554*
(Stone Brewing Company)

Stoudt's Double India Pale Ale (90 IBU)
(Stoudt's Brewing Company)

Summit India Pale Ale (25 SRM, 60 IBU) – *page 556*
(Summit Brewing Company)

Sweetwater Brewing IPA
(Sweetwater Brewing)

Terrapin Rye Squared (80 IBU)
(Terrapin Beer Company)

The Palisade Brewery Red Truck IPA
(The Palisade Brewery)

The Raj India Pal Ale
(Four Peaks Brewing Company)

Thirsty Dog Hoppus Maximus (43 IBU)
(Thirsty Dog Brewing Company)

Thomas Creek IPA (45.8 IBU)
(Thomas Creek Brewery)

Thomas Hooker Hop Meadow IPA (10.5 SRM, 73 IBU)
(Thomas Hooker Brewing Company)

Three Floyds Brewing Dreadnaught IPA (100 IBU)
(Three Floyds Brewing Company)

Traditional IPA (56 IBU) – *page 516*
(The Long Trail Brewing Company)

Traverse Brewing Batch 500 IPA
(Traverse Brewing Company)

Tremont Brewing Tremont IPA
(Tremont Brewery/Atlantic Coast Brewing Company)

Tuppers' Hop Pocket Ale
(Old Dominion Brewing Company)

Twisted Pine Hoppy Boy
(Twisted Pine Brewing Company)

Two Brothers Heavy Handed India Pale Ale (September-December)
(Two Brothers Brewing Company)

Two Brothers Hop Juice Double India Pale Ale (100.1 IBU)
  (Limited Release)
(Two Brothers Brewing Company)

Tyranena Brewing Company Bitter Women IPA (9 SRM, 68 IBU)
(Tyranena Brewing Company)

Tyranena Brewing Company Brewers Gone Wild! Bitter
(Tyranena Brewing Company)

Women From Hell Extra IPA
(Tyranena Brewing Company)

Tyranena Brewing Company Brewers Gone Wild! Hop Whore Imperial IPA
(Tyranena Brewing Company)

Uinta Brewing Trader IPA
(Uinta Brewing Company)

Upland Brewing Company Dragonfly India Pale Ale (40 IBU)
(Upland Brewing Company)

Victory HopDevil Ale (50-60 IBU) – *page 569*
(Victory Brewing Company)

Viking Brewing Queen Victoria's Secret
(Viking Brewing)

Wachusett IPA
(Wachusett Brewing Company)

Wagner Valley Brewing Indian Pale Ale
(Wagner Valley Brewing Company)

Waimea Brewing Captain Cook's Original IPA (55 IBU)
(Waimea Brewing Company)

Weyerbacher Brewing Double Simcoe
(Weyerbacher Brewing Company)

Weyerbacher Brewing Eleven
(Weyerbacher Brewing Company)

Weyerbacher Brewing Hops Infusion India Pale Ale
(Weyerbacher Brewing Company)

Widmer Brothers Brewing Company Broken Halo IPA (10 SRM, 52 IBU)
(Widmer Brothers Brewing Company)

Wildcat IPA (75 IBU)
(Snoqualmie Falls Brewing Company)

Williamsburg AleWerks Drake Tail India Pale Ale
(Williamsburg AleWerks)

Wipeout IPA
(Port Brewing Company)

Wolaver's Organic India Pale Ale (55 IBU) – *page 573*
(Otter Creek Brewing Company)

Woodstock India Pale Ale (11 SRM, 77.6 IBU)
(Woodstock Beer)

Yards Brewing India Pale Ale
(Yards Brewing)

Irish Ale

Alpine Beer Mchenney's Irish Red (10.7 IBU)
(Alpine Beer Company)

Bitter Root Brewing Amber
(Bitter Root Brewing)

Boulevard Brewing Irish Ale (28 IBU)
(Boulevard Brewing Company)

Central Waters Reserve Irish Red Ale
(Central Waters Brewing Company)

Cooper's Cave Ale Company Radeau Red Ale (35 IBU) – *page 487*
(Cooper's Cave Ale Company, LTD.)

Crooked River Irish Red Ale
(Wild Goose Brewery, LLC)

Diamond Bear Irish Red Ale (31 IBU)
(Diamond Bear Brewing Company)

Dick's Irish Ale
(Dick's Brewing Company)

Dragonmead Erik the Red Irish Style Amber Ale (20.5 IBU)
(Dragonmead Microbrewery)

Dunedin Brewery Drop Kick Monday's Erin Red Ale
(Dunedin Brewery)

Golden Valley Red Thistle Ale (40 IBU)
(Golden Valley Brewery)

Great Lakes Brewing Conway's Irish Ale (25 IBU)
(Great Lakes Brewing Company)

Jack's Irish Red Ale
(Jack Russell Brewing)

King Irish Red Ale
(King Brewing Company)

McSorley's Irish Ale
(Pabst Brewing Company)

Moylan's Paddy's Irish Style Red Ale
(Moylan's Brewing Company)

Newport Storm Thunderhead Irish Red (32 SRM, 31IBU)
(Coastal Extreme Brewing Company, LLC)

Rocky Bay Brewing Katie's Celtic Red Ale
(Rocky Bay Brewing Company)

The Palisade Brewery Farmer's Friend
(The Palisade Brewery)

Thomas Hooker Irish Red (17.7 SRM, 22 IBU)
(Thomas Hooker Brewing Company)

Three Floyds Brewing Brian Boru
(Three Floyds Brewing Company)

Irish Dry Stout

Appalachian Brewing Susquehanna Stout
(Appalachian Brewing Company)

Back Road Brewery Belle Gunness Stout
(Back Road Brewery)

Boulevard Brewing Dry Stout (28 IBU)
(Boulevard Brewing Company)

Central Waters Reserve Irish Dry Stout
(Central Waters Brewing Company)

Cooper's Cave Ale Company Sagamore Stout (30 IBU)
(Cooper's Cave Ale Company, LTD.)

Dragonmead Earl's Spit Stout
(Dragonmead Microbrewery)

Elmwood Brewing Dry Stout
(Elmwood Brewing Company)

English Ales Black Hound Stout
(English Ales Brewery)

Founders Classic Dry Stout
(Mishawaka Brewing Company)

Frankenmuth Irish Dry Stout
(Frankenmuth Brewery)

Keweenaw Brewing R.A.M. Stout
(Keweenaw Brewing Company)

Lakefront Snake Chaser Stout (55 SRM, 26 IBU)
(Lakefront Brewery, Inc.)

Maine Coast Brewing Black Irish Style Stout
(Maine Coast Brewing)

Paper City Brewing Riley's Stout
(Paper City Brewery Company)

Rio Grande Brewing Stout (42 IBU)
(Rio Grande Brewing Company)

Russian River Brewing Sanctification (27 IBU)
(Russian River Brewing Company)

Shipyard Brewing Bluefin Stout
(Shipyard Brewing Company)

Starr Hill Dark Starr Stout
(Starr Hill Brewery)

Yazoo Brewing Onward Stout
(Yazoo Brewing)

Kölsch

Alaskan Summer Ale (8 SRM, 18 IBU)
(Alaskan Brewing Company)

August Schell Brewing Zommerfest (4 SRM, 25 IBU)
(August Schell Brewing Company)

Ballast Point Yellowtail Pale Ale (22-28 IBU) – *page 465*
(Ballast Point Brewing Company)

Berkshire Brewing Gold Spike Ale
(Berkshire Brewing Company)

Big Sky Brewing Crystal Ale – *page 468*
(Big Sky Brewing Company)

Colorado Kölsch (3.9 SRM, 18.8 IBU)
(Steamworks Brewing Company)

Crooked River Kölsch Ale
(Wild Goose Brewery, LLC)

Dragonmead Kaiser's Kölsch
(Dragonmead Microbrewery)

Drake's Blonde Ale
(Drake's Brewing Company)

Farmhouse Kölsch Bier
(Farmhouse Brewing Company)

Four Peaks Kölsch
(Four Peaks Brewing Company)

Glacier Brewing Golden Grizzly Ale (5.8 SRM, 14.6 IBU)
(Glacier Brewing)

Great Beer Hollywood Blonde
(Great Beer Company)

Harpoon Summer (28 IBU)
(Harpoon Brewery)

Heiner Brau Kölsch
(Heiner Brau)

High & Mighty Brewing Beer of the Gods
(High & Mighty Brewing Company)

Ice Harbor Brewing Columbia Kölsch
(Ice Harbor Brewing Company)

Island Brewing Blonde (25 IBU)
(Island Brewing Company)

Lake Superior Brewing Kayak Kölsch
(Lake Superior Brewing Company)

Lexington Brewing Kentucky Light
(Alltech's Lexington Brewing Company)

Mammoth Brewing Company Gold
(Mammoth Brewing Company)

Mishawaka Kölsch
(Mishawaka Brewing Company)

Pyramid Brewery Curve Ball Kölsch (18 IBU) – *page 531*
(Pyramid Brewery)

R.J. Rockers Liberty Light (4 SRM, 25 IBU)
(R.J. Rockers Brewing Company)

Saint Arnold Brewing Fancy Lawnmower Beer (20 IBU)
(Saint Arnold Brewing Company)

Sand Creek Brewing Groovy Brew (6 SRM, 6.5 IBU)
(Sand Creek Brewing Company, LLC)

Shiner Kölsch
(The Spoetzl Brewing (Gambrinus))

Twisted Pine Blond Ale
(Twisted Pine Brewing Company)

Uinta Brewing Summer Solstice Kölsch – *page 568*
(Uinta Brewing Company)

Weeping Radish Kölsch (5 SRM, 23.8 IBU)
(The Weeping Radish Brewery)

Lambic

New Glarus Brewing Belgian Red
(New Glarus Brewing)

BEER STYLES INDEX

New Glarus Brewing Raspberry Tart
(New Glarus Brewing)

Samuel Adams Cranberry Lambic (13.5 SRM, 22 IBU)
(The Boston Beer Company)

Two Brothers Project Opus
(Two Brothers Brewing Company)

Light Ale

Anchor Brewing Small Beer
(Anchor Brewing Company)

Barley Creek Light
(Barley Creek Brewing Company)

Bayhawk Ales Beach Blonde (9.5 IBU)
(Bayhawk Ales, Inc.)

Black Mountain Frog Light
(The Black Mountain/Chili Beer Brewing Company)

Cisco Brewers Sankaty Light
(Cisco Brewers, Inc.)

Eel River Brewing California Blonde Ale
(Eel River Brewing Company)

Eel River Brewing Organic Extra Pale Ale
(Eel River Brewing Company)

Harvest (24 IBU) – *page 515*
(The Long Trail Brewing Company)

Indian Wells Mojave Gold
(Indian Wells Brewing)

Michigan Brewing Golden Ale
(Michigan Brewing Company, Inc.)

Redhook Ale Brewery Sunrye Summer Ale (4.6 SRM, 16 IBU)
(Redhook Ale Brewery)

Shiner Light
(The Spoetzl Brewing (Gambrinus))

Traverse Brewing Torch Lake Light Ale
(Traverse Brewing Company)

Milk Stout

Duck-Rabbit Milk Stout
(Duck-Rabbit Craft Brewery)

Keegan Ales Mother's Milk (29.7 SRM, 25.4 IBU)
(Keegan Ales)

Lake Louie Brewing Milk Stout
(Lake Louie Brewing, LLC)

Lancaster Brewing Milk Stout (22 IBU)
(Lancaster Brewing Company)

Left Hand Brewing Milk Stout (22 IBU) – *page 512*
(Left Hand Brewing Company)

Ska Brewing Steel Toe Stout – *page 549*
(Ska Brewing Company)

Slab City Brewing Milkhouse Stout
(Slab City Brewing)

Widmer Brothers Brewing Company Snowplow Milk Stout
(80 SRM, 26 IBU)
(Widmer Brothers Brewing Company)

Oatmeal Stout

Alaskan Stout (11 SRM, 28 IBU)
(Alaskan Brewing Company)

Anderson Valley Barney Flats Oatmeal Stout (13 IBU) – *page 452*
(Anderson Valley Brewing Company)

Arcadia Brewing Ales Starboard Stout (29 IBU)
(Arcadia Brewing Company)

Barley Island Brewing Bourbon Barrel-Aged Oatmeal Stout
(Barley Island Brewing Company)

Barley Island Brewing Brass Knuckles Oatmeal Stout
(52.4 SRM, 24.4 IBU)
(Barley Island Brewing Company)

Blue Point Brewing Oatmeal Stout (30 IBU)
(Blue Point Brewing)

Breckenridge Oatmeal Stout (31 IBU)
(Breckenridge Brewery)

Bristol Brewing Winter Warlock Oatmeal Stout (44 IBU)
(Bristol Brewing Company)

Church Brew Works Blast Furnace Stout (30 IBU)
(The Church Brew Works)

Cooperstown Brewing Strike Out Stout
(Cooperstown Brewing Company)

Dark Horse One Oatmeal Stout Ale
(Dark Horse Brewing Company)

Dragonmead Reverend Fred's Oatmeal
(Dragonmead Microbrewery)

El Toro Negro Oatmeal Stout
(El Toro Brewing)

Ellicottville Brewing Black Jack Oatmeal Stout
(Ellicottville Brewing Company)

Erie Brewing Drake's Crude Oatmeal Stout (19 IBU)
(Erie Brewing)

Flying Bison Brewing Blackbird Oatmeal Stout
(Flying Bison Brewing Company)

Four Peaks Oatmeal Stout
(Four Peaks Brewing Company)

Golden City Oatmeal Stout
(Golden City Brewery)

Goose Island Oatmeal Stout (80 SRM, 30 IBU)
(Goose Island Beer Company)

Gray's Brewing Oatmeal Stout
(Gray Brewing)

Hood Canal Brewing Big Beef Oatmeal Stout
(Hood Canal Brewing)

Lake Superior Brewing Sir Duluth Oatmeal Stout
(Lake Superior Brewing Company)

Lost Coast 8 Ball Stout (48 IBU)
(Lost Coast Brewery & Café)

Mercury Brewing Ipswich Oatmeal Stout (69 IBU)
(Mercury Brewing Company)

Millstream Brewing Colony Oatmeal Stout
(Millstream Brewing Company)

New Glarus Brewing Road Slush Oatmeal Stout
(New Glarus Brewing)

Nimbus Oatmeal Stout (36 SRM, 45 IBU) – *page 525*
(Nimbus Brewing Company)

Sand Creek Brewing Oscar's Chocolate Oatmeal Stout – *page 539*
(107 SRM, 30 IBU)
(Sand Creek Brewing Company, LLC)

Seabright Brewery Oatmeal Stout
(Seabright Brewery)

Sebago Brewing Lake Trout Stout (171.5 SRM, 31.4 IBU)
(Sebago Brewing Company)

Squatters Captain Bastard's Oatmeal Stout
(Utah Brewers Cooperative/ Wasatch)

Terrapin Wake-N-Bake Coffee Oatmeal Imperial Stout (75 IBU)
(Terrapin Beer Company)

Tractor Brewing Double Plow Oatmeal Stout
(Tractor Brewing Company)

Tröegs Brewing Oatmeal Stout (60 IBU)
(Tröegs Brewing Company)

Trout River Brewing Chocolate Oatmeal Stout
(Trout River Brewing Company)

Wagner Valley Brewing Caywood Oatmeal Stout
(Wagner Valley Brewing Company)

Wild Goose Oatmeal Stout (50 SRM, 45 IBU)
(Wild Goose Brewery, LLC)

Wolaver's Organic Oatmeal Stout (40 IBU)
(Otter Creek Brewing Company)

Yellowstone Valley Black Widow Oatmeal Stout
(Yellowstone Valley Brewing)

Old Ale

Alaskan Winter Ale (17 SRM, 27 IBU)
(Alaskan Brewing Company)

Big Sky Brewing Powder Hound Winter Ale
(Big Sky Brewing Company)

Blue Ridge HopFest
(Wild Goose Brewery, LLC)

Dogfish Head Midas Touch Golden Elixir (12 IBU)
(Dogfish Head Craft Brewery)

El Toro "Yo" Winter Brew
(El Toro Brewing)

Erie Brewing RailBender Ale (26 IBU)
(Erie Brewing)

Founders Brewing Curmudgeon Old Ale (50 IBU)
(Founders Brewing Company)

Hair of the Dog Brewing Adam (50 IBU)
(Hair of the Dog Brewing Company)

Healthy Brew Snowman's Revenge
(Healthy Brew)

Independence Brewing Jasperilla Old Ale (29 IBU)
(Independence Brewing)

Island Brewing Jubilee Ale (30 IBU)
(Island Brewing Company)

King Two Fisted Old Ale
(King Brewing Company)

Lancaster Brewing Winter Warmer
(Lancaster Brewing Company)

Mercury Brewing Ipswich Winter Ale (35 IBU)
(Mercury Brewing Company)

Middle Ages Old Marcus Ale
(Middle Ages Brewing Company)

Saint Arnold Brewing Christmas Ale (35 IBU)
(Saint Arnold Brewing Company)

Smuttynose Brewing Really Old Brown Dog Old Ale
(Smuttynose Brewing Company)

Southampton 10th Anniversary Old Ale
(Southampton Publick House)

Southern Tier Brewing Old Man Winter Warmer
(Southern Tier Brewing Company)

Other Stout

Barley Creek Renovator Stout
(Barley Creek Brewing Company)

Barley Island Brewing Black Majic Java Stout
(Barley Island Brewing Company)

BBC Jefferson's Reserve Bourbon Barrel Stout (40+ SRM, 15 IBU)
(Bluegrass Brewing Company)

Big Daddy Espresso Stout
(Twisted Pine Brewing Company)

Blue Ridge Steeple Stout
(Wild Goose Brewery, LLC)

Brooklyn Black Chocolate Stout (70 IBU)
(Brooklyn Brewery)

Carolina Beer Cottonwood Almond Stout
(Carolina Beer & Beverage Company)

Dark Horse Special Reserve Black Bier Ale
(Dark Horse Brewing Company)

Dark Horse Too Cream Stout
(Dark Horse Brewing Company)

Dark Horse Tres Blueberry Stout
(Dark Horse Brewing Company)

Deschutes Obsidian Stout (50 IBU)
(Deschutes Brewery)

Dick's Cream Stout
(Dick's Brewing Company)

Dominion Oak Barrel Stout
(Old Dominion Brewing Company)

Dragonmead Willy's Oompa-Loompa
(Dragonmead Microbrewery)

Fordham Brewing Oyster Stout
(Fordham Brewing Company)

Founders Brewing Breakfast Stout (25 IBU)
(Founders Brewing Company)

Founders Brewing Kentucky Breakfast (25 IBU)
(Founders Brewing Company)

Hale's Cream Stout
(Hale's Ales)

High & Mighty Brewing Two-Headed Beast
(High & Mighty Brewing Company)

Highland Brewing Black Mocha Stout (25 IBU)
(Highland Brewing)

Island Brewing Starry Night Stout (50 IBU)
(Island Brewing Company)

Jolly Pumpkin Madrugada Obscura "Dark Dawn"
(Jolly Pumpkin Artisan Ales)

Lagunitas Brewing Cappuccino Stout
(Lagunitas Brewing)

Sacramento Brewing Russian Imperial Stout
(Sacramento Brewing Company Inc)

Short's Brew Mystery Stout
(Short's Brewing Company)

Snipes Mountain Brewing Crazy Ivan's Imperial Stout
(Snipes Mountain Brewing Company)

Three Floyds Brewing Black Sun Stout
(Three Floyds Brewing Company)

Viking Brewing Hot Chocolate
(Viking Brewing)

Porter

Alaskan Smoked Porter (92 SRM, 45 IBU)
(Alaskan Brewing Company)

Anchor Brewing Porter
(Anchor Brewing Company)

Anderson Valley Deependers Porter (17 IBU)
(Anderson Valley Brewing Company)

Andrews St. Nick Porter
(Andrews Brewing Company)

Arcadia Brewing Ales London Porter (42 IBU)
(Arcadia Brewing Company)

Atlanta Brewing Red Brink Winter Brew - Double-Chocolate Oatmeal Porter
(Atlanta Brewing Company)

Atlantic Brewing Coal Porter
(Atlantic Brewing Company)

Atwater Shaman's Porter
(Atwater Block Brewery)

Avery Brewing New World Porter (45 IBU)
(Avery Brewing Company)

Back Road Brewery Autumn Ale
(Back Road Brewery)

Backcountry Brewery Peak One Porter (70.6 SRM, 35 IBU)
(Backcountry Brewery)

Badger Porter (62 SRM, 21 IBU)
(Sand Creek Brewing Company, LLC)

Ballast Point Black Marlin Porter
(Ballast Point Brewing Company)

Bayhawk Ales Chocolate Porter (35 IBU)
(Bayhawk Ales, Inc.)

BBC Dark Star Porter (35 SRM, 35 IBU)
(Bluegrass Brewing Company)

Beachside Porter
(Florida Beer Company)

Berkshire Brewing Drayman's Porter
(Berkshire Brewing Company)

Bitter Root Brewing Porter (30 SRM, 35 IBU)
(Bitter Root Brewing)

Black Bear Porter
(Stone Coast Brewing Company)

Black Mountain South of the Border Porter
(The Black Mountain/Chili Beer Brewing Company)

Blacksnake Porter
(Nine G Brewing Company, Inc.)

Blue Point Brewing Porter (26 IBU)
(Blue Point Brewing)

Blue Ridge Porter
(Wild Goose Brewery, LLC)

Boulder Beer Planet Porter (45 SRM, 26 IBU)
(Boulder Beer Company)

Boulevard Brewing Bully! Porter (47 IBU)
(Boulevard Brewing Company)

Breckenridge Vanilla Porter (16 IBU)
(Breckenridge Brewery)

Buckeye Brewing Vanilla Bean Porter
(Buckeye Brewing)

Butte Creek Organic Porter
(Butte Creek Brewing)

Cascade Lakes Monkey Face Porter (34 IBU)
(Cascade Lakes Brewing Company)

Central Waters Mud Puppy Porter
(Central Waters Brewing Company)

Cisco Brewers Moor Porter
(Cisco Brewers, Inc.)

City Winter Porter
(City Brewery)

Concord Porter (32 IBU)
(Concord Brewery, Inc.)

Cooper's Cave Ale Company Pathfinder's Porter (53 IBU)
(Cooper's Cave Ale Company, LTD.)

Cooperstown Brewing Benchwarmer Porter
(Cooperstown Brewing Company)

Crooked River Robust Porter
(Wild Goose Brewery, LLC)

Defiant Brewing Porter
(The Defiant Brewing Company)

Deschutes Black Butte Porter (30 IBU) – *page 490*
(Deschutes Brewery)

Diamond Bear Party Porter (38 IBU)
(Diamond Bear Brewing Company)

Dick's Danger Ale – *page 491*
(Dick's Brewing Company)

Dick's Lave Rock Porter
(Dick's Brewing Company)

Dick's Smoked Porter
(Dick's Brewing Company)

Dragonmead Honey Porter
(Dragonmead Microbrewery)

Dragonmead Woody's Perfect Porter
(Dragonmead Microbrewery)

Duck-Rabbit Baltic Porter (in NC only)
(Duck-Rabbit Craft Brewery)

Duck-Rabbit Porter
(Duck-Rabbit Craft Brewery)

Eel River Brewing Organic Porter
(Eel River Brewing Company)

Eel River Brewing Ravensbrau Porter
(Eel River Brewing Company)

English Ales Black Prince Porter
(English Ales Brewery)

Estes Park Porter
(Estes Park Brewery)

Etna Old Grind Porter
(Etna Brewing Company)

Falls Brewing Falls Porter
(Falls Brewing Company)

Farmhouse Stone Fence Porter
(Farmhouse Brewing Company)

Fish Tale Mudshark Porter
(Fish Brewing Company)

Flying Dog Road Scottish Porter (38 SRM, 26 IBU)
(Flying Dog Brewery, LLC)

Flying Fish Brewing Imperial Espresso Porter
(Flying Fish Brewing)

Flying Fish Brewing Porter
(Flying Fish Brewing)

Founders Brewing Porter (40 IBU)
(Founders Brewing Company)

Geary's London Porter
(D L Geary Brewing Company)

Golden Valley Dundee Porter (26 IBU)
(Golden Valley Brewery)

Gonzo Imperial Porter (135 SRM, 80 IBU)
(Flying Dog Brewery, LLC)

Great Divide Brewing Saint Bridget's Porter (27.5 IBU)
(Great Divide Brewing Company)

Great Lakes Brewing Edmund Fitzgerald Porter (37 IBU)
(Great Lakes Brewing Company)

Hale's Troll Porter
(Hale's Ales)

Highland Brewing Oatmeal Porter (32 IBU)
(Highland Brewing)

Hood Canal Brewing Southpoint Porter
(Hood Canal Brewing)

Island Brewing London Porter (35 IBU)
(Island Brewing Company)

Ithaca Beer Gorges Smoked Porter
(Ithaca Beer Company, Inc.)

Jack's London Porter
(Jack Russell Brewing)

Keweenaw Brewing Coal Porter
(Keweenaw Brewing Company)

King Pontiac Porter
(King Brewing Company)

Kodiak Island Night Watch Porter
(Kodiak Island Brewing Company (Kegs/ Growlers))

Kona Brewing Pipeline Porter (85 SRM, 30 IBU)
(Kona Brewing LLC)

Lake Louie Brewing Dino's Dark
(Lake Louie Brewing, LLC)

Lake Louie Brewing Tommy's Porter
(Lake Louie Brewing, LLC)

Left Hand Brewing Black Jack Porter (27 IBU)
(Left Hand Brewing Company)

Left Hand Brewing Smokejumper Imperial Porter (67 IBU)
(Left Hand Brewing Company)

Legend Brewing Porter
(Legend Brewing Company)

MacTarnahan's Brewing Blackwatch Cream Porter
(MacTarnahan's Brewing Company)

Mad Anthony Old Fort Porter
(Mad Anthony Brewing Company)

Mad River Steelhead Scotch Porter (39.1 IBU)
(Mad River Brewing)

Magic Hat Brewing Ravell (63.6 SRM, 22 IBU)
(Magic Hat Brewing Company)

Maine Coast Brewing Eden Porter
(Maine Coast Brewing)

Mantorville Brewing Stagecoach Double Barrel Porter
(Mantorville Brewing Company, LLC)

Mantorville Brewing Stagecoach Smoked Porter
(Mantorville Brewing Company, LLC)

Marin Brewing Point Reyes Porter
(Marin Brewing Company)

Mercury Brewing Dog Pound Porter
(Mercury Brewing Company)

Mercury Brewing Ipswich Porter (48 IBU)
(Mercury Brewing Company)

Mercury Brewing Stone Cat Pumpkin Porter (25 IBU)
(Mercury Brewing Company)

Michelob Porter
(Anheuser-Busch, Inc.)

Michigan Brewing Peninsula Porter
(Michigan Brewing Company, Inc.)

Midnight Sun Arctic Rhino Coffee Porter (20 IBU)
(Midnight Sun Brewing Company)

Mount Hood Brewing Double T Porter
(Mount Hood Brewing Company)

Mount Hood Brewing Hogsback
(Mount Hood Brewing Company)

Mount Hood Brewing Multorporter
(Mount Hood Brewing Company)

New Knoxville Brewing Porter
(New Knoxville Brewing Company)

Newport Storm Blizzard Porter (49 SRM, 30 IBU)
(Coastal Extreme Brewing Company, LLC)

Oaken Barrel Brewing Snake Pit Porter
(Oaken Barrel Brewing Company)

Odell Brewing Cutthroat Porter
(Odell Brewing Company)

O'Fallon Smoked Porter
(O'Fallon Brewery)

Oregon Trail Ginseng Porter
(Oregon Trail Brewery)

Orlando Brewing Blackwater Ale
(Orlando Brewing Partners, Inc. (Kegs/ Growlers))

Otter Creek Brewing Stovepipe Porter (30 IBU)
(Otter Creek Brewing Company)

Palmetto Brewing Porter
(Palmetto Brewing Company, Inc.)

Perseus Porter (25 IBU)
(Elysian Brewing Company)

R.J. Rockers Bald Eagle Brown (18 SRM, 25 IBU)
(R.J. Rockers Brewing Company)

Ramapo Valley Brewery Suffern Station Porter
(Ramapo Valley Brewery)

Real Ale Brewing Shade Grown Coffee Porter
(Real Ale Brewing Company)

Redhook Ale Brewery Blackhook Porter (51 SRM, 40 IBU)
(Redhook Ale Brewery)

Rock Art Brewery Midnight Madness Smoked Porter (27 IBU)
(Rock Art Brewery, LLC)

Rogue Mocha Porter (54 IBU)
(Rogue Ales)

Ruby Mountain Brewing Bristlecone Brown Porter
(Ruby Mountain Brewing Company)

Rush River Brewing Lost Arrow Porter
(Rush River Brewing (Kegs))

Sam Adams George Washington Porter
(The Boston Beer Company)

Samuel Adams Holiday Porter (55 SRM, 40 IBU)
(The Boston Beer Company)

Samuel Adams Honey Porter
(The Boston Beer Company)

Santa Fe Brewing Santa Fe State Pen Porter (77 SRM, 55 IBU)
(Santa Fe Brewing Company)

Saranac Caramel Porter
(The Matt Brewing)

Scuttlebutt Porter (20 IBU)
(Scuttlebutt Brewing Company)

Sea Dog Riverdriver Hazelnut Porter
(The Sea Dog Brewing Company)

Sebago Brewing Midnight Porter (98.0 SRM, 35.7 IBU)
(Sebago Brewing Company)

Shastafarian Porter
(Mt.Shasta Brewing Company)

Sierra Nevada Porter (50 SRM, 39 IBU)
(Sierra Nevada Brewing Company)

Siletz Brewing Company Black Diamond Imperial Porter (76.1 SRM, 45 IBU)
(Siletz Brewing Company, Inc.)

Silver Gulch Pick Axe Porter (29 IBU)
(Silver Gulch Brewing & Bottling)

Ska Brewing Nefarious Ten Pin Imperial Porter – *page 547*
(Ska Brewing Company)

Ska Brewing Ten Pin Porter
(Ska Brewing Company)

SLO Brewing Cole Porter
(Downtown Brewing Company)

Smuttynose Brewing Baltic Porter
(Smuttynose Brewing Company)

Smuttynose Brewing Robust Porter (15 IBU)
(Smuttynose Brewing Company)

Snipes Mountain Brewing Porter
(Snipes Mountain Brewing Company)

Southampton Imperial Porter
(Southampton Publick House)

Southern Tier Brewing Porter
(Southern Tier Brewing Company)

Sprecher Brewing Generation Porter (26 IBU)
(Sprecher Brewing)

Springfield Brewing Porter (30 IBU)
(Springfield Brewing Company)

St. George Brewing Company Porter (81.1 SRM, 32 IBU)
(St.George Brewing Company)

Steam Train Porter (28 IBU)
(Snoqualmie Falls Brewing Company)

Stegmaier Porter
(The Lion Brewery, Inc.)

Stone Smoked Porter (53 IBU)
(Stone Brewing Company)

Summit Great Northern Porter (63 SRM, 50 IBU) – *page 556*
(Summit Brewing Company)

Thirsty Dog Old Leghumper (24 IBU)
(Thirsty Dog Brewing Company)

Thomas Creek Porter (40 IBU)
(Thomas Creek Brewery)

Thomas Hooker Imperial Porter (30 SRM, 61 IBU)
(Thomas Hooker Brewing Company)

Three Floyds Brewing Christmas Porter
(Three Floyds Brewing Company)

Three Threads Porter
(Far West Brewing Company)

Total Disorder Porter (60 SRM, 22 IBU)
(Big Horn Brewing (CB Potts))

Total Eclipse Black Ale
(Hoppy Brewing Company)

Traverse Brewing Power Island Porter
(Traverse Brewing Company)

Tyranena Brewing Company Brewers Gone Wild! Who's Your Daddy?
  Imperial Porter
(Tyranena Brewing Company)

Tyranena Brewing Company Chief Black Hawk Porter (59 SRM, 35 IBU)
(Tyranena Brewing Company)

Uinta Brewing King's Peak Porter
(Uinta Brewing Company)

Upland Brewing Company Bad Elmer's Porter (24 IBU)
(Upland Brewing Company)

Viking Brewing Whole Stein
(Viking Brewing)

Wachusett Black Shack Porter
(Wachusett Brewing Company)

Waimea Brewing Pakala Porter (22 IBU)
(Waimea Brewing Company)

Wasatch Polygamy Porter
(Utah Brewers Cooperative/ Wasatch)

Weyerbacher Brewing Black Hole
(Weyerbacher Brewing Company)

Wild Goose Porter (40 SRM, 55 IBU)
(Wild Goose Brewery, LLC)

Williamsburg AleWerks Washington's Porter
(Williamsburg AleWerks)

Yards Brewing General Washington Tavern Porter
(Yards Brewing)

Yazoo Brewing Sly Rye Porter
(Yazoo Brewing)

Ybor Gold Gaspar's Porter
(Florida Beer Company)

Yuengling Dark Brewed Porter
(D.G. Yuengling & Son, Inc.)

Rauchbier

Baron Rauchbier
(Baron Brewing)

Rogue Smoke Ale (48 IBU)
(Rogue Ales)

Red Ale

Abita Brewing Red Ale
(Abita Brewing Company)

Atlanta Brewing Red Brick Ale – *page 463*
(Atlanta Brewing Company)

Back Road Brewery Pecker Head Red (19 SRM, 37 IBU)
(Back Road Brewery)

Bear Republic Brewing Red Rocket Ale (65+ IBU)
(Bear Republic Brewing Company)

Berghoff Famous Red Ale (21 IBU)
(Joseph Huber Brewing Company, Inc.)

Bison Brewing Organic Red Ale (16 SRM, 25 IBU)
(Bison Brewing)

Boulevard Brewing Nutcracker Ale (31 IBU)
(Boulevard Brewing Company)

Butte Creek Roland's Red
(Butte Creek Brewing)

Carolina Beer Cottonwood Irish Style Red Ale
(Carolina Beer & Beverage Company)

Catawba Valley Indian Head Red
(Catawba Valley Brewing)

Central Waters Ouisconsing Red Ale
(Central Waters Brewing Company)

Crested Butte Brewery Red Lady Ale
(Crested Butte Brewery)

Dixie Brewing Crimson Voodoo Ale
(Dixie Brewing Company)

Dragonmead Corktown Red
(Dragonmead Microbrewery)

Edenton Brewing King David's Red
(Edenton Brewing Company)

Ellicottville Brewing German Red
(Ellicottville Brewing Company)

Etna Phoenix Red
(Etna Brewing Company)

Fort Collins Retro Red
(The Fort Collins Brewery)

Founders Brewing Red's Rye (68 IBU)
(Founders Brewing Company)

Four Horsemen Irish Ale
(Mishawaka Brewing Company)

Fred Red Ale
(Blue & Gray Brewing Company, Inc.)

Goose Island Kilgubbin Red Ale (20 SRM, 25 IBU)
(Goose Island Beer Company)

Great Lakes Brewing Nosferatu (75 IBU)
(Great Lakes Brewing Company)

Harpoon Hibernian Ale (25 IBU)
(Harpoon Brewery)

Hedgerow Red
(Far West Brewing Company)

Hoptown Paint the Town Red (25 IBU)
(Hoptown Brewery)

Ice Harbor Brewing Runaway Red Ale (25 IBU)
(Ice Harbor Brewing Company)

Iron Horse Loco-Motive Ale
(Iron Horse Brewery)

Ithaca Beer Company CascaZilla
(Ithaca Beer Company, Inc.)

Karl Strauss Brewing Red Trolley Ale (30 SRM, 17 IBU)
(Karl Strauss Breweries)

Kelley Brothers Inferno Red
(Kelley Brothers Brewing Company)

King Big Red
(King Brewing Company)

Lagunitas Brewing Imperial Red Ale
(Lagunitas Brewing)

Landmark Colonel Hops Red Ale
(Landmark Beer Company)

Landmark Colonel Hops Red Ale
(Landmark Beer Company)

Legacy Brewing Hedonism Red Ale (110 IBU)
(Legacy Brewing Company)

Lizard Head Red (12.4 SRM, 27.8 IBU)
(Steamworks Brewing Company)

Mad River Jamaica Red (42 IBU)
(Mad River Brewing)

Mantorville Brewing Stagecoach Amber Ale
(Mantorville Brewing Company LLC)

Maritime Pacific Flagship Red Ale
(Maritime Pacific Brewing Company)

Mendocino Brewing Red Tail Ale
(Mendocino Brewing Company)

Nectar Ales Red Nectar
(Nectar Ales)

New Holland Red Tulip
(New Holland Brewing Company)

Nimbus Red Ale (14 SRM, 29 IBU) – *page 524*
(Nimbus Brewing Company)

Pony Express Tornado Red Ale
(Pony Express Brewing Company)

ReaperAle Redemption Red Ale (35 IBU)
(ReaperAle, Inc.)

Rock Art Brewery American Red Ale (14 IBU)
(Rock Art Brewery, LLC)

Rogue Santa's Private Reserve (44 IBU)
(Rogue Ales)

Rogue St.Rogue Red (44 IBU)
(Rogue Ales)

Sacramento Brewing Red Horse Ale
(Sacramento Brewing Company Inc)

Santa Cruz Mountain Brewing Nicky 666
(Santa Cruz Mountain Brewing)

Seabright Brewery Resolution Red
(Seabright Brewery)

Sebago Brewing Runabout Red Ale (26.24 SRM, 37.3 IBU)
(Sebago Brewing Company)

Sharkbite Red Ale
(Port Brewing Company)

Shenandoah Brewing Skyland Red Ale
(Shenandoah Brewing Company)

Siletz Brewing Company Red Ale (19.1 SRM, 42.3 IBU)
(Siletz Brewing Company, Inc.)

Ska Brewing Pinstripe Red Ale – *page 547*
(Ska Brewing Company)

Sonora Brewing Top Down Red Ale
(Sonoran Brewing Company (Kegs/ Growlers))

Stony Face Red Ale
(Hoppy Brewing Company)

Terrapin Big Hoppy Monster (75 IBU)
(Terrapin Beer Company)

Thomas Creek Red Ale (14 IBU) – *page 563*
(Thomas Creek Brewery)

Tractor Brewing Farmer's Tan – Red Ale – *page 564*
(Tractor Brewing Company)

Trout River Brewing Rainbow Red Ale
(Trout River Brewing Company)

Twisted Pine Red Mountain Ale
(Twisted Pine Brewing Company)

Wachusett Octoberfest
(Wachusett Brewing Company)

Warbird Brewing T-6 Red Ale (14.5 SRM, 15 IBU)
(Warbird Brewing Company)

Widmer Brothers Brewing Company W '06 N.W. Red Ale (50 IBU)
(Widmer Brothers Brewing Company)

Woodstock Inn Brewery Red Rack Ale
(Woodstock Inn Brewery)

Scottish Ale

Alesmith Brewing Wee Heavy
(Alesmith Brewing Company)

BEER STYLES INDEX

ALES

Appalachian Brewing Jolly Scot Scottish Ale
(Appalachian Brewing Company)

Bristol Brewing Laughing Lab Scottish Ale (19 IBU)
(Bristol Brewing Company)

Carolina Beer Cottonwood Lift your Kilt Scottish Ale
(Carolina Beer & Beverage Company)

Dillion DAM Olde Forster's Scotch Ale
(Dillion DAM Brewery)

Dragonmead 90 Shilling
(Dragonmead Microbrewery)

Empyrean Ales Burning Skye Scottish Ale (7 SRM, 13 IBU)
(Empyrean Brewing)

Glacier Brewing St. Arnold's Autumn Ale (19.4 SRM, 47.3 IBU)
(Glacier Brewing)

Great Divide Brewing Ridgeline Amber (27 IBU)
(Great Divide Brewing Company)

Gritty McDuff's Scottish Ale (25 IBU)
(Gritty McDuff's Brewing Company, LLC)

Heinzelmannchen Kilted Gnome Scottish Ale
(Heinzelmannchen Brewery (Kegs/ Growlers))

Hibernator (25 IBU) – *page 516*
(The Long Trail Brewing Company)

Kiltlifter Scottish-Style Ale – *page 501*
(Four Peaks Brewing Company)

Kodiak Island North Pacific Ale
(Kodiak Island Brewing Company (Kegs/ Growlers))

Lake Louie Brewing Warped Speed Scotch Ale
(Lake Louie Brewing, LLC)

Lewis & Clark Back Country Scottish Ale
(Lewis & Clark Brewing)

Mercury Brewing Stone Cat Scotch Ale (18 IBU)
(Mercury Brewing Company)

Middle Ages The Duke of Winship Scottish Style Ale
(Middle Ages Brewing Company)

Paper City Brewing Winter Palace Wee Heavy
(Paper City Brewery Company)

Pike Brewing Company Kilt Lifter Scotch Ale
(Pike Brewing Company)

Rocky Bay Black Castle Ale
(Rocky Bay Brewing Company)

SLO Olde Highland Ale
(Downtown Brewing Company)

Three Floyds Brewing Robert the Bruce Scottish Ale (35 IBU)
(Three Floyds Brewing Company)

Trout River Brewing Scottish Ale
(Trout River Brewing Company)

Wachusett Winter Ale
(Wachusett Brewing Company)

Whitstran Brewing Highlander Scottish Style Ale (16 IBU)
(Whitstran Brewing Company)

Seasonally Produced

Bayhawk Ales Stout (30 IBU)
(Bayhawk Ales, Inc.)

Blue Ridge Snowball's Chance
(Wild Goose Brewery, LLC)

Brewmasters Limited Edition Series - Unfiltered IPA (56 IBU)
(The Long Trail Brewing Company)

Butte Creek Christmas Cranberry Ale
(Butte Creek Brewing)

Butte Creek Spring Ale
(Butte Creek Brewing)

Carolina Beer Cottonwood Pumpkin Spiced Ale
(Carolina Beer & Beverage Company)

Catawba Valley King Coconut Porter
(Catawba Valley Brewing)

Catawba Valley King Don's Original Pumpkin Ale
(Catawba Valley Brewing)

Deschutes Twilight Ale (35 IBU)
(Deschutes Brewery)

Dogfish Head Aprihop (55 IBU)
(Dogfish Head Craft Brewery)

Beer Styles Index Seasonally Produced (continued)

Dogfish Head Punkin Ale (24 IBU)
(Dogfish Head Craft Brewery)

Dragonmead Andromeda Heather Ale
(Dragonmead Microbrewery)

Dragonmead Castlebrite Apricot Ale
(Dragonmead Microbrewery)

Dragonmead Jul 01
(Dragonmead Microbrewery)

Dragonmead Lil's Grumpkin Pumpkin Ale
(Dragonmead Microbrewery)

Dragonmead Redwing Raspberry Wheat Beer
(Dragonmead Microbrewery)

Full Sail Brewing Holiday Wassail Ale
(Full Sail Brewing Company)

Great Divide Brewing Fresh Hop Pale Ale (55 IBU)
(Great Divide Brewing Company)

Great Divide Brewing Hibernation Ale (37 IBU)
(Great Divide Brewing Company)

Hoppy Claus Holiday Ale
(Hoppy Brewing Company)

Jack Russell's Harvest Apple Ale
(Jack Russell Brewing)

Jack's Blueberry Beer
(Jack Russell Brewing)

Jolly Pumpkin Maracaibo Especial
(Jolly Pumpkin Artisan Ales)

Lakefront Holiday Spice Lager Beer (12 SRM, 14 IBU)
(Lakefront Brewery, Inc.)

Leavenworth Beers Nosferatu Red Ale (55 IBU)
(Fish Brewing Company)

Lion Brewing Pocono Caramel Porter
(Lion Brewery)

Lost Coast Winterbraun (45 IBU)
(Lost Coast Brewery & Café)

Midnight Sun Co Ho Ho Imperial IPA (85 IBU)
(Midnight Sun Brewing Company)

Otter Creek Brewing Oktoberfest (19 IBU)
(Otter Creek Brewing Company)

Shipyard Brewing Prelude Special Ale
(Shipyard Brewing Company)

Southern Tier Brewing Harvest Ale
(Southern Tier Brewing Company)

Stone Anniversary Ale
(Stone Brewing Company)

Tröegs Brewing Mad Elf (15 IBU)
(Tröegs Brewing Company)

Special Ale

Anchor Brewing Liberty Ale
(Anchor Brewing Company)

Beermann's Honey Brew
(Beermann's Beerwerks)

Black Mountain Gold
(The Black Mountain/Chili Beer Brewing Company)

Cooperstown Brewing Pride Of Milford Special Ale
(Cooperstown Brewing Company)

Dragonmead Bill's Witbier
(Dragonmead Microbrewery)

Dragonmead Lady Guinevere's Golden Belgian Style
(Dragonmead Microbrewery)

Empyrean Ales Dark Side Vanilla Porter (75 SRM, 19 IBU)
(Empyrean Brewing)

Geary's Hampshire Special Ale
(D L Geary Brewing Company)

Indian Wells Irish Green Ale
(Indian Wells Brewing)

Moylander: Double IPA
(Moylan's Brewing Company)

Moylan's Hopsickle Imperial Triple Hoppy Ale
(Moylan's Brewing Company)

North Coast Old Stock Ale (36 IBU)
(North Coast Brewing Company)

Yards Brewing Extra Special Ale – *page 574*
(Yards Brewing)

Stout

Alesmith Brewing Speedway Stout
(Alesmith Brewing Company)

Avery Brewing Mephistopheles' Stout (107 IBU)
(Avery Brewing Company)

Avery Brewing Out of Bounds Stout (51 IBU)
(Avery Brewing Company)

Backside Stout (28.5 SRM, 42.1 IBU)
(Steamworks Brewing Company)

Bar Harbor Brewing Cadillac Mountain Stout
(Bar Harbor Brewing Company)

Bison Brewing Organic Chocolate Stout (45 SRM, 30 IBU)
(Bison Brewing)

Bourbon County Stout (100 SRM, 60 IBU)
(Goose Island Beer Company)

BridgePort Black Strap Stout (30 IBU)
(BridgePort Brewing Company (Gambrinus))

Carolina Brewing Winter Stout
(Carolina Brewing)

Catawba Valley Honust Injun Stout
(Catawba Valley Brewing)

Central Coast Brewing Stenner Stout Ale
(Central Coast Brewing)

Cisco Brewers Captain Swain's Extra Stout
(Cisco Brewers, Inc.)

Dark Horse Fore Smoked Stout
(Dark Horse Brewing Company)

Defiant Brewing Stephano's Stout
(The Defiant Brewing Company)

Dragonstooth Stout (36 IBU)
(Elysian Brewing Company)

Dunedin Brewery Leonard Croon's Old Mean Stout
(Dunedin Brewery)

Estes Park Samson Stout
(Estes Park Brewery)

Fish Tale Trout Stout
(Fish Brewing Company)

Fort Collins Chocolate Stout
(The Fort Collins Brewery)

Glacier Brewing Slurry Bomber Stout (44 SRM, 36.6 IBU)
(Glacier Brewing)

Gritty McDuff's Black Fly Stout (16 IBU)
(Gritty McDuff's Brewing Company, LLC)

Healthy Brew Strong Stout
(Healthy Brew)

Heinzelmannchen Black Forest Stout
(Heinzelmannchen Brewery (Kegs/ Growlers))

Hyland's Sturbridge Stout
(Pioneer Brewing Company)

Ice Harbor Brewing Sternwheeler Stout (30 IBU)
(Ice Harbor Brewing Company)

Indian Wells Piute Stout
(Indian Wells Brewing)

Ithaca Beer Company Finger Lakes Stout
(Ithaca Beer Company, Inc.)

King Mocha Java Stout
(King Brewing Company)

Lagunitas Brewing IPA Maximus
(Lagunitas Brewing)

Lakefront Fuel Café Stout (45 SRM, 20 IBU)
(Lakefront Brewery, Inc.)

Mad River Steelhead Extra Stout (32.7 IBU)
(Mad River Brewing)

Marin Brewing San Quentin's Breakout Stout
(Marin Brewing Company)

Mendocino Brewing Black Hawk Stout
(Mendocino Brewing Company)

BEER STYLES INDEX Stout *(continued)*

Michigan Brewing Superior Stout
(Michigan Brewing Company, Inc.)

Middle Ages Black Heart Stout
(Middle Ages Brewing Company)

Moo Thunder Stout (25 IBU)
(Butternuts Beer & Ale)

New Holland The Poet
(New Holland Brewing Company)

Newport Storm Cyclone Series - Derek Stout
(Coastal Extreme Brewing Company, LLC)

North Coast Old No. 38 Stout (46 IBU)
(North Coast Brewing Company)

Old Courthouse Stout
(Trailhead Brewing Company)

Pike Brewing Company XXXXX Stout
(Pike Brewing Company)

R.J. Rockers Star Spangled Stout (60 SRM, 25 IBU)
(R.J. Rockers Brewing Company)

ReaperAle Mortality Stout (30 IBU)
(ReaperAle, Inc.)

Rock Art Brewery Stump Jumper Stout (40 IBU)
(Rock Art Brewery, LLC)

Rocky Bay Brewing Nor' Easter Stout
(Rocky Bay Brewing Company)

Rogue Chocolate Stout (69 IBU)
(Rogue Ales)

Rogue Shakespeare Stout (69 IBU)
(Rogue Ales)

Saint Arnold Brewing Winter Stout (36 IBU)
(Saint Arnold Brewing Company)

Samuel Adams Cream Stout (80 SRM, 28 IBU)
(The Boston Beer Company)

Santa Cruz Mountain Brewing Organic Devout Stout – *page 540*
(Santa Cruz Mountain Brewing)

Shenandoah Brewing Stony Man Stout
(Shenandoah Brewing Company)

Sierra Nevada Stout (70 SRM, 53 IBU)
(Sierra Nevada Brewing Company)

Siletz Brewing Company Oatmeal Cream Stout (87.2 SRM, 64.1 IBU)
(Siletz Brewing Company, Inc.)

Snake River Zonker Stout (36 IBU)
(Snake River Brewing Company)

South Shore Brewery Rhodes' Scholar Stout
(South Shore Brewery)

Sprecher Brewing Irish Stout (26 IBU)
(Sprecher Brewing)

Stonewall Stout
(Blue & Gray Brewing Company, Inc.)

Traverse Brewing Stout
(Traverse Brewing Company)

Twisted Pine Twisted Stout
(Twisted Pine Brewing Company)

Whitstran Brewing O2O Heavy Water Stout (63 IBU)
(Whitstran Brewing Company)

Yards Brewing Love Stout
(Yards Brewing)

Summer

Anchor Brewing Summer Ale
(Anchor Brewing Company)

Blue Point Brewing Summer Ale (16 IBU)
(Blue Point Brewing)

Breckenridge Summerbright Ale (15 IBU)
(Breckenridge Brewery)

Carolina Beer Cottonwood American Wheat
(Carolina Beer & Beverage Company)

Carolina Brewing Summer Ale
(Carolina Brewing)

Flying Fish Brewing Farmhouse Summer Ale
(Flying Fish Brewing)

Founders Brewing Rubaeus (24 IBU)
(Founders Brewing Company)

Geary's Summer Ale
(D L Geary Brewing Company)

Goose Island Summertime (4 SRM, 25 IBU)
(Goose Island Beer Company)

Indian Wells Vette's Honey Ale
(Indian Wells Brewing)

Mercury Brewing Ipswich Summer Ale (23 IBU)
(Mercury Brewing Company)

Mercury Brewing Stone Cat Wheat Beer
(Mercury Brewing Company)

New Belgium Skinny Dip
(New Belgium Brewing Company)

Pete's WickedRally Cap Ale(22 IBU)
(Pete's Brewing (Gambrinus))

River Horse Summer Blonde – *page 534*
(River Horse Brewing Company)

Rock Art Brewery River Runner Summer Ale (12 IBU)
(Rock Art Brewery, LLC)

Samuel Adams Summer Ale (7.5 SRM, 10 IBU) – *page 475*
(The Boston Beer Company)

Saranac 12 Beers of Summer
(The Matt Brewing)

Sea Dog Summer Ale
(The Sea Dog Brewing Company)

Shipyard Brewing Summer
(Shipyard Brewing Company)

Tremont Brewing Tremont Summer
(Tremont Brewery/Atlantic Coast Brewing Company)

Viking Brewing Lime Twist
(Viking Brewing)

Weizen Beer

Angel City Vitzen (5 SRM,15 IBU)
(Angel City Brewing)

Atwater Hefeweizen
(Atwater Block Brewery)

Avery Brewing Thirteen
(Avery Brewing Company)

Baron Berliner-Weisse
(Baron Brewing)

Baron Uber-Weisse
(Baron Brewing)

Bayern Brewing Flathead Lake Monster Lager
(Bayern Brewing)

Bayern Brewing Killarney
(Bayern Brewing)

Bayern Brewing Trout Slayer
(Bayern Brewing)

Buzzards Bay Brewing Weizen Dopplebock (17 IBU)
(Buzzards Bay Brewing Company)

Diamond Bear Honey Weiss (21 IBU)
(Diamond Bear Brewing Company)

Dominion Summer Wheat
(Old Dominion Brewing Company)

Rahr Brewing Summer Time Wheat (4 SRM, 18 IBU)
(Rahr & Sons Brewing Company)

Sand Creek Brewing Woody's Wheat (12 SRM, 6 IBU)
(Sand Creek Brewing Company, LLC)

Santa Fe Brewing Santa Fe Wheat (3.5 SRM, 23 IBU)
(Santa Fe Brewing Company)

Smuttynose Brewing Summer Weizen
(Smuttynose Brewing Company)

Smuttynose Brewing Weizenheimer
(Smuttynose Brewing Company)

Southern Tier Brewing Heavy Weizen
(Southern Tier Brewing Company)

Stoudt's Weizen (12 IBU)
(Stoudt's Brewing Company)

Summit Hefe Weizen (5 SRM, 18 IBU)
(Summit Brewing Company)

Upland Brewing Company Valley Weizen (9.8 IBU)
(Upland Brewing Company)

Weeping Radish Weizen (3.3 SRM, 15.2 IBU)
(The Weeping Radish Brewery)

Wild Dog Weizenbock Ale (25 SRM, 30 IBU)
(Flying Dog Brewery, LLC)

Wheat Ale

Abita Brewing Wheat
(Abita Brewing Company)

Allagash Brewing White Beer (18 IBU)
(Allagash Brewing Company)

Anderson Valley High Rollers Wheat Beer (5 IBU)
(Anderson Valley Brewing Company)

Appalachian Brewing Water Gap Wheat
(Appalachian Brewing Company)

Arcadia Brewing Ales Whitsun (17 IBU)
(Arcadia Brewing Company)

Atlantic Brewing Mount Desert Island Ginger
(Atlantic Brewing Company)

Backcountry Brewery Wheeler Wheat (3.6 SRM, 18 IBU)
(Backcountry Brewery)

Berkshire Brewing River Ale
(Berkshire Brewing Company)

Bitchin' Betty Citrus Wheat Beer
(Nine G Brewing Company, Inc.)

Black Mountain Juanderful Wheat
(The Black Mountain/Chili Beer Brewing Company)

Blackbeary Wheat (8 IBU) – *page 514*
(The Long Trail Brewing Company)

Boulevard Brewing Unfiltered Wheat Beer (13 IBU) – *page 479*
(Boulevard Brewing Company)

Bristol Brewing Beehive Honey Wheat (16 IBU)
(Bristol Brewing Company)

Bristol Brewing Edge City Wit Bier (18 IBU)
(Bristol Brewing Company)

Butte Creek Creekside Wheat
(Butte Creek Brewing)

Capital Brewery Island Wheat – *page 483*
(Capital Brewery Company, Inc.)

Catawba Valley King Karma Ale
(Catawba Valley Brewing)

Central Coast Brewing Honey Wheat Ale
(Central Coast Brewing)

City Brewery Golden Leaf Unfiltered Wheat
(City Brewery)

Coeur d'Alene Brewing Honeymoon Wheat
(Coeur D'Alene Brewing Company)

Columbus Brewing Ohio Honey Wheat
(Columbus Brewing Company)

Crabtree Brewing Twisted Creek Wheat
(Crabtree Brewing Company)

Dunedin Brewery Lowland Wheat Ale (5 SRM, 11.5 IBU)
(Dunedin Brewery)

Dunedin Brewery Razzbeery Wheat Ale (7 SRM, 12 IBU)
(Dunedin Brewery)

Dunedin Brewery Summer Apricot Wheat Ale (5 SRM, 11 IBU)
(Dunedin Brewery)

Durango Brewing Wheat Beer (10 IBU)
(Durango Brewing Company)

El Toro William Jones Wheat
(El Toro Brewing)

Ellicottville Brewing Blueberry Wheat – *page 494*
(Ellicottville Brewing Company)

English Ales Monterey Bay Wheat
(English Ales Brewery)

Estes Park Raspberry Wheat
(Estes Park Brewery)

Estes Park Stinger Wild Honey Wheat
(Estes Park Brewery)

Beer Styles Index

Fort Collins Major Tom's Pomegranate Wheat – *page 500*
(The Fort Collins Brewery)

Four Plus DUNK'L Amber Wheat (15 SRM, 24 IBU)
(Four Plus Brewing Company)

Goose Island 312 Urban Wheat Ale (4 SRM, 15 IBU)
(Goose Island Beer Company)

Grand Teton Workhorse Wheat (10.4 IBU)
(Grand Teton Brewing Company)

Harbor City Brewing Harvest Wheat
(Harbor City Brewing, Inc.)

Healthy Brew Wheat Serenity
(Healthy Brew)

Heinnieweisse Weissbier (11 IBU)
(Butternuts Beer & Ale)

Henry Weinhard's Summer Wheat
(SAB Miller Corporation)

Hoptown Wheathopper Red Wheat Ale
(Hoptown Brewery)

Independence Brewing Freestyle Wheat Beer (15 IBU)
(Independence Brewing)

Lang Creek Taildragger Honey Wheat (8 IBU)
(Lang Creek Brewery)

Left Hand Brewing Haystack Wheat (14 IB)
(Left Hand Brewing Company)

Leinenkugel's Sunset Wheat
(Jacob Leinenkugel Brewing Company)

Lion Brewing Pocono Summer Wheat
(Lion Brewery)

Magic Hat Brewing Hocus Pocus(4.5 SRM, 13 IBU)
(Magic Hat Brewing Company)

Marin Brewing Hefe Doppel Weizen
(Marin Brewing Company)

Marin Brewing Hefe Weiss
(Marin Brewing Company)

Marin Brewing Star Brew
(Marin Brewing Company)

Michigan Brewing Wheatland Wheat Beer
(Michigan Brewing Company, Inc.)

Middle Ages Winter Wheat
(Middle Ages Brewing Company)

Millstream Brewing Wheat
(Millstream Brewing Company)

New Belgium Sunshine Wheat (3.3 SRM, 14.5 IBU)
(New Belgium Brewing Company)

New Holland Zoomer Wheat Ale
(New Holland Brewing Company)

New Knoxville Brewing Honey Wheat
(New Knoxville Brewing Company)

New South White Ale
(New South Brewing Company (Kegs/ Growlers))

North Coast Blue Star Great American Wheat Beer (17 IBU)
(North Coast Brewing Company)

Odell Brewing Easy Street Wheat
(Odell Brewing Company)

O'Fallon Wheat
(O'Fallon Brewery)

Otter Creek Brewing Otter Summer Ale
(Otter Creek Brewing Company)

Pony Express Original Wheat
(Pony Express Brewing Company)

Pyramid Brewery Amber Weizen (17 IBU) – *page 530*
(Pyramid Brewery)

Pyramid Brewery Apricot Weizen (11 IBU) – *page 530*
(Pyramid Brewery)

Ramapo Valley Brewery Ramapo Razz Ale
(Ramapo Valley Brewery)

Rock Art Brewery Vermont Maple Wheat (8 IBU)
(Rock Art Brewery, LLC)

Saint Arnold Brewing Texas Wheat (18 IBU)
(Saint Arnold Brewing Company)

Sam Adams James Madison Dark Wheat Ale
(The Boston Beer Company)

171

Samuel Adams Cherry Wheat (8 SRM, 23 IBU)
(The Boston Beer Company)

Sheepscot Valley Brewing Monhegan Wheat
(Sheepscot Valley Brewing Company)

Shenandoah Brewing White Water Wheat
(Shenandoah Brewing Company)

Sierra Nevada Wheat Beer (5 SRM, 26 IBU)
(Sierra Nevada Brewing Company)

Slab City Brewing Shawano Gold
(Slab City Brewing)

Sly Fox Royal Weisse (11 IBU)
(Sly Fox Brewing Company)

Sonora Brewing C.I.A. - Citrus Infused Ale
(Sonoran Brewing Company (Kegs/ Growlers))

Southern Tier Brewing Hop Sun Summer Ale
(Southern Tier Brewing Company)

Spring Heat Spiced Wheat – *page 458*
(Anheuser-Busch, Inc.)

Springfield Brewing Unfiltered Wheat (15 IBU)
(Springfield Brewing Company)

Sweetwater Brewing Sweetwater Blue
(Sweetwater Brewing)

Thomas Creek Multi Grain Ale (19.4 IBU)
(Thomas Creek Brewery)

Three Floyds Brewing Gumballhead
(Three Floyds Brewing Company)

Tommyknocker Jack Whacker Wheat Ale
(Tommyknocker Brewery)

Tractor Brewing Haymaker - Honey Wheat Ale
(Tractor Brewing Company)

Traverse Brewing Voss Wend Wheat
(Traverse Brewing Company)

Twisted Pine Raspberry Wheat Ale
(Twisted Pine Brewing Company)

Upland Brewing Company Wheat Ale (11 IBU)
(Upland Brewing Company)

Victory Sunrise Weissbier (13-18 IBU)
(Victory Brewing Company)

Viking Brewing Weathertop Wheat
(Viking Brewing)

Wachusett Summer Breeze
(Wachusett Brewing Company)

Wagner Valley Brewing Grace House Wheat
(Wagner Valley Brewing Company)

Wall Street Wheat Ale
(Mishawaka Brewing Company)

Weyerbacher Brewing HefeWeizen
(Weyerbacher Brewing Company)

Williamsburg AleWerks Colonial Wheat Ale
(Williamsburg AleWerks)

Ybor Gold Wheat Ale
(Florida Beer Company)

Yellowstone Valley Grizzly Wulff Wheat
(Yellowstone Valley Brewing)

Winter

Abita Brewing Christmas Ale
(Abita Brewing Company)

Alesmith Brewing YuleSmith Holiday Ale
(Alesmith Brewing Company)

Anchor Brewing Christmas Ale
(Anchor Brewing Company)

Anderson Valley Winter Solstice (5 IBU)
(Anderson Valley Brewing Company)

August Schell Brewing Snowstorm
(August Schell Brewing Company)

Avalanche Winter Ale (48 IBU)
(Snoqualmie Falls Brewing Company)

Back Road Brewery Christmas Ale
(Back Road Brewery)

BEER STYLES INDEX

Berghoff Hazelnut Winterfest Ale (20 IBU)
(Joseph Huber Brewing Company, Inc.)

Berkshire Brewing Cabin Fever Ale
(Berkshire Brewing Company)

Bifrost Winter Ale (42 IBU)
(Elysian Brewing Company)

Blue Point Brewing Winter Ale (16 IBU)
(Blue Point Brewing)

Boulder Beer Never Summer Ale (36.9 SRM, 45 IBU)
(Boulder Beer Company)

Boundary Bay Cabin Fever
(Boundary Bay Brewing Company)

BridgePort Ebenezer Ale (40 IBU)
(BridgePort Brewing Company (Gambrinus))

Butte Creek Winter Ale
(Butte Creek Brewing)

Capital Brewery Winter Skal
(Capital Brewery Company, Inc.)

Carolina Beer Cottonwood Frostbite Ale
(Carolina Beer & Beverage Company)

Carolina Beer Cottonwood Low Down Brown
(Carolina Beer & Beverage Company)

Cisco Brewers Celebration Libation
(Cisco Brewers, Inc.)

Clay Pipe Brewing Pursuit of Happiness Winter Warmer
(12 SRM, 46 IBU)
(Clay Pipe Brewing Company)

Conductor (11 SRM, 96 IBU)
(Steamworks Brewing Company)

Crooked River Yuletide
(Wild Goose Brewery, LLC)

Deschutes Jubelale (60 IBU)
(Deschutes Brewery)

Dick's Double Diamond Winter Ale
(Dick's Brewing Company)

Dillion DAM Winter Warmer
(Dillion DAM Brewery)

Dunedin Brewery Christmas Farm Ale (11 SRM, 37 IBU)
(Dunedin Brewery)

English Ales Edinburgh Winter Ale
(English Ales Brewery)

Erie Brewing Red Ryder Big Beer (35 IBU)
(Erie Brewing)

Flying Dog K9 Winter Cruiser (35 SRM, 30 IBU)
(Flying Dog Brewery, LLC)

Founders Brewing Black Rye (64 IBU)
(Founders Brewing Company)

Geary's Winter
(D L Geary Brewing Company)

Golden Valley Tannen Bomb (50 IBU)
(Golden Valley Brewery)

Goose Island Christmas Ale (30 SRM, 55 IBU)
(Goose Island Beer Company)

Gordon Biersch Winter Bock (24 IBU)
(Gordon Biersch Brewery)

Great Lakes Brewing Christmas Ale (40 IBU)
(Great Lakes Brewing Company)

Hale's Wee Heavy Winter Ale
(Hale's Ales)

Jack's Olde Ale
(Jack Russell Brewing)

Jackson's Winter Ale
(Stone Coast Brewing Company)

Leavenworth Beers Snowblind Winter Warmer
(Fish Brewing Company)

New Belgium 2 Below (14.7 SRM, 28 IBU)
(New Belgium Brewing Company)

Northern Lights Winter Ale
(The Northern Lights Brewing Company)

Odell Brewing Isolation Ale
(Odell Brewing Company)

Paper City Brewing Winter Lager
(Paper City Brewery Company)

R.J. Rockers First Snow Ale (8 SRM, 30 IBU)
(R.J. Rockers Brewing Company)

Ramapo Valley BreweryChristmas Ale
(Ramapo Valley Brewery)

Redhook Ale Brewery Winter Hook Winter Ale
(21.7 SRM, 27.6 IBU)
(Redhook Ale Brewery)

Samuel Adams 375 Colonial Ale
(The Boston Beer Company)

Samuel Adams Old Fezziwig Ale (37.5 SRM, 25 IBU)
(The Boston Beer Company)

Samuel Adams Winter Lager (25 SRM, 22 IBU) – *page 476*
(The Boston Beer Company)

Saranac 12 Beers of Winter
(The Matt Brewing)

Scuttlebutt 10 Below (22 IBU)
(Scuttlebutt Brewing Company)

Sea Dog Winter Ale
The Sea Dog Brewing Company

Sebago Brewing Slick Nick Winter Ale (21.1 SRM, 38.7 IBU)
(Sebago Brewing Company)

Shipyard Brewing Longfellow
(Shipyard Brewing Company)

Siletz Brewing Company Winter Warmer (38.5 SRM, 53.8 IBU)
(Siletz Brewing Company, Inc.)

Smuttynose Brewing Winter Ale
(Smuttynose Brewing Company)

Spiced Winter Ale (Nov. - Jan.)
(Blue & Gray Brewing Company, Inc.)

Sprecher Brewing Winter Brew (0 IBU)
(Sprecher Brewing)

Spruce Goose (16.1 SRM, 21 IBU)
(Steamworks Brewing Company)

Stoudt's Winter Ale
(Stoudt's Brewing Company)

Summit Winter Ale (45 SRM, 35 IBU) – *page 557*
(Summit Brewing Company)

Sweetwater Brewing Sweetwater Festive Ale
(Sweetwater Brewing)

Tremont Brewing Winter
(Tremont Brewery/Atlantic Coast Brewing Company)

Viking Brewing JuleOL
(Viking Brewing)

Weeping Radish Christmas Bier (21.2 SRM, 33.7 IBU)
(The Weeping Radish Brewery)

Weyerbacher Brewing Winter Ale
(Weyerbacher Brewing Company)

Wild Goose Snow Goose (16 SRM, 28 IBU)
(Wild Goose Brewery, LLC)

Winterfest
(Molson Coors Brewing Company)

Winter's Bourbon Cask Ale – *page 458*
(Anheuser-Busch, Inc.)

Amber Lager

Atwater Rost
(Atwater Block Brewery)

Bayern Brewing Amber
(Bayern Brewing)

Boulevard Brewing Bob's '47 (27 IBU)
(Boulevard Brewing Company)

Brooklyn Lager (28-30 IBU)
(Brooklyn Brewery)

Central Coast Brewing Old Mission Ale
(Central Coast Brewing)

Dominion Lager
(Old Dominion Brewing Company)

Fort Collins Edgar Lager
(The Fort Collins Brewery)

Genesee Red Lager
(High Falls Brewing)

Great Lakes Brewing Eliot Ness Amber Lager (35 IBU)
(Great Lakes Brewing Company)

Great Northern Brewing Bear Naked Amber (43 IBU)
(Great Northern Brewing Company)

Great Northern Brewing Hellroaring Amber Lager (18 IBU)
(Great Northern Brewing Company)

Indian Wells Orange Blossom Amber
(Indian Wells Brewing)

James Page Brewing Iron Ranger Amber Lager
(James Page Brewing Company, LLC)

Lakefront Riverwest Stein (15 SRM, 36 IBU)
(Lakefront Brewery, Inc.)

Lion Brewing Pocono Lager
(Lion Brewery)

Mad Anthony Auburn Lager
(Mad Anthony Brewing Company)

Michigan Brewing Sunset Amber Lager
(Michigan Brewing Company, Inc.)

OK Ale
(Electric Beer Company)

Point Classic Amber
(Stevens Point Brewery)

Rahr Brewing Rahr's Red (17 SRM, 22 IBU)
(Rahr & Sons Brewing Company)

Ramstein Munich Amber Lager
(High Point Wheat Beer Company)

Saranac Adirondack Lager
(The Matt Brewing)

Terre Haute Brewing Champagne Velvet Amber
(Terre Haute Brewing Company)

The Palisade Brewery Orchard Amber Ale
(The Palisade Brewery)

Twisted Pine American Amber Ale
(Twisted Pine Brewing Company)

Weeping Radish Fest (11.2 SRM, 24 IBU)
(The Weeping Radish Brewery)

Ybor Gold Amber Lager
(Florida Beer Company)

Yuengling Traditional Lager – *page 489*
(D.G. Yuengling & Son, Inc.)

ZeigenBock
(Anheuser-Busch, Inc.)

Bock

Abita Bock
(Abita Brewing Company)

Anchor Brewing Bock Beer
(Anchor Brewing Company)

Atwater Winter Bock
(Atwater Block Brewery)

Back Road Brewery Koza Brada Bock (17 SRM, 15 IBU)
(Back Road Brewery)

Baron Bock
(Baron Brewing)

Bayern Brewing Maibock
(Bayern Brewing)

Berghoff Famous Bock Beer (24 IBU)
(Joseph Huber Brewing Company, Inc.)

Bristol Brewing Edge City Pale Bock (31 IBU)
(Bristol Brewing Company)

Carolina Brewing Spring Bock
(Carolina Brewing)

Deschutes Broken Top Bock
(Deschutes Brewery)

Dragonmead Bishop Bob's Holy Smoke
(Dragonmead Microbrewery)

Dragonmead Bock Tubock
(Dragonmead Microbrewery)

Dragonmead Tayken Abock
(Dragonmead Microbrewery)

Erie Brewing Fallenbock (18 IBU)
(Erie Brewing)

Frankenmuth Winter Bock
(Frankenmuth Brewery)

Gluek Brewing Honey Bock
(Gluek Brewing Company)

Gluek Brewing Red Bock
(Gluek Brewing Company)

Golden Valley Geist Bock (35 IBU)
(Golden Valley Brewery)

Gordon Biersch Blonde Bock (23 IBU)
(Gordon Biersch Brewery)

Huber Bock Beer (23 IBU)
(Joseph Huber Brewing Company, Inc.)

Illuminator Dock Street Bock (27 SRM, 28 IBU)
(The Dock Street Brewery Company)

Indian Wells Lobotomy Bock
(Indian Wells Brewing)

Knuckleball Bock
(Stone Coast Brewing Company)

Lake Superior Brewing Split Rock Bock
(Lake Superior Brewing Company)

Lakefront Bock Beer (18 SRM, 24 IBU)
(Lakefront Brewery, Inc.)

Lancaster Brewing Spring Bock
(Lancaster Brewing Company)

Leavenworth Beers Spring Bock Lager
(Fish Brewing Company)

Michigan Brewing Celis Pale Bock
(Michigan Brewing Company, Inc.)

Millstream Brewing Schokolade Bock
(Millstream Brewing Company)

New Glarus Brewing Uff-da Bock
(New Glarus Brewing)

New Holland Blue Goat Doppelbock
(New Holland Brewing Company)

Nicolet Brewing Winter Fest Beer
(Nicolet Brewing)

Pandora's Bock
(Elysian Brewing Company)

Paper City Brewing Goats Peak Bock (20 IBU)
(Paper City Brewery Company)

Penn Oktoberfest
(Penn Brewery (Pennsylvania Brewing))

Penn St. Nikolaus Bock Bier
(Penn Brewery (Pennsylvania Brewing))

Pioneer Oderbolz Bock (12.9 SRM, 25 IBU)
(Sand Creek Brewing Company, LLC)

Point Spring Bock
(Stevens Point Brewery)

Rio Grande Brewing Elfego Bock (26 IBU)
(Rio Grande Brewing Company)

Rock Art Brewery Hell's Bock (75 IBU)
(Rock Art Brewery, LLC)

Saint Arnold Brewing Spring Bock (24 IBU)
(Saint Arnold Brewing Company)

Samuel Adams Chocolate Bock (75 SRM, 16 IBU)
(The Boston Beer Company)

Shiner Bock
(The Spoetzl Brewing (Gambrinus))

Siletz Brewing Company Wooly Bully (16.8 SRM, 38.2 IBU)
(Siletz Brewing Company, Inc.)

Southampton May Bock
(Southampton Publick House)

St. George Brewing Fall Bock (28 IBU)
(St.George Brewing Company)

Stegmaier Brewhouse Bock – *page 561*
(The Lion Brewery, Inc.)

Terre Haute Brewing Champagne Velvet Bock
(Terre Haute Brewing Company)

Thomas Creek Jingle Bell Bock (38.1 IBU)
(Thomas Creek Brewery)

Tommyknocker Butt Head Bock
(Tommyknocker Brewery)

Victory Moonglow Weizenbock (18-23 IBU)
(Victory Brewing Company)

Dark Lager

August Schell Brewing Caramel Bock (30.8 SRM, 17 IBU)
(August Schell Brewing Company)

August Schell Brewing Dark (23 SRM, 8 IBU)
(August Schell Brewing Company)

Barley Creek Angler Black Widow Lager
(Barley Creek Brewing Company)

Baron Schwarzbier (SRM 25, IBU 13)
(Baron Brewing)

Berghoff Genuine Dark Beer (21 IBU)
(Joseph Huber Brewing Company, Inc.)

Climax Hoffmann Bavarian Dark
(Climax Brewing Company)

Durango Brewing Dark Lager (17 IBU)
(Durango Brewing Company)

Fort Collins The Kidd Lager
(The Fort Collins Brewery)

Frankenmuth Mitternacht Munchner Dark Lager
(Frankenmuth Brewery)

Great Northern Brewing Fred's Black Lager (23 IBU)
(Great Northern Brewing Company)

Great Northern Brewing Snow Ghost (16 IBU)
(Great Northern Brewing Company)

Henry Weinhard's Classic Dark
(SAB Miller Corporation)

Leinenkugel's Creamy Dark
(Jacob Leinenkugel Brewing Company)

Mercury Brewing Stone Cat Winter Lager (35 IBU)
(Mercury Brewing Company)

Michelob AmberBock – *page 460*
(Anheuser-Busch, Inc.)

Nicolet Brewing Dark Pilsner
(Nicolet Brewing)

Penn Dark Lager
(Penn Brewery (Pennsylvania Brewing))

Pittsburgh Brewing Augustiner Dark
(Pittsburgh Brewing Company)

Rahr Brewing Ugly Pug (30 SRM, 24 IBU)
(Rahr & Sons Brewing Company)

Rock Art Brewery Trail Cutter Dark Lager (12 IBU)
(Rock Art Brewery, LLC)

Roslyn Brewing Roslyn Dark Lager Beer
(Roslyn Brewing Company)

Samuel Adams Black Lager (50 SRM, 19 IBU)
(The Boston Beer Company)

Saranac Black Forest
(The Matt Brewing)

Sly Fox Dunkel Lager (21 IBU)
(Sly Fox Brewing Company)

BEER STYLES INDEX Dark Lager (continued)

Sprecher Brewing Black Bavarian (32 IBU)
(Sprecher Brewing)

Viking Brewing Morketid
(Viking Brewing)

Weeping Radish Black Radish (22.6 SRM, 27 IBU) – *page 570*
(The Weeping Radish Brewery)

Doppelbock/Triplebock/Quadrupel

Atwater Voodoo Vator Dopplebock
(Atwater Block Brewery)

Back Road Brewery Aviator Dopplebock
(Back Road Brewery)

Baron Doppelbock
(Baron Brewing)

Baron Liberator Doppelbock (SRM 25, IBU 20)
(Baron Brewing)

Bayern Brewing Doppelbock
(Bayern Brewing)

Blue Ridge Subliminator Dopplebock
(Wild Goose Brewery, LLC)

Brew Masters' Private Reserve – *page 461*
(Anheuser-Busch, Inc.)

Capital Brewery Blonde Dopplelbock
(Capital Brewery Company, Inc.)

Christian Moerlein Doppelbock
(Christian Moerlein Brewing Company)

Dominion Spring Brew
(Old Dominion Brewing Company)

Elmwood Brewing Dopple Bock
(Elmwood Brewing Company)

Fish Tale Detonator Doppelbock Lager
(Fish Brewing Company)

Heiner Weihnachtsbock
(Heiner Brau)

Hoffmann Doppel Bock – *page 485*
(Climax Brewing Company)

King Annihilater Doppel Bock
(King Brewing Company)

Lancaster Brewing Doppel Bock
(Lancaster Brewing Company)

Left Hand Brewing Goosinator (27 IBU)
(Left Hand Brewing Company)

Left Hand Brewing Ryebock Lager (17 IBU)
(Left Hand Brewing Company)

Leinenkugel's Big Butt Doppelbock
(Jacob Leinenkugel Brewing Company)

Nicolet Brewing Prostrator Doppelbock
(Nicolet Brewing)

Oak Pond Brewing Storyteller Doppelbock
(Oak Pond Brewery)

Ramstein Winter Wheat ((70 SRM, 20 IBU)
(High Point Wheat Beer Company)

Rio Grande Brewing Bock Holiday (30 IBU)
(Rio Grande Brewing Company)

Samuel Adams Double Bock (38 SRM, 25 IBU)
(The Boston Beer Company)

Samuel Adams Triple Bock (200 SRM, 31 IBU)
(The Boston Beer Company)

Samuel Adams Utopias (34 SRM, 25 IBU)
(The Boston Beer Company)

Sly Fox Instigator Doppelbock (20 IBU)
(Sly Fox Brewing Company)

Sprecher Brewing Dopple Bock (31 IBU)
(Sprecher Brewing)

Sudwerk Doppelbock
(Sudwerk)

Thomas Creek Dopplebock (20.7 IBU)
(Thomas Creek Brewery)

Thomas Hooker Liberator Doppelbock (20.4 SRM, 27 IBU)
(Thomas Hooker Brewing Company)

Tröegs Brewing Troegenater Double Bock (25 IBU) – *page 566*
(Tröegs Brewing Company)

Two Brothers Incinerator Dopplebock (32 IBU)
(Two Brothers Brewing Company)

Tyranena Brewing Company Shantytown Doppelbock (28 SRM, 23 IBU)
(Tyranena Brewing Company)

Victory Victorious Doppelbock
(Victory Brewing Company)

Viking Brewing Invader
(Viking Brewing)

Wagner Valley Brewing Sled Dog Dopplebock
(Wagner Valley Brewing Company)

Fordham Brewing Copperhead Ale
(Fordham Brewing Company)

Golden City Red Ale
(Golden City Brewery)

Long Trail Ale (30 IBU) – *page 513*
(The Long Trail Brewing Company)

Sunday River Alt
(Stone Coast Brewing Company)

Tyranena Brewing Company Headless Man Amber Alt (14 SRM, 25 IBU)
(Tyranena Brewing Company)

Dry Lager

Bud Dry
(Anheuser-Busch, Inc.)

Dunkelweizen

Angel City Dunkel (24 SRM, 20 IBU)
(Angel City Brewing)

Baron Dunkel-Weisse
(Baron Brewing)

Elmwood Brewing Dunkle Weizen
(Elmwood Brewing Company)

Leavenworth Beers Blind Pig Dunkle Weizen Ale (25 IBU)
(Fish Brewing Company)

Ramstein Classic Wheat Beer (60 SRM, 12.5 IBU)
(High Point Wheat Beer Company)

Shiner Dunkelweizen
(The Spoetzl Brewing (Gambrinus))

Dusseldorf-Style Altbeir

August Schell Brewing Schmaltz's Alt (49 SRM, 21 IBU)
(August Schell Brewing Company)

Double Bag (25 IBU) – *page 514*
(The Long Trail Brewing Company)

Dragonmead Dragon Slayer Altbier Style
(Dragonmead Microbrewery)

Helles Bock/Maibock Pale Lager

Ambrosia Maibock
(Elysian Brewing Company)

Atwater Mai Bock
(Atwater Block Brewery)

August Schell Brewing Maifest (8.3 SRM, 25 IBU)
(August Schell Brewing Company)

Baron Helles Bock
(Baron Brewing)

Baron Munich Helles Lager
(Baron Brewing)

Berkshire Brewing Maibock Lager
(Berkshire Brewing Company)

Bourbon Street Bock
(Big Easy Brewing Company)

Capital Brewery Maibock
(Capital Brewery Company, Inc.)

Climax Hoffmann Helles
(Climax Brewing Company)

Dragonmead Tuhelles Enbock
(Dragonmead Microbrewery)

Edenton Brewing Helles Angel
(Edenton Brewing Company)

Erie Brewing Golden Fleece Maibock Lager (21 IBU)
(Erie Brewing)

Flying Dog Heller Hound Mai Bock (9 SRM, 26 IBU)
(Flying Dog Brewery, LLC)

Fordham Brewing Fordham Lager
(Fordham Brewing Company)

Gordon Biersch Maibock- Lager (Restaurants Only)
(Gordon Biersch Brewery)

Heiner Brau Maibock
(Heiner Brau)

Lakefront Big Easy Beer (6 SRM, 24 IBU)
(Lakefront Brewery, Inc.)

Millstream Brewing Maifest
(Millstream Brewing Company)

Paper City Brewing Summer Brew
(Paper City Brewery Company)

Penn Maibock
(Penn Brewery (Pennsylvania Brewing))

Rahr Brewing Bucking Bock - Miabock (10 SRM, 30 IBU)
(Rahr & Sons Brewing Company)

Ramstein Maibock Lager Beer (37 IBU)
(High Point Wheat Beer Company)

Rogue Dead Guy Ale (40 IBU) – *page 537*
(Rogue Ales)

Scuttlebutt Weizenbock (23 IBU)
(Scuttlebutt Brewing Company)

Smuttynose Brewing Maibock
(Smuttynose Brewing Company)

Sprecher Brewing Mai Bock (24 IBU)
(Sprecher Brewing)

Stoudt's Blonde Double Maibock (35 IBU)
(Stoudt's Brewing Company)

Stoudt's Gold Lager (25 IBU)
(Stoudt's Brewing Company)

Summit Maibock (10 SRM, 30 IBU)
(Summit Brewing Company)

Tyranena Brewing Company Fighting Finches Mai Bock (10 SRM, 25 IBU)
(Tyranena Brewing Company)

Upland Brewing Company Maibock
(Upland Brewing Company)

Victory St. Boisterous (20-25 IBU)
(Victory Brewing Company)

Viking Brewing J.S. Bock
(Viking Brewing)

Weeping Radish Corolla Gold (4.6 SRM, 15.2 IBU)
(The Weeping Radish Brewery)

Weeping Radish Maibock (9.4 SRM, 31.5 IBU)
(The Weeping Radish Brewery)

Ice Lager

Bud Ice
(Anheuser-Busch, Inc.)

Busch Ice
(Anheuser-Busch, Inc.)

Hurricane Ice
(Anheuser-Busch, Inc.)

Natural Ice
(Anheuser-Busch, Inc.)

Genesee Ice
(High Falls Brewing)

Gluek Ice
(Gluek Brewing Company)

Gluek Northern Reserve Ice Lager
(Gluek Brewing Company)

Keystone Ice
(Molson Coors Brewing Company)

Mickey's Ice
(SAB Miller Corporation)

Milwaukee's Best Ice
(SAB Miller Corporation)

Old Milwaukee Ice
(Pabst Brewing Company)

Pittsburgh Brewing American Ice
(Pittsburgh Brewing Company)

Schmidt's Ice
(Pabst Brewing Company)

Lager

Abita Brewing Amber
(Abita Brewing Company)

Abita Brewing Golden
(Abita Brewing Company)

Angel City Lager (3.5 SRM, 20 IBU)
(Angel City Brewing)

Appalachian Brewing Mountain Lager
(Appalachian Brewing Company)

Atwater Hell Pale Lager
(Atwater Block Brewery)

August Schell Brewing Original (2.8 SRM, 12.5 IBU)
(August Schell Brewing Company)

Bayhawk Ales O.C. Lager (14 IBU)
(Bayhawk Ales, Inc.)

Beachside American Lager
(Florida Beer Company)

Berghoff Original Lager Beer (20 IBU)
(Joseph Huber Brewing Company, Inc.)

Berghoff Solstice Wit Beer (11 IBU)
(Joseph Huber Brewing Company, Inc.)

Blatz
(Pabst Brewing Company)

Blue & Gray Classic Lager
(Blue & Gray Brewing Company, Inc.)

Blue Point Brewing Toasted Lager (28 IBU) – *page 471*
(Blue Point Brewing Company)

Blue Ridge Amber Lager
(Wild Goose Brewery, LLC)

Bootie Beer
(Bootie Beer Company)

Buckeye Brewing Cleveland Lager
(Buckeye Brewing)

Budweiser
(Anheuser-Busch, Inc.)

Busch
(Anheuser-Busch, Inc.)

Cancun
(Zuma Brewing Company)

Cape Ann Brewing Fisherman's Brew (30 IBU)
(Cape Ann Brewing)

Capital Brewery Bavarian Lager
(Capital Brewery Company, Inc.)

Carling Black Label
(Pabst Brewing Company)

Chelada Bud
(Anheuser-Busch, Inc.)

Christian Moerlein Select Lager
(Christian Moerlein Brewing Company)

Cisco Brewers Summer of Lager
(Cisco Brewers, Inc.)

City Lager
(City Brewery)

Clipper City McHenry Old Baltimore Style Beer
(Clipper City Brewing Company)

Coffaro Italian Style Beer
(Coffaro Beer Company)

Coors
(Molson Coors Brewing Company)

Coors Extra Gold
(Molson Coors Brewing Company)

Cricket Hill Brewing East Coast Lager – *page 488*
(Cricket Hill Brewing Company)

Crooked River Select Lager
(Wild Goose Brewery, LLC)

Dave's Electric Beer
(Electric Beer Company)

Defiant Brewing Pearl River Lager
(The Defiant Brewing Company)

Diamond Bear Southern Blonde (28 IBU)
(Diamond Bear Brewing Company)

Dixie Brewing Blackened Voodoo Lager
(Dixie Brewing Company)

Dixie Brewing Dixie Beer
(Dixie Brewing Company)

Dragonmead Drei Kronen 1308
(Dragonmead Microbrewery)

Dragonmead Tafelbeir Lager
(Dragonmead Microbrewery)

Ellicottville Brewing Toasted Lager
(Ellicottville Brewing Company)

Esquire Extra Premium
(Jones Brewing Company)

Estes Park Staggering Elk
(Estes Park Brewery)

Firestone Walker Lager (4 SRM, 24 IBU)
(Firestone Walker Brewing Company)

Flying Bison Brewing Buffalo Lager
(Flying Bison Brewing Company)

Flying Dog Tire Bite Golden Ale (4 SRM, 17.5 IBU)
(Flying Dog Brewery, LLC)

Fort Collins Z Lager
(The Fort Collins Brewery)

Full Sail Brewing Session Premium Lager
(Full Sail Brewing Company)

Genesee Beer
(High Falls Brewing)

George Killian's Irish Red Lager
(Molson Coors Brewing Company)

Gluek Northern Golden Lager
(Gluek Brewing Company)

Gluek Stite Golden Lager – *page 504*
(Gluek Brewing Company)

Great Lakes Brewing Dortmunder Golden Lager (30 IBU) – *page 505*
(Great Lakes Brewing Company)

Great Northern Brewing Big Fog Amber Lager (43 IBU)
(Great Northern Brewing Company)

Great Northern Brewing Fred's Black Lager (23 IBU)
(Great Northern Brewing Company)

Great Northern Brewing Hellroaring Amber Lager (19 IBU)
(Great Northern Brewing Company)

Great Northern Brewing Snow Ghost Winter Lager (15 IBU)
(Great Northern Brewing Company)

Great Northern Brewing Wild Huckleberry Wheat Lager (12 IBU)
(Great Northern Brewing Company)

Great Northern Brewing Wild Huckleberry Wheat Lager (12 IBU)
(Great Northern Brewing Company)

Hamm's
(SAB Miller Corporation)

Heiner Brau Kellerbier
(Heiner Brau)

Henry Weinhard's Northwest Trail Blonde Lager
(SAB Miller Corporation)

Henry Weinhard's Private Reserve
(SAB Miller Corporation)

Huber Premium Beer (14 IBU)
(Joseph Huber Brewing Company, Inc.)

Huebert Brewing Huebert's Old Tyme Lager
(Huebert Brewing)

Hurricane Reef Lager
(Florida Beer Company)

Icehouse
(SAB Miller Corporation)

Icehouse 5.0
(SAB Miller Corporation)

Indian Wells Mojave Red
(Indian Wells Brewing)

Island Brewing Tropical Lager
(Island Brewing Company)

Jack's Huntsmans Lager
(Jack Russell Brewing)

Joseph Huber Brewing Wisconsin Club
(Joseph Huber Brewing Company, Inc.)

JW DunDee's American Amber Lager
(High Falls Brewing)

JW DunDee's Honey Brown Lager
(High Falls Brewing)

Karl Strauss Brewing Amber Lager (15 SRM, 15 IBU) – *page 509*
(Karl Strauss Breweries)

Key West Golden Lager
(Florida Beer Company)

Keystone
(Molson Coors Brewing Company)

King Continental Lager
(King Brewing Company)

King Loranger Lager
(King Brewing Company)

Kona Brewing Longboard Island Lager (6 SRM, 25 IBU)
(Kona Brewing LLC)

LaCrosse Lager
(City Brewery)

Land Shark Lager
(Anheuser-Busch, Inc.)

Legend Brewing Lager
(Legend Brewing Company)

Leinenkugel's Original
(Jacob Leinenkugel Brewing Company)

Lewis & Clark Lager
(Lewis & Clark Brewing)

Lionshead
(Lion Brewery)

Loki Lager
(Elysian Brewing Company)

Lone Star
(Pabst Brewing Company)

Mad Anthony Gabby Blonde Lager
(Mad Anthony Brewing Company)

Magic Hat Brewing Mother Lager (3.2 SRM, 17 IBU)
(Magic Hat Brewing Company)

Mehana Brewing Hawaii Lager
(Mehana Brewing Company, Inc.)

Mendocino Brewing Red Tail Lager
(Mendocino Brewing Company)

Michelob
(Anheuser-Busch, Inc.)

Michelob Golden Draft
(Anheuser-Busch, Inc.)

Miller Geniune Draft
(SAB Miller Corporation)

Miller High Life
(SAB Miller Corporation)

Milwaukee's Best
(SAB Miller Corporation)

Mississippi Mud Lager
(Mississippi Brewing Company)

Narragansett Beer
(The Narragansett Brewing Company)

National Bohemian
(Pabst Brewing Company)

New Glarus Brewing Totally Naked
(New Glarus Brewing)

New Glarus Brewing Yokel
(New Glarus Brewing)

New South Lager
(New South Brewing Company (Kegs/ Growlers))

New South Oktoberfest
(New South Brewing Company (Kegs/ Growlers))

Nicolet Brewing Blonde
(Nicolet Brewing)

Oak Creek Golden Lager
(Oak Creek Brewing Company)

Old German
(Latrobe Brewing)

Old Milwaukee
(Pabst Brewing Company)

Old Style
(Pabst Brewing Company)

Olde Saratoga Brewing Saratoga Lager
(Olde Saratoga Brewing Company)

Olympia
(Pabst Brewing Company)

Pabst Blue Ribbon
(Pabst Brewing Company)

Palmetto Brewing Amber Lager
(Palmetto Brewing Company, Inc.)

Palmetto Brewing Lager
(Palmetto Brewing Company, Inc.)

Paper City Brewing 1 Eared Monkey
(Paper City Brewery Company)

Paper City Brewing Denogginator
(Paper City Brewery Company)

Paper City Brewing Dorado
(Paper City Brewery Company)

Paper City Brewing Golden Lager
(Paper City Brewery Company)

Paper City Brewing P.C. Blue
(Paper City Brewery Company)

Paper City Brewing Red Hat Razzberry
(Paper City Brewery Company)

Pearl
(Pabst Brewing Company)

Penn Crew Lager
(Penn Brewery (Pennsylvania Brewing))

Peroni Nastro Azzurro
(SAB Miller Corporation)

Piels
(Pabst Brewing Company)

Pilsner Urquell
(SAB Miller Corporation)

Pittsburgh Brewing American
(Pittsburgh Brewing Company)

Pittsburgh Brewing Augustiner Amber Lager
(Pittsburgh Brewing Company)

Pittsburgh Brewing Iron City Beer Premium Lager
(Pittsburgh Brewing Company)

Pittsburgh Brewing Old German
(Pittsburgh Brewing Company)

Point Special Lager
(Stevens Point Brewery)

Pony Express Gold Beer
(Pony Express Brewing Company)

Rahr Brewing Blonde Lager (3 SRM, 19 IBU)
(Rahr & Sons Brewing Company)

Rainer
(Pabst Brewing Company)

Ramstein Golden Lager (6 SRM, 22 IBU)
(High Point Wheat Beer Company)

Red Dog
(SAB Miller Corporation)

Rheingold Beer
(Rheingold Brewing Company)

Rhinelander (13 IBU)
(Joseph Huber Brewing Company, Inc.)

River Horse Lager
(River Horse Brewing Company)

Rogue Kells Irish Lager (28 IBU)
(Rogue Ales)

Rolling Rock Extra Pale
(Anheuser-Busch, Inc.)

Roslyn Brewing Brookside Pale Lager
(Roslyn Brewing Company)

Samuel Adams Boston Lager (11 SRM, 30 IBU) – *page 473*
(The Boston Beer Company)

Saranac Lager
(The Matt Brewing)

Schaefer
(Pabst Brewing Company)

Schlitz
(Pabst Brewing Company)

Schmidt's
(Pabst Brewing Company)

Sebago Brewing Northern Light Ale
(Sebago Brewing Company)

Sierra Nevada Summerfest (6 SRM, 30 IBU)
(Sierra Nevada Brewing Company)

Siletz Brewing Company Lovin Lager (11.6 SRM, 34.3 IBU)
(Siletz Brewing Company, Inc.)

Ska Brewing Mexican Logger
(Ska Brewing Company)

Special Export
(Pabst Brewing Company)

Springfield Brewing Munich Lager (23 IBU)
(Springfield Brewing Company)

St.Ides
(Pabst Brewing Company)

Stag
(Pabst Brewing Company)

Starr Hill Jomo Lager
(Starr Hill Brewery)

Steam Engine Lager (12.3 SRM, 21.9 IBU)
(Steamworks Brewing Company)

Stegmaier 1857 American Lager
(The Lion Brewery, Inc.)

Stegmaier Gold Medal
(The Lion Brewery Inc.)

Steinlager
(High Falls Brewing)

Stoney's Beer
(Jones Brewing Company)

Stoney's Harvest Gold
(Jones Brewing Company)

Straub
(Straub Brewing)

Stroh's
(Pabst Brewing Company)

Sudwerk Lager
(Sudwerk)

Sunday River Lager
(Stone Coast Brewing Company)

Thirsty Dog Balto Heroic Lager (17 IBU)
(Thirsty Dog Brewing Company)

Thomas Hooker Munich Golden Lager (3 SRM, 15 IBU)
(Thomas Hooker Brewing Company)

Tiger Town Beer
(Big Easy Brewing Company)

Tommyknocker Alpine Glacier Lager
(Tommyknocker Brewery)

Tommyknocker Ornery Amber Lager
(Tommyknocker Brewery)

Two Brothers Dog Days Dortmunder Style Lager (May-August)
(Two Brothers Brewing Company)

Uinta Brewing Gelande Amber Lager
(Uinta Brewing Company)

Victory Lager (17-22 IBU)
(Victory Brewing Company)

Victory St. Victorious (20-25 IBU)
(Victory Brewing Company)

Waimea Brewing Luau Lager (20 IBU)
(Waimea Brewing Company)

Wasatch 1st Amendment Lager
(Utah Brewers Cooperative/ Wasatch)

Wiedenmayer Jersey Lager
(Wiedenmayer Brewing Company)

Wild Hop Lager – *page 457*
(Anheuser-Busch, Inc.)

Wild Hop Organic Lager
(Anheuser-Busch, Inc.)

Yuengling Premium Beer
(D.G. Yuengling & Son, Inc.)

Light Lager

Abita Light
(Abita Brewing Company)

August Schell Brewing Light (2.2 SRM, 8 IBU)
(August Schell Brewing Company)

Beachside Sun Light
(Florida Beer Company)

Beermann's Lincoln Lager - Helles Lager
(Beermann's Beerwerks)

Bootie Light
(Bootie Beer Company)

Bud Ice Light
(Anheuser-Busch, Inc.)

Bud Light
(Anheuser-Busch, Inc.)

Budweiser Select
(Anheuser-Busch, Inc.)

Busch Light
(Anheuser-Busch, Inc.)

Carolina Beer Carolina Light
(Carolina Beer & Beverage Company)

Chelada Bud Light
(Anheuser-Busch, Inc.)

Christian Moerlein Select Light
(Christian Moerlein Brewing Company)

City Light
(City Brewery)

Coors Light
(Molson Coors Brewing Company)

Dixie Brewing Jazz Amber Light
(Dixie Brewing Company)

Edison The Independent Light Beer – *page 522*
(New Century Brewing Company)

Engineer Light Lager (4 SRM, 21.5 IBU)
(Steamworks Brewing Company)

Fordham Brewing C126 Light
(Fordham Brewing Company)

Frankenmuth Mel-O-Dry Light Lager
(Frankenmuth Brewery)

Genny Light
(High Falls Brewing)

Gluek Golden Light
(Gluek Brewing Company)

Gluek Northern Reserve Low Carb Light
(Gluek Brewing Company)

Hamm's Special Light
(SAB Miller Corporation)

Huber Light Beer (7 IBU)
(Joseph Huber Brewing Company, Inc.)

Icehouse Light
(SAB Miller Corporation)

Indian Wells Mojave Silver
(Indian Wells Brewing)

Jack Russell's All American Premium Lager
(Jack Russell Brewing)

Karl Strauss Brewing Endless Summer Light (6 SRM, 15 IBU)
(Karl Strauss Breweries)

Keystone Light
(Molson Coors Brewing Company)

KUL Lite
(City Brewery)

LaCrosse Light
(City Brewery)

Leinenkugel's Light
(Jacob Leinenkugel Brewing Company)

Lion Brewing Pocono Light
(Lion Brewery)

Lone Star Light
(Pabst Brewing Company)

Michelob Golden Draft Light
(Anheuser-Busch, Inc.)

Michelob Light
(Anheuser-Busch, Inc.)

Michelob Ultra
(Anheuser-Busch, Inc.)

Michelob Ultra Amber
(Anheuser-Busch, Inc.)

Miller Geniune Draft Light
(SAB Miller Corporation)

Miller High Life Light
(SAB Miller Corporation)

Miller Lite
(SAB Miller Corporation)

Milwaukee's Best Light
(SAB Miller Corporation)

Natural Light
(Anheuser-Busch, Inc.)

Old Milwaukee Light
(Pabst Brewing Company)

Old Style Light
(Pabst Brewing Company)

Pabst Blue Ribbon Light
(Pabst Brewing Company)

Piels Light
(Pabst Brewing Company)

Pittsburgh Brewing American Light
(Pittsburgh Brewing Company)

Pittsburgh Brewing IC Light
(Pittsburgh Brewing Company)

Point Honey Light
(Stevens Point Brewery)

Point Premier Light
(Stevens Point Brewery)

Rainer Light
(Pabst Brewing Company)

Red Bell Brewing Philadelphia Original Light Lager
(Red Bell Brewery & Pub)

Rhinelander Light (8.5 IBU)
(Joseph Huber Brewing Company, Inc.)

Rock Green Light
(Anheuser-Busch, Inc.)

Rocky Bay Brewing Schooner Point Lager
(Rocky Bay Brewing Company)

Sam Adams Light (11 SRM, 10 IBU) – *page 474*
(The Boston Beer Company)

Schmidt's Light
(Pabst Brewing Company)

Shipyard Brewing Light
(Shipyard Brewing Company)

Southpaw Light
(SAB Miller Corporation)

Special Export Light
(Pabst Brewing Company)

Stampede Light
(Stampde Brewing Company)

Stoney's Light
(Jones Brewing Company)

Straub Light
(Straub Brewing)

Stroh's Light
(Pabst Brewing Company)

Weeping Radish Corolla Light (2.7 SRM, 11.8 IBU)
(The Weeping Radish Brewery)

Ybor Gold Light
(Florida Beer Company)

Yuengling Light Beer
(D.G. Yuengling & Son, Inc.)

Yuengling Light Lager
(D.G. Yuengling & Son, Inc.)

Munich Dunkel

Atwater Dunkel Dark Lager
(Atwater Block Brewery)

Bayern Brewing Schwarzbier
(Bayern Brewing)

Capital Brewery Munich Dark
(Capital Brewery Company, Inc.)

Christian Moerlein Select Dunkel
(Christian Moerlein Brewing Company)

Church Brew Works Pious Monk Dunkel (20 IBU)
(The Church Brew Works)

Harpoon Munich Dark (35 IBU)
(Harpoon Brewery)

Lakefront Eastside Dark (22 SRM, 15 IBU)
(Lakefront Brewery, Inc.)

Northern Lights Chocolate Dunkel
(The Northern Lights Brewing Company)

Oak Pond Brewing Laughing Loon Lager
(Oak Pond Brewery)

Penn Gold
(Penn Brewery (Pennsylvania Brewing))

Saranac Season's Best
(The Matt Brewing)

Oktoberfest/Marzen

Abita Fall Fest
(Abita Brewing Company)

Appalachian Brewing Kipona Fest Lager
(Appalachian Brewing Company)

Atwater Bloktoberfest
(Atwater Block Brewery)

August Schell Brewing Octoberfest (14 SRM, 20 IBU)
(August Schell Brewing Company)

Avery Brewing The Kaiser Imperial Oktoberfest (24 IBU)
(Avery Brewing Company)

Back Road Brewery Maple Gold City
(Back Road Brewery)

Barley Creek Harvest Moon Oktoberfest
(Barley Creek Brewing Company)

Baron Oktoberfest (SRM 13, IBU 15)
(Baron Brewing)

Bayern Brewing Oktoberfest
(Bayern Brewing)

Berghoff Oktoberfest Beer (21 IBU)
(Joseph Huber Brewing Company, Inc.)

Berkshire Brewing Ocktoberfest Lager
(Berkshire Brewing Company)

Blue Point Brewing Octoberfest (28 IBU)
(Blue Point Brewing)

Bristol Brewing Edge City Octoberfest (24 IBU)
(Bristol Brewing Company)

Brooklyn Oktoberfest (20 IBU)
(Brooklyn Brewery)

Buckeye Brewing Martian Marzen Lager
(Buckeye Brewing)

Capital Brewery Autumnal Fire
(Capital Brewery Company, Inc.)

Capital Brewery Oktoberfest
(Capital Brewery Company, Inc.)

Carolina Brewing Oktoberfest Lager
(Carolina Brewing)

Central Waters Reserve Oktoberfest
(Central Waters Brewing Company)

Christian Moerlein Oktoberfest
(Christian Moerlein Brewing Company)

City Festbier
(City Brewery)

Climax Hoffmann Oktoberfest
(Climax Brewing Company)

Clipper City BaltoMärzHon
(Clipper City Brewing Company)

Diamond Bear Rocktoberfest (32 IBU)
(Diamond Bear Brewing Company)

Dick's Harvest Ale
(Dick's Brewing Company)

Dominion Octoberfest
(Old Dominion Brewing Company)

Dragonmead Oktoberfest Marzen
(Dragonmead Microbrewery)

E.J. Phair Marzen
(E.J. Phair Brewing)

Elmwood Brewing Oktoberfest
(Elmwood Brewing Company)

Flying Dog Dogtoberfest (20 SRM, 30 IBU)
(Flying Dog Brewery, LLC)

Flying Fish Brewing Oktoberfish
(Flying Fish Brewing)

Frankenmuth Oktoberfest
(Frankenmuth Brewery)

Glacier Brewing Select Oktoberfest (16.2 SRM, 4.4 IBU) – *page 503*
(Glacier Brewing)

Gluek Stite Amber Red Reserve
(Gluek Brewing Company)

Goose Island Oktoberfest (15 SRM, 25 IBU)
(Goose Island Beer Company)

Gordon Biersch Festbier (Restaurants Only)
(Gordon Biersch Brewery)

Gordon Biersch Marzen (18 IBU)
(Gordon Biersch Brewery)

Harpoon Octoberfest (30 IBU)
(Harpoon Brewery)

Harvest Moon Festbier (24 IBU)
(Snoqualmie Falls Brewing Company)

Heiner Brau Maerzen
(Heiner Brau)

Heiner Brau Mardi Gras Festbier
(Heiner Brau)

Heiner Brau Octoberfest Bier
(Heiner Brau)

Heinzelmannchen Oktoberfest
(Heinzelmannchen Brewery (Kegs/ Growlers))

Indian Wells Oktoberfest
(Indian Wells Brewing)

Karl Strauss Brewing Oktoberfest (9 SRM, 27 IBU)
(Karl Strauss Breweries)

King Festbier
(King Brewing Company)

Lake Superior Brewing Oktoberfest
(Lake Superior Brewing Company)

Lakefront Oktoberfest (10 SRM, 24 IBU)
(Lakefront Brewery, Inc.)

Lancaster Brewing Oktoberfest
(Lancaster Brewing Company)

Leavenworth Beers Oktoberfest Bier
(Fish Brewing Company)

Legend Brewing Legend Oktoberfest (25 IBU)
(Legend Brewing Company)

Leinenkugel's Oktoberfest
(Jacob Leinenkugel Brewing Company)

Mercury Brewing Stone Cat Octoberfest (24 IBU)
(Mercury Brewing Company)

Michelob Marzen
(Anheuser-Busch, Inc.)

Millstream Brewing Oktoberfest
(Millstream Brewing Company)

Newport Storm Regenschauer Oktoberfest (14 SRM, 17 IBU)
(Coastal Extreme Brewing Company, LLC)

Nicolet Brewing Oktoberfest
(Nicolet Brewing)

Oak Pond Brewing Oktoberfest
(Oak Pond Brewery)

Paper City Brewing Summit House Oktoberfest (23 IBU)
(Paper City Brewery Company)

Penn Marzen
(Penn Brewery (Pennsylvania Brewing))

Pioneer Black River Red (23 SRM, 25 IBU)
(Sand Creek Brewing Company, LLC)

Ramapo Valley Brewery Octoberfest
(Ramapo Valley Brewery)

Rocky Bay Brewing Seasider Oktoberfest
(Rocky Bay Brewing Company)

Saint Arnold Brewing Oktoberfest (24 IBU)
(Saint Arnold Brewing Company)

Samuel Adams Octoberfest (20 SRM, 17 IBU) – *page 474*
(The Boston Beer Company)

Saranac Octoberfest
(The Matt Brewing)

Shiner 96 Marzen Style Ale
(The Spoetzl Brewing (Gambrinus))

Sly Fox Oktoberfest (25 IBU)
(Sly Fox Brewing Company)

Smuttynose Brewing Octoberfest
(Smuttynose Brewing Company)

Sprecher Brewing Oktoberfest (15 IBU)
(Sprecher Brewing)

Stegmaier Oktoberfest
(The Lion Brewery, Inc.)

Stoudt's Oktoberfest (24 IBU)
(Stoudt's Brewing Company)

Sudwerk Marzen
(Sudwerk)

Summit Oktoberfest (14 SRM, 25 IBU)
(Summit Brewing Company)

Thomas Creek Octoberfest (18.9 IBU)
(Thomas Creek Brewery)

Thomas Hooker Octoberfest (10SRM, 11 IBU)
(Thomas Hooker Brewing Company)

Tyranena Brewing Company Gemuetlichkeit Oktoberfest (13 SRM, 22 IBU)
(Tyranena Brewing Company)

Victory Festbier (15-20 IBU)
(Victory Brewing Company)

Viking Brewing Copperhead
(Viking Brewing)

Viking Brewing Rauch
(Viking Brewing)

Von Steuben Oktoberfest (Sept. - Oct)
(Blue & Gray Brewing Company, Inc.)

Weeping Radish Marzen (11.2 SRM, 28.4 IBU)
(The Weeping Radish Brewery)

Weyerbacher Brewing Autumn Fest
(Weyerbacher Brewing Company)

Widmer Brothers Brewing Company OKTO (22 SRM, 25 IBU)
(Widmer Brothers Brewing Company)

Pilsner

Abita Brewing 20th Anniversary Pilsner
(Abita Brewing Company)

Angel City Pilz (3.5 SRM, 22 IBU)
(Angel City Brewing)

Anheuser World Lager
(Anheuser-Busch, Inc.)

Appalachian Brewing Peregrine Pilsner
(Appalachian Brewing Company)

Atwater Pilsner
(Atwater Block Brewery)

BEER STYLES INDEX

August Schell Brewing Pilsner (3.1 SRM, 27 IBU)
(August Schell Brewing Company)

Back Road Brewery Millennium Lager
(Back Road Brewery)

Backcountry Brewery Ptarmigan Pilsner (3.1 SRM, 42 IBU)
(Backcountry Brewery)

Baron Pils (SRM 2.5, IBU 35)
(Baron Brewing)

Bayern Brewing Pilsner
(Bayern Brewing)

Berghoff Classic Pilsner (10 IBU)
(Joseph Huber Brewing Company, Inc.)

Brooklyn Pilsner (30 IBU)
(Brooklyn Brewery)

Buckeye Brewing Czech Pilsner
(Buckeye Brewing)

Butte Creek Organic Pilsner
(Butte Creek Brewing)

Butte Creek Summer Pilsner
(Butte Creek Brewing)

Buzzards Bay Brewing Lager (35 IBU)
(Buzzards Bay Brewing Company)

Capital Brewery Special Pilsner
(Capital Brewery Company, Inc.)

Defiant Brewing Pilsner
(The Defiant Brewing Company)

Dogfish Head Golden Shower Imperial Pilsner (80 IBU)
(Dogfish Head Craft Brewery)

Dragonmead Squire Pilsen
(Dragonmead Microbrewery)

E.J. Phair Pilsner
(E.J. Phair Brewing)

Erie Brewing Presque Isle Pilsner (18 IBU)
(Erie Brewing)

Farmhouse Hayloft Pils
(Farmhouse Brewing Company)

Frankenmuth German Style Pilsner
(Frankenmuth Brewery)

Glacier Brewing Port Polson Pilsner (3.5 SRM, 13.1 IBU)
(Glacier Brewing)

Gluek Stite Golden Pilsner
(Gluek Brewing Company)

Golden Valley Red Hills Pilsner (38 IBU)
(Golden Valley Brewery)

Gordon Biersch Pilsner (28 IBU)
(Gordon Biersch Brewery)

Grand Teton Paradise Pilsner
(Grand Teton Brewing Company)

Great Northern Brewing Buckin' Horse Pilsner (32 IBU)
(Great Northern Brewing Company)

Heavy Seas Brewing Small Craft Warning Über Pils
(Clipper City Brewing Company)

Heinzelmannchen Gopher Ale
(Heinzelmannchen Brewery (Kegs/ Growlers))

Hudepohl 14 – K
(Wild Goose Brewery, LLC)

Hurricane Reef Caribbean Pilsner
(Florida Beer Company)

Hyland's Sturbridge Farmhand Ale
(Pioneer Brewing Company)

Indian Wells Eastern Sierra Lager
(Indian Wells Brewing)

Josef Bierbitzch Golden Pilsner
(The Academy of Fine Beers, LLC)

Karl Strauss Brewing Woodie Gold (5 SRM, 18 IBU)
(Karl Strauss Breweries)

KUL
(City Brewery)

La Tropical
(Florida Beer Company)

Lagunitas Brewing Czech Style Pilsner
(Lagunitas Brewing)

Lakefront Klisch Pilsner (4 SRM, 32 IBU)
(Lakefront Brewery, Inc.)

Lancaster Brewing Gold Star Pilsner (IBU)
(Lancaster Brewing Company)

Latrobe Pilsner
(Latrobe Brewing)

Leavenworth Beers Friesian Pilsner (40 IBU)
(Fish Brewing Company)

Left Hand Brewing Polestar Pilsner (33 IBU)
(Left Hand Brewing Company)

Legend Brewing Pilsner (40 IBU)
(Legend Brewing Company)

Michigan Brewing Petoskey Pilsner
(Michigan Brewing Company, Inc.)

Millstream Brewing German Pilsner
(Millstream Brewing Company)

Nashoba Valley Brewery Bolt 117 Lager (25 IBU)
(Nashoba Valley Brewery)

New Belgium Blue Paddle Pilsner (4.8 SRM, 32.5 IBU)
(New Belgium Brewing Company)

New England Brewing Elm City Lager
(New England Brewing Company)

Nicolet Brewing Classic Pilsner
(Nicolet Brewing)

North Coast Scrimshaw Pilsner Style Beer (22 IBU)
(North Coast Brewing Company)

Odell Brewing Double Pilsner
(Odell Brewing Company)

Otter Creek Brewing Vermont Lager (26 IBU)
(Otter Creek Brewing Company)

Penn Kaiser Pils
(Penn Brewery (Pennsylvania Brewing))

Penn Pilsner
(Penn Brewery (Pennsylvania Brewing)) – *page 528*

Pig's Eye Pilsner
(Pig's Eye Brewing Company)

Rahr Brewing Pecker Wrecker Imperial Pilsner (8 SRM, 62 IBU)
(Rahr & Sons Brewing Company)

Rio Grande Brewing Desert Pils (24 IBU)
(Rio Grande Brewing Company)

Rogue Morimoto Imperial Pilsner (74 IBU)
(Rogue Ales)

Rogue Uberfest Pilsner (35 IBU)
(Rogue Ales)

Saint Arnold Brewing Summer Pils (41 IBU)
(Saint Arnold Brewing Company)

Samuel Adams Imperial Pilsner (20 SRM, 110 IBU)
(The Boston Beer Company)

Shorts Brew The Curl (50 IBU)
(Short's Brewing Company)

Sierra Blanca Brewing Pilsner
(Sierra Blanca Brewing Company)

Silver Gulch Coldfoot Pilsner Lager (22 IBU)
(Silver Gulch Brewing & Bottling)

Sly Fox Pikeland Pils (44 IBU)
(Sly Fox Brewing Company)

Smuttynose Brewing Portsmouth Lager (15 IBU)
(Smuttynose Brewing Company)

South Shore Brewery Honey Pils
(South Shore Brewery)

Squatters Provo Girl Pilsner
(Utah Brewers Cooperative/ Wasatch)

Stoudt's Pils (40 IBU)
(Stoudt's Brewing Company)

Sudwerk Pilsner
(Sudwerk)

Summer Beer (28 IBU)
(Snoqualmie Falls Brewing Company)

Summit Grand Pilsner (5 SRM, 25 IBU) – *page 558*
(Summit Brewing Company)

Terrapin All American Imperial Pilsner (75 IBU)
(Terrapin Beer Company)

Terre Haute Brewing Champagne Velvet Pilsner
(Terre Haute Brewing Company)

Thomas Creek Pilsner (18.2 IBU)
(Thomas Creek Brewery)

Tröegs Brewing Sunshine Pils (45 IBU)
(Tröegs Brewing Company)

Tuppers' Hop Pocket Pils
(Old Dominion Brewing Company)

Uinta Brewing Club Pils Pilsner
(Uinta Brewing Company)

Victory Prima Pils (40-50 IBU)
(Victory Brewing Company)

Viking Brewing Blonde
(Viking Brewing)

Viking Brewing Sylvan Springs
(Viking Brewing)

Wagner Valley Brewing Mill Street Pilsner
(Wagner Valley Brewing Company)

Woodstock Pilsner (2.4 SRM, 18.2 IBU)
(Woodstock Beer)

Pilsner Light

Diamond Bear Ultra Blonde (18 IBU)
(Diamond Bear Brewing Company)

Gluek Stite Light Lager
(Gluek Brewing Company)

Key West Pilsner Light
(Florida Beer Company)

Pig's Eye Lean
(Pig's Eye Brewing Company)

Specialty Beer

Dominion Winter Brew
(Old Dominion Brewing Company)

Michelob Celebrate Chocolate – *page 461*
(Anheuser-Busch, Inc.)

Michelob Celebrate Vanilla Oak
(Anheuser-Busch, Inc.)

Michelob Honey Lager – *page 460*
(Anheuser-Busch, Inc.)

Newport Storm Annual Limited Release
(Coastal Extreme Brewing Company, LLC)

Saranac Trail Mix
(The Matt Brewing)

The Raven Christmas Lager
(B.W. Beer Works USA)

The Raven Special Lager
(B.W. Beer Works USA)

Vienna-Style Lager

August Schell Brewing FireBrick (15.2 SRM, 23 IBU)
(August Schell Brewing Company)

Buzzards Bay Brewing Octoberfest
(Buzzards Bay Brewing Company)

DAM DAM Straight Lager
(Dillion DAM Brewery)

Indian Wells Springfest Lager
(Indian Wells Brewing)

Lancaster Brewing Franklinfest Lager 17 IBU)
(Lancaster Brewing Company)

Leinenkugel's Red Lager
(Jacob Leinenkugel Brewing Company)

Millstream Brewing Schild Brau Amber
(Millstream Brewing Company)

Morena
(Zuma Brewing Company)

Pioneer Lager (12 SRM, 15 IBU)
(Sand Creek Brewing Company, LLC)

Rahr Brewing Buffalo Batt Beer (20 SRM, 24 IBU)
(Rahr & Sons Brewing Company)

Ruby Mountain Brewing Vienna Style Lager
(Ruby Mountain Brewing Company)

Silver Gulch Fairbanks Lager (21 IBU)
(Silver Gulch Brewing & Bottling)

Snake River Lager (18 IBU)
(Snake River Brewing Company)

St. George Brewing Company Vienna Lager (22 IBU)
(St.George Brewing Company)

Viking Brewing Vienna Woods
(Viking Brewing)

Wagner Valley Brewing Dockside Amber Lager
(Wagner Valley Brewing Company)

Barleywine

Alaskan Big Nugget Barley Wine
(Alaskan Brewing Company)

Alesmith Brewing Old Numbskull
(Alesmith Brewing Company)

Anchor Brewing Old Foghorn Barleywine Style Ale
(Anchor Brewing Company)

Atlantic Brewing Brother Adam's Honey Bragget
(Atlantic Brewing Company)

Avery Brewing Hog Heaven Barley Wine (104 IBU)
(Avery Brewing Company)

Avery Brewing Samael's Oak Aged Ale (41 IBU)
(Avery Brewing Company)

Back Road Brewery No. Nine Barley-Style Ale
(Back Road Brewery)

Barley Creek Old '99 Barley Wine
(Barley Creek Brewing Company)

BBC Bearded Pat's Barleywine (18 SRM, 100+ IBU)
(Bluegrass Brewing Company)

Berkshire Brewing Holidale
(Berkshire Brewing Company)

Berkshire Brewing Raspberry Strong Ale
(Berkshire Brewing Company)

Bison Brewing Organic Barleywine (30 SRM, 87 IBU)
(Bison Brewing)

Bitter Root Brewing Winter Ale
(Bitter Root Brewing)

Blue Point Brewing Old Howling Bastard (78 IBU)
(Blue Point Brewing)

Boulder Beer Killer Penguin Barleywine (34.5 SRM, 42 IBU)
(Boulder Beer Company)

Boundary BayBarley Wine
(Boundary Bay Brewing Company)

BridgePort Old Knucklehead (60 IBU)
(BridgePort Brewing Company (Gambrinus))

Bristol Brewing Old No. 23 Barley Wine (67 IBU)
(Bristol Brewing Company)

Brooklyn Monster Ale (70 IBU)
(Brooklyn Brewery)

Central Waters Kosmyk Charlie Y2K Catastrophe Ale
(Central Waters Brewing Company)

Cisco Brewers Baggywrinkle Barleywine
(Cisco Brewers, Inc.)

Dick's Barley Wine Ale
(Dick's Brewing Company)

Dogfish Head Old School Barleywine
(Dogfish Head Craft Brewery)

Dominion Millennium
(Old Dominion Brewing Company)

Double Bastard Ale (100+ IBU)
(Stone Brewing Company)

Dragonmead Copper Shield Bitter Harvest
(Dragonmead Microbrewery)

Dragonmead Excalibur Barley Wine
(Dragonmead Microbrewery)

Duck-Rabbit Barleywine Ale (in NC only)
(Duck-Rabbit Craft Brewery)

El Toro Bravo
(El Toro Brewing)

English Ales Brew 66
(English Ales Brewery)

Fish Tale Leviathan Barleywine
(Fish Brewing Company)

Flying Dog Horn Dog Barley Wine Style Ale (95 SRM, 45 IBU)
(Flying Dog Brewery, LLC)

Golden City Centurion Barley Wine Ale
(Golden City Brewery)

Great Divide Brewing Old Ruffian Barley Wine
(Great Divide Brewing Company)

Green Flash Barleywine
(Green Flash Brewing)

Beer Styles Index   Barleywine (continued)

Hair of the Dog Brewing Doggie Claws (70 IBU)
(Hair of the Dog Brewing Company)

Heavy Seas Brewing Below Decks
(Clipper City Brewing Company)

Ice Harbor Brewing Barley Wine Style Ale (84 IBU)
(Ice Harbor Brewing Company)

Kodiak Island Island Fog Barley Wine
(Kodiak Island Brewing Company (Kegs/ Growlers))

Lagunitas Brewing Olde GnarlyWine
(Lagunitas Brewing)

Lake Superior Brewing Old Man Winter Warmer
(Lake Superior Brewing Company)

Left Hand Brewing Widdershins Barleywine (70 IBU)
(Left Hand Brewing Company)

Mad River John Barleycorn Barleywine Style Ale (96 IBU)
(Mad River Brewing)

Marin Brewing "Old Dipsea" Barleywine Style Ale
(Marin Brewing Company)

Mercury Brewing Stone Cat Barley Wine
(Mercury Brewing Company)

Middle Ages Druid Fluid Barley Wine
(Middle Ages Brewing Company)

Midnight Sun Arctic Devil Barley Wine
(Midnight Sun Brewing Company)

Moylan's Old Blarney Barleywine Style Ale
(Moylan's Brewing Company)

Nashoba Valley Brewery Barleywine Ale (72 IBU)
(Nashoba Valley Brewery)

Odell Brewing Curmudgeons NIP
(Odell Brewing Company)

Pike Brewing Company Old Bawdy Barley Wine
(Pike Brewing Company)

Real Ale Brewing Sisyphus Barleywine Ale
(Real Ale Brewing Company)

Rock Art Brewery Ridge Runner Mild Barleywine (23 IBU)
(Rock Art Brewery, LLC)

Rogue Old Crustacean Barleywine (110 IBU)
(Rogue Ales)

Saint Arnold Brewing Barleywine
(Saint Arnold Brewing Company)

Samuel Adams Millennium (30 SRM, 27 IBU)
(The Boston Beer Company)

Santa Fe Brewing Santa Fe Chicken Killer Barley Wine
(29 SRM, 86 IBU)
(Santa Fe Brewing Company)

Sierra Nevada Bigfoot Ale (38 SRM, 100 IBU)
(Sierra Nevada Brewing Company)

Siletz Brewing Company Noggin Knocker (83.6 SRM, 67.9 IBU)
(Siletz Brewing Company, Inc.)

Smuttynose Brewing Barleywine Style Ale
(Smuttynose Brewing Company)

Sonora Brewing Old Saguaro Barley Wine
(Sonoran Brewing Company (Kegs/ Growlers))

Sprecher Brewing Barley Wine (46 IBU)
(Sprecher Brewing)

Sprecher Brewing Bourbon Barrel Barley Wine (46 IBU)
(Sprecher Brewing)

Stone Old Guardian Barley Wine (95 IBU)
(Stone Brewing Company)

Thomas Hooker Old Marley Barley Wine (16 SRM, 74 IBU)
(Thomas Hooker Brewing Company)

Three Floyds Brewing Behemoth Barleywine
(Three Floyds Brewing Company)

Two Brothers Bare Tree Weiss Wine (December)
(Two Brothers Brewing Company)

Tyranena Brewing Company Brewers Gone Wild! Spank Me Baby
  Barley Wine
(Tyranena Brewing Company)

Uinta Brewing Anniversary Barley Wine
(Uinta Brewing Company)

Beer Styles Index

Victory Old Horizontal Ale (60+ IBU)
(Victory Brewing Company)

Viking Brewing Berserk
(Viking Brewing)

Weyerbacher Brewing Blithering Idiot
(Weyerbacher Brewing Company)

Weyerbacher Brewing Insanity
(Weyerbacher Brewing Company)

Whitstran Brewing Friar's Penance Barley Wine (96 IBU)
(Whitstran Brewing Company)

Williamsburg AleWerks Winter Barleywine
(Williamsburg AleWerks)

Black & Tan

Berkshire Brewing "Shabadoo" Black & Tan Ale
(Berkshire Brewing Company)

Gluek Stite Black and Tan
(Gluek Brewing Company)

Gray's Brewing Black & Tan
(Gray Brewing)

Lion Brewing Pocono Black & Tan
(Lion Brewery)

McSorley's Black & Tan
(Pabst Brewing Company)

Mississippi Mud Black & Tan
(Mississippi Brewing Company)

Saranac Black & Tan
(The Matt Brewing)

Shenandoah Brewing Black and Tan Beer
(Shenandoah Brewing Company)

Stoney's Black And Tan
(Jones Brewing Company)

Yuengling Black and Tan
(D.G. Yuengling & Son, Inc.)

Caffeinated Beer

Berkshire Brewing Coffeehouse Porter
(Berkshire Brewing Company)

Bud Extra
(Anheuser-Busch, Inc.)

Dogfish Head Chicory Stout (22 IBU)
(Dogfish Head Craft Brewery)

Moonshot
(New Century Brewing Company)

Natty Up
(Anheuser-Busch, Inc.)

Sparks
(SAB Miller Corporation)

Sparks Light
(SAB Miller Corporation)

Sparks Plus 6%
(SAB Miller Corporation)

Sparks Plus 7%
(SAB Miller Corporation)

California Common Beer/Steam Ale

Anchor Brewing Steam – *page 450*
(Anchor Brewing Company)

Eel River Brewing Climax California Classic
(Eel River Brewing Company)

Rio Grande Brewing Outlaw Lager (35 IBU)
(Rio Grande Brewing Company)

Whitstran Brewing Steamy Cream California Common Ale
(14 IBU)
(Whitstran Brewing Company)

Cream Ale

Anderson Valley Summer Solstice Cerveza Crema (4 IBU)
(Anderson Valley Brewing Company)

Central Coast Brewing Cream Ale
(Central Coast Brewing)

City Cream Ale
(City Brewery)

Climax Brewing Cream Ale
(Climax Brewing Company)

Dragonmead Lancelot's Cream Ale
(Dragonmead Microbrewery)

Elmwood Brewing Lawnmower
(Elmwood Brewing Company)

Frankenmuth Original Geyer's American Cream Ale
(Frankenmuth Brewery)

Genesee Cream Ale
(High Falls Brewing)

Hale's Cream Ale
(Hale's Ales)

Hale's Cream H.S.B.
(Hale's Ales)

Little Kings Cream Ale
(Wild Goose Brewery, LLC)

Northern Lights Creme Ale
(The Northern Lights Brewing Company)

Pete's Wicked Wanderlust Cream Ale (18 IBU)
(Pete's Brewing (Gambrinus))

South Shore Brewery Herbal Cream Ale
(South Shore Brewery)

Sprecher Brewing Micro-Light Ale (6 IBU)
(Sprecher Brewing)

St.Croix Cream
(St. Croix Beer Company)

Thomas Creek Vanilla Cream Ale (15.8 IBU)
(Thomas Creek Brewery)

Fruit or Vegetable Beer

21st Amendment Brewery Watermelon Wheat (17 IBU)
(21st Amendment)

Abita Brewing Purple Haze
(Abita Brewing Company)

Alpine Mandarin Nectar (4.1IBU)
(Alpine Beer Company)

Atlantic Brewing Bar Harbor Blueberry Ale
(Atlantic Brewing Company)

Back Road Brewery Blueberry Ale
(Back Road Brewery)

Bar Harbor Brewing Bar Harbor Peach
(Bar Harbor Brewing Company)

Bar Harbor Brewing Ginger Mild Brew
(Bar Harbor Brewing Company)

Bayhawk Ales Honey Blonde (9 IBU)
(Bayhawk Ales, Inc.)

Bethlehem Brew Works Pumpkin Ale
(The Bethlehem Brew Works)

Billy's Chilies Beer
(Twisted Pine Brewing Company)

Black Dog Honey Raspberry Ale (12 IBU)
Spanish Peaks Brewing Company/United States Beverage

Black Mountain Cave Creek Chili Beer – *page 469*
(The Black Mountain/Chili Beer Brewing Company)

BluCreek Blueberry Ale (9 SRM, 25 IBU)
(BluCreek Brewing)

Blue Moon Pumpkin Ale
(Molson Coors Brewing Company)

Blue Point Brewing Blueberry Ale (14 IBU)
(Blue Point Brewing)

Buffalo Bill's Brewery Orange Blossom Cream Ale
(Buffalo Bill's Brewery)

Buffalo Bill's Brewery Pumpkin Ale
(Buffalo Bill's Brewery)

Cisco Brewers Bailey's Ale
(Cisco Brewers, Inc.)

Coeur d'Alene Brewing Huckleberry Ale
(Coeur D'Alene Brewing Company)

Columbus Brewing Apricot Ale
(Columbus Brewing Company)

Cranberry Special Ale
(Sand Creek Brewing Company, LLC)

Crooked River Pumpkin Harvest Ale
(Wild Goose Brewery, LLC)

Dark Horse Raspberry Ale
(Dark Horse Brewing Company)

Defiant Brewing The Horseman's Ale
(The Defiant Brewing Company)

Dogfish Head Fort
(Dogfish Head Craft Brewery)

Dogfish Head Raison D'Etre (25 IBU)
(Dogfish Head Craft Brewery)

El Toro Peach Ale
(El Toro Brewing)

Four Peaks Arizona Peach
(Four Peaks Brewing Company)

Four Plus PUNK'N Pumpkin Harvest Ale (13 SRM, 118 IBU)
(Four Plus Brewing Company)

Gena's Honey Blonde Ale
(El Toro Brewing)

Glacier Brewing Flathead Cherry Ale (3.8 SRM, 12 IBU)
(Glacier Brewing)

Gray's Brewing Honey Ale
(Gray Brewing)

Great Divide Brewing Wild Raspberry Ale (21 IBU)
(Great Divide Brewing Company)

Harbor City Brewing Raspberry Brown Ale
(Harbor City Brewing, Inc.)

Harpoon UFO Raspberry Hefeweizen (12 IBU)
(Harpoon Brewery)

Hurricane Reef Raspberry Wheat
(Florida Beer Company)

Indian Wells Raspberry Ale
(Indian Wells Brewing)

Island Brewing Avocado Ale
(Island Brewing Company)

Ithaca Beer Company Apricot Wheat
(Ithaca Beer Company, Inc.)

King Cherry Ale
(King Brewing Company)

Lakefront Cherry Lager (10 SRM, 12 IBU)
(Lakefront Brewery, Inc.)

Lakefront Pumpkin Lager (12 SRM, 12 IBU)
(Lakefront Brewery, Inc.)

Lancaster Brewing Strawberry Wheat (16 IBU)
(Lancaster Brewing Company)

Leinenkugel's Apple Spice
(Jacob Leinenkugel Brewing Company)

Leinenkugel's Berry Weiss
(Jacob Leinenkugel Brewing Company)

Maine Coast Brewing Wild Blueberry Ale
(Maine Coast Brewing)

Marin Brewing Blueberry Ale
(Marin Brewing Company)

Marin Brewing Raspberry Trail Ale
(Marin Brewing Company)

Marin Brewing Stinson Beach Peach
(Marin Brewing Company)

Mercury Brewing Eagle Brook Saloon's Blueberry Ale (14 IBU)
(Mercury Brewing Company)

Mercury Brewing Stone Cat Blueberry
(Mercury Brewing Company)

Michelob ULTRA Lime
(Anheuser-Busch, Inc.)

Michelob ULTRA Orange
(Anheuser-Busch, Inc.)

Michelob ULTRA Pomegranate
(Anheuser-Busch, Inc.)

Michigan Brewing Celis Raspberry
(Michigan Brewing Company, Inc.)

BEER STYLES INDEX Fruit or Vegetable Beer (continued)

Middle Ages Apricot Ale
(Middle Ages Brewing Company)

Middle Ages Raspberry Ale
(Middle Ages Brewing Company)

Morimoto Black Obi Soba (30 IBU)
(Rogue Ales)

Moylan's Wheat Berry Ale
(Moylan's Brewing Company)

Nashoba Valley Brewery Blackberry Ale
(Nashoba Valley Brewery)

New Holland Ichabod
(New Holland Brewing Company)

Newport Storm Rhode Island Blueberry (9 SRM, 11 IBU)
(Coastal Extreme Brewing Company, LLC)

Night Owl Pumpkin Ale
(Elysian Brewing Company)

Northern Lights Blueberry Creme Ale
(The Northern Lights Brewing Company)

Oaken Barrel Brewing Razz-Wheat
(Oaken Barrel Brewing Company)

O'Fallon Cherry Chocolate Beer
(O'Fallon Brewery)

O'Fallon Pumpkin Ale
(O'Fallon Brewery)

O'Fallon Wheach
(O'Fallon Brewery)

Oxford Raspberry
(Clipper City Brewing Company)

Pete's Wicked Strawberry Blonde(19 IBU)
(Pete's Brewing (Gambrinus))

Post Road Pumpkin Ale (24 IBU)
(Brooklyn Brewery)

Raspberry Wheat Ale
(Mishawaka Brewing Company)

Riverboat Raspberry Fruit Beer
(Trailhead Brewing Company)

Rogue Morimoto Soba Ale (30 IBU)
(Rogue Ales)

Sea Dog Apricot Wheat Beer
(The Sea Dog Brewing Company)

Sea Dog Blue Paw Wild Blueberry Wheat Ale – *page 542*
(The Sea Dog Brewing Company)

Sea Dog Pumpkin Ale
(The Sea Dog Brewing Company)

Sea Dog Raspberry Wheat Beer
(The Sea Dog Brewing Company)

Sebago Brewing Bass Ackwards Berryblue Ale (13.3 SRM, 16.1 IBU)
(Sebago Brewing Company)

Shipyard Brewing Pumpkinhead Ale
(Shipyard Brewing Company)

Siletz Brewing Company Spruce Ale (25.7 SRM, 35.2 IBU)
(Siletz Brewing Company, Inc.)

SLO Brewing Blueberry Ale
(Downtown Brewing Company)

Sly Fox Black Raspberry Reserve (16 IBU)
(Sly Fox Brewing Company)

Smuttynose Brewing Pumpkin Ale
(Smuttynose Brewing Company)

Southampton Pumpkin Ale
(Southampton Publick House)

Tequiza
(Anheuser-Busch, Inc.)

Tommyknocker Tundrabeary Ale
(Tommyknocker Brewery)

Trailhead Spiced Pumpkin Ale
(Trailhead Brewing Company)

Wachusett Blueberry
(Wachusett Brewing Company)

Wasatch Pumpkin Ale
(Utah Brewers Cooperative/ Wasatch)

Wasatch Raspberry Wheat Beer
(Utah Brewers Cooperative/ Wasatch)

Wild Blue
(Anheuser-Busch, Inc.)

Wild Goose Pumpkin Patch (16 SRM, 28 IBU)
(Wild Goose Brewery, LLC)

Gluten Free

Bard's Tale Dragon's Gold Sorghum Lager (4 SRM, 35 IBU) – *page 466*
(Bard's Tale Beer Company)

Lakefront New Grist (2 SRM, 8 IBU)
(Lakefront Brewery, Inc.)

Ramapo Valley Brewery Honey Lager
(Ramapo Valley Brewery)

Redbridge Lager – *page 456*
(Anheuser-Busch, Inc.)

Herb & Spice Beer

Atwater Vanilla Java Porter
(Atwater Block Brewery)

Baron Roggen
(Baron Brewing)

Bison Brewing Organic Gingerbread Ale (35 SRM, 25 IBU)
(Bison Brewing)

Bison Brewing Organic Honey-Basil (6 SRM, 24 IBU)
(Bison Brewing)

BluCreek (Honey) Herbal Ale (9.3 SRM, 20 IBU)
(BluCreek Brewing)

Dick's Rye Ale
(Dick's Brewing Company)

Dragonmead Dragon Daze Hemp Ale
(Dragonmead Microbrewery)

Harpoon Winter Warmer (22 IBU)
(Harpoon Brewery)

Highland Brewing Cold Mountain Winter Ale
(Highland Brewing)

Jack's Pumpkin Spice Ale– *page 457*
(Anheuser-Busch, Inc.)

Left Hand Brewing JuJu Ginger Ale (17 IBU)
(Left Hand Brewing Company)

Leinenkugel's Honey Weiss
(Jacob Leinenkugel Brewing Company)

MacTarnahan's Oregon Honey Beer (16 IBU)
(MacTarnahan's Brewing Company)

Marin Brewing Hoppy Holidaze Flavored Ale
(Marin Brewing Company)

O'Fallon Blackberry Scottish Ale
(O'Fallon Brewery)

Rio Grande Brewing Pancho Verde Chile Cerveza (12 IBU)
(Rio Grande Brewing Company)

Rogue Chamomellow Ale (34 IBU)
(Rogue Ales)

Salmon Fly Honey Rye
(Madison River Brewing Company)

Sam Adams Traditional Ginger Honey Ale
(The Boston Beer Company)

Siletz Brewing Company Chocolate Porter (86.9 SRM, 41.7 IBU)
(Siletz Brewing Company, Inc.)

St.Croix Maple Ale
(St.Croix Beer Company)

St.Croix Serrano Pepper Ale
(St.Croix Beer Company)

Two Brothers Cane and Ebel (Limited Release)
(Two Brothers Brewing Company)

Weyerbacher Brewing Decadence
(Weyerbacher Brewing Company)

Weyerbacher Brewing Imperial Pumpkin Ale
(Weyerbacher Brewing Company)

Yards Brewing Poor Richard's Tavern Spruce
(Yards Brewing)

BEER STYLES INDEX

Malt Liquor

City Slicker Malt Liquor
(City Brewery)

Colt 45
(Pabst Brewing Company)

Country Club Malt Liquor
(Pabst Brewing Company)

Haffenreffer's Private Stock
(Pabst Brewing Company)

Hurricane High Gravity (HG)
(Anheuser-Busch, Inc.)

Hurricane Malt Liquor
(Anheuser-Busch, Inc.)

King Cobra
(Anheuser-Busch, Inc.)

Lionshead Malt Liquor
(Lion Brewery)

Magnum Malt Liquor
(SAB Miller Corporation)

Mickey's Malt Liquor
(SAB Miller Corporation)

Old English 800 Malt Liquor
(SAB Miller Corporation)

Olde English HG800
(SAB Miller Corporation)

Olde English HG800 7.5
(SAB Miller Corporation)

Pig's Eye Pitt Bull
(Pig's Eye Brewing Company)

Rogue Dad's Little Helper Malt Liquor (25 IBU)
(Rogue Ales)

Schlitz Bull Ice
(Pabst Brewing Company)

Schlitz Malt Liquor
(Pabst Brewing Company)

Schlitz Red Bull
(Pabst Brewing Company)

Steel Reserve High Gravity
(SAB Miller Corporation)

Steel Reserve Triple
(SAB Miller Corporation)

Viking Brewing HoneyMoon
(Viking Brewing)

No Applicable Style Category

Demolition (5 SRM, 55 IBU)
(Goose Island Beer Company)

Dogfish Head Red & White
(Dogfish Head Craft Brewery)

Great Divide Brewing Samurai
(Great Divide Brewing Company)

Harpoon 100 BBL Series
(Harpoon Brewery)

Magic Hat Brewing #9 (9 SRM, 18 IBU)
(Magic Hat Brewing Company)

Matilda (13 SRM, 32 IBU)
(Goose Island Beer Company)

Non-Alcohol Malt Beverage

Busch NA
(Anheuser-Busch, Inc.)

Coors Non-Alcoholic
(Molson Coors Brewing Company)

Genesee NA
(High Falls Brewing)

O'Doul's
(Anheuser-Busch, Inc.)

O'Doul's Amber
(Anheuser-Busch, Inc.)

Old Milwaukee Non-Alcoholic
(Pabst Brewing Company)

Pabst Blue Ribbon Non-Alcoholic
(Pabst Brewing Company)

Sharp's
(SAB Miller Corporation)

Other Ale

Abita Brewing Restoration Ale
(Abita Brewing Company)

Allagash Brewing Curieux
(Allagash Brewing Company)

Allagash Brewing Interlude
(Allagash Brewing Company)

Allagash Brewing Odyssey
(Allagash Brewing Company)

Arrogant Bastard Ale
(Stone Brewing Company)

Baron Dampf Bier
(Baron Brewing)

Bear Republic Brewing Hop Rod Rye (90+ IBU)
(Bear Republic Brewing Company)

Capital Brewery Fest Beer
(Capital Brewery Company, Inc.)

Dogfish Head Immort Ale (40 IBU)
(Dogfish Head Craft Brewery)

El Toro Keller Bier
(El Toro Brewing)

Fish Tale Thornton Creek Ale
(Fish Brewing Company)

Hale's O'Brien's Harvest Ale
(Hale's Ales)

Helmar Big League Brew
(Helmar Brewing Company)

Indian Wells Sidewinder Missile Ale
(Indian Wells Brewing)

Lagunitas Brewing Number 10 Ale
(Lagunitas Brewing)

Lake Louie Brewing Coon Rock Cream Ale
(Lake Louie Brewing, LLC)

Lake Placid Craft Brewing Moose Island Ale
(Lake Placid Craft Brewing)

Left Hand Brewing Twin Sisters (87 IBU)
(Left Hand Brewing Company)

Lexington Brewing Kentucky Bourbon Barrel Aged Ale
(Alltech's Lexington Brewing Company)

Magic Hat Brewing Jinx (22 SRM, 20 IBU)
(Magic Hat Brewing Company)

Magic Hat Brewing Roxy Rolles
(Magic Hat Brewing Company)

Maritime Pacific Nightwatch Dark
(Maritime Pacific Brewing Company)

Mehana Brewing Humback Blue Beer
(Mehana Brewing Company, Inc.)

Mehana Brewing Roy's Private Reserve
(Mehana Brewing Company, Inc.)

Mercury Brewing Stone Cat Ale
(Mercury Brewing Company)

New Belgium Springboard
(New Belgium Brewing Company)

New Glarus Brewing Spotted Cow
(New Glarus Brewing)

New Holland Pilgrim's Dole
(New Holland Brewing Company)

Northern Lights Crystal Bitter
(The Northern Lights Brewing Company)

Old Viscosity Ale
(Port Brewing Company)

Oregon Trail Beaver Tail
(Oregon Trail Brewery)

Orlando Brewing Mild Ale
(Orlando Brewing Partners, Inc. (Kegs/ Growlers))

Pike Brewing Company Naughty Nellie Ale
(Pike Brewing Company)

Rainer Ale
(Pabst Brewing Company)

Ramapo Valley Brewery Copper Ale
(Ramapo Valley Brewery)

Ramapo Valley Brewery Skull Crusher
(Ramapo Valley Brewery)

Real Ale Brewing Full Moon Pale Rye Ale
(Real Ale Brewing Company)

ReaperAle Ritual Dark Ale (50 IBU)
(ReaperAle, Inc.)

Redhook Ale Brewery Late Harvest Autumn Ale (21 SRM, 32 IBU)
(Redhook Ale Brewery)

Rock Art Brewery Infusco (25 IBU)
(Rock Art Brewery, LLC)

Rock Art Brewery Stock Ale (18 IBU)
(Rock Art Brewery, LLC)

Rock Art Brewery Sunny and 75 (10 IBU)
(Rock Art Brewery, LLC)

Rock Art Brewery The Riddler (32 IBU)
(Rock Art Brewery, LLC)

Rock Art Brewery The Vermonster (100 IBU)
(Rock Art Brewery, LLC)

Rogue Chipotle Ale (35 IBU)
(Rogue Ales)

Russian River Brewing Beatification
(Russian River Brewing Company)

Russian River Brewing Sanctification (27 IBU)
(Russian River Brewing Company)

Sam Adams 1790 Root Beer Brew
(The Boston Beer Company)

Shmaltz Brewing Jewbelation
(Shmaltz Brewing Company)

Slab City Brewing Xenabock
(Slab City Brewing)

Smuttynose Brewing Wheat Wine Ale
(Smuttynose Brewing Company)

Southampton Secret Ale
(Southampton Publick House)

Sprecher Brewing Mbege Ale (10 IBU)
(Sprecher Brewing)

Sprecher Brewing Shakparo Ale (9 IBU)
(Sprecher Brewing)

Spilker Ales Hopluia Ale
(Spilker Ales)

Sudwerk Leatherneck
(Sudwerk)

Victory 'Hop' Wallop (70+ IBU)
(Victory Brewing Company)

Viking Brewing Mj0d
(Viking Brewing)

Scotch Ale

Arcadia Brewing Ales Scotch Ale (28 IBU)
(Arcadia Brewing Company)

Boundary Bay Scotch
(Boundary Bay Brewing Company)

Copper John Scotch Ale
(Madison River Brewing Company)

Dark Horse Scotty Karate Scotch Ale
(Dark Horse Brewing Company)

Dogfish Head Indian Brown Ale (50 IBU)
(Dogfish Head Craft Brewery)

Duck-Rabbit Wee Heavy Scotch Style Ale (in NC Only)
(Duck-Rabbit Craft Brewery)

Dunedin Brewery Highland Games Ale (20 SRM, 39 IBU)
(Dunedin Brewery)

Highland Brewing Tasgall Ale (27 IBU)
(Highland Brewing)

Middle Ages Highlander Scotch Ale
(Middle Ages Brewing Company)

Middle Ages Kilt Tilter Scotch Style Ale
(Middle Ages Brewing Company)

Moylan's Kilt Lifter Scotch Ale
(Moylan's Brewing Company)

Sacramento Brewing Sacsquatch Ale
(Sacramento Brewing Company Inc)

Samuel Adams Scotch Ale (28.5 SRM, 35 IBU)
(The Boston Beer Company)

Sheepscot Valley Brewing Pemaquid Ale
(Sheepscot Valley Brewing Company)

Shenandoah Brewing Old Rag Mountain Ale
(Shenandoah Brewing Company)

Sly Fox Gang Aft Angley (20 IBU)
(Sly Fox Brewing Company)

Smuttynose Brewing Scotch Style Ale
(Smuttynose Brewing Company)

Sprecher Brewing Bourbon Barrel Scotch Ale (21 IBU)
(Sprecher Brewing)

Sprecher Brewing Piper's Scotch Ale (21 IBU)
(Sprecher Brewing)

Weyerbacher Brewing Scotch Ale
(Weyerbacher Brewing Company)

Brewery	AK	AL	AR	AZ	CA	CO	CT	DC	DE	FL	GA	HI	IA	ID	IL	IN	KS	KY	LA	MA	MD	ME	MI	MN	MO	MS	MT	NC	NE	ND	NH	NJ	NM	NV	NY	OH	OK	OR	PA	RI	SC	SD	TN	TX	UT	VA	VT	WA	WI	WV	WY
21st Amendment (Contact Brewery)																																																			
Abbey Beverage Company																																	X																		
Abita Brewing Company		X	X	X	X		X	X		X	X				X	X	X	X	X	X	X		X		X	X		X					X	X	X	X	X		X		X		X	X		X			X		
Alaskan Brewing Company	X			X	X									X													X		X									X										X			X
Alesmith Brewing Company (Contact Brewery)																																																			
Allagash Brewing Company					X	X	X			X					X	X				X	X	X	X								X	X			X	X	X		X	X				X		X	X				
Alltech's Lexington Brewing Company																		X												X												X									
Alpine Beer Company					X																																														
Anchor Brewing Company	X	X	X	X	X	X	X	X	X	X	X	X	X	X	X	X	X	X	X	X	X	X	X	X	X	X	X	X	X	X	X	X	X	X	X	X	X	X	X	X	X	X	X	X	X	X	X	X	X	X	X
Anderson Valley Brewing				X	X	X	X			X					X	X	X						X		X			X			X	X		X	X		X	X	X					X	X			X			
Andrews Brewing Company																						X																													
Angel City Brewing					X																																														
Angry Minnow Brewing																							X	X																									X		
Anheuser-Busch, Inc.	X	X	X	X	X	X	X	X	X	X	X	X	X	X	X	X	X	X	X	X	X	X	X	X	X	X	X	X	X	X	X	X	X	X	X	X	X	X	X	X	X	X	X	X	X	X	X	X	X	X	X
Appalachian Brewing Company																																							X												
Arbor Brewing Company																							X																												
Arcadia Brewing Company															X			X					X	X	X									X			X								X						
Atlanta Brewing Company											X																																								
Atlantic Brewing Company																						X																													
Atwater Block Brewery						X									X	X							X												X				X									X		
August Schell Brewing Company													X										X	X						X									X			X							X		
Avery Brewing Company			X	X	X	X				X	X					X	X	X	X	X	X		X	X					X						X	X				X	X		X	X	X			X	X		X
Back Road Brewery															X																																				
Backcountry Brewery						X																																													
Ballast Point Brewing Company (San Diego, Orange, LA)					X																																														

Brewery	AK	AL	AR	AZ	CA	CO	CT	DC	DE	FL	GA	HI	IA	ID	IL	IN	KS	KY	LA	MA	MD	ME	MI	MN	MO	MS	MT	NC	NE	ND	NH	NJ	NM	NV	NY	OH	OK	OR	PA	RI	SC	SD	TN	TX	UT	VA	VT	WA	WI	WV	WY
Baltimore-Washington Beer Works								X							X					X	X																		X	X						X					
Bar Harbor Brewing Company																						X																													
Bard's Tale Beer Company				X	X	X		X			X			X	X	X	X			X				X	X			X	X		X	X		X	X		X	X	X	X			X	X	X	X		X			
Barley Creek Brewing Company																															X							X													
Barley Island Brewing Company (Contact Brewery)																																																			
Baron Brewing																																																X			
Barrel House Brewing Company (Contact Brewery)																																																			
Bayern Brewing														X													X											X													
Bayhawk Ales, Inc.			X	X								X																						X												X					
Bear Republic Brewing Company				X	X	X			X						X				X		X	X		X				X				X		X											X			X	X		
Beautiful Brews, Inc. (Contact Brewery)																																																			
Beermann's Beerwerks					X																																														
Bell's Brewery, Inc.															X	X							X	X	X			X							X															X	
Berkshire Brewing Company							X													X																			X								X				
Big Easy Brewing Company																			X																																
Big Horn Brewing (CB Potts)					X																																														X
Big Sky Brewing Company	X			X	X										X									X		X		X	X						X								X					X	X	X	X
Bison Brewing				X						X	X					X												X						X		X									X				X		
Bitter Root Brewing														X														X																							
Blucreek Brewing										X					X									X										X															X		
Blue & Gray Brewing Company, Inc.																																														X					
Blue Point Brewing																				X	X											X			X				X	X											
Bluegrass Beer Company							X											X		X														X									X			X					
Bonnema Brewing Company (Contact Brewery)																																																			
Bootie Beer Company										X																																									
Boulder Beer Company			X			X	X			X					X	X	X	X		X				X				X	X		X	X		X	X		X	X	X		X		X		X			X		X	
Boulevard Brewing Company		X								X			X		X		X						X	X				X	X				X					X											X		X
Boundary Bay Brewing Company																																																X			
Breckenridge Brewery		X			X						X				X	X	X	X					X	X	X				X	X		X			X	X							X		X			X		X	X
Brewery Ommegang	X			X	X	X	X	X	X	X	X			X	X	X		X	X	X	X	X	X	X	X			X	X		X	X		X	X	X		X	X	X					X		X	X	X	X	X

Availability by State *Continued*

Brewery	AK	AL	AR	AZ	CA	CO	CT	DC	DE	FL	GA	HI	IA	ID	IL	IN	KS	KY	LA	MA	MD	ME	MI	MN	MO	MS	MT	NC	NE	ND	NH	NJ	NM	NV	NY	OH	OK	OR	PA	RI	SC	SD	TN	TX	UT	VA	VT	WA	WI	WV	WY
BridgePort Brewing Company	X	X		X	X	X					X				X		X			X	X	X	X	X								X					X	X					X	X				X			
Bristol Brewing Company					X																																														
Brooklyn Brewery							X	X	X	X										X	X	X									X		X	X					X	X	X					X					
Buckeye Brewing (Contact Brewery)																																																			
Butte Creek Brewing					X																																														
Butternuts Beer & Ale																																X	X																		
Buzzards Bay Brewing Company							X													X		X																	X								X			
Caldera Brewing Company																																X		X																	
Cape Ann Brewing																				X		X										X																			
Capital Brewery													X		X									X																									X		
Carolina Beer & Beverage Company											X																	X													X		X			X				
Carolina Brewing																												X																							
Cascade Lakes Brewing Company (Contact Brewery)																																																			
Casco Bay Brewing Company							X													X		X									X				X				X											
Catawba Valley Brewing																												X															X			X				
Central Coast Brewing					X																																														
Central Waters Brewing Company																																																	X		
Charleston Brewing Company											X																	X															X								
Charlesville Brewing Company																									X																										
Christian Moerlein Brewing Company (Contact Brewery)																																																			
Cisco Brewers, Inc.							X	X												X	X											X		X	X																
City Brewery													X		X									X										X					X												X
Clay Pipe Brewing Company																					X																														
Climax Brewing Company																																X		X				X												
Clipper City Brewing Company							X	X	X	X	X				X	X			X	X	X	X						X				X	X						X	X						X				
Coast Range Brewing (Contact Brewery)																																																			
Coastal Extreme Brewing Company, LLC							X													X																				X						X				
Coeur d'Alene Brewing Company (Contact Brewery)																																																			
Coffaro Beer Company																																X		X				X												
Columbus Brewing Company (Contact Brewery)																																																			

Brewery	AK	AL	AR	AZ	CA	CO	CT	DC	DE	FL	GA	HI	IA	ID	IL	IN	KS	KY	LA	MA	MD	ME	MI	MN	MO	MS	MT	NC	NE	ND	NH	NJ	NM	NV	NY	OH	OK	OR	PA	RI	SC	SD	TN	TX	UT	VA	VT	WA	WI	WV	WY
Concord Brewery, Inc.																				x																				x											
Cooper's Cave Ale Company, LTD.																																			x																	
Cooperstown Brewing Company							x													x											x				x				x	x											
Cottrell Brewing Company							x																																	x											
Crabtree Brewing Company (Contact Brewery)																																																			
Crested Butte Brewery						x																																												x	
Cricket Hill Brewing Company																																x			x				x												
D G Yuengling & Son Inc.		x						x	x	x											x							x				x			x				x				x			x					
D L Geary Brewing Company							x												x	x	x	x						x	x		x				x				x	x	x					x	x				
Dark Horse Brewing Company															x								x																												
Deschutes Brewery	x			x	x	x				x				x										x			x		x	x					x													x			x
Diamond Bear Brewing Company			x																					x																											
Dick's Brewing Company																																						x										x			
Dillon DAM Brewery						x																																													
Dixie Brewing Company (Contact Brewery)																																																			
Dogfish Head Craft Brewery	x			x		x	x	x	x	x	x				x	x	x			x	x	x						x				x		x	x			x	x	x			x	x	x	x	x	x	x		
Downtown Brewing Company					x																																														
Dragonmead Microbrewery																							x																												
Drakes Brewing Company					x																																														
Duck-Rabbit Craft Brewery																												x													x		x								
Dunedin Brewery										x																																									
Durango Brewing Company						x																																													
Edenton Brewing Company																												x									x									x					
Eel River Brewing Company		x		x	x					x				x															x					x					x	x								x			x
EJ Phair Brewing					x																																														
El Toro Brewing					x																																													x	
Electric Beer Company (Contact Brewery)																																																			
Ellicottville Brewing Company (Contact Brewery)																																		x	x																
Elmwood Brewing Company (Contact Brewery)																																																			
Elysian Brewing Company	x													x																					x													x			

Brewery	AK	AL	AR	AZ	CA	CO	CT	DC	DE	FL	GA	HI	IA	ID	IL	IN	KS	KY	LA	MA	MD	ME	MI	MN	MO	MS	MT	NC	NE	ND	NH	NJ	NM	NV	NY	OH	OK	OR	PA	RI	SC	SD	TN	TX	UT	VA	VT	WA	WI	WV	WY
Empyrean Brewing																													X																						
English Ales Brewery					X																																														
Erie Brewing																																X	X						X												
Estes Park Brewery						X											X																									X								X	
Etna Brewing Company (Contact Brewery)																																																			
Falls Brewing Company																																																		X	
Far West Brewing Company																																																X			
Firestone Walker Brewing Company					X																							X																							
Fish Brewing Company																																																X			
Fletcher Street Brewing Company																							X																												
Florida Beer Company		X								X	X										X														X												X				
Flying Bison Brewing Company																																			X																
Flying Dog Brewery LLC	X	X	X	X	X	X	X	X		X	X	X	X	X		X	X	X	X	X	X	X	X	X	X		X	X	X	X	X	X	X	X	X	X	X	X	X				X	X		X					
Flying Fish Brewing									X	X											X											X							X												
Fordham Brewing Company									X												X											X							X							X					
Founders Brewing Company (Contact Brewery)																																																			
Four Peaks Brewing Company				X																																															
Four Plus Brewing Company					X										X																			X											X	X					
Franconia Notch Brewing Company																				X											X									X											
Frankenmuth Brewery (Contact Brewery)																																																			
Frederick Brewing Company					X				X						X	X	X	X			X				X										X	X		X	X							X				X	X
Freeport Brewing Company																						X																													
Full Sail Brewing Company	X			X	X	X				X		X												X							X				X	X		X	X				X	X		X					X
Glacier Brewing																											X																								
Gluek Brewing Company																								X																										X	
Gold Hill Brewery					X																																														
Golden City Brewery						X																																													
Golden Valley Brewery (Contact Brewery)																																																			
Goose Island Beer Company (Contact Brewery)																																																			
Gordon Biersch Brewery				X	X					X																								X	X																

Availability by State *Continued*

Brewery	AK	AL	AR	AZ	CA	CO	CT	DC	DE	FL	GA	HI	IA	ID	IL	IN	KS	KY	LA	MA	MD	ME	MI	MN	MO	MS	MT	NC	NE	ND	NH	NJ	NM	NV	NY	OH	OK	OR	PA	RI	SC	SD	TN	TX	UT	VA	VT	WA	WI	WV	WY
Grand Teton Brewing Company					✗									✗													✗																		✗						✗
Gray Brewing (Contact Brewery)															✗																																			✗	
Great Beer Company					✗																																														
Great Divide Brewing Company				✗		✗				✗	✗				✗	✗	✗	✗		✗	✗			✗	✗			✗	✗	✗					✗	✗	✗	✗	✗	✗			✗	✗		✗		✗	✗		
Great Lakes Brewing Company															✗	✗							✗												✗	✗			✗										✗	✗	
Great Northern Brewing Company															✗												✗																						✗		
Great Northern Brewing Company																											✗																								
Great Sex Brewing, Inc.					✗	✗																	✗																												
Green Bay Brewing Company																																																	✗		
Green Flash Brewing (Contact Brewery)																																																			
Gritty McDuff's Brewing Company																				✗		✗									✗	✗			✗												✗				
Hair Of The Dog Brewing Company					✗																										✗		✗															✗			
Hale's Ales (Contact Brewery)																																																			
Happy Valley Brewing Company					✗																																														
Harbor City Brewing, Inc. (Contact Brewery)																																																			
Harlem Brewing Company (Contact Brewery)																																																			
Harpoon Brewery							✗	✗	✗	✗					✗			✗		✗	✗	✗	✗					✗			✗	✗			✗	✗			✗	✗	✗		✗			✗	✗		✗		
Healthy Brew (Contact Brewery)																																																			
Heiner Brau																			✗																																
Heinzelmannchen Brewery (Kegs/ Growlers)																												✗																							
Helmar Brewing Company (Contact Brewery)																																																			
High & Mighty Brewing Company (Contact Brewery)																																																			
High Falls Brewing	✗	✗	✗			✗	✗			✗	✗	✗			✗	✗	✗	✗	✗	✗	✗	✗	✗	✗	✗	✗	✗	✗	✗		✗	✗	✗	✗	✗	✗	✗	✗	✗	✗	✗		✗	✗		✗	✗	✗	✗		
High Point Wheat Beer Company																															✗	✗							✗												
Highland Brewing										✗																		✗													✗		✗								
Hood Canal Brewing (Contact Brewery)																																																			
Hoppy Brewing Company					✗																																														
Hoptown Brewery					✗																																														
Hornpout Brewing (Contact Brewery)																																																			
Huebert Brewing																																					✗														

Brewery	AK	AL	AR	AZ	CA	CO	CT	DC	DE	FL	GA	HI	IA	ID	IL	IN	KS	KY	LA	MA	MD	ME	MI	MN	MO	MS	MT	NC	NE	ND	NH	NJ	NM	NV	NY	OH	OK	OR	PA	RI	SC	SD	TN	TX	UT	VA	VT	WA	WI	WV	WY
Ice Harbor Brewing Company																																						X										X			
Independence Brewing																																												X							
Indian Wells Brewing (Contact Brewery)																																																			
Iron Horse Brewery																																																X			
Island Brewing Company					X																																														
Ithaca Beer Company, Inc.																																			X																
Jack Russell Brewing					X																																														
Jacob Leinenkugel Brewing Company				X											X	X	X	X					X	X	X				X	X					X	X						X							X	X	
James Page Brewing Company, LLC															X									X																									X		
Jarre Creek Ranch Brewery					X																																														
Jolly Pumpkin Artisan Ales	X				X					X	X				X	X		X					X	X											X	X													X		
Jones Brewing Company (Contact Brewery)																																																			
Joseph Huber Brewing Company, Inc.																																																	X		
Karl Strauss Breweries					X																																														
Keegan Ales																																			X																
Kelley Brothers Brewing Company					X																																														
Keoki Brewing Company												X																																							
Kettle House Brewing Company																											X																								
Keweenaw Brewing Company																							X																												
King Brewing Company (Contact Brewery)																																																			
Kodiak Island Brewing Company	X																																																		
Kona Brewing LLC	X			X	X					X		X		X				X							X				X	X		X			X				X				X			X		X			X
LaConner Brewing Company (Contact Brewery)																																																			
Lagunitas Brewing				X	X	X		X							X					X														X	X				X				X			X		X	X		
Lake Louie Brewing, LLC																																																		X	
Lake Placid Craft Brewing																				X												X			X					X	X						X			
Lake Superior Brewing Company																								X																										X	
Lakefront Brewery, Inc.				X	X	X				X					X	X					X			X	X							X	X	X					X	X			X			X			X	X	
Lancaster Brewing Company																					X											X							X							X					
Landmark Beer Company																																			X																

Availability by State *Continued*

Brewery	AK	AL	AR	AZ	CA	CO	CT	DC	DE	FL	GA	HI	IA	ID	IL	IN	KS	KY	LA	MA	MD	ME	MI	MN	MO	MS	MT	NC	NE	ND	NH	NJ	NM	NV	NY	OH	OK	OR	PA	RI	SC	SD	TN	TX	UT	VA	VT	WA	WI	WV	WY
Landmark Beer Company																																			X																
Lang Creek Brewery														X													X											X											X		
Latrobe Brewing (Contact Brewery)																																																			
Left Coast Brewing					X																																														
Left Handed Brewing Company		X		X		X				X	X			X	X	X	X			X				X							X	X	X	X			X						X	X		X					X
Legacy Brewing Company																												X											X												
Legend Brewing Company																																														X					
Lion Brewery																																							X												
The Long Trail Brewing Company							X											X		X											X	X			X					X							X				
Lost Coast Brewery & Café				X	X				X				X	X			X	X										X			X	X	X	X				X	X				X			X			X	X	
Mac Tarnahan's Brewing Company	X		X	X	X		X				X	X	X	X	X	X							X	X	X			X	X		X	X		X		X		X	X		X		X	X	X	X	X	X	X	X	X
Mad Anthony Brewing Company																X																																			
Mad River Brewing			X	X	X				X					X															X					X					X	X						X			X		
Madison River Brewing Company (Contact Brewery)																																																			
Magic Hat Brewing Company							X		X		X								X	X	X										X	X							X	X						X	X				
Maine Coast Brewing																						X																													
Mammoth Brewing Company					X																																														
Mantorville Brewing Company LLC																								X																											
Marin Brewing Company					X																																	X													
Maritime Pacific Brewing Company																																																X			
Mehana Brewing Company, Inc.				X	X						X																																								
Mendocino Brewing Company (Contact Brewery)																																																			
Mercury Brewing							X												X													X											X								
Michigan Brewing Company, Inc.															X				X				X										X	X			X	X							X	X					
Middle Ages Brewing Company (Contact Brewery)																																																			
Midnight Sun Brewing Company	X																																					X													
Millstream Brewing Company													X		X																																			X	
Minhas Craft Brewery (Contact Brewery)																																																			
Mishawaka Brewing Company																X																																			
Mississippi Brewing Company (Contact Brewery)																																																			

214

Brewery	AK	AL	AR	AZ	CA	CO	CT	DC	DE	FL	GA	HI	IA	ID	IL	IN	KS	KY	LA	MA	MD	ME	MI	MN	MO	MS	MT	NC	NE	ND	NH	NJ	NM	NV	NY	OH	OK	OR	PA	RI	SC	SD	TN	TX	UT	VA	VT	WA	WI	WV	WY
Moab Brewery																																													X						
Molson Coors Brewing Company	X	X	X	X	X	X	X	X	X	X	X	X	X	X	X	X	X	X	X	X	X	X	X	X	X	X	X	X	X	X	X	X	X	X	X	X	X	X	X	X	X	X	X	X	X	X	X	X	X	X	X
Mount Hood Brewing Company																																						X														
Moylan's Brewing Company				X	X															X															X	X		X	X												
Mt. Shasta Brewing Company (Contact Brewery)																																																			
Mudshark Brewing Company				X																																															
Nashoba Valley Brewery (Contact Brewery)																																																			
Nectar Ales					X																							X																								
New Belgium Brewing Company			X	X	X	X									X				X						X	X			X	X				X							X					X			X		X
New Century Brewing Company															X	X		X		X					X							X			X								X								
New England Brewing Company							X																																												
New Glarus Brewing																																																	X		
New Holland Brewing Company															X	X							X												X				X												
New Knoxville Brewing Company (Contact Brewery)																																																			
New River Brewing Company																												X																		X			X	
New South Brewing Company																												X													X										
Nicolet Brewing (Contact Brewery)																																																			
Nimbus Brewing Company				X	X	X																												X																	
Nine G Brewing Company, Inc.																X																																			
North Coast Brewing Company				X	X	X	X			X	X	X	X	X	X			X	X	X			X	X	X	X					X	X	X	X	X	X	X	X	X		X		X			X			X	X	
O'Fallon Brewery						X				X					X	X	X	X					X	X	X																									X	
Oak Creek Brewing Company				X																																		X													
Oak Pond Brewery																						X																													
Oaken Barrel Brewing Company																X																																			
Oceanside Ale Works (Contact Brewery)																																																			
Odell Brewing Company						X											X							X			X		X				X									X									X
Old Dominion Brewing Company								X		X											X							X							X				X							X				X	
Olde Saratoga Brewing Company																																			X																
Olde Town Brewing (Contact Brewery)																																																			
Oregon Trail Brewery (Contact Brewery)																																																			

Brewery	AK	AL	AR	AZ	CA	CO	CT	DC	DE	FL	GA	HI	IA	ID	IL	IN	KS	KY	LA	MA	MD	ME	MI	MN	MO	MS	MT	NC	NE	ND	NH	NJ	NM	NV	NY	OH	OK	OR	PA	RI	SC	SD	TN	TX	UT	VA	VT	WA	WI	WV	WY
Orlando Brewing Partners, Inc. (Contact Brewery)																																																			
Oskar Blues Grill & Brew				✗		✗				✗					✗					✗								✗				✗	✗	✗					✗							✗			✗	✗	
Otter Creek Brewing Company					✗		✗							✗						✗					✗			✗			✗	✗			✗	✗	✗	✗	✗	✗						✗	✗	✗	✗		
Pabst Brewing Company	✗	✗	✗	✗	✗	✗	✗	✗	✗	✗	✗	✗	✗	✗	✗	✗	✗	✗	✗	✗	✗	✗	✗	✗	✗	✗	✗	✗	✗	✗	✗	✗	✗	✗	✗	✗	✗	✗	✗	✗	✗	✗	✗	✗	✗	✗	✗	✗	✗	✗	✗
Palmetto Brewing Company, Inc.																																									✗										
Paper City Brewery Company	✗												✗							✗																					✗										
Peak Organic Brewing Company (Contact Brewery)																																																			
Pelican Pub & Brewery (Contact Brewery)																																																			
Penn Brewery (Pennsylvania Brewing)					✗				✗	✗											✗											✗							✗												
Pennichuck Brewing Company																				✗											✗								✗												
Pete's Brewing	✗	✗	✗	✗	✗	✗	✗	✗	✗	✗	✗	✗	✗	✗	✗	✗	✗	✗	✗	✗	✗	✗	✗	✗	✗	✗	✗	✗	✗	✗	✗	✗	✗	✗	✗	✗	✗	✗	✗	✗	✗	✗	✗	✗	✗	✗	✗	✗	✗	✗	✗
Pig's Eye Brewing Company				✗		✗				✗					✗									✗					✗										✗				✗			✗				✗	
Pike Brewing Company (Contact Brewery)																																																			
Pioneer Brewing Company																				✗																															
Pisgah Brewing Company																												✗																							
Pittsburgh Brewing Company (Contact Brewery)	✗			✗		✗	✗	✗		✗	✗				✗		✗	✗	✗	✗	✗		✗	✗	✗	✗		✗	✗		✗	✗			✗	✗	✗	✗	✗		✗		✗	✗		✗				✗	✗
Pony Express Brewing Company										✗						✗									✗				✗																					✗	
Port Brewing Company				✗	✗															✗																			✗												
Port Townsend Brewing Company																																																✗			
Pyramid Brewery	✗			✗	✗	✗				✗	✗	✗	✗	✗	✗						✗		✗	✗	✗			✗	✗	✗					✗	✗	✗	✗				✗	✗	✗	✗	✗	✗	✗	✗		✗
R.J. Rockers Brewing Company																												✗													✗										
Ramapo Valley Brewery					✗					✗					✗					✗												✗		✗					✗										✗		
Rarh & Sons Brewing Company																																												✗							
Real Ale Brewing Company (Contact Brewery)																																																			
ReaperAle, Inc.				✗	✗				✗																							✗		✗											✗						
Red Bell Brewery & Pub									✗																							✗							✗												
Red Lodge Ales Brewing Company																											✗																								
Redhook Ale Brewery, Inc.	✗	✗	✗	✗	✗	✗	✗	✗	✗	✗	✗	✗	✗	✗	✗	✗	✗	✗	✗	✗	✗	✗	✗	✗	✗	✗	✗	✗	✗	✗	✗	✗	✗	✗	✗	✗	✗	✗	✗	✗	✗		✗	✗	✗	✗	✗	✗	✗	✗	✗
Rheingold Brewing Company (Contact Brewery)																																																			
Rio Grande Brewing Company (Contact Brewery)																																																			

Brewery	AK	AL	AR	AZ	CA	CO	CT	DC	DE	FL	GA	HI	IA	ID	IL	IN	KS	KY	LA	MA	MD	ME	MI	MN	MO	MS	MT	NC	NE	ND	NH	NJ	NM	NV	NY	OH	OK	OR	PA	RI	SC	SD	TN	TX	UT	VA	VT	WA	WI	WV	WY
River Horse Brewing Company							x		x											x	x											x		x	x				x												
Rock Art Brewery, LLC																																x															x				
Rocky Bay Brewing Company																						x																													
Rocky Coulee Brewing Company																																																x			
Rogue Ales	x	x	x	x	x	x	x	x	x	x	x	x	x	x	x	x	x	x	x	x	x	x	x	x	x	x	x	x	x	x	x	x	x	x	x	x	x	x	x	x	x	x	x	x	x	x	x	x	x	x	x
Roslyn Brewing Company (Contact Brewery)																																																			
Ruby Mountain Brewing Company														x																				x																	
Rush River Brewing (Contact Brewery)																								x																									x		
Russian River Brewing Company					x				x																														x												
SAB Miller Corp	x	x	x	x	x	x	x	x	x	x	x	x	x	x	x	x	x	x	x	x	x	x	x	x	x	x	x	x	x	x	x	x	x	x	x	x	x	x	x	x	x	x	x	x	x	x	x	x	x	x	x
Sacramento Brewing Company, Inc.					x																																														
Saint Arnold Brewing Company																																												x							
Sand Creek Brewing Company, LLC															x								x																										x		
Santa Cruz Mountain Brewing					x																																														
Santa Fe Brewing Company				x	x	x																											x	x		x									x	x					
Schlafly Beer															x	x		x					x		x																										
Scuttlebutt Brewing Company																																																x			
Seabright Brewery					x																																														
Sebago Brewing Company																				x		x																													
Sheepscot Valley Brewing Company																						x																													
Shenandoah Brewing Company (Contact Brewery)									x																																					x					
Sherwood Forest Brewers																				x																															
Shipyard Brewing Company	x	x	x	x	x	x	x	x	x	x	x	x	x	x	x	x	x	x	x	x	x	x	x	x	x	x	x	x	x	x	x	x	x	x	x	x	x	x	x	x	x	x	x	x	x	x	x	x	x	x	x
Shmaltz Brewing Company				x	x	x	x	x	x	x					x	x	x			x	x		x	x				x				x		x	x			x	x		x		x			x			x		
Short's Brewing Company																							x																												
Sierra Blanca Brewing Company																																	x																		
Sierra Nevada Brewing Company	x	x	x	x	x	x	x	x	x	x	x	x	x	x	x	x	x	x	x	x	x	x	x	x	x	x	x	x	x	x	x	x	x	x	x	x	x	x	x	x	x	x	x	x	x	x	x	x	x	x	x
Siletz Brewing Company, Inc.																																		x				x													
Silver Gulch Brewing & Bottling	x																																																		
SKA Brewing Company				x		x									x														x				x																		

217

Availability by State *Continued*

Brewery	AK	AL	AR	AZ	CA	CO	CT	DC	DE	FL	GA	HI	IA	ID	IL	IN	KS	KY	LA	MA	MD	ME	MI	MN	MO	MS	MT	NC	NE	ND	NH	NJ	NM	NV	NY	OH	OK	OR	PA	RI	SC	SD	TN	TX	UT	VA	VT	WA	WI	WV	WY
Skagit River Brewery (Contact Brewery)																																																			
Slab City Brewing																																																	X		
Sly Fox Brewing Company																																							X												
Smuttynose Brewing Company							X		X											X	X	X									X			X	X				X	X							X	X	X		
Snake River Brewing Company					X									X													X							X											X			X			X
Snipes Mountain Brewing Company														X																								X										X			
Snoqualmie Falls Brewing Company																																																X			
Snowshoe Brewing Company (Contact Brewery)																																																			
Sonora Brewing Company (Contact Brewery)																																																			
South Hampton Publick House						X													X												X		X						X	X											
South Shore Brewery																							X	X																								X		
Southern Tier Brewing Company						X	X								X	X			X				X											X	X				X	X							X		X		
Spanish Peaks Brewing Company/ United States Beverage	X	X	X	X	X	X	X	X	X	X	X	X	X	X	X	X	X	X	X	X	X	X	X	X	X	X	X	X	X	X	X	X	X	X	X	X	X	X	X	X	X	X	X	X	X	X	X	X	X	X	X
Speakeasy Ales & Lagers, Inc.				X	X			X							X								X									X		X	X	X			X	X							X				
Spilker Ales																													X																						
Sprecher Brewing		X	X	X	X									X		X	X	X	X		X	X		X	X	X									X											X			X	X	
Springfield Brewing Company																									X																										
St. Croix Beer Company																								X																								X		
St. George Brewing Company																												X													X					X					
Stampede Brewing Company (Contact Brewery)																																																			
Starr Hill Brewer (Contact Brewery)																																																			
Steamworks Brewing Company (Contact Brewery)																																																			
Stevens Point Brewery										X			X	X	X	X								X	X					X												X							X		
Stone Brewing Company	X			X	X	X		X		X					X				X	X												X	X	X	X	X	X						X	X		X		X			
Stone Coast Brewing Company						X									X					X		X										X			X								X		X						
Stoudt's Brewing Company					X			X		X	X									X	X		X									X		X	X				X							X					
Straub Brewing																																				X		X													
Streich's Brewing Company, LLC (Contact Brewery)																																																			
Sudwerk Restaurant and Brewer (Contact Brewery)																																																			
Summit Brewing Company					X					X					X	X			X				X	X			X		X	X								X				X							X		

Brewery	AK	AL	AR	AZ	CA	CO	CT	DC	DE	FL	GA	HI	IA	ID	IL	IN	KS	KY	LA	MA	MD	ME	MI	MN	MO	MS	MT	NC	NE	ND	NH	NJ	NM	NV	NY	OH	OK	OR	PA	RI	SC	SD	TN	TX	UT	VA	VT	WA	WI	WV	WY
Surly Brewing Company																								X																											
Sweetwater Brewing		X								X	X													X																	X		X								
Telegraph Brewing Company					X																																														
Terminal Gravity Brewing (Contact Brewery)																																																			
Terrapin Beer Company		X								X														X																	X		X								
Terre Haute Brewing																X																																			
The Academy of Fine Beers, LLC				X	X					X						X					X			X										X																	
The Bethlehem Brew Works (Contact Brewery)																																																			
The Black Mountain /Chili Beer Brewing Company		X		X	X	X				X	X				X	X	X	X	X	X					X	X		X			X	X		X	X								X	X	X			X	X		
The Boston Beer Company	X	X	X	X	X	X	X	X	X	X	X	X	X	X	X	X	X	X	X	X	X	X	X	X	X	X	X	X	X	X	X	X	X	X	X	X	X	X	X	X	X	X	X	X	X	X	X	X	X	X	X
The Church Brew Works																																							X												
The Defiant Brewing Company (Contact Brewery)																																																			
The Dock Street Brewery Company								X																								X							X												
The Fort Collins Brewery						X									X	X					X				X			X											X						X			X		X
The Matt Brewing							X	X	X	X					X	X					X								X	X		X	X				X	X	X							X	X			X	
The Narragansett Brewing Company																				X																				X											
The Northern Lights Brewing Company														X																																	X				
The Palisade Brewery (Contact Brewery)			X																																																
The Sea Dog Brewing Company	X	X	X	X	X	X	X	X	X	X	X	X	X	X	X	X	X	X	X	X	X	X	X	X	X	X	X	X	X	X	X	X	X	X	X	X	X	X	X	X	X	X	X	X	X	X	X	X	X	X	X
The Spoetzl Brewing	X	X	X	X	X	X				X	X				X	X	X	X	X		X		X	X	X	X	X	X				X	X		X	X	X				X		X	X	X	X			X		X
The Weeping Radish Brewery								X													X		X									X														X					
Thirsty Dog Brewing Company															X			X			X															X			X												
Thomas Creek Brewery									X												X																						X	X							
Three Floyds Brewing Company									X						X	X	X															X			X		X	X								X			X		
Tommyknocker Brewery				X											X	X		X	X						X				X	X	X	X	X	X	X										X	X				X	X
Tractor Brewing Company																																	X	X																	
Trailhead Brewing Company																									X																										
Traverse Brewing Company																							X																												
Tremont Brewery/Atlantic Coast Brewing Company	X	X	X	X	X	X	X	X	X	X	X	X	X	X	X	X	X	X	X	X	X	X	X	X	X	X	X	X	X	X	X	X	X	X	X	X	X	X	X	X	X	X	X	X	X	X	X	X	X	X	X
Tröegs Brewing Company									X												X											X							X							X					

Brewery	AK	AL	AR	AZ	CA	CO	CT	DC	DE	FL	GA	HI	IA	ID	IL	IN	KS	KY	LA	MA	MD	ME	MI	MN	MO	MS	MT	NC	NE	ND	NH	NJ	NM	NV	NY	OH	OK	OR	PA	RI	SC	SD	TN	TX	UT	VA	VT	WA	WI	WV	WY
Trout Brook Brewing Company							X				X									X											X								X												
Trout River Brewing Company																															X				X												X				
Tuckerman Brewing																				X											X																				
Tuscan Brewing Company				X																																															
Twisted Pine Brewing Company (Contact Brewery)																																																			
Two Brothers Brewing Company															X	X			X	X			X											X															X		
Tyranena Brewing Company																																																	X		
Uinta Brewing Company					X									X													X																		X	X					
Upland Brewing Company (Contact Brewery)																																																			
Utah Brewers Cooperative																																													X						
Victory Brewing Company					X		X		X						X				X	X			X				X					X			X	X			X	X			X			X					
Viking Brewing																								X																									X		
Wachusett Brewing Company																				X															X																
Wagner Valley Brewing Company																																			X				X												
Waimea Brewing Company					X							X																																							
Warbird Brewing Company (Contact Brewery)																X																																			
Weyerbacher Brewing Company								X											X	X												X			X	X			X	X						X					
Whitstran Brewing Company																																																X			
Widmer Brothers Brewing Company	X	X		X	X	X	X	X	X	X	X	X	X	X	X	X	X	X		X	X	X	X	X	X	X	X	X			X	X	X	X	X		X	X	X	X	X				X	X	X	X	X	X	X
Wiedenmayer Brewing Company (Contact Brewery)																																																			
Williamsburg AleWerks (Contact Brewery)																																																			
Woodstock Beer											X																																								
Woodstock Inn Brewery																															X																				
Yards Brewing							X	X	X												X											X							X							X					
Yazoo Brewing																																											X								
Yellowstone Valley Brewing						X																		X			X							X								X								X	X
Zuma Brewing Company (Cancun Brewery)											X																																	X							

GEOGRAPHIC BREWERY INDEX

This section lists by state the breweries indexed in *The Essential Reference of Domestic Brewers and Their Bottled Brands (DBBB)*.

Each brewery listing provides the brewery's name, address, phone number, company web site (if available), and a listing of each brewery's currently offered brands. The brewery and the brand listing is followed by the number of the page on which the brand appears as a full portfolio listing.

GEOGRAPHIC BREWER INDEX (Alphabetical)

Alaskan Brewing Company – *page 448*

AK

5429 Shaune Drive
Juneau, AK 99801
907-780-5866
www.alaskanbeer.com

BRANDS:
Alaskan Amber (22 SRM, 18 IBU) – *page 448*
Alaskan Big Nugget Barley Wine
Alaskan ESB (26 SRM, 35 IBU)
Alaskan IPA (12 SRM, 55 IBU)
Alaskan Pale (8.5 SRM, 24 IBU)
Alaskan Smoked Porter (92 SRM, 45 IBU)
Alaskan Stout (11 SRM, 28 IBU)
Alaskan Summer Ale (8 SRM, 18 IBU)
Alaskan Winter Ale (17 SRM, 27 IBU)

States Available: AK, AZ, CA, ID, MT, NV, OR, OR, WA, WY

Kodiak Island Brewing Company (Kegs/Growlers)

338 Shelikof
Kodiak, AK 99615
907-486-2537
www.kodiakbrewery.com

BRANDS:
Kodiak Island Cloud Peak Hefeweizen
Kodiak Island Island Fog Barley Wine
Kodiak Island Liquid Sunshine
Kodiak Island Night Watch Porter
Kodiak Island North Pacific Ale
Kodiak Island Sweet Georgia Brown

States Available: AK

Midnight Sun Brewing Company – *page 520*

7329 Arctic Boulevard, Suite #A
Anchorage, AK 99518
907-344-1179
www.midnightsunbrewing.com

BRANDS:
Midnight Sun Arctic Devil Barley Wine
Midnight Sun Arctic Rhino Coffee Porter (20 IBU)
Midnight Sun Co Ho Ho Imperial IPA (85 IBU)
Midnight Sun Epluche-Culotte (20 IBU)
Midnight Sun Kodiak Brown Ale (24 IBU)
Midnight Sun La Miatresse du Moine (40 IBU)
Midnight Sun Saison of the Sun (27 IBU)
Midnight Sun Sockeye Red IPA (70 IBU) – *page 520*

States Available: AK, OR

Silver Gulch Brewing & Bottling

P.O. Box 82125
Fairbanks, AK 99708-2125
907-452-2739
www.silvergulch.com

BRANDS:
Silver Gulch Coldfoot Pilsner Lager (22 IBU)
Silver Gulch Copper Creek Amber Ale (24 IBU)
Silver Gulch Fairbanks Lager (21 IBU)
Silver Gulch Old 55 Pale Ale
Silver Gulch Pick Axe Porter (29 IBU)

States Available: AK

GEOGRAPHIC BREWER INDEX (Alphabetical)

The following brewers distribute their brands in Alaska:

Alaskan Brewing Company	Pete's Brewing
Anchor Brewing Company	Pittsburgh Brewing Company
Anheuser-Busch, Inc.	Pyramid Brewery
Big Sky Brewing Company	Redhook Ale Brewery
Brewery Ommegang	Rogue Ales
BridgePort Brewing Company	SAB Miller Corp
Deschutes Brewery	Shipyard Brewing Company
Dogfish Head Craft Brewery	Sierra Nevada Brewing Company
Elysian Brewing Company	Silver Gulch Brewing & Bottling
Flying Dog Brewery, LLC	Spanish Peaks Brewing Company/
Full Sail Brewing Company	United States Beverage
Jolly Pumpkin Artisan Ales	Stone Brewing Company
Kodiak Island Brewing Company	The Boston Beer Company
Kona Brewing, LLC	The Sea Dog Brewing Company
MacTarnahan's Brewing Company	The Spoetzl Brewing
Midnight Sun Brewing Company	Tremont Brewery/Atlantic Coast Brewing
Molson Coors Brewing Company	Company
Pabst Brewing Company	Widmer Brothers Brewing Company
Paper City Brewery Company	

Olde Towne Brewing 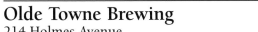 AL

214 Holmes Avenue
Huntsville, AL 35801
256-564-7404
www.oldetownebrewery.com

BRANDS:
Olde Towne Amber
Olde Towne Pale Ale

States Available: Contact Brewery

The following brewers distribute their brands in Alabama:

Anchor Brewing Company	SAB Miller Corp
Abita Brewing Company	Shipyard Brewing Company
Anheuser-Busch, Inc.	Sierra Nevada Brewing Company
BridgePort Brewing Company	Spanish Peaks Brewing Company/
D.G. Yuengling & Son, Inc.	United States Beverage
Eel River Brewing Company	Sprecher Brewing
Florida Beer Company	Sweetwater Brewing
Flying Dog Brewery, LLC	Terrapin Beer Company
High Falls Brewing	The Black Mountain/Chili Beer Company
Left Handed Brewing Company	The Boston Beer Company
Molson Coors Brewing Company	The Sea Dog Brewing Company
Pabst Brewing Company	The Spoetzl Brewing
Pete's Brewing	Tremont Brewery/Atlantic Coast Brewing
Redhook Ale Brewery	Company
Rogue Ales	Widmer Brothers Brewing Company

Diamond Bear Brewing Company  AR

323C Cross Street
Little Rock, AR 72201
501-708-2739
www.diamondbear.com

BRANDS:
Diamond Bear Honey Weiss (21 IBU)
Diamond Bear Irish Red Ale (31 IBU)
Diamond Bear Pale Ale (33 IBU)
Diamond Bear Party Porter (38 IBU)
Diamond Bear Presidential IPA (57 IBU)
Diamond Bear Rocktoberfest (32 IBU)
Diamond Bear Southern Blonde (28 IBU)
Diamond Bear Ultra Blonde (18 IBU)

States Available: AR, MO

The following brewers distribute their brands in Arkansas:

Abita Brewing Company	Redhook Ale Brewery
Anchor Brewing Company	Rogue Ales
Anheuser-Busch, Inc.	SAB Miller Corp
Boulevard Brewing Company	Shipyard Brewing Company
Breckenridge Brewery	Sierra Nevada Brewing Company
Diamond Bear Brewing Company	Spanish Peaks Brewing Company/
Flying Dog Brewery, LLC	United States Beverage
High Falls Brewing	Sprecher Brewing
MacTarnahan's Brewing Company	The Boston Beer Company
Molson Coors Brewing Company	The Palisade Brewery
New Belgium Brewing Company	The Sea Dog Brewing Company
Pabst Brewing Company	The Spoetzl Brewing
Pete's Brewing	Tremont Brewery/Atlantic Coast Brewing
Pyramid Brewery	Company

GEOGRAPHIC BREWER INDEX (Alphabetical)

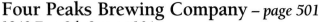

AZ

Electric Beer Company
1326 Highway 92 #8, P.O. Box 354
Bisbee, AZ 85603
520-432-5465
www.electricbrewing.com

BRANDS:
Dave's Electric Beer
OK Ale

States Available: Contact Brewery

Four Peaks Brewing Company – *page 501*
1340 East 8th Street #104
Tempe, AZ 85281
480-303-9967
www.fourpeaks.com

BRANDS:
Four Peaks Arizona Peach
Four Peaks Hefeweizen
Four Peaks Kölsch
Four Peaks Oatmeal Stout
Hopknot IPA
Kiltlifter Scottish-Style Ale – *page 501*
The Raj India Pal Ale
8th Street Ale

States Available: AZ

Mudshark Brewing Company
210 Swanson Avenue
Lake Havasu City, AZ 86403
928-453-2981
www.mudsharkbrewingco.com

BRANDS:
Mudshark Brewery Full Moon Belgian White Ale
Mudshark Brewery Dry Heat Hefeweizen (3.6 SRM, 18 IBU)

States Available: AZ

Nimbus Brewing Company – *page 523*
3850 E. 44th Street
Tucson, AZ 85713
520-745-9175
www.nimbusbeer.com

BRANDS:
Nimbus Blonde Ale (4 SRM, 12 IBU) – *page 523*
Nimbus Brown Ale (21 SRM, 26 IBU) – *page 525*
Nimbus Oatmeal Stout (36 SRM, 45 IBU) – *page 525*
Nimbus "Old Monkeyhine" English Strong (16 SRM, 35 IBU) – *page 526*
Nimbus Pale Ale (8 SRM, 40 IBU) – *page 524*
Nimbus Red Ale (14 SRM, 29 IBU) – *page 524*

States Available: AZ, CA

Oak Creek Brewing Company
450 Jordan Road, Suite 7
Sedona, AZ 86336-4100
520-204-1300
www.oakcreekbrew.com

BRANDS:
Oak Creek Amber Ale
Oak Creek Golden Lager
Oak Creek Hefeweizen
Oak Creek Nut Brown Ale
Oak Creek Pale Ale

States Available: AZ

Sonoran Brewing Company (Kegs/Growlers)
10426 East Jomax Road
Scottsdale, AZ 85255
602-484-7775
www.sonorabrew.com

BRANDS:
Sonora Brewing Burning Bird Pale Ale
Sonora Brewing C.I.A. - Citrus Infused Ale
Sonora Brewing Desert Amber
Sonora Brewing India Pale Ale
Sonora Brewing Mandarin Orange Hefeweizen
Sonora Brewing Old Saguaro Barley Wine
Sonora Brewing Top Down Red Ale

States Available: Contact Brewery

(The Black Mountain/Chili Beer Brewing Company) – *page 469*

6245 E.Cave Creek Road
Cave Creek, AZ 85331-9046
602-488-4742
www.chilibeer.com

BRANDS:
Black Mountain Cave Creek Chili Beer – *page 469*
Black Mountain Frog Light
Black Mountain Gold
Black Mountain Juanderful Wheat
Black Mountain Ocotillo Amber
Black Mountain South of the Border Porter

States Available: AL, AZ, CA, CO, FL, GA, IA, IL, IN, KS, KY, MA, MN, MO, ND, NE, NJ, NY, OH, TN, TX, VA, WA, WI

The following brewers distribute their brands in Arizona:

Abita Brewing Company	North Coast Brewing Company
Alaskan Brewing Company	Oak Creek Brewing Company
Anchor Brewing Company	Oskar Blues Grill & Brew
Anderson Valley Brewing	Pabst Brewing Company
Anheuser-Busch, Inc.	Pete's Brewing
Avery Brewing Company	Pig's Eye Brewing Company
Bayhawk Ales Inc.	Pittsburgh Brewing Company
Bear Republic Brewing Company	Port Brewing Company
Boulder Beer Company	Pyramid Brewery
Brewery Ommegang	ReaperAle, Inc.
BridgePort Brewing Company	Redhook Ale Brewery
Deschutes Brewery	Rogue Ales
Dogfish Head Craft Brewery	SAB Miller Corp
Eel River Brewing Company	Santa Fe Brewing Company
Flying Dog Brewery, LLC	Shipyard Brewing Company
Four Peaks Brewing Company	Shmaltz Brewing Company
Frederick Brewing Company	Sierra Nevada Brewing Company
Full Sail Brewing Company	Ska Brewing Company
Gordon Biersch Brewery	Spanish Peaks Brewing Company/
Great Divide Brewing Company	United States Beverage
High Falls Brewing	Speakeasy Ales & Lagers, Inc.
Hoppy Brewing Company	Sprecher Brewing
Kona Brewing, LLC	Stone Brewing Company
Lagunitas Brewing	The Academy of Fine Beers, LLC
Left Handed Brewing Company	The Black Mountain/Chili Beer Company
Lost Coast Brewery & Café	The Boston Beer Company
Mad River Brewing	The Sea Dog Brewing Company
Molson Coors Brewing Company	The Spoetzl Brewing
Moylan's Brewing Company	Tremont Brewery/Atlantic Coast Brewing
Mudshark Brewing Company	Company
New Belgium Brewing Company	Widmer Brothers Brewing Company
Nimbus Brewing Company	

21st Amendment

563 2nd Street
San Francisco, CA 94107
415-369-0900
www.21st-amendment.com

BRANDS:
21st Amendment Brewery IPA (75 IBU)
21st Amendment Brewery Watermelon Wheat (17 IBU)

States Available: Contact Brewery

Alesmith Brewing Company

9368 Cabot Drive
San Diego, CA 92126
858-549-9888
www.alesmith.com

BRANDS:
Alesmith Brewing Horny Devil
Alesmith Brewing IPA
Alesmith Brewing Old Numbskull
Alesmith Brewing Special Bitter
Alesmith Brewing Speedway Stout
Alesmith Brewing Wee Heavy
Alesmith Brewing X-Extra Pale Ale
Alesmith Brewing YuleSmith Holiday Ale

States Available: Contact Brewery

Alpine Beer Company – *page 449*

2351 Alpine Boulevard
Alpine, CA 91901
619-445-2337
www.alpinebeerco.com

BRANDS:
Alpine Ale (38 IBU)
Alpine Beer Mchenney's Irish Red (10.7 IBU)
Alpine Beer Pure Hoppiness – *page 449*
Alpine Mandarin Nectar (4.1 IBU)

States Available: CA

CA

GEOGRAPHIC BREWER INDEX (Alphabetical)

Anchor Brewing Company – *page 450*

1705 Mariposa Street
San Francisco, CA 94107-2334
415-863-8350
www.anchorbrewing.com

BRANDS:
Anchor Brewing Bock Beer
Anchor Brewing Christmas Ale
Anchor Brewing Liberty Ale
Anchor Brewing Old Foghorn Barleywine Style Ale
Anchor Brewing Porter
Anchor Brewing Small Beer
Anchor Brewing Steam – *page 450*
Anchor Brewing Summer Ale

States Available: All 50 States

Anderson Valley Brewing Company – *page 451*

17700 Highway 253
Boonville, CA 95415
707-895-2337
www.avbc.com

BRANDS:
Anderson Valley Barney Flats Oatmeal Stout (13 IBU) – *page 452*
Anderson Valley Boont ESB Ale – *page 453*
Anderson Valley Boont Amber Ale (15 IBU) – *page 451*
Anderson Valley Brother David's Abbey Style Double (28 IBU)
Anderson Valley Brother David's Abbey Style Triple (26 IBU)
Anderson Valley Deependers Porter (17 IBU)
Anderson Valley High Rollers Wheat Beer (5 IBU)
Anderson Valley Hop Ottin' IPA (82 IBU) – *page 452*
Anderson Valley Poleeko Gold Pale Ale (34 IBU)
Anderson Valley Summer Solstice Cerveza Crema (4 IBU)
Anderson Valley Winter Solstice (5 IBU)

States Available: AZ, CO, CT, DE, ID, IL, IN, MA, MD, MI, NC, NJ, NM, NY,
        OH, OR, PA, RI, UT, VA, WA

Angel City Brewing – *page 454*

833 W. Torrance Blvd., Suite #105
Torrance, CA 90502
310-329-8881
www.angelcitybrewing.com

BRANDS:
Angel City Abbey (18 SRM, 30 IBU)
Angel City Ale (12 SRM, 30 IBU) – *page 454*
Angel City Dunkel (24 SRM, 20 IBU)
Angel City IPA (5.5 SRM, 45 IBU)
Angel City Lager (3.5 SRM, 20 IBU)
Angel City Pilz (3.5 SRM, 22 IBU)
Angel City Vitzen (5 SRM,15 IBU)

States Available: CA

Ballast Point Brewing Company – *page 465*

10051 Old Grove Road, Suite B
San Diego, CA 92131-1654
619-298-2337
www.ballastpoint.com

BRANDS:
Ballast Point Big Eye IPA
Ballast Point Black Marlin Porter
Ballast Point Calico Amber Ale
Ballast Point Wahoo Wheat Beer
Ballast Point Yellowtail Pale Ale (22 - 28 IBU) – *page 465*

States Available: CA (San Diego, Orange, L.A.)

GEOGRAPHIC BREWER INDEX (Alphabetical)

Bayhawk Ales, Inc.
2000 Main St Suite A
Irvine, CA 92614-7202
949-442-7565
www.bayhawkales.com

BRANDS:
Bayhawk Ales Amber Ale (23 IBU)
Bayhawk Ales Beach Blonde (9.5 IBU)
Bayhawk Ales California Pale Ale (CPA) (49 IBU)
Bayhawk Ales Chocolate Porter (35 IBU)
Bayhawk Ales Hefe Weizen (13 IBU)
Bayhawk Ales Honey Blonde (9 IBU)
Bayhawk Ales IPA (64 IBU)
Bayhawk Ales O.C. Lager (14 IBU)
Bayhawk Ales Stout (30 IBU)

States Available: AZ, CA, HI, NV, TX

Bear Republic Brewing Company
345 Healdsburg Avenue
Healdsburg, CA 95448
707-431-7258
www.bearrepublic.com

BRANDS:
Bear Republic Brewing Big Bear Stout Ale (68 IBU)
Bear Republic Brewing Hop Rod Rye (90+ IBU)
Bear Republic Brewing Pete Brown's Tribute Ale
Bear Republic Brewing Racer 5 (69 IBU)
Bear Republic Brewing Red Rocket Ale (65+ IBU)
Bear Republic Brewing Special XP Pale Ale (55 IBU)

States Available: AZ, CA, CO, DE, IL, KY, MA, MD, MI, NC, NY, OR, VA,
WA, WI

Beermann's Beerwerks
8284 Industrial Avenue
Roseville, CA 95678
916-781-2337
www.beermanns.com

BRANDS:
Beermann's Hefe Weizen
Beermann's Honey Brew
Beermann's India Pale Ale
Beermann's Lincoln Lager – Helles Lager
Beermann's Rip Roarin' Red – Red Ale

States Available: CA

Bison Brewing
2598 Telegraph Avenue
Berkeley, CA 94704
510-697-1537
www.bisonbrew.com

BRANDS:
Bison Brewing Organic Barleywine (30 SRM, 87 IBU)
Bison Brewing Organic Belgain Ale (30 SRM, 87 IBU)
Bison Brewing Organic Chocolate Stout (45 SRM, 30 IBU)
Bison Brewing Organic Farmhouse (7 SRM, 24 IBU)
Bison Brewing Organic Gingerbread Ale (35 SRM, 25 IBU)
Bison Brewing Organic Honey-Basil (6 SRM, 24 IBU)
Bison Brewing Organic IPA (12 SRM, 59 IBU)
Bison Brewing Organic Red Ale (16 SRM, 25 IBU)
Bison Brewing Organic Winter (32 SRM, 27 IBU)

States Available: CA, FL, GA, IN, NC, OH, OR, VA, WA

Bonnema Brewing Company

6900 El Camino Real
Atascadero, CA 93423
805-462-3660

BRANDS:
Bonnema Brewing Marzen
Bonnema Brewing Mudhole Porter
Bonnema Brewing Pozo Pale Ale
Bonnema Brewing Raspberry Wheat
Bonnema Brewing Red Kroeker Ale
Bonnema Brewing Whalerock Wheat
Bonnema Brewing White Christmas
Gold Hill Gold Trail Pale Ale

States Available: Contact Brewery

Buffalo Bill's Brewery

1082 B Street
Hayward, CA 94541
510-886-9823
www.buffalobillsbrewery.com

BRANDS:
Buffalo Bill's Brewery Orange Blossom Cream Ale
Buffalo Bill's Brewery Pumpkin Ale

States Available: Contact Brewery

Butte Creek Brewing

945 West Second Street
Chico, CA 95928
530-894-7906
www.buttecreek.com

BRANDS:
Butte Creek Christmas Cranberry Ale
Butte Creek Creekside Wheat
Butte Creek Gold Ale
Butte Creek Mt. Shasta Extra Pale Ale
Butte Creek Organic Ale
Butte Creek Organic India Pale Ale
Butte Creek Organic Pilsner
Butte Creek Organic Porter
Butte Creek Roland's Red
Butte Creek Spring Ale
Butte Creek Summer Pilsner
Butte Creek Winter Ale

States Available: CA

Central Coast Brewing

1422 Monterey Street
San Luis Obispo, CA 93401
805-783-2739
www.centralcoastbrewing.com

BRANDS:
Central Coast Brewing Cream Ale
Central Coast Brewing Golden Glow Ale
Central Coast Brewing Honey Wheat Ale
Central Coast Brewing Old Mission Ale
Central Coast Brewing Stenner Stout Ale
Central Coast Brewing Topless Blonde Ale

States Available: CA

Downtown Brewing Company
1119 Garden Street
San Luis Obispo, CA 93401
805-543-1843
www.slobrews.com

BRANDS:
SLO Brewing Amber Ale
SLO Brewing Blueberry Ale
SLO Brewing Cole Porter
SLO Brewing Extra Pale Ale
SLO Olde Highland Ale

States Available: CA

Drake's Brewing Company
1933 Davis St Suite 177
San Leandro, CA 94577-1256
510-562-0866
www.drinkdrakes.com

BRANDS:
Drake's Amber Ale
Drake's Blonde Ale
Drake's Hefe-Weizen
Drake's IPA

States Available: CA

E.J. Phair Brewing
975-E Detroit Avenue
Concord, CA 94518
925-680-4523
www.ejphair.com

BRANDS:
E.J. Phair India Pale Ale
E.J. Phair Marzen
E.J. Phair Pale Ale
E.J. Phair Pilsner

States Available: CA

Eel River Brewing Company
1777 Alamar Way
Fortuna, CA 95540
707-725-2739
www.climaxbeer.com

BRANDS:
Eel River Brewing California Blonde Ale
Eel River Brewing Climax California Classic
Eel River Brewing Organic Amber Ale
Eel River Brewing Organic Extra Pale Ale
Eel River Brewing Organic India Pale Ale
Eel River Brewing Organic Porter
Eel River Brewing Ravensbrau India Pale Ale
Eel River Brewing Ravensbrau Porter

States Available: AL, AZ, CA, FL, ID, MT, NV, OR, WA, WY

El Toro Brewing
17370 Hill Road
Morgan Hill, CA 95037
408-778-2739

BRANDS:
El Toro Bravo
El Toro Deuce Imperial IPA
El Toro IPA
El Toro Keller Bier
El Toro Negro Oatmeal Stout
El Toro Oro Golden Ale
El Toro Peach Ale
El Toro Poppy Jasper Amber Ale
El Toro William Jones Wheat
El Toro "Yo" Winter Brew
Gena's Honey Blonde Ale

States Available: CA, WI

GEOGRAPHIC BREWER INDEX (Alphabetical)

English Ales Brewery
223-A Reindollar Avenue
Marina, CA 93933
831-883-3000
www.englishalesbrewery.com

BRANDS:
English Ales Black Hound Stout
English Ales Black Prince Porter
English Ales Brew 66
English Ales Dragon Slayer India Pale Ale
English Ales Edinburgh Winter Ale
English Ales English Pale Ale
English Ales Jubilee Golden Ale
English Ales Monk's Brown Ale
English Ales Monterey Bay Wheat
English Ales Ramsey's Fat Lip Ale
English Ales Triple B (Borthwick's Best Bitter)
English Ales Victory ESB

States Available: CA

Etna Brewing Company
131 Callahan Street
Etna, CA 96027
530-467-5277
www.etnabrew.com

BRANDS:
Etna Classic Gold
Etna Old Grind Porter
Etna Phoenix Red

States Available: Contact Brewery

Farmhouse Brewing Company
7050 Monterey Street
Gilroy, CA 95020
408-842-1000
www.farmhousebrewing.com

BRANDS:
Farmhouse Hayloft Pils
Farmhouse Kölsch Bier
Farmhouse Oasthouse IPA
Farmhouse Saison 7
Farmhouse Stone Fence Porter
Farmhouse Two Tractor Pale Ale

States Available: Contact Brewery

Firestone Walker Brewing Company
1400 Ramada Drive
Paso Robles, CA 93446
805-238-2556
www.firestonewalker.com

BRANDS:
Firestone Walker Double Barrel Ale (16 SRM, 32 IBU)
Firestone Walker Lager (4 SRM, 24 IBU)
Firestone Walker Pale Ale (7 SRM, 38 IBU)
Firestone Walker Walker's Reserve (75 SRM, 45 IBU)

States Available: CA, NV

Gold Hill Brewery
5660 Vineyard Lane
Placerville, CA 95667
530-626-6522
www.goldhillvineyard.com

BRANDS:
Gold Hill 49'er Red
Gold Hill Axe Pic n Stout
Gold Hill Gold Strike Light
Gold Hill Hank's Porter
Gold Hill Old Miners Scotch Ale

States Available: CA

GEOGRAPHIC BREWER INDEX (Alphabetical)

Gordon Biersch Brewery
41 Hugus Alley At One Colorada
Pasadena, CA 91103
626-449-0052
www.gordonbiersch.com

BRANDS:
Gordon Biersch Blonde Bock (23 IBU)
Gordon Biersch Festbier (Restaurants Only)
Gordon Biersch Hefeweizen (12 IBU)
Gordon Biersch Maibock - Lager (Restaurants Only)
Gordon Biersch Marzen (18 IBU)
Gordon Biersch Pilsner (28 IBU)
Gordon Biersch Winter Bock (24 IBU)

States Available: AZ, CA, HI, NV, OH

Great Beer Company
21119 Superior Street
Chatsworth, CA 91311-4309
818-718-2739
www.greatbeerco.com

BRANDS:
Great Beer Hollywood Blonde

States Available: CA

Great Sex Brewing, Inc. – *page 506*
12763 Encanto Way
Redding, CA 96003
530-275-2705
www.greatsexbrewing.com

BRANDS:
Great Sex Brewing Adam and Eve Ale – *page 506*

States Available: CA, CO, NV

Green Flash Brewing Company
1430 Vantage Court #104a
Vista, CA 92083
760-597-9012
www.greenflashbrew.com

BRANDS:
Green Flash Barleywine
Green Flash Belgian Style Trippel
Green Flash Extra Pale Ale
Green Flash Imperial IPA
Green Flash Nut Brown Ale
Green Flash Ruby Red Ale
Green Flash West Coast IPA

States Available: Contact Brewery

Happy Valley Brewing Company
6452 Happy Valley Road
Somerset, CA 95684
530-644-4733
www.happyvalleybrewing.com

BRANDS:
Happy Valley Brewing Mission Ale Double
Happy Valley Brewing Mission Ale Wit

States Available: CA

Hoppy Brewing Company
6300 Folsom Boulevard
Sacramento, CA 95819
916-451-6328
www.hoppy.com

BRANDS:
Hoppy Claus Holiday Ale
Hoppy Face Amber Ale
Liquid Sunshine Blonde Ale
Stony Face Red Ale
Total Eclipse Black Ale

States Available: CA

GEOGRAPHIC BREWER INDEX (Alphabetical)

Hoptown Brewery

3015 Hopyard Road, Suite D
Pleasanton, CA 94588-5253
925-426-5665
www.hoptownbrewing.com

BRANDS:
Hoptown Brown Nose Ale
Hoptown DUIPA Imperial Ale
Hoptown ESB
Hoptown Golden Ale
Hoptown IPA
Hoptown Old Yeltsin
Hoptown Paint the Town Red (25 IBU)
Hoptown Paleface Pale Ale
Hoptown Wheathopper Red Wheat Ale

States Available: CA

Indian Wells Brewing

2565 North Highway 14
Inyokern, CA 93527
760-377-5989
www.mojave-red.com

BRANDS:
Indian Wells Desert Pale Ale
Indian Wells Eastern Sierra Lager
Indian Wells Irish Green Ale
Indian Wells Lobotomy Bock
Indian Wells Mojave Gold
Indian Wells Mojave Red
Indian Wells Mojave Silver
Indian Wells Oktoberfest
Indian Wells Orange Blossom Amber
Indian Wells Piute Stout
Indian Wells Raspberry Ale
Indian Wells Sidewinder Missile Ale
Indian Wells Springfest Lager
Indian Wells Vette's Honey Ale

States Available: Contact Brewery

Island Brewing Company

5049 Sixth Street
Carpinteria, CA 93013
805-745-8272
www.islandbrewingcompany.com

BRANDS:
Island Brewing Avocado Ale
Island Brewing Blonde (25 IBU)
Island Brewing Island Pale Ale (60 IBU)
Island Brewing Jubilee Ale (30 IBU)
Island Brewing London Porter (35 IBU)
Island Brewing Nut Brown Ale (25 IBU)
Island Brewing Paradise Pale Ale (35 IBU)
Island Brewing Starry Night Stout (50 IBU)
Island Brewing Tropical Lager
Island Brewing Weiss (15 IBU)

States Available: CA

Jack Russell Brewing

2380 Larson Drive
Camino, CA 95709
530-644-4722
www.jackrussellbrewing.com

BRANDS:
Captain Boomer's IPA
Jack Russell's All American Premium Lager
Jack Russell's Harvest Apple Ale
Jack's Best Bitter Ale
Jack's Blackberry Abbey Ale
Jack's Blueberry Beer
Jack's Brown Ale
Jack's Farmhouse Ale
Jack's Huntsmans Lager
Jack's Irish Red Ale
Jack's London Porter
Jack's Olde Ale
Jack's Raspberry Imperial Stout
Jack's Scottish Ale
Jack's Whitewater Pale Ale

States Available: CA

GEOGRAPHIC BREWER INDEX (Alphabetical)

Karl Strauss Breweries – *page 509*

1044 Wall Street
La Jolla, CA 92037
858-551-2739
www.karlstrauss.com

BRANDS:
Karl Strauss Brewing Amber Lager (15 SRM, 15 IBU) – *page 509*
Karl Strauss Brewing Endless Summer Light (6 SRM, 15 IBU)
Karl Strauss Brewing Oktoberfest (9 SRM, 27 IBU)
Karl Strauss Brewing Red Trolley Ale (30 SRM, 17 IBU)
Karl Strauss Brewing Stargazer IPA (14 SRM, 40 IBU)
Karl Strauss Brewing Woodie Gold (5 SRM, 18 IBU)

States Available: Southern CA

Kelley Brothers Brewing Company

112 East Yosemite Avenue
Manteca, CA 95336
209-825-1727
www.kelleybrewing.com

BRANDS:
Kelley Brothers Four Towers IPA
Kelley Brothers Inferno Red

States Available: CA

Lagunitas Brewing

1280 North McDowell Boulevard
Petaluma, CA 94954
707-769-4495
www.lagunitas.com

BRANDS:
Lagunitas Brewing Brown Shugga
Lagunitas Brewing Cappuccino Stout
Lagunitas Brewing Czech Style Pilsner
Lagunitas Brewing Dogtown Pale Ale
Lagunitas Brewing Imperial Red Ale
Lagunitas Brewing Imperial Stout
Lagunitas Brewing India Pale Ale
Lagunitas Brewing IPA Maximus
Lagunitas Brewing Number 10 Ale
Lagunitas Brewing Olde GnarlyWine
Lagunitas Brewing The Censored Rich Copper Ale

States Available: AZ, CA, CO, DC, ID, MA, NV, NY, OR, TX, VA, WA

Left Coast Brewing

1245 Puerta Del Sol
San Clemente, CA 92673
949-481-0731
www.leftcoastbrewing.com

BRANDS:
Left Coast Gold
Left Coast Hefeweizen
Left Coast India Pale Ale
Left Coast Pale Ale

States Available: Southern CA

Lost Coast Brewery & Café – *page 517*

617 4th Street
Eureka, CA 95501-1013
707-445-4480
www.lostcoast.com

BRANDS:
Lost Coast 8 Ball Stout (48 IBU)
Lost Coast Alleycat Amber (35 IBU)
Lost Coast Downtown Brown (33 IBU)
Lost Coast Great White (27 IBU) – *page 517*
Lost Coast Indica IPA (62 IBU)
Lost Coast Raspberry Brown
Lost Coast Winterbraun (45 IBU)

States Available: AZ, CA, FL, IA, ID, IN, KS, NC, NM, NV, NY, OR, PA, TN, VA, WA, WI

Mad River Brewing – *page 518*

P.O. Box 767, 193 Taylor Way
Blue Lake, CA 95525
707-668-4151
www.madriverbrewing.com

BRANDS:
Mad River Jamaica Red (42 IBU)
Mad River Jamaica Sunset West Indies Pale Ale (65 IBU)
Mad River John Barleycorn Barleywine Style Ale (96 IBU)
Mad River Steelhead Extra Pale Ale (24.6 IBU) – *page 518*
Mad River Steelhead Extra Stout (32.7 IBU)
Mad River Steelhead Scotch Porter (39.1 IBU)

States Available: AZ, CA, CO, FL, ID, NC, NV, OR, PA, VA, WI

233

Mammoth Brewing Company

P.O. Box 611
Mammoth Lakes, CA 93546
760-934-2337
www.mammothbrewingco.com

BRANDS:
Mammoth Brewing Company Amber
Mammoth Brewing Company Double Nut Brown
Mammoth Brewing Company Gold
Mammoth Brewing Company India Pale Ale
Mammoth Brewing Company Pale Ale

States Available: CA

Marin Brewing Company

1809 Larkspur Landing Circle
Larkspur, CA 94939-1801
415-461-4677
www.marinbrewing.com

BRANDS:
Marin Brewing Albion Amber Ale
Marin Brewing Blueberry Ale
Marin Brewing Hefe Doppel Weizen
Marin Brewing Hefe Weiss
Marin Brewing Hoppy Holidaze Flavored Ale
Marin Brewing India Pale Ale
Marin Brewing Mt. Tam Pale Ale
Marin Brewing "Old Dipsea" Barleywine Style Ale
Marin Brewing Point Reyes Porter
Marin Brewing Raspberry Trail Ale
Marin Brewing San Quentin's Breakout Stout
Marin Brewing Star Brew
Marin Brewing Stinson Beach Peach
Marin Brewing Tripel Dipsea
Marin Brewing White Knuckle Ale

States Available: CA, OR

Mendocino Brewing Company

1601 Airport Road
Ukiah, CA 94582
707-463-6610
www.mendobrew.com

BRANDS:
Mendocino Brewing Black Hawk Stout
Mendocino Brewing Blue Heron Pale Ale
Mendocino Brewing Eye of the Hawk
Mendocino Brewing Peregrine Golden Ale
Mendocino Brewing Red Tail Ale
Mendocino Brewing Red Tail Lager
Mendocino Brewing White Hawk Select IPA

States Available: Contact Brewery (in 38 States)

Moylan's Brewing Company

15 Rowland Way
Novato, CA 94945
415- 898-4677
www.moylans.com

BRANDS:
Moylan's Celts Golden Ale
Moylan's Hopsickle Imperial Triple Hoppy Ale
Moylan's India Pale Ale
Moylan's Kilt Lifter Scotch Ale
Moylan's Old Blarney Barleywine Style Ale
Moylan's Paddy's Irish Style Red Ale
Moylan's Ryan O'Sullivan's Imperial Stout
Moylan's Tipperary Pale Ale
Moylan's Wheat Berry Ale
Moylander Double IPA

States Available: AZ, CA, MA, NY, OH, OR, RI

Mt. Shasta Brewing Company

360 College Avenue
Weed, CA 96094
530-938-2394
www.mtshastabrewingcompany.com

BRANDS:
Abner Weed Amber Ale
Brewers Creek Pale Ale
Mountain High IPA
Shastafarian Porter
Weed Golden Ale

States Available: Contact Brewery

Nectar Ales

620 McMurray Road
Buellton, CA 93427
805-686-1557
www.nectarales.com

BRANDS:
Nectar Ales IPA Nectar
Nectar Ales Pale Nectar
Nectar Ales Red Nectar

States Available: CA, NV

North Coast Brewing Company

455 N Main Street
Fort Bragg, CA 95437-3215
707-964-2739
www.northcoastbrewing.com

BRANDS:
North Coast ACME California Pale Ale (21 IBU)
North Coast ACME IPA (52 IBU)
North Coast Blue Star Great American Wheat Beer (17 IBU)
North Coast Brewing Brother Thelonious
North Coast Old No. 38 Stout (46 IBU)
North Coast Old Rasputin Russian Imperial Stout (75 IBU)
North Coast Old Stock Ale (36 IBU)
North Coast Pranqster Belgian Style Golden Ale (20 IBU)
North Coast Ruedrich's Red Seal Ale (45 IBU)
North Coast Scrimshaw Pilsner Style Beer (22 IBU)

States Available: AZ, CA, CO, CT, FL, GA, HI, IA, ID, IL, KY, LA, MA, MN, MO, MT, NC, NJ, NM, NV, NY, OH, OK, OR, PA, SC, TN, TX, VA, WA, WI

Oceanside Ale Works

3800 Oceanic Drive, #105
Oceanside, CA 92056
760-758-2064
www.oceansidealeworks.com

BRANDS:
Oceanside Ale Works Pier View Pale Ale
Oceanside Ale Works San Luis Rey Red

States Available: Contact Brewery

Geographic Brewer Index (Alphabetical)

Port Brewing Company

155 Mata Way
San Marcos, CA 92069
760-891-0272
www.lostabbey.com

BRANDS:
High Tide Fresh Hop IPA
Old Viscosity Ale
Santa's Little Helper Imperial Stout
Sharkbite Red Ale
The Lost Abbey Avant Garde (24 IBU)
The Lost Abbey Cuvee de Tomme
The Lost Abbey Judgment Day
The Lost Abbey Lost & Found Abbey Ale (19 IBU)
The Lost Abbey Red Barn Ale
The Lost Abbey The Angel's Share
Wipeout IPA

States Available: AZ, CA, MA

ReaperAle, Inc.

26741 Portola Parkway, 1E #476
Foothill Ranch, CA 92610
949-223-0122
www.reaperale.com

BRANDS:
ReaperAle Deathly Pale Ale (45 IBU)
ReaperAle Inevitable Ale (22 IBU)
ReaperAle Mortality Stout (30 IBU)
ReaperAle Redemption Red Ale (35 IBU)
ReaperAle Ritual Dark Ale (50 IBU)
ReaperAle Sleighor Double IPA (105 IBU)

States Available: AZ, CA, DE, NJ, PA, VA

Russian River Brewing Company

725 4th Street
Santa Rosa, CA 95404
707-545-BEER
www.russianriverbrewing.com

BRANDS:
Russian River Brewing Beatification
Russian River Brewing Damnation (25 IBU)
Russian River Brewing Depuration (27 IBU)
Russian River Brewing Redemption (23 IBU)
Russian River Brewing Salvation (22 IBU)
Russian River Brewing Sanctification (27 IBU)
Russian River Brewing Supplication (27 IBU)
Russian River Brewing Temptation (27 IBU)

States Available: CA, DC, PA

Sacramento Brewing Company Inc.

2713 El Paseo Lane
Sacramento, CA 95821
916-485-4677
www.sacbrew.com

BRANDS:
Sacramento Brewing Hefeweizen
Sacramento Brewing India Pale Ale
Sacramento Brewing Red Horse Ale
Sacramento Brewing River Otter Ale
Sacramento Brewing Russian Imperial Stout
Sacramento Brewing Sacsquatch Ale

States Available: CA

GEOGRAPHIC BREWER INDEX (Alphabetical)

Santa Cruz Mountain Brewing – *page 540*
402 Ingallis Street, Suite 27
Santa Cruz, CA 95060
831-425-4900
www.santacruzmountainbrewing.com

BRANDS:
Santa Cruz Mountain Brewing India Pale Ale
Santa Cruz Mountain Brewing Nicky 666
Santa Cruz Mountain Brewing Organic Amber Ale – *page 541*
Santa Cruz Mountain Brewing Organic Devout Stout – *page 540*
Santa Cruz Mountain Brewing Organic Dread Brown Ale – *page 541*
Santa Cruz Mountain Brewing Pale Ale
Santa Cruz Mountain Brewing Wilder Wheat

States Available: CA, HI, OR, WA

Seabright Brewery
519 Seabright Avenue
Santa Cruz, CA 95060
831-426-2793
www.seabrightbrewery.com

BRANDS:
Seabright Brewery Blur IPA
Seabright Brewery Oatmeal Stout
Seabright Brewery Resolution Red

States Available: CA

Shmaltz Brewing Company – *page 545*
912 Cole Street, #338
San Francisco, CA 94117
415-339-7462
www.shmaltz.com

BRANDS:
Shmaltz Brewing Bittersweet Lenny's R.I.P.A.
Shmaltz Brewing Genesis 10:10
Shmaltz Brewing Genesis Ale – *page 545*
Shmaltz Brewing Jewbelation
Shmaltz Brewing Messiah Bold

States Available: AZ, CA, CO, CT, DC, DE, FL, GA, ID, IL, IN, KY, MA, MD,
MI, MO, NC, NJ, NY, OH, PA, SC, TN, VA, WI

Snowshoe Brewing Company
2050 Highway 4
Arnold, CA 95223
209-795-2272
www.snowshoebrewing.com

BRANDS:
Snowshoe Brewing Grizzly Brown Ale
Snowshoe Brewing Snoweizen Wheat Ale
Snowshoe Brewing Thompson Pale Ale

States Available: Contact Brewery

Sierra Nevada Brewing Company
1075 E 20th Street
Chico, CA 95928-6722
530-893-3520
www.sierranevada.com

BRANDS:
Sierra Nevada Bigfoot Ale (38 SRM, 100 IBU)
Sierra Nevada Celebration Ale 21 SRM, 70 IBU)
Sierra Nevada Pale Ale (12 SRM, 38 IBU)
Sierra Nevada Porter (50 SRM, 39 IBU)
Sierra Nevada Stout (70 SRM, 53 IBU)
Sierra Nevada Summerfest (6 SRM, 30 IBU)
Sierra Nevada Wheat Beer (5 SRM, 26 IBU)

States Available: All 50 States

Speakeasy Ales & Lagers, Inc.
1195 Evans Avenue, Suite A
San Francisco, CA 94124
415-642-3371
www.goodbeer.com

BRANDS:
Speakeasy Big Daddy IPA
Speakeasy Double Daddy Imperial IPA
Speakeasy Prohibition Ale
Speakeasy Untouchable Pale Ale

States Available: AZ, CA, DC, IL, MI, NJ, NV, NY, OH, OR, PA, VA

Stone Brewing Company – *page 554*

1999 Citracado Parkway
Escondido, CA 92029
760-471-4999 Ext. 1561
www.stonebrew.com

BRANDS:
Arrogant Bastard Ale
Double Bastard Ale (100+ IBU)
Stone Anniversary Ale
Stone Imperial Russian Stout (90 IBU)
Stone IPA (77 IBU)
Stone Levitation Ale (45 IBU)
Stone Old Guardian Barley Wine (95 IBU)
Stone Pale Ale (41 IBU)
Stone Ruination IPA (100+ IBU) – *page 554*
Stone Smoked Porter (53 IBU)
Stone Vertical Epic Ale

States Available: AK, AZ, CA, CO, DC, ID, IN, KY, MA, NJ, NM, NV, NY, OH, OR, PA, TN, TX, VA, WA

Sudwerk

2001 Second Street
Davis, CA 95616
530-756-2739
www.sudwerk.com

BRANDS:
Sudwerk Doppelbock
Sudwerk Hefe-Weizen
Sudwerk Lager
Sudwerk Leatherneck
Sudwerk Marzen
Sudwerk Pilsner

States Available: Contact Brewery

Telegraph Brewing Company

416 North Salsipuedes Street
Santa Barbara, CA 93103
805-963-5018
www.telegraphbrewing.com

BRANDS:
Telegraph Brewing California Ale
Telegraph Brewing Golden Wheat Ale
Telegraph Brewing Stock Porter

States Available: CA

The Academy of Fine Beers, LLC

435 Fernleaf
Corona Del Mar, CA 92625
949-862-5808
www.bierbitzch.com

BRANDS:
Josef Bierbitzch Golden Pilsner

States Available: AZ, CA, GA, IL, MI, NE, NV

Tuscan Brewing Company

25009 Kauffman Avenue
Red Bluff, CA 96080
530-529-9318
www.tuscanbrewery.com

BRANDS:
Tuscan Paradise Pale Ale
Tuscan Sundown Brown

States Available: CA

GEOGRAPHIC BREWER INDEX (Alphabetical)

The following brewers distribute their brands in California:

Abita Brewing Company
Alaskan Brewing Company
Allagash Brewing Company
Alpine Beer Company
Anchor Brewing Company
Anderson Valley Brewing
Angel City Brewing
Anheuser-Busch, Inc.
Avery Brewing Company
Ballast Point Brewing Company (San Diego, Orange, LA)
Bard's Tale Beer Company
Bayhawk Ales Inc.
Bear Republic Brewing Company
Beermann's Beerwerks
Big Sky Brewing Company
Bison Brewing
Brewery Ommegang
BridgePort Brewing Company
Butte Creek Brewing
Central Coast Brewing
Deschutes Brewery
Downtown Brewing Company
Drakes Brewing Company
Eel River Brewing Company
EJ Phair Brewing
El Toro Brewing
English Ales Brewery
Firestone Walker Brewing Company
Flying Dog Brewery, LLC
Four Plus Brewing Company
Full Sail Brewing Company
Gordon Biersch Brewery
Grand Teton Brewing Company
Great Beer Company
Great Sex Brewing,Inc.
Hair of the Dog Brewing Company
Happy Valley Brewing Company
Hoptown Brewery
Island Brewing Company
Jack Russell Brewing
Jolly Pumpkin Artisan Ales
Karl Strauss Breweries
Kelley Brothers Brewing Company
Kona Brewing, LLC
Lagunitas Brewing
Lakefront Brewery Inc.
Left Coast Brewing
Lost Coast Brewery & Café

MacTarnahan's Brewing Company
Mad River Brewing
Mammoth Brewing Company
Marin Brewing Company
Mehana Brewing Company Inc.
Molson Coors Brewing Company
Moylan's Brewing Company
Nectar Ales
New Belgium Brewing Company
Nimbus Brewing Company
North Coast Brewing Company
Otter Creek Brewing Company
Pabst Brewing Company
Penn Brewery (Pennsylvania Brewing)
Pete's Brewing
Port Brewing Company
Pyramid Brewery
Ramapo Valley Brewery
ReaperAle, Inc.
Redhook Ale Brewery
Rogue Ales
Russian River Brewing Company
SAB Miller Corp
Sacramento Brewing Company Inc.
Santa Cruz Mountain Brewing
Santa Fe Brewing Company
Seabright Brewery
Shipyard Brewing Company
Shmaltz Brewing Company
Sierra Nevada Brewing Company
Spanish Peaks Brewing Company/ United States Beverage
Speakeasy Ales & Lagers, Inc.
Sprecher Brewing
Stone Brewing Company
Stoudt's Brewing Company
The Academy of Fine Beers, LLC
The Black Mountain/Chili Beer Company
The Boston Beer Company
The Sea Dog Brewing Company
The Spoetzl Brewing
Tremont Brewery/Atlantic Coast Brewing Company
Tuscan Brewery
Uinta Brewing Company
Victory Brewing Company
Waimea Brewing Company
Widmer Brothers Brewing Company

Avery Brewing Company – *page 464*

5763 Arapahoe Avenue, Unit E
Boulder, CO 80303
303-440-4324
www.averybrewing.com

<u>BRANDS:</u>
Avery Brewing 14'er ESB (37 IBU)
Avery Brewing Ellie's Brown (17 IBU)
Avery Brewing Hog Heaven Barley Wine (104 IBU)
Avery Brewing IPA (69 IBU) – *page 464*
Avery Brewing Karma Belgian Ale (10 IBU)
Avery Brewing Mephistopheles' Stout (107 IBU)
Avery Brewing New World Porter (45 IBU)
Avery Brewing Old Jubilation (30 IBU)
Avery Brewing Out of Bounds Stout (51 IBU)
Avery Brewing Red Point Amber Ale (22 IBU)
Avery Brewing Salvation (25 IBU)
Avery Brewing Samael's Oak Aged Ale (41 IBU)
Avery Brewing The Beast Belgian Grand Cru (68 IBU)
Avery Brewing The Czar Russian Imperial Stout (60 IBU)
Avery Brewing The Kaiser Imperial Oktoberfest (24 IBU)
Avery Brewing The Maharaja Imperial IPA (102 IBU)
Avery Brewing The Reverend Belgian Quadupel (10 IBU)
Avery Brewing Thirteen
Avery Brewing Twelve
Avery Brewing White Rascal Belgian-Style White Ale (10 IBU)

States Available: AZ, CA, CO, CT, DC, FL, GA, IL, IN, KS, KY, MA, MD, MI, MN, NC, NJ, NM, OH, OR, PA, TN, TX, VA, WA, WI, WY

Backcountry Brewery

710 Main Street
Frisco, CO 080443
970-668-2337
www.backcountrybrewery.com

<u>BRANDS:</u>
Backcountry Brewery Peak One Porter (70.6 SRM, 35 IBU)
Backcountry Brewery Ptarmigan Pilsner (3.1 SRM, 42 IBU)
Backcountry Brewery Switchback Amber (16 SRM, 28 IBU)
Backcountry Brewery Telemark IPA (10.8 SRM, 60 IBU)
Backcountry Brewery Wheeler Wheat (3.6 SRM, 18 IBU)

States Available: CO

GEOGRAPHIC BREWER INDEX (Alphabetical)

Big Horn Brewing (CB Potts)
1427 West Elizabeth Street
Ft. Collins, CO 80521
970-221-5954
www.cbpotts.com

BRANDS:
Big Horn Blonde (5 SRM, 20 IBU)
Big Horn Hefeweizen (7 SRM, 12 IBU)
Big Red AIPA (15 SRM, 60 IBU)
Buttface Amber Ale (22 SRM, 22 IBU)
Total Disorder Porter (60 SRM, 22 IBU)

States Available: CO, WY

Boulder Beer Company – *page 477*
2880 Wilderness Place
Boulder, CO 80301-2258
303-444-8448
www.boulderbeer.com

BRANDS:
Boulder Beer Buffalo Gold Golden Ale   (10.3 SRM, 22 IBU)
Boulder Beer Hazed & Infused Dry-Hopped Ale (19.7 SRM, 38 IBU) – *page 477*
Boulder Beer Killer Penguin Barleywine (34.5 SRM, 42 IBU)
Boulder Beer Mojo India Pale Ale (12 SRM, 63 IBU)
Boulder Beer Mojo Risin' Double IPA (12 SRM, 80 IBU)
Boulder Beer Never Summer Ale (36.9 SRM, 45 IBU)
Boulder Beer Pass Time Pale Ale (13.8 SRM, 23 IBU)
Boulder Beer Planet Porter (45 SRM, 26 IBU)
Boulder Beer Singletrack Copper Ale (13.3 SRM, 30 IBU)
Boulder Beer Sundance Amber (19.6 SRM, 29 IBU)
Boulder Beer Sweaty Betty Blonde Wheat Beer (4 SRM, 12 IBU)

States Available: AZ, CO, CT, FL, IL, IN, KS, KY, MA, MN, ND, NE, NJ, NM,
NY, OH, OR, PA, RI, SD, UT, WA, WY

Breckenridge Brewery
471 Kalamath Street
Denver, CO 80204
303-623-BREW
www.breckenridgebrewery.com

BRANDS:
Breckenridge Autumn Ale (21 IBU)
Breckenridge Avalanche Ale (19 IBU)
Breckenridge Christmas Ale (22 IBU)
Breckenridge Hefe Proper (9 IBU)
Breckenridge Oatmeal Stout (31 IBU)
Breckenridge Summerbright Ale (15 IBU)
Breckenridge Vanilla Porter (16 IBU)
Trademark Pale Ale (40 IBU)
471 IPA (70 IBU)

States Available: AR, CO, IA, IL, IN, KS, KY, MI, MN, MO, ND, NE, NM, OH,
OK, TX, VA, WI, WY

Bristol Brewing Company
1647 South Tejon
Colorado Springs, CO 80906
719-633-2555
www.bristolbrewing.com

BRANDS:
Bristol Brewing Beehive Honey Wheat (16 IBU)
Bristol Brewing Edge City Octoberfest (24 IBU)
Bristol Brewing Edge City Pale Bock (31 IBU)
Bristol Brewing Edge City Wit Bier (18 IBU)
Bristol Brewing Laughing Lab Scottish Ale (19 IBU)
Bristol Brewing Mass Transit Ale (21 IBU)
Bristol Brewing Old No. 23 Barley Wine (67 IBU)
Bristol Brewing Red Rocket Pale Ale (28 IBU)
Bristol Brewing Winter Warlock Oatmeal Stout (44 IBU)

States Available: CO

GEOGRAPHIC BREWER INDEX (Alphabetical)

Crabtree Brewing Company

625 3rd Street (#D)
Greely, CO 80634
970-356-0516
www.crabtreebrewing.com

BRANDS:
Crabtree Brewing Downtown Nut Brown
Crabtree Brewing Twisted Creek Wheat

States Available: Contact Brewery

Crested Butte Brewery

1600 West Evans Avenue, Suite L
Englewood, CO 80110
720-884-1023
www.cbbrewery.com

BRANDS:
Crested Butte Brewery Paradise Crisp Golden Ale
Crested Butte Brewery Red Lady Ale
Crested Butte Brewery White Buffalo Peace Ale

States Available: CO, WA

Dillion DAM Brewery

100 Little Dam Street
Dillon, CO 80435
866-326-6196

BRANDS:
DAM DAM Straight Lager
Dillion DAM Extra Pale Ale
Dillion DAM Olde Forster's Scotch Ale
Dillion DAM Winter Warmer
Sweet George's Brown Ale

States Available: CO

Durango Brewing Company

3000 Main Street
Durango, CO 81301
970-247-3396
www.durangobrewing.com

BRANDS:
Durango Brewing Amber Ale (20 IBU)
Durango Brewing Dark Lager (17 IBU)
Durango Brewing Derail Ale
Durango Brewing Ian's Pale Ale (57 IBU)
Durango Brewing Wheat Beer (10 IBU)

States Available: CO

Estes Park Brewery

470 Prospect Drive, P.O. Box 2136
Estes Park, CO 80517
970-586-5421
www.epbrewery.net

BRANDS:
Estes Park Gold
Estes Park Porter
Estes Park Raspberry Wheat
Estes Park Renegade
Estes Park Samson Stout
Estes Park Staggering Elk
Estes Park Stinger Wild Honey Wheat
Estes Park Trail Ridge Red

States Available: CO, KS, SD, WI

GEOGRAPHIC BREWER INDEX (Alphabetical)

Flying Dog Brewery, LLC – *page 498*

2401 Blake Street
Denver, CO 80205-2199
303-292-5027
www.flyingdogales.com

BRANDS:
Doggie Style Pale Ale
  (19 SRM, 36 IBU) – *page 498*
Dogtoberfest (20 SRM, 30 IBU)
Heller Hound Mai Bock (9 SRM, 26 IBU)
Horn Dog Barley Wine Style Ale (95 SRM, 45 IBU)
In Heat Wheat (5 SRM, 13 IBU)
K9 Winter Cruiser (35 SRM, 30 IBU)
Old Scratch Amber (21 SRM, 20 IBU)
Road Scottish Porter (38 SRM, 26 IBU)
Snake Dog IPA (11 SRM, 60 IBU)
Tire Bite Golden Ale (4 SRM, 17.5 IBU)
Gonzo Imperial Porter (135 SRM, 80 IBU)
Wild Dog Colorado Saison (8 SRM, 20 IBU)
Wild Dog Weizenbock Ale (25 SRM, 30 IBU)

States Available: AK, AL, AR, AZ, CA, CO, CT, DC, DE, FL, GA, HI, IA, IL, IN, KS, KY, LA, MA, MD, ME, MI, MN, MS, NC, ND, NE, NH, NJ, NM, NV, NY, OH, OK, OR, PA, SC, TN, TX, VT

Golden City Brewery

920 12th Street
Golden, CO 80401-1181
303-279-8092

BRANDS:
Golden City Centurion Barley Wine Ale
Golden City IPA
Golden City Mad Molly Brown Ale
Golden City Oatmeal Stout
Golden City Pale Ale
Golden City Red Ale

States Available: CO

Great Divide Brewing Company

2201 Arapahoe Street
Denver, CO 80205
303-296-9460
www.greatdivide.com

BRANDS:
Great Divide Brewing Denver Pale Ale (40 IBU)
Great Divide Brewing Fresh Hop Pale Ale (55 IBU)
Great Divide Brewing Hercules Double IPA (85 IBU)
Great Divide Brewing Hibernation Ale (37 IBU)
Great Divide Brewing HotShot ESB (32 IBU)
Great Divide Brewing Oak Aged Yeti Imperial Stout (75 IBU)
Great Divide Brewing Old Ruffian Barley Wine
Great Divide Brewing Ridgeline Amber (27 IBU)
Great Divide Brewing Saint Bridget's Porter (27.5 IBU)
Great Divide Brewing Samurai
Great Divide Brewing Titan IPA (65 IBU)
Great Divide Brewing Wild Raspberry Ale (21 IBU)
Great Divide Brewing Yeti Imperial Stout (75 IBU)

States Available: AZ, CO, FL, GA, IA, IL, IN, KS, KY, MA, MD, MI, MN, NC, NJ, NY, OH, OK, OR, PA, RI, TN, TX, VA, WA, WI

Left Hand Brewing Company – *page 512*

1265 Boston Avenue
Longmont, CO 80501
303-772-0258
www.lefthandbrewing.com

BRANDS:
Left Hand Brewing Black Jack Porter (27 IBU)
Left Hand Brewing Chainsaw Ale (55 IBU)
Left Hand Brewing Deep Cover Brown (20 IBU)
Left Hand Brewing Goosinator (27 IBU)
Left Hand Brewing Haystack Wheat (14 IB)
Left Hand Brewing Imperial Stout (65 IBU)
Left Hand Brewing Jackman's Pale Ale (42 IBU)
Left Hand Brewing JuJu Ginger Ale (17 IBU)
Left Hand Brewing Milk Stout (22 IBU) – *page 512*
Left Hand Brewing Polestar Pilsner (33 IBU)
Left Hand Brewing Ryebock Lager (17 IBU)
Left Hand Brewing Sawtooth Ale (27 IBU)
Left Hand Brewing Smokejumper Imperial Porter (67 IBU)
Left Hand Brewing Snowbound Ale (16 IBU)
Left Hand Brewing St. Vrain Ale (20 IBU)
Left Hand Brewing Twin Sisters (87 IBU)
Left Hand Brewing Warrior IPA (60 IBU)
Left Hand Brewing Widdershins Barleywine (70 IBU)

States Available: AL, AZ, CO, FL, GA, IA, IL, IN, KY, MA, MN, NC, NJ, NM, OH, OK, PA, TN, TX, VA, WI

Molson Coors Brewing Company

P.O. Box 4030, MS#N8470
Golden, CO 80401-0030
303-279-6565
www.coors.com

BRANDS:
Blue Moon Belgian White
Blue Moon Pumpkin Ale
Coors
Coors Extra Gold
Coors Light
Coors Non-Alcoholic
George Killian's Irish Red Lager
Keystone
Keystone Ice
Keystone Light
Winterfest

States Available: All 50 States

New Belgium Brewing Company – *page 521*

500 Linden Street
Fort Collins, CO 80524-2457
970-221-0524
www.newbelgium.com

BRANDS:
New Belgium 2 Below (14.7 SRM, 28 IBU)
New Belgium 1554 Brussels Style Black Ale (45.7 SRM, 21 IBU)
New Belgium Abbey Belgian Style Ale (27.9 SRM, 20 IBU)
New Belgium Blue Paddle Pilsner (4.8 SRM, 32.5 IBU)
New Belgium Fat Tire Amber Ale (12.9 SRM, 18.5 IBU) – *page 521*
New Belgium Saison Harvest Ale
New Belgium Skinny Dip
New Belgium Springboard
New Belgium Sunshine Wheat (3.3 SRM, 14.5 IBU)
New Belgium Trippel Belgian Style Ale (7.9 SRM, 25 IBU)

States Available: AR, AZ, CA, CO, ID, KS, MO, MT, NE, NM, NV, OR, TX, WA, WY

GEOGRAPHIC BREWER INDEX (Alphabetical)

Odell Brewing Company

800 E Lincoln Avenue
Fort Collins, CO 80524
970-489-9070
www.odellbrewing.com

BRANDS:
Odell Brewing 5 Barrel Pale Ale
Odell Brewing 90 Shilling
Odell Brewing Curmudgeons NIP
Odell Brewing Cutthroat Porter
Odell Brewing Double Pilsner
Odell Brewing Easy Street Wheat
Odell Brewing Isolation Ale
Odell Brewing Levity Amber

States Available: CO, KS, MO, NE, NM, SD, WY

Oskar Blues Grill & Brew

303 Main Street
Lyons, CO 80540
303-823-6685
www.oskarblues.com

BRANDS:
Oskar Blues Grill & Brew Dale's Pale Ale (65 IBU)
Oskar Blues Grill & Brew Gordon (35 IBU)
Oskar Blues Grill & Brew Leroy (90 IBU)
Oskar Blues Grill & Brew Old Chub (30 IBU)

States Available: AZ, CO, GA, ID, MA, NC, NJ, NM, NY, PA, VA, WA, WI

Ska Brewing Company – *page 546*

545 Turner Drive
Durango, CO 81301
970-247-5792
www.skabrewing.com

BRANDS:
Ska Brewing Buster Nut Brown Ale (19 SRM, 30 IBU) – *page 548*
Ska Brewing Decadent Imperial I.P.A. (14 SRM, 100 IBU) – *page 546*
Ska Brewing Mexican Logger
Ska Brewing Nefarious Ten Pin Imperial Porter (37 SRM, 77 IBU) – *page 547*
Ska Brewing Pinstripe Red Ale (10 SRM, 42 IBU) – *page 547*
Ska Brewing Special ESB (in cans) (8 SRM, 58 IBU) – *page 549*
Ska Brewing Steel Toe Stout (41 SRM, 29 IBU) – *page 549*
Ska Brewing Ten Pin Porter
Ska Brewing True Blonde Ale (4 SRM, 40 IBU) – *page 548*
Ska Brewing True Blonde Dubbel

States Available: CO, NC, NM

Steamworks Brewing Company

801 East Second Avenue
Durango, CO 81301
970-259-9200
www.steamworksbrewing.com

BRANDS:
Backside Stout (28.5 SRM, 42.1 IBU)
Colorado Kölsch (3.9 SRM, 18.8 IBU)
Conductor (11 SRM, 96 IBU)
Engineer Light Lager (4 SRM, 21.5 IBU)
Lizard Head Red (12.4 SRM, 27.8 IBU)
Spruce Goose (16.1 SRM, 21 IBU)
Steam Engine Lager (12.3 SRM, 21.9 IBU)
Third Eye Pale Ale (8.8 SRM, 59 IBU)

States Available: Contact Brewery

The Fort Collins Brewery – *page 500*

196 Alps Road #2-237
1900 E. Lincoln Avenue, #B
Fort Collins, CO 80524
970-472-1499
www.fortcollinsbrewery.com

BRANDS:
Fort Collins Chocolate Stout
Fort Collins Edgar Lager
Fort Collins Major Tom's Pomegranate Wheat – *page 500*
Fort Collins Retro Red
Fort Collins The Kidd Lager
Fort Collins Z Lager

States Available: CO, IA, IN, MD, NC, NM, SC, VA, WI, WY

The Palisade Brewery

P.O. Box 1535
Palisade, CO 81526
970-464-7257
www.palisadebrewery.com

BRANDS:
The Palisade Brewery Farmer's Friend
The Palisade Brewery Orchard Amber Ale
The Palisade Brewery PAL Beer
The Palisade Brewery Red Truck IPA

States Available: Contact Brewery

Tommyknocker Brewery

1401 Miner Street
Idaho Springs, CO 80452
303-567-4419
www.tommyknocker.com

BRANDS:
Tommyknocker Alpine Glacier Lager
Tommyknocker Butt Head Bock
Tommyknocker Imperial Nut Brown Ale
Tommyknocker Jack Whacker Wheat Ale
Tommyknocker Maple Nut Brown Ale
Tommyknocker Ornery Amber Lager
Tommyknocker Pick Axe Pale Ale
Tommyknocker Tundrabeary Ale

States Available: CO, IL, IN, KY, MN, ND, NE, OH, TX, VA, WI, WY

Twisted Pine Brewing Company

3201 Walnut Street
Boulder, CO 80301
303-786-9270
www.isidb.com/twisted

BRANDS:
Big Daddy Espresso Stout
Billy's Chilies Beer
Twisted Pine American Amber Ale
Twisted Pine Blond Ale
Twisted Pine Honey Brown Ale
Twisted Pine Hoppy Boy
Twisted Pine Raspberry Wheat Ale
Twisted Pine Red Mountain Ale
Twisted Pine Twisted Stout

States Available: Contact Brewery

GEOGRAPHIC BREWER INDEX (Alphabetical)

The following brewers distribute their brands in Colorado:

Allagash Brewing Company
Anchor Brewing Company
Anderson Valley Brewing
Anheuser-Busch, Inc.
Atwater Block Brewery
Avery Brewing Company
Backcountry Brewery
Bard's Tale Beer Company
Bear Republic Brewing Company
Big Horn Brewing (CB Potts)
Big Sky Brewing Company
Boulder Beer Company
Breckenridge Brewery
Brewery Ommegang
BridgePort Brewing Company
Bristol Brewing Company
Crested Butte Brewery
Deschutes Brewery
Dillion DAM Brewery
Dogfish Head Craft Brewery
Durango Brewing Company
Estes Park Brewery
Flying Dog Brewery, LLC
Full Sail Brewing Company
Golden City Brewery
Great Divide Brewing Company
Great Sex Brewing,Inc.
High Falls Brewing
Jacob Leinenkugel Brewing Company
Jarre Creek Ranch Brewery
Lagunitas Brewing
Lakefront Brewery Inc.
Left Handed Brewing Company
MacTarnahan's Brewing Company
Mad River Brewing

Mehana Brewing Company Inc.
Molson Coors Brewing Company
New Belgium Brewing Company
North Coast Brewing Company
O'Fallon Brewery
Odell Brewing Company
Oskar Blues Grill & Brew
Pabst Brewing Company
Pete's Brewing
Pig's Eye Brewing Company
Pittsburgh Brewing Company
Pyramid Brewery
Redhook Ale Brewery
Rogue Ales
SAB Miller Corp
Santa Fe Brewing Company
Shipyard Brewing Company
Shmaltz Brewing Company
Sierra Nevada Brewing Company
Ska Brewing Company
Snake River Brewing Company
Spanish Peaks Brewing Company/
   United States Beverage
Stone Brewing Company
Summit Brewing Company
The Black Mountain/Chili Beer Company
The Boston Beer Company
The Fort Collins Brewery
The Sea Dog Brewing Company
The Spoetzl Brewing
Tommyknocker Brewery
Tremont Brewery/Atlantic Coast Brewing
   Company
Widmer Brothers Brewing Company
Yellowstone Valley Brewing

CT

Cottrell Brewing Company

100 Mechanic Street
Pawcatuck, CT 06379
860-599-8213
www.cottrellbrewing.com

BRANDS:
Cottrell Brewing Old Yankee Ale

States Available: CT, RI

Rheingold Brewing Company

372 Danbury Road, Suite 163
Wilton, CT 06897
212-481-1018
www.rheingoldbeer.com

BRANDS:
Rheingold Beer

States Available: Contact Brewery

Spanish Peaks Brewing Company/
United States Beverage

700 Canal Street
Stamford, CT 06902
203-961-8215
www.blackdogales.com

BRANDS:
Black Dog Ale (36 IBU)
Black Dog American Pale Ale (50 IBU)
Black Dog Honey Raspberry Ale (12 IBU)
Black Dog Summer White Ale

States Available: All 50 States

Streich's Brewing Company, LLC

53 Richard Street Route 68
West Hartford, CT 06119
860-233-4545

BRANDS:
Streich's Brewing Naughty Fish Pale Ale

States Available: Contact Brewery

GEOGRAPHIC BREWER INDEX (Alphabetical)

Thomas Hooker Brewing Company

P.O. Box 271062
West Hartford, CT 06127-1062
860-951-2739
www.troutbrookbeer.com

BRANDS:
Thomas Hooker American Pale Ale (7.6 SRM, 31 IBU)
Thomas Hooker Blonde Ale (1.93 SRM, 11 IBU)
Thomas Hooker Hop Meadow IPA (10.5 SRM, 73 IBU)
Thomas Hooker Imperial Porter (30 SRM, 61 IBU)
Thomas Hooker Irish Red (17.7 SRM, 22 IBU)
Thomas Hooker Liberator Doppelbock (20.4 SRM, 27 IBU)
Thomas Hooker Munich Golden Lager (3 SRM, 15 IBU)
Thomas Hooker Octoberfest (10 SRM, 11 IBU)
Thomas Hooker Old Marley Barley Wine (16 SRM, 74 IBU)

States Available: CT, GA, MA, NY, PA, RI

The following brewers distribute their brands in Connecticut:

Abita Brewing Company	North Coast Brewing Company
Allagash Brewing Company	Otter Creek Brewing Company
Anchor Brewing Company	Pabst Brewing Company
Anderson Valley Brewing	Pete's Brewing
Anheuser-Busch, Inc.	Pittsburgh Brewing Company
Avery Brewing Company	Redhook Ale Brewery
Bard's Tale Beer Company	River Horse Brewing Company
Berkshire Brewing Company	Rogue Ales
Bluegrass Beer Company	SAB Miller Corp
Boulder Beer Company	Shipyard Brewing Company
Brewery Ommegang	Shmaltz Brewing Company
Brooklyn Brewery	Sierra Nevada Brewing Company
Buzzards Bay Brewing Company	Smuttynose Brewing Company
Casco Bay Brewing Company	South Hampton Publick House
Cisco Brewers Inc.	Southern Tier Brewing Company
Clipper City Brewing Company	Spanish Peaks Brewing Company/
Coastal Extreme Brewing Company LLC	United States Beverage
Cooperstown Brewing Company	Stone Coast Brewing Company
Cottrell Brewing Company	The Boston Beer Company
D L Geary Brewing Company	The Long Trail Brewing Company
Dogfish Head Craft Brewery	The Matt Brewing
Flying Dog Brewery, LLC	The Sea Dog Brewing Company
Harpoon Brewery	Tremont Brewery/Atlantic Coast Brewing
High Falls Brewing	Company
Lakefront Brewery Inc.	Trout Brook Brewing Company
Magic Hat Brewing Company	Victory Brewing Company
Mercury Brewing Company	Widmer Brothers Brewing Company
Molson Coors Brewing Company	Yards Brewing
New England Brewing Company	

Dogfish Head Craft Brewery – *page 492*

DE

6 Cannery Village Center
Milton, DE 19968-1327
888-836-4347
www.dogfish.com

BRANDS:
Dogfish Head 60 Minute IPA (60 IBU) – *page 492*
Dogfish Head 90 Minute Imperial IPA (90 IBU)
Dogfish Head 120 Minute Imperial IPA (120 IBU)
Dogfish Head Aprihop (55 IBU)
Dogfish Head Au Courant
Dogfish Head Black & Blue
Dogfish Head Burton Baton
Dogfish Head Chicory Stout (22 IBU)
Dogfish Head Fort
Dogfish Head Golden Shower Imperial Pilsner (80 IBU)
Dogfish Head Immort Ale (40 IBU)
Dogfish Head Indian Brown Ale (50 IBU)
Dogfish Head Midas Touch Golden Elixir (12 IBU)
Dogfish Head Old School Barleywine
Dogfish Head Punkin Ale (24 IBU)
Dogfish Head Raison D'Etre (25 IBU)
Dogfish Head Red & White
Dogfish Head Shelter Pale Ale (25 IBU)
Dogfish Head Snowblown Ale (33 IBU)
Dogfish Head World Wide Stout (80 IBU)

States Available: AK, AZ, CO, CT, DC, DE, FL, GA, IL, IN, KY, MA, MD, ME, NC, NJ, NY, OH, OR, PA, RI, TN, TX, VA, VT, WA, WI

Fordham Brewing Company

1284 Mcd Drive
Dover, DE 19901-4639
302-678-4810
www.fordhambrewing.com

BRANDS:
Fordham Brewing C126 Light
Fordham Brewing Copperhead Ale
Fordham Brewing Fordham Lager
Fordham Brewing Oyster Stout
Fordham Brewing Tavern Ale

States Available: DE, MD, NC, NJ, PA, VA

GEOGRAPHIC BREWER INDEX (Alphabetical)

The following brewers distribute their brands in Delaware:

Anchor Brewing Company	Red Bell Brewery & Pub
Anderson Valley Brewing	Redhook Ale Brewery
Anheuser-Busch, Inc.	River Horse Brewing Company
Bard's Tale Beer Company	Rogue Ales
Bear Republic Brewing Company	SAB Miller Corp
Brewery Ommegang	Shipyard Brewing Company
Brooklyn Brewery	Shmaltz Brewing Company
Clipper City Brewing Company	Sierra Nevada Brewing Company
D.G. Yuengling & Son, Inc.	Smuttynose Brewing Company
Dogfish Head Craft Brewery	Spanish Peaks Brewing Company/
Flying Dog Brewery, LLC	United States Beverage
Flying Fish Brewing	The Boston Beer Company
Fordham Brewing Company	The Dock Street Brewery Company
Harpoon Brewery	The Matt Brewing
High Falls Brewing	The Sea Dog Brewing Company
Magic Hat Brewing Company	Tremont Brewery/Atlantic Coast Brewing
Molson Coors Brewing Company	Company
Pabst Brewing Company	Tröegs Brewing Company
Penn Brewery (Pennsylvania Brewing)	Victory Brewing Company
Pete's Brewing	Widmer Brothers Brewing Company
ReaperAle, Inc.	Yards Brewing

FL

Beautiful Brews, Inc.

1200 Holland Drive
Boca Raton, FL 33432
561-241-7373

BRANDS:
Beautiful Brews Honey Amber Rose

States Available: Contact Brewery

Bootie Beer Company

620 North Demming Drive #100
Winter Park, FL 32789
407-319-1999
www.bootiebeer.com

BRANDS:
Bootie Beer
Bootie Light

States Available: FL

Coffaro Beer Company

5769 N Andrews Way
Fort Lauderdale, FL 33309-2364
732- 261-4888
www.coffarobeer.com

BRANDS:
Coffaro Italian Style Beer

States Available: NJ, NY, PA

Dunedin Brewery – *page 493*

937 Douglas Avenue
Dunedin, FL 34698
727-736-0606
www.dunedinbrewery.com

BRANDS:
Dunedin Brewery Beach Tale Brown Ale   (21 SRM, 41 IBU)   – *page 493*
Dunedin Brewery Celtic Gold Ale (5 SRM, 25 IBU)
Dunedin Brewery Christmas Farm Ale (11 SRM, 37 IBU)
Dunedin Brewery Drop Kick Monday's Erin Red Ale
Dunedin Brewery Highland Games Ale (20 SRM, 39 IBU)
Dunedin Brewery Leonard Croon's Old Mean Stout
Dunedin Brewery Lowland Wheat Ale (5 SRM, 11.5 IBU)
Dunedin Brewery Oktoberfest Ale (10 SRM, 15 IBU)
Dunedin Brewery Piper's Pale Ale (7 SRM, 37 IBU)
Dunedin Brewery Razzbeery Wheat Ale (7 SRM, 12 IBU)
Dunedin Brewery Redhead Red Ale (11 SRM, 30 IBU)
Dunedin Brewery Summer Apricot Wheat Ale (5 SRM, 11 IBU)
Dunedin Brewery Summer Buzz

States Available: FL

GEOGRAPHIC BREWER INDEX (Alphabetical)

Florida Beer Company – *page 497*

725 Silver Palm Avenue
Melbourne, FL 32901
321-728-3412
www.floridabeer.com

BRANDS:
Beachside American Lager
Beachside Porter
Beachside Sun Light
Hurricane Reef Caribbean Pilsner
Hurricane Reef Lager
Hurricane Reef Pale Ale
Hurricane Reef Raspberry Wheat
Key West Golden Lager
Key West Pilsner Light
Key West Sunset Ale – *page 497*
La Tropical
Ybor Gold Amber Lager
Ybor Gold Brown Ale
Ybor Gold Gaspar's Porter
Ybor Gold Light
Ybor Gold Wheat Ale

States Available: AL, FL, GA, NC, NY, VA

Orlando Brewing Partners, Inc. (Kegs/Growlers)

1301 Atlanta Avenue
Orlando, FL 32806
407-872-1117
www.orlandobrewing.com

BRANDS:
Orlando Brewing Blackwater Ale
Orlando Brewing Blonde Ale (2.9 SRM, 10.2 IBU)
Orlando Brewing Mild Ale
Orlando Brewing Olde Pelican Ale
Orlando Brewing Pale Ale (7.6 SRM, 28.3 IBU)

States Available: Contact Brewery

The following brewers distribute their brands in Florida:

Abita Brewing Company	Molson Coors Brewing Company
Allagash Brewing Company	North Coast Brewing Company
Anchor Brewing Company	Pabst Brewing Company
Anheuser-Busch, Inc.	Penn Brewery (Pennsylvania Brewing)
Avery Brewing Company	Pete's Brewing
Bison Brewing	Pittsburgh Brewing Company
Blucreek Brewing	Ramapo Valley Brewery
Bootie Beer Company	Redhook Ale Brewery
Boulder Beer Company	Rogue Ales
Brewery Ommegang	SAB Miller Corp
D.G. Yuengling & Son, Inc.	Shipyard Brewing Company
Dogfish Head Craft Brewery	Shmaltz Brewing Company
Dunedin Brewery	Sierra Nevada Brewing Company
Eel River Brewing Company	Spanish Peaks Brewing Company/
Florida Beer Company	United States Beverage
Flying Dog Brewery, LLC	Stoudt's Brewing Company
Great Divide Brewing Company	Sweetwater Brewing
Harpoon Brewery	The Black Mountain/Chili Beer Company
High Falls Brewing	The Boston Beer Company
Jolly Pumpkin Artisan Ales	The Sea Dog Brewing Company
Kona Brewing, LLC	The Spoetzl Brewing
Lakefront Brewery Inc.	Tremont Brewery/Atlantic Coast Brewing
Left Handed Brewing Company	Company
Lost Coast Brewery & Café	Widmer Brothers Brewing Company
Mad River Brewing	

Atlanta Brewing Company – *page 463*

GA

2323 Defoor Hills Rd. NW
Atlanta, GA 30318
(404) 881-0300
www.atlantabrewing.com

BRANDS:
Atlanta Brewing PeachTree Pale Ale
Atlanta Brewing Red Brick Ale – *page 463*
Atlanta Brewing Red Brick Blonde
Atlanta Brewing Red Brick Summer Brew – Hefeweizen
Atlanta Brewing Red Brink Winter Brew – Double-Chocolate Oatmeal Porter

States Available: GA

GEOGRAPHIC BREWER INDEX (Alphabetical)

New River Brewing Company
2015 Afond Court
Atlanta, GA 30341
770-841-2953
www.newriverbrewing.com

BRANDS:
New River Pale Ale (6.5 SRM, 35 IBU)
States Available: NC, VA, WV

Sweetwater Brewing Company – *page 559*
195 Ottley Drive
Atlanta, GA 30324
404-691-2537
www.sweetwaterbrew.com

BRANDS:
Sweetwater Brewing 420 Extra Pale Ale – *page 559*
Sweetwater Brewing IPA
Sweetwater Brewing Sweet Georgia Brown
Sweetwater Brewing Sweetwater Blue
Sweetwater Brewing Sweetwater Festive Ale
States Available: AL, FL, GA, NC, SC, TN

Terrapin Beer Company – *page 560*
196 Alps Road #2-237
Athens, GA 30606
706-202-4467
www.terrapinbeer.com

BRANDS:
Terrapin All American Imperial Pilsner (75 IBU)
Terrapin Big Hoppy Monster (75 IBU)
Terrapin Golden Ale (21 IBU)
Terrapin Rye Pale Ale (45 IBU) – *page 560*
Terrapin Rye Squared (80 IBU)
Terrapin Wake-N-Bake Coffee Oatmeal Imperial Stout (75 IBU)
States Available: AL, GA, NC, SC, TN

Woodstock Beer
1951 Canton Road NE, Suite 250
Marietta, GA 30066
770-795-1432
www.woodstockbrands.com

BRANDS:
Woodstock India Pale Ale (11 SRM, 77.6 IBU)
Woodstock Pilsner (2.4 SRM, 18.2 IBU)
States Available: Contact Brewery

Zuma Brewing Company
900 Wendell Court
Atlanta, GA 30336
404-691-6535
www.zumaimporting.com

BRANDS:
Cancun
Morena
States Available: GA, TN

GEOGRAPHIC BREWER INDEX (Alphabetical)

The following brewers distribute their brands in Georgia:

Abita Brewing Company
Anchor Brewing Company
Anheuser-Busch, Inc.
Atlanta Brewing Company
Avery Brewing Company
Bison Brewing
Brewery Ommegang
BridgePort Brewing Company
Brooklyn Brewery
Carolina Beer & Beverage Company
Charleston Brewing Company
Clipper City Brewing Company
Dogfish Head Craft Brewery
Florida Beer Company
Flying Dog Brewery, LLC
Great Divide Brewing Company
Harpoon Brewery
High Falls Brewing
Highland Brewing
Jolly Pumpkin Artisan Ales
Left Handed Brewing Company
Molson Coors Brewing Company
North Coast Brewing Company
Old Dominion Brewing Company
Oskar Blues Grill & Brew
Pabst Brewing Company
Pete's Brewing

Pittsburgh Brewing Company
Redhook Ale Brewery
Rogue Ales
SAB Miller Corp
Shipyard Brewing Company
Shmaltz Brewing Company
Sierra Nevada Brewing Company
Spanish Peaks Brewing Company/
    United States Beverage
Stevens Point Brewery
Stoudt's Brewing Company
Sweetwater Brewing
Terrapin Beer Company
The Academy of Fine Beers, LLC
The Black Mountain/Chili Beer Company
The Boston Beer Company
The Matt Brewing
The Sea Dog Brewing Company
The Spoetzl Brewing
Thomas Creek Brewery
Trout Brook Brewing Company
Tremont Brewery/Atlantic Coast Brewing
    Company
Widmer Brothers Brewing Company
Woodstock Beer
Zuma Brewing Company (Cancun
    Brewery)

Keoki Brewing Company

HI

2976 Aukele Street, B-7
Linhue, HI 96766
808-245-8884
www.keokibrewing.com

BRANDS:
Keoki Gold
Keoki Sunset

States Available: HI

Kona Brewing, LLC

75-5629 Kuakini Highway
Kailua-Kona, HI 96740
808-334-1133
www.konabrewingco.com

BRANDS:
Kona Brewing Big Wave Golden Ale (8 SRM, 20 IBU)
Kona Brewing Fire Rock Pale Ale (14 SRM, 36 IBU)
Kona Brewing Longboard Island Lager (6 SRM, 25 IBU)
Kona Brewing Pipeline Porter (85 SRM, 30 IBU)

States Available: AK, AZ, CA, FL, HI (Big Wave HI Only), ID, KY, MT, NJ,
    NM, NY, OR, UT, WA, WY

Mehana Brewing Company, Inc.

275 E Kawili Street
Hilo, HI 96720-5074
808-934-8211
www.mehana.com

BRANDS:
Mehana Brewing Hawaii Lager
Mehana Brewing Humpback Blue Beer
Mehana Brewing Mauna Kea Pale Ale
Mehana Brewing Roy's Private Reserve
Mehana Brewing Volcano Red Ale

States Available: CA (Southern), CO, HI

Waimea Brewing Company

9400 Kaumualii Highway, P.O. Box 667
Waimea, HI 96796
425-443-3255
www.waimeabrewing.com

BRANDS:
Waimea Brewing Captain Cook's Original IPA (55 IBU)
Waimea Brewing Luau Lager (20 IBU)
Waimea Brewing Na Pali Pale Ale (26 IBU)
Waimea Brewing Pakala Porter (22 IBU)
Waimea Brewing Wai'ale'ale Ale (18 IBU)
Waimea Brewing Waimea Bay Pale Ale (40 IBU)

States Available: CA, HI

GEOGRAPHIC BREWER INDEX (Alphabetical)

The following brewers distribute their brands in Hawaii:

Anchor Brewing Company	Pete's Brewing
Anheuser-Busch, Inc.	Pyramid Brewery
Bayhawk Ales Inc.	Redhook Ale Brewery
Deschutes Brewery	Rogue Ales
Flying Dog Brewery, LLC	SAB Miller Corp
Full Sail Brewing Company	Shipyard Brewing Company
Gordon Biersch Brewery	Sierra Nevada Brewing Company
Keoki Brewing Company	Spanish Peaks Brewing Company/
Kona Brewing, LLC	United States Beverage
MacTarnahan's Brewing Company	The Boston Beer Company
Magic Hat Brewing Company	The Sea Dog Brewing Company
Mehana Brewing Company Inc.	Tremont Brewery/Atlantic Coast Brewing
Molson Coors Brewing Company	Company
North Coast Brewing Company	Waimea Brewing Company
Pabst Brewing Company	Widmer Brothers Brewing Company

The following brewers distribute their brands in Iowa:

Anchor Brewing Company	Pony Express Brewing Company
Anheuser-Busch, Inc.	Pyramid Brewery
August Schell Brewing Company	Ramapo Valley Brewery
Bard's Tale Beer Company	Redhook Ale Brewery
Boulevard Brewing Company	Rogue Ales
Breckenridge Brewery	SAB Miller Corp
Capital Brewery Company, Inc.	Shipyard Brewing Company
City Brewery	Sierra Nevada Brewing Company
Flying Dog Brewery, LLC	Spanish Peaks Brewing Company/
Great Divide Brewing Company	United States Beverage
Jacob Leinenkugel Brewing Company	Sprecher Brewing
Left Handed Brewing Company	Stevens Point Brewery
Lost Coast Brewery & Café	Summit Brewing Company
MacTarnahan's Brewing Company	The Black Mountain/Chili Beer Company
Millstream Brewing Company	The Boston Beer Company
Molson Coors Brewing Company	The Fort Collins Brewery
North Coast Brewing Company	The Matt Brewing
O'Fallon Brewery	The Sea Dog Brewing Company
Pabst Brewing Company	The Spoetzl Brewing
Paper City Brewery Company	Three Floyds Brewing Company
Pete's Brewing	Tremont Brewery/Atlantic Coast Brewing
Pig's Eye Brewing Company	Company
Pittsburgh Brewing Company	Widmer Brothers Brewing Company

Millstream Brewing Company

IA

835 48th Avenue, P.O. Box 284
Amana, IA 52203-0284
319-622-3672
www.millstreambrewing.com

BRANDS:
Millstream Brewing Colony Oatmeal Stout
Millstream Brewing German Pilsner
Millstream Brewing John's Generations White Ale
Millstream Brewing Maifest
Millstream Brewing Oktoberfest
Millstream Brewing Schild Brau Amber
Millstream Brewing Schokolade Bock
Millstream Brewing Warsh Pail Ale
Millstream Brewing Wheat

States Available: IA, IL, WI

Coeur d'Alene Brewing Company

ID

209 Lakeside Avenue
Coeur D'Alene, ID 83814
208-664-2739
www.cdabrewing.com

BRANDS:
Coeur d'Alene Brewing Centennial Pale Ale
Coeur d'Alene Brewing Honeymoon Wheat
Coeur d'Alene Brewing Huckleberry Ale
Coeur d'Alene Brewing Lake Side British Ale

States Available: ID

GEOGRAPHIC BREWER INDEX (Alphabetical)

Grand Teton Brewing Company

430 Old Jackson Hole Highway
Victor, ID 83455
888-899-1656
www.grandtetonbrewing.com

BRANDS:
Black Cauldron Imperial Stout
Grand Teton Bitch Creek ESB (51 IBU)
Grand Teton Double IPA
Grand Teton Old Faithful Ale (23 IBU)
Grand Teton Paradise Pilsner
Grand Teton Sweetgrass IPA (58 IBU)
Grand Teton Teton Ale (24 IBU)
Grand Teton Workhorse Wheat (10.4 IBU)

States Available: CA, ID, MT, UT, WY

The following brewers distribute their brands in Idaho:

Alaskan Brewing Company	Oskar Blues Grill & Brew
Anchor Brewing Company	Pabst Brewing Company
Anderson Valley Brewing	Pete's Brewing
Anheuser-Busch, Inc.	Pyramid Brewery
Bayern Brewing	Redhook Ale Brewery
Big Sky Brewing Company	Rogue Ales
Bitter Root Brewing	Ruby Mountain Brewing Company
Brewery Ommegang	SAB Miller Corp
BridgePort Brewing Company	Shipyard Brewing Company
Deschutes Brewery	Shmaltz Brewing Company
Eel River Brewing Company	Sierra Nevada Brewing Company
Elysian Brewing Company	Snake River Brewing Company
Four Plus Brewing Company	Snipes Mountain Brewing Company
Full Sail Brewing Company	Spanish Peaks Brewing Company/
Grand Teton Brewing Company	United States Beverage
Great Northern Brewing Company	Stone Brewing Company
Kona Brewing, LLC	The Boston Beer Company
Lang Creek Brewery	The Northern Lights Brewing Company
Lost Coast Brewery & Café	The Sea Dog Brewing Company
MacTarnahan's Brewing Company	The Spoetzl Brewing
Mad River Brewing	Tremont Brewery/Atlantic Coast Brewing
Molson Coors Brewing Company	Company
New Belgium Brewing Company	Uinta Brewing Company
North Coast Brewing Company	Widmer Brothers Brewing Company

Elmwood Brewing Company

118 East Main Street
Elmwood, IL 61529
309-742-4200
www.elmwoodbrewing.com

BRANDS:
Elmwood Brewing Amber Ale
Elmwood Brewing Dopple Bock
Elmwood Brewing Dry Stout
Elmwood Brewing Dunkle Weizen
Elmwood Brewing Lawnmower
Elmwood Brewing Nut Brown
Elmwood Brewing Oktoberfest
Elmwood Brewing Pale Ale

States Available: Contact Brewery

Goose Island Beer Company

1800 West Fulton Street
Chicago, IL 60612
312-226-1119
www.gooseisland.com

BRANDS:
Bourbon County Stout (100 SRM, 60 IBU)
Demolition (5 SRM, 55 IBU)
Goose Island 312 Urban Wheat Ale (4 SRM, 15 IBU)
Goose Island Christmas Ale (30 SRM, 55 IBU)
Goose Island Honker's Ale (15 SRM, 32 IBU)
Goose Island India Pale Ale (10 SRM, 58 IBU)
Goose Island Kilgubbin Red Ale (20 SRM, 25 IBU)
Goose Island Nut Brown Ale (50 SRM, 29 IBU)
Goose Island Oatmeal Stout (80 SRM, 30 IBU)
Goose Island Oktoberfest (15 SRM, 25 IBU)
Goose Island Summertime (4 SRM, 25 IBU)
Imperial IPA (12 SRM, 90 IBU)
Matilda (13 SRM, 32 IBU)
Pere Jacques (32 SRM, 26 IBU)

States Available: Contact Brewery

253

GEOGRAPHIC BREWER INDEX (Alphabetical)

Two Brothers Brewing Company – *page 567*

30W 114 Butterfield Road
Warrenville, IL 60555
630-393-4800
www.twobrosbrew.com

BRANDS:

Two Brothers Bare Tree Weiss Wine (December)
Two Brothers Brown Project OPUS
Two Brothers Cane and Ebel (Limited Release)
Two Brothers Dog Days Dortmunder Style Lager (May-August)
Two Brothers Domaine Dupage French Country Ale (24 IBU) – *page 567*
Two Brothers Ebel's Weiss Beer (15 IBU)
Two Brothers Heavy Handed India Pale Ale (September-December)
Two Brothers Hop Juice Double India Pale Ale (100.1 IBU) (Limited Release)
Two Brothers Monarch White (March)
Two Brothers Northwind Imperial Stout (Winter)
Two Brothers Prairie Path Golden Ale (29 IBU)
Two Brothers The Bitter End Pale Ale (36 IBU)

States Available: IL, IN, MA, MI, OH, WI

The following brewers distribute their brands in Illinois:

Abita Brewing Company	New Century Brewing Company
Allagash Brewing Company	New Holland Brewing Company
Anchor Brewing Company	North Coast Brewing Company
Anderson Valley Brewing	O'Fallon Brewery
Anheuser-Busch, Inc.	Otter Creek Brewing Company
Atwater Block Brewery	Pabst Brewing Company
Avery Brewing Company	Pete's Brewing
Baltimore-Washington Beer Works	Pyramid Brewery
Bard's Tale Beer Company	Ramapo Valley Brewery
Bear Republic Brewing Company	Redhook Ale Brewery
Blucreek Brewing	Rogue Ales
Boulder Beer Company	SAB Miller Corp
Boulevard Brewing Company	Sand Creek Brewing Company, LLC
Breckenridge Brewery	Shipyard Brewing Company
Brewery Ommegang	Shmaltz Brewing Company
Capital Brewery Company, Inc.	Sierra Nevada Brewing Company
City Brewery	Ska Brewing Company
Clipper City Brewing Company	Spanish Peaks Brewing Company/
Dogfish Head Craft Brewery	United States Beverage
Flying Dog Brewery, LLC	Speakeasy Ales & Lagers, Inc.
Frederick Brewing Company	Sprecher Brewing
Gray Brewing	Stevens Point Brewery
Great Divide Brewing Company	Stone Coast Brewing Company
Great Lakes Brewing Company	Summit Brewing Company
High Falls Brewing	The Academy of Fine Beers, LLC
Jacob Leinenkugel Brewing Company	The Black Mountain/Chili Beer Company
James Page Brewing Company, LLC	The Boston Beer Company
Jolly Pumpkin Artisan Ales	The Sea Dog Brewing Company
Lagunitas Brewing	Three Floyds Brewing Company
Lakefront Brewery Inc.	Tommyknocker Brewery
Left Handed Brewing Company	Tremont Brewery/Atlantic Coast Brewing
MacTarnahan's Brewing Company	Company
Michigan Brewing Company, Inc.	Two Brothers Brewing Company
Millstream Brewing Company	Victory Brewing Company
Molson Coors Brewing Company	Widmer Brothers Brewing Company

GEOGRAPHIC BREWER INDEX (Alphabetical)

IN

Back Road Brewery

1315 Michigan Avenue
La Porte, IN 46350
219-362-7623
www.backroadbrewery.com

BRANDS:
Back Road Brewery American Pale Ale (8 SRM, 30 IBU)
Back Road Brewery Autumn Ale
Back Road Brewery Aviator Dopplebock (26 SRM, 15 IBU)
Back Road Brewery Back Road Ale (14 SRM, 13 IBU)
Back Road Brewery Belgian-Style Wit (2 SRM, 7 IBU)
Back Road Brewery Belle Gunness Stout (40 SRM, 45 IBU)
Back Road Brewery Blueberry Ale (14 SRM, 13 IBU)
Back Road Brewery Christmas Ale
Back Road Brewery Koza Brada Bock (17 SRM, 15 IBU)
Back Road Brewery Maple Gold City (17 SRM, 23 IBU)
Back Road Brewery Midwest IPA (12 SRM, 70 IBU)
Back Road Brewery Millennium Lager (4 SRM, 9 IBU)
Back Road Brewery No. 9 Barley-Style Ale (25 SRM, 83 IBU)
Back Road Brewery Pecker Head Red (19 SRM, 37 IBU)

States Available: IN

Barley Island Brewing Company

639 Conner Street (Hwy 32)
Nobelsville, IN 46062
317-770-5280
www.barleyisland.com

BRANDS:
Barley Island Brewing Bar Fly India Pale Ale (7.8 SRM, 60 IBU)
Barley Island Brewing Black Majic Java Stout
Barley Island Brewing Blind Tiger Pale Ale (7.1 SRM, 32.6 IBU)
Barley Island Brewing Bourbon Barrel-Aged Oatmeal Stout
Barley Island Brewing Brass Knuckles Oatmeal Stout (52.4 SRM, 24.4 IBU)
Barley Island Brewing Dirty Helen Brown Ale (17.8 SRM, 24.5 IBU)
Barley Island Brewing Sheet Metal Blonde

States Available: Contact Brewery

Mad Anthony Brewing Company

2002 Broadway
Ft. Wayne, IN 46802
219-426-2537
www.madbrew.com

BRANDS:
Mad Anthony Auburn Lager
Mad Anthony Gabby Blonde Lager
Mad Anthony Old Fort Porter
Mad Anthony Pale Ale

States Available: IN

Mishawaka Brewing Company

3703 North Main Street
Mishawaka, IN 46545
574-256-9993
www.mishawakabrewingcompany.com

BRANDS:
Founders Classic Dry Stout
Four Horsemen Irish Ale
Hop Head Ale
INDIAna Pale Ale
Lake Effect Pale Ale
Mishawaka Kölsch
Raspberry Wheat Ale
Seven Mules Kick-Ass Ale
Wall Street Wheat Ale

States Available: IN

Nine G Brewing Company, Inc.

1115 West Sample Street
South Bend, IN 46619
574-282-2337
www.ninegbrewing.com

BRANDS:
Bitchin' Betty Citrus Wheat Beer
Blacksnake Porter
Infidel Imperial India Pale Ale
Wingman Amber Ale

States Available: IN

GEOGRAPHIC BREWER INDEX (Alphabetical)

Oaken Barrel Brewing Company

50 North Airport Parkway, Suite L
Greenwood, IN 46143-1438
317-887-2287
www.oakenbarrel.com

BRANDS:
Oaken Barrel Brewing Alabaster
Oaken Barrel Brewing Gnaw Bone Pale Ale
Oaken Barrel Brewing Indiana Amber Ale
Oaken Barrel Brewing Razz-Wheat
Oaken Barrel Brewing Snake Pit Porter

States Available: IN

Terre Haute Brewing Company

401-02 South 9th Street, P.O. Box 2027
Terre Haute, IN 47807
812-234-2800
www.cvbeer.com

BRANDS:
Terre Haute Brewing Champagne Velvet Amber
Terre Haute Brewing Champagne Velvet Bock
Terre Haute Brewing Champagne Velvet Pilsner

States Available: IN

Three Floyds Brewing Company

9750 Indiana Parkway
Munster, IN 46321
219-922-3565
www.threefloyds.com

BRANDS:
Three Floyds Brewing Alpha King (66 IBU)
Three Floyds Brewing Behemoth Barleywine
Three Floyds Brewing Black Sun Stout
Three Floyds Brewing Brian Boru
Three Floyds Brewing Christmas Porter
Three Floyds Brewing Dreadnaught IPA (100 IBU)
Three Floyds Brewing Gumballhead
Three Floyds Brewing Pride & Joy Mild Ale (21 IBU)
Three Floyds Brewing Rabbid Rabbit Saison
Three Floyds Brewing Robert the Bruce Scottish Ale (35 IBU)

States Available: DC, IA, IL, IN, NJ, OH, PA, RI, VA, WI

Upland Brewing Company

350 West 11th Street
Bloomington, IN 12411
812-336-BEER
www.uplandbeer.com

BRANDS:
Upland Brewing Company Amber (28 IBU)
Upland Brewing Company Bad Elmer's Porter (24 IBU)
Upland Brewing Company Dragonfly India Pale Ale (40 IBU)
Upland Brewing Company Maibock
Upland Brewing Company Pale Ale (19 IBU)
Upland Brewing Company Valley Weizen (9.8 IBU)
Upland Brewing Company Wheat Ale (11 IBU)

States Available: Contact Brewery

Warbird Brewing Company

10510 Majic Port Lane
Fort Wayne, IN 46819
260-459-2400
www.warbirdbrewing.com

BRANDS:
Warbird Brewing P47 Warbird Wheat (6 SRM, 18 IBU)
Warbird Brewing T-6 Red Ale (14.5 SRM, 15 IBU)

States Available: Contact Brewery

The following brewers distribute their brands in Indiana:

Abita Brewing Company	Nine G Brewing Company, Inc.
Allagash Brewing Company	O'Fallon Brewery
Anchor Brewing Company	Oaken Barrel Brewing Company
Anderson Valley Brewing	Pabst Brewing Company
Anheuser-Busch, Inc.	Pete's Brewing
Arcadia Brewing Company	Pig's Eye Brewing Company
Atwater Block Brewery	Pittsburgh Brewing Company
Avery Brewing Company	Pyramid Brewery
Back Road Brewery	Redhook Ale Brewery
Bard's Tale Beer Company	Rogue Ales
Bell's Brewery, Inc.	SAB Miller Corp
Bison Brewing	Shipyard Brewing Company
Bluegrass Beer Company	Shmaltz Brewing Company
Boulder Beer Company	Sierra Nevada Brewing Company
Breckenridge Brewery	Spanish Peaks Brewing Company/
Brewery Ommegang	United States Beverage
Clipper City Brewing Company	Sprecher Brewing
Dark Horse Brewing Company	Stevens Point Brewery
Dogfish Head Craft Brewery	Stone Brewing Company
Flying Dog Brewery, LLC	Summit Brewing Company
Frederick Brewing Company	Terre Haute Brewing
Great Divide Brewing Company	The Black Mountain/Chili Beer Company
Harpoon Brewery	The Boston Beer Company
High Falls Brewing	The Fort Collins Brewery
Jacob Leinenkugel Brewing Company	The Matt Brewing
Jolly Pumpkin Artisan Ales	The Sea Dog Brewing Company
Lakefront Brewery Inc.	Thirsty Dog Brewing Company
Left Handed Brewing Company	Three Floyds Brewing Company
Lost Coast Brewery & Café	Tommyknocker Brewery
MacTarnahan's Brewing Company	Tremont Brewery/Atlantic Coast Brewing
Mad Anthony Brewing Company	Company
Mishawaka Brewing Company	Two Brothers Brewing Company
Molson Coors Brewing Company	Warbird Brewing Company
New Century Brewing Company	Widmer Brothers Brewing Company
New Holland Brewing Company	

Pony Express Brewing Company

KS

311 N Burch Street
Olathe, KS 66061-3649
913-764-7669
www.ponygold.com

BRANDS:
Pony Express Gold Beer
Pony Express Original Wheat
Pony Express Rattlesnake Pale Ale
Pony Express Tornado Red Ale

States Available: IA, KS, MI, NE, WI

The following brewers distribute their brands in Kansas:

Abita Brewing Company	Pete's Brewing
Anchor Brewing Company	Pittsburgh Brewing Company
Anheuser-Busch, Inc.	Pony Express Brewing Company
Avery Brewing Company	Pyramid Brewery
Bard's Tale Beer Company	Redhook Ale Brewery
Boulder Beer Company	Rogue Ales
Boulevard Brewing Company	SAB Miller Corp
Breckenridge Brewery	Shipyard Brewing Company
BridgePort Brewing Company	Sierra Nevada Brewing Company
Estes Park Brewery	Spanish Peaks Brewing Company/
Flying Dog Brewery, LLC	United States Beverage
Frederick Brewing Company	Sprecher Brewing
Great Divide Brewing Company	Stevens Point Brewery
High Falls Brewing	The Black Mountain/Chili Beer Company
Jacob Leinenkugel Brewing Company	The Boston Beer Company
Lost Coast Brewery & Café	The Matt Brewing
MacTarnahan's Brewing Company	The Sea Dog Brewing Company
Molson Coors Brewing Company	The Spoetzl Brewing
New Belgium Brewing Company	Tremont Brewery/Atlantic Coast Brewing
O'Fallon Brewery	Company
Odell Brewing Company	Widmer Brothers Brewing Company
Pabst Brewing Company	

GEOGRAPHIC BREWER INDEX (Alphabetical)

Alltech's Lexington Brewing Company  KY

401 Cross Street
Lexington, KY 40508
859-887-3406
www.kentuckylight.com

BRANDS:
Lexington Brewing Kentucky Ale
Lexington Brewing Kentucky Bourbon Barrel Aged Ale
Lexington Brewing Kentucky Light

States Available: KY, NE, SD

Bluegrass Brewing Company – *page 472*

636 E. Main Street
Louisville, KY 40202
502-584-2739
www.bbcbrew.com

BRANDS:
BBC Altbier (14 SRM, 30 IBU)
BBC American Pale Ale (14 SRM, 52 IBU) – *page 472*
BBC Bearded Pat's Barleywine (18 SRM, 100+ IBU)
BBC Bluegrass Gold (3 SRM, 10 IBU)
BBC Dark Star Porter (35 SRM, 35 IBU)
BBC Hell For Certain (16 SRM, 25 IBU)
BBC Jefferson's Reserve Bourbon Barrel Stout (40+ SRM, 15 IBU)
BBC Nut Brown Ale (22SRM, 28 IBU)
BBC White Wedding Ale (4 SRM, 10 IBU)

States Available: CT, IN, KY, OH, TN, VA

The following brewers distribute their brands in Kentucky:

Abita Brewing Company	O'Fallon Brewery
Alltech's Lexington Brewing Company	Pabst Brewing Company
Anchor Brewing Company	Pete's Brewing
Anheuser-Busch, Inc.	Pittsburgh Brewing Company
Arcadia Brewing Company	Pyramid Brewery
Avery Brewing Company	Redhook Ale Brewery
Bard's Tale Beer Company	Rogue Ales
Bear Republic Brewing Company	SAB Miller Corp
Bluegrass Beer Company	Schlafly Beer
Boulder Beer Company	Shipyard Brewing Company
Breckenridge Brewery	Shmaltz Brewing Company
Brewery Ommegang	Sierra Nevada Brewing Company
Clipper City Brewing Company	Spanish Peaks Brewing Company/United
Dogfish Head Craft Brewery	States Beverage
Flying Dog Brewery LLC	Sprecher Brewing
Frederick Brewing Company	Stone Brewing Company
Great Divide Brewing Company	Summit Brewing Company
Great Lakes Brewing Company	The Black Mountain/Chili Beer Company
Harpoon Brewery	The Boston Beer Company
High Falls Brewing	The Sea Dog Brewing Company
Jacob Leinenkugel Brewing Company	The Spoetzl Brewing
Jolly Pumpkin Artisan Ales	Thirsty Dog Brewing Company
Kona Brewing LLC	Tommyknocker Brewery
Left Handed Brewing Company	Tremont Brewery/Atlantic Coast Brewing
Molson Coors Brewing Company	Company
North Coast Brewing Company	Widmer Brothers Brewing Company

Abita Brewing Company  LA

P.O. Box 1510
Abita Springs, LA 70420
985-898-3544
www.abita.com

BRANDS:
Abita Bock
Abita Brewing 20th Anniversary Pilsner
Abita Brewing Amber
Abita Brewing Christmas Ale
Abita Brewing Golden
Abita Brewing Purple Haze
Abita Brewing Red Ale
Abita Brewing Restoration Ale
Abita Brewing Turbodog
Abita Brewing Wheat
Abita Fall Fest
Abita Light

States Available: AL, AR, AZ, CA, CT, DC, FL, GA, IL, IN, KS, KY, LA, MA, MD,
MI, MO, MS, NC, NJ, NV, NY, OH, OK, PA, SC, TN, TX, VA, WI

GEOGRAPHIC BREWER INDEX (Alphabetical)

Big Easy Brewing Company

5200 Taravella Road
Marreor, LA 70072
504-347-8200
www.bigeasybeer.com

BRANDS:
Bourbon Street Bock
Mojo Red Ale
Tiger Town Beer

States Available: LA

Dixie Brewing Company

2401 Tulane Avenue
New Orleans, LA 70119-7444
504-822-8711

BRANDS:
Dixie Brewing Blackened Voodoo Lager
Dixie Brewing Crimson Voodoo Ale
Dixie Brewing Dixie Beer
Dixie Brewing Jazz Amber Light

States Available: Contact Brewery

Heiner Brau

P.O. 4238, 226 East Lockwood Street
Covington, LA 70434-4238
985-893-2884
www.heinerbrau.net

BRANDS:
Heiner Brau Hefe Weisse
Heiner Brau Kellerbier
Heiner Brau Kölsch
Heiner Brau Maerzen
Heiner Brau Maibock
Heiner Brau Mardi Gras Festbier
Heiner Brau Octoberfest Bier
Heiner Weihnachtsbock

States Available: Contact Brewery

The following brewers distribute their brands in Louisiana:

Abita Brewing Company	Redhook Ale Brewery
Anchor Brewing Company	Rogue Ales
Anheuser-Busch, Inc.	SAB Miller Corp
Big Easy Brewing Company	Shipyard Brewing Company
Brewery Ommegang	Sierra Nevada Brewing Company
Flying Dog Brewery, LLC	Spanish Peaks Brewing Company/
Heiner Brau	United States Beverage
High Falls Brewing	The Boston Beer Company
Molson Coors Brewing Company	The Sea Dog Brewing Company
North Coast Brewing Company	The Spoetzl Brewing
Pabst Brewing Company	Tremont Brewery/Atlantic Coast Brewing
Pete's Brewing	Company

Berkshire Brewing Company – *page 467*

MA

P.O. Box 251
South Deerfield, MA 01373
413-665-6600
www.berkshirebrewingcompany.com

BRANDS:
Berkshire Brewing Berkshire Traditional Pale Ale
Berkshire Brewing Cabin Fever Ale
Berkshire Brewing Coffeehouse Porter
Berkshire Brewing Drayman's Porter
Berkshire Brewing Gold Spike Ale
Berkshire Brewing Hefeweizen
Berkshire Brewing Holidale
Berkshire Brewing Imperial Stout
Berkshire Brewing Lost Sailor India Pale Ale
Berkshire Brewing Maibock Lager
Berkshire Brewing Ocktoberfest Lager
Berkshire Brewing Raspberry Strong Ale
Berkshire Brewing River Ale
Berkshire Brewing "Shabadoo" Black & Tan Ale
Berkshire Brewing Steel Rail Extra Pale Ale – *page 467*

States Available: CT, MA, RI, VT

GEOGRAPHIC BREWER INDEX (Alphabetical)

Buzzards Bay Brewing Company

98 Horseneck Road
Westport, MA 02790
508-636-2288
www.buzzardsbrew.com

BRANDS:
Buzzards Bay Brewing Hefe-Weizen (40 IBU)
Buzzards Bay Brewing Lager (35 IBU)
Buzzards Bay Brewing Octoberfest
Buzzards Bay Brewing Pale Ale (47 IBU)
Buzzards Bay Brewing Weizen Dopplebock (17 IBU)

States Available: CT, MA, ME, RI, VT

Cape Ann Brewing

27 Commercial Street
Glouchester, MA 01930
978-282-0772
www.capeannbrewing.com

BRANDS:
Cape Ann Brewing Fisherman's Brew (30 IBU)
Cape Ann Brewing Fisherman's IPA (64 IBU)

States Available: MA, ME, NY

Cisco Brewers, Inc.

5 Bartlett Farm Road
Nantucket, MA 02554
508-325-5929
www.ciscobrewers.com

BRANDS:
Cisco Brewers Baggywrinkle Barleywine
Cisco Brewers Bailey's Ale
Cisco Brewers Captain Swain's Extra Stout
Cisco Brewers Celebration Libation
Cisco Brewers Moor Porter
Cisco Brewers Sankaty Light
Cisco Brewers Summer of Lager
Cisco Brewers Whale's Tale Pale Ale

States Available: CT, DC, DE, MA, MD, NJ, NY, RI

Concord Brewery, Inc.

199 Cabot Street
Lowell, MA 01854
978-937-1200
www.concordbrew.com

BRANDS:
Concord Grape Ale (16 IBU)
Concord IPA (38 IBU)
Concord North Woods Ale (38 IBU)
Concord Pale Ale (26 IBU)
Concord Porter (32 IBU)
Rapscallion Blessing (36 IBU)
Rapscallion Creation (18 IBU)
Rapscallion Premier (26 IBU)

States Available: MA, RI

Harpoon Brewery – *page 508*

306 Northern Avenue
Boston, MA 02210
617-574-9551
www.harpoonbrewery.com

BRANDS:
Harpoon 100 BBL Series
Harpoon Ale (24 IBU)
Harpoon Brown Ale
Harpoon Hibernian Ale (25 IBU)
Harpoon IPA (42 IBU) – *page 508*
Harpoon Munich Dark (35 IBU)
Harpoon Octoberfest (30 IBU)
Harpoon Summer (28 IBU)
Harpoon UFO Hefeweizen (19 IBU)
Harpoon UFO Raspberry Hefeweizen (12 IBU)
Harpoon Winter Warmer (22 IBU)

States Available: CT, DC, DE, FL, GA, IN, KY, MA, MD, ME, MI, NC, NH, NJ, NY, OH, PA, RI, SC, TN, VA, VT, WV

High & Mighty Brewing Company

108 Cabot Street
Holyoke, MA 01040
www.highandmigtybrewing.com

BRANDS:
High & Mighty Brewing Beer of the Gods
High & Mighty Brewing Two-Headed Beast
High & Mighty Brewing XPA

States Available: Contact Brewery

Mercury Brewing Company – *page 519*

23 Hayward Street
Ipswich, MA 01938
978-356-3329
www.mercurybrewing.com

BRANDS:
Farmington River Blonde Ale
Farmington River Mahogany Ale
Mercury Brewing Dog Pound Porter
Mercury Brewing Eagle Brook Saloon's Blueberry Ale (14 IBU)
Mercury Brewing Ipswich Dark Ale (40 IBU)
Mercury Brewing Ipswich Harvest Ale (40 IBU)
Mercury Brewing Ipswich IPA (60 IBU)
Mercury Brewing Ipswich Nut Brown (25 IBU)
Mercury Brewing Ipswich Oatmeal Stout (69 IBU)
Mercury Brewing Ipswich Original Ale (30 IBU) – *page 519*
Mercury Brewing Ipswich Porter (48 IBU)
Mercury Brewing Ipswich Summer Ale (23 IBU)
Mercury Brewing Ipswich Winter Ale (35 IBU)
Mercury Brewing Stone Cat Ale
Mercury Brewing Stone Cat Barley Wine
Mercury Brewing Stone Cat Blonde (25 IBU)
Mercury Brewing Stone Cat Blueberry
Mercury Brewing Stone Cat ESB (35 IBU)
Mercury Brewing Stone Cat IPA (55 IBU)
Mercury Brewing Stone Cat Octoberfest (24 IBU)
Mercury Brewing Stone Cat Pumpkin Porter (25 IBU)
Mercury Brewing Stone Cat Scotch Ale (18 IBU)
Mercury Brewing Stone Cat Wheat Beer
Mercury Brewing Stone Cat Winter Lager (35 IBU)

States Available: CT, Stone Cat - MA / Ipswich Ale - MA, NJ, RI

Nashoba Valley Brewery

100 Wattaquadoc Hill Road
Bolton, MA 01740
978-779-5521
www.nashobawinery.com

BRANDS:
Nashoba Valley Brewery Barleywine Ale (72 IBU)
Nashoba Valley Brewery Belgian Double
Nashoba Valley Brewery Belgian Pale Ale (26 IBU)
Nashoba Valley Brewery Blackberry Ale
Nashoba Valley Brewery Bolt 117 Lager (25 IBU)
Nashoba Valley Brewery Heron Ale (30 IBU)
Nashoba Valley Brewery Imperial Stout
Nashoba Valley Brewery IPA (50 IBU)
Nashoba Valley Brewery Peach Lambic (15 IBU)

States Available: Contact Brewery

New Century Brewing Company – *page 522*

P.O. Box 1498
Boston, MA 02117
781-963-4007
www.edisonbeer.com

BRANDS:
Moonshot
Edison The Independent Light Beer – *page 522*

States Available: IL, IN, MA, MI, NJ, OH, VA

GEOGRAPHIC BREWER INDEX (Alphabetical)

Paper City Brewery Company

108 Cabot Street
Holyoke, MA 01040
413-535-1588
www.papercity.com

BRANDS:
Paper City Brewing 1 Eared Monkey
Paper City Brewing Banchee Extra Pale Ale
Paper City Brewing Blonde Hop Monster
Paper City Brewing Cabot Street Summer Wheat
Paper City Brewing Denogginator
Paper City Brewing Dorado
Paper City Brewing Goats Peak Bock (20 IBU)
Paper City Brewing Golden Lager
Paper City Brewing Holyoke Dam Ale
Paper City Brewing India's Pale Ale
Paper City Brewing Ireland Parish Golden Ale
Paper City Brewing Nut Brown
Paper City Brewing P.C. Blue
Paper City Brewing Red Hat Razzberry
Paper City Brewing Riley's Stout
Paper City Brewing Summer Brew
Paper City Brewing Summer Time Pale Ale
Paper City Brewing Summit House Oktoberfest (23 IBU)
Paper City Brewing Winter Lager
Paper City Brewing Winter Palace Wee Heavy

States Available: CT, MA, RI

Peak Organic Brewing Company

3 Little's Brook Ct #55
Burlington, MA 01803
520-360-8412
www.peakbrewing.com

BRANDS:
Peak Organic Amber Ale
Peak Organic Nut Brown Ale
Peak Organic Pale Ale

States Available: Contact Brewery

Pioneer Brewing Company

199 Arnold Road
Sturbridge, MA 01566
508-347-7500
www.hylandbrew.com

BRANDS:
Hyland's Sturbridge Amber Ale
Hyland's Sturbridge American Pale Ale
Hyland's Sturbridge Farmhand Ale
Hyland's Sturbridge Stout

States Available: MA

Sherwood Forest Brewers

655 Farm Road
Marlborough, MA 01752
877-272-4376
www.sherwoodbrewers.com

BRANDS:
Sherwood Forest Archer's Ale

States Available: MA

GEOGRAPHIC BREWER INDEX (Alphabetical)

The Boston Beer Company – *page 473*

30 Germania Street
Boston, MA 02130
617-368-5000
www.samueladams.com

BRANDS:
Sam Adams 1790 Root Beer Brew
Sam Adams George Washington Porter
Sam Adams James Madison Dark Wheat Ale
Sam Adams Light (11 SRM, 10 IBU) – *page 474*
Sam Adams Traditional Ginger Honey Ale
Samuel Adams 375 Colonial Ale
Samuel Adams Black Lager (50 SRM, 19 IBU)
Samuel Adams Boston Ale (14 SRM, 32 IBU)
Samuel Adams Boston Lager (11 SRM, 30 IBU) – *page 473*
Samuel Adams Brown Ale (26 SRM, 18 IBU)
Samuel Adams Cherry Wheat (8 SRM, 23 IBU)
Samuel Adams Chocolate Bock (75 SRM, 16 IBU)
Samuel Adams Cranberry Lambic (13.5 SRM, 22 IBU)
Samuel Adams Cream Stout (80 SRM, 28 IBU)
Samuel Adams Double Bock (38 SRM, 25 IBU)
Samuel Adams Hefeweizen (7 SRM, 14 IBU)
Samuel Adams Holiday Porter (55 SRM, 40 IBU)
Samuel Adams Honey Porter
Samuel Adams Imperial Pilsner (20 SRM, 110 IBU)
Samuel Adams Millennium (30 SRM, 27 IBU)
Samuel Adams Octoberfest (20 SRM, 17 IBU) – *page 474*
Samuel Adams Old Fezziwig Ale (37.5 SRM, 25 IBU)
Samuel Adams Pale Ale (8 SRM, 23 IBU)
Samuel Adams Scotch Ale (28.5 SRM, 35 IBU)
Samuel Adams Summer Ale (7.5 SRM, 10 IBU) – *page 475*
Samuel Adams Triple Bock (200 SRM, 31 IBU)
Samuel Adams Utopias (34 SRM, 25 IBU)
Samuel Adams White Ale (8 SRM, 12 IBU) – *page 475*
Samuel Adams Winter Lager (25 SRM, 22 IBU)– *page 476*

States Available: All 50 States

Tremont Brewery/Atlantic Coast Brewing Company – *page 565*

P.O. Box 52328
Boston, MA 02205
800-347-1150
www.tremontale.com

BRANDS:
Tremont Brewing Tremont Ale (14 SRM, 40 IBU) – *page 565*
Tremont Brewing Tremont IPA 11.8 SRM, 50 IBU)
Tremont Brewing Tremont Summer (7 SRM, 22 IBU)
Tremont Brewing Tremont Winter (23 SRM, 39 IBU)

States Available: All 50 States

Wachusett Brewing Company

175 State Road East, Route 2A
Westminster, MA 01473-1208
978-874-9965
www.wachusettbrew.com

BRANDS:
Wachusett Black Shack Porter
Wachusett Blueberry
Wachusett Country Ale
Wachusett Green Monsta
Wachusett IPA
Wachusett Nut Brown Ale
Wachusett Octoberfest
Wachusett Quinn's Amber Ale
Wachusett Summer Breeze
Wachusett Winter Ale

States Available: MA, NY (Blueberry only)

GEOGRAPHIC BREWER INDEX (Alphabetical)

The following brewers distribute their brands in Massachusetts:

Abita Brewing Company	Otter Creek Brewing Company
Allagash Brewing Company	Pabst Brewing Company
Anchor Brewing Company	Paper City Brewery Company
Anderson Valley Brewing	Pete's Brewing
Anheuser-Busch, Inc.	Pioneer Brewing Company
Avery Brewing Company	Pittsburgh Brewing Company
Baltimore-Washington Beer Works	Port Brewing Company
Bard's Tale Beer Company	Ramapo Valley Brewery
Bear Republic Brewing Company	Redhook Ale Brewery
Berkshire Brewing Company	River Horse Brewing Company
Blue Point Brewing	Rogue Ales
Boulder Beer Company	SAB Miller Corp
Brewery Ommegang	Sebago Brewing Company
Brooklyn Brewery	Sherwood Forest Brewers
Buzzards Bay Brewing Company	Shipyard Brewing Company
Cape Ann Brewing	Shmaltz Brewing Company
Casco Bay Brewing Company	Sierra Nevada Brewing Company
Cisco Brewers Inc.	Smuttynose Brewing Company
Clipper City Brewing Company	South Hampton Publick House
Coastal Extreme Brewing Company LLC	Southern Tier Brewing Company
Concord Brewery, Inc.	Spanish Peaks Brewing Company/
Cooperstown Brewing Company	United States Beverage
D L Geary Brewing Company	Sprecher Brewing
Dogfish Head Craft Brewery	Stone Brewing Company
Flying Dog Brewery, LLC	Stone Coast Brewing Company
Franconia Notch Brewing Company	Stoudt's Brewing Company
Great Divide Brewing Company	The Black Mountain/Chili Beer Company
Gritty McDuff's Brewing Company	The Boston Beer Company
Harpoon Brewery	The Long Trail Brewing Company
High Falls Brewing	The Matt Brewing
Lagunitas Brewing	The Narragansett Brewing Company
Lake Placid Craft Brewing	The Sea Dog Brewing Company
Left Handed Brewing Company	Tommyknocker Brewery
Magic Hat Brewing Company	Tremont Brewery/Atlantic Coast Brewing
Mercury Brewing Company	Company
Michigan Brewing Company, Inc.	Trout Brook Brewing Company
Molson Coors Brewing Company	Tuckerman Brewing
Moylan's Brewing Company	Two Brothers Brewing Company
New Century Brewing Company	Victory Brewing Company
North Coast Brewing Company	Wachusett Brewing Company
Nutfield Brewing Company	Weyerbacher Brewing Company
Oskar Blues Grill & Brew	Widmer Brothers Brewing Company

MD

B.W. Beer Works USA

P.O. Box 9829
Baltimore, MD 21284-9829
410-321-1892
www.ravenbeer.com

BRANDS:

The Raven Christmas Lager
The Raven Special Lager

States Available: DC, IL, MA, MD, PA, SC, VA

Clay Pipe Brewing Company

1203 New Windsor Road
Westminster, MD 21157
410-871-9333
www.cpbrewing.com

BRANDS:

Clay Pipe Brewing Blackfin Pale Ale (8.0 SRM)
Clay Pipe Brewing Blue Tractor Ale (28 IBU)
Clay Pipe Brewing Pursuit of Happiness Winter Warmer (12 SRM, 46 IBU)
Hop-ocalypse India Pale Ale (50 IBU)

States Available: MD

Clipper City Brewing Company – *page 486*

4615 Hollins Ferry Road, Suite B
Baltimore, MD 21227
410-247-7822
www.clippercitybeer.com

BRANDS:
Clipper City BaltoMärzHon
Clipper City Brewing Gold Ale
Clipper City Brewing Pale Ale
Clipper City McHenry Old Baltimore Style Beer
Heavy Seas Brewing Below Decks
Heavy Seas Brewing "Holy Sheet"
Heavy Seas Brewing Loose Cannon Hop³ Ale – *page 486*
Heavy Seas Brewing Peg Leg Stout
Heavy Seas Brewing Red Sky at Night Saison Ale
Heavy Seas Brewing Small Craft Warning Über Pils
Heavy Seas Brewing Winter Storm "Category 5" Ale
Oxford Hefeweizen
Oxford Raspberry

States Available: CT, DC, DE, FL, GA, IL, IN, KY, MA, ME, MD, NC, NY, OH,
OH, PA, RI, VA

Wild Goose Brewery, LLC – *page 572*

4607 Wedgewood Boulevard
Frederick, MD 21703-7120
301-694-7899
www.wildgoosebrewery.com

BRANDS:
Blue Ridge Amber Lager
Blue Ridge ESB Red Ale
Blue Ridge Golden Ale
Blue Ridge HopFest
Blue Ridge Porter
Blue Ridge Snowball's Chance
Blue Ridge Steeple Stout
Blue Ridge Subliminator Dopplebock
Crooked River ESB
Crooked River Irish Red Ale
Crooked River Kolsch Ale
Crooked River Pumpkin Harvest Ale
Crooked River Robust Porter
Crooked River Select Lager
Crooked River Yuletide
Hudepohl 14 – K
Little Kings Cream Ale
Wild Goose Amber (20 SRM, 25 IBU)
Wild Goose India Pale Ale (10 SRM, 50 IBU) – *page 572*
Wild Goose Nut Brown Ale (35 SRM, 20 IBU)
Wild Goose Oatmeal Stout (50 SRM, 45 IBU)
Wild Goose Porter (40 SRM, 55 IBU)
Wild Goose Pumpkin Patch (16 SRM, 28 IBU)
Wild Goose Snow Goose (16 SRM, 28 IBU)

States Available: Wild Goose/ Blue Ridge: MD, AZ, CANADA, DC, IL, IN, IN,
KS, KY, KY, MI, NC, OH, OH, OK, PA, PA, SC Crooked
River: Ohio Only Little Kings: MD, VA, WV, WY

GEOGRAPHIC BREWER INDEX (Alphabetical)

Frederick Brewing Company

4607 Wedgewood Boulevard
Frederick, MD 21703-7120
301-694-7899
www.frederickbrewing.com

BRANDS:
Blue Ridge Amber Lager
Blue Ridge ESB Red Ale
Blue Ridge Golden Ale
Blue Ridge HopFest
Blue Ridge Porter
Blue Ridge Snowball's Chance
Blue Ridge Steeple Stout
Blue Ridge Subliminator Dopplebock
Crooked River ESB
Crooked River Irish Red Ale
Crooked River Kölsch Ale
Crooked River Pumpkin Harvest Ale
Crooked River Robust Porter
Crooked River Select Lager
Crooked River Yuletide
Hudepohl 14 – K
Little Kings Cream Ale
Wild Goose Amber
Wild Goose India Pale Ale
Wild Goose Nut Brown Ale
Wild Goose Oatmeal Stout
Wild Goose Porter
Wild Goose Pumpkin
Wild Goose Snow Goose

States Available: Wild Goose/Blue Ridge: MD, PA, WV, KY, VA, NC, OH, DC, IN, SC Crooked River: Ohio Only Little Kings: MD, PA, OH, KY, WY, AZ, IN, IL, MI, KS, OK, CANADA

The following brewers distribute their brands in Maryland:

Abita Brewing Company	Pabst Brewing Company
Allagash Brewing Company	Penn Brewery
Anchor Brewing Company	Pete's Brewing
Anderson Valley Brewing	Pittsburgh Brewing Company
Anheuser-Busch, Inc.	Pyramid Brewery
Avery Brewing Company	Redhook Ale Brewery
Baltimore-Washington Beer Works	River Horse Brewing Company
Bear Republic Brewing Company	Rogue Ales
Blue Point Brewing	SAB Miller Corp
Brewery Ommegang	Shipyard Brewing Company
Brooklyn Brewery	Shmaltz Brewing Company
Cisco Brewers Inc.	Sierra Nevada Brewing Company
Clay Pipe Brewing Company	Smuttynose Brewing Company
Clipper City Brewing Company	Spanish Peaks Brewing Company/
D.G. Yuengling & Son, Inc.	United States Beverage
D L Geary Brewing Company	Sprecher Brewing
Dogfish Head Craft Brewery	Stoudt's Brewing Company
Flying Dog Brewery, LLC	The Boston Beer Company
Flying Fish Brewing	The Fort Collins Brewery
Fordham Brewing Company	The Sea Dog Brewing Company
Frederick Brewing Company	The Spoetzl Brewing
Great Divide Brewing Company	The Weeping Radish Brewery
Harpoon Brewery	Thirsty Dog Brewing Company
High Falls Brewing	Tremont Brewery/Atlantic Coast Brewing
Lakefront Brewery Inc.	Company
Lancaster Brewing Company	Victory Brewing Company
Magic Hat Brewing Company	Weyerbacher Brewing Company
Molson Coors Brewing Company	Widmer Brothers Brewing Company
Old Dominion Brewing Company	Yards Brewing

GEOGRAPHIC BREWER INDEX (Alphabetical)

Allagash Brewing Company
ME

100 Industrial Way
Portland, ME 04103
207-878-5385
www.allagash.com

BRANDS:
Allagash Brewing 11th Anniversary
Allagash Brewing Curieux
Allagash Brewing Dubbel (27 IBU)
Allagash Brewing Four (37 IBU)
Allagash Brewing Interlude
Allagash Brewing Musette
Allagash Brewing Odyssey
Allagash Brewing Tripel (30 IBU)
Allagash Brewing Victoria Ale
Allagash Brewing White Beer (18 IBU)
Allagash Grand Cru (30 IBU)

States Available: CA, CO, CT, FL, IN, MA, MD, ME, ME, NC, NJ, NY, OH, OR, PA, RI, TX, VA, VT

Andrews Brewing Company

353 High Street
Lincolnville, ME 04846
207-763-3305
www.drinkmainebeer.com

BRANDS:
Andrew's Brown Ale
Andrew's English Pale Ale
Andrew's St. Nick Porter
Andrew's Summer Golden Ale

States Available: ME, CA, CO, CT, FL, IN, IL, MD, MA, NJ, NY, NC, OH, OR, PA, RI, TX, VT, VA

Atlantic Brewing Company

15 Knox Road
Bar Harbor, ME 04609-7720
207-288-2337
www.atlanticbrewing.com

BRANDS:
Atlantic Brewing Bar Harbor Blueberry Ale
Atlantic Brewing Bar Harbor Real Ale
Atlantic Brewing Brother Adam's Honey Bragget
Atlantic Brewing Coal Porter
Atlantic Brewing Mount Desert Island Ginger
Atlantic Brewing Special Old Bitter Ale

States Available: ME

Bar Harbor Brewing Company

135 Otter Creek Drive
Bar Harbor, ME 04609
207-288-4592
www.barharborbrewing.com

BRANDS:
Bar Harbor Brewing Bar Harbor Peach
Bar Harbor Brewing Cadillac Mountain Stout
Bar Harbor Brewing Ginger Mild Brew
Bar Harbor Brewing Harbor Lighthouse Ale
Bar Harbor Brewing Thunder Hole Ale

States Available: ME

GEOGRAPHIC BREWER INDEX (Alphabetical)

D L Geary Brewing Company

38 Evergreen Drive
Portland, ME 04103-1066
207-878-2337
www.gearybrewing.com

BRANDS:
Geary's Autumn Ale
Geary's Hampshire Special Ale
Geary's London Porter
Geary's Pale Ale
Geary's Summer Ale
Geary's Winter

States Available: CT, MA, MD, ME, MI, NC, NH, NJ, NY, OH, PA, RI, SC, VA, VT

Freeport Brewing Company

46 Durham Road
Freeport, ME 04032
207-767-2577

BRANDS:
Brown Hound Brown Ale

States Available: ME

Gritty McDuff's Brewing Company, LLC – *page 507*

396 Fore Street
Portland, ME 04101
207-772-2739
www.grittys.com

BRANDS:
Gritty McDuff's Best Bitter (25 IBU)
Gritty McDuff's Best Brown Ale (16 IBU)
Gritty McDuff's Black Fly Stout (16 IBU)
Gritty McDuff's Christmas Ale (28.5 IBU)
Gritty McDuff's Halloween Ale
Gritty McDuff's Original Pub Style Ale (20 IBU) – *page 507*
Gritty McDuff's Scottish Ale (25 IBU)
Gritty McDuff's Vacationland Summer Ale (22 IBU)

States Available: MA, ME, NH, NJ, NY, VT

Maine Coast Brewing

102 Eden Street
Bar Harbor, ME 04609
207-288-4914
http://www.bhmaine.com/MCBCPrimary.html

BRANDS:
Jack's Best Brown
Maine Coast Brewing Black Irish Style Stout
Maine Coast Brewing Eden Porter
Maine Coast Brewing Wild Blueberry Ale

States Available: ME

GEOGRAPHIC BREWER INDEX (Alphabetical)

Oak Pond Brewery

101 Oak Pond Road
Skowhegan, ME 04976
207-474-3233
www.oakpondbrewery.com

BRANDS:
Oak Pond Brewing Dooryard Ale
Oak Pond Brewing Laughing Loon Lager
Oak Pond Brewing Nut Brown Ale
Oak Pond Brewing Oktoberfest
Oak Pond Brewing Storyteller Doppelbock
Oak Pond Brewing White Fox Ale

States Available: ME

Rocky Bay Brewing Company

230 Park Street
Rockland, ME 04841
207-596-0300
www.rockybaybrewing.com

BRANDS:
Rocky Bay Brewing Foghorn Ale
Rocky Bay Brewing Seasider Oktoberfest
Rocky Bay Brewing Whitecap Ale
Rocky Bay Black Castle Ale
Rocky Bay Brewing Nor' Easter Stout
Rocky Bay Brewing Schooner Point Lager
Rocky Bay Brewing Katie's Celtic Red Ale

States Available: ME

Sebago Brewing Company – *page 543*

48 Sanford Drive
Gorham, ME 04038
207-856-2537
www.sebagobrewing.com

BRANDS:
Sebago Brewing Bass Ackwards Berryblue Ale (13.3 SRM, 16.1 IBU)
Sebago Brewing Boathouse Brown Ale (49.5 SRM, 24.4 IBU)
Sebago Brewing Frye's Leap India Pale Ale (11.5 SRM, 54.4 IBU) – *page 543*
Sebago Brewing Hefe-Weizen (4.6 SRM, 19.8 IBU)
Sebago Brewing Lake Trout Stout (171.5 SRM, 31.4 IBU)
Sebago Brewing Midnight Porter (98.0 SRM, 35.7 IBU)
Sebago Brewing Northern Light Ale
Sebago Brewing Runabout Red Ale (26.24 SRM, 37.3 IBU)
Sebago Brewing Slick Nick Winter Ale (21.1 SRM, 38.7 IBU)

States Available: MA, ME

Sheepscot Valley Brewing Company

74 Hollywood Boulevard
Whitefield, ME 04353
207-549-5530
www.photo-ne.com/sheepscot/sheepscot4.html

BRANDS:
Sheepscot Valley Brewing Boothbay Special Bitter
Sheepscot Valley Brewing Damariscotta Double Brown
Sheepscot Valley Brewing Monhegan Wheat
Sheepscot Valley Brewing Pemaquid Ale

States Available: ME

The Shipyard Brewing Company – *page 544*

86 Newbury Street
Portland, ME 04103
207-761-0807
www.shipyard.com

BRANDS:
Shipyard Brewing Bluefin Stout (110 SRM, 42 IBU)
Shipyard Brewing Brown (19 SRM, 28 IBU)
Shipyard Brewing Chamberland Pale Ale (7.5 SRM, 35 IBU)
Shipyard Brewing Export Ale (8.5 SRM, 29 IBU)
Shipyard Brewing IPA (11 SRM, 50 IBU)
Shipyard Brewing Light (3.5 SRM, 46 IBU)
Shipyard Brewing Longfellow (47 SRM, 40 IBU)
Shipyard Brewing Old Thumper Extra Special Ale (12 SRM, 34 IBU)
Shipyard Brewing Prelude Special Ale (29 SRM, 46 IBU)
Shipyard Brewing Pumpkinhead Ale (6 SRM, 14 IBU)
Shipyard Brewing Summer (6.5 SRM, 27 IBU)

States Available: All 50 States

Stone Coast Brewing Company

23 Rice Street
Portland, ME 04103
207-347-5729
www.stonecoast.com

BRANDS:
Black Bear Porter
Jackson's Winter Ale
Knuckleball Bock
Stone Coast 420 India Pale Ale
Sunday River Alt
Sunday River Lager
Sunday River Sunsplash Golden Ale

States Available: CT, IL, MA, ME, NH, NY, RI, VT

The Sea Dog Brewing Company – *page 542*

26 Front Street
Bangor, ME 04401
207-947-8009
www.seadogbrewing.com

BRANDS:
Sea Dog Apricot Wheat Beer (6 SRM, 8 IBU)
Sea Dog Old East India Pale Ale (18 SRM, 44 IBU)
Sea Dog Pumpkin Ale (6 SRM, 14 IBU)
Sea Dog Raspberry Wheat (6.4 SRM, 8.2 IBU)
Sea Dog Riverdriver Hazelnut Porter (54 SRM, 35 IBU)
Sea Dog Summer Ale (6 SRM, 14 IBU)
Sea Dog Wild Blueberry Wheat Ale – *page 542*
Sea Dog Winter Ale (23 SRM, 39 IBU)

States Available: All 50 States

The following brewers distribute their brands in Maine:

Allagash Brewing Company	Pabst Brewing Company
Anchor Brewing Company	Pete's Brewing
Andrews Brewing Company	Redhook Ale Brewery
Anheuser-Busch, Inc.	Rocky Bay Brewing Company
Atlantic Brewing Company	Rogue Ales
Bar Harbor Brewing Company	SAB Miller Corp
Brewery Ommegang	Sebago Brewing Company
Buzzards Bay Brewing Company	Sheepscot Valley Brewing Company
Cape Ann Brewing	Shipyard Brewing Company
Casco Bay Brewing Company	Sierra Nevada Brewing Company
D L Geary Brewing Company	Smuttynose Brewing Company
Dogfish Head Craft Brewery	Spanish Peaks Brewing Company/
Flying Dog Brewery, LLC	United States Beverage
Gritty McDuff's Brewing Company	Stone Coast Brewing Company
Harpoon Brewery	The Boston Beer Company
High Falls Brewing	The Long Trail Brewing Company
Jolly Pumpkin Artisan Ales	The Sea Dog Brewing Company
Maine Coast Brewing	Tremont Brewery/Atlantic Coast Brewing
Magic Hat Brewing Company	Company
Molson Coors Brewing Company	Tröegs Brewing Company
Oak Pond Brewery	Widmer Brothers Brewing Company

GEOGRAPHIC BREWER INDEX (Alphabetical)

MI

Arbor Brewing Company

720 Norris Street
Ypsilanti, MI 49198
734-480-2739
www.cornerbrewery.com

BRANDS::
Arbor Brewing Bavarian Bliss Hefeweizen
Arbor Brewing Brasserie Blonde Belgian
Arbor Brewing Olde Number 23 Alt Bier
Arbor Brewing Red Snapper Special Bitter
Arbor Brewing Sacred Cow IPA

States Available: MI

Arcadia Brewing Company – *page 462*

103 West Michigan Avenue
Battle Creek, MI 49017
269-963-9690
www.arcadiabrewingcompany.com

BRANDS:
Arcadia Brewing Ales Amber Ale (34 IBU)
Arcadia Brewing Ales Angler's Ale (34 IBU)
Arcadia Brewing Ales Battle Creek Special Reserve (23 IBU)
Arcadia Brewing Ales HopMouth (76 IBU)
Arcadia Brewing Ales Imperial Stout (59 IBU)
Arcadia Brewing Ales India Pale Ale (41 IBU) – *page 462*
Arcadia Brewing Ales London Porter (42 IBU)
Arcadia Brewing Ales Nut Brown Ale (26 IBU)
Arcadia Brewing Ales Scotch Ale (28 IBU)
Arcadia Brewing Ales Starboard Stout (29 IBU)
Arcadia Brewing Ales Whitsun (17 IBU)

States Available: IL, KY, MI, MN, MO, NJ, OH, PA, NY, VA

Atwater Block Brewery

237 Jos Campau Street
Detroit, MI 48207
313-877-9205
www.atwaterbeer.com

BRANDS:
Atwater Bloktoberfest
Atwater Dunkel Dark Lager
Atwater Hefeweizen
Atwater Hell Pale Lager
Atwater Mai Bock
Atwater Pilsner
Atwater Rost
Atwater Salvation IPA
Atwater Shaman's Porter
Atwater Vanilla Java Porter
Atwater Voodoo Vator Dopplebock
Atwater Winter Bock

States Available: CO, IL, IN, MI, OH, PA, WI

Bell's Brewery, Inc.

8939 Krum Avenue
Galesburg, MI 49053
269-382-2338
www.bellsbeer.com

BRANDS:
(Non-participating Brewery – Please consult brewery)

States Available: IL, IN, KY, MI, MN, MO, ND, OH, WI

Dark Horse Brewing Company

511 South Kalamazoo Street
Marshall, MI 49068
269-781-9940
www.darkhorsebrewery.com

BRANDS:
Dark Horse 750 ml Imperial Stout
Dark Horse Belgian Amber Ale
Dark Horse Crooked Tree IPA
Dark Horse Double Crooked Tree IPA
Dark Horse Fore Smoked Stout
Dark Horse One Oatmeal Stout Ale
Dark Horse Raspberry Ale
Dark Horse Sapient Trip Ale
Dark Horse Scotty Karate Scotch Ale
Dark Horse Special Reserve Black Bier Ale
Dark Horse Too Cream Stout
Dark Horse Tres Blueberry Stout

States Available: IN, MI

Dragonmead Microbrewery

14600 East Eleven Mile Road
Warren, MI 48089
586-776-9428
www.dragonmead.com

BRANDS:
Dragonmead 90 Shilling
Dragonmead Andromeda Heather Ale
Dragonmead Armageddon Grand Cru
Dragonmead Big Larry's Pale Ale
Dragonmead Bill's Witbier
Dragonmead Bishop Bob's Holy Smoke
Dragonmead Bock Tubock
Dragonmead Breath Of The Dragon English Bitter
Dragonmead Broken Paddle India Pale Ale
Dragonmead Bronze Griffin Belgian Style
Dragonmead Castlebrite Apricot Ale
Dragonmead Copper Shield Bitter Harvest
Dragonmead Corktown Red

Dragonmead Crooked Door Amber Ale
Dragonmead Crown Jewels IPA (57 IBU)
Dragonmead Crusader Dark Mild Ale
Dragonmead Dead Monk Abbey Ale
Dragonmead Dragon Daze Hemp Ale
Dragonmead Dragon Slayer Altbier Style
Dragonmead Drei Kronen 1308
Dragonmead Dubbel Dragon Ale
Dragonmead Earl's Spit Stout
Dragonmead Erik the Red Irish Style Amber Ale (20.5 IBU)
Dragonmead Excalibur Barley Wine
Dragonmead Final Absolution Belgian Style (30 IBU)
Dragonmead Honey Porter
Dragonmead Imperial Stout
Dragonmead Inquisition Pale Ale
Dragonmead Jul 01
Dragonmead Kaiser's Kölsch
Dragonmead Lady Guinevere's Golden Belgian Style
Dragonmead Lancelot's Cream Ale
Dragonmead Larry's Lionheart Pale
Dragonmead Lil's Grumpkin Pumpkin Ale
Dragonmead London Brown Ale
Dragonmead Mariann's Honey Brown
Dragonmead Nagelweiss Wheat
Dragonmead Oktoberfest Marzen
Dragonmead Redwing Raspberry Wheat Beer
Dragonmead Reverend Fred's Oatmeal
Dragonmead Sir William's Extra Special Bitter (43 IBU)
Dragonmead Squire Pilsen
Dragonmead Tafelbeir Lager
Dragonmead Tayken Abock
Dragonmead Tuhelles Enbock
Dragonmead Under The Kilt Wee Heavy (30 IBU)
Dragonmead Wench Water Belgian Pale Ale
Dragonmead Willy's Oompa-Loompa
Dragonmead Woody's Perfect Porter

States Available: MI

272

Fletcher Street Brewing Company

124 West Fletcher Street
Alpena, MI 40707
800-848-3221
www.fletcherstreetbrewing.com

BRANDS:
Alpena Wheat Ale
Lumber Lager Red
Paper Maker Light
Paper Maker Pilsner
Pewabic Pale Ale
Sanctuary Stout
Thunder Bay Bock

States Available: MI

Founders Brewing Company

648 Monroe NW
Grand Rapids, MI 49503
616 776-1195
www.foundersbrewing.com

BRANDS:
Founders Brewing Bad Habit Belgium Quad
Founders Brewing Black Rye (64 IBU)
Founders Brewing Blushing Monk
Founders Brewing Breakfast Stout (25 IBU)
Founders Brewing Centennial IPA (46 IBU)
Founders Brewing Curmudgeon Old Ale (50 IBU)
Founders Brewing Devil Dancer Triple IPA (24 IBU)
Founders Brewing Dirty Bastard (50 IBU)
Founders Brewing Imperial Stout (25 IBU)
Founders Brewing Kentucky Breakfast (25 IBU)
Founders Brewing Pale Ale (32 IBU)
Founders Brewing Porter (40 IBU)
Founders Brewing Red's Rye (68 IBU)
Founders Brewing Rubaeus (24 IBU)

States Available: Contact Brewery

Frankenmuth Brewery

425 South Main Street
Frankenmuth, MI 48734
989-652-6183
www.frankenmuthbrewery.com

BRANDS:
Frankenmuth German Style Pilsner
Frankenmuth Hefeweizen
Frankenmuth Irish Dry Stout
Frankenmuth Mel-O-Dry Light Lager
Frankenmuth Mitternacht Munchner Dark Lager
Frankenmuth Oktoberfest
Frankenmuth Old Detroit Amber Ale
Frankenmuth Original Geyer's American Cream Ale
Frankenmuth Pioneer Pale Ale
Frankenmuth Winter Bock

States Available: Contact Brewery

Helmar Brewing Company

87 Oakdale Boulevard
Pleasant Ridge, MI 48069
248-882-0834
www.helmarbrewing.com

BRANDS:
Helmar Big League Brew

States Available: Contact Brewery

GEOGRAPHIC BREWER INDEX (Alphabetical)

Jolly Pumpkin Artisan Ales

3115 Broad Street
Dexter, MI 48130
734-426-4962
www.jollypumpkin.com

BRANDS:
Jolly Pumpkin Bam Biere
Jolly Pumpkin Biere de Mars
Jolly Pumpkin Calabaza Blanca
Jolly Pumpkin Fuego del Otono "Autumn Fire"
Jolly Pumpkin La Roja
Jolly Pumpkin Luciernaga "The Firefly"
Jolly Pumpkin Madrugada Obscura "Dark Dawn"
Jolly Pumpkin Maracaibo Especial
Jolly Pumpkin Oro de Calabaza

States Available: AK, CA, FL, GA, IL, IN, ME, MI, NY, OH, WI

Keweenaw Brewing Company

408 Shelden Avenue
Houghton, MI 49931
906-482-5596
www.keweenawbrewing.com

BRANDS:
Keweenaw Brewing Coal Porter
Keweenaw Brewing Empress Hefeweizen
Keweenaw Brewing Hilde's Brown Ale
Keweenaw Brewing Magnum Pale Ale
Keweenaw Brewing Pickaxe Blonde Ale
Keweenaw Brewing R.A.M. Stout
Keweenaw Brewing Red Jacket Amber Ale

States Available: MI

King Brewing Company

985 Oakland Avenue
Pontiac, MI 48340
248-745-5900
www.kingbrewing.com

BRANDS:
King Annihilater Doppel Bock
King Big Red
King Cherry Ale
King Continental Lager
King Crown Brown Ale
King Festbier
King Hefeweizen
King IPA
King Irish Red Ale
King King's Gold
King Loranger Lager
King Mocha Java Stout
King Pale Ale
King Pontiac Porter
King Red Ox Amber Ale
King Royal Amber
King Two Fisted Old Ale

States Available: Contact Brewery

GEOGRAPHIC BREWER INDEX (Alphabetical)

Michigan Brewing Company, Inc.
1093 Highview Drive
Webberville, MI 48892
517-521-3600
www.michiganbrewing.com

BRANDS:
Michigan Brewing Celis Grand Cru
Michigan Brewing Celis Pale Bock
Michigan Brewing Celis Raspberry
Michigan Brewing Celis White
Michigan Brewing Golden Ale
Michigan Brewing High Seas IPA
Michigan Brewing Mackinac Pale Ale
Michigan Brewing Nut Brown Ale
Michigan Brewing Peninsula Porter
Michigan Brewing Petoskey Pilsner
Michigan Brewing Sunset Amber Lager
Michigan Brewing Superior Stout
Michigan Brewing Wheatland Wheat Beer

States Available: IL, MA, MI, NY, OH, OR, PA, TX, VA

New Holland Brewing Company
66 East 8th Street
Holland, MI 49423
616-355-6422
www.newhollandbrew.com

BRANDS:
New Holland Black Tulip
New Holland Blue Goat Doppelbock
New Holland Dragon's Milk
New Holland Ichabod
New Holland Mad Hatter
New Holland Pilgrim's Dole
New Holland Red Tulip
New Holland Sundog
New Holland The Poet
New Holland Zoomer Wheat Ale

States Available: IL, IN, MI, OH, PA

Short's Brewing Company
121 North Bridge Street
Bellaire, MI 49615
231-533-6622
www.shortsbrewing.com

BRANDS:
Short's Brew Mystery Stout
Shorts Brew The Curl (50 IBU)

States Available: MI

Traverse Brewing Company
11550 US 31 South
Williamsburg, MI 49690
231-264-9343

BRANDS:
Traverse Brewing Batch 500 IPA
Traverse Brewing Manitou Amber Ale
Traverse Brewing Old Mission Lighthouse Ale
Traverse Brewing Power Island Porter
Traverse Brewing Sleeping Bear Brown Ale
Traverse Brewing Stout
Traverse Brewing Torch Lake Light Ale
Traverse Brewing Voss Wend Wheat

States Available: MI

GEOGRAPHIC BREWER INDEX (Alphabetical)

The following brewers distribute their brands in Michigan:

Abita Brewing Company
Anchor Brewing Company
Anderson Valley Brewing
Angry Minnow Brewing
Anheuser-Busch, Inc.
Arcadia Brewing Company
Atwater Block Brewery
August Schell Brewing Company
Avery Brewing Company
Bear Republic Brewing Company
Bell's Brewery, Inc.
Breckenridge Brewery
Brewery Ommegang
BridgePort Brewing Company
Brooklyn Brewery
D L Geary Brewing Company
Dark Horse Brewing Company
Dragonmead Microbrewery
Flying Dog Brewery, LLC
Frederick Brewing Company
Great Divide Brewing Company
Great Lakes Brewing Company
Harpoon Brewery
High Falls Brewing
Jacob Leinenkugel Brewing Company
Jolly Pumpkin Artisan Ales
Keweenaw Brewing Company
Lakefront Brewery Inc.
MacTarnahan's Brewing Company
Michigan Brewing Company, Inc.
Molson Coors Brewing Company
New Century Brewing Company

New Holland Brewing Company
O'Fallon Brewery
Pabst Brewing Company
Pete's Brewing
Pittsburgh Brewing Company
Pony Express Brewing Company
Pyramid Brewery
Redhook Ale Brewery
Rogue Ales
SAB Miller Corp
Sand Creek Brewing Company, LLC
Shipyard Brewing Company
Shmaltz Brewing Company
Short's Brewing Company
Sierra Nevada Brewing Company
South Shore Brewery
Southern Tier Brewing Company
Spanish Peaks Brewing Company/
   United States Beverage
Speakeasy Ales & Lagers, Inc.
Sprecher Brewing
Stoudt's Brewing Company
Summit Brewing Company
The Academy of Fine Beers, LLC
The Boston Beer Company
The Sea Dog Brewing Company
Traverse Brewing Company
Tremont Brewery/Atlantic Coast Brewing
   Company
Two Brothers Brewing Company
Widmer Brothers Brewing Company

August Schell Brewing Company — MN

1860 Schell Road
New Ulm, MN 56073-0128
507-354-5528
www.schellsbrewery.com

BRANDS:
August Schell Brewing Caramel Bock (30.8 SRM, 17 IBU)
August Schell Brewing Dark (23 SRM, 8 IBU)
August Schell Brewing FireBrick (15.2 SRM, 23 IBU)
August Schell Brewing Hefeweizen (3.4 SRM, 12 IBU)
August Schell Brewing Light (2.2 SRM, 8 IBU)
August Schell Brewing Maifest (8.3 SRM, 25 IBU)
August Schell Brewing Octoberfest (14 SRM, 20 IBU)
August Schell Brewing Original (2.8 SRM, 12.5 IBU)
August Schell Brewing Pale Ale (14 SRM, 35 IBU)
August Schell Brewing Pilsner (3.1 SRM, 27 IBU)
August Schell Brewing Schmaltz's Alt (49 SRM, 21 IBU)
August Schell Brewing Snowstorm
August Schell Brewing Zommerfest (4 SRM, 25 IBU)

States Available: IA, MI, MN, ND, PA, SD, WI

Gluek Brewing Company – *page 504*

219 N Red River Avenue, P.O. Box 476
Cold Spring, MN 56320-0476
320-685-8686
www.gluek.com

BRANDS:
Gluek Brewing Honey Bock
Gluek Brewing Red Bock
Gluek Golden Light
Gluek Ice
Gluek Northern Golden Lager
Gluek Northern Reserve Ice Lager
Gluek Northern Reserve Low Carb Light
Gluek Stite Amber Red Reserve
Gluek Stite Black and Tan
Gluek Stite Golden Lager
Gluek Stite Golden Pilsner – *page 504*
Gluek Stite Light Lager

States Available: MN, WI

GEOGRAPHIC BREWER INDEX (Alphabetical)

Lake Superior Brewing Company

2711 West Superior Street
Duluth, MN 55806
218-723-4000
www.lakesuperiorbrewing.com

BRANDS:
Lake Superior Brewing 7 Bridges Brown
Lake Superior Brewing Kayak Kölsch
Lake Superior Brewing Mesabi Red
Lake Superior Brewing Oktoberfest
Lake Superior Brewing Old Man Winter Warmer
Lake Superior Brewing Sir Duluth Oatmeal Stout
Lake Superior Brewing Special Ale
Lake Superior Brewing Split Rock Bock
Lake Superior Brewing St. Louis Bay IPA
Lake Superior Brewing Windward Wheat

States Available: MN, WI

Mantorville Brewing Company, LLC

501 North Main Street
Mantorville, MN 55955
651-387-0708
www.mantorvillebeer.com

BRANDS:
Mantorville Brewing Stagecoach Amber Ale
Mantorville Brewing Stagecoach Double Barrel Porter
Mantorville Brewing Stagecoach Smoked Porter

States Available: Contact Brewery

Pig's Eye Brewing Company

10107 Bridgewater Parkway
St. Paul, MN 55129
651-734-1661
www.pigseyebeer.com

BRANDS:
Pig's Eye Lean
Pig's Eye Pilsner
Pig's Eye Pitt Bull

States Available: AZ, CO, IA, IN, MN, ND, OK, PA, SD, WI

St. Croix Beer Company

P.O. Box 16545
St. Paul, MN 55116
651-387-0708
www.stcroixbeer.com

BRANDS:
St. Croix Cream
St. Croix Maple Ale
St. Croix Serrano Pepper Ale

States Available: MN, WI

Summit Brewing Company – *page 555*

910 Montreal Circle
St. Paul, MN 55102
651-265-7800
www.summitbrewing.com

BRANDS:
Summit ESB (26 SRM, 50 IBU) – *page 557*
Summit Extra Pale Ale (13 SRM, 42 IBU) – *page 555*
Summit Grand Pilsner (5 SRM, 25 IBU) – *page 558*
Summit Great Northern Porter (63 SRM, 50 IBU) – *page 556*
Summit Hefe Weizen (5 SRM, 18 IBU)
Summit India Pale Ale (25 SRM, 60 IBU) – *page 556*
Summit Maibock (10 SRM, 30 IBU)
Summit Oktoberfest (14 SRM, 25 IBU)
Summit Scandia Ale (5.5 SRM, 17 IBU) – *page 558*
Summit Winter Ale (45 SRM, 35 IBU) – *page 557*

States Available: CO, IA, IL, IN, KY, MI, MN, MT, ND, NE, OH, PA, SD, WI

Surly Brewing Company

4811 Dusharme Drive
Brooklyn Center, MN 55429
763-535-3330
www.surlybrewing.com

BRANDS:
Surly Brewing Bender
Surly Brewing Furious

States Available: MN

GEOGRAPHIC BREWER INDEX (Alphabetical)

The following brewers distribute their brands in Minnesota:

Anchor Brewing Company
Angry Minnow Brewing
Anheuser-Busch, Inc.
Arcadia Brewing Company
August Schell Brewing Company
Avery Brewing Company
Bard's Tale Beer Company
Bell's Brewery, Inc.
Big Sky Brewing Company
Blucreek Brewing
Boulder Beer Company
Boulevard Brewing Company
Breckenridge Brewery
BridgePort Brewing Company
Capital Brewery Company, Inc.
City Brewery
Deschutes Brewery
Flying Dog Brewery, LLC
Four Plus Brewing Company
Full Sail Brewing Company
Gluek Brewing Company
Great Divide Brewing Company
High Falls Brewing
Jacob Leinenkugel Brewing Company
James Page Brewing Company, LLC
Lake Superior Brewing Company
Lakefront Brewery Inc.
Left Handed Brewing Company
MacTarnahan's Brewing Company
Molson Coors Brewing Company
North Coast Brewing Company
O'Fallon Brewery

Pabst Brewing Company
Pete's Brewing
Pig's Eye Brewing Company
Pittsburgh Brewing Company
Pyramid Brewery
Redhook Ale Brewery
Rogue Ales
Rush River Brewing (Contact Brewery)
SAB Miller Corp
Shipyard Brewing Company
Sierra Nevada Brewing Company
South Shore Brewery
Spanish Peaks Brewing Company/
    United States Beverage
Sprecher Brewing
St. Croix Beer Company
Stevens Point Brewery
Summit Brewing Company
The Black Mountain/Chili Beer Company
The Boston Beer Company
The Fort Collins Brewery
The Sea Dog Brewing Company
The Spoetzl Brewing
Tommyknocker Brewery
Tremont Brewery/Atlantic Coast Brewing
    Company
Uinta Brewing Company
Victory Brewing Company
Viking Brewing
Widmer Brothers Brewing Company
Yellowstone Valley Brewing

Anheuser-Busch, Inc. – *page 455*

MO

One Busch Place
St. Louis, MO 63118
314-577-2000
www.anheuser-busch.com

<u>BRANDS:</u>
Anheuser World Lager
Beach Bum Blonde Ale – *page 459*
Brew Masters' Private Reserve – *page 461*
Bud Dry
Bud Extra
Bud Ice
Bud Ice Light
Bud Light
Budweiser
Budweiser NA
Budweiser Select
Busch
Busch Ice
Busch Light
Busch NA
Chelada Bud
Chelada Bud Light
Hurricane High Gravity (HG)
Hurricane Ice
Hurricane Malt Liquor
Jack's Pumpkin Spice Ale – *page 457*
King Cobra
Land Shark Lager
Michelob – *page 459*
Michelob AmberBock – *page 460*
Michelob Bavarian-Style Wheat
Michelob Celebrate Chocolate – *page 461*
Michelob Celebrate Vanilla
Michelob Golden Draft
Michelob Golden Draft Light
Michelob Honey Lager – *page 460*
Michelob Light
Michelob Marzen
Michelob Pale Ale
Michelob Porter
Michelob Ultra

GEOGRAPHIC BREWER INDEX (Alphabetical)

Michelob ULTRA Amber
Michelob ULTRA Lime
Michelob ULTRA Orange
Michelob ULTRA Pomegranate
Natty Up
Natural Ice
Natural Light
O'Doul's
O'Doul's Amber
Redbridge Lager – *page 456*
Rock Green Light
Rolling Rock Extra Pale
Spring Heat Spiced Wheat – *page 458*
Stone Mill Pale Ale – *page 456*
Tequiza
Wild Blue
Wild Hop Lager – *page 457*
Wild Hop Organic Lager
Winter's Bourbon Cask Ale – *page 458*
ZeigenBock

States Available: All 50 States

Bard's Tale Beer Company – *page 466*

211 NW Ward Road
Lee's Summit, MO 64063
203-831-8899
www.bardsbeer.com

BRANDS:
Bard's Tale Dragon's Gold Sorghum Lager (4 SRM, 35 IBU) – *page 466*

States Available: CA, CO, CT, DE, IA, IL, IN, KS, KY, MA, MN, MO, NC, NE, NH, NJ, NV, NY, OH, OR, PA, RI, SC, TX, UT, VA, VT

Boulevard Brewing Company – *page 478*

2501 Southwest Boulevard
Kansas City, MO 64108
816-474-7095
www.boulevard.com

BRANDS:
Boulevard Brewing Bob's '47 (27 IBU)
Boulevard Brewing Bully! Porter (47 IBU)
Boulevard Brewing Dry Stout (28 IBU)
Boulevard Brewing Irish Ale (28 IBU)
Boulevard Brewing Lunar Ale – *page 478*
Boulevard Brewing Nutcracker Ale (31 IBU)
Boulevard Brewing Pale Ale (31 IBU) – *page 479*
Boulevard Brewing Unfiltered Wheat Beer (13 IBU) – *page 479*
Boulevard Brewing ZÔN (12 IBU)

States Available: AR, IA, IL, KS, MN, MO, ND, NE, OK, SD, WY

Charleville Brewing Company

1693 Boyd Road
Ste. Geneviev, MO 63670
573-756-4537
www.charlevillevineyard.com

BRANDS:
Charleville Brewing Amber Ale
Charleville Brewing Belgium Wheat
Charleville Brewing Lager

States Available: MO

GEOGRAPHIC BREWER INDEX (Alphabetical)

O'Fallon Brewery

26 West Industrial Drive
O' Fallon, MO 63366
636-474-2337
www.ofallonbrewery.com

BRANDS:
O'Fallon 5-Day IPA (in MO only)
O'Fallon Blackberry Scottish Ale
O'Fallon Cherry Chocolate Beer
O'Fallon Gold (in MO only)
O'Fallon Light
O'Fallon Pumpkin Ale
O'Fallon Smoked Porter
O'Fallon Summer Brew (in MO only)
O'Fallon Wheach
O'Fallon Wheat

States Available: CO, IA, IL, IN, KS, KY, MI, MN, MO, WI

Schlafly Beer

2100 Locust Street
St. Louis, MO 63103
314-241-2337
www.schlafly.com

BRANDS:
Schlafly American Pale Ale (50 IBU)
Schlafly Christmas Ale
Schlafly Coffee Stout (40 IBU)
Schlafly Hefeweizen
Schlafly IPA
Schlafly Irish Extra Stout (45 IU)
Schlafly No. 15 (15 IBU)
Schlafly Oatmeal Stout (40 IBU)
Schlafly Oktoberfest (25 IBU)
Schlafly Pale Ale (27 IBU)
Schlafly Pilsner (35 IBU) (Pilsner)
Schlafly Pumpkin Ale (16 IBU)
Schlafly Raspberry Hefeweizen
Schlafly Saison (22 IBU)
Schlafly Scotch Ale (25 IBU)
Schlafly Summer Kölsch (25 IBU)
Schlafly Winter ESB (45 IBU) (ESB

States Available: IL, IN, KY, MI, MO

Springfield Brewing Company

305 South Market
Springfield, MO 65806
417-832-8277
www.springfieldbrewingco.com

BRANDS:
Springfield Brewing Munich Lager (23 IBU)
Springfield Brewing Pale Ale (25 IBU)
Springfield Brewing Porter (30 IBU)
Springfield Brewing Unfiltered Wheat (15 IBU)

States Available: MO

GEOGRAPHIC BREWER INDEX (Alphabetical)

Trailhead Brewing Company

921 South Riverside Drive
St. Charles, MO 63302
636-946-2739
www.trailheadbrewing.com

BRANDS:
Missouri Brown Dark Ale
Old Courthouse Stout
Riverboat Raspberry Fruit Beer
Trailblazer Blonde Ale
Trailhead Red Amber Ale
Trailhead Spiced Pumpkin Ale

States Available: MO

The following brewers distribute their brands in Missouri:

Abita Brewing Company	Pete's Brewing
Anchor Brewing Company	Pittsburgh Brewing Company
Anderson Valley Brewing	Pyramid Brewery
Anheuser-Busch, Inc.	Redhook Ale Brewery
Arcadia Brewing Company	Rogue Ales
Bard's Tale Beer Company	SAB Miller Corp
Bell's Brewery, Inc.	Shipyard Brewing Company
Boulevard Brewing Company	Shmaltz Brewing Company
Breckenridge Brewery	Sierra Nevada Brewing Company
Brewery Ommegang	Spanish Peaks Brewing Company/
BridgePort Brewing Company	United States Beverage
Diamond Bear Brewing Company	Sprecher Brewing
High Falls Brewing	Springfield Brewing Company
Jacob Leinenkugel Brewing Company	Stevens Point Brewery
MacTarnahan's Brewing Company	The Black Mountain/Chili Beer Company
Molson Coors Brewing Company	The Boston Beer Company
New Belgium Brewing Company	The Sea Dog Brewing Company
North Coast Brewing Company	The Spoetzl Brewing
Odell Brewing Company	Trailhead Brewing Company
O'Fallon Brewery	Tremont Brewery/Atlantic Coast Brewing
Otter Creek Brewing Company	Company
Pabst Brewing Company	Widmer Brothers Brewing Company

MT

Bayern Brewing

1507 Montana Street
Missoula, MT 59801
406-721-1482
www.bayernbrewery.com

BRANDS:
Bayern Brewing Amber
Bayern Brewing Doppelbock
Bayern Brewing Flathead Lake Monster Lager
Bayern Brewing Hefeweizen
Bayern Brewing Killarney
Bayern Brewing Maibock
Bayern Brewing Oktoberfest
Bayern Brewing Pilsner
Bayern Brewing Schwarzbier
Bayern Brewing Trout Slayer

States Available: ID, MT, OR

Big Sky Brewing Company – *page 468*

5417 Trumpeter Way
Missoula, MT 59808-7170
406-549-2777
www.bigskybrew.com

BRANDS:
Big Sky Brewing Crystal Ale – *page 468*
Big Sky Brewing IPA
Big Sky Brewing Moose Drool Brown Ale
Big Sky Brewing Powder Hound Winter Ale
Big Sky Brewing Scape Goat Pale Ale
Big Sky Brewing Summer Honey Seasonal Ale

States Available: AK, CA, CO, ID, MN, MT, ND, NV, OR, SD, WA, WI, WY

GEOGRAPHIC BREWER INDEX (Alphabetical)

Bitter Root Brewing
101 Marcus Street
Hamilton, MT 59840
406-363-7468
www.bitterrootbrewing.com

BRANDS:
Bitter Root Brewing Amber
Bitter Root Brewing India Pale Ale (7.5 SRM, 50 IBU)
Bitter Root Brewing Nut Brown (20 SRM, 25 IBU)
Bitter Root Brewing Pale Ale (10 SRM, 35 IBU)
Bitter Root Brewing Porter (30 SRM, 35 IBU)
Bitter Root Brewing Sawtooth Ale (5 SRM, 20 IBU)
Bitter Root Brewing Winter Ale

States Available: ID, MT

Glacier Brewing – *page 503*
6 Tenth Avenue East
Polson, MT 59860
406-883-2595
www.glacierbrewing.com

BRANDS:
Glacier Brewing Flathead Cherry Ale (3.8 SRM, 12 IBU)
Glacier Brewing Golden Grizzly Ale (5.8 SRM, 14.6 IBU)
Glacier Brewing Northfork Amber Ale (14 SRM, IBU 22.3)
Glacier Brewing Port Polson Pilsner (3.5 SRM, 13.1 IBU)
Glacier Brewing Select Dunkel Hefeweizen (13.4 SRM, 14.3 IBU)
Glacier Brewing Select Oktoberfest (16.2 SRM, 4.4 IBU) – *page 503*
Glacier Brewing Slurry Bomber Stout (44 SRM, 36.6 IBU)
Glacier Brewing St. Arnold's Autumn Ale (19.4 SRM, 47.3 IBU)

States Available: MT (Western)

Great Northern Brewing Company
2 Central Avenue
Whitefish, MT 59937
406-863-1000
www.greatnorthernbrewing.com

BRANDS:
Great Northern Brewing Bear Naked Amber (43 IBU)
Great Northern Brewing Big Fog Amber Lager (43 IBU)
Great Northern Brewing Buckin' Horse Pilsner (32 IBU)
Great Northern Brewing Fred's Black Lager (23 IBU)
Great Northern Brewing Fred's Black Lager (23 IBU)
Great Northern Brewing Going To The Sun Pale Ale (33 IBU)
Great Northern Brewing Going To The Sun Pale Ale (33 IBU)
Great Northern Brewing Hellroaring Amber Lager (18 IBU)
Great Northern Brewing Hellroaring Amber Lager (19 IBU)
Great Northern Brewing Snow Ghost (16 IBU)
Great Northern Brewing Snow Ghost Winter Lager (15 IBU)
Great Northern Brewing Wheatfish Hefeweizen (12 IBU)
Great Northern Brewing Wheatfish Hefeweizen (12 IBU)
Great Northern Brewing Wild Huckleberry Wheat Lager (12 IBU)
Great Northern Brewing Wild Huckleberry Wheat Lager (12 IBU)

States Available: ID, MT, WA

Kettle House Brewing Company
602 Myrtle Street
Missoula, MT 59801
406-728-1660
www.kettlehouse.com

BRANDS:
Double Haul IPA

States Available: MT

GEOGRAPHIC BREWER INDEX (Alphabetical)

Lang Creek Brewery – *page 511*
655 Lang Creek Road
Marion, MT 59925
406-858-2200
www.langcreekbrewery.com

BRANDS:
Lang Creek Huckleberry N' Honey (8 IBU)
Lang Creek Taildragger Honey Wheat (8 IBU)
Lang Creek Tri-Motor Amber (26 IBU) – *page 511*
Lang Creek Windsock Pale Ale (27 IBU)

States Available: ID, MT, OR, WA

Lewis & Clark Brewing
939 Getchell Street
Helena, MT 59601
406-442-5960
www.lewisandclarkbrewing.com

BRANDS:
Lewis & Clark Back Country Scottish Ale
Lewis & Clark Lager
Lewis & Clark Miner's Gold Hefe-Weizen
Lewis & Clark Tumbleweed IPA
Yellowstone Beer

States Available: MT

Madison River Brewing Company
20900 Frontage Road, Building B
Belgrade, MT 59714
406-388-0322
www.madisonriverbrewing.com

BRANDS:
Copper John Scotch Ale
Irresistible E.S.B.
Salmon Fly Honey Rye
Hopper Pale Ale

States Available: Contact Brewery

Red Lodge Ales Brewing Company
417 North Broadway
Red Lodge, MT 59068
406-446-4607

BRANDS:
Red Lodge Ales Glacier Ale
Red Lodge Ales Hefeweizen

States Available: MT

Yellowstone Valley Brewing
2132-B First Avenue N
Billings, MT 59101
406-245-0918
www.yellowstonevalleybrew.com

BRANDS:
Yellowstone Valley Black Widow Oatmeal Stout
Yellowstone Valley Grizzly Wulff Wheat
Yellowstone Valley Renegade Red ESB
Yellowstone Valley Wild Fly Ale

States Available: CO, MN, MT, ND, OK, SD, WI, WY

GEOGRAPHIC BREWER INDEX (Alphabetical)

The following brewers distribute their brands in Montana:

Alaskan Brewing Company	Pabst Brewing Company
Anchor Brewing Company	Pete's Brewing
Anheuser-Busch, Inc.	Pyramid Brewery
Bayern Brewing	Red Lodge Ales Brewing Company
Big Sky Brewing Company	Redhook Ale Brewery
Bitter Root Brewing	Rogue Ales
BridgePort Brewing Company	SAB Miller Corp
Deschutes Brewery	Shipyard Brewing Company
Eel River Brewing Company	Sierra Nevada Brewing Company
Full Sail Brewing Company	Snake River Brewing Company
Glacier Brewing	Spanish Peaks Brewing Company/
Grand Teton Brewing Company	United States Beverage
Great Northern Brewing Company	Summit Brewing Company
Great Northern Brewing Company	The Boston Beer Company
Kona Brewing, LLC	The Sea Dog Brewing Company
Lang Creek Brewery	The Spoetzl Brewing
MacTarnahan's Brewing Company	Tremont Brewery/Atlantic Coast Brewing
Molson Coors Brewing Company	Company
New Belgium Brewing Company	Widmer Brothers Brewing Company
North Coast Brewing Company	Yellowstone Valley Brewing

Carolina Beer & Beverage Company – *page 484* NC

110 Barley Park Lane
Mooresville, NC 28115-1183
888-601-2739
www.carolinablonde.com

BRANDS:
Carolina Beer Carolina Blonde – *page 484*
Carolina Beer Carolina Light
Carolina Beer Cottonwood Almond Stout
Carolina Beer Cottonwood American Wheat
Carolina Beer Cottonwood Endo IPA
Carolina Beer Cottonwood Frostbite Ale
Carolina Beer Cottonwood Irish Style Red Ale
Carolina Beer Cottonwood Lift your Kilt Scottish Ale
Carolina Beer Cottonwood Low Down Brown
Carolina Beer Cottonwood Pumpkin Spiced Ale

States Available: GA, NC, SC, TN, VA

Carolina Brewing

140 Thomas Mill Road
Mooresville, NC 28115-1183
Holly Springs, NC 27540-9372
919-557-2337
www.carolinabrew.com

BRANDS:
Carolina Brewing IPA
Carolina Brewing Nut Brown Ale
Carolina Brewing Oktoberfest Lager
Carolina Brewing Pale Ale
Carolina Brewing Spring Bock
Carolina Brewing Summer Ale
Carolina Brewing Winter Stout

States Available: NC

Catawba Valley Brewing

212 S. Gree Street
Morganton, NC 28655
828-584-9400
www.cvbc.homestead.com/about.html

BRANDS:
Catawba Valley Brewing Buffalo Nickel Ale
Catawba Valley Brown Bear Ale
Catawba Valley Firewater IPA
Catawba Valley Honust Injun Stout
Catawba Valley Indian Head Red
Catawba Valley King Coconut Porter
Catawba Valley King Don's Original Pumpkin Ale
Catawba Valley King Karma Ale

States Available: NC, SC, TN

GEOGRAPHIC BREWER INDEX (Alphabetical)

Duck-Rabbit Craft Brewery

4519 West Pine Street
Farmville, NC 27828
252-753-7745
www.duckrabbitbrewery.com

BRANDS:
Duck-Rabbit Amber Ale
Duck-Rabbit Baltic Porter (in NC only)
Duck-Rabbit Barleywine Ale (in NC only)
Duck-Rabbit Brown Ale
Duck-Rabbit Milk Stout
Duck-Rabbit Porter
Duck-Rabbit Russian Imperial Stout (in NC only)
Duck-Rabbit Wee Heavy Scotch Style Ale (in NC Only)

States Available: NC, SC, TN

Edenton Brewing Company

1249-A Wicker Drive
Raleigh, NC 27604
919-834-0045
www.edentonbrewing.com

BRANDS:
Edenton Brewing Helles Angel
Edenton Brewing Horniblow's Tavern
Edenton Brewing Joseph Hewes
Edenton Brewing King David's Red
Edenton Brewing Uncle Nut's

States Available: NC, PA, VA

Heinzelmannchen Brewery (Kegs/Growlers)

545 Mill Street, P.O. Box 2075
Sylva, NC 28779
828-631-4466
www.yourgnometownbrewery.com

BRANDS:
Heinzelmannchen Ancient Days Honey Blonde Ale
Heinzelmannchen Black Forest Stout
Heinzelmannchen Gopher Ale
Heinzelmannchen Kilted Gnome Scottish Ale
Heinzelmannchen Middleworld Brown Ale
Heinzelmannchen Oktoberfest
Heinzelmannchen Weise Gnome Hefeweizen Style Ale

States Available: NC

Highland Brewing

42 Biltmore Avenue, P.O. Box 2351
Asheville, NC 28802
828-255-8240
www.highlandbrewing.com

BRANDS:
Highland Brewing Black Mocha Stout (25 IBU)
Highland Brewing Cold Mountain Winter Ale
Highland Brewing Gaelic Ale (32 IBU)
Highland Brewing Kashmir IPA (60 IBU)
Highland Brewing Oatmeal Porter (32 IBU)
Highland Brewing St. Terese's Pale Ale (24 IBU)
Highland Brewing Tasgall Ale (27 IBU)

States Available: GA, NC, SC, TN

GEOGRAPHIC BREWER INDEX (Alphabetical)

Pisgah Brewing Company

150 Eastside Business Park
Black Mountain, NC 28711
828-582-2175
www.pisgahbrewing.com

BRANDS:
Pisgah Equinox (47.5 IBU)
Pisgah Pale Ale (31.8 IBU)
Pisgah Porter
Pisgah Solstice
Pisgah Stout
Vortex I (133 IBU)

States Available: NC

The Weeping Radish Brewery – *page 570*

Highway 64, P.O. Box 471
Manteo, NC 27954
252-491-5205
www.weepingradish.com

BRANDS:
Weeping Radish Altier (12.2 SRM, 47.2 IBU)
Weeping Radish Black Radish (22.6 SRM, 27 IBU) – *page 570*
Weeping Radish Christmas Bier (21.2 SRM, 33.7 IBU)
Weeping Radish Corolla Gold (4.6 SRM, 15.2 IBU)
Weeping Radish Corolla Light (2.7 SRM, 11.8 IBU)
Weeping Radish Fest (11.2 SRM, 24 IBU)
Weeping Radish Kölsch (5 SRM, 23.8 IBU)
Weeping Radish Maibock (9.4 SRM, 31.5 IBU)
Weeping Radish Marzen (11.2 SRM, 28.4 IBU)
Weeping Radish Weizen (3.3 SRM, 15.2 IBU)

States Available: DC, MD, NC, PA, VA

The following brewers distribute their brands in North Carolina:

Abita Brewing Company	Molson Coors Brewing Company
Allagash Brewing Company	New River Brewing Company
Anchor Brewing Company	New South Brewing Company
Anderson Valley Brewing	North Coast Brewing Company
Anheuser-Busch, Inc.	Old Dominion Brewing Company
Avery Brewing Company	Oskar Blues Grill & Brew
Bard's Tale Beer Company	Otter Creek Brewing Company
Bear Republic Brewing Company	Pabst Brewing Company
Bison Brewing	Pete's Brewing
Brewery Ommegang	Pittsburgh Brewing Company
BridgePort Brewing Company	Pyramid Brewery
Brooklyn Brewery	R.J. Rockers Brewing Company
Carolina Beer & Beverage Company	Redhook Ale Brewery
Carolina Brewing	Rogue Ales
Catawba Valley Brewing	SAB Miller Corp
Charleston Brewing Company	Shipyard Brewing Company
Clipper City Brewing Company	Shmaltz Brewing Company
D.G. Yuengling & Son, Inc.	Sierra Nevada Brewing Company
D L Geary Brewing Company	Ska Brewing Company
Dogfish Head Craft Brewery	Smuttynose Brewing Company
Duck-Rabbit Craft Brewery	Spanish Peaks Brewing Company/
Edenton Brewing Company	United States Beverage
Florida Beer Company	St.George Brewing Company
Flying Dog Brewery, LLC	Sweetwater Brewing
Fordham Brewing Company	Terrapin Beer Company
Frederick Brewing Company	The Boston Beer Company
Great Divide Brewing Company	The Fort Collins Brewery
Harpoon Brewery	The Sea Dog Brewing Company
Heinzelmannchen Brewery (Kegs/	The Spoetzl Brewing
Growlers)	The Weeping Radish Brewery
High Falls Brewing	Thomas Creek Brewery
Highland Brewing	Tommyknocker Brewery
Lakefront Brewery Inc.	Tremont Brewery/Atlantic Coast Brewing
Left Handed Brewing Company	Company
Lost Coast Brewery & Café	Victory Brewing Company
Mad River Brewing	Widmer Brothers Brewing Company

GEOGRAPHIC BREWER INDEX (Alphabetical)

Empyrean Brewing – page 495

NE

729 Q Street
Lincoln, NE 68508
402-434-5959
www.empyreanbrewingco.com

BRANDS:
Empyrean Ales Burning Skye Scottish Ale (7 SRM, 13 IBU)
Empyrean Ales Chaco Canyon Honey Gold (5 SRM, 23 IBU)
Empyrean Ales Dark Side Vanilla Porter (75 SRM, 19 IBU)
Empyrean Ales Luna Sea ESB (10 SRM, 31 IBU) – *page 495*
Empyrean Ales Third Stone Brown (18 SRM, 13 IBU)

States Available: NE

Spilker Ales

300 W 4th Street
Cortland, NE 68331
402-798-7445
www.spilkerales.com

BRANDS:
Spilker Ales Hopluia Ale

States Available: NE

The following brewers distribute their brands in Nebraska:

Alltech's Lexington Brewing Company	Pyramid Brewery
Anchor Brewing Company	Redhook Ale Brewery
Anheuser-Busch, Inc.	Rogue Ales
Bard's Tale Beer Company	SAB Miller Corp
Big Sky Brewing Company	Shipyard Brewing Company
Boulder Beer Company	Sierra Nevada Brewing Company
Boulevard Brewing Company	Spanish Peaks Brewing Company/
Breckenridge Brewery	United States Beverage
Brewery Ommegang	Spilker Ales
Empyrean Brewing	Summit Brewing Company
Flying Dog Brewery, LLC	The Academy of Fine Beers, LLC
High Falls Brewing	The Black Mountain/Chili Beer Company
Jacob Leinenkugel Brewing Company	The Boston Beer Company
MacTarnahan's Brewing Company	The Sea Dog Brewing Company
Molson Coors Brewing Company	The Spoetzl Brewing
New Belgium Brewing Company	Tommyknocker Brewery
Odell Brewing Company	Tremont Brewery/Atlantic Coast Brewing
Pabst Brewing Company	Company
Pete's Brewing	Widmer Brothers Brewing Company
Pony Express Brewing Company	

Franconia Notch Brewing Company

NH

686 Main Street
Bethlehem, NH 03574
603-444-6258
www.4front.com/brewery

BRANDS:
Franconia Notch Brewing Grail Pale Ale
Franconia Notch Brewing River Driver Ale

States Available: MA, NH, RI

Pennichuck Brewing Company

127 Elm Street, Unit C
Milford, NH 03055
603-672-2750
www.pennichuckbrewing.com

BRANDS:
Pennichuck Brewing 2-6-0 Mogul
Pennichuck Brewing Engine Number 5
Pennichuck Brewing Pozharnik Espresso Russian Imperial Stout
Pennichuck Brewing The Big O

States Available: NH, RI. MA

GEOGRAPHIC BREWER INDEX (Alphabetical)

Smuttynose Brewing Company

225 Heritage Avenue
Portsmouth, NH 03801-5610
603-436-4026
www.smuttynose.com

BRANDS:
Smuttynose Brewing Baltic Porter
Smuttynose Brewing Barleywine Style Ale
Smuttynose Brewing Big A IPA
Smuttynose Brewing Farmhouse Ale
Smuttynose Brewing Imperial Stout
Smuttynose Brewing Imperial IPA
Smuttynose Brewing IPA (65 IBU)
Smuttynose Brewing Maibock
Smuttynose Brewing Octoberfest
Smuttynose Brewing Old Brown Dog Ale (15 IBU)
Smuttynose Brewing Portsmouth Lager (15 IBU)
Smuttynose Brewing Pumpkin Ale
Smuttynose Brewing Really Old Brown Dog Old Ale
Smuttynose Brewing Robust Porter (15 IBU)
Smuttynose Brewing S'muttonator Doppelbock
Smuttynose Brewing Scotch Style Ale
Smuttynose Brewing Shoals Pale Ale (30 IBU)
Smuttynose Brewing Summer Weizen
Smuttynose Brewing Weizenheimer
Smuttynose Brewing Wheat Wine Ale
Smuttynose Brewing Winter Ale

States Available: CT, DE, MA, MD, ME, NC, NH, NJ, NY, PA, RI, VA, VT, WI

Tuckerman Brewing

64 Hobbs Street
Conway, NH 03818-1058
603-447-5400
www.tuckermanbrewing.com

BRANDS:
Tuckerman Brewing Headwall Alt
Tuckerman Brewing Pale Ale

States Available: MA, NH

Woodstock Inn Brewery

135 Main Street, P.O. Box 118
North Woodstock, NH 03262
603-745-3951
www.woodstockinnnh.com

BRANDS:
Woodstock Inn Brewery Pig's Ear Brown Ale
Woodstock Inn Brewery Red Rack Ale

States Available: NH

The following brewers distribute their brands in New Hampshire:

Anchor Brewing Company	SAB Miller Corp
Anheuser-Busch, Inc.	Shipyard Brewing Company
Bard's Tale Beer Company	Sierra Nevada Brewing Company
Brewery Ommegang	Smuttynose Brewing Company
Casco Bay Brewing Company	Spanish Peaks Brewing Company/
D L Geary Brewing Company	United States Beverage
Flying Dog Brewery, LLC	Stone Coast Brewing Company
Franconia Notch Brewing Company	The Boston Beer Company
Gritty McDuff's Brewing Company	The Long Trail Brewing Company
Harpoon Brewery	The Matt Brewing
High Falls Brewing	The Sea Dog Brewing Company
Molson Coors Brewing Company	Tremont Brewery/Atlantic Coast Brewing
Nutfield Brewing Company	Company
Otter Creek Brewing Company	Trout River Brewing Company
Pabst Brewing Company	Tuckerman Brewing
Pete's Brewing	Widmer Brothers Brewing Company
Redhook Ale Brewery	Woodstock Inn Brewery
Rogue Ales	

GEOGRAPHIC BREWER INDEX (Alphabetical)

Climax Brewing Company – *page 485*

NJ

112 Valley Road
Roselle Park, NJ 07204-1402
908-620-9585
www.climaxbrewing.com

BRANDS:
Climax Brewing Cream Ale
Climax Brewing Extra Special Bitter Ale
Climax Brewing India Pale Ale
Climax Brewing Nut Brown Ale
Climax Hoffmann Bavarian Dark
Hoffmann Doppel Bock – *page 485*
Climax Hoffmann Helles
Climax Hoffmann Oktoberfest

States Available: NJ, NY, PA

Cricket Hill Brewing Company, Inc. – *page 488*

24 Kulick Road
Fairfield, NJ 07004
973-276-9415
www.crickethillbrewery.com

BRANDS:
Cricket Hill Brewing American Ale
Cricket Hill Brewing East Coast Lager – *page 488*
Cricket Hill Brewing Colonel Blides Altbier
Cricket Hill Brewing Hopnotic IPA

States Available: NJ, NY, PA

Flying Fish Brewing – *page 499*

1940 Olney Avenue
Cherry Hill, NJ 08003
856-489-0061
www.flyingfish.com

BRANDS:
Flying Fish Brewing Belgian Abbey Dubbel
  (21.2 SRM, 38.7 IBU) – *page 499*
Flying Fish Brewing ESB Ale (12.2 SRM, 25.3 IBU)
Flying Fish Brewing Extra Pale Ale (12.2 SRM, 14.4 IBU)
Flying Fish Brewing Farmhouse Summer Ale
Flying Fish Brewing Grand Cru Winter Reserve
Flying Fish Brewing Hopfish (21.2 SRM, 18.8 IBU)
Flying Fish Brewing Imperial Espresso Porter
Flying Fish Brewing Oktoberfish
Flying Fish Brewing Porter

States Available: DC, DE, MD, NJ, PA

High Point Wheat Beer Company

22 Park Place
Butler, NJ 07405
973-838-7400
www.ramsteinbeer.com

BRANDS:
Ramstein Blonde Wheat (8 SRM, 12.5 IBU)
Ramstein Classic Wheat Beer (60 SRM, 12.5 IBU)
Ramstein Golden Lager (6 SRM, 22 IBU)
Ramstein Maibock Lager Beer (37 IBU)
Ramstein Munich Amber Lager
Ramstein Winter Wheat ((70 SRM, 20 IBU)

States Available: NJ, NY, PA

GEOGRAPHIC BREWER INDEX (Alphabetical)

River Horse Brewing Company – *page 534*

80 Lambert Lane
Lambertville, NJ 08530
609-397-7776
www.riverhorse.com

BRANDS:
River Horse Belgian Frostbite Winter Ale
River Horse Hop Hazard Pale Ale
River Horse Lager
River Horse Special Ale
River Horse Summer Blonde – *page 534*
River Horse Tripel Horse

States Available: CT, DE, MA, MD, NJ, NY (NYC, Long Island), OH, PA

Wiedenmayer Brewing Company

P.O. Box 67
Bedminster, NJ 07921
908-470-4000
www.wiedenmayerbrewing.com

BRANDS:
Wiedenmayer Jersey Lager

States Available: Contact Brewery

The following brewers distribute their brands in New Jersey:

Abita Brewing Company
Allagash Brewing Company
Anchor Brewing Company
Anderson Valley Brewing
Anheuser-Busch, Inc.
Arcadia Brewing Company
Avery Brewing Company
Bard's Tale Beer Company
Barley Creek Brewing Company
Blue Point Brewing
Boulder Beer Company
Brewery Ommegang
Brooklyn Brewery
Butternuts Beer & Ale
Caldera Brewing Company
Cisco Brewers Inc.
Climax Brewing Company
Coffaro Beer Company
Cooperstown Brewing Company
Cricket Hill Brewing Company
D.G. Yuengling & Son, Inc.
D L Geary Brewing Company
Dogfish Head Craft Brewery
Flying Dog Brewery, LLC
Flying Fish Brewing
Fordham Brewing Company
Great Divide Brewing Company
Gritty McDuff's Brewing Company
Harpoon Brewery
High Falls Brewing
High Point Wheat Beer Company
Kona Brewing, LLC
Lake Placid Craft Brewing
Lancaster Brewing Company
Left Handed Brewing Company
Legacy Brewing Company
Lost Coast Brewery & Café
MacTarnahan's Brewing Company
Magic Hat Brewing Company
Molson Coors Brewing Company
New Century Brewing Company

North Coast Brewing Company
Oskar Blues Grill & Brew
Otter Creek Brewing Company
Pabst Brewing Company
Pete's Brewing
Pittsburgh Brewing Company
Ramapo Valley Brewery
ReaperAle, Inc.
Red Bell Brewery & Pub
Redhook Ale Brewery
River Horse Brewing Company
Rock Art Brewery, LLC
Rogue Ales
SAB Miller Corp
Shipyard Brewing Company
Shmaltz Brewing Company
Sierra Nevada Brewing Company
Smuttynose Brewing Company
South Hampton Publick House
Spanish Peaks Brewing Company/
    United States Beverage
Speakeasy Ales & Lagers, Inc.
Stone Brewing Company
Stoudt's Brewing Company
The Black Mountain/Chili Beer Company
The Boston Beer Company
The Dock Street Brewery Company
The Long Trail Brewing Company
The Matt Brewing
The Sea Dog Brewing Company
Three Floyds Brewing Company
Tommyknocker Brewery
Tremont Brewery/Atlantic Coast Brewing
    Company
Tröegs Brewing Company
Uinta Brewing Company
Victory Brewing Company
Weyerbacher Brewing Company
Widmer Brothers Brewing Company
Yards Brewing

GEOGRAPHIC BREWER INDEX (Alphabetical)

NM

Abbey Beverage Company
Our Lady of Guadalupe Abbey, P.O. Box 1080
Pecos, NM 87552
505-757-6415

BRANDS:
Monk's Ale

States Available: NM

Rio Grande Brewing Company
3760 Hawkins NE
Albuquerque, NM 87109
505-343-0903
www.riograndebrewing.com

BRANDS:
Rio Grande Brewing Bock Holiday (30 IBU)
Rio Grande Brewing Desert Pils (24 IBU)
Rio Grande Brewing Elfego Bock (26 IBU)
Rio Grande Brewing IPA (76 IBU)
Rio Grande Brewing Outlaw Lager (35 IBU)
Rio Grande Brewing Pancho Verde Chile Cerveza (12 IBU)
Rio Grande Brewing Stout (42 IBU)
Rio Grande Brewing Sunchaser Ale (32 IBU)

States Available: NM

Santa Fe Brewing Company
35 Fire Place
Santa Fe, NM 87508
505-424-3333
www.santafebrewing.com

BRANDS:
Santa Fe Brewing Santa Fe Chicken Killer Barley Wine (29 SRM, 86 IBU)
Santa Fe Brewing Santa Fe Nut Brown Ale (33 SRM, 18 IBU)
Santa Fe Brewing Santa Fe Pale Ale (13 SRM, 48 IBU)
Santa Fe Brewing Santa Fe State Pen Porter (77 SRM, 55 IBU)
Santa Fe Brewing Santa Fe Wheat (3.5 SRM, 23 IBU)

States Available: AZ, CA, CO, NM, NV, OK, TX, UT

Sierra Blanca Brewing Company
503 12th Street, P.O. Box 308
Carrizozo, NM 88301
505-648-6606
www.sierrablancabrewery.com

BRANDS:
Sierra Blanca Brewing Alien Amber Ale
Sierra Blanca Brewing Nut Brown
Sierra Blanca Brewing Pale Ale
Sierra Blanca Brewing Pilsner

States Available: NM

Tractor Brewing Company – *page 564*
120 Nelson Lane
Los Lunas, NM 87031-8299
505-866-0477
www.getplowed.com

BRANDS:
Tractor Brewing Double Plow Oatmeal Stout
Tractor Brewing Farmer's Tan - Red Ale – *page 564*
Tractor Brewing Haymaker - Honey Wheat Ale
Tractor Brewing Sod Buster Pale Ale

States Available: NM, NY

GEOGRAPHIC BREWER INDEX (Alphabetical)

The following brewers distribute their brands in New Mexico:

Abbey Beverage Company
Anchor Brewing Company
Anderson Valley Brewing
Anheuser-Busch, Inc.
Avery Brewing Company
Boulder Beer Company
Breckenridge Brewery
BridgePort Brewing Company
Deschutes Brewery
Flying Dog Brewery, LLC
Full Sail Brewing Company
Great Divide Brewing Company
High Falls Brewing
Kona Brewing, LLC
Lost Coast Brewery & Café
Left Handed Brewing Company
Molson Coors Brewing Company
New Belgium Brewing Company
North Coast Brewing Company
Odell Brewing Company
Oskar Blues Grill & Brew
Pabst Brewing Company
Pete's Brewing
Pittsburgh Brewing Company
Pyramid Brewery
Redhook Ale Brewery
Rogue Ales
SAB Miller Corp
Santa Fe Brewing Company
Shipyard Brewing Company
Sierra Blanca Brewing Company
Sierra Nevada Brewing Company
Ska Brewing Company
Spanish Peaks Brewing Company/
    United States Beverage
Stone Brewing Company
The Boston Beer Company
The Sea Dog Brewing Company
The Spoetzl Brewing
Tommyknocker Brewery
Tractor Brewing Company
Tremont Brewery/Atlantic Coast Brewing
    Company
Widmer Brothers Brewing Company

The following brewers distribute their brands in Nevada:

Abita Brewing Company
Alaskan Brewing Company
Anchor Brewing Company
Anheuser-Busch, Inc.
Bard's Tale Beer Company
Bayhawk Ales Inc.
Brewery Ommegang
Deschutes Brewery
Eel River Brewing Company
Firestone Walker Brewing Company
Flying Dog Brewery, LLC
Four Plus Brewing Company
Full Sail Brewing Company
Great Sex Brewing, Inc.
High Falls Brewing
Lagunitas Brewing
Lakefront Brewery Inc.
Lost Coast Brewery & Café
MacTarnahan's Brewing Company
Mad River Brewing
Molson Coors Brewing Company
Nectar Ales
New Belgium Brewing Company
North Coast Brewing Company
Pabst Brewing Company
Pete's Brewing
Pyramid Brewery
Redhook Ale Brewery
Rogue Ales
Ruby Mountain Brewing Company
SAB Miller Corp
Santa Fe Brewing Company
Shipyard Brewing Company
Sierra Nevada Brewing Company
Spanish Peaks Brewing Company/
    United States Beverage
Speakeasy Ales & Lagers, Inc.
Stone Brewing Company
The Academy of Fine Beers, LLC
The Boston Beer Company
The Sea Dog Brewing Company
The Spoetzl Brewing
Tremont Brewery/Atlantic Coast Brewing
    Company
Widmer Brothers Brewing Company

Ruby Mountain Brewing Company NV

HC-60 Route 100
Clover Valley, NV 89835-0100
775-752-2337
www.rubymountainbrewing.com

BRANDS:
Ruby Mountain Brewing Angel Creek Amber Ale
Ruby Mountain Brewing Bristlecone Brown Porter
Ruby Mountain Brewing Vienna Style Lager
Ruby Mountain Brewing Wild West Hefeweizen

States Available: ID, NV

Blue Point Brewing – page 471 NY

161 River Avenue
Patchogue, NY 11772
631-475-6944
www.bluepointbrewing.com

BRANDS:
Blue Point Brewing Blueberry Ale (14 IBU)
Blue Point Brewing Cherry Imperial Stout (67 IBU)
Blue Point Brewing ESB (35 IBU)
Blue Point Brewing Golden Ale (16 IBU)
Blue Point Brewing Hefeweizen (15 IBU)
Blue Point Brewing Hoptical Illusion (60 IBU)
Blue Point Brewing Oatmeal Stout (30 IBU)
Blue Point Brewing Octoberfest (28 IBU)
Blue Point Brewing Old Howling Bastard (78 IBU)
Blue Point Brewing Pale Ale (36 IBU)
Blue Point Brewing Porter (26 IBU)
Blue Point Brewing Summer Ale (16 IBU)
Blue Point Brewing Toasted Lager (28 IBU) – page 471
Blue Point Brewing Winter Ale (16 IBU)

States Available: MA, MD, NJ, NY, PA, RI

Brewery Ommegang – *page 480*
656 County Highway 33
Cooperstown, NY 13326
607-544-1800
www.ommegang.com

BRANDS:
Hennepin Farmhouse Saison Ale
Ommegang Abbey Ale Dubbel
Ommegang Witte Ale
Rare Vos Amber Ale
Three Philosophers Quadrupel Ale – *page 480*

States Available: AK, AZ, CA, CO, CT, DC, DE, FL, GA, ID, IL, IN, KY, LA,
MA, MD, ME, MI, MO, NC, NE, NH, NJ, NV, NY, OH, OR,
PA, RI, TX, VA, VT, WA, WI

Brooklyn Brewery
79 North Eleventh Street
Brooklyn, NY 11211
718-486-7422
www.brooklynbrewery.com

BRANDS:
Brooklyn Black Chocolate Stout (70 IBU)
Brooklyn Brown Ale (30 IBU)
Brooklyn East India Pale Ale (40 IBU)
Brooklyn Lager (28-30 IBU)
Brooklyn Monster Ale (70 IBU)
Brooklyn Oktoberfest (20 IBU)
Brooklyn Pennant Ale (26 IBU)
Brooklyn Pilsner (30 IBU)
Brooklyn Weisse (13 IBU)
Post Road Pumpkin Ale (24 IBU)

States Available: CT, DC, DE, GA, MA, MD, MI, NC, NJ, NY, OH, PA, RI,
SC, VA

Butternuts Beer & Ale – *page 481*
4021 State Highway 51
Garrattsville, NY 13342
607-263-5070
www.butternutsbeerandale.com

BRANDS:
Heinnieweisse Weissbier (11 IBU)
Moo Thunder Stout (25 IBU)
Porkslap Pale Ale (24 IBU) – *page 481*
Snapperhead IPA (40 IBU)

States Available: NJ, NY

Cooper's Cave Ale Company, LTD. – *page 487*
2 Sagamore Street
Glens Falls, NY 12801
518-792-0007
www.cooperscaveale.com

BRANDS:
Cooper's Cave Ale Company Bumppo's Brown Ale
 (35 IBU)
Cooper's Cave Ale Company Pale Ale (55 IBU)
Cooper's Cave Ale Company Pathfinder's Porter (53 IBU)
Cooper's Cave Ale Company Radeau Red Ale (35 IBU) – *page 487*
Cooper's Cave Ale Company Sagamore Stout (30 IBU)
Cooper's Cave Ale Company Tavern Ale (30 IBU)

States Available: NY

Cooperstown Brewing Company
110 River Street, P.O. Box 276
Milford, NY 13807
607-286-9330
www.cooperstownbrewing.com

BRANDS:
Cooperstown Brewing Back Yard India Pale Ale
Cooperstown Brewing Benchwarmer Porter
Cooperstown Brewing Nine Man Ale
Cooperstown Brewing Old Slugger Pale Ale
Cooperstown Brewing Pride Of Milford Special Ale
Cooperstown Brewing Strike Out Stout

States Available: CT, MA, NJ, NY, PA, RI

GEOGRAPHIC BREWER INDEX (Alphabetical)

Ellicottville Brewing Company – *page 494*

28A Monroe Street
Ellicottville, New York 14731
716-699-2537
www.ellicottvillebrewing.com

BRANDS:
Ellicottville Brewing Black Jack Oatmeal Stout
Ellicottville Brewing Blueberry Wheat – *page 494*
Ellicottville Brewing German Red
Ellicottville Brewing Nut Brown
Ellicottville Brewing American Pale Ale
Ellicottville Brewing Toasted Lager

States Available: Contact Brewery

Flying Bison Brewing Company

491 Ontario Street
Buffalo, NY 14207-1641
716-837-1557
www.flyingbisonbrewing.com

BRANDS:
Flying Bison Brewing Aviator Red
Flying Bison Brewing Barnstormer Pale Ale
Flying Bison Brewing Blackbird Oatmeal Stout
Flying Bison Brewing Buffalo Lager
Flying Bison Brewing Dawn Patrol Gold

States Available: NY (Western)

Harlem Brewing Company

360 West 125th Street
New York, NY 10027
888-559-6735
www.harlembrewingcompany.com

BRANDS:
Sugar Hill Golden Ale

States Available: Contact Brewery

High Falls Brewing

445 St. Paul Street
Rochester, NY 14605
585-263-9446
www.highfalls.com

BRANDS:
Genesee Beer
Genesee Cream Ale
Genesee Ice
Genesee NA
Genesee Red Lager
Genny Light
JW DunDee's American Amber Lager
JW DunDee's American Pale Ale
JW DunDee's Honey Brown Lager
Michael Shea's Irish Amber
Steinlager

States Available: AL, AR, AZ, CO, CT, DE, FL, GA, IL, IN, KS, KY, LA, MA, MD, ME, MI, MN, MO, NC, NE, NH, NJ, NM, NV, NY, OH, OK, OR, PA, RI, SC, TN, TX, VA, VT, WA, WI

Ithaca Beer Company, Inc.

600 Elmira Road
Ithaca, NY 14850-8745
607-273-0766
www.ithacabeer.com

BRANDS:
Ithaca Beer Company Apricot Wheat
Ithaca Beer Company CascaZilla
Ithaca Beer Company Double IPA
Ithaca Beer Company Finger Lakes Stout
Ithaca Beer Company Flower Power India Pale Ale
Ithaca Beer Company Nut Brown
Ithaca Beer Company Pale Ale
Ithaca Beer Company Partly Sunny
Ithaca Beer Company Winterizer
Ithaca Beer Gorges Smoked Porter

States Available: NY

GEOGRAPHIC BREWER INDEX (Alphabetical)

Keegan Ales

20 Saint James Street
Kingston, NY 12401
845-331-BREW
www.keeganales.com

BRANDS:
Keegan Ales Hurricane Kitty (8.9 SRM, 69.9 IBU)
Keegan Ales Mother's Milk (29.7 SRM, 25.4 IBU)
Keegan Ales Old Capital (3.5 SRM, 11.1 INU)

States Available: NY

Lake Placid Craft Brewing

1472 Military Turnpike
Plattsburgh, NY 12901
518-563-3340
www.ubuale.com

BRANDS:
Lake Placid Craft Brewing 46'er India Pale Ale
Lake Placid Craft Brewing Barkeater Amber Ale
Lake Placid Craft Brewing Moose Island Ale
Lake Placid Craft Brewing Ubu Ale

States Available: MA, NJ, NY, PA, RI, VT

Landmark Beer Company *– page 510*

3650 James Street, Room 105
Syracuse, NY 13206
315-720-2013
www.landmarkbrewing.com

BRANDS:
Landmark Colonel Hops Red Ale
Landmark India Pale Ale
Landmark Vanilla Bean Brown Ale *– page 510*

States Available: NY

Middle Ages Brewing Company

120 Wilkinson Street, Suite 3, P.O. Box 1164
Syracuse, NY 13204-2490
315-476-4250
www.middleagesbrewing.com

BRANDS:
Middle Ages Apricot Ale
Middle Ages Beast Bitter
Middle Ages Black Heart Stout
Middle Ages Dragonslayer Imperial Stout
Middle Ages Druid Fluid Barley Wine
Middle Ages Grail Ale
Middle Ages Highlander Scotch Ale
Middle Ages Impaled Ale
Middle Ages Kilt Tilter Scotch Style Ale
Middle Ages Old Marcus Ale
Middle Ages Raspberry Ale
Middle Ages Swallow Wheat
Middle Ages Syracuse Pale Ale
Middle Ages The Duke of Winship Scottish Style Ale
Middle Ages Tripel Crown
Middle Ages Wailing Wench
Middle Ages Winter Wheat
Middle Ages Wizard's Winter Ale

States Available: Contact Brewery

Mississippi Brewing Company

Utica, NY 13502-4092

BRANDS:
Mississippi Mud Black & Tan
Mississippi Mud Lager

States Available: Contact Brewery

Olde Saratoga Brewing Company

131 Excelsior Avenue
Saratoga Springs, NY 12866
518-581-0492
www.oldesaratogabrew.com

BRANDS:
Olde Saratoga Brewing Saratoga Lager

States Available: NY

Ramapo Valley Brewery

P.O. Box 1031, 143 Route 59, Building 6
Hilburn, NY 10931
845-369-7827
www.ramapovalleybrewery.com

BRANDS:

Ramapo Valley Brewery Copper Ale
Ramapo Valley Brewery Honey Lager
Ramapo Valley Brewery India Pale Ale
Ramapo Valley Brewery Octoberfest
Ramapo Valley Brewery Ramapo Razz Ale
Ramapo Valley Brewery Skull Crusher
Ramapo Valley Brewery Suffern Station Porter
Ramapo Valley Brewery Christmas Ale

States Available: CA, FL, IA, IL, MA, NJ, NY, PA, VT

Southampton Publick House – *page 551*

40 Bowden Square
Southampton, NY 11968
631-283-2800
www.publick.com

BRANDS:

Southampton 10th Anniversary Old Ale
Southampton Abbot 12
Southampton Biere de Garde
Southampton Double White Ale – *page 551*
Southampton Grand Cru
Southampton Imperial Porter
Southampton IPA
Southampton May Bock
Southampton Pumpkin Ale
Southampton Saison
Southampton Secret Ale
Southampton Triple

States Available: CT, MA, NJ, NY, PA, RI

Southern Tier Brewing Company – *page 552*

2051A Stoneman Circle
Lakewood, NY 14750-0166
716-763-5479
www.southerntierbrewing.com

BRANDS:

Southern Tier Brewing Belgian Tripel Ale
Southern Tier Brewing Big Red Imperial Red
Southern Tier Brewing Black Water Series Imperial Stout
Southern Tier Brewing Harvest Ale
Southern Tier Brewing Heavy Weizen
Southern Tier Brewing Hop Sun Summer Ale
Southern Tier Brewing Imperial IPA – *page 552*
Southern Tier Brewing Old Man Winter Warmer
Southern Tier Brewing Phin & Matt's
Southern Tier Brewing Porter

States Available: CT, DC, IN, IL, MA, MD, MI, NY, OH, PA, RI, WI, VA

The Defiant Brewing Company

6 East Dexter Plaza
Pearl River, NY 10965
845-920-8602
www.Defiantbrewing.com

BRANDS:

Defiant Brewing 3
Defiant Brewing Big Thumper Ale
Defiant Brewing Christmas Ale
Defiant Brewing ESB
Defiant Brewing Inspiration Ale
Defiant Brewing Little Thumper Ale
Defiant Brewing Pearl River Lager
Defiant Brewing Pilsner
Defiant Brewing Porter
Defiant Brewing Stephano's Stout
Defiant Brewing The Horseman's Ale

States Available: Contact Brewery

GEOGRAPHIC BREWER INDEX (Alphabetical)

The Matt Brewing – *page 562*

811 Edward Street
Utica, NY 13502-4092
315-624-2400
www.saranac.com/products

BRANDS:
Saranac 12 Beers of Summer
Saranac 12 Beers of Winter
Saranac Adirondack Lager
Saranac Black & Tan
Saranac Black Forest
Saranac Caramel Porter
Saranac India Pale Ale
Saranac Lager
Saranac Octoberfest
Saranac Pale Ale – *page 562*
Saranac Season's Best
Saranac Trail Mix

States Available: CT, DC, DE, GA, IA, IN, KS, MA, NH, NJ, NY, OH, PA, RI,
SC, VA, VT, WV

Wagner Valley Brewing Company

9322 Route 414
Lodi, NY 14860
607-582-6450
www.wagnervineyards.com

BRANDS:
Wagner Valley Brewing Caywood Oatmeal Stout
Wagner Valley Brewing Dockside Amber Lager
Wagner Valley Brewing Grace House Wheat
Wagner Valley Brewing Indian Pale Ale
Wagner Valley Brewing Mill Street Pilsner
Wagner Valley Brewing Sled Dog Dopplebock
Wagner Valley Brewing Tripellbock Reserve

States Available: NY, RI

The following brewers distribute their brands in New York:

Abita Brewing Company	Magic Hat Brewing Company
Allagash Brewing Company	Michigan Brewing Company, Inc.
Anchor Brewing Company	Molson Coors Brewing Company
Anderson Valley Brewing	Moylan's Brewing Company
Anheuser-Busch, Inc.	North Coast Brewing Company
Bard's Tale Beer Company	Olde Saratoga Brewing Company
Bear Republic Brewing Company	Oskar Blues Grill & Brew
Blue Point Brewing	Otter Creek Brewing Company
Boulder Beer Company	Pabst Brewing Company
Brewery Ommegang	Penn Brewery
Brooklyn Brewery	Pete's Brewing
Butternuts Beer & Ale	Pittsburgh Brewing Company
Cape Ann Brewing	Ramapo Valley Brewery
Cisco Brewers Inc.	Redhook Ale Brewery
Climax Brewing Company	River Horse Brewing Company
Clipper City Brewing Company	Rogue Ales
Coffaro Beer Company	SAB Miller Corp
Cooper's Cave Ale Company, LTD.	Shipyard Brewing Company
Cooperstown Brewing Company	Shmaltz Brewing Company
Cricket Hill Brewing Company	Sierra Nevada Brewing Company
D.G. Yuengling & Son, Inc.	Smuttynose Brewing Company
D L Geary Brewing Company	South Hampton Publick House
Dogfish Head Craft Brewery	Southern Tier Brewing Company
Erie Brewing	Spanish Peaks Brewing Company/
Florida Beer Company	United States Beverage
Flying Bison Brewing Company	Speakeasy Ales & Lagers, Inc.
Flying Dog Brewery, LLC	Stone Brewing Company
Gordon Biersch Brewery	Stone Coast Brewing Company
Great Divide Brewing Company	Stoudt's Brewing Company
Great Lakes Brewing Company	The Black Mountain/Chili Beer Company
Gritty McDuff's Brewing Company	The Boston Beer Company
Hair of the Dog Brewing Company	The Long Trail Brewing Company
Harpoon Brewery	The Matt Brewing
High Falls Brewing	The Sea Dog Brewing Company
High Point Wheat Beer Company	Tommyknocker Brewery
Ithaca Beer Company Inc.	Tremont Brewery/Atlantic Coast Brewing
Jolly Pumpkin Artisan Ales	Company
Keegan Ales	Trout Brook Brewing Company
Kona Brewing, LLC	Victory Brewing Company
Lagunitas Brewing	Wachusett Brewing Company
Lake Placid Craft Brewing	Wagner Valley Brewing Company
Lakefront Brewery Inc.	Weyerbacher Brewing Company
Landmark Beer Company	Widmer Brothers Brewing Company
Lost Coast Brewery & Café	

Barrel House Brewing Company OH

544-B West Liberty Street
Cincinnati, OH 45214
513-421-2337
www.barrelhouse.malz.com

BRANDS::

Barrel House Belgian Style Winter Ale
Barrel House Boss Cox Double Dark IPA
Barrel House Cumberland Pale Ale
Barrel House Duveneck's Dortmunder Style Lager
Barrel House Hocking Hills HefeWeizen
Barrel House Red Leg Ale

States Available: Contact Brewery

Christian Moerlein Brewing Company

3400 Yankee Road
Cincinnati, OH 45200
513-771-0690
www.christianmoerlein.com

BRANDS:

Christian Moerlein Doppelbock
Christian Moerlein Hefeweisen
Christian Moerlein Oktoberfest
Christian Moerlein Select Dunkel
Christian Moerlein Select Lager
Christian Moerlein Select Light

States Available: Contact Brewer

Columbus Brewing Company

535 Short Street
Columbus, OH 43215-5614
614-224-3626
www.columbusbrewing.com

BRANDS:

Columbus Brewing 90 Schilling Ale
Columbus Brewing Apricot Ale
Columbus Brewing Ohio Honey Wheat
Columbus Brewing Pale Ale

States Available: Contact Brewery

Great Lakes Brewing Company – *page 505*

2516 Market Avenue
Cleveland, OH 44113
216-771-4404
www.greatlakesbrewing.com

BRANDS:

Great Lakes Brewing Burning River Pale Ale
(45 IBU)
Great Lakes Brewing Christmas Ale (40 IBU)
Great Lakes Brewing Commodore Perry India Pale Ale (80 IBU)
Great Lakes Brewing Conway's Irish Ale (25 IBU)
Great Lakes Brewing Dortmunder Golden Lager (30 IBU) – *page 505*
Great Lakes Brewing Edmund Fitzgerald Porter (37 IBU)
Great Lakes Brewing Eliot Ness Amber Lager (35 IBU)
Great Lakes Brewing Holy Moses White Ale (30 IBU)
Great Lakes Brewing Moondog Ale (25 IBU)
Great Lakes Brewing Nosferatu (75 IBU)

States Available: IL, KY, MI, NY, OH, PA, WI, WV

Thirsty Dog Brewing Company

P.O. Box 31043
Independence, OH 44131
216-447-9336
www.thirstydog.com

BRANDS:

Thirsty Dog Balto Heroic Lager (17 IBU)
Thirsty Dog Hoppus Maximus (43 IBU)
Thirsty Dog Old Leghumper (24 IBU)
Thirsty Dog Siberian Night (58 IBU)

States Available: IN, KY, MD, OH, PA

GEOGRAPHIC BREWER INDEX (Alphabetical)

The following brewers distribute their brands in Ohio:

Abita Brewing Company
Allagash Brewing Company
Anchor Brewing Company
Anderson Valley Brewing
Anheuser-Busch, Inc.
Arcadia Brewing Company
Atwater Block Brewery
Avery Brewing Company
Bard's Tale Beer Company
Bell's Brewery, Inc.
Bison Brewing
Blucreek Brewing
Bluegrass Beer Company
Boulder Beer Company
Breckenridge Brewery
Brewery Ommegang
Brooklyn Brewery
Casco Bay Brewing Company
City Brewery
Clipper City Brewing Company
D L Geary Brewing Company
Dogfish Head Craft Brewery
Erie Brewing
Flying Dog Brewery, LLC
Frederick Brewing Company
Gordon Biersch Brewery
Great Divide Brewing Company
Great Lakes Brewing Company
Harpoon Brewery
High Falls Brewing
Jacob Leinenkugel Brewing Company
Jolly Pumpkin Artisan Ales
Lakefront Brewery Inc.
Left Handed Brewing Company
MacTarnahan's Brewing Company
Michigan Brewing Company, Inc.
Molson Coors Brewing Company
Moylan's Brewing Company
New Century Brewing Company
New Holland Brewing Company

North Coast Brewing Company
Old Dominion Brewing Company
Otter Creek Brewing Company
Pabst Brewing Company
Pete's Brewing
Pittsburgh Brewing Company
Pyramid Brewery
Redhook Ale Brewery
River Horse Brewing Company
Rogue Ales
SAB Miller Corp
Shipyard Brewing Company
Shmaltz Brewing Company
Sierra Nevada Brewing Company
Siletz Brewing Company, Inc.
Snake River Brewing Company
Southern Tier Brewing Company
Spanish Peaks Brewing Company/
    United States Beverage
Speakeasy Ales & Lagers, Inc.
Sprecher Brewing
Stone Brewing Company
Stoudt's Brewing Company
Straub Brewing
Summit Brewing Company
The Black Mountain/Chili Beer Company
The Boston Beer Company
The Matt Brewing
The Sea Dog Brewing Company
The Spoetzl Brewing
Thirsty Dog Brewing Company
Three Floyds Brewing Company
Tommyknocker Brewery
Tremont Brewery/Atlantic Coast Brewing
    Company
Two Brothers Brewing Company
Victory Brewing Company
Weyerbacher Brewing Company
Widmer Brothers Brewing Company

OK

Huebert Brewing
421 SW 26th Street
Oklahoma City, OK 73109
405-634-6528
http://groups.msn.com/HuebertBrewingCompany

<u>BRANDS:</u>
Huebert Brewing Huebert's Old Tyme Lager

States Available: OK

The following brewers distribute their brands in Okalahoma:

Great Divide Brewing Company
Abita Brewing Company
Anchor Brewing Company
Anheuser-Busch, Inc.
Boulevard Brewing Company
Breckenridge Brewery
BridgePort Brewing Company
Flying Dog Brewery, LLC
Frederick Brewing Company
Full Sail Brewing Company
High Falls Brewing
Huebert Brewing
Jacob Leinenkugel Brewing Company
Left Handed Brewing Company
Molson Coors Brewing Company
North Coast Brewing Company

Pabst Brewing Company
Pete's Brewing
Pig's Eye Brewing Company
Pittsburgh Brewing Company
Pyramid Brewery
Rogue Ales
SAB Miller Corp
Santa Fe Brewing Company
Shipyard Brewing Company
Sierra Nevada Brewing Company
The Boston Beer Company
The Sea Dog Brewing Company
The Spoetzl Brewing
Tremont Brewery/Atlantic Coast Brewing
    Company
Yellowstone Valley Brewing

OR

BridgePort Brewing Company (Gambrinus)
1313 NorthWest Marshall
Portland, OR 97209
503-241-7179
www.bridgeportbrew.com

<u>BRANDS:</u>
Beer Town Brown (20 IBU)
BridgePort Black Strap Stout (30 IBU)
BridgePort Blue Heron Pale Ale (25 IBU)
BridgePort Ebenezer Ale (40 IBU)
BridgePort ESB (30 IBU)
BridgePort IPA (60 IBU)
BridgePort Old Knucklehead (60 IBU)
BridgePort Ropewalker (18 IBU)

States Available: AK, AL, AZ, CA, CO, GA, ID, KS, MI, MN, MO,
    MT, NC, NM, OK, OR, TN, TX, WA

299

GEOGRAPHIC BREWER INDEX (Alphabetical)

Caldera Brewing Company – *page 482*
540 Clover Lane
Ashland, OR 97520
541-482-4677
www.calderabrewing.com
BRANDS:
Caldera Brewing Pale Ale – *page 482*
States Available: OR

Cascade Lakes Brewing Company
2141 South West First Street
Redmond, OR 97756
541-923-3110
www.cascadelakes.com
BRANDS:
Cascade Lakes 20" Brown (35 IBU)
Cascade Lakes Angus MacDougal's Amber (30 IBU)
Cascade Lakes Blonde Bombshell (26 IBU)
Cascade Lakes IPA (65 IBU)
Cascade Lakes Monkey Face Porter (34 IBU)
Cascade Lakes Pine Marten Pale Ale (38 IBU)
Cascade Lakes Rooster Tail Ale (20 IBU)

States Available: Contact Brewery

Deschutes Brewery – *page 490*
901 SW Simpson Avenue
Bend, OR 97702
541-385-8606
www.deschutesbrewery.com
BRANDS:
Deschutes Bachelor ESB (50 IBU)
Deschutes Black Butte Porter (30 IBU) – *page 490*
Deschutes Bond Street Brown
Deschutes Broken Top Bock
Deschutes Buzzsaw Brown (30 IBU)
Deschutes Cascade Ale (28 IBU)
Deschutes Cinder Cone Red Ale (55 IBU)
Deschutes Hop Henge India Pale Ale (85 IBU)
Deschutes Hop Trip Pale Ale (35 IBU)
Deschutes Inversion IPA (75 IBU)
Deschutes Jubelale (60 IBU)
Deschutes Mirror Pond Pale Ale (40 IBU)
Deschutes Obsidian Stout (50 IBU)
Deschutes Quail Springs IPA
Deschutes The Abyss
Deschutes Twilight Ale (35 IBU)

States Available: AK, AZ, CA (Northern), CO, HI, ID, MT, NM, NV (Western), OR, WA, WY

Full Sail Brewing Company – *page 502*
506 Columbia Street
Hood River, OR 97031-2000
541- 386-2247
www.fullsailbrewing.com
BRANDS:
Full Sail Brewing Amber – *page 502*
Full Sail Brewing Holiday Wassail Ale
Full Sail Brewing IPA
Full Sail Brewing Pale Ale
Full Sail Brewing Rip Curl
Full Sail Brewing Session Premium Lager

States Available: AK, AZ, CA, CO, HI, ID, MN, MT, NM, NV, OK, OR, TX, UT, WA, WY

GEOGRAPHIC BREWER INDEX (Alphabetical)

Golden Valley Brewery

980 North East 4th Street
McMinnville, OR 97128
503-472-2739
www.goldenvalleybrewery.com

BRANDS:
Golden Valley American Pale Ale (38 IBU)
Golden Valley Black Panther Imperial Stout (48 IBU)
Golden Valley Chehalem Moutain IPA (55 IBU)
Golden Valley Dundee Porter (26 IBU)
Golden Valley Geist Bock (35 IBU)
Golden Valley Red Hills Pilsner (38 IBU)
Golden Valley Red Thistle Ale (40 IBU)
Golden Valley Tannen Bomb (50 IBU)

States Available: Contact Brewery

Hair of the Dog Brewing Company

4509 SE 23rd Avenue
Portland, OR 97202-4771
503-232-6585
www.hairofthedog.com

BRANDS:
Hair of the Dog Brewing Adam (50 IBU)
Hair of the Dog Brewing Doggie Claws (70 IBU)
Hair of the Dog Brewing Fred (65 IBU)
Hair of the Dog Brewing Rose (17 IBU)
Hair of the Dog Brewing Ruth

States Available: CA, NY, OR, WA

MacTarnahan's Brewing Company

2730 NW 31st Avenue
Portland, OR 97210
503-226-7623
www.macsbeer.com

BRANDS:
MacTarnahan's Brewing Blackwatch Cream Porter
MacTarnahan's Brewing Mac's Amber Ale (30 IBU)
MacTarnahan's Oregon Honey Beer (16 IBU)

States Available: AK, AK, AR, CA, CO, DC, HI, IA, ID, IL, IN, KS, MI, MN, MO, MT, NE, NJ, NV, OH, OR, OR, PA, SC, SC, TN, TX, VA, VT, WA, WI

Mount Hood Brewing Company

P.O. Box 56
Government Camp, OR 97028
503-622-0768
www.mthoodbrewing.com

BRANDS:
Mount Hood Brewing Cascadian Pale Ale
Mount Hood Brewing Cloudcap Amber Ale
Mount Hood Brewing Double T Porter
Mount Hood Brewing Highland Meadow Blonde Ale
Mount Hood Brewing Hogsback
Mount Hood Brewing Ice Axe IPA
Mount Hood Brewing Imperial Ice Axxe
Mount Hood Brewing Multorporter

States Available: OR

Oregon Trail Brewery

341 SW Second Street
Corvallis, OR 97333
541-758-3527
www.oregontrailbrewery.com

BRANDS:
Oregon Trail Beaver Tail
Oregon Trail Brown Ale
Oregon Trail Ginseng Porter
Oregon Trail IPA
Oregon Trail Wit

States Available: Contact Brewery

Pelican Pub & Brewery

P.O. Box 189, 33180 Cape Kiwanda Drive
Pacific City, OR 97135
503-965-7007
www.pelicanbrewery.com

BRANDS:
India Pelican Ale (85 IBU)

States Available: Contact Brewery

Rogue Ales – *page 537*
2320 OSU Drive
Newport, OR 97365
541-867-3660
www.rogue.com

BRANDS:
Morimoto Black Obi Soba (30 IBU)
Rogue American Amber Ale (53 IBU)
Rogue Brutal Bitter (59 IBU)
Rogue Chamomellow Ale (34 IBU)
Rogue Chipotle Ale (35 IBU)
Rogue Chocolate Stout (69 IBU)
Rogue Dad's Little Helper Malt Liquor (25 IBU)
Rogue Dead Guy Ale (40 IBU) – *page 537*
Rogue Half-E-Weizen (34 IBU)
Rogue Hazelnut Brown Nectar (33 IBU)
Rogue I2PA Imperial India Pale Ale (74 IBU)
Rogue Imperial Stout (88 IBU)
Rogue Juniper Pale Ale (34 IBU)
Rogue Kells Irish Lager (28 IBU)
Rogue Mocha Porter (54 IBU)
Rogue Monk Madness Ale (108 IBU)
Rogue Morimoto Imperial Pilsner (74 IBU)
Rogue Morimoto Soba Ale (30 IBU)
Rogue Old Crustacean Barleywine (110 IBU)
Rogue Oregon Golden Ale (35 IBU)
Rogue Santa's Private Reserve (44 IBU)
Rogue Shakespeare Stout (69 IBU)
Rogue Smoke Ale (48 IBU)
Rogue St.Rogue Red (44 IBU)
Rogue Uberfest Pilsner (35 IBU)
Rogue Younger's Special Bitter (35 IBU)

States Available: All 50 States

Siletz Brewing Company, Inc.
P.O. Box 116
Siletz, OR 97380
541-444-7012
www.siletzbrewing.com

BRANDS:
Siletz Brewing Company Amber Ale (24.3 SRM, 53.5 IBU)
Siletz Brewing Company Black Diamond Imperial Porter (76.1 SRM, 45 IBU)
Siletz Brewing Company Chocolate Porter (86.9 SRM, 41.7 IBU)
Siletz Brewing Company Lovin Lager (11.6 SRM, 34.3 IBU)
Siletz Brewing Company Noggin Knocker (83.6 SRM, 67.9 IBU)
Siletz Brewing Company Oatmeal Cream Stout (87.2 SRM, 64.1 IBU)
Siletz Brewing Company Paddle Me IPA (12 SRM, 76.8 IBU)
Siletz Brewing Company Red Ale (19.1 SRM, 42.3 IBU)
Siletz Brewing Company Spruce Ale (25.7 SRM, 35.2 IBU)
Siletz Brewing Company Winter Warmer (38.5 SRM, 53.8 IBU)
Siletz Brewing Company Wooly Bully (16.8 SRM, 38.2 IBU)

States Available: OH, OR

Terminal Gravity Brewing
803 South East School Street
Enterprise, OR 97828
541-426-0518
www.terminalgravitybrewing.com

BRANDS:

States Available: Contact Brewery

Widmer Brothers Brewing Company – *page 571*
929 N Russell Street
Portland, OR 97227-1733
503-281-2438
www.widmer.com

BRANDS:
Broken Halo IPA (10 SRM, 52 IBU)
Drop Top Amber Ale (14 SRM, 20 IBU)
OKTO (22 SRM, 25 IBU)
Snowplow Milk Stout (80 SRM, 26 IBU)
Summit Pale Ale (17 SRM, 34 IBU)
W '06 N.W. Red Ale (50 IBU)
Widmer Hefeweizen (7 SRM, 32 IBU) – *page 571*

States Available: AR, LA, ND, OK, TX, Not in UT

GEOGRAPHIC BREWER INDEX (Alphabetical)

The following brewers distribute their brands in Oregon:

Alaskan Brewing Company
Allagash Brewing Company
Anchor Brewing Company
Anderson Valley Brewing
Anheuser-Busch, Inc.
Avery Brewing Company
Bard's Tale Beer Company
Bayern Brewing
Bear Republic Brewing Company
Big Sky Brewing Company
Bison Brewing
Boulder Beer Company
Brewery Ommegang
BridgePort Brewing Company
Caldera Brewing Company
Deschutes Brewery
Dick's Brewing Company
Dogfish Head Craft Brewery
Eel River Brewing Company
Elysian Brewing Company
Flying Dog Brewery, LLC
Full Sail Brewing Company
Great Divide Brewing Company
Hair of the Dog Brewing Company
High Falls Brewing
Ice Harbor Brewing Company
Kona Brewing, LLC
Lagunitas Brewing
Lang Creek Brewery
Lost Coast Brewery & Café
MacTarnahan's Brewing Company
Mad River Brewing

Marin Brewing Company
Michigan Brewing Company, Inc.
Midnight Sun Brewing Company
Molson Coors Brewing Company
Mount Hood Brewing Company
Moylan's Brewing Company
New Belgium Brewing Company
North Coast Brewing Company
Otter Creek Brewing Company
Pabst Brewing Company
Pete's Brewing
Pittsburgh Brewing Company
Pyramid Brewery
Redhook Ale Brewery
Rogue Ales
SAB Miller Corp
Shipyard Brewing Company
Sierra Nevada Brewing Company
Siletz Brewing Company, Inc.
Snipes Mountain Brewing Company
Spanish Peaks Brewing Company/
    United States Beverage
Speakeasy Ales & Lagers, Inc.
Stone Brewing Company
The Boston Beer Company
The Sea Dog Brewing Company
The Spoetzl Brewing
Tremont Brewery/Atlantic Coast Brewing
    Company
Trout River Brewing Company
Victory Brewing Company
Widmer Brothers Brewing Company

Appalachian Brewing Company

PA

50 North Cameron Street
Harrisburg, PA 17101
717-221-1080
www.abcbrew.com

BRANDS:
Appalachian Brewing Hoppy Trail IPA
Appalachian Brewing Jolly Scot Scottish Ale
Appalachian Brewing Kipona Fest Lager
Appalachian Brewing Mountain Lager
Appalachian Brewing Peregrine Pilsner
Appalachian Brewing Purist Pale Ale
Appalachian Brewing Susquehanna Stout
Appalachian Brewing Water Gap Wheat

States Available: PA

Barley Creek Brewing Company

Sullivan Trail and Camelback Road
Tannerville, PA 18372
570-629-9399
www.barleycreek.com

BRANDS:
Barley Creek Angler Black Widow Lager
Barley Creek Antler Brown Ale
Barley Creek Atlas Ale
Barley Creek Harvest Moon Oktoberfest
Barley Creek Light
Barley Creek Navigator Gold
Barley Creek Old '99 Barley Wine
Barley Creek Renovator Stout
Barley Creek Rescue India Pale Ale

States Available: NJ, PA

303

GEOGRAPHIC BREWER INDEX (Alphabetical)

D.G. Yuengling & Son, Inc. – *page 489*
540 Clover Lane
5TH & Mahantongo Streets
Pottsville, PA 17901
570-622-4141
www.yuengling.com

BRANDS:
Yuengling Black and Tan
Yuengling Dark Brewed Porter
Yuengling Light Beer
Yuengling Light Lager
Yuengling Lord Chesterfield Ale
Yuengling Premium Beer
Yuengling Traditional Lager – *page 489*

States Available: AL, DC, DE, FL, MD, NC, NJ, NY, PA, SC, VA

Erie Brewing
1213 Veshecco Drive
Erie, PA 16501
814-459-7741
www.eriebrewingco.com

BRANDS:
Erie Brewing Drake's Crude Oatmeal Stout (19 IBU)
Erie Brewing Fallenbock (18 IBU)
Erie Brewing German Wheat (16 IBU)
Erie Brewing Golden Fleece Maibock Lager (21 IBU)
Erie Brewing Heritage Alt (15 IBU)
Erie Brewing Mad Anthony's Ale (13 IBU)
Erie Brewing Presque Isle Pilsner (18 IBU)
Erie Brewing RailBender Ale (26 IBU)
Erie Brewing Red Ryder Big Beer (35 IBU)
Erie Brewing Sunshine Wit (17 IBU)

States Available: NY (Western), OH (Eastern), PA

Jones Brewing Company
254 Second Street, P.O. Box 746
Smithton, PA 15479
724-872-6626
www.stoneysbeer.com

BRANDS:
Esquire Extra Premium
Stoney's Beer
Stoney's Black And Tan
Stoney's Harvest Gold
Stoney's Light

States Available: Contact Brewery

Lancaster Brewing Company
302-304 North Plum Street
Lancaster, PA 17602
717-391-6258
www.lancasterbrewing.com

BRANDS:
Lancaster Brewing Amish Four Grain Pale Ale (28 IBU)
Lancaster Brewing Doppel Bock
Lancaster Brewing Franklinfest Lager 17 IBU)
Lancaster Brewing Gold Star Pilsner (33 IBU)
Lancaster Brewing Hop Hog IPA (55 IBU)
Lancaster Brewing Milk Stout (22 IBU)
Lancaster Brewing Oktoberfest
Lancaster Brewing Spring Bock
Lancaster Brewing Strawberry Wheat (16 IBU)
Lancaster Brewing Winter Warmer

States Available: MD, NJ, PA, VA

Latrobe Brewing
119 Jefferson St
Latrobe, PA 15650-1474
724-539-3394
www.rollingrock.com

BRANDS:
Latrobe Pilsner
Old German

States Available: Contact Brewery

GEOGRAPHIC BREWER INDEX (Alphabetical)

The Lion Brewery, Inc. – *page 561*

545 Canal Street
Reading, PA 19602
610-376-9996

BRANDS:
Legacy Brewing Hedonism Red Ale (110 IBU)
Legacy Brewing Midnight Wit Ale (17 IBU)

States Available: NJ, PA

Lion Brewery

700 North Pennsylvania Avenue
Wilkes Barre, PA 18705
570-823-8662
www.lionbrewery.com

BRANDS:
Lion Brewing Pocono Black & Tan
Lion Brewing Pocono Caramel Porter
Lion Brewing Pocono Lager
Lion Brewing Pocono Light
Lion Brewing Pocono Pale Ale
Lion Brewing Pocono Summer Wheat
Lionshead
Lionshead Malt Liquor
Stegmaier 1857 American Lager
Stegmaier Brewhouse Bock – *page 561*
Stegmaier Gold Medal
Stegmaier Oktoberfest
Stegmaier Porter

States Available: CT, DE, NJ, NY, PA

Penn Brewery (Pennsylvania Brewing) – *page 528*

800 Vinial Street
Pittsburgh, PA 15212-5128
412-237-9400
www.pennbrew.com

BRANDS:
Penn Crew Lager
Penn Dark Lager
Penn Gold
Penn Kaiser Pils
Penn Maibock
Penn Marzen
Penn Oktoberfest
Penn Pilsner – *page 528*
Penn St. Nikolaus Bock Bier
Penn Weizen

States Available: CA, DE, FL, MD, NY, PA

Pittsburgh Brewing Company

3340 Liberty Avenue
Pittsburgh, PA 15201
412-692-1136
www.pittsburghbrewingco.com

BRANDS:
Pittsburgh Brewing American
Pittsburgh Brewing American Ice
Pittsburgh Brewing American Light
Pittsburgh Brewing Augustiner Amber Lager
Pittsburgh Brewing Augustiner Dark
Pittsburgh Brewing IC Light
Pittsburgh Brewing Iron City Beer Premium Lager
Pittsburgh Brewing Old German

States Available: AK, AZ, CO, CT, DC, FL, GA, IA, IN, KS, KY, MA, MD, MI, MN, MO, MS, NC, ND, NJ, NM, OH, OK, OR, PA, SC, TN, TX, VA, WI, WV

GEOGRAPHIC BREWER INDEX (Alphabetical)

Red Bell Brewery & Pub

4421 Main Street
Philadelphia, PA 19127
215-482-9494
www.redbell.com

BRANDS:
Red Bell Brewing Philadelphia Original Light Lager
States Available: DE, NJ, PA

Sly Fox Brewing Company

519 Kimberton Road
Phoenixville, PA 19460
610-935-4540
www.slyfoxbeer.com

BRANDS:
Sly Fox Black Raspberry Reserve (16 IBU)
Sly Fox Christmas Ale (16 IBU)
Sly Fox Dunkel Lager (21 IBU)
Sly Fox Gang Aft Angley (20 IBU)
Sly Fox Ichor (20 IBU)
Sly Fox Incubus (39 IBU)
Sly Fox Instigator Doppelbock (20 IBU)
Sly Fox Odyssey (90 IBU)
Sly Fox Oktoberfest (25 IBU)
Sly Fox Phoenix Pale Ale (40 IBU)
Sly Fox Pikeland Pils (44 IBU)
Sly Fox Route 113 India Pale Ale (113 IBU)
Sly Fox Royal Weisse (11 IBU)
Sly Fox Saison VOS (32 IBU)

States Available: PA

Stoudt's Brewing Company

2800 North Reading Road, Route 272
Adamstown, PA 19501
717-484-4386
www.stoudtsbeer.com

BRANDS:
Stoudt's Abbey Triple (37 IBU)
Stoudt's American Pale Ale (40 IBU)
Stoudt's Blonde Double Maibock (35 IBU)
Stoudt's Double India Pale Ale (90 IBU)
Stoudt's Fat Dog Stout (55 IBU)
Stoudt's Gold Lager (25 IBU)
Stoudt's Oktoberfest (24 IBU)
Stoudt's Pils (40 IBU)
Stoudt's Scarlet Lady Ale (32 IBU)
Stoudt's Weizen (12 IBU)
Stoudt's Winter Ale
States Available: CA, DC, FL, GA, MA, MD, MI, NJ, NY, OH, PA, VA

Straub Brewing

303 Sorg Street
St. Mary's, PA 15857
814-834-2875
www.straubbeer.com

BRANDS:
Straub
Straub Light
States Available: OH, PA

The Bethlehem Brew Works

569 Main Street
Bethlehem, PA 18018
610-882-1300
www.thebrewworks.com

BRANDS:
Bethlehem Brew Works Pumpkin Ale
Bethlehem Brew Works Rude Elf's Reserve
States Available: Contact Brewery

GEOGRAPHIC BREWER INDEX (Alphabetical)

The Church Brew Works

3525 Liberty Avenue
Pittsburgh, PA 15201
412-688-8200
www.churchbrew.com

BRANDS:
Church Brew Works Blast Furnace Stout (30 IBU)
Church Brew Works Celestial Gold (18 IBU)
Church Brew Works Millenium Trippel Ale
Church Brew Works Pious Monk Dunkel (20 IBU)
Church Brew Works Pipe Organ Pale Ale (30 IBU)
Church Brew Works Quadzilla

States Available: PA

The Dock Street Brewery Company

P.O. Box 301
Gladwyne, PA 19035
www.dockstreetbeer.com

BRANDS:
Dock Street Amber (16 SRM, 28 IBU)
Illuminator Dock Street Bock (27 SRM, 28 IBU)

States Available: DE, NJ, PA

Tröegs Brewing Company – *page 566*

800 Paxton Street
Harrisburg, PA 17104
717-232-1297
www.troegs.com

BRANDS:
Tröegs Brewing Dreamweaver Wheat (15 IBU)
Tröegs Brewing Hopback Amber (55 IBU)
Tröegs Brewing Mad Elf (15 IBU)
Tröegs Brewing Nugget Nectar (93 IBU)
Tröegs Brewing Oatmeal Stout (60 IBU)
Tröegs Brewing Pale Ale (45 IBU)
Tröegs Brewing Rugged Trail Ale (28 IBU)
Tröegs Brewing Sunshine Pils (45 IBU)
Tröegs Brewing Troegenater Double Bock (25 IBU) – *page 566*

States Available: DE, MD, NJ, PA, VA

Victory Brewing Company – *page 569*

420 Acorn Lane
Downingtown, PA 19335
610-873-0881
www.victorybeer.com

BRANDS:
Victory Festbier (15-20 IBU)
Victory Golden Monkey (20-25 IBU)
Victory HopDevil Ale (50-60 IBU) – *page 569*
Victory 'Hop' Wallop (70+ IBU)
Victory Lager (17-22 IBU)
Victory Moonglow Weizenbock (18-23 IBU)
Victory Old Horizontal Ale (60+ IBU)
Victory Prima Pils (40-50 IBU)
Victory St. Boisterous (20-25 IBU)
Victory St. Victorious (20-25 IBU)
Victory Storm King (70+ IBU)
Victory Sunrise Weissbier (13-18 IBU)
Victory Throwback Lager
Victory V Saison (25-30 IBU)
Victory V Twelve (25-30 IBU)
Victory Victorious Doppelbock
Victory Whirlwind Witbier (13-18 IBU)

States Available: CA, CT, DE, IL, MA, MD, MN, NC, NJ, NY, OH, OR, PA, TX, VA

GEOGRAPHIC BREWER INDEX (Alphabetical)

Weyerbacher Brewing Company

905g Line Street
Easton, PA 18042-7379
610-559-5561
www.weyerbacher.com

BRANDS:
Weyerbacher Brewing Autumn Fest
Weyerbacher Brewing Black Hole
Weyerbacher Brewing Blanche
Weyerbacher Brewing Blithering Idiot
Weyerbacher Brewing Decadence
Weyerbacher Brewing Double Simcoe
Weyerbacher Brewing Eleven
Weyerbacher Brewing ESB Ale
Weyerbacher Brewing HefeWeizen
Weyerbacher Brewing Heresy Imperial Stout
Weyerbacher Brewing Hops Infusion India Pale Ale
Weyerbacher Brewing Imperial Pumpkin Ale
Weyerbacher Brewing Insanity
Weyerbacher Brewing Merry Monk's Ale
Weyerbacher Brewing Old Heathen
Weyerbacher Brewing Prophecy
Weyerbacher Brewing QUAD
Weyerbacher Brewing Raspberry Imperial Stout
Weyerbacher Brewing Scotch Ale
Weyerbacher Brewing Winter Ale

States Available: DC, MA, MD, NJ, NY, OH, PA, RI, VA

Yards Brewing – *page 574*

2439 Amber Street
Philadelphia, PA 19125
215-634-2600
www.yardsbrewing.com

BRANDS:
Yards Brewing Extra Special Ale – *page 574*
Yards Brewing General Washington Tavern Porter
Yards Brewing India Pale Ale
Yards Brewing Love Stout
Yards Brewing Philadelphia Pale Ale
Yards Brewing Poor Richard's Tavern Spruce
Yards Brewing Saison
Yards Brewing Thomas Jefferson Tavern Ale

States Available: CT, DC, DE, MD, NJ, PA, VA

GEOGRAPHIC BREWER INDEX (Alphabetical)

The following brewers distribute their brands in Pennsylvania:

Abita Brewing Company
Allagash Brewing Company
Anchor Brewing Company
Anderson Valley Brewing
Anheuser-Busch, Inc.
Appalachian Brewing Company
Arcadia Brewing Company
Atwater Block Brewery
August Schell Brewing Company
Avery Brewing Company
Baltimore-Washington Beer Works
Bard's Tale Beer Company
Barley Creek Brewing Company
Blue Point Brewing
Boulder Beer Company
Brewery Ommegang
Brooklyn Brewery
City Brewery
Climax Brewing Company
Clipper City Brewing Company
Coffaro Beer Company
Cooperstown Brewing Company
Cricket Hill Brewing Company
D.G. Yuengling & Son, Inc.
D L Geary Brewing Company
Dogfish Head Craft Brewery
Edenton Brewing Company
Eel River Brewing Company
Erie Brewing
Flying Dog Brewery, LLC
Flying Fish Brewing
Fordham Brewing Company
Frederick Brewing Company
Great Divide Brewing Company
Great Lakes Brewing Company
Harpoon Brewery
High Falls Brewing
High Point Wheat Beer Company
Lake Placid Craft Brewing
Lancaster Brewing Company
Left Handed Brewing Company
Legacy Brewing Company
Lion Brewery
Lost Coast Brewery & Café
MacTarnahan's Brewing Company
Mad River Brewing
Magic Hat Brewing Company
Michigan Brewing Company, Inc.
Molson Coors Brewing Company
New Holland Brewing Company

North Coast Brewing Company
Oak Creek Brewing Company
Old Dominion Brewing Company
Oskar Blues Grill & Brew
Otter Creek Brewing Company
Pabst Brewing Company
Penn Brewery
Pete's Brewing
Pig's Eye Brewing Company
Pittsburgh Brewing Company
Port Brewing Company
Pyramid Brewery
Ramapo Valley Brewery
ReaperAle, Inc.
Red Bell Brewery & Pub
Redhook Ale Brewery
River Horse Brewing Company
Rogue Ales
Russian River Brewing Company
SAB Miller Corp
Shipyard Brewing Company
Shmaltz Brewing Company
Sierra Nevada Brewing Company
Sly Fox Brewing Company
Smuttynose Brewing Company
South Hampton Publick House
Southern Tier Brewing Company
Spanish Peaks Brewing Company/
    United States Beverage
Speakeasy Ales & Lagers, Inc.
Stone Brewing Company
Stoudt's Brewing Company
Straub Brewing
Summit Brewing Company
The Boston Beer Company
The Church Brew Works
The Dock Street Brewery Company
The Matt Brewing
The Sea Dog Brewing Company
The Weeping Radish Brewery
Thirsty Dog Brewing Company
Three Floyds Brewing Company
Tremont Brewery/Atlantic Coast Brewing
    Company
Tröegs Brewing Company
Victory Brewing Company
Weyerbacher Brewing Company
Widmer Brothers Brewing Company
Yards Brewing

Coastal Extreme Brewing Company, LLC

RI

P.O. Box 628
Newport, RI 02840-0006
401-849-5232
www.newportstorm.com/index.asp

BRANDS:
Newport Storm Annual Limited Release
Newport Storm Blizzard Porter (49 SRM, 30 IBU)
Newport Storm Cyclone Series - Derek Stout
Newport Storm Hurricane Amber Ale (16 SRM, 24 IBU)
Newport Storm Maelstrom IPA (13 SRM, 48 IBU)
Newport Storm Regenschauer Oktoberfest (14 SRM, 17 IBU)
Newport Storm Rhode Island Blueberry (9 SRM, 11 IBU)
Newport Storm Thunderhead Irish Red (32 SRM, 31IBU)

States Available: CT, MA, RI, VA

The Narragansett Brewing Company

60 Ship Street
Providence, RI 02903
401-437-8970
www.narragansettbeer.com

BRANDS:
Narragansett Beer

States Available: MA, RI

GEOGRAPHIC BREWER INDEX (Alphabetical)

The following brewers distribute their brands in Rhode Island:

Allagash Brewing Company	Moylan's Brewing Company
Anchor Brewing Company	Otter Creek Brewing Company
Anderson Valley Brewing	Pabst Brewing Company
Anheuser-Busch, Inc.	Paper City Brewery Company
Bard's Tale Beer Company	Pete's Brewing
Berkshire Brewing Company	Redhook Ale Brewery
Blue Point Brewing	Rogue Ales
Boulder Beer Company	SAB Miller Corp
Brewery Ommegang	Shipyard Brewing Company
Brooklyn Brewery	Sierra Nevada Brewing Company
Buzzards Bay Brewing Company	Smuttynose Brewing Company
Casco Bay Brewing Company	South Hampton Publick House
Cisco Brewers Inc.	Southern Tier Brewing Company
Clipper City Brewing Company	Spanish Peaks Brewing Company/
Coastal Extreme Brewing Company LLC	United States Beverage
Concord Brewery, Inc.	Stone Coast Brewing Company
Cooperstown Brewing Company	The Boston Beer Company
Cottrell Brewing Company	The Long Trail Brewing Company
D L Geary Brewing Company	The Matt Brewing
Dogfish Head Craft Brewery	The Narragansett Brewing Company
Franconia Notch Brewing Company	The Sea Dog Brewing Company
Great Divide Brewing Company	Three Floyds Brewing Company
Harpoon Brewery	Tremont Brewery/Atlantic Coast Brewing
High Falls Brewing	Company
Lake Placid Craft Brewing	Trout Brook Brewing Company
Lakefront Brewery Inc.	Wagner Valley Brewing Company
Magic Hat Brewing Company	Weyerbacher Brewing Company
Mercury Brewing Company	Widmer Brothers Brewing Company
Molson Coors Brewing Company	

Charleston Brewing Company

SC

557 East Bay Street, Suite #21482
Charleston, SC 29403
843-200-0070
www.charlestonbrewing.com

BRANDS:
Charleston Brewing East Bay IPA
Charleston Brewing Half Moon Hefeweizen

States Available: GA, NC, SC

New South Brewing Company (Kegs/Growlers)

851 Campbell Street
Myrtle Beach, SC 29577
843-916-2337
www.newsouthbrewing.com

BRANDS:
New South India Pale Ale
New South Lager
New South Nut Brown Ale
New South Oktoberfest
New South White Ale

States Available: NC, SC

Palmetto Brewing Company, Inc.

289 Huger Street
Charleston, SC 29403-4522
803-937-0903

BRANDS:
Palmetto Brewing Amber Lager
Palmetto Brewing Lager
Palmetto Brewing Pale Ale
Palmetto Brewing Porter

States Available: SC

R.J. Rockers Brewing Company

113D Belton Drive
Spartanburg, SC 29302
864-587-1435
www.rjrockers.com

BRANDS:
R.J. Rockers Bald Eagle Brown (18 SRM, 25 IBU)
R.J. Rockers Buckwheat (4 SRM, 18 IBU)
R.J. Rockers First Snow Ale (8 SRM, 30 IBU)
R.J. Rockers Liberty Light (4 SRM, 25 IBU)
R.J. Rockers Patriot Pale Ale (6 SRM, 40 IBU)
R.J. Rockers Star Spangled Stout (60 SRM, 25 IBU)

States Available: NC, SC

Thomas Creek Brewery – *page 563*

2054 Piedmont Highway
Greenville, SC 29605-4840
864-605-1166
www.thomascreekbeer.com

BRANDS:
Thomas Creek Amber Ale (19.7 IBU)
Thomas Creek Dopplebock (20.7 IBU)
Thomas Creek IPA (45.8 IBU)
Thomas Creek Jingle Bell Bock (38.1 IBU)
Thomas Creek Multi Grain Ale (19.4 IBU)
Thomas Creek Octoberfest (18.9 IBU)
Thomas Creek Pilsner (18.2 IBU)
Thomas Creek Porter (40 IBU)
Thomas Creek Red Ale (14 IBU) – *page 563*
Thomas Creek Vanilla Cream Ale (15.8 IBU)

States Available: GA, NC, SC, TN

The following brewers distribute their brands in South Carolina:

Abita Brewing Company	Pete's Brewing
Anchor Brewing Company	Pittsburgh Brewing Company
Anheuser-Busch, Inc.	R.J. Rockers Brewing Company
Baltimore-Washington Beer Works	Redhook Ale Brewery
Bard's Tale Beer Company	Rogue Ales
Brooklyn Brewery	SAB Miller Corp
Carolina Beer & Beverage Company	Shipyard Brewing Company
Catawba Valley Brewing	Shmaltz Brewing Company
Charleston Brewing Company	Sierra Nevada Brewing Company
D.G. Yuengling & Son, Inc.	Spanish Peaks Brewing Company/
D L Geary Brewing Company	United States Beverage
Duck-Rabbit Craft Brewery	St.George Brewing Company
Flying Dog Brewery, LLC	Sweetwater Brewing
Frederick Brewing Company	Terrapin Beer Company
Harpoon Brewery	The Boston Beer Company
High Falls Brewing	The Fort Collins Brewery
Highland Brewing	The Matt Brewing
MacTarnahan's Brewing Company	The Sea Dog Brewing Company
Molson Coors Brewing Company	The Spoetzl Brewing
New South Brewing Company	Thomas Creek Brewery
North Coast Brewing Company	Tremont Brewery/Atlantic Coast Brewing
Otter Creek Brewing Company	Company
Pabst Brewing Company	Widmer Brothers Brewing Company
Palmetto Brewing Company Inc.	

New Knoxville Brewing Company

TN

708 E Depot Avenue
Knoxville, TN 37917-7611
865-522-0029
www.newknoxvillebrewery.com

BRANDS:
New Knoxville Brewing Honey Wheat
New Knoxville Brewing India Pale Ale
New Knoxville Brewing Porter
New Knoxville Brewing Traditional Pale Ale
New Knoxville Brewing XX Pale Ale

States Available: Contact Brewery

Yazoo Brewing

1200 Clinton Street, #110
Nashville, TN 37203
615-320-0290
www.yazoobrew.com

BRANDS:
Yazoo Brewing Amarillo Pale Ale
Yazoo Brewing Dos Perros
Yazoo Brewing Hefeweizen
Yazoo Brewing Onward Stout
Yazoo Brewing Sly Rye Porter
Yazoo Brewing Yazoo ESB

States Available: IN

GEOGRAPHIC BREWER INDEX (Alphabetical)

The following brewers distribute their brands in Tennessee:

Abita Brewing Company	Pyramid Brewery
Anchor Brewing Company	Redhook Ale Brewery
Anheuser-Busch, Inc.	Rogue Ales
Avery Brewing Company	SAB Miller Corp
Bluegrass Beer Company	Shipyard Brewing Company
BridgePort Brewing Company	Shmaltz Brewing Company
Carolina Beer & Beverage Company	Sierra Nevada Brewing Company
Catawba Valley Brewing	Spanish Peaks Brewing Company/
Dogfish Head Craft Brewery	United States Beverage
Duck-Rabbit Craft Brewery	Stone Brewing Company
Flying Dog Brewery, LLC	Sweetwater Brewing
Great Divide Brewing Company	Terrapin Beer Company
Harpoon Brewery	The Black Mountain/Chili Beer Company
High Falls Brewing	The Boston Beer Company
Highland Brewing	The Sea Dog Brewing Company
Lakefront Brewery Inc.	The Spoetzl Brewing
Left Handed Brewing Company	Thomas Creek Brewery
Lost Coast Brewery & Café	Tremont Brewery/Atlantic Coast Brewing
MacTarnahan's Brewing Company	Company
Molson Coors Brewing Company	Widmer Brothers Brewing Company
North Coast Brewing Company	Yazoo Brewing
Pabst Brewing Company	Zuma Brewing Company (Cancun
Pete's Brewing	Brewery)
Pittsburgh Brewing Company	

Healthy Brew
6435 Nine Mile Bridge Road
Fort Worth, TX 76135
817-238-1334
www.healthybrew.com

<u>BRANDS:</u>
Healthy Brew 1-Day IPA
Healthy Brew Easy Amber
Healthy Brew Snowman's Revenge
Healthy Brew Strong Stout
Healthy Brew Wheat Serenity

States Available: Contact Brewery

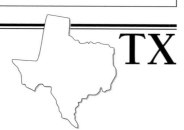

Independence Brewing
3913 Todd Lane #607
Austin, TX 78744
512-797-7879
www.independencebrewing.com

<u>BRANDS:</u>
Independence Brewing Bootlegger Brown Ale (14 IBU)
Independence Brewing Freestyle Wheat Beer (15 IBU)
Independence Brewing Jasperilla Old Ale (29 IBU)
Independence Brewing Pale Ale (39 IBU)

States Available: TX

Pabst Brewing Company
P.O. Box 792627
San Antonio, TX 78279
210-226-0231
www.pabst.com

<u>BRANDS:</u>
Ballantine Ale
Blatz
Carling Black Label
Colt 45
Country Club Malt Liquor
Haffenreffer's Private Stock
Lone Star
Lone Star Light
McSorley's Black & Tan
McSorley's Irish Ale
National Bohemian
Old Milwaukee
Old Milwaukee Ice
Old Milwaukee Light
Old Milwaukee Non-Alcoholic
Old Style
Old Style Light
Olympia
Pabst Blue Ribbon
Pabst Blue Ribbon Light
Pabst Blue Ribbon Non-Alcoholic
Pearl
Piels
Piels Light
Rainer
Rainer Ale

GEOGRAPHIC BREWER INDEX (Alphabetical)

Rainer Light
Schaefer
Schlitz
Schlitz Bull Ice
Schlitz Malt Liquor
Schlitz Red Bull
Schmidt's
Schmidt's Ice
Schmidt's Light
Special Export
Special Export Light
St.Ides
Stag
Stroh's
Stroh's Light

States Available: All 50 States

Pete's Brewing (Gambrinus)

14800 San Pedro Avenue, Third Floor
San Antonio, TX 78232
210-490-9128
www.peteswicked.com

BRANDS:
Pete's Wicked Ale (18 IBU)
Pete's Wicked Strawberry Blonde(19 IBU)
Pete's Wicked Wanderlust Cream Ale (18 IBU)
Pete's Wicked Rally Cap Ale (22 IBU)

States Available: All 50 States

Rahr & Sons Brewing Company

701 Galveston Avenue
Fort Worth, TX 76104
817-810-9266
www.rahrbrewing.com

BRANDS:
Rahr Brewing Blonde Lager (3 SRM, 19 IBU)
Rahr Brewing Bucking Bock – Miabock (10 SRM, 30 IBU)
Rahr Brewing Buffalo Batt Beer (20 SRM, 24 IBU)
Rahr Brewing Pecker Wrecker Imperial Pilsner (8 SRM, 62 IBU)
Rahr Brewing Rahr's Red (17 SRM, 22 IBU)
Rahr Brewing Summer Time Wheat (4 SRM, 18 IBU)
Rahr Brewing Ugly Pug (30 SRM, 24 IBU)

States Available: TX

Real Ale Brewing Company

405 Third Street
Blanco, TX 78606
830-833-2534
www.realalebrewing.com

BRANDS:
Real Ale Brewing Brewhouse Brown Ale
Real Ale Brewing Fireman's #4 Blonde Ale
Real Ale Brewing Full Moon Pale Rye Ale
Real Ale Brewing Rio Blanco Pale Ale
Real Ale Brewing Shade Grown Coffee Porter
Real Ale Brewing Sisyphus Barleywine Ale

States Available: Contact Brewery

Saint Arnold Brewing Company – *page 538*

2522 Fairway Park Drive
Houston, TX 77092-7607
713-686-9494
www.saintarnold.com

BRANDS:
Saint Arnold Brewing Abbey American Quadruppel
Saint Arnold Brewing Amber Ale (31 IBU) – *page 538*
Saint Arnold Brewing Barleywine
Saint Arnold Brewing Brown Ale (24 IBU)
Saint Arnold Brewing Christmas Ale (35 IBU)
Saint Arnold Brewing Double IPA
Saint Arnold Brewing Elissa IPA (60 IBU)
Saint Arnold Brewing Fancy Lawnmower Beer (20 IBU)
Saint Arnold Brewing Oktoberfest (24 IBU)
Saint Arnold Brewing Spring Bock (24 IBU)
Saint Arnold Brewing Summer Pils (41 IBU)
Saint Arnold Brewing Texas Wheat (18 IBU)
Saint Arnold Brewing Winter Stout (36 IBU)

States Available: TX

GEOGRAPHIC BREWER INDEX (Alphabetical)

Stampede Brewing Company

100 Highland Park Village #200
Dallas, TX 75205
214-295-3255
www.stampedebeer.com

BRANDS:

Stampede Light

States Available: Contact Brewery

The Spoetzl Brewing (Gambrinus)

603 East Brewery Street
Shiner, TX 77984
361-594-3383
www.shiner.com

BRANDS:

Shiner 96 Marzen Style Ale
Shiner Blonde
Shiner Bock
Shiner Dunkelweizen
Shiner Hefeweizen
Shiner Kölsch
Shiner Light

States Available: AK, AL, AR, AZ, CA, CO, FL, GA, IA, ID, KS, KY, LA, MD,
MN, MO, MS, MT, NC, NE, NM, NV, OH, OK, OR, SC, TN,
TX, UT, VA, WA, WY

The following brewers distribute their brands in Texas:

Abita Brewing Company	Pabst Brewing Company
Allagash Brewing Company	Pete's Brewing
Anchor Brewing Company	Pittsburgh Brewing Company
Anheuser-Busch, Inc.	Pyramid Brewery
Avery Brewing Company	Rarh & Sons Brewing Company
Bard's Tale Beer Company	Redhook Ale Brewery
Bayhawk Ales Inc.	Rogue Ales
Breckenridge Brewery	SAB Miller Corp
Brewery Ommegang	Saint Arnold Brewing Company
BridgePort Brewing Company	Santa Fe Brewing Company
Dogfish Head Craft Brewery	Shipyard Brewing Company
Flying Dog Brewery, LLC	Sierra Nevada Brewing Company
Full Sail Brewing Company	Spanish Peaks Brewing Company/
Great Divide Brewing Company	United States Beverage
High Falls Brewing	Stone Brewing Company
Independence Brewing	The Black Mountain/Chili Beer Company
Lagunitas Brewing	The Boston Beer Company
Left Handed Brewing Company	The Sea Dog Brewing Company
MacTarnahan's Brewing Company	The Spoetzl Brewing
Michigan Brewing Company, Inc.	Tommyknocker Brewery
Molson Coors Brewing Company	Tremont Brewery/Atlantic Coast Brewing
New Belgium Brewing Company	Company
North Coast Brewing Company	Victory Brewing Company

Four Plus Brewing Company
UT

1722 South Fremont Drive (2375 West)
Salt Lake City, UT 84104
801-467-0909

BRANDS:

Four Plus DUNK'L Amber Wheat (15 SRM, 24 IBU)
Four Plus Monkshine Belgian Style Pale Ale (9 SRM, 19 IBU)
Four Plus PUNK'N Pumpkin Harvest Ale (13 SRM, 118 IBU)
Four Plus WILDFIRE Extra Pale Ale (8 SRM, 41 IBU)

States Available: CA, ID, NV, UT, VA

GEOGRAPHIC BREWER INDEX (Alphabetical)

Moab Brewery

685 South Main Street
Moab, UT 84532
435-259-6333
www.themoabbrewery.com

BRANDS:

Dead Horse Amber Ale

Scorpion Pale Ale

States Available: UT

Uinta Brewing Company – *page 568*

1722 South Fremont Drive (2375 West)
Salt Lake City, UT 84104
801-467-0909
www.uintabrewing.com

BRANDS:

Uinta Brewing Anglers Pale Ale (10 SRM, 39 IBU)

Uinta Brewing Anniversary Barley Wine (18 SRM, 72 IBU)

Uinta Brewing Blue Sky Pilsner (4 SRM, 20 IBU)

Uinta Brewing Bristlecone Brown Ale

Uinta Brewing Cutthroat Pale Ale (14 SRM, 22 IBU)

Uinta Brewing Gelande Amber Lager (15 SRM, 22 IBU)

Uinta Brewing Golden Spike Hefeweizen (8 SRM, 18 IBU)

Uinta Brewing King's Peak Porter (32 SRM, 25 IBU)

Uinta Brewing Solstice Kölsch (5 SRM, 25 IBU) – *page 568*

Uinta Brewing Trader IPA (10 SRM, 42 IBU)

States Available: CA, ID, NV, UT, VA

Utah Brewers Cooperative/Wasatch

1763 South 300 West
Salt Lake City, UT 84115
801-466-8855
www.utahbeers.com

BRANDS:

Chasing Tail Golden Ale

Squatters Captain Bastard's Oatmeal Stout

Squatters Full Suspension Pale Ale

Squatters Hefeweizen

Squatters India Pale Ale

Squatters Provo Girl Pilsner

Wasatch 1st Amendment Lager

Wasatch Apricot Hefe-Weizen

Wasatch Bobsled Brown Ale

Wasatch Evolution Amber Ale

Wasatch Polygamy Porter

Wasatch Pumpkin Ale

Wasatch Raspberry Wheat Beer

Wasatch Special Reserve Pale Ale

States Available: UT

The following brewers distribute their brands in Utah:

Anchor Brewing Company	SAB Miller Corp
Anderson Valley Brewing	Santa Fe Brewing Company
Anheuser-Busch, Inc.	Shipyard Brewing Company
Bard's Tale Beer Company	Sierra Nevada Brewing Company
Boulder Beer Company	Snake River Brewing Company
Four Plus Brewing Company	Spanish Peaks Brewing Company/
Full Sail Brewing Company	United States Beverage
Grand Teton Brewing Company	The Boston Beer Company
Kona Brewing, LLC	The Sea Dog Brewing Company
Moab Brewery	The Spoetzl Brewing
Molson Coors Brewing Company	Tremont Brewery/Atlantic Coast Brewing
Pabst Brewing Company	Company
Pete's Brewing	Uinta Brewing Company
Pyramid Brewery	Utah Brewers Cooperative
Rogue Ales	

GEOGRAPHIC BREWER INDEX (Alphabetical)

Blue & Gray Brewing Company, Inc.

VA

3321A Dill Smith Drive
Fredricksburg, VA 22408
540-538-2379
www.blueandgraybrewingco.com

BRANDS:
Blue & Gray Classic Lager
Falmouth American Pale Ale
Fred Red Ale
Spiced Winter Ale (Nov. - Jan.)
Stonewall Stout
Von Steuben Oktoberfest (Sept. - Oct)

States Available: VA

Legend Brewing Company

321 W Seventh Street
Richmond, VA 23224-2307
804-232-8871
www.legendbrewing.com

BRANDS:
Legend Brewing Brown Ale
Legend Brewing Golden IPA (35 IBU)
Legend Brewing Lager
Legend Brewing Legend Oktoberfest (25 IBU)
Legend Brewing Legend Pale Ale
Legend Brewing Pilsner (40 IBU)
Legend Brewing Porter

States Available: VA

Old Dominion Brewing Company

44633 Guiliford Drive
Ashburn, VA 20147
703-742-9100
www.olddominion.com

BRANDS:
Dominion Ale
Dominion Lager
Dominion Millennium
Dominion Oak Barrel Stout
Dominion Octoberfest
Dominion Pale Ale
Dominion Spring Brew
Dominion Summer Wheat
Dominion Winter Brew
New River Pale Ale
Tuppers' Hop Pocket Ale
Tuppers' Hop Pocket Pils

States Available: DC, GA, MD, NC, OH, – Tuppers' and New River Only, PA, VA, WV

Shenandoah Brewing Company

652 S Pickett Street
Alexandria, VA 22034
703-823-9508
www.shenandoahbrewing.com

BRANDS:
Shenandoah Brewing Big Meadow Pale Ale
Shenandoah Brewing Black and Tan Beer
Shenandoah Brewing Old Rag Mountain Ale
Shenandoah Brewing Skyland Red Ale
Shenandoah Brewing Stony Man Stout
Shenandoah Brewing White Water Wheat

States Available: DC, VA

GEOGRAPHIC BREWER INDEX (Alphabetical)

St. George Brewing Company – *page 553*

204 Challenger Way
Hampton, VA 23666
757-865-7781
www.stgeorgebrewingco.com

BRANDS:
St. George Brewing Company Golden Ale (6.9 SRM, 33 IBU)
St. George Brewing Company IPA (9 SRM, 50 IBU) – *page 553*
St. George Brewing Company Pale Ale
St. George Brewing Company Porter (81.1 SRM, 32 IBU)
St. George Brewing Company Vienna Lager (22 IBU)
St. George Brewing Fall Bock (28 IBU)

States Available: NC, SC, VA

Starr Hill Brewery

5391 Three Notched Road
Crozet, VA 22932
434-823-5671
www.starrhillbeer.com

BRANDS:
Starr Hill Amber Ale
Starr Hill Dark Starr Stout
Starr Hill Jomo Lager
Starr Hill Pale Ale

States Available: Contact Brewery

Williamsburg AleWerks

189-B Ewell Road
Williamsburg, VA 23188
757-220-3670
www.williamsburgalewerks.com

BRANDS:
Williamsburg AleWerks Brown Ale
Williamsburg AleWerks Chesapeake Pale Ale
Williamsburg AleWerks Colonial Wheat Ale
Williamsburg AleWerks Drake Tail India Pale Ale
Williamsburg AleWerks Washington's Porter
Williamsburg AleWerks Winter Barleywine

States Available: Contact Brewery

The following brewers distribute their brands in Virginia:

Abita Brewing Company	North Coast Brewing Company
Allagash Brewing Company	Old Dominion Brewing Company
Anchor Brewing Company	Oskar Blues Grill & Brew
Anderson Valley Brewing	Otter Creek Brewing Company
Anheuser-Busch, Inc.	Pabst Brewing Company
Avery Brewing Company	Pete's Brewing
Baltimore-Washington Beer Works	Pittsburgh Brewing Company
Bard's Tale Beer Company	Pyramid Brewery
Bear Republic Brewing Company	ReaperAle, Inc.
Bison Brewing	Redhook Ale Brewery
Blue & Gray Brewing Company, Inc.	Rogue Ales
Bluegrass Beer Company	SAB Miller Corp
Breckenridge Brewery	Shenandoah Brewing Company
Brewery Ommegang	Shipyard Brewing Company
Brooklyn Brewery	Shmaltz Brewing Company
Carolina Beer & Beverage Company	Sierra Nevada Brewing Company
Clipper City Brewing Company	Smuttynose Brewing Company
Coastal Extreme Brewing Company LLC	Spanish Peaks Brewing Company/
D.G. Yuengling & Son, Inc.	United States Beverage
D L Geary Brewing Company	Speakeasy Ales & Lagers, Inc.
Dogfish Head Craft Brewery	Sprecher Brewing
Edenton Brewing Company	St.George Brewing Company
Florida Beer Company	Stone Brewing Company
Fordham Brewing Company	Stoudt's Brewing Company
Four Plus Brewing Company	The Black Mountain/Chili Beer Company
Frederick Brewing Company	The Boston Beer Company
Great Divide Brewing Company	The Fort Collins Brewery
Harpoon Brewery	The Matt Brewing
High Falls Brewing	The Sea Dog Brewing Company
Lagunitas Brewing	The Spoetzl Brewing
Lakefront Brewery Inc.	The Weeping Radish Brewery
Lancaster Brewing Company	Three Floyds Brewing Company
Left Handed Brewing Company	Tommyknocker Brewery
Legend Brewing Company	Tremont Brewery/Atlantic Coast Brewing
Lost Coast Brewery & Café	Company
MacTarnahan's Brewing Company	Tröegs Brewing Company
Mad River Brewing	Uinta Brewing Company
Magic Hat Brewing Company	Victory Brewing Company
Michigan Brewing Company, Inc.	Weyerbacher Brewing Company
Molson Coors Brewing Company	Widmer Brothers Brewing Company
New Century Brewing Company	Yards Brewing
New River Brewing Company	

GEOGRAPHIC BREWER INDEX (Alphabetical)

VT

Hornpout Brewing
1713 Industrial Parkway #106
Lyndonville, VT 05851
802-748-2198

BRANDS:
Hornpout No Limit Amber Ale
Hornpout Pale Ale

States Available: Contact Brewery

The Long Trail Brewing Company – *page 513*
Jct. Route 4 & 100A, P.O. Box 168
Bridgewater Corners, VT 05035-0168
802-672-5011
www.longtrail.com

BRANDS:
Blackberry Wheat (8 IBU) – *page 514*
Brewmasters Limited Edition Series – Unfiltered IPA
  (56 IBU) – *page 514*
Double Bag (25 IBU)
Harvest (24 IBU) – *page 515*
Hefeweizen (14 IBU) – *page 515*
Hibernator (25 IBU) – *page 516*
Hit the Trail (25 IBU)
Long Trail Ale (30 IBU) – *page 513*
Traditional IPA (56 IBU) – *page 516*

States Available: CT, MA, ME, NH, NJ, NY, RI, VT

Magic Hat Brewing Company
5 Bartlett Bay Road
South Burlington, VT 05403-7727
802-658-2739
www.magichat.net

BRANDS:
Magic Hat Brewing #9 (9 SRM, 18 IBU)
Magic Hat Brewing Blind Faith (12.5 SRM, 40 IBU)
Magic Hat Brewing Circus Boy (5 SRM, 18 IBU)
Magic Hat Brewing Fat Angel (9.2 SRM, 29 IBU)
Magic Hat Brewing HI.P.A. (6.8 SRM, 45 IBU)
Magic Hat Brewing Hocus Pocus(4.5 SRM, 13 IBU)
Magic Hat Brewing Jinx (22 SRM, 20 IBU)
Magic Hat Brewing Mother Lager (3.2 SRM, 17 IBU)
Magic Hat Brewing Participation Ale (54 SRM, 28 IBU)
Magic Hat Brewing Ravell (63.6 SRM, 22 IBU)
Magic Hat Brewing Roxy Rolles

States Available: CT, DE, MA, MD, ME, NH, NJ, NY, PA, RI, VA, VT

Otter Creek Brewing Company – *page 527*
793 Exchange Street
Middlebury, VT 05753
800-473-0727
www.ottercreekbrewing.com

BRANDS:
Otter Creek Brewing Alpine Ale (36 IBU)
Otter Creek Brewing Anniversary IPA
Otter Creek Brewing Copper Ale (21 IBU) – *page 527*
Otter Creek Brewing ESB
Otter Creek Brewing Oktoberfest (19 IBU)
Otter Creek Brewing Otter Summer Ale
Otter Creek Brewing Pale Ale (23 IBU)
Otter Creek Brewing Stovepipe Porter (30 IBU)
Otter Creek Brewing Vermont Lager (26 IBU)
Wolaver's Organic Brown Ale (21 IBU) – *page 573*
Wolaver's Organic India Pale Ale (55 IBU)
Wolaver's Organic Oatmeal Stout (40 IBU)
Wolaver's Organic Pale Ale (34 IBU)
Wolaver's Organic Wit Bier

States Available: CA, CT, IL, MA, MO, NC, NH, NJ, NY, OH, OR, PA, RI, VA, VT, WA, WI

GEOGRAPHIC BREWER INDEX (Alphabetical)

Rock Art Brewery, LLC – *page 535*

254 Wilkens Street
Morrisville, VT 05661
802-888-9400
www.rockartbrewery.com

BRANDS:
Rock Art Brewery American Red Ale (14 IBU)
Rock Art Brewery Brown Bear Ale (11 IBU)
Rock Art Brewery Hell's Bock (75 IBU)
Rock Art Brewery India Pale Ale (22 IBU)
Rock Art Brewery Infusco (25 IBU)
Rock Art Brewery Magnumus ete Tomahawkus (80 IBU) – *page 535*
Rock Art Brewery Midnight Madness Smoked Porter (27 IBU)
Rock Art Brewery Ridge Runner Mild Barleywine (23 IBU)
Rock Art Brewery River Runner Summer Ale (12 IBU)
Rock Art Brewery Stock Ale (18 IBU)
Rock Art Brewery Stump Jumper Stout (40 IBU)
Rock Art Brewery Sunny and 75 (10 IBU)
Rock Art Brewery The Riddler (32 IBU)
Rock Art Brewery The Vermonster (100 IBU)
Rock Art Brewery Trail Cutter Dark Lager (12 IBU)
Rock Art Brewery Vermont Maple Wheat (8 IBU)
Rock Art Brewery Whitetail Ale (28 IBU)

States Available: Central NJ, VT

Trout River Brewing Company

P.O. Box 165
Lyndonville, VT 05851
802-626-9396
www.troutriverbrewing.com

BRANDS:
Trout River Brewing Chocolate Oatmeal Stout
Trout River Brewing Hoppin' Mad Trout
Trout River Brewing Rainbow Red Ale
Trout River Brewing Scottish Ale

States Available: NH, OR, VT

The following brewers distribute their brands in Vermont:

Allagash Brewing Company	Ramapo Valley Brewery
Anchor Brewing Company	Redhook Ale Brewery
Anheuser-Busch, Inc.	Rock Art Brewery, LLC
Bard's Tale Beer Company	Rogue Ales
Berkshire Brewing Company	SAB Miller Corp
Brewery Ommegang	Shipyard Brewing Company
Buzzards Bay Brewing Company	Sierra Nevada Brewing Company
D L Geary Brewing Company	Smuttynose Brewing Company
Dogfish Head Craft Brewery	Spanish Peaks Brewing Company/
Flying Dog Brewery, LLC	United States Beverage
Gritty McDuff's Brewing Company	Stone Coast Brewing Company
Harpoon Brewery	The Boston Beer Company
High Falls Brewing	The Long Trail Brewing Company
Lake Placid Craft Brewing	The Matt Brewing
MacTarnahan's Brewing Company	The Sea Dog Brewing Company
Magic Hat Brewing Company	Tremont Brewery/Atlantic Coast Brewing
Molson Coors Brewing Company	Company
Otter Creek Brewing Company	Trout River Brewing Company
Pabst Brewing Company	Widmer Brothers Brewing Company
Pete's Brewing	

Baron Brewing

WA

1605 South 93rd Street, Bldg E Unit L
Seattle, WA 98108
206-764-1213
www.baronbeer.com

BRANDS:
Baron Bavarian Weizen
Baron Berliner-Weisse
Baron Bock
Baron Dampf Bier
Baron Doppelbock
Baron Dunkel-Weisse
Baron Dusseldof Altbier
Baron Hefe-Weisse (SRM 5, IBU 15)
Baron Helles Bock
Baron Liberator Doppelbock (SRM 25, IBU 20)
Baron Munich Helles Lager
Baron Oktoberfest (SRM 13, IBU 15)
Baron Pils (SRM 2.5, IBU 35)
Baron Rauchbier
Baron Roggen
Baron Schwarzbier (SRM 25, IBU 13)
Baron Uber-Weisse

States Available: WA

GEOGRAPHIC BREWER INDEX (Alphabetical)

Boundary Bay Brewing Company

1107 Railroad Avenue
Bellingham, WA 98225
360-647-5593
www.bbaybrewery.com

BRANDS:
Boundary Bay Best Bitter
Boundary Bay Cabin Fever
Boundary Bay Inside Passage Ale
Boundary Bay Scotch
Boundary BayBarley Wine

States Available: WA

Dick's Brewing Company – page 491

540 Clover Lane
5945 Prather Road
Centralla, WA 98531
800-586-7760
www.dicksbeer.com

BRANDS:
Bottleworks India Pale Ale
Dick's Barley Wine Ale
Dick's Belgian Double
Dick's Belgian Tripel
Dick's Best Bitter
Dick's Cream Stout
Dick's Danger Ale – *page 491*
Dick's Double Diamond Winter Ale
Dick's Grand Cru
Dick's Harvest Ale
Dick's Imperial Stout
Dick's India Pale Ale
Dick's Irish Ale
Dick's Lave Rock Porter
Dick's Mountain Ale
Dick's Pale Ale
Dick's Rye Ale
Dick's Silk Lady
Dick's Smoked Porter
Dick's Working Man's Brown Ale

States Available: OR, WA

Elysian Brewing Company

1221 East Pike Street
Seattle, WA 98122
206-860-1920
www.elysianbrewing.com

BRANDS:
Ambrosia Maibock
Avatar Jasmine IPA
Bete Blanche Belgian-Style Tripel (31 IBU)
Bifrost Winter Ale (42 IBU)
Dragonstooth Stout (36 IBU)
Elysian Fields Pale Ale (36 IBU)
Immortal India Pale Ale (42 IBU)
Loki Lager
Night Owl Pumpkin Ale
Pandora's Bock
Perseus Porter (25 IBU)
Saison Elysee
The Wise Extra Special Bitter (39 IBU)
Zephyrus Pilsner (38 IBU)

States Available: AK, ID, OR, WA

Far West Brewing Company

7289 West Lake Sammamish Parkway NE
Redmond, WA 98052
425-883-2432
www.farwestbrewing.com

BRANDS:
Hedgerow Red
Ranger IPA
Three Threads Porter

States Available: WA

GEOGRAPHIC BREWER INDEX (Alphabetical)

Fish Brewing Company – *page 496*

515 Jefferson Street SE
Olympia, WA 98501
360-943-3650
www.fishbrewing.com

BRANDS:
Fish Tale Blonde Ale (15 IBU)
Fish Tale Detonator Doppelbock Lager (44 IBU)
Fish Tale Leviathan Barleywine (62 IBU)
Fish Tale Monkfish Belgian-style Triple Ale (32 IBU)
Fish Tale Mudshark Porter (24 IBU)
Fish Tale Old Woody English Old Ale
Fish Tale Organic Amber Ale (22 IBU)
Fish Tale Organic India Pale Ale (53 IBU) – *page 496*
Fish Tale Poseidon's Imperial Stout (79 IBU)
Fish Tale Thornton Creek Ale (45 IBU)
Fish Tale Trout Stout (31 IBU)
Fish Tale Wild Salmon Organic Pale Ale (32 IBU)
Fish Tale Winterfish Ale (70 IBU)
Leavenworth Beers Blind Pig Dunkle Weizen Ale (25 IBU)
Leavenworth Beers Friesian Pilsner (40 IBU)
Leavenworth Beers Hodgson's India Pale Ale (80 IBU)
Leavenworth Beers Ingall's Extra Special Bitter (64IBU)
Leavenworth Beers Nosferatu Red Ale (55 IBU)
Leavenworth Beers Oktoberfest Bier (23 IBU)
Leavenworth Beers Snowblind Winter Warmer
Leavenworth Beers Spring Bock Lager
Leavenworth Beers Whistling Pig Hefeweizen (22 IBU)

States Available: WA

Hale's Ales

4301 Leary Way NW
Seattle, WA 98107
206-706-1544
www.halesales.com

BRANDS:
Hale's Cream Ale
Hale's Cream H.S.B.
Hale's Cream Stout
Hale's Drawbridge Blonde
Hale's Irish Style Nut Brown Ale
Hale's Mongoose IPA
Hale's O'Brien's Harvest Ale
Hale's Pale American Ale
Hale's Red Menance Big Amber
Hale's Troll Porter
Hale's Wee Heavy Winter Ale

States Available: Contact Brewery

Hood Canal Brewing

26499 Bond Road North East
Kingston, WA 98346
360-267-8316
www.hoodcanalbrewery.com

BRANDS:
Hood Canal Brewing Agate Pass Amber
Hood Canal Brewing Big Beef Oatmeal Stout
Hood Canal Brewing Dabob Bay India Pale Ale
Hood Canal Brewing Dosewallipps Special Ale
Hood Canal Brewing Southpoint Porter

States Available: Contact brewery

Geographic Brewer Index (Alphabetical)

Ice Harbor Brewing Company

206 North Benton Street
Kennewick, WA 99336-3665
509-582-5340
www.iceharbor.com

BRANDS:
Ice Harbor Brewing Barley Wine Style Ale (84 IBU)
Ice Harbor Brewing Columbia Kölsch
Ice Harbor Brewing Harvest Pale Ale (40 IBU)
Ice Harbor Brewing Runaway Red Ale (25 IBU)
Ice Harbor Brewing Sternwheeler Stout (30 IBU)

States Available: OR, WA

Iron Horse Brewery

1000 Prospect Street, Suite 4
Ellensburg, WA 98926
509-933-3134
www.iron-horse-brewery.com

BRANDS:
Iron Horse Brown Ale
Iron Horse India Pale Ale
Iron Horse Loco-Motive Ale
Iron Horse Rodeo Extra Pale Ale

States Available: WA

LaConner Brewing Company

117 South First Street
LaConner, WA 98257
360-466-1415

BRANDS:
Skagit Sculler's IPA

States Available: Contact Brewery

Maritime Pacific Brewing Company

1514 North West Leary Way
Seattle, WA 98107
206-782-6181
www.maritimebrewery.citysearch.com

BRANDS:
Maritime Pacific Flagship Red Ale
Maritime Pacific Imperial Pale
Maritime Pacific Islander Pale
Maritime Pacific Nightwatch Dark

States Available: WA

Pike Brewing Company

1415 First Avenue
Seattle, WA 98101
206-622-6044
www.pikebrewing.com

BRANDS:
Pike Brewing Company India Pale Ale
Pike Brewing Company Kilt Lifter Scotch Ale
Pike Brewing Company Monk's Uncle
Pike Brewing Company Naughty Nellie Ale
Pike Brewing Company Old Bawdy Barley Wine
Pike Brewing Company Pale Ale
Pike Brewing Company Tandem
Pike Brewing Company XXXXX Stout

States Available: AK, ID, MT, OR, UT, WA

Port Townsend Brewing Company

330 10th Street
Port Townsend, WA 98368
360-385-9967
www.porttownsendbrewing.com

BRANDS:
Port Townsend Dry-Hopped IPA
Port Townsend Reel Amber

States Available: WA

GEOGRAPHIC BREWER INDEX (Alphabetical)

Pyramid Brewery – *page 529*
91 South Royal Brougham Way
Seattle, WA 98134
206-682-8322
www.pyramidbrew.com

BRANDS:
Pyramid Brewery Amber Weizen (17 IBU) – *page 530*
Pyramid Brewery Apricot Weizen (11 IBU) – *page 530*
Pyramid Brewery Curve Ball Kölsch (18 IBU) – *page 531*
Pyramid Brewery Hefe Weizen (18 IBU) – *page 529*
Pyramid Brewery Snow Cap Ale (47 IBU) – *page 532*
Pyramid Brewery ThunderHead IPA (67 IBU) – *page 531*

States Available: AK, AR, AZ, CA, CO, HI, IA, ID, IL, IN, KS, KY, MD, MI, MN, MO, MT, NC, NE, NM, NV, OH, OK, OR, PA, TN, TX, UT, VA, WA, WY

Redhook Ale Brewery, Inc. – *page 533*
14300 NE 145th Street
Woodinville, WA 98072
425-483-3232
www.redhook.com

BRANDS:
Redhook Ale Brewery Blackhook Porter (51 SRM, 40 IBU)
Redhook Ale Brewery Blonde Ale (8.1 SRM, 18.3 IBU)
Redhook Ale Brewery Copperhook Spring Ale (11SRM, 20 IBU)
Redhook Ale Brewery ESB (13.2 SRM, 28 IBU) – *page 533*
Redhook Ale Brewery IPA (8.4 SRM, 38.5 IBU)
Redhook Ale Brewery Late Harvest Autumn Ale (21 SRM, 32 IBU)
Redhook Ale Brewery Sunrye Summer Ale (4.6 SRM, 16 IBU)
Redhook Ale Brewery Winter Hook Winter Ale (21.7 SRM, 27.6 IBU)

States Available: 48 States (NOT UT, OK)

Rocky Coulee Brewing Company – *page 536*
205 North First Street
Odessa, WA 99159
509-345-2216
www.rockycouleebrewingco.com

BRANDS:
Fireweed Honey Blonde – *page 536*

States Available: WA

Roslyn Brewing Company
208 Pennsylvania Avenue, P.O. Box 24
Roslyn, WA 98941
509-649-2232
www.roslynbrewery.com

BRANDS:
Roslyn Brewing Brookside Pale Lager
Roslyn Brewing Roslyn Dark Lager Beer

States Available: WA

Scuttlebutt Brewing Company
1524 W. Marine View Drive
Everett, WA 98201
425-257-9316
www.scuttlebuttbrewing.com

BRANDS:
Scuttlebutt 10 Below (22 IBU)
Scuttlebutt Amber Ale (23 IBU)
Scuttlebutt Gale Force IPA (96 IBU)
Scuttlebutt Homeport Blonde (17 IBU)
Scuttlebutt Porter (20 IBU)
Scuttlebutt Weizenbock (23 IBU)

States Available: WA

Skagit River Brewery
404 South 3rd Street
Mount Vernon, WA 98273
360-336-2884
www.skagitbrew.com

BRANDS:
Skagit River Brewing Sculler's IPA

States Available: Contact Brewery

GEOGRAPHIC BREWER INDEX (Alphabetical)

Snipes Mountain Brewing Company

905 Yakima Valley Highway, P.O. Box 274
Sunnyside, WA 98944
509-837-2739
www.snipesmountain.com

BRANDS:

Snipes Mountain Brewing Coyote Moon
Snipes Mountain Brewing Crazy Ivan's Imperial Stout
Snipes Mountain Brewing Extra Blonde Ale
Snipes Mountain Brewing Harvest Ale
Snipes Mountain Brewing Hefeweizen
Snipes Mountain Brewing India Pale Ale
Snipes Mountain Brewing Porter
Snipes Mountain Brewing Red Sky Ale
Snipes Mountain Brewing Roza Reserve
Snipes Mountain Brewing Sunnyside Pale Ale

States Available: ID, OR, WA

Snoqualmie Falls Brewing Company

8032 Falls Avenue South East, P.O. Box 924
Snoqualmie, WA 98065
425-831-2357
www.fallsbrew.com

BRANDS:

Avalanche Winter Ale (48 IBU)
Copperhead Pale Ale (32 IBU)
Harvest Moon Festbier (24 IBU)
PGA (Perfectly Great Amber) (23 IBU)
Spring Fever (32 IBU)
Steam Train Porter (28 IBU)
Summer Beer (28 IBU)
Wildcat IPA (75 IBU)

States Available: WA

The Northern Lights Brewing Company

1003 East Trent Avenue
Spokane, WA 99202
509-244-4909
www.nwbrewpage.com

BRANDS:

Northern Lights Blueberry Creme Ale
Northern Lights Chocolate Dunkel
Northern Lights Creme Ale
Northern Lights Crystal Bitter
Northern Lights Pale Ale
Northern Lights Winter Ale

States Available: ID, WA

Whitstran Brewing Company

2800 Lee Road, Ste B
Prosser, WA 99350
509-786-3883

BRANDS:

11th Hour Pale Ale (46 IBU)
Friar Lawrence Belgium-Style Ale (18 IBU)
Friar's Decadence Chocolate Chocolate Imperial Stout (55 IBU)
Friar's Penance Barley Wine (96 IBU)
Highlander Scottish Style Ale (16 IBU)
Horse Heaven Hefe Bavarian Style Hefeweizen (14 IBU)
O2O Heavy Water Stout (63 IBU)
Over-The-Edge Dry-Hopped Pale Ale (46 IBU)
Steamy Cream California Common Ale (14 IBU)

States Available: WA

GEOGRAPHIC BREWER INDEX (Alphabetical)

The following brewers distribute their brands in Washington:

Alaskan Brewing Company
Anchor Brewing Company
Anderson Valley Brewing
Anheuser-Busch, Inc.
Avery Brewing Company
Baron Brewing
Bear Republic Brewing Company
Big Sky Brewing Company
Bison Brewing
Boulder Beer Company
Boundary Bay Brewing Company
Brewery Ommegang
BridgePort Brewing Company
Crested Butte Brewery
Deschutes Brewery
Dick's Brewing Company
Dogfish Head Craft Brewery
Eel River Brewing Company
Elysian Brewing Company
Far West Brewing Company
Fish Brewing Company
Full Sail Brewing Company
Great Divide Brewing Company
Great Northern Brewing Company
Hair of the Dog Brewing Company
High Falls Brewing
Ice Harbor Brewing Company
Iron Horse Brewery
Kona Brewing, LLC
Lagunitas Brewing
Lakefront Brewery Inc.
Lang Creek Brewery

Lost Coast Brewery & Café
MacTarnahan's Brewing Company
Maritime Pacific Brewing Company
Molson Coors Brewing Company
New Belgium Brewing Company
North Coast Brewing Company
Oskar Blues Grill & Brew
Otter Creek Brewing Company
Pabst Brewing Company
Pete's Brewing
Port Townsend Brewing Company
Pyramid Brewery
Redhook Ale Brewery
Rogue Ales
SAB Miller Corp
Scuttlebutt Brewing Company
Shipyard Brewing Company
Sierra Nevada Brewing Company
Snipes Mountain Brewing Company
Snoqualmie Falls Brewing Company
Sprecher Brewing
Stone Brewing Company
The Black Mountain/Chili Beer Company
The Boston Beer Company
The Northern Lights Brewing Company
The Sea Dog Brewing Company
The Spoetzl Brewing
Tremont Brewery/Atlantic Coast Brewing Company
Whitstran Brewing Company
Widmer Brothers Brewing Company

WI

Angry Minnow Brewing
10440 Florida Avenue
Hayward, WI 54843
715-934-3055
www.angryminnow.com

BRANDS:
Angry Minnow Honey Wheat Pale Ale
States Available: MI, MN, WI

BluCreek Brewing – *page 470*
2310 Daniels Street, Suite 148
Madison, WI 53718
608-204-0868
www.blucreek.com

BRANDS:
BluCreek (Honey) Herbal Ale (9.3 SRM, 20 IBU)
BluCreek Altbier (12 SRM, 30 IBU)
BluCreek Blueberry Ale (9 SRM, 25 IBU)
BluCreek Zen IPA (7.2 SRM, 41.5 IBU) – *page 470*

States Available: FL, IL, MN, OH, WI

Capital Brewery Company, Inc. – *page 483*
7734 Terrace Avenue
Middleton, WI 53562
608-836-7100
www.capital-brewery.com

BRANDS:
Capital Brewery Autumnal Fire
Capital Brewery Bavarian Lager (22 IBU)
Capital Brewery Blonde Dopplelbock
Capital Brewery Brown Ale (25 IBU)
Capital Brewery Fest Beer
Capital Brewery Island Wheat – *page 483*
Capital Brewery Maibock (25 IBU)
Capital Brewery Munich Dark (28 IBU)
Capital Brewery Oktoberfest (23 IBU)
Capital Brewery Special Pilsner (32 IBU)
Capital Brewery Winter Skal (25 IBU)
Capital Brewery Wisconsin Amber (25 IBU)

States Available: IA, IL, MN, WI

GEOGRAPHIC BREWER INDEX (Alphabetical)

Central Waters Brewing Company

701 Main Street
Junction City, WI 54443
715-457-3322

BRANDS:
Central Waters Happy Heron Pale Ale
Central Waters Junc Town Brown Ale
Central Waters Kosmyk Charlie Y2K Catastrophe Ale
Central Waters Lac Du Bay IPA
Central Waters Mud Puppy Porter
Central Waters Ouisconsing Red Ale
Central Waters Reserve Bourbon Barrel Stout
Central Waters Reserve Irish Dry Stout
Central Waters Reserve Irish Red Ale
Central Waters Reserve Oktoberfest
Central Waters Satin Solstice Imperial Stout
Central Waters White Water Weizen

States Available: WI

City Brewery

925 South Third Street
La Crosse, WI 54601
608-785-4200
www.citybrewery.com

BRANDS:
City Brewery Golden Leaf Unfiltered Wheat
City Cream Ale
City Festbier
City Lager
City Light
City Pale Ale
City Slicker Malt Liquor
City Winter Porter
KUL
KUL Lite
LaCrosse Lager
LaCrosse Light

States Available: IA, IL, MN, OH, PA, WI

Falls Brewing Company

782 N. Main Street, P.O. Box 10
Oconte Falls, WI 54154
920-846-4844
www.fallsbrewing.com

BRANDS:
Falls Brewing Falls Dirty Blonde Ale
Falls Brewing Falls Hot Tail Ale
Falls Brewing Falls Nut Brown Ale
Falls Brewing Falls Porter

States Available: WI

Gray Brewing

2424 West Court Street
Janesville, WI 53545
608-752-3552
www.graybrewing.com

BRANDS:
Gray's Brewing Black & Tan
Gray's Brewing Honey Ale
Gray's Brewing Oatmeal Stout
Gray's Brewing Pale Ale

States Available: IL, WI

Green Bay Brewing Company

313 Dousman
Green Bay, WI 54303
920-438-8050
www.hinterlandbeer.com

BRANDS:
Hinterland Pale Ale

States Available: WI

GEOGRAPHIC BREWER INDEX (Alphabetical)

Harbor City Brewing, Inc.
535 W Grand Avenue
Port Washington, WI 53074-2102
262-284-3118

BRANDS:
Harbor City Brewing Full Tilt IPA
Harbor City Brewing Harvest Wheat
Harbor City Brewing Main Street Brown Ale
Harbor City Brewing Mile Rock Amber Ale
Harbor City Brewing Raspberry Brown Ale

States Available: Contact Brewery

Jacob Leinenkugel Brewing Company
124 East Elm Street, P.O. Box 337
Chippewa Falls, WI 54729-0337
888-534-6437
www.leinie.com

BRANDS:
Leinenkugel's Apple Spice
Leinenkugel's Berry Weiss
Leinenkugel's Big Butt Doppelbock
Leinenkugel's Creamy Dark
Leinenkugel's Honey Weiss
Leinenkugel's Light
Leinenkugel's Oktoberfest
Leinenkugel's Original
Leinenkugel's Red Lager
Leinenkugel's Sunset Wheat

States Available: CO, IA, IL, IN, KS, KY, MI, MN, MO, ND, NE, OH, OK, SD, WI, WV

James Page Brewing Company, LLC
2617 Water Street
Stevens Point, WI 54481
715-344-9310
www.pagebrewing.com

BRANDS:
James Page Brewing Burly Brown Ale
James Page Brewing Iron Ranger Amber Lager
James Page Brewing Voyageur Extra Pale Ale

States Available: IL, MN, WI

Joseph Huber Brewing Company, Inc.
1208 14th Avenue
Monroe, WI 53566-0277
608-325-3191
www.huberbrewery.com

BRANDS:
Berghoff Classic Pilsner (10 IBU)
Berghoff Famous Bock Beer (24 IBU)
Berghoff Famous Red Ale (21 IBU)
Berghoff Genuine Dark Beer (21 IBU)
Berghoff Hazelnut Winterfest Ale (20 IBU)
Berghoff Hefe-Weizen (14 IBU)
Berghoff Oktoberfest Beer (21 IBU)
Berghoff Original Lager Beer (20 IBU)
Berghoff Pale Ale (43 IBU)
Berghoff Solstice Wit Beer (11 IBU)

States Available: WI

Lake Louie Brewing, LLC
7556 Pine Road
Arena, WI 53503
608-753-2675
www.lakelouie.com

BRANDS:
Lake Louie Brewing Arena Premium
Lake Louie Brewing Brother Tim Tripel
Lake Louie Brewing Coon Rock Cream Ale
Lake Louie Brewing Dino's Dark
Lake Louie Brewing Milk Stout
Lake Louie Brewing Prairie Moon Belgian Style Farmhouse Ale
Lake Louie Brewing Tommy's Porter
Lake Louie Brewing Warped Speed Scotch Ale

States Available: WI

GEOGRAPHIC BREWER INDEX (Alphabetical)

Lakefront Brewery, Inc.

1872 N Commerce Street
Milwaukee, WI 53212-3701
414-372-8800
www.lakefrontbrewery.com

BRANDS:
Lakefront Big Easy Beer (6 SRM, 24 IBU)
Lakefront Bock Beer (18 SRM, 24 IBU)
Lakefront Cattail Ale (5 SRM, 15 IBU)
Lakefront Cherry Lager (10 SRM, 12 IBU)
Lakefront Cream City Pale Ale (14 SRM, 40 IBU)
Lakefront Eastside Dark (22 SRM, 15 IBU)
Lakefront Fuel Café Stout (45 SRM, 20 IBU)
Lakefront Holiday Spice Lager Beer (12 SRM, 14 IBU)
Lakefront Klisch Pilsner (4 SRM, 32 IBU)
Lakefront New Grist (2 SRM, 8 IBU)
Lakefront Oktoberfest (10 SRM, 24 IBU)
Lakefront Organic ESB (12 SRM, 36 IBU)
Lakefront Pumpkin Lager (12 SRM, 12 IBU)
Lakefront Riverwest Stein (15 SRM, 36 IBU)
Lakefront Snake Chaser Stout (55 SRM, 26 IBU)
Lakefront White Beer (3 SRM, 15 IBU)

States Available: CA, CO, CT, FL, IL, IN, MD, MI, MN, NC, NV, NY, OH, RI, TN, VA, WA, WI

Minhas Craft Brewery

1208 14th Avenue
Monroe, WI 53566-0277
608-325-3191
www.minhasbrewery.com

BRANDS:
Extreme Rockhead Malt Liquor
Hi Test Malt Liquor
Huber Bock Beer (23 IBU)
Huber Light Beer (7 IBU)
Huber Premium Beer (14 IBU)
Mountain Creek Classic Lager
Rhinelander (13 IBU)
Wisconsin Club

States Available: WI

New Glarus Brewing

119 Elmer Road
New Glarus, WI 53574
608-527-5850
www.newglarusbrewing.com

BRANDS:
New Glarus Brewing Belgian Red
New Glarus Brewing Copper Kettle Weiss
New Glarus Brewing Enigma
New Glarus Brewing Fat Squirrel
New Glarus Brewing Hop Hearty Ale
New Glarus Brewing Raspberry Tart
New Glarus Brewing Road Slush Oatmeal Stout
New Glarus Brewing Spotted Cow
New Glarus Brewing Totally Naked
New Glarus Brewing Uff-da Bock
New Glarus Brewing Yokel

States Available: WI

Nicolet Brewing

3578 Brewery Lane, P.O. Box 650
Florence, WI 54121-0650
715-528-5244

BRANDS:
Nicolet Brewing Blonde
Nicolet Brewing Classic Pilsner
Nicolet Brewing Prostrator Doppelbock
Nicolet Brewing Winter Fest Beer
Nicolet Brewing Oktoberfest
Nicolet Brewing Dark Pilsner

States Available: Contact Brewery

Oconomowoc Brewing Company

750 E Wisconsin Avenue
Oconomowoc, WI 53066-3045
262-560-0388

BRANDS:
Oconomowoc Brewing Black Forest Lager
Oconomowoc Brewing German Style Kölsch
Oconomowoc Brewing Oktoberfest
Oconomowoc Brewing Winter Brew

States Available: Contact Brewery

Rush River Brewing (Kegs)

W 4001 120th Avenue
Maiden Rock, WI 54750
715-448-2035
www.rushriverbeer.com

BRANDS:
Rush River Brewing BubbleJack IPA
Rush River Brewing Lost Arrow Porter
Rush River Brewing Small Axe Golden Ale
Rush River Brewing The Unforgiven Amber Ale

States Available: MN, WI

SAB Miller Corporation

3939 W Highland Boulevard
Milwaukee, WI 53208-2816
312-577-1754
www.sabmiller.com

BRANDS:
Hamm's
Hamm's Special Light
Henry Weinhard's Blue Boar Pale Ale
Henry Weinhard's Classic Dark
Henry Weinhard's Hefeweizen
Henry Weinhard's Northwest Trail Blonde Lager
Henry Weinhard's Private Reserve
Henry Weinhard's Summer Wheat
Icehouse
Icehouse 5.0
Icehouse Light
Magnum Malt Liquor
Mickey's Ice
Mickey's Malt Liquor
Miller Geniune Draft
Miller Geniune Draft Light
Miller High Life
Miller High Life Light
Miller Lite
Milwaukee's Best
Milwaukee's Best Ice
Milwaukee's Best Light
Old English 800 Malt Liquor
Olde English HG800
Olde English HG800 7.5
Peroni Nastro Azzurro
Pilsner Urquell
Red Dog
Sharp's
Southpaw Light
Sparks
Sparks Light
Sparks Plus 6%
Sparks Plus 7%
Steel Reserve High Gravity
Steel Reserve Triple

States Available: All 50 States

Sand Creek Brewing Company, LLC – *page 539*

320 South Pierce Street, P.O. Box 187
Black River Falls, WI 54615
715-284-7553
www.sandcreekbrewing.com

BRANDS:
Badger Porter (62 SRM, 21 IBU)
Cranberry Special Ale
Pioneer Black River Red (23 SRM, 25 IBU)
Pioneer Lager (12 SRM, 15 IBU)
Pioneer Oderbolz Bock (12.9 SRM, 25 IBU)
Sand Creek Brewing English Style Special Ale (13.4 SRM, 25 IBU)
Sand Creek Brewing Golden Ale (5.8 SRM, 11 IBU)
Sand Creek Brewing Groovy Brew (6 SRM, 6.5 IBU)
Sand Creek Brewing Oscar's Chocolate Oatmeal Stout
 (107 SRM, 30 IBU) – *page 539*
Sand Creek Brewing Wild Ride IPA (8.2 SRM, 64 IBU)
Sand Creek Brewing Woody's Wheat (12 SRM, 6 IBU)

States Available: IL, MN, WI

Slab City Brewing

West 3590 Pit Lane
Bonduel, WI 54107
715-758-2337
www.slabcitybeer.com

BRANDS:
Slab City Brewing Esker Alt
Slab City Brewing Milkhouse Stout
Slab City Brewing Old 47 Pale Ale
Slab City Brewing Shawano Gold
Slab City Brewing W.C. Bitter
Slab City Brewing Xenabock

States Available: WI

South Shore Brewery

808 West Main Street
Ashland, WI 54806
715-682-4200
www.southshorebrewery.com

BRANDS:
South Shore Brewery Herbal Cream Ale
South Shore Brewery Honey Pils
South Shore Brewery Nut Brown Ale
South Shore Brewery Rhoades' Scholar Stout

States Available: MI, MN, WI

Sprecher Brewing

701 West Glendale Avenue
Glendale, WI 53209
414-964-7837
www.sprecherbrewery.com

BRANDS:
Sprecher Brewing Abbey Triple (13 IBU)
Sprecher Brewing Barley Wine (46 IBU)
Sprecher Brewing Black Bavarian (32 IBU)
Sprecher Brewing Bourbon Barrel Barley Wine (46 IBU)
Sprecher Brewing Bourbon Barrel Scotch Ale (21 IBU)
Sprecher Brewing Dopple Bock (31 IBU)
Sprecher Brewing Generation Porter (26 IBU)
Sprecher Brewing Hefe' Weiss (11 IBU)
Sprecher Brewing Imperial Stout (32 IBU)
Sprecher Brewing India Pale Ale (88 IBU)
Sprecher Brewing Irish Stout (26 IBU)
Sprecher Brewing Mai Bock (24 IBU)
Sprecher Brewing Mbege Ale (10 IBU)
Sprecher Brewing Micro-Light Ale (6 IBU)
Sprecher Brewing Oktoberfest (15 IBU)
Sprecher Brewing Piper's Scotch Ale (21 IBU)
Sprecher Brewing Pub Ale (17 IBU)
Sprecher Brewing Shakparo Ale (9 IBU)
Sprecher Brewing Special Amber (22 IBU)
Sprecher Brewing Winter Brew (0 IBU)

States Available: AL, AR, AZ, CA, IA, IL, IN, KS, KY, MA, MD, MI, MN, MO,
OH, VA, WA, WI

Stevens Point Brewery

2617 Water Street
Stevens Point, WI 54481
715-344-9310
www.pointbeer.com

BRANDS:
Point Cascade Pale Ale
Point Classic Amber
Point Honey Light
Point Premier Light
Point Special Lager
Point Spring Bock
Point White Bière

States Available: GA, IA, IL, IN, KS, MN, MO, ND, SD, WI

Tyranena Brewing Company

1025 Owen Street, P.O. Box 736
Lake Mills, WI 53551
920-648-8699
www.tyranena.com

BRANDS:
Bitter Women IPA (9 SRM, 68 IBU)
Brewers Gone Wild! Bitter Women From Hell Extra IPA
Brewers Gone Wild! Hop Whore Imperial IPA
Brewers Gone Wild! Spank Me Baby Barley Wine
Brewers Gone Wild! Who's Your Daddy? Imperial Porter
Chief Black Hawk Porter (59 SRM, 35 IBU)
Fargo Brothers Hefeweizen (8 SRM, 12 IBU)
Fighting Finches Mai Bock (10 SRM, 25 IBU)
Gemuetlichkeit Oktoberfest (13 SRM, 22 IBU)
Headless Man Amber Alt (14 SRM, 25 IBU)
Rocky's Revenge (26 SRM, 30 IBU)
Shantytown Doppelbock (28 SRM, 23 IBU)
Stone Tepee Pale Ale (6 SRM, 32 IBU)
Three Beaches Honey Blonde (9 SRM,68 IBU)

States Available: WI

Viking Brewing

234 Dallas Street West
Dallas, WI 54733
715-837-1824
www.vikingbrewing.com

BRANDS:
Viking Brewing Abby Normal
Viking Brewing Berserk
Viking Brewing Big Swede
Viking Brewing Blonde
Viking Brewing Copperhead
Viking Brewing Dim Whit
Viking Brewing Honey Pale Ale
Viking Brewing Honey Moon
Viking Brewing Hot Chocolate
Viking Brewing Invader
Viking Brewing J.S. Bock
Viking Brewing JuleOL
Viking Brewing Lime Twist
Viking Brewing Mj0d
Viking Brewing Morketid
Viking Brewing Queen Victoria's Secret
Viking Brewing Rauch
Viking Brewing Sylvan Springs
Viking Brewing Vienna Woods
Viking Brewing Weathertop Wheat
Viking Brewing Whole Stein

States Available: MN, WI

GEOGRAPHIC BREWER INDEX (Alphabetical)

William Kuether Brewing Company

360 Fourth Street, P.O. Box 127
Clear Lake, WI 54005
715-263-4333
www.sconnieales.com

BRANDS:
William Kuether Brewing Hefeweizen
William Kuether Brewing Pils
William Kuether Brewing Sconnie Badger Brown Ale
William Kuether Brewing Sconnie Harvest Moon
William Kuether Brewing Sconnie Pale Ale
William Kuether Brewing Sconnie Rustic Trail Amber Ale
William Kuether Brewing Sconnie Tall Blonde Ale

States Available: MN, WI

The following brewers distribute their brands in Wisconsin:

Abita Brewing Company	North Coast Brewing Company
Anchor Brewing Company	O'Fallon Brewery
Angry Minnow Brewing	Oskar Blues Grill & Brew
Anheuser-Busch, Inc.	Otter Creek Brewing Company
Arcadia Brewing Company	Pabst Brewing Company
Atwater Block Brewery	Pete's Brewing
August Schell Brewing Company	Pig's Eye Brewing Company
Avery Brewing Company	Pittsburgh Brewing Company
Bear Republic Brewing Company	Pony Express Brewing Company
Bell's Brewery, Inc.	Redhook Ale Brewery
Big Sky Brewing Company	Rogue Ales
Blucreek Brewing	Rush River Brewing (Contact Brewery)
Breckenridge Brewery	SAB Miller Corp
Brewery Ommegang	Sand Creek Brewing Company, LLC
Capital Brewery Company, Inc.	Shipyard Brewing Company
Central Waters Brewing Company	Shmaltz Brewing Company
City Brewery	Sierra Nevada Brewing Company
Dogfish Head Craft Brewery	Slab City Brewing
El Toro Brewing	Smuttynose Brewing Company
Estes Park Brewery	Snake River Brewing Company
Falls Brewing Company	South Shore Brewery
Gluek Brewing Company	Spanish Peaks Brewing Company/
Gray Brewing (Contact Brewery)	United States Beverage
Great Divide Brewing Company	Sprecher Brewing
Great Lakes Brewing Company	St. Croix Beer Company
Green Bay Brewing Company	Stevens Point Brewery
High Falls Brewing	Summit Brewing Company
Jacob Leinenkugel Brewing Company	The Black Mountain/Chili Beer Company
James Page Brewing Company, LLC	The Boston Beer Company
Jolly Pumpkin Artisan Ales	The Fort Collins Brewery
Joseph Huber Brewing Company Inc.	The Sea Dog Brewing Company
Lake Louie Brewing, LLC	Three Floyds Brewing Company
Lake Superior Brewing Company	Tommyknocker Brewery
Lakefront Brewery Inc.	Tremont Brewery/Atlantic Coast Brewing
Lost Coast Brewery & Café	Company
MacTarnahan's Brewing Company	Two Brothers Brewing Company
Mad River Brewing	Tyranena Brewing Company
Millstream Brewing Company	Viking Brewing
Molson Coors Brewing Company	Widmer Brothers Brewing Company
New Glarus Brewing	Yellowstone Valley Brewing

GEOGRAPHIC BREWER INDEX (Alphabetical)

Snake River Brewing Company – *page 550*

WY

P.O. Box 3317, 265 South Millward
Jackson Hole, WY 83001
307-739-2337
www.snakeriverbrewing.com

BRANDS:
Snake River Lager (18 IBU)
Snake River OB-1 Organic Ale (22 IBU) – *page 550*
Snake River Pale Ale (32 IBU)
Snake River Zonker Stout (36 IBU)

States Available: CO, ID, MT, OH, UT, WI, WY

The following brewers distribute their brands in Wyoming:

Alaskan Brewing Company	Pabst Brewing Company
Anchor Brewing Company	Pete's Brewing
Anheuser-Busch, Inc.	Pyramid Brewery
Avery Brewing Company	Redhook Ale Brewery
Big Horn Brewing (CB Potts)	Rogue Ales
Big Sky Brewing Company	SAB Miller Corp
Boulder Beer Company	Shipyard Brewing Company
Boulevard Brewing Company	Snake River Brewing Company
Breckenridge Brewery	Spanish Peaks Brewing Company/
Deschutes Brewery	United States Beverage
Eel River Brewing Company	The Boston Beer Company
Frederick Brewing Company	The Fort Collins Brewery
Full Sail Brewing Company	The Sea Dog Brewing Company
Grand Teton Brewing Company	The Spoetzl Brewing
Kona Brewing, LLC	Tommyknocker Brewery
Left Handed Brewing Company	Tremont Brewery/Atlantic Coast Brewing
Molson Coors Brewing Company	Company
New Belgium Brewing Company	Widmer Brothers Brewing Company
Odell Brewing Company	Yellowstone Valley Brewing

It's not "just beer"
Commentary by Michael Kuderka

Beer Quest? – Hopping Around the Country to Arrive at Beer's Ultimate Destination...

Creating the ultimate beer resource for beer sellers and beer lovers has meant hours in front of the computer, hours on the phone, hours at the post office, and luckily for me a few hours here and there for road trips to the actual breweries for some fantastic brewery tours.

Enjoying and appreciating beer is all about experiencing the wide variety of styles and flavors that our US Breweries have to offer. And, very honestly there is nothing like tasting exceptionally fresh beer at its source. When one goes on a brewery tour, not only are you able to see, smell, and taste what goes into creating a great beer, but you gain an even greater appreciation for the differences between beer styles by having the ability to try any number of the brands that a brewery is producing at the time of your visit.

Also, "and I cannot overstate this enough" if you really want to "see America," you should search out these beer tours. Most of the breweries I have visited are not by any means on the "scenic side" of town. Very often zoning laws, space and facility requirements place these breweries either in the heart of the city in which they are located, or in the more industrial part of town. Many a hotel concierge has been surprised when street names that they have never heard of suddenly pop up as valid searches on MapQuest, and they will attempt to talk you out of venturing off to visit these unfamiliar boulevards – don't listen!

The Essential Reference of Domestic Brewers and Their Bottled Brands and the book's "Online Companion" document over 400 breweries and over 3000 of the brands of beer which they bottle. We have not even come close to visiting 1/5 of these breweries in person, but we definitely have developed our own personal "top ten" to tour:

The Boston Beer Company
Boston, MA

The home of Samuel Adams beers, located in the Jamaica Plain section of Boston, gives you a good appreciation for the quality ingredients that go into a great beer – hops, malt, barley, wheat and so forth. The tour ends in a beautiful Victorian style bar room, where very often Samuel Adams will let you try brands that are still in development. Some of the brands that you might want to sample are Samuel Adams Octoberfest, Samuel Adams Winter Lager, or Samuel Adams Boston Ale.

617-522-9080; http://www.samueladams.com

Anchor Brewing Company
San Francisco, CA

Tradition rules here atop one of San Francisco's many hills. Beers are made in a beautiful handcrafted copper brewhouse, a throwback to the simple, traditional ways of yesteryear. A fantastic building with a good deal of personality, and a tour that begins and ends in the bar/waiting room. Some of the brands you might want to try are Anchor Brewing Steam, Anchor Brewing Liberty Ale, or Anchor Brewing Christmas Ale.

415-863-8350; http://www.anchorbrewing.com

Atlanta Brewing Company
Atlanta, GA

If you are in Atlanta, without the kids, and are looking for a great time, Atlanta Brewing has the brewery, the beer and even live local music. The brewery, located in midtown Atlanta, is best-known for its Red Brick line of ales and specifically its Peach Tree Pale Ale, and offers tours which, include live music, and a full tasting sessions – plus a great pint glass!

404-275-6701; http://www.atlantabrewing.com

Boulevard Brewing Company
Kansas City, MO

This place is hopping! Boulevard, founded about 20 years ago when John McDonald installed a vintage Bavarian brewhouse in a turn-of-the-century brick building on Kansas City's historic Southwest Boulevard, is the largest specialty brewer in the Midwest. Visitors can take a walking tour of the plant, and sample some of the brands manufactured there, including Pale Ale, Unfiltered Wheat Beer, Bully! Porter, and Dry Stout. They have a excellent gift shop.

816-474-7095; http://www.boulevard.com

Yards Brewing
Philadelphia, PA

If you love historic landmarks, which I do, Yards Brewing is your kind of place. About five years ago Yards resurrected a huge building which once housed the Weisbrod and Hess Oriental Brewing Company (think Reingold beer), founded in the 1880s but done in by Prohibition in the late 1930s. You'll know from the second you enter this place that it was designed and constructed to do one thing: brew beer. Among Yards brands: General Washington Tavern Porter and Thomas Jefferson Tavern Ale.

215-634-2600; http://www.yardsbrewing.com

The Long Trail Brewing Company
Bridgewater Corners, VT

An idyllic setting adds immeasurably to the experience of this brewery. Built alongside the picturesque Ottauquechee River in the Green Mountains of central Vermont, the Long Trail Visitors Center was designed and inspired by the Munich Hofbrau House in Germany. There is something extremely relaxing about listening to the rush of a river, after a self-guided tour and a sampling of Long Trail Ale. Enjoy one great afternoon and try some of their brands, such as the Long Trail Ale, Long Trail Blackberry Wheat or the Long Trail Double Bag.

802-672-5011; http://www.longtrail.com

New Belgium Brewing Company
Fort Collins, CO

New Belgium is one of nation's most beautiful breweries, but that's not what really sets it apart. Along with learning about its brewing process and its brands (Fat Tire, Sunshine and Blue Paddle, to name a few), visitors will be inspired by the brewery's very progressive environmental efforts. We aren't just talking about recycling bottles. New Belgium utilizes wind power in their brewery, along with other environmentally friendly heating and cooling equipment.

970-221-0524; http://www.newbelgium.com

Saint Arnold Brewing Company
Houston, TX

Located in downtown Houston, there are no reservations needed for this tour, little walking required, and it was packed when we where there. The tasting area, which is in the center of the brewery's activities, has Oktoberfest-like picnic tables and a tour that gives a great overview of the brewing process and the Saint Arnold's history (plus something I treasure, a really great tasting glass). Saint Arnold Brewing Company, now operating for twelve years, is Texas' oldest craft Brewery. Some of the brands that Saint Arnold Brewing is known for are the Elissa, the Spring Bock , and the Saint Arnold Brewing Double IPA.

713-686-9494; http://www.saintarnold.com

River Horse Brewing Company
Lambertville, NJ

Located in historic Lambertville, NJ, on the banks of the Delaware River, is River Horse Brewing Company, just a few miles north of where George Washington made his famous Christmas crossing. This Brewery offers a relatively short self-tour, but you'll want to keep hanging around for the various River Horse brands. You might want to try the Summer Blonde, the ESB, and the Tripel Horse. The town also bills itself as "The Antique Capital of New Jersey," so there are plenty of other things to do while you are there.

609-397-7776; http://www.riverhorse.com

Hale's Ales
Seattle, WA

No official tour here, for the layout is such that visitors walk through the brewery to get to the popular brew pub. The wrap-around bar is absolutely gorgeous. Hale's is a great first stop in a town famous for its breweries and a state that produces much of the US-grown hops. Brands to try while you are there include Hale's Pale American Ale, Hale's Drawbridge Blonde, and Hale's Cream Ale.

206-706-1544; http://www.halesales.com

Anheuser-Busch, Inc.
St. Louis, MO – Fairfield, CA – Fort Collins, CO – Jacksonville, FL – Merrimack, NH

Once you have experienced brewing on the craft and micro-brewing scale, it is almost mind-numbing to experience brewing on its grandest scale. Anheuser-Busch brews the majority of the beer consumed in the United States, and the tradition, history, and innovation (plus the shear volume) is really something to see. The Anheuser-Busch brands are well known, and some of their newer brands are Wild Blue, Jack's Pumpkin Spice Ale, Wild Hop Organic Lager, Stone Mill Pale Ale and Winter's Bourbon Cask Ale.

314-577-2626;
http://www.budweisertours.com/home.htm

VI HOW SUPPLIED

How a bottled brand is available is great information to have as a retailer, bar or restaurant owner, or if you happen to have (like I do) that dual tap kegerator installed in your basement bar.

The "How Supplied Section" of the book is designed to quickly give you a better idea of how each of the brewer's individual bottled brands is available. Very often brands that are available in 12 once bottles can also be found in 22 once bottles, as well as 1/6, and 1/2 kegs. Note that how a brand is supplied is an important component of any product's promotional effort and that the availability of specific configurations (bottle vs. keg and specific container size) can vary from region to region and with any changes in a brand's promotional plan.

How Supplied *Continued*

Locally available bottle and keg sizes may vary.

Brewery / Brand Name	Contact Brewery	Cans	7 oz	8 1/2 oz	10 oz	12 oz	16 oz	20 oz	22 oz	24 oz	1/2 liter	25 oz	32 oz	64 oz	1 liter	1 1/2 liter	375 ml	500 ml	750 ml	40 oz	2 liter	Growlers/Jugs	3 liter	1/6 Keg	1/4 Keg	1/2 Keg	Keg (Non-Specified Size)
21st Amendment Brewery																											
21st Amendment Brewery IPA		✗																									
21st Amendment Brewery Watermelon Wheat		✗																									
Abbey Beverage Company																											
Monk's Ale	✗																										
Abita Brewing Company																											
Abita Bock						✗																					
Abita Brewing 20th Anniversary Pilsner						✗																					
Abita Brewing Amber						✗																					
Abita Brewing Christmas Ale						✗																					
Abita Brewing Golden						✗																					
Abita Brewing Purple Haze						✗																				✗	
Abita Brewing Red Ale						✗																					
Abita Brewing Restoration Ale						✗																					
Abita Brewing Turbodog						✗																				✗	
Abita Brewing Wheat						✗																					
Abita Fall Fest	✗																										
Abita Light						✗																					
Alaskan Brewing Company																											
Alaskan Amber						✗				✗															✗	✗	
Alaskan Big Nugget Barley Wine						✗																			✗	✗	
Alaskan ESB						✗																			✗	✗	
Alaskan Pale						✗																			✗	✗	
Alaskan Smoked Porter						✗																			✗	✗	
Alaskan Stout						✗																			✗	✗	
Alaskan Summer Ale						✗																			✗	✗	
Alaskan Winter Ale						✗																			✗	✗	
Alesmith Brewing Company																											
Alesmith Brewing IPA																			✗								
Alesmith Brewing Old Numbskull																			✗								
Alesmith Brewing Special Bitter																			✗								
Alesmith Brewing Speedway Stout																			✗								

338

Brewery Brand Name	Contact Brewery	Cans	7 oz	8 1/2 oz	10 oz	12 oz	16 oz	20 oz	22 oz	24 oz	1/2 liter	25 oz	32 oz	64 oz	1 liter	1 1/2 liter	375 ml	500 ml	750 ml	40 oz	2 liter	Growlers/ Jugs	3 liter	1/6 Keg	1/4 Keg	1/2 Keg	Keg (Non-Specified Size)
Alesmith Brewing Wee Heavy																			✗								
Alesmith Brewing X-Extra Pale Ale																			✗								
Alesmith Brewing YuleSmith Holiday Ale																			✗								
Alesmith Brewing Horny Devil																			✗								
Allagash Brewing Company																											
Allagash Brewing 11th Anniversary																			✗					✗			
Allagash Brewing Curieux																			✗					✗			
Allagash Brewing Dubbel						✗													✗					✗		✗	
Allagash Brewing Four																			✗					✗			
Allagash Brewing Interlude																			✗					✗			
Allagash Brewing Musette																			✗					✗			
Allagash Brewing Odyssey																			✗					✗			
Allagash Brewing Tripel																			✗					✗		✗	
Allagash Brewing Victoria Ale																			✗					✗			
Allagash Brewing White Beer						✗													✗					✗		✗	
Allagash Grand Cru						✗													✗					✗		✗	
Alltech's Lexington Brewing Company																											
Lexington Brewing Kentucky Ale						✗																					
Lexington Brewing Kentucky Bourbon Barrel Aged Ale	✗																										
Lexington Brewing Kentucky Light						✗																					
Alpine Beer Company																											
Alpine Ale									✗													✗		✗		✗	
Alpine Beer Mchenney's Irish Red									✗													✗		✗		✗	
Alpine Beer Pure Hoppiness									✗													✗		✗		✗	
Alpine Mandarin Nectar									✗													✗		✗		✗	
Anchor Brewing Company																											
Anchor Brewing Bock Beer						✗			✗															✗		✗	
Anchor Brewing Christmas Ale						✗										✗								✗		✗	
Anchor Brewing Liberty Ale						✗			✗															✗		✗	
Anchor Brewing Old Foghorn Barleywine Style Ale						✗																		✗		✗	
Anchor Brewing Porter						✗			✗															✗		✗	
Anchor Brewing Small Beer									✗															✗		✗	

Locally available bottle and keg sizes may vary.

Brewery / Brand Name	Contact Brewery	Cans	7 oz	8 1/2 oz	10 oz	12 oz	16 oz	20 oz	22 oz	24 oz	1/2 liter	25 oz	32 oz	64 oz	1 liter	1 1/2 liter	375 ml	500 ml	750 ml	40 oz	2 liter	Growlers/Jugs	3 liter	1/6 Keg	1/4 Keg	1/2 Keg	Keg (Non-Specified Size)
Anchor Brewing Steam						✗			✗															✗		✗	
Anchor Brewing Summer Ale						✗			✗															✗		✗	
Anderson Valley Brewing Company																											
Anderson Valley Barney Flats Oatmeal Stout						✗			✗															✗		✗	
Anderson Valley Belk's ESB Ale						✗			✗															✗		✗	
Anderson Valley Boon Amber Ale						✗			✗															✗		✗	
Anderson Valley Brother David's Abbey Style Double																			✗					✗		✗	
Anderson Valley Brother David's Abbey Style Triple																			✗					✗		✗	
Anderson Valley Deependers Porter									✗																	✗	
Anderson Valley High Rollers Wheat Beer									✗															✗		✗	
Anderson Valley Hop Ottin' IPA						✗			✗															✗		✗	
Anderson Valley Poleeko Gold Pale Ale						✗			✗															✗		✗	
Anderson Valley Summer Solstice Cerveza Crema						✗																		✗		✗	
Anderson Valley Winter Solstice						✗			✗															✗		✗	
Andrews Brewing Company																											
Andrews English Pale Ale	✗																										
Andrews Northern Brown Ale	✗																										
Andrews St. Nick Porter	✗																										
Andrews Summer Golden Ale	✗																										
Angel City Brewing																											
Angel City Abbey									✗															✗		✗	
Angel City Ale						✗			✗															✗		✗	
Angel City Dunkel									✗															✗		✗	
Angel City IPA									✗															✗		✗	
Angel City Lager																								✗		✗	
Angel City Pilz									✗															✗		✗	
Angel City Vitzen									✗															✗		✗	
Angry Minnow Brewing																											
Angry Minnow Honey Wheat Pale Ale						✗																		✗	✗	✗	
Anheuser-Busch, Inc.																											
Anheuser World Lager						✗	✗																	✗		✗	
Beach Bum Blonde Ale						✗																		✗		✗	

340

Locally available bottle and keg sizes may vary.

Brewery Brand Name	Contact Brewery	Cans	7 oz	8 1/2 oz	10 oz	12 oz	16 oz	20 oz	22 oz	24 oz	1/2 liter	25 oz	32 oz	64 oz	1 liter	1 1/2 liter	375 ml	500 ml	750 ml	40 oz	2 liter	Growlers/Jugs	3 liter	1/6 Keg	1/4 Keg	1/2 Keg	Keg (Non-Specified Size)
Brew Masters' Private Reserve													X														
Bud Dry		X				X							X														
Bud Extra		X			X																						
Bud Ice		X				X	X		X	X			X							X						X	
Bud Ice Light		X				X																					
Bud Light		X	X			X	X		X	X			X							X				X	X	X	
Budweiser		X	X			X	X		X	X			X							X				X	X	X	
Budweiser NA		X																									
Budweiser Select		X				X	X		X	X										X				X	X	X	
Busch		X	X			X			X				X							X					X	X	
Busch Ice		X																		X							
Busch Light		X				X			X				X							X					X	X	
Busch NA		X																									
Chelada Bud		X																									
Chelada Bud Light		X																									
Hurricane High Gravity (HG)		X																		X							
Hurricane Ice		X																									
Hurricane Malt Liquor		X											X							X							
Jack's Pumpkin Spice Ale						X																		X		X	
King Cobra		X							X				X							X							
Land Shark Lager						X																					
Michelob		X	X			X	X			X														X	X	X	
Michelob AmberBock		X				X																		X	X	X	
Michelob Bavarian-Style Wheat						X																					
Michelob Celebrate Chocolate										X																	
Michelob Celebrate Vanilla										X																	
Michelob Golden Draft		X				X																				X	
Michelob Golden Draft Light		X				X	X																		X	X	
Michelob Honey Lager						X																					
Michelob Light		X	X			X	X			X														X	X	X	
Michelob Marzen						X																					
Michelob Pale Ale						X																					

341

How Supplied *Continued*

Locally available bottle and keg sizes may vary.

Brewery / Brand Name	Contact Brewery	Cans	7 oz	8 1/2 oz	10 oz	12 oz	16 oz	20 oz	22 oz	24 oz	1/2 liter	25 oz	32 oz	64 oz	1 liter	1 1/2 liter	375 ml	500 ml	750 ml	40 oz	2 liter	Growlers/Jugs	3 liter	1/6 Keg	1/4 Keg	1/2 Keg	Keg (Non-Specified Size)
Michelob Porter						X																					
Michelob Ultra		X	X			X	X			X														X	X	X	
Michelob ULTRA Amber		X				X																		X		X	
Michelob ULTRA Lime						X																					
Michelob ULTRA Orange						X																					
Michelob ULTRA Pomegranate						X																					
Natty Up		X																									
Natural Ice		X				X			X				X							X						X	
Natural Light		X	X			X			X				X													X	
O'Doul's		X				X																				X	
O'Doul's Amber		X				X																				X	
Redbridge Lager						X																					
Rock Green Light		X	X			X																			X	X	
Rolling Rock Extra Pale		X	X			X																			X	X	
Spring Heat Spiced Wheat						X																		X		X	
Stone Mill Pale Ale						X																		X			
Tequiza						X																					
Wild Blue						X																					
Wild Hop Lager						X																		X			
Winter's Bourbon Cask Ale						X																		X		X	
ZeigenBock						X																			X	X	
Appalachian Brewing Company																											
Appalachian Brewing Hoppy Trail IPA						X																		X			
Appalachian Brewing Jolly Scot Scottish Ale						X																				X	
Appalachian Brewing Kipona Fest Lager						X																				X	
Appalachian Brewing Mountain Lager						X																				X	
Appalachian Brewing Peregrine Pilsner						X																		X		X	
Appalachian Brewing Purist Pale Ale						X																				X	
Appalachian Brewing Susquehanna Stout						X																				X	
Appalachian Brewing Water Gap Wheat						X																				X	
Arbor Brewing Company																											
Arbor Brewing Bavarian Bliss Hefeweizen						X																					

Locally available bottle and keg sizes may vary.

Brewery Brand Name	Contact Brewery	Cans	7 oz	8 1/2 oz	10 oz	12 oz	16 oz	20 oz	22 oz	24 oz	1/2 liter	25 oz	32 oz	64 oz	1 liter	1 1/2 liter	375 ml	500 ml	750 ml	40 oz	2 liter	Growlers/ Jugs	3 liter	1/6 Keg	1/4 Keg	1/2 Keg	Keg (Non-Specified Size)
Arbor Brewing Brasserie Blonde Belgian						✗																					
Arbor Brewing Olde Number 23 Alt Bier						✗																					
Arbor Brewing Red Snapper Special Bitter						✗																					
Arbor Brewing Sacred Cow I.P.A.						✗																					
Arcadia Brewing Company																											
Arcadia Brewing Ales Amber Ale						✗																		✗		✗	
Arcadia Brewing Ales Angler's Ale						✗																		✗		✗	
Arcadia Brewing Ales Battle Creek Special Reserve						✗																		✗		✗	
Arcadia Brewing Ales HopMouth						✗																		✗		✗	
Arcadia Brewing Ales Imperial Stout						✗																		✗		✗	
Arcadia Brewing Ales India Pale Ale						✗																		✗		✗	
Arcadia Brewing Ales London Porter						✗																		✗		✗	
Arcadia Brewing Ales Nut Brown Ale						✗																		✗		✗	
Arcadia Brewing Ales Scotch Ale						✗																		✗		✗	
Arcadia Brewing Ales Starboard Stout						✗																		✗		✗	
Arcadia Brewing Ales Whitsun						✗																		✗		✗	
Atlanta Brewing Company																											
Atlanta Brewing PeachTree Pale Ale						✗																		✗		✗	
Atlanta Brewing Red Brick Ale						✗																		✗		✗	
Atlanta Brewing Red Brick Blonde						✗																		✗		✗	
Atlanta Brewing Red Brick Summer Brew — Hefeweizen						✗																		✗		✗	
Red Brick Winter Brew — Double-Chocolate Oatmeal Porter						✗																		✗		✗	
Atlantic Brewing Company																											
Atlantic Brewing Bar Harbor Blueberry Ale						✗																					
Atlantic Brewing Bar Harbor Real Ale						✗																					
Atlantic Brewing Brother Adam's Honey Bragget						✗																					
Atlantic Brewing Coal Porter						✗																					
Atlantic Brewing Mount Desert Island Ginger						✗																					
Atlantic Brewing Special Old Bitter Ale						✗																					
Atwater Block Brewery																											
Atwater Voodoo Vator Dopplebock						✗																					
Atwater Bloktoberfest						✗																					

343

How Supplied *Continued*

Locally available bottle and keg sizes may vary.

Brewery / Brand Name	Contact Brewery	Cans	7 oz	8 1/2 oz	10 oz	12 oz	16 oz	20 oz	22 oz	24 oz	1/2 liter	25 oz	32 oz	64 oz	1 liter	1 1/2 liter	375 ml	500 ml	750 ml	40 oz	2 liter	Growlers/Jugs	3 liter	1/6 Keg	1/4 Keg	1/2 Keg	Keg (Non-Specified Size)
Atwater Dunkel Dark Lager						✗																					
Atwater Hefeweizen						✗																					
Atwater Hell Pale Lager						✗																					
Atwater Mai Bock						✗																					
Atwater Pilsner						✗																					
Atwater Rost						✗																					
Atwater Salvation IPA						✗																					
Atwater Shaman's Porter						✗																					
Atwater Vanilla Java Porter						✗																					
Atwater Winter Bock						✗																					
August Schell Brewing Company																											
August Schell Brewing Caramel Bock						✗																		✗		✗	
August Schell Brewing Dark						✗																		✗	✗	✗	
August Schell Brewing FireBrick		✗				✗																		✗		✗	
August Schell Brewing Hefeweizen						✗																		✗		✗	
August Schell Brewing Light		✗				✗																			✗	✗	
August Schell Brewing Maifest						✗																		✗		✗	
August Schell Brewing Octoberfest						✗																		✗		✗	
August Schell Brewing Original		✗				✗																			✗	✗	
August Schell Brewing Pale Ale						✗																				✗	
August Schell Brewing Pilsner						✗																		✗		✗	
August Schell Brewing Schmaltz's Alt						✗																		✗		✗	
August Schell Brewing Snowstorm						✗																		✗		✗	
August Schell Brewing Zommerfest						✗																		✗		✗	
Avery Brewing Company																											
Avery Brewing 14'er ESB						✗																		✗		✗	
Avery Brewing Ellie's Brown						✗																		✗		✗	
Avery Brewing Hog Heaven Barley Wine									✗															✗		✗	
Avery Brewing IPA						✗																		✗		✗	
Avery Brewing Karma Belgian Ale						✗			✗															✗		✗	
Avery Brewing Mephistopheles' Stout						✗																		✗		✗	
Avery Brewing New World Porter						✗																		✗		✗	

Brewery Brand Name	Contact Brewery	Cans	7 oz	8 1/2 oz	10 oz	12 oz	16 oz	20 oz	22 oz	24 oz	1/2 liter	25 oz	32 oz	64 oz	1 liter	1 1/2 liter	375 ml	500 ml	750 ml	40 oz	2 liter	Growlers/Jugs	3 liter	1/6 Keg	1/4 Keg	1/2 Keg	Keg (Non-Specified Size)
Avery Brewing Old Jubilation						✗																		✗		✗	
Avery Brewing Out of Bounds Stout						✗																		✗		✗	
Avery Brewing Red Point Amber Ale						✗																		✗		✗	
Avery Brewing Salvation									✗															✗		✗	
Avery Brewing Samael's Oak Aged Ale						✗																		✗		✗	
Avery Brewing The Beast Belgian Grand Cru						✗			✗															✗		✗	
Avery Brewing The Czar Russian Imperial Stout									✗															✗		✗	
Avery Brewing The Kaiser Imperial Oktoberfest									✗															✗		✗	
Avery Brewing The Maharaja Imperial IPA									✗															✗		✗	
Avery Brewing The Reverend Belgian Quadupel									✗															✗		✗	
Avery Brewing Thirteen									✗															✗		✗	
Avery Brewing Twelve									✗															✗		✗	
Avery Brewing White Rascal Belgian-Style White Ale						✗																		✗		✗	
B.W. Beer Works USA																											
The Raven Christmas Lager																			✗								
The Raven Special Lager						✗																					
Back Road Brewery																											
Back Road Brewery American Pale Ale						✗																		✗	✗	✗	
Back Road Brewery Autumn Ale						✗																		✗	✗	✗	
Back Road Brewery Aviator Dopplebock						✗																		✗	✗	✗	
Back Road Brewery Back Road Ale						✗																		✗	✗	✗	
Back Road Brewery Belgian-Style Wit						✗																		✗	✗	✗	
Back Road Brewery Belle Gunness Stout						✗																		✗	✗	✗	
Back Road Brewery Blueberry Ale						✗																		✗	✗	✗	
Back Road Brewery Christmas Ale						✗																		✗	✗	✗	
Back Road Brewery Koza Brada Bock						✗																		✗	✗	✗	
Back Road Brewery Maple Gold City						✗																		✗	✗	✗	
Back Road Brewery Midwest IPA						✗																		✗	✗	✗	
Back Road Brewery Millennium Lager						✗																		✗	✗	✗	
Back Road Brewery No. 9 Barley-Style Ale						✗																		✗	✗	✗	
Back Road Brewery Pecker Head Red						✗																		✗	✗	✗	

Locally available bottle and keg sizes may vary.

Brewery / Brand Name	Contact Brewery	Cans	7 oz	8 1/2 oz	10 oz	12 oz	16 oz	20 oz	22 oz	24 oz	1/2 liter	25 oz	32 oz	64 oz	1 liter	1 1/2 liter	375 ml	500 ml	750 ml	40 oz	2 liter	Growlers/ Jugs	3 liter	1/6 Keg	1/4 Keg	1/2 Keg	Keg (Non-Specified Size)
Backcountry Brewery																											
Backcountry Brewery Peak One Porter									✗																		
Backcountry Brewery Ptarmigan Pilsner									✗																		
Backcountry Brewery Switchback Amber									✗																		
Backcountry Brewery Telemark IPA									✗																		
Backcountry Brewery Wheeler Wheat									✗																		
Ballast Point Brewing Company																											
Ballast Point Big Eye IPA										✗																✗	
Ballast Point Black Marlin Porter										✗																✗	
Ballast Point Calico Amber Ale										✗																✗	
Ballast Point Wahoo Wheat Beer										✗																✗	
Ballast Point Yellowtail Pale Ale						✗				✗																✗	
Bar Harbor Brewing																											
Bar Harbor Brewing Cadillac Mountain Stout									✗																		
Bar Harbor Brewing Ginger Mild Brew									✗																		
Bar Harbor Brewing Harbor Lighthouse Ale									✗																		
Bar Harbor Brewing Thunder Hole Ale									✗																		
Bard's Tale Beer Company																											
Bard's Tale Dragon's Gold Sorghum Lager						✗																					
Barley Creek Brewing Company																											
Barley Creek Angler Black Widow Lager						✗																					
Barley Creek Antler Brown Ale						✗			✗																	✗	
Barley Creek Atlas Ale	✗																										
Barley Creek Harvest Moon Oktoberfest	✗																										
Barley Creek Light	✗																										
Barley Creek Navigator Gold						✗																					
Barley Creek Old '99 Barley Wine	✗																										
Barley Creek Renovator Stout	✗																										
Barley Creek Rescue India Pale Ale						✗																					
Barley Island Brewing Company																											
Barley Island Brewing Bar Fly India Pale Ale						✗																				✗	
Barley Island Brewing Black Majic Java Stout						✗																				✗	

Locally available bottle and keg sizes may vary.

Brewery / Brand Name	Contact Brewery	Cans	7 oz	8 1/2 oz	10 oz	12 oz	16 oz	20 oz	22 oz	24 oz	1/2 liter	25 oz	32 oz	64 oz	1 liter	1 1/2 liter	375 ml	500 ml	750 ml	40 oz	2 liter	Growlers/Jugs	3 liter	1/6 Keg	1/4 Keg	1/2 Keg	Keg (Non-Specified Size)
Barley Island Brewing Blind Tiger Pale Ale						X																				X	
Barley Island Brewing Bourbon Barrel-Aged Oatmeal Stout	X								X																		
Barley Island Brewing Brass Knuckles Oatmeal Stout						X																				X	
Barley Island Brewing Dirty Helen Brown Ale						X																			X	X	
Barley Island Brewing Sheet Metal Blonde						X																				X	
Baron Brewing																											
Baron Bavarian Weizen	X																										
Baron Berliner-Weisse	X																										
Baron Bock	X																										
Baron Dampf Bier	X																										
Baron Doppelbock	X																										
Baron Dunkel-Weisse	X																										
Baron Dusseldof Altbier	X																										
Baron Hefe-Weisse	X																										
Baron Helles Bock	X																										
Baron Liberator Doppelbock	X																										
Baron Munich Helles Lager	X																										
Baron Oktoberfest	X																										
Baron Pils	X																										
Baron Rauchbier	X																										
Baron Roggen	X																										
Baron Schwarzbier	X																										
Baron Uber-Weisse	X																										
Barrel House Brewing Company																											
Barrel House Belgian Style Winter Ale									X																		
Barrel House Boss Cox Double Dark IPA									X																		
Barrel House Cumberland Pale Ale									X																		
Barrel House Duveneck's Dortmunder Style Lager									X																		
Barrel House Hocking Hills Hefe Weizen									X																		
Barrel House Red Leg Ale									X																		
Bayern Brewing																											
Bayern Brewing Amber	X																										

347

Locally available bottle and keg sizes may vary.

Brewery Brand Name	Contact Brewery	Cans	7 oz	8 1/2 oz	10 oz	12 oz	16 oz	20 oz	22 oz	24 oz	1/2 liter	25 oz	32 oz	64 oz	1 liter	1 1/2 liter	375 ml	500 ml	750 ml	40 oz	2 liter	Growlers/ Jugs	3 liter	1/6 Keg	1/4 Keg	1/2 Keg	Keg (Non-Specified Size)
Bayern Brewing Doppelbock	X																										
Bayern Brewing Flathead Lake Monster Lager	X																										
Bayern Brewing Hefeweizen						X																					
Bayern Brewing Killarney	X																										
Bayern Brewing Maibock	X																										
Bayern Brewing Oktoberfest	X																										
Bayern Brewing Pilsner	X																										
Bayern Brewing Schwarzbier	X																										
Bayern Brewing Trout Slayer						X																					
Bayhawk Ales, Inc.																											
Bayhawk Ales Amber Ale																								X		X	
Bayhawk Ales Beach Blonde																								X		X	
Bayhawk Ales California Pale Ale									X															X		X	
Bayhawk Ales Chocolate Porter									X															X		X	
Bayhawk Ales Hefe Weizen																								X		X	
Bayhawk Ales Honey Blonde																								X		X	
Bayhawk Ales IPA																								X		X	
Bayhawk Ales O.C. Lager																								X		X	
Bayhawk Ales Stout																								X		X	
Bear Republic Brewing Company																											
Bear Republic Brewing Big Bear Stout Ale									X																		
Bear Republic Brewing Hop Rod Rye	X																										
Bear Republic Brewing Pete Brown's Tribute Ale	X																										
Bear Republic Brewing Racer 5	X																										
Bear Republic Brewing Red Rocket Ale									X																		
Bear Republic Brewing Special XP Pale Ale	X																										
Beautiful Brews, Inc.																											
Beautiful Brews Honey Amber Rose						X																					
Beermann's Beerwerks																											
Beermann's Hefe Weizen	X																										
Beermann's Honey Brew	X																										
Beermann's India Pale Ale	X																										

Locally available bottle and keg sizes may vary.

Brewery Brand Name	Contact Brewery	Cans	7 oz	8 1/2 oz	10 oz	12 oz	16 oz	20 oz	22 oz	24 oz	1/2 liter	25 oz	32 oz	64 oz	1 liter	1 1/2 liter	375 ml	500 ml	750 ml	40 oz	2 liter	Growlers/ Jugs	3 liter	1/6 Keg	1/4 Keg	1/2 Keg	Keg (Non-Specified Size)
Beermann's Lincoln Lager — Helles Lager						✗																					
Beermann's Rip Roarin' Red - Red Ale						✗																					
Berkshire Brewing Company																											
Berkshire Brewing "Shabadoo" Black & Tan Ale										✗																✗	
Berkshire Brewing Berkshire Traditional Pale Ale										✗																✗	
Berkshire Brewing Cabin Fever Ale										✗																✗	
Berkshire Brewing Coffeehouse Porter										✗																✗	
Berkshire Brewing Drayman's Porter										✗																✗	
Berkshire Brewing Gold Spike Ale										✗																✗	
Berkshire Brewing Hefeweizen										✗																✗	
Berkshire Brewing Holidale										✗																✗	
Berkshire Brewing Imperial Stout										✗																✗	
Berkshire Brewing Lost Sailor India Pale Ale										✗																✗	
Berkshire Brewing Maibock Lager										✗																✗	
Berkshire Brewing Ocktoberfest Lager										✗																✗	
Berkshire Brewing Raspberry Strong Ale										✗																✗	
Berkshire Brewing River Ale										✗																✗	
Berkshire Brewing Steel Rail Extra Pale Ale						✗				✗																✗	
Big Easy Brewing Company																											
Bourbon Street Bock						✗																					
Mojo Red Ale						✗																					
Tiger Town Beer						✗																					
Big Horn Brewing (CB Potts)																											
Big Horn Hefeweizen						✗																		✗	✗	✗	
Big Red IPA						✗																		✗	✗	✗	
Buttface Amber Ale						✗																		✗	✗	✗	
Colorado Blonde						✗																		✗	✗	✗	
Total Disorder Porter						✗																		✗	✗	✗	
Big Sky Brewing Company																											
Big Sky Brewing Crystal Ale						✗																					✗
Big Sky Brewing IPA						✗																					✗
Big Sky Brewing Moose Drool Brown Ale						✗																					✗

349

Locally available bottle and keg sizes may vary.

Brewery Brand Name	Contact Brewery	Cans	7 oz	8 1/2 oz	10 oz	12 oz	16 oz	20 oz	22 oz	24 oz	1/2 liter	25 oz	32 oz	64 oz	1 liter	1 1/2 liter	375 ml	500 ml	750 ml	40 oz	2 liter	Growlers/Jugs	3 liter	1/6 Keg	1/4 Keg	1/2 Keg	Keg (Non Specified Size)
Big Sky Brewing Powder Hound Winter Ale						X																					X
Big Sky Brewing Scape Goat Pale Ale						X																					X
Big Sky Brewing Summer Honey Seasonal Ale						X																					X
Bison Brewing																											
Bison Brewing Organic Barleywine									X															X		X	
Bison Brewing Organic Belgain Ale									X																	X	
Bison Brewing Organic Chocolate Stout						X			X															X		X	
Bison Brewing Organic Farmhouse																		X								X	
Bison Brewing Organic Gingerbread Ale									X															X		X	
Bison Brewing Organic Honey-Basil									X															X		X	
Bison Brewing Organic IPA						X			X															X		X	
Bison Brewing Organic Red Ale									X															X		X	
Bison Brewing Organic Winter									X																		
Bitter Root Brewing																											
Bitter Root Brewing Amber									X															X		X	
Bitter Root Brewing India Pale Ale									X															X		X	
Bitter Root Brewing Nut Brown									X															X		X	
Bitter Root Brewing Pale Ale									X															X		X	
Bitter Root Brewing Porter									X															X		X	
Bitter Root Brewing Sawtooth Ale									X															X		X	
Bitter Root Brewing Winter Ale									X															X			
BluCreek Brewing																											
BluCreek (Honey) Herbal Ale						X																					X
BluCreek Altbier						X																					X
BluCreek Blueberry Ale						X																		X		X	
BluCreek Zen IPA						X																					X
Blue & Gray Brewing Company, Inc.																											
Blue & Gray Classic Lager						X			X																		
Falmouth American Pale Ale						X			X																		
Fred Red Ale						X			X																		
Spiced Winter Ale						X			X																		
Stonewall Stout						X			X																		

Brewery Brand Name	Contact Brewery	Cans	7 oz	8 1/2 oz	10 oz	12 oz	16 oz	20 oz	22 oz	24 oz	1/2 liter	25 oz	32 oz	64 oz	1 liter	1 1/2 liter	375 ml	500 ml	750 ml	40 oz	2 liter	Growlers/ Jugs	3 liter	1/6 Keg	1/4 Keg	1/2 Keg	Keg (Non-Specified Size)
Von Steuben Oktoberfest						✗			✗																		
Blue Point Brewing																											
Blue Point Brewing Blueberry Ale						✗																✗		✗		✗	
Blue Point Brewing Cherry Imperial Stout																						✗		✗		✗	
Blue Point Brewing ESB																						✗		✗		✗	
Blue Point Brewing Golden Ale																						✗		✗		✗	
Blue Point Brewing Hefeweizen																						✗		✗		✗	
Blue Point Brewing Hoptical Illusion						✗																✗		✗		✗	
Blue Point Brewing Oatmeal Stout																						✗		✗		✗	
Blue Point Brewing Octoberfest																						✗		✗		✗	
Blue Point Brewing Old Howling Bastard												✗										✗		✗		✗	
Blue Point Brewing Pale Ale																						✗		✗		✗	
Blue Point Brewing Porter																						✗		✗		✗	
Blue Point Brewing Summer Ale						✗			✗													✗		✗		✗	
Blue Point Brewing Toasted Lager						✗																✗		✗		✗	
Blue Point Brewing Winter Ale						✗																✗		✗		✗	
Bluegrass Brewing Company																											
BBC Altbier						✗																		✗		✗	
BBC American Pale Ale						✗																		✗		✗	
BBC Bearded Pat's Barleywine						✗																		✗		✗	
BBC Bluegrass Gold						✗																		✗		✗	
BBC Dark Star Porter						✗																		✗		✗	
BBC Hell For Certain						✗																		✗		✗	
BBC Jefferson's Reserve Bourbon Barrel Stout						✗																		✗		✗	
BBC Nut Brown Ale						✗																		✗		✗	
BBC White Wedding Ale						✗																		✗		✗	
Bonnema Brewing Company																											
Bonnema Brewing Marzen	✗																										
Bonnema Brewing Mudhole Porter	✗																										
Bonnema Brewing Pozo Pale Ale	✗																										
Bonnema Brewing Raspberry Wheat	✗																										
Bonnema Brewing Red Kroeker Ale	✗																										

351

Locally available bottle and keg sizes may vary.

Brewery Brand Name	Contact Brewery	Cans	7 oz	8 1/2 oz	10 oz	12 oz	16 oz	20 oz	22 oz	24 oz	1/2 liter	25 oz	32 oz	64 oz	1 liter	1 1/2 liter	375 ml	500 ml	750 ml	40 oz	2 liter	Growlers/Jugs	3 liter	1/6 Keg	1/4 Keg	1/2 Keg	Keg (Non-Specified Size)
Bonnema Brewing Whalerock Wheat	X																										
Bonnema Brewing White Christmas	X																										
Bootie Beer Company																											
Bootie Beer						X																					
Bootie Light						X																					
Boulder Beer Company																											
Boulder Beer Buffalo Gold Golden Ale						X																				X	
Boulder Beer Hazed & Infused Dry-Hopped Ale						X			X															X		X	
Boulder Beer Killer Penguin Barleywine									X															X			
Boulder Beer Mojo India Pale Ale						X			X																	X	
Boulder Beer Mojo Risin' Double IPA									X																	X	
Boulder Beer Never Summer Ale						X			X																	X	
Boulder Beer Pass Time Pale Ale						X																				X	
Boulder Beer Planet Porter						X																				X	
Boulder Beer Singletrack Copper Ale						X																		X		X	
Boulder Beer Sundance Amber						X																				X	
Boulder Beer Sweaty Betty Blonde Wheat Beer						X			X																	X	
Boulevard Brewing Company																											
Boulevard Brewing Bob's '47						X																		X		X	
Boulevard Brewing Bully! Porter						X																		X		X	
Boulevard Brewing Dry Stout						X																		X		X	
Boulevard Brewing Irish Ale						X																		X		X	
Boulevard Brewing Nutcracker Ale						X																		X		X	
Boulevard Brewing Pale Ale						X																		X		X	
Boulevard Brewing Unfiltered Wheat Beer						X																		X		X	
Boulevard Brewing ZÔN						X																		X		X	
Boundary Bay Brewing Company																											
Boundary Bay Best Bitter									X																		
Boundary Bay Cabin Fever									X																		
Boundary Bay Inside Passage Ale									X																		
Boundary Bay Scotch									X																		
Boundary Bay Barley Wine									X																		

Brewery / Brand Name	Contact Brewery	Cans	7 oz	8 1/2 oz	10 oz	12 oz	16 oz	20 oz	22 oz	24 oz	1/2 liter	25 oz	32 oz	64 oz	1 liter	1 1/2 liter	375 ml	500 ml	750 ml	40 oz	2 liter	Growlers/Jugs	3 liter	1/6 Keg	1/4 Keg	1/2 Keg	Keg (Non-Specified Size)
Breckenridge Brewery																											
471 IPA						✗																					
Breckenridge Autumn Ale						✗																					
Breckenridge Avalanche Ale						✗																					
Breckenridge Christmas Ale						✗																					
Breckenridge Hefe Proper						✗																					
Breckenridge Oatmeal Stout						✗																					
Breckenridge Summerbright Ale						✗																					
Breckenridge Vanilla Porter						✗																					
Trademark Pale Ale						✗																					
Brewery Ommegang																											
Hennepin Farmhouse Saison Ale						✗						✗							✗					✗	✗	✗	
Ommegang Abbey Ale Dubbel						✗						✗							✗					✗	✗	✗	
Ommegang Witte Ale						✗						✗							✗					✗	✗	✗	
Rare Vos Amber Ale						✗						✗							✗					✗	✗	✗	
Three Philosophers Quadrupel Ale						✗						✗							✗					✗	✗	✗	
BridgePort Brewing Company																											
Beer Town Brown	✗																										
BridgePort Black Strap Stout	✗																										
BridgePort Blue Heron Pale Ale						✗																					
BridgePort Ebenezer Ale	✗																										
BridgePort ESB	✗																										
BridgePort IPA	✗																										
BridgePort Old Knucklehead	✗																										
BridgePort Ropewalker						✗																					
Bristol Brewing Company																											
Bristol Brewing Beehive Honey Wheat						✗																					
Bristol Brewing Edge City Octoberfest									✗																		
Bristol Brewing Edge City Pale Bock									✗																		
Bristol Brewing Edge City Wit Bier									✗																		✗
Bristol Brewing Laughing Lab Scottish Ale						✗																					✗
Bristol Brewing Mass Transit Ale						✗																					✗

Brewery Brand Name	Contact Brewery	Cans	7 oz	8 1/2 oz	10 oz	12 oz	16 oz	20 oz	22 oz	24 oz	1/2 liter	25 oz	32 oz	64 oz	1 liter	1 1/2 liter	375 ml	500 ml	750 ml	40 oz	2 liter	Growlers/ Jugs	3 liter	1/6 Keg	1/4 Keg	1/2 Keg	Keg (Non-Specified Size)
Bristol Brewing Old No. 23 Barley Wine						✗																					
Bristol Brewing Red Rocket Pale Ale						✗																					✗
Bristol Brewing Winter Warlock Oatmeal Stout						✗																					✗
Brooklyn Brewery																											
Brooklyn Black Chocolate Stout						✗																		✗	✗		
Brooklyn Brown Ale						✗																		✗	✗		
Brooklyn East India Pale Ale						✗																		✗	✗		
Brooklyn Lager						✗																		✗	✗		
Brooklyn Monster Ale						✗																		✗	✗		
Brooklyn Oktoberfest						✗																		✗	✗		
Brooklyn Pennant Ale						✗																		✗	✗		
Brooklyn Pilsner						✗																		✗	✗		
Brooklyn Weisse						✗																		✗	✗		
Post Road Pumpkin Ale						✗																					
Buckeye Brewing																											
Buckeye Brewing Cleveland Lager	✗																										
Buckeye Brewing Czech Pilsner	✗																										
Buckeye Brewing Hippie I.P.A	✗																										
Buckeye Brewing Ho Ho Ho Magical Dubbel	✗																										
Buckeye Brewing Martian Marzen Lager	✗																										
Buckeye Brewing Seventy-Six	✗																										
Buckeye Brewing Vanilla Bean Porter	✗																										
Buckeye Brewing Wheat Cloud	✗																										
Buffalo Bill's Brewery																											
Buffalo Bill's Brewery Orange Blossom Cream Ale						✗																					
Buffalo Bill's Brewery Pumpkin Ale						✗																					
Butte Creek Brewing																											
Butte Creek Christmas Cranberry Ale	✗																										
Butte Creek Creekside Wheat	✗																										
Butte Creek Gold Ale	✗																										
Butte Creek Mt. Shasta Extra Pale Ale	✗																										
Butte Creek Organic Ale						✗																					

Locally available bottle and keg sizes may vary.

Brewery / Brand Name	Contact Brewery	Cans	7 oz	8 1/2 oz	10 oz	12 oz	16 oz	20 oz	22 oz	24 oz	1/2 liter	25 oz	32 oz	64 oz	1 liter	1 1/2 liter	375 ml	500 ml	750 ml	40 oz	2 liter	Growlers/ Jugs	3 liter	1/6 Keg	1/4 Keg	1/2 Keg	Keg (Non-Specified Size)
Butte Creek Organic India Pale Ale	✗																										
Butte Creek Organic Pilsner	✗																										
Butte Creek Organic Porter						✗																					
Butte Creek Roland's Red						✗																					
Butte Creek Spring Ale	✗																										
Butte Creek Summer Pilsner	✗																										
Butte Creek Winter Ale	✗																										
Butternuts Beer & Ale																											
Heinnieweisse Weissbier		✗																						✗			
Moo Thunder Stout		✗																						✗			
Porkslap Pale Ale		✗																						✗			
Snapperhead IPA		✗																						✗			
Buzzards Bay Brewing Company																											
Buzzards Bay Brewing Hefe-Weizen						✗																					
Buzzards Bay Brewing Lager						✗																					
Buzzards Bay Brewing Octoberfest						✗																					
Buzzards Bay Brewing Pale Ale						✗																					
Buzzards Bay Brewing Weizen Dopplebock						✗																					
Caldera Brewing Company																											
Caldera Brewing Pale Ale		✗																									
Cape Ann Brewing																											
Cape Ann Brewing Fisherman's Brew						✗																			✗	✗	
Cape Ann Brewing Fisherman's IPA						✗																			✗	✗	
Capital Brewery																											
Capital Brewery Autumnal Fire						✗																		✗		✗	
Capital Brewery Bavarian Lager						✗																				✗	
Capital Brewery Blonde Dopplebock						✗																		✗		✗	
Capital Brewery Brown Ale						✗																					
Capital Brewery Fest Beer						✗																		✗	✗	✗	
Capital Brewery Island Wheat		✗				✗																		✗		✗	
Capital Brewery Maibock						✗																		✗	✗	✗	
Capital Brewery Munich Dark						✗																					

355

Locally available bottle and keg sizes may vary.

Brewery / Brand Name	Contact Brewery	Cans	7 oz	8 1/2 oz	10 oz	12 oz	16 oz	20 oz	22 oz	24 oz	1/2 liter	25 oz	32 oz	64 oz	1 liter	1 1/2 liter	375 ml	500 ml	750 ml	40 oz	2 liter	Growlers/Jugs	3 liter	1/6 Keg	1/4 Keg	1/2 Keg	Keg (Non-Specified Size)
Capital Brewery Oktoberfest						X																		X	X	X	
Capital Brewery Special Pilsner						X																					
Capital Brewery Winter Skal						X																		X	X	X	
Capital Brewery Wisconsin Amber		X				X																		X	X	X	
Carolina Beer & Beverage Company																											
Carolina Beer Carolina Blonde						X																		X		X	
Carolina Beer Carolina Light						X																		X		X	
Carolina Beer Cottonwood Almond Stout						X																		X		X	
Carolina Beer Cottonwood American Wheat						X																		X		X	
Carolina Beer Cottonwood Endo IPA						X																		X		X	
Carolina Beer Cottonwood Frostbite Ale						X																		X		X	
Carolina Beer Cottonwood Irish Style Red Ale						X																		X		X	
Carolina Beer Cottonwood Lift Your Kilt Scottish Ale						X																		X		X	
Carolina Beer Cottonwood Low Down Brown						X																		X		X	
Carolina Beer Cottonwood Pumpkin Spiced Ale						X																		X		X	
Carolina Brewing																											
Carolina Brewing IPA						X																		X	X	X	
Carolina Brewing Nut Brown Ale						X																		X	X	X	
Carolina Brewing Oktoberfest Lager						X																		X	X	X	
Carolina Brewing Pale Ale						X																		X	X	X	
Carolina Brewing Spring Bock						X																		X	X	X	
Carolina Brewing Summer Ale						X																		X	X	X	
Carolina Brewing Winter Stout						X																		X	X	X	
Cascade Lakes Brewing Company																											
Cascade Lakes 20" Brown						X																					
Cascade Lakes Angus MacDougal's Amber						X																					
Cascade Lakes Blonde Bombshell						X																					
Cascade Lakes IPA						X																					
Cascade Lakes Monkey Face Porter						X																					
Cascade Lakes Pine Marten Pale Ale						X																					
Cascade Lakes Rooster Tail Ale						X																					

Locally available bottle and keg sizes may vary.

Brewery Brand Name	Contact Brewery	Cans	7 oz	8 1/2 oz	10 oz	12 oz	16 oz	20 oz	22 oz	24 oz	1/2 liter	25 oz	32 oz	64 oz	1 liter	1 1/2 liter	375 ml	500 ml	750 ml	40 oz	2 liter	Growlers/Jugs	3 liter	1/6 Keg	1/4 Keg	1/2 Keg	Keg (Non-Specified Size)
Catawba Valley Brewing																											
Catawba Valley Brewing Buffalo Nickle Ale																											✗
Catawba Valley Brown Bear Ale																											✗
Catawba Valley Firewater IPA																											✗
Catawba Valley Honust Injun Stout																											✗
Catawba Valley Indian Head Red																											✗
Catawba Valley King Coconut Porter																											✗
Catawba Valley King Don's Original Pumpkin Ale																											✗
Catawba Valley King Karma Ale																											✗
Central Coast Brewing																											
Central Coast Brewing Cream Ale									✗																	✗	
Central Coast Brewing Golden Glow Ale									✗																	✗	
Central Coast Brewing Honey Wheat Ale									✗																	✗	
Central Coast Brewing Old Mission Ale									✗																	✗	
Central Coast Brewing Stenner Stout Ale									✗																	✗	
Central Coast Brewing Topless Blonde Ale									✗																	✗	
Central Waters Brewing Company																											
Central Waters Happy Heron Pale Ale						✗																			✗		
Central Waters Junc Town Brown Ale						✗																			✗		
Central Waters Kosmyk Charlie Y2K Catastrophe Ale						✗																			✗		
Central Waters Lac Du Bay IPA						✗																			✗		
Central Waters Mud Puppy Porter						✗																			✗		
Central Waters Ouisconsing Red Ale						✗																			✗		
Central Waters Reserve Bourbon Barrel Stout						✗																			✗		
Central Waters Reserve Irish Dry Stout						✗																			✗		
Central Waters Reserve Irish Red Ale						✗																			✗		
Central Waters Reserve Oktoberfest						✗																			✗		
Central Waters Satin Solstice Imperial Stout						✗																			✗		
Central Waters White Water Weizen						✗																			✗		
Charleston Brewing Company																											
Charleston Brewing East Bay IPA						✗																					✗
Charleston Brewing Half Moon Hefeweizen						✗																					✗

357

Brewery / Brand Name	Contact Brewery	Cans	7 oz	8 1/2 oz	10 oz	12 oz	16 oz	20 oz	22 oz	24 oz	1/2 liter	25 oz	32 oz	64 oz	1 liter	1 1/2 liter	375 ml	500 ml	750 ml	40 oz	2 liter	Growlers/Jugs	3 liter	1/6 Keg	1/4 Keg	1/2 Keg	Keg (Non-Specified Size)
Charleville Brewing Amber Ale															X												
Charleville Brewing Belgium Wheat															X												
Charleville Brewing Lager															X												
Christian Moerlein Brewing Company																											
Christian Moerlein Doppelbock	X																										
Christian Moerlein Hefeweisen	X																										
Christian Moerlein Oktoberfest	X																										
Christian Moerlein Select Dunkel	X																										
Christian Moerlein Select Lager						X																					
Christian Moerlein Select Light						X																					
Cisco Brewers, Inc.																											
Cisco Brewers Baggywrinkle Barleywine						X													X								X
Cisco Brewers Bailey's Ale						X													X								X
Cisco Brewers Captain Swain's Extra Stout						X													X								X
Cisco Brewers Celebration Libation						X													X								X
Cisco Brewers Moor Porter						X													X								X
Cisco Brewers Sankaty Light						X													X								X
Cisco Brewers Summer of Lager						X													X								X
Cisco Brewers Whale's Tale Pale Ale						X													X								X
City Brewery																											
City Brewery Golden Leaf Unfiltered Wheat						X																					
City Cream Ale						X																					
City Festbier						X																					
City Lager		X				X																					
City Light		X				X																					
City Pale Ale						X																					
City Slicker Malt Liquor						X																					
City Winter Porter						X																					
KUL		X				X																					
KUL Lite		X				X																					
LaCrosse Lager		X				X																					
LaCrosse Light		X				X																					

How Supplied *Continued*

Locally available bottle and keg sizes may vary.

Brewery / Brand Name	Contact Brewery	Cans	7 oz	8 1/2 oz	10 oz	12 oz	16 oz	20 oz	22 oz	24 oz	1/2 liter	25 oz	32 oz	64 oz	1 liter	1 1/2 liter	375 ml	500 ml	750 ml	40 oz	2 liter	Growlers/Jugs	3 liter	1/6 Keg	1/4 Keg	1/2 Keg	Keg (Non-Specified Size)
Clay Pipe Brewing Company																											
Clay Pipe Brewing Blackfin Pale Ale						✗																					
Clay Pipe Brewing Blue Tractor Ale						✗																					
Clay Pipe Brewing Pursuit of Happiness Winter Warmer						✗																					
Hop-ocalypse India Pale Ale						✗																					
Climax Brewing Company																											
Climax Brewing Cream Ale																						✗		✗		✗	
Climax Brewing Extra Special Bitter Ale																						✗		✗		✗	
Climax Brewing India Pale Ale																						✗		✗		✗	
Climax Brewing Nut Brown Ale																						✗		✗		✗	
Climax Hoffmann Bavarian Dark																						✗		✗		✗	
Climax Hoffmann Helles																						✗		✗		✗	
Climax Hoffmann Oktoberfest																						✗		✗		✗	
Clipper City Brewing Company																											
Clipper City BaltoMärzHon						✗																		✗		✗	
Clipper City Brewing Gold Ale						✗																		✗		✗	
Clipper City Brewing Pale Ale						✗																		✗		✗	
Clipper City McHenry Old Baltimore Style Beer						✗																		✗		✗	
Heavy Seas Brewing Below Decks						✗																		✗		✗	
Heavy Seas Brewing "Holy Sheet"						✗																		✗		✗	
Heavy Seas Brewing Loose Cannon						✗																		✗		✗	
Heavy Seas Brewing Peg Leg Stout						✗																		✗		✗	
Heavy Seas Brewing Red Sky at Night Saison Ale						✗																		✗		✗	
Heavy Seas Brewing Small Craft Warning Über Pils						✗																		✗		✗	
Heavy Seas Brewing Winter Storm "Category 5" Ale						✗																		✗		✗	
Oxford Hefeweizen						✗																		✗		✗	
Oxford Raspberry						✗																		✗		✗	
Coastal Extreme Brewing Company, LLC																											
Newport Storm Annual Limited Release						✗																					
Newport Storm Blizzard Porter						✗																					
Newport Storm Cyclone Series - Derek Stout						✗																					
Newport Storm Hurricane Amber Ale						✗																					

Locally available bottle and keg sizes may vary.

Brewery / Brand Name	Contact Brewery	Cans	7 oz	8 1/2 oz	10 oz	12 oz	16 oz	20 oz	22 oz	24 oz	1/2 liter	25 oz	32 oz	64 oz	1 liter	1 1/2 liter	375 ml	500 ml	750 ml	40 oz	2 liter	Growlers/Jugs	3 liter	1/6 Keg	1/4 Keg	1/2 Keg	Keg (Non-Specified Size)
Newport Storm Maelstrom IPA						✗																					
Newport Storm Regenschauer Oktoberfest						✗																					
Newport Storm Rhode Island Blueberry						✗																					
Newport Storm Thunderhead Irish Red						✗																					
Coeur d'Alene Brewing Company																											
Coeur d'Alene Brewing Centennial Pale Ale	✗																										
Coeur d'Alene Brewing Honeymoon Wheat	✗																										
Coeur d'Alene Brewing Huckleberry Ale	✗																										
Coeur d'Alene Brewing Lake Side British Ale	✗																										
Coffaro Beer Company																											
Coffaro Italian Style Beer	✗																										
Columbus Brewing Company																											
Columbus Brewing 90 Schilling Ale	✗																										
Columbus Brewing Apricot Ale	✗																										
Columbus Brewing Ohio Honey Wheat	✗																										
Columbus Brewing Pale Ale	✗																										
Concord Brewery, Inc.																											
Concord Porter						✗																					✗
Concord Grape Ale						✗																					✗
Concord IPA						✗																					✗
Concord North Woods Ale						✗																					✗
Concord Pale Ale						✗																					✗
Rapscallion Blessing						✗																					✗
Rapscallion Creation						✗																					✗
Rapscallion Premier						✗																					✗
Cooper's Cave Ale Company, LTD.																											
Cooper's Cave Ale Company Bumppo's Brown Ale									✗													✗		✗	✗	✗	
Cooper's Cave Ale Company Pale Ale									✗													✗		✗	✗	✗	
Cooper's Cave Ale Company Pathfinder's Porter									✗													✗		✗	✗	✗	
Cooper's Cave Ale Company Radeau Red Ale									✗													✗		✗	✗	✗	
Cooper's Cave Ale Company Sagamore Stout									✗													✗		✗	✗	✗	
Cooper's Cave Ale Company Tavern Ale									✗													✗		✗	✗	✗	

Locally available bottle and keg sizes may vary.

Brewery / Brand Name	Contact Brewery	Cans	7 oz	8 1/2 oz	10 oz	12 oz	16 oz	20 oz	22 oz	24 oz	1/2 liter	25 oz	32 oz	64 oz	1 liter	1 1/2 liter	375 ml	500 ml	750 ml	40 oz	2 liter	Growlers/Jugs	3 liter	1/6 Keg	1/4 Keg	1/2 Keg	Keg (Non-Specified Size)
Cooperstown Brewing Company																											
Cooperstown Brewing Back Yard India Pale Ale						X																					
Cooperstown Brewing Benchwarmer Porter						X																					
Cooperstown Brewing Nine Man Ale						X																					
Cooperstown Brewing Old Slugger Pale Ale						X																					
Cooperstown Brewing Pride Of Milford Special Ale						X																					
Cooperstown Brewing Strike Out Stout						X																					
Cottrell Brewing Company																											
Cottrell Brewing Old Yankee Ale						X																			X	X	
Crabtree Brewing Company																											
Crabtree Brewing Downtown Nut Brown						X			X													X			X	X	
Crabtree Brewing Twisted Creek Wheat						X			X													X			X	X	
Crested Butte Brewery																											
Crested Butte Brewery Paradise Crisp Golden Ale	X																										
Crested Butte Brewery Red Lady Ale	X																										
Crested Butte Brewery White Buffalo Peace Ale	X																										
Cricket Hill Brewing Company																											
Cricket Hill Brewing American Ale						X																		X		X	
Cricket Hill Brewing Colonel Blides Altbier																								X		X	
Cricket Hill Brewing East Coast Lager						X																		X		X	
Cricket Hill Brewing Hopnotic IPA						X																		X		X	
D.G. Yuengling & Son, Inc.																											
Yuengling Black and Tan		X				X																			X	X	
Yuengling Dark Brewed Porter						X																			X	X	
Yuengling Light Beer		X				X				X															X	X	
Yuengling Light Lager		X				X				X															X	X	
Yuengling Lord Chesterfield Ale		X				X																					
Yuengling Premium Beer		X				X				X			X												X	X	
Yuengling Traditional Lager		X				X			X				X												X	X	
D L Geary Brewing Company																											
Geary's Autumn Ale						X																					
Geary's Hampshire Special Ale						X																					

361

How Supplied *Continued*   Locally available bottle and keg sizes may vary.

Brewery Brand Name	Contact Brewery	Cans	7 oz	8 1/2 oz	10 oz	12 oz	16 oz	20 oz	22 oz	24 oz	1/2 liter	25 oz	32 oz	64 oz	1 liter	1 1/2 liter	375 ml	500 ml	750 ml	40 oz	2 liter	Growlers/Jugs	3 liter	1/6 Keg	1/4 Keg	1/2 Keg	Keg (Non-Specified Size)
Geary's London Porter						✗																					
Geary's Pale Ale						✗																					
Geary's Summer Ale						✗																					
Geary's Winter						✗																					
Dark Horse Brewing Company																											
Dark Horse 750 ml Imperial Stout						✗																		✗		✗	
Dark Horse Belgian Amber Ale						✗																		✗		✗	
Dark Horse Crooked Tree IPA						✗																		✗		✗	
Dark Horse Double Crooked Tree IPA						✗																				✗	
Dark Horse Fore Smoked Stout						✗																		✗		✗	
Dark Horse One Oatmeal Stout Ale						✗																		✗		✗	
Dark Horse Raspberry Ale						✗																		✗		✗	
Dark Horse Sapient Trip Ale						✗																		✗		✗	
Dark Horse Scotty Karate Scotch Ale						✗																		✗		✗	
Dark Horse Special Reserve Black Bier Ale						✗																		✗		✗	
Dark Horse Too Cream Stout						✗																		✗		✗	
Dark Horse Tres Blueberry Stout						✗																		✗		✗	
Deschutes Brewery																											
Deschutes Bachelor ESB						✗																		✗	✗	✗	
Deschutes Black Butte Porter						✗				✗														✗	✗	✗	
Deschutes Bond Street Brown						✗				✗														✗	✗	✗	
Deschutes Broken Top Bock						✗																		✗	✗	✗	
Deschutes Buzzsaw Brown						✗																		✗	✗	✗	
Deschutes Cascade Ale						✗																		✗	✗	✗	
Deschutes Cinder Cone Red Ale						✗																		✗	✗	✗	
Deschutes Hop Hennch India Pale Ale						✗																		✗	✗	✗	
Deschutes Hop Trip Pale Ale						✗				✗														✗	✗	✗	
Deschutes Inversion IPA						✗																		✗	✗	✗	
Deschutes Jubelale						✗																		✗	✗	✗	
Deschutes Mirror Pond Pale Ale						✗																		✗	✗	✗	
Deschutes Obsidian Stout						✗																		✗	✗	✗	
Deschutes Quail Springs IPA						✗																		✗	✗	✗	

Locally available bottle and keg sizes may vary.

Brewery / Brand Name	Contact Brewery	Cans	7 oz	8 1/2 oz	10 oz	12 oz	16 oz	20 oz	22 oz	24 oz	1/2 liter	25 oz	32 oz	64 oz	1 liter	1 1/2 liter	375 ml	500 ml	750 ml	40 oz	2 liter	Growlers/Jugs	3 liter	1/6 Keg	1/4 Keg	1/2 Keg	Keg (Non-Specified Size)
Deschutes The Abyss										✗														✗	✗	✗	
Deschutes Twilight Ale						✗																		✗	✗	✗	
Diamond Bear Brewing Company																											
Diamond Bear Honey Weiss						✗																		✗		✗	
Diamond Bear Irish Red Ale						✗																		✗		✗	
Diamond Bear Pale Ale						✗																		✗		✗	
Diamond Bear Party Porter	✗																							✗		✗	
Diamond Bear Presidential IPA						✗																		✗		✗	
Diamond Bear Rocktoberfest	✗																							✗		✗	
Diamond Bear Southern Blonde						✗																		✗		✗	
Diamond Bear Ultra Blonde	✗																										
Dick's Brewing Company																											
Bottleworks India Pale Ale						✗																		✗	✗	✗	
Dick's Barley Wine Ale						✗																		✗	✗	✗	
Dick's Belgian Double						✗																		✗	✗	✗	
Dick's Belgian Tripel						✗																		✗	✗	✗	
Dick's Best Bitter						✗																		✗	✗	✗	
Dick's Cream Stout						✗																		✗	✗	✗	
Dick's Danger Ale						✗																		✗	✗	✗	
Dick's Double Diamond Winter Ale						✗																		✗	✗	✗	
Dick's Grand Cru						✗																		✗	✗	✗	
Dick's Harvest Ale						✗																		✗	✗	✗	
Dick's Imperial Stout						✗																		✗	✗	✗	
Dick's India Pale Ale						✗																		✗	✗	✗	
Dick's Irish Ale						✗																		✗	✗	✗	
Dick's Lave Rock Porter						✗																		✗	✗	✗	
Dick's Mountain Ale						✗																		✗	✗	✗	
Dick's Pale Ale						✗																					
Dick's Rye Ale						✗																					
Dick's Silk Lady						✗																					
Dick's Smoked Porter									✗																		
Dick's Working Man's Brown Ale						✗																					

Brewery / Brand Name	Contact Brewery	Cans	7 oz	8 1/2 oz	10 oz	12 oz	16 oz	20 oz	22 oz	24 oz	1/2 liter	25 oz	32 oz	64 oz	1 liter	1 1/2 liter	375 ml	500 ml	750 ml	40 oz	2 liter	Growlers/Jugs	3 liter	1/6 Keg	1/4 Keg	1/2 Keg	Keg (Non-Specified Size)
Dillion DAM Brewery																											
DAM DAM Straight Lager	✗																										
Dillion DAM Extra Pale Ale	✗																										
Dillion DAM Olde Forster's Scotch Ale	✗																										
Dillion DAM Winter Warmer	✗																										
Sweet George's Brown Ale	✗																										
Dixie Brewing Company																											
Dixie Brewing Blackened Voodoo Lager	✗																										
Dixie Brewing Crimson Voodoo Ale	✗																										
Dixie Brewing Dixie Beer	✗																										
Dixie Brewing Jazz Amber Light	✗																										
Dogfish Head Craft Brewery																											
Dogfish Head 120 Minute Imperial IPA						✗																					
Dogfish Head 60 Minute IPA						✗																		✗		✗	
Dogfish Head 90 Minute Imperial IPA						✗																		✗		✗	
Dogfish Head Aprihop						✗																		✗		✗	
Dogfish Head Au Courant						✗																					
Dogfish Head Black & Blue									✗																		
Dogfish Head Burton Baton						✗																					
Dogfish Head Chicory Stout						✗																		✗		✗	
Dogfish Head Fort						✗																					
Dogfish Head Golden Shower Imperial Pilsner																			✗								
Dogfish Head Immort Ale						✗																					
Dogfish Head Indian Brown Ale						✗																		✗		✗	
Dogfish Head Midas Touch Golden Elixir						✗																					
Dogfish Head Old School Barleywine						✗																					
Dogfish Head Punkin Ale						✗																				✗	
Dogfish Head Raison D'Etre						✗																		✗		✗	
Dogfish Head Red & White									✗																		
Dogfish Head Shelter Pale Ale						✗																		✗		✗	
Dogfish Head Snowblown Ale	✗																										
Dogfish Head World Wide Stout						✗																					

Locally available bottle and keg sizes may vary.

Brewery / Brand Name	Contact Brewery	Cans	7 oz	8 1/2 oz	10 oz	12 oz	16 oz	20 oz	22 oz	24 oz	1/2 liter	25 oz	32 oz	64 oz	1 liter	1 1/2 liter	375 ml	500 ml	750 ml	40 oz	2 liter	Growlers/Jugs	3 liter	1/6 Keg	1/4 Keg	1/2 Keg	Keg (Non-Specified Size)
Downtown Brewing Company																											
SLO Brewing Amber Ale						✗																					
SLO Brewing Blueberry Ale						✗																					
SLO Brewing Cole Porter						✗																					
SLO Brewing Extra Pale Ale						✗																					
SLO Olde Highland Ale						✗																					
Dragonmead Microbrewery																											
Dragonmead 90 Shilling																								✗	✗	✗	
Dragonmead Andromeda Heather Ale																								✗	✗	✗	
Dragonmead Armageddon Grand Cru																								✗	✗	✗	
Dragonmead Big Larry's Pale Ale																								✗	✗	✗	
Dragonmead Bill's Witbier																								✗	✗	✗	
Dragonmead Bishop Bob's Holy Smoke																								✗	✗	✗	
Dragonmead Bock Tubock																								✗	✗	✗	
Dragonmead Breath Of The Dragon English Bitter																								✗	✗	✗	
Dragonmead Broken Paddle India Pale Ale																								✗	✗	✗	
Dragonmead Bronze Griffin Belgian Style																								✗	✗	✗	
Dragonmead Castlebrite Apricot Ale																								✗	✗	✗	
Dragonmead Copper Shield Bitter Harvest																								✗	✗	✗	
Dragonmead Corktown Red																								✗	✗	✗	
Dragonmead Crooked Door Amber Ale																								✗	✗	✗	
Dragonmead Crown Jewels IPA						✗																		✗	✗	✗	
Dragonmead Crusader Dark Mild Ale																								✗	✗	✗	
Dragonmead Dead Monk Abbey Ale																								✗	✗	✗	
Dragonmead Dragon Daze Hemp Ale																								✗	✗	✗	
Dragonmead Dragon Slayer Altbier Style																								✗	✗	✗	
Dragonmead Drei Kronen 1308																								✗	✗	✗	
Dragonmead Dubbel Dragon Ale																								✗	✗	✗	
Dragonmead Earl's Spit Stout																								✗	✗	✗	
Dragonmead Erik the Red Irish Style Amber Ale						✗																		✗	✗	✗	
Dragonmead Excalibur Barley Wine																								✗	✗	✗	
Dragonmead Final Absolution Belgian Style						✗																		✗	✗	✗	

365

Locally available bottle and keg sizes may vary.

Brewery Brand Name	Contact Brewery	Cans	7 oz	8 1/2 oz	10 oz	12 oz	16 oz	20 oz	22 oz	24 oz	1/2 liter	25 oz	32 oz	64 oz	1 liter	1 1/2 liter	375 ml	500 ml	750 ml	40 oz	2 liter	Growlers/ Jugs	3 liter	1/6 Keg	1/4 Keg	1/2 Keg	Keg (Non-Specified Size)
Dragonmead Honey Porter																								✗	✗	✗	
Dragonmead Imperial Stout																								✗	✗	✗	
Dragonmead Inquisition Pale Ale																								✗	✗	✗	
Dragonmead Jul 01																								✗	✗	✗	
Dragonmead Kaiser's Kolsch																								✗	✗	✗	
Dragonmead Lady Guinevere's Golden Belgian Style																								✗	✗	✗	
Dragonmead Lancelot's Cream Ale																								✗	✗	✗	
Dragonmead Larry's Lionheart Pale																								✗	✗	✗	
Dragonmead Lil's Grumpkin Pumpkin Ale																								✗	✗	✗	
Dragonmead London Brown Ale																								✗	✗	✗	
Dragonmead Mariann's Honey Brown																								✗	✗	✗	
Dragonmead Nagelweiss Wheat																								✗	✗	✗	
Dragonmead Oktoberfest Marzen																								✗	✗	✗	
Dragonmead Redwing Raspberry Wheat Beer																								✗	✗	✗	
Dragonmead Reverend Fred's Oatmeal																								✗	✗	✗	
Dragonmead Sir William's Extra Special Bitter						✗																		✗	✗	✗	
Dragonmead Squire Pilsen																								✗	✗	✗	
Dragonmead Tafelbeir Lager																								✗	✗	✗	
Dragonmead Tayken Abock																								✗	✗	✗	
Dragonmead Tuhelles Enbock																								✗	✗	✗	
Dragonmead Under The Kilt Wee Heavy						✗																		✗	✗	✗	
Dragonmead Wench Water Belgian Pale Ale																								✗	✗	✗	
Dragonmead Willy's Oompa-Loompa																								✗	✗	✗	
Dragonmead Woody's Perfect Porter																								✗	✗	✗	
Drake's Brewing Company																											
Drake's Amber Ale						✗																		✗	✗	✗	
Drake's Blonde Ale						✗																		✗	✗	✗	
Drake's Hefe-Weizen						✗																		✗	✗	✗	
Drake's IPA						✗																		✗	✗	✗	
Duck-Rabbit Craft Brewery																											
Duck-Rabbit Amber Ale						✗																		✗		✗	
Duck-Rabbit Baltic Porter (in NC only)						✗																		✗		✗	

Locally available bottle and keg sizes may vary.

Brewery Brand Name	Contact Brewery	Cans	7 oz	8 1/2 oz	10 oz	12 oz	16 oz	20 oz	22 oz	24 oz	1/2 liter	25 oz	32 oz	64 oz	1 liter	1 1/2 liter	375 ml	500 ml	750 ml	40 oz	2 liter	Growlers/ Jugs	3 liter	1/6 Keg	1/4 Keg	1/2 Keg	Keg (Non-Specified Size)
Duck-Rabbit Barleywine Ale (in NC only)						✗																		✗		✗	
Duck-Rabbit Brown Ale						✗																		✗		✗	
Duck-Rabbit Milk Stout						✗																		✗		✗	
Duck-Rabbit Porter						✗																		✗		✗	
Duck-Rabbit Russian Imperial Stout (in NC only)						✗																		✗		✗	
Duck-Rabbit Wee Heavy Scotch Style Ale (in NC only)						✗																		✗		✗	
Dunedin Brewery																											
Dunedin Brewery Beach Tale Brown Ale							✗																	✗		✗	
Dunedin Brewery Celtic Gold Ale							✗																	✗		✗	
Dunedin Brewery Christmas Farm Ale							✗																	✗		✗	
Dunedin Brewery Drop Kick Monday's Erin Red Ale							✗																	✗		✗	
Dunedin Brewery Highland Games Ale							✗																	✗		✗	
Dunedin Brewery Leonard Croon's Old Mean Stout							✗																	✗		✗	
Dunedin Brewery Lowland Wheat Ale							✗																	✗		✗	
Dunedin Brewery Oktoberfest Ale							✗																	✗		✗	
Dunedin Brewery Piper's Pale Ale							✗																	✗		✗	
Dunedin Brewery Razzbeery Wheat Ale							✗																	✗		✗	
Dunedin Brewery Redhead Red Ale							✗																	✗		✗	
Dunedin Brewery Summer Apricot Wheat Ale							✗																	✗		✗	
Dunedin Brewery Summer Buzz							✗																	✗		✗	
Durango Brewing Company																											
Durango Brewing Amber Ale		✗																									
Durango Brewing Dark Lager		✗																									
Durango Brewing Derail Ale		✗																									
Durango Brewing Ian's Pale Ale		✗																									
Durango Brewing Wheat Beer		✗																									
E.J. Phair Brewing																											
E.J. Phair India Pale Ale						✗																					✗
E.J. Phair Marzen						✗																					✗
E.J. Phair Pale Ale						✗																					✗
E.J. Phair Pilsner						✗																					✗

Locally available bottle and keg sizes may vary.

Brewery / Brand Name	Contact Brewery	Cans	7 oz	8 1/2 oz	10 oz	12 oz	16 oz	20 oz	22 oz	24 oz	1/2 liter	25 oz	32 oz	64 oz	1 liter	1 1/2 liter	375 ml	500 ml	750 ml	40 oz	2 liter	Growlers/Jugs	3 liter	1/6 Keg	1/4 Keg	1/2 Keg	Keg (Non-Specified Size)
Edenton Brewing Company																											
Edenton Brewing Helles Angel	X																										
Edenton Brewing Horniblow's Tavern						X																					
Edenton Brewing Joseph Hewes	X																										
Edenton Brewing King David's Red	X																										
Edenton Brewing Uncle Nut's						X																					
Eel River Brewing Company																											
Eel River Brewing California Blonde Ale						X																					
Eel River Brewing Climax California Classic						X																					
Eel River Brewing Organic Amber Ale						X																					
Eel River Brewing Organic Extra Pale Ale						X																					
Eel River Brewing Organic India Pal Ale						X																					
Eel River Brewing Organic Porter						X																					
Eel River Brewing Ravensbrau India Pale Ale						X																					
Eel River Brewing Ravensbrau Porter						X																					
El Toro Brewing																											
El Toro "Yo" Winter Brew	X																										
El Toro Bravo	X																										
El Toro Deuce Imperial IPA	X																										
El Toro IPA	X																										
El Toro Keller Bier	X																										
El Toro Negro Oatmeal Stout	X																										
El Toro Oro Golden Ale	X																										
El Toro Peach Ale	X																										
El Toro Poppy Jasper Amber Ale	X																										
El Toro William Jones Wheat	X																										
Gena's Honey Blonde Ale	X																										
Electric Beer Company																											
Dave's Electric Beer	X																										
OK Ale	X																										
Ellicottville Brewing Company																											
Ellicottville Brewing Black Jack Oatmeal Stout	X																										

Brewery / Brand Name	Contact Brewery	Cans	7 oz	8 1/2 oz	10 oz	12 oz	16 oz	20 oz	22 oz	24 oz	1/2 liter	25 oz	32 oz	64 oz	1 liter	1 1/2 liter	375 ml	500 ml	750 ml	40 oz	2 liter	Growlers/ Jugs	3 liter	1/6 Keg	1/4 Keg	1/2 Keg	Keg (Non-Specified Size)
Ellicottville Brewing Blueberry Wheat						✗																		✗		✗	
Ellicottville Brewing German Red	✗																										
Ellicottville Brewing Nut Brown						✗																		✗		✗	
Ellicottville Brewing American Pale Ale						✗																		✗		✗	
Ellicottville Brewing Toasted Lager	✗																										
Elmwood Brewing Company																											
Elmwood Brewing Amber Ale						✗																					
Elmwood Brewing Dopple Bock						✗																					
Elmwood Brewing Dry Stout						✗																					
Elmwood Brewing Dunkle Weizen						✗																					
Elmwood Brewing Lawnmower						✗																					
Elmwood Brewing Nut Brown						✗																					
Elmwood Brewing Oktoberfest						✗																					
Elmwood Brewing Pale Ale						✗																					
Elysian Brewing Company																											
Ambrosia Maibock									✗																		
Avatar Jasmine IPA									✗																		
Bete Blanche Belgian-Style Tripel									✗																		
Bifrost Winter Ale									✗																		
Dragonstooth Stout									✗																		
Elysian Fields Pale Ale									✗																		
Immortal India Pale Ale									✗																		
Loki Lager									✗																		
Night Owl Pumpkin Ale									✗																		
Pandora's Bock									✗																		
Perseus Porter									✗																		
Saison Elysee									✗																		
The Wise Extra Special Bitter									✗																		
Zephyrus Pilsner									✗																		
Empyrean Brewing																											
Empyrean Ales Burning Skye Scottish Ale						✗																		✗		✗	
Empyrean Ales Chaco Canyon Honey Gold						✗																		✗		✗	

369

Locally available bottle and keg sizes may vary.

Brewery Brand Name	Contact Brewery	Cans	7 oz	8 1/2 oz	10 oz	12 oz	16 oz	20 oz	22 oz	24 oz	1/2 liter	25 oz	32 oz	64 oz	1 liter	1 1/2 liter	375 ml	500 ml	750 ml	40 oz	2 liter	Growlers/Jugs	3 liter	1/6 Keg	1/4 Keg	1/2 Keg	Keg (Non-Specified Size)
Empyrean Ales Dark Side Vanilla Porter						X																		X		X	
Empyrean Ales Luna Sea ESB						X																		X		X	
Empyrean Ales Third Stone Brown						X																		X		X	
English Ales Brewery																											
English Ales Black Hound Stout	X																										
English Ales Black Prince Porter	X																										
English Ales Brew 66	X																										
English Ales Dragon Slayer India Pale Ale	X																										
English Ales Edinburgh Winter Ale	X																										
English Ales English Pale Ale	X																										
English Ales Jubilee Golden Ale	X																										
English Ales Monk's Brown Ale	X																										
English Ales Monterey Bay Wheat	X																										
English Ales Ramsey's Fat Lip Ale	X																										
English Ales Triple B (Borthwick's Best Bitter)	X																										
English Ales Victory ESB	X																										
Erie Brewing																											
Erie Brewing Drake's Crude Oatmeal Stout						X																		X		X	
Erie Brewing Fallenbock						X																		X		X	
Erie Brewing German Wheat						X																		X		X	
Erie Brewing Golden Fleece Maibock Lager						X																		X		X	
Erie Brewing Heritage Alt						X																		X		X	
Erie Brewing Mad Anthony's Ale						X																		X		X	
Erie Brewing Presque Isle Pilsner						X																		X		X	
Erie Brewing RailBender Ale						X																		X		X	
Erie Brewing Red Ryder Big Beer						X																		X		X	
Erie Brewing Sunshine Wit						X																		X		X	
Estes Park Brewery																											
Estes Park Gold						X																					
Estes Park Porter						X																					
Estes Park Raspberry Wheat						X																					
Estes Park Renegade										X																	

Locally available bottle and keg sizes may vary.

Brewery / Brand Name	Contact Brewery	Cans	7 oz	8 1/2 oz	10 oz	12 oz	16 oz	20 oz	22 oz	24 oz	1/2 liter	25 oz	32 oz	64 oz	1 liter	1 1/2 liter	375 ml	500 ml	750 ml	40 oz	2 liter	Growlers/ Jugs	3 liter	1/6 Keg	1/4 Keg	1/2 Keg	Keg (Non-Specified Size)
Estes Park Samson Stout										✗																	
Estes Park Staggering Elk						✗																					
Estes Park Stinger Wild Honey Wheat						✗																					
Estes Park Trail Ridge Red						✗				✗																	
Etna Brewing Company																											
Etna Classic Gold						✗																					
Etna Old Grind Porter						✗																					
Etna Phoenix Red						✗																					
Falls Brewing Company																											
Falls Brewing Falls Dirty Blonde Ale						✗																					
Falls Brewing Falls Hot Tail Ale						✗																					
Falls Brewing Falls Nut Brown Ale						✗																					
Falls Brewing Falls Porter						✗																					
Far West Brewing Company (Contact Brewery)																											
Hedgerow Red	✗																										
Ranger IPA	✗																										
Three Threads Porter	✗																										
Farmhouse Brewing Company																											
Farmhouse Hayloft Pils	✗																										
Farmhouse Kölsch Bier	✗																										
Farmhouse Oasthouse IPA	✗																										
Farmhouse Saison 7	✗																										
Farmhouse Stone Fence Porter	✗																										
Farmhouse Two Tractor Pale Ale	✗																										
Firestone Walker Brewing Company																											
Firestone Walker Double Barrel Ale						✗																		✗			✗
Firestone Walker Lager						✗																		✗			✗
Firestone Walker Pale Ale						✗																		✗			✗
Firestone Walker Walker's Reserve	✗																										
Fish Brewing Company																											
Fish Tale Blonde Ale						✗																					✗
Fish Tale Detonator Doppelbock Lager						✗			✗																		✗

Brewery / Brand Name	Contact Brewery	Cans	7 oz	8 1/2 oz	10 oz	12 oz	16 oz	20 oz	22 oz	24 oz	1/2 liter	25 oz	32 oz	64 oz	1 liter	1 1/2 liter	375 ml	500 ml	750 ml	40 oz	2 liter	Growlers/ Jugs	3 liter	1/6 Keg	1/4 Keg	1/2 Keg	Keg (Non-Specified Size)
Fish Tale Leviathan Barleywine						X			X																		X
Fish Tale Monkfish Belgian-style Triple Ale						X			X																		X
Fish Tale Mudshark Porter	X																										X
Fish Tale Old Woody English Old Ale						X			X																		X
Fish Tale Organic Amber Ale						X																					X
Fish Tale Organic India Pale Ale						X																					X
Fish Tale Poseidon's Imperial Stout						X			X																		X
Fish Tale Thornton Creek Ale	X																										X
Fish Tale Trout Stout						X																					X
Fish Tale Wild Salmon Organic Pale Ale						X																					X
Fish Tale Winterfish Ale						X																					X
Leavenworth Beers Blind Pig Dunkle Weizen Ale						X																					X
Leavenworth Beers Friesian Pilsner	X																										X
Leavenworth Beers Hodgson's India Pale Ale	X																										X
Leavenworth Beers Ingall's Extra Special Bitter	X																										X
Leavenworth Beers Nosferatu Red Ale	X																										X
Leavenworth Beers Oktoberfest Bier	X																										X
Leavenworth Beers Snowblind Winter Warmer	X																										X
Leavenworth Beers Spring Bock Lager	X																										X
Leavenworth Beers Whistling Pig Hefeweizen						X																					X
Fletcher Street Brewing Company																											
Alpena Wheat Ale						X																					X
Lumber Lager Red						X																					X
Paper Maker Light						X																					X
Paper Maker Pilsner						X																					X
Pewabic Pale Ale						X																					X
Sanctuary Stout						X																					X
Thunder Bay Bock						X																					X
Florida Beer Company																											
Beachside American Lager						X																		X		X	
Beachside Porter						X																		X		X	
Beachside Sun Light						X																		X		X	

Locally available bottle and keg sizes may vary.

Brewery / Brand Name	Contact Brewery	Cans	7 oz	8 1/2 oz	10 oz	12 oz	16 oz	20 oz	22 oz	24 oz	1/2 liter	25 oz	32 oz	64 oz	1 liter	1 1/2 liter	375 ml	500 ml	750 ml	40 oz	2 liter	Growlers/ Jugs	3 liter	1/6 Keg	1/4 Keg	1/2 Keg	Keg (Non-Specified Size)
Hurricane Reef Caribbean Pilsner						X																		X		X	
Hurricane Reef Lager	X																							X		X	
Hurricane Reef Pale Ale						X																		X		X	
Hurricane Reef Raspberry Wheat						X																		X		X	
Key West Golden Lager	X																							X		X	
Key West Pilsner Light						X																		X		X	
Key West Sunset Ale						X																		X		X	
La Tropical						X																		X		X	
Ybor Gold Amber Lager						X																		X		X	
Ybor Gold Brown Ale																								X		X	
Ybor Gold Gaspar's Porter						X																		X		X	
Ybor Gold Light						X																		X		X	
Ybor Gold Wheat Ale						X																		X		X	
Flying Bison Brewing Company																											
Flying Bison Brewing Aviator Red						X																		X			
Flying Bison Brewing Barnstormer Pale Ale						X																					
Flying Bison Brewing Blackbird Oatmeal Stout	X																										
Flying Bison Brewing Buffalo Lager						X																					
Flying Bison Brewing Dawn Patrol Gold	X																										
Flying Dog Brewery, LLC																											
Flying Dog Doggie Style Pale Ale						X																		X		X	
Flying Dog Dogtoberfest						X																		X		X	
Flying Dog Heller Hound Mai Bock						X																		X		X	
Flying Dog Horn Dog Barley Wine Style Ale						X																		X		X	
Flying Dog In Heat Wheat						X																		X		X	
Flying Dog K9 Winter Cruiser						X																		X		X	
Flying Dog Old Scratch Amber						X																		X		X	
Flying Dog Road Scottish Porter						X																		X		X	
Flying Dog Snake Dog IPA						X																		X		X	
Flying Dog Tire Bite Golden Ale						X																		X		X	
Gonzo Imperial Porter						X													X					X		X	
Wild Dog Colorado Saison						X																		X		X	

How Supplied *Continued*

Locally available bottle and keg sizes may vary.

Brewery / Brand Name	Contact Brewery	Cans	7 oz	8 1/2 oz	10 oz	12 oz	16 oz	20 oz	22 oz	24 oz	1/2 liter	25 oz	32 oz	64 oz	1 liter	1 1/2 liter	375 ml	500 ml	750 ml	40 oz	2 liter	Growlers/Jugs	3 liter	1/6 Keg	1/4 Keg	1/2 Keg	Keg (Non-Specified Size)
Wild Dog Weizenbock Ale						✗													✗					✗		✗	
Flying Fish Brewing																											
Flying Fish Brewing Belgian Abbey Dubbel						✗																		✗		✗	
Flying Fish Brewing ESB Ale						✗																		✗		✗	
Flying Fish Brewing Extra Pale Ale						✗																		✗		✗	
Flying Fish Brewing Farmhouse Summer Ale						✗																		✗		✗	
Flying Fish Brewing Grand Cru Winter Reserve						✗																		✗		✗	
Flying Fish Brewing Hopfish						✗																		✗		✗	
Flying Fish Brewing Imperial Espresso Porter						✗																		✗		✗	
Flying Fish Brewing Oktoberfish						✗																		✗		✗	
Flying Fish Brewing Porter						✗																		✗		✗	
Fordham Brewing Company																											
Fordham Brewing C126 Light						✗																		✗		✗	
Fordham Brewing Copperhead Ale						✗																		✗		✗	
Fordham Brewing Fordham Lager						✗																		✗		✗	
Fordham Brewing Oyster Stout	✗																										
Fordham Brewing Tavern Ale	✗																										
Founders Brewing Company																											
Founders Brewing Bad Habit Belgium Quad																								✗		✗	
Founders Brewing Black Rye																								✗		✗	
Founders Brewing Blushing Monk																								✗		✗	
Founders Brewing Breakfast Stout						✗																		✗		✗	
Founders Brewing Centennial IPA						✗																		✗		✗	
Founders Brewing Curmudgeon Old Ale						✗																		✗		✗	
Founders Brewing Devil Dancer Triple IPA						✗																		✗		✗	
Founders Brewing Dirty Bastard						✗																		✗		✗	
Founders Brewing Imperial Stout						✗																		✗		✗	
Founders Brewing Kentucky Breakfast																								✗		✗	
Founders Brewing Pale Ale						✗																		✗		✗	
Founders Brewing Porter						✗																		✗		✗	
Founders Brewing Red's Rye						✗																		✗		✗	
Founders Brewing Rubaeus						✗																		✗		✗	

374

Locally available bottle and keg sizes may vary.

Brewery / Brand Name	Contact Brewery	Cans	7 oz	8 1/2 oz	10 oz	12 oz	16 oz	20 oz	22 oz	24 oz	1/2 liter	25 oz	32 oz	64 oz	1 liter	1 1/2 liter	375 ml	500 ml	750 ml	40 oz	2 liter	Growlers/Jugs	3 liter	1/6 Keg	1/4 Keg	1/2 Keg	Keg (Non-Specified Size)
Four Peaks Brewing Company																											
8th Street Ale						✗																		✗	✗	✗	
Four Peaks Arizona Peach																								✗	✗	✗	
Four Peaks Hefeweizen																								✗	✗	✗	
Four Peaks Kolsch																								✗	✗	✗	
Four Peaks Oatmeal Stout																								✗	✗	✗	
Hopknot IPA																								✗	✗	✗	
Kiltlifter Scottish-Style Ale						✗																		✗	✗	✗	
The Raj India Pal Ale																								✗	✗	✗	
Four Plus Brewing Company																											
Four Plus DUNK'L Amber Wheat						✗																		✗		✗	
Four Plus Monkshine Belgian Style Pale Ale						✗																		✗		✗	
Four Plus PUNK'N Pumpkin Harvest Ale						✗																		✗		✗	
Four Plus WILDFIRE Extra Pale Ale						✗																		✗		✗	
Franconia Notch Brewing Company																											
Franconia Notch Brewing Grail Pale Ale	✗																										
Franconia Notch Brewing River Driver Ale	✗																										
Frankenmuth Brewery																											
Frankenmuth German Style Pilsner						✗																					✗
Frankenmuth Hefeweizen						✗																					✗
Frankenmuth Irish Dry Stout						✗																					✗
Frankenmuth Mel-O-Dry Light Lager						✗																					✗
Frankenmuth Mitternacht Munchner Dark Lager						✗																					✗
Frankenmuth Oktoberfest						✗																					✗
Frankenmuth Old Detroit Amber Ale						✗																					✗
Frankenmuth Original Geyer's American Cream Ale						✗																					✗
Frankenmuth Pioneer Pale Ale						✗																					✗
Frankenmuth Winter Bock						✗																					✗
Freeport Brewing Company																											
Brown Hound Brown Ale									✗																		
Full Sail Brewing Company																											
Full Sail Brewing Amber						✗																		✗	✗	✗	

375

Brewery / Brand Name	Contact Brewery	Cans	7 oz	8 1/2 oz	10 oz	12 oz	16 oz	20 oz	22 oz	24 oz	1/2 liter	25 oz	32 oz	64 oz	1 liter	1 1/2 liter	375 ml	500 ml	750 ml	40 oz	2 liter	Growlers/Jugs	3 liter	1/6 Keg	1/4 Keg	1/2 Keg	Keg (Non-Specified Size)
Full Sail Brewing Holiday Wassail Ale						X																		X	X	X	
Full Sail Brewing IPA						X																		X	X	X	
Full Sail Brewing Pale Ale						X																		X	X	X	
Full Sail Brewing Rip Curl						X																		X	X	X	
Full Sail Brewing Session Premium Lager						X																		X	X	X	
Glacier Brewing																											
Glacier Brewing Flathead Cherry Ale						X																					X
Glacier Brewing Golden Grizzly Ale						X																					X
Glacier Brewing Northfork Amber Ale						X																					X
Glacier Brewing Port Polson Pilsner						X																					X
Glacier Brewing Select Dunkel Hefeweizen						X																					X
Glacier Brewing Select Oktoberfest						X																					X
Glacier Brewing Slurry Bomber Stout						X																					X
Glacier Brewing St. Arnold's Autumn Ale						X																					X
Gluek Brewing Company																											
Gluek Brewing Honey Bock		X																						X		X	
Gluek Brewing Red Bock		X																									
Gluek Golden Light		X																									
Gluek Golden Pilsner		X																						X		X	
Gluek Ice		X																									
Gluek Northern Golden Lager		X																						X		X	
Gluek Northern Reserve Ice Lager		X																									
Gluek Northern Reserve Low Carb Light		X																									
Gluek Stite						X																					
Gluek Stite Amber Red Reserve						X																					
Gluek Stite Black and Tan						X																					
Gluek Stite Light Lager						X																					
Gold Hill Brewery																											
Gold Hill 49'er Red						X								X													
Gold Hill Axe Pic n Stout						X								X													
Gold Hill Gold Strike Light						X								X													
Gold Hill Gold Trail Pale Ale						X								X													

Locally available bottle and keg sizes may vary.

Brewery / Brand Name	Contact Brewery	Cans	7 oz	8 1/2 oz	10 oz	12 oz	16 oz	20 oz	22 oz	24 oz	1/2 liter	25 oz	32 oz	64 oz	1 liter	1 1/2 liter	375 ml	500 ml	750 ml	40 oz	2 liter	Growlers/Jugs	3 liter	1/6 Keg	1/4 Keg	1/2 Keg	Keg (Non-Specified Size)
Gold Hill Hank's Porter						✗								✗													
Gold Hill Old Miners Scotch Ale						✗								✗													
Golden City Brewery																											
Golden City Centurion Barley Wine Ale	✗																										
Golden City IPA	✗																										
Golden City Mad Molly Brown Ale									✗																		
Golden City Oatmeal Stout	✗																										
Golden City Pale Ale	✗																										
Golden City Red Ale									✗																		
Golden Valley Brewery																											
Golden Valley American Pale Ale						✗																					✗
Golden Valley Black Panther Imperial Stout									✗																		✗
Golden Valley Chehalem Mountain IPA									✗																		✗
Golden Valley Dundee Porter									✗																		✗
Golden Valley Geist Bock						✗																					✗
Golden Valley Red Hills Pilsner									✗																		✗
Golden Valley Red Thistle Ale						✗																					✗
Golden Valley Tannen Bomb						✗																					✗
Goose Island Beer Company																											
Bourbon County Stout						✗																					
Demolition						✗																		✗			
Goose Island 312 Urban Wheat Ale						✗																		✗		✗	
Goose Island Christmas Ale						✗																		✗		✗	
Goose Island Honker's Ale						✗																		✗		✗	
Goose Island India Pale Ale						✗																		✗		✗	
Goose Island Kilgubbin Red Ale						✗																		✗		✗	
Goose Island Nut Brown Ale						✗																					
Goose Island Oatmeal Stout						✗																					
Goose Island Oktoberfest						✗																		✗		✗	
Goose Island Summertime						✗																		✗		✗	
Imperial IPA						✗																		✗			
Matilda						✗																		✗			

377

How Supplied *Continued*

Locally available bottle and keg sizes may vary.

Brewery / Brand Name	Contact Brewery	Cans	7 oz	8 1/2 oz	10 oz	12 oz	16 oz	20 oz	22 oz	24 oz	1/2 liter	25 oz	32 oz	64 oz	1 liter	1 1/2 liter	375 ml	500 ml	750 ml	40 oz	2 liter	Growlers/ Jugs	3 liter	1/6 Keg	1/4 Keg	1/2 Keg	Keg (Non-Specified Size)
Pere Jacques						X																		X			
Gordon Biersch Brewery																											
Gordon Biersch Blonde Bock						X																				X	
Gordon Biersch Festbier (Restaurants Only)						X																					
Gordon Biersch Hefeweizen						X																		X		X	
Gordon Biersch Maibock- Lager (Restaurants Only)						X																					
Gordon Biersch Marzen							X																	X		X	
Gordon Biersch Pilsner						X																		X		X	
Gordon Biersch Winter Bock						X																				X	
Grand Teton Brewing Company																											
Black Cauldron Imperial Stout						X																		X	X		
Grand Teton Bitch Creek ESB						X																		X	X		
Grand Teton Double IPA															X									X	X		
Grand Teton Old Faithful Ale						X																		X	X		
Grand Teton Paradise Pilsner						X																		X	X		
Grand Teton Sweetgrass IPA						X																		X	X		
Grand Teton Teton Ale						X																		X	X		
Grand Teton Workhorse Wheat						X																		X	X		
Gray's Brewing																											
Gray's Brewing Black & Tan						X																					
Gray's Brewing Honey Ale						X																					
Gray's Brewing Oatmeal Stout						X																					
Gray's Brewing Pale Ale						X																					
Great Beer Company																											
Great Beer Hollywood Blonde						X																					
Great Divide Brewing Company																											
Great Divide Brewing Denver Pale Ale						X																					X
Great Divide Brewing Fresh Hop Pale Ale									X																		X
Great Divide Brewing Hercules Double IPA						X			X																		X
Great Divide Brewing Hibernation Ale						X																					X
Great Divide Brewing HotShot ESB						X																					X
Great Divide Brewing Oak Aged Yeti Imperial Stout									X																		X

378

How Supplied *Continued*

Locally available bottle and keg sizes may vary.

Brewery Brand Name	Contact Brewery	Cans	7 oz	8 1/2 oz	10 oz	12 oz	16 oz	20 oz	22 oz	24 oz	1/2 liter	25 oz	32 oz	64 oz	1 liter	1 1/2 liter	375 ml	500 ml	750 ml	40 oz	2 liter	Growlers/Jugs	3 liter	1/6 Keg	1/4 Keg	1/2 Keg	Keg (Non-Specified Size)
Great Divide Brewing Old Ruffian Barley Wine									X																		X
Great Divide Brewing Ridgeline Amber						X											X										X
Great Divide Brewing Saint Bridget's Porter						X																					X
Great Divide Brewing Samurai																											X
Great Divide Brewing Titan IPA						X																					X
Great Divide Brewing Wild Raspberry Ale						X																					X
Great Divide Brewing Yeti Imperial Stout									X																		X
Great Lakes Brewing Company																											
Great Lakes Brewing Burning River Pale Ale						X																		X		X	
Great Lakes Brewing Christmas Ale						X																		X		X	
Great Lakes Brewing Commodore Perry India Pale Ale						X																		X		X	
Great Lakes Brewing Conway's Irish Ale						X																		X		X	
Great Lakes Brewing Dortmunder Golden Lager						X																		X		X	
Great Lakes Brewing Edmund Fitzgerald Porter						X																		X		X	
Great Lakes Brewing Eliot Ness Amber Lager						X																		X		X	
Great Lakes Brewing Holy Moses White Ale						X																		X		X	
Great Lakes Brewing Moondog Ale						X																		X		X	
Great Lakes Brewing Nosferatu						X																		X		X	
Great Northern Brewing Company																											
Great Northern Brewing Bear Naked Amber						X																		X		X	
Great Northern Brewing Big Fog Amber Lager						X																		X	X	X	
Great Northern Brewing Buckin' Horse Pilsner						X																		X	X	X	
Great Northern Brewing Fred's Black Lager						X																		X	X	X	
Great Northern Brewing Going To The Sun Pale Ale						X																		X	X	X	
Great Northern Brewing Hellroaring Amber Lager						X																		X	X	X	
Great Northern Brewing Snow Ghost						X																		X		X	
Great Northern Brewing Snow Ghost Winter Lager						X																		X	X	X	
Great Northern Brewing Wheatfish Hefeweizen						X																		X	X	X	
Great Northern Brewing Wild Huckleberry Wheat Lager						X																		X		X	
Great Sex Brewing, Inc.																											
Great Sex Brewing Adam and Eve Ale						X																				X	

379

Brewery Brand Name	Contact Brewery	Cans	7 oz	8 1/2 oz	10 oz	12 oz	16 oz	20 oz	22 oz	24 oz	1/2 liter	25 oz	32 oz	64 oz	1 liter	1 1/2 liter	375 ml	500 ml	750 ml	40 oz	2 liter	Growlers/Jugs	3 liter	1/6 Keg	1/4 Keg	1/2 Keg	Keg (Non-Specified Size)
Green Bay Brewing Company																											
Hinterland Pale Ale						X																					X
Green Flash Brewing																											
Green Flash Barleywine									X															X	X	X	
Green Flash Belgian Style Trippel									X															X	X	X	
Green Flash Extra Pale Ale						X																		X	X	X	
Green Flash Imperial IPA									X															X	X	X	
Green Flash Nut Brown Ale						X																		X	X	X	
Green Flash Ruby Red Ale						X																		X	X	X	
Green Flash West Coast IPA						X																		X	X	X	
Gritty McDuff's Brewing Company																											
Gritty McDuff's Best Bitter						X																		X	X	X	
Gritty McDuff's Best Brown Ale						X																			X	X	
Gritty McDuff's Black Fly Stout						X																			X	X	
Gritty McDuff's Christmas Ale						X																			X	X	
Gritty McDuff's Halloween Ale						X																			X	X	
Gritty McDuff's Original Pub Style Ale						X			X																X	X	
Gritty McDuff's Scottish Ale						X																			X	X	
Gritty McDuff's Vacationland Summer Ale						X																			X	X	
Hair of the Dog Brewing Company																											
Hair of the Dog Brewing Adam						X										X							X				
Hair of the Dog Brewing Doggie Claws						X										X							X				
Hair of the Dog Brewing Fred						X										X							X				
Hair of the Dog Brewing Rose						X										X							X				
Hair of the Dog Brewing Ruth						X										X							X				
Hale's Ales																											
Hale's Cream Ale	X																										
Hale's Cream H.S.B.	X																										
Hale's Cream Stout	X																										
Hale's Drawbridge Blonde	X																										
Hale's Irish Style Nut Brown Ale	X																										
Hale's Mongoose IPA									X																		

Locally available bottle and keg sizes may vary.

Brewery / Brand Name	Contact Brewery	Cans	7 oz	8 1/2 oz	10 oz	12 oz	16 oz	20 oz	22 oz	24 oz	1/2 liter	25 oz	32 oz	64 oz	1 liter	1 1/2 liter	375 ml	500 ml	750 ml	40 oz	2 liter	Growlers/Jugs	3 liter	1/6 Keg	1/4 Keg	1/2 Keg	Keg (Non-Specified Size)
Hale's O'Brien's Harvest Ale	X																										
Hale's Pale American Ale						X																					
Hale's Red Menance Big Amber									X																		
Hale's Troll Porter	X																										
Hale's Wee Heavy Winter Ale						X																					
Happy Valley Brewing Company																											
Happy Valley Brewing Mission Ale Double	X																										
Happy Valley Brewing Mission Ale Wit	X																										
Harbor City Brewing, Inc.																											
Harbor City Brewing Full Tilt IPA	X																										
Harbor City Brewing Harvest Wheat	X																										
Harbor City Brewing Main Street Brown Ale	X																										
Harbor City Brewing Mile Rock Amber Ale	X																										
Harbor City Brewing Raspberry Brown Ale	X					X																					
Harlem Brewing Company																											
Sugar Hill Golden Ale						X																					
Harpoon Brewery																											
Harpoon 100 BBL Series						X																				X	
Harpoon Ale						X																			X	X	
Harpoon Hibernian Ale						X																			X	X	
Harpoon Brown Ale						X																			X	X	
Harpoon IPA						X			X																X	X	
Harpoon Munich Dark						X																			X	X	
Harpoon Octoberfest						X																			X	X	
Harpoon Summer						X																			X	X	
Harpoon UFO Hefeweizen						X			X																X	X	
Harpoon UFO Raspberry Hefeweizen						X																					
Harpoon Winter Warmer						X																			X	X	
Healthy Brew																											
Healthy Brew 1-Day IPA						X																					
Healthy Brew Easy Amber						X																					
Healthy Brew Snowman's Revenge						X																					

381

Brewery Brand Name	Contact Brewery	Cans	7 oz	8 1/2 oz	10 oz	12 oz	16 oz	20 oz	22 oz	24 oz	1/2 liter	25 oz	32 oz	64 oz	1 liter	1 1/2 liter	375 ml	500 ml	750 ml	40 oz	2 liter	Growlers/Jugs	3 liter	1/6 Keg	1/4 Keg	1/2 Keg	Keg (Non-Specified Size)
Healthy Brew Strong Stout						X																					
Healthy Brew Wheat Serenity						X																					
Heiner Brau																											
Heiner Brau Hefe Weisse	X																										
Heiner Brau Kellerbier	X																										
Heiner Brau Kolsch	X																										
Heiner Brau Maerzen	X																										
Heiner Brau Maibock	X																										
Heiner Brau Mardi Gras Festbier	X																										
Heiner Brau Octoberfest Bier	X																										
Heiner Weihnachtsbock	X																										
Heinzelmannchen Brewery																											
Heinzelmannchen Ancient Days Honey Blonde Ale																											X
Heinzelmannchen Black Forest Stout																											X
Heinzelmannchen Gopher Ale																											X
Heinzelmannchen Kilted Gnome Scottish Ale																											X
Heinzelmannchen Middleworld Brown Ale																											X
Heinzelmannchen Oktoberfest																											X
Heinzelmannchen Weise Gnome Hefeweizen Style Ale																											X
Helmar Brewing Company																											
Helmar Big League Brew							X																				
High & Mighty Brewing Company																											
High & Mighty Brewing Beer of the Gods							X																				
High & Mighty Brewing Two-Headed Beast							X																				
High & Mighty Brewing XPA							X																				
High Falls Brewing																											
Genesee Beer		X																									
Genesee Cream Ale		X																									
Genesee Ice		X																									
Genesee NA		X																									
Genesee Red Lager	X																										
Genny Light		X																									

Brewery Brand Name	Contact Brewery	Cans	7 oz	8 1/2 oz	10 oz	12 oz	16 oz	20 oz	22 oz	24 oz	1/2 liter	25 oz	32 oz	64 oz	1 liter	1 1/2 liter	375 ml	500 ml	750 ml	40 oz	2 liter	Growlers/ Jugs	3 liter	1/6 Keg	1/4 Keg	1/2 Keg	Keg (Non-Specified Size)
JW DunDee's American Amber Lager						✗																					
JW DunDee's American Pale Ale						✗																					
JW DunDee's Honey Brown Lager						✗																					
Michael Shea's Irish Amber						✗																					
Steinlager						✗																					
High Point Wheat Beer Company																											
Ramstein Blonde Wheat						✗																					
Ramstein Classic Wheat Beer						✗																					
Ramstein Golden Lager																											
Ramstein Maibock Lager Beer																								✗		✗	
Ramstein Munich Amber Lager																											✗
Ramstein Winter Wheat						✗																					
Highland Brewing																											
Highland Brewing Black Mocha Stout						✗																					
Highland Brewing Cold Mountain Winter Ale	✗																										
Highland Brewing Gaelic Ale						✗																					
Highland Brewing Kashmir IPA						✗																					
Highland Brewing Oatmeal Porter						✗																					
Highland Brewing St. Terese's Pale Ale						✗																					
Highland Brewing Tasgall Ale						✗																					
Hood Canal Brewing																											
Hood Canal Brewing Agate Pass Amber							✗																				
Hood Canal Brewing Big Beef Oatmeal Stout							✗																				
Hood Canal Brewing Dabob Bay India Pale Ale							✗																				
Hood Canal Brewing Dosewallipps Special Ale							✗																				
Hood Canal Brewing Southpoint Porter							✗																				
Hoppy Brewing Company																											
Hoppy Claus Holiday Ale									✗																		✗
Hoppy Face Amber Ale									✗																		✗
Liquid Sunshine Blonde Ale									✗																		✗
Stony Face Red Ale									✗																		✗
Total Eclipse Black Ale									✗																		✗

Brewery Brand Name	Contact Brewery	Cans	7 oz	8 1/2 oz	10 oz	12 oz	16 oz	20 oz	22 oz	24 oz	1/2 liter	25 oz	32 oz	64 oz	1 liter	1 1/2 liter	375 ml	500 ml	750 ml	40 oz	2 liter	Growlers/Jugs	3 liter	1/6 Keg	1/4 Keg	1/2 Keg	Keg (Non-Specified Size)
Hoptown Brewery																											
Hoptown Brown Nose Ale	✗																										
Hoptown DUIPA Imperial Ale	✗																										
Hoptown ESB	✗																										
Hoptown Golden Ale	✗																										
Hoptown IPA	✗																										
Hoptown Old Yeltsin	✗																										
Hoptown Paint the Town Red	✗																										
Hoptown Paleface Pale Ale	✗																										
Hoptown Wheathopper Red Wheat Ale	✗																										
Hornpout Brewing																											
Hornpout No Limit Amber Ale	✗																										
Hornpout Pale Ale	✗																										
Huebert Brewing																											
Huebert Brewing Huebert's Old Tyme Lager	✗																										
Hyland Orchard and Brewery																											
Hyland's Sturbridge Amber Ale									✗																		
Hyland's Sturbridge American Pale Ale									✗																		
Hyland's Sturbridge Farmhand Ale									✗																		
Hyland's Sturbridge Stout									✗																		
Ice Harbor Brewing Company																											
Ice Harbor Brewing Barley Wine Style Ale						✗																				✗	
Ice Harbor Brewing Columbia Kölsch						✗																				✗	
Ice Harbor Brewing Harvest Pale Ale						✗																				✗	
Ice Harbor Brewing Runaway Red Ale						✗																				✗	
Ice Harbor Brewing Sternwheeler Stout						✗																				✗	
Independence Brewing																											
Independence Brewing Bootlegger Brown Ale						✗																					
Independence Brewing Freestyle Wheat Beer						✗																					
Independence Brewing Jasperilla Old Ale						✗																					
Independence Brewing Pale Ale						✗																					

Locally available bottle and keg sizes may vary.

Brewery / Brand Name	Contact Brewery	Cans	7 oz	8 1/2 oz	10 oz	12 oz	16 oz	20 oz	22 oz	24 oz	1/2 liter	25 oz	32 oz	64 oz	1 liter	1 1/2 liter	375 ml	500 ml	750 ml	40 oz	2 liter	Growlers/ Jugs	3 liter	1/6 Keg	1/4 Keg	1/2 Keg	Keg (Non-Specified Size)
Indian Wells Brewing																											
Indian Wells Desert Pale Ale						X																					
Indian Wells Eastern Sierra Lager	X																										
Indian Wells Irish Green Ale						X																					
Indian Wells Lobotomy Bock						X																					
Indian Wells Mojave Gold						X																					
Indian Wells Mojave Red						X																					
Indian Wells Mojave Silver						X																					
Indian Wells Oktoberfest						X																					
Indian Wells Orange Blossom Amber						X																					
Indian Wells Piute Stout						X																					
Indian Wells Raspberry Ale						X																					
Indian Wells Sidewinder Missile Ale	X																										
Indian Wells Springfest Lager						X																					
Indian Wells Vette's Honey Ale	X																										
Iron Horse Brewery																											
Iron Horse Brown Ale						X																					
Iron Horse India Pale Ale						X																					
Iron Horse Loco-Motive Ale						X																					
Iron Horse Rodeo Extra Pale Ale						X																					
Island Brewing Company																											
Island Brewing Avocado Ale									X																		X
Island Brewing Blonde									X																		X
Island Brewing Island Pale Ale									X																		X
Island Brewing Jubilee Ale									X																		X
Island Brewing London Porter									X																		X
Island Brewing Nut Brown Ale									X																		X
Island Brewing Paradise Pale Ale									X																		X
Island Brewing Starry Night Stout									X																		X
Island Brewing Tropical Lager									X																		X
Island Brewing Weiss									X																		X

Locally available bottle and keg sizes may vary.

Brewery / Brand Name	Contact Brewery	Cans	7 oz	8 1/2 oz	10 oz	12 oz	16 oz	20 oz	22 oz	24 oz	1/2 liter	25 oz	32 oz	64 oz	1 liter	1 1/2 liter	375 ml	500 ml	750 ml	40 oz	2 liter	Growlers/Jugs	3 liter	1/6 Keg	1/4 Keg	1/2 Keg	Keg (Non-Specified Size)
Ithaca Beer Company, Inc.																											
Ithaca Beer Company Apricot Wheat						✗																					
Ithaca Beer Company CascaZilla						✗																					
Ithaca Beer Company Double IPA						✗																					
Ithaca Beer Company Finger Lakes Stout						✗																					
Ithaca Beer Company Flower Power India Pale Ale						✗																					
Ithaca Beer Company Nut Brown						✗																					
Ithaca Beer Company Pale Ale						✗																					
Ithaca Beer Company Partly Sunny						✗																					
Ithaca Beer Company Winterizer						✗																					
Ithaca Beer Gorges Smoked Porter						✗																					
Jack Russell Brewing																											
Captain Boomer's IPA						✗																		✗		✗	
Jack Russell's All American Premium Lager						✗																				✗	
Jack Russell's Harvest Apple Ale						✗																		✗		✗	
Jack's Farmhouse Ale						✗																		✗		✗	
Jack's Best Bitter Ale						✗																		✗		✗	
Jack's Blackberry Abbey Ale						✗																		✗		✗	
Jack's Blueberry Beer						✗																		✗		✗	
Jack's Brown Ale						✗																		✗		✗	
Jack's Huntsman's Lager						✗																		✗		✗	
Jack's Irish Red Ale						✗																		✗		✗	
Jack's London Porter						✗																		✗		✗	
Jack's Olde Ale						✗																		✗		✗	
Jack's Raspberry Imperial Stout						✗																		✗		✗	
Jack's Scottish Ale						✗																		✗		✗	
Jack's Whitewater Pale Ale						✗																		✗		✗	
Jacob Leinenkugel Brewing Company																											
Leinenkugel's Apple Spice						✗																					
Leinenkugel's Berry Weiss						✗																					
Leinenkugel's Big Butt Doppelbock						✗																					
Leinenkugel's Creamy Dark						✗																					

Locally available bottle and keg sizes may vary.

Brewery / Brand Name	Contact Brewery	Cans	7 oz	8 1/2 oz	10 oz	12 oz	16 oz	20 oz	22 oz	24 oz	1/2 liter	25 oz	32 oz	64 oz	1 liter	1 1/2 liter	375 ml	500 ml	750 ml	40 oz	2 liter	Growlers/Jugs	3 liter	1/6 Keg	1/4 Keg	1/2 Keg	Keg (Non-Specified Size)
Leinenkugel's Honey Weiss						✗																					
Leinenkugel's Light						✗																					
Leinenkugel's Oktoberfest						✗																					
Leinenkugel's Original						✗																					
Leinenkugel's Red Lager						✗																					
Leinenkugel's Sunset Wheat						✗																					
James Page Brewing Company, LLC																											
James Page Brewing Burly Brown Ale						✗																					
James Page Brewing Iron Ranger Amber Lager		✗				✗																			✗	✗	
James Page Brewing Voyageur Extra Pale Ale		✗				✗																					
Jolly Pumpkin Artisan Ales																											
Jolly Pumpkin Bam Biere						✗																					
Jolly Pumpkin Biere de Mars																			✗								
Jolly Pumpkin Calabaza Blanca						✗													✗								
Jolly Pumpkin Fuego del Otono "Autumn Fire"																			✗								
Jolly Pumpkin La Roja						✗													✗								
Jolly Pumpkin Luciernaga "The Firefly"												✗							✗								
Jolly Pumpkin Madrugada Obscura "Dark Dawn"																			✗								
Jolly Pumpkin Maracaibo Especial																			✗								
Jolly Pumpkin Oro de Calabaza												✗							✗								
Jones Brewing Company																											
Esquire Extra Premium	✗																										
Stoney's Beer							✗																				
Stoney's Black And Tan	✗																										
Stoney's Harvest Gold	✗																										
Stoney's Light							✗																				
Joseph Huber Brewing Company, Inc.																											
Berghoff Classic Pilsner						✗																					
Berghoff Famous Bock Beer						✗																					
Berghoff Famous Red Ale						✗																					
Berghoff Genuine Dark Beer						✗																					
Berghoff Hazelnut Winterfest Ale						✗																					

Locally available bottle and keg sizes may vary.

Brewery / Brand Name	Contact Brewery	Cans	7 oz	8 1/2 oz	10 oz	12 oz	16 oz	20 oz	22 oz	24 oz	1/2 liter	25 oz	32 oz	64 oz	1 liter	1 1/2 liter	375 ml	500 ml	750 ml	40 oz	2 liter	Growlers/Jugs	3 liter	1/6 Keg	1/4 Keg	1/2 Keg	Keg (Non-Specified Size)
Berghoff Hefe-Weizen						X																					
Berghoff Oktoberfest Beer						X																					
Berghoff Original Lager Beer						X																					
Berghoff Pale Ale						X																					
Berghoff Solstice Wit Beer						X																					
Karl Strauss Breweries																											
Karl Strauss Brewing Amber Lager						X				X															X	X	
Karl Strauss Brewing Endless Summer Light						X																			X	X	
Karl Strauss Brewing Oktoberfest						X																			X	X	
Karl Strauss Brewing Red Trolley Ale						X																			X	X	
Karl Strauss Brewing Stargazer IPA						X																			X	X	
Karl Strauss Brewing Woodie Gold						X																			X	X	
Keegan Ales																											
Keegan Ales Hurricane Kitty						X								X										X	X	X	
Keegan Ales Mother's Milk						X								X										X	X	X	
Keegan Ales Old Capital						X								X										X	X	X	
Kelley Brothers Brewing Company																											
Kelley Brothers Four Towers IPA	X																										
Kelley Brothers Inferno Red	X																										
Keoki Brewing Company																											
Keoki Gold						X																		X		X	
Keoki Sunset						X																		X		X	
Kettle House Brewing Company																											
Double Haul IPA		X																									
Keweenaw Brewing Company																											
Keweenaw Brewing Coal Porter																											X
Keweenaw Brewing Empress Hefeweizen																											X
Keweenaw Brewing Hilde's Brown Ale																											X
Keweenaw Brewing Magnum Pale Ale																											X
Keweenaw Brewing Pickaxe Blonde Ale		X																									X
Keweenaw Brewing R.A.M. Stout																											X
Keweenaw Brewing Red Jacket Amber Ale		X																									X

388

Locally available bottle and keg sizes may vary.

Brewery / Brand Name	Contact Brewery	Cans	7 oz	8 1/2 oz	10 oz	12 oz	16 oz	20 oz	22 oz	24 oz	1/2 liter	25 oz	32 oz	64 oz	1 liter	1 1/2 liter	375 ml	500 ml	750 ml	40 oz	2 liter	Growlers/Jugs	3 liter	1/6 Keg	1/4 Keg	1/2 Keg	Keg (Non-Specified Size)
King Brewing Company																											
King Annihilater Doppel Bock						✗																					
King Big Red						✗																					
King Cherry Ale						✗																					
King Continental Lager						✗																					
King Crown Brown Ale						✗																					
King Festbier						✗																					
King Hefeweizen						✗																					
King IPA						✗																					
King Irish Red Ale						✗																					
King King's Gold						✗																					
King Loranger Lager						✗																					
King Mocha Java Stout						✗																					
King Pale Ale						✗																					
King Pontiac Porter						✗																					
King Red Ox Amber Ale						✗																					
King Royal Amber						✗																					
King Two Fisted Old Ale						✗																					
Kodiak Island Brewing Company																											
Kodiak Island Cloud Peak Hefeveizen																											✗
Kodiak Island Island Fog Barley Wine																											✗
Kodiak Island Liquid Sunshine																											✗
Kodiak Island Night Watch Porter																											✗
Kodiak Island North Pacific Ale																											✗
Kodiak Island Sweet Georgia Brown																											✗
Kona Brewing, LLC																											
Kona Brewing Big Wave Golden Ale						✗																		✗		✗	
Kona Brewing Fire Rock Pale Ale						✗																		✗		✗	
Kona Brewing Longboard Island Lager						✗																		✗		✗	
Kona Brewing Pipeline Porter						✗																		✗		✗	
LaConner Brewing Company																											
Skagit Sculler's IPA									✗																		

389

Locally available bottle and keg sizes may vary.

Brewery / Brand Name	Contact Brewery	Cans	7 oz	8 1/2 oz	10 oz	12 oz	16 oz	20 oz	22 oz	24 oz	1/2 liter	25 oz	32 oz	64 oz	1 liter	1 1/2 liter	375 ml	500 ml	750 ml	40 oz	2 liter	Growlers/Jugs	3 liter	1/6 Keg	1/4 Keg	1/2 Keg	Keg (Non-Specified Size)
Lagunitas Brewing																											
Lagunitas Brewing Brown Shugga									X																		
Lagunitas Brewing Cappuccino Stout									X																		
Lagunitas Brewing Czech Style Pilsner						X																					X
Lagunitas Brewing Dogtown Pale Ale						X																					X
Lagunitas Brewing Imperial Red Ale									X																		X
Lagunitas Brewing Imperial Stout									X																		
Lagunitas Brewing India Pale Ale						X																					
Lagunitas Brewing IPA Maximus									X																		
Lagunitas Brewing Number 10 Ale									X																		
Lagunitas Brewing Olde GnarlyWine									X																		
Lagunitas Brewing The Censored Rich Copper Ale						X																					
Lake Louie Brewing, LLC																											
Lake Louie Brewing Arena Premium						X																				X	
Lake Louie Brewing Brother Tim Tripel						X																				X	
Lake Louie Brewing Coon Rock Cream Ale						X																				X	
Lake Louie Brewing Dino's Dark						X																				X	
Lake Louie Brewing Milk Stout						X																				X	
Lake Louie Brewing Prairie Moon Belgian Style Farmhouse Ale						X																				X	
Lake Louie Brewing Tommy's Porter						X																				X	
Lake Louie Brewing Warped Speed Scotch Ale						X																				X	
Lake Placid Craft Brewing 46'er India Pale Ale						X																					
Lake Placid Craft Brewing Barkeater Amber Ale						X																					
Lake Placid Craft Brewing Moose Island Ale						X																					
Lake Placid Craft Brewing Ubu Ale						X																					
Lake Superior Brewing Company																											
Lake Superior Brewing 7 Bridges Brown						X																					X
Lake Superior Brewing Kayak Kölsch						X																					X
Lake Superior Brewing Mesabi Red						X																					X
Lake Superior Brewing Oktoberfest						X																					X
Lake Superior Brewing Old Man Winter Warmer						X																					X
Lake Superior Brewing Sir Duluth Oatmeal Stout						X																					X

Locally available bottle and keg sizes may vary.

Brewery Brand Name	Contact Brewery	Cans	7 oz	8 1/2 oz	10 oz	12 oz	16 oz	20 oz	22 oz	24 oz	1/2 liter	25 oz	32 oz	64 oz	1 liter	1 1/2 liter	375 ml	500 ml	750 ml	40 oz	2 liter	Growlers/Jugs	3 liter	1/6 Keg	1/4 Keg	1/2 Keg	Keg (Non-Specified Size)
Lake Superior Brewing Special Ale						✗																					✗
Lake Superior Brewing Split Rock Bock						✗																					✗
Lake Superior Brewing St. Louis Bay IPA						✗																					✗
Lake Superior Brewing Windward Wheat						✗																					✗
Lakefront Brewery, Inc.																											
Lakefront Big Easy Beer						✗																			✗	✗	
Lakefront Bock Beer						✗																			✗	✗	
Lakefront Cattail Ale						✗																			✗	✗	
Lakefront Cherry Lager						✗																			✗	✗	
Lakefront Cream City Pale Ale						✗																			✗	✗	
Lakefront Eastside Dark						✗																			✗	✗	
Lakefront Fuel Café Stout						✗																			✗	✗	
Lakefront Holiday Spice Lager Beer						✗																			✗	✗	
Lakefront Klisch Pilsner						✗																			✗	✗	
Lakefront New Grist						✗																			✗	✗	
Lakefront Oktoberfest						✗																			✗	✗	
Lakefront Organic ESB						✗																			✗	✗	
Lakefront Pumpkin Lager						✗																			✗	✗	
Lakefront Riverwest Stein						✗																			✗	✗	
Lakefront Snake Chaser Stout						✗																			✗	✗	
Lakefront White Beer						✗																			✗	✗	
Lancaster Brewing Company																											
Lancaster Brewing Amish Four Grain Pale Ale						✗																		✗		✗	
Lancaster Brewing Doppel Bock						✗																					
Lancaster Brewing Franklinfest Lager						✗																					
Lancaster Brewing Gold Star Pilsner						✗																		✗		✗	
Lancaster Brewing Hop Hog IPA						✗																		✗		✗	
Lancaster Brewing Milk Stout						✗																		✗		✗	
Lancaster Brewing Oktoberfest						✗																					
Lancaster Brewing Spring Bock						✗																					
Lancaster Brewing Strawberry Wheat						✗																		✗		✗	
Lancaster Brewing Winter Warmer						✗																		✗		✗	

Locally available bottle and keg sizes may vary.

Brewery / Brand Name	Contact Brewery	Cans	7 oz	8 1/2 oz	10 oz	12 oz	16 oz	20 oz	22 oz	24 oz	1/2 liter	25 oz	32 oz	64 oz	1 liter	1 1/2 liter	375 ml	500 ml	750 ml	40 oz	2 liter	Growlers/Jugs	3 liter	1/6 Keg	1/4 Keg	1/2 Keg	Keg (Non-Specified Size)
Landmark Beer Company																											
Landmark Colonel Hops Red Ale						X																			X	X	
Landmark India Pale Ale						X																			X	X	
Landmark Vanilla Bean Brown Ale						X																			X	X	
Lang Creek Brewery																											
Lang Creek Huckleberry N' Honey						X																			X	X	
Lang Creek Taildragger Honey Wheat						X																			X	X	
Lang Creek Tri-Motor Amber						X																			X	X	
Lang Creek Windsock Pale Ale						X																			X	X	
Latrobe Brewing																											
Latrobe Pilsner	X																										
Old German	X																										
Left Coast Brewing																											
Left Coast Gold	X																										
Left Coast Hefeweizen	X																										
Left Coast India Pale Ale	X																										
Left Coast Pale Ale	X																										
Left Hand Brewing Company																											
Left Hand Brewing Black Jack Porter						X																					X
Left Hand Brewing Chainsaw Ale																			X								X
Left Hand Brewing Deep Cover Brown						X																					X
Left Hand Brewing Goosinator																			X								X
Left Hand Brewing Haystack Wheat						X																					X
Left Hand Brewing Imperial Stout						X			X										X								X
Left Hand Brewing Jackman's Pale Ale						X																					X
Left Hand Brewing JuJu Ginger Ale																											X
Left Hand Brewing Milk Stout						X			X																		X
Left Hand Brewing Polestar Pilsner						X																					X
Left Hand Brewing Ryebock Lager																			X								X
Left Hand Brewing Sawtooth Ale						X			X																		X
Left Hand Brewing Smokejumper Imperial Porter																			X								X
Left Hand Brewing Snowbound Ale									X																		X

Locally available bottle and keg sizes may vary.

Brewery / Brand Name	Contact Brewery	Cans	7 oz	8 1/2 oz	10 oz	12 oz	16 oz	20 oz	22 oz	24 oz	1/2 liter	25 oz	32 oz	64 oz	1 liter	1 1/2 liter	375 ml	500 ml	750 ml	40 oz	2 liter	Growlers/Jugs	3 liter	1/6 Keg	1/4 Keg	1/2 Keg	Keg (Non-Specified Size)
Left Hand Brewing St. Vrain Ale																			X								
Left Hand Brewing Twin Sisters																			X								X
Left Hand Brewing Warrior IPA									X																		X
Left Hand Brewing Widdershins Barleywine																			X								X
Legacy Brewing Company																											
Legacy Brewing Hedonism Red Ale						X																		X		X	
Legacy Brewing Midnight Wit Ale						X																		X		X	
Legend Brewing Company																											
Legend Brewing Brown Ale									X																	X	
Legend Brewing Golden IPA									X																	X	
Legend Brewing Lager									X																	X	
Legend Brewing Legend Oktoberfest									X																	X	
Legend Brewing Legend Pale Ale									X																	X	
Legend Brewing Pilsner									X																	X	
Legend Brewing Porter									X																	X	
Lewis & Clark Brewing																											
Lewis & Clark Back Country Scottish Ale						X																					X
Lewis & Clark Lager						X																					X
Lewis & Clark Miner's Gold Hefe-Weizen						X																					X
Lewis & Clark Tumbleweed IPA						X																					X
Yellowstone Beer						X																					X
Lion Brewery																											
Lion Brewing Pocono Black & Tan						X																		X		X	
Lion Brewing Pocono Caramel Porter						X																		X		X	
Lion Brewing Pocono Lager						X																		X		X	
Lion Brewing Pocono Light						X																		X		X	
Lion Brewing Pocono Pale Ale						X																		X		X	
Lion Brewing Pocono Summer Wheat						X																		X		X	
Lionshead						X																		X		X	
Lionshead Malt Liquor						X																		X		X	
Stegmaier 1857 American Lager						X																		X		X	
Stegmaier Brewhouse Bock						X																		X		X	

393

How Supplied *Continued*

Locally available bottle and keg sizes may vary.

Brewery Brand Name	Contact Brewery	Cans	7 oz	8 1/2 oz	10 oz	12 oz	16 oz	20 oz	22 oz	24 oz	1/2 liter	25 oz	32 oz	64 oz	1 liter	1 1/2 liter	375 ml	500 ml	750 ml	40 oz	2 liter	Growlers/Jugs	3 liter	1/6 Keg	1/4 Keg	1/2 Keg	Keg (Non-Specified Size)
Stegmaier Gold Medal						✗																		✗		✗	
Stegmaier Oktoberfest						✗																		✗		✗	
Stegmaier Porter						✗																		✗		✗	
The Long Trail Brewing Company																											
Blackberry Wheat						✗																		✗		✗	
Brewmasters Limited Edition Series — Unfiltered IPA						✗																		✗		✗	
Double Bag						✗			✗															✗		✗	
Harvest						✗																		✗		✗	
Hefeweizen						✗																		✗		✗	
Hibernator						✗																		✗		✗	
Hit the Trail						✗																		✗		✗	
Long Trail Ale						✗			✗															✗		✗	
Traditional IPA						✗																		✗		✗	
Lost Coast Brewery & Café																											
Lost Coast 8 Ball Stout						✗				✗														✗	✗	✗	
Lost Coast Alleycat Amber						✗				✗														✗	✗	✗	
Lost Coast Downtown Brown						✗				✗														✗	✗	✗	
Lost Coast Great White						✗				✗														✗	✗	✗	
Lost Coast Indica IPA						✗				✗														✗	✗	✗	
Lost Coast Raspberry Brown										✗														✗	✗	✗	
Lost Coast Winterbraun						✗				✗														✗	✗	✗	
MacTarnahan's Brewing Company																											
MacTarnahan's Brewing Blackwatch Cream Porter						✗																					
MacTarnahan's Brewing Mac's Amber Ale						✗																					
MacTarnahan's Oregon Honey Beer						✗																					
Mad Anthony Brewing Company																											
Mad Anthony Auburn Lager						✗																				✗	
Mad Anthony Gabby Blonde Lager						✗																				✗	
Mad Anthony Old Fort Porter						✗																				✗	
Mad Anthony Pale Ale						✗																				✗	
Mad River Brewing																											
Mad River Jamaica Red						✗																		✗	✗	✗	

Locally available bottle and keg sizes may vary.

Brewery / Brand Name	Contact Brewery	Cans	7 oz	8 1/2 oz	10 oz	12 oz	16 oz	20 oz	22 oz	24 oz	1/2 liter	25 oz	32 oz	64 oz	1 liter	1 1/2 liter	375 ml	500 ml	750 ml	40 oz	2 liter	Growlers/Jugs	3 liter	1/6 Keg	1/4 Keg	1/2 Keg	Keg (Non-Specified Size)
Mad River Jamaica Sunset West Indies Pale Ale						✗																		✗	✗	✗	
Mad River John Barleycorn Barleywine Style Ale						✗																		✗	✗	✗	
Mad River Steelhead Extra Pale Ale						✗				✗														✗	✗	✗	
Mad River Steelhead Extra Stout						✗																		✗	✗	✗	
Mad River Steelhead Scotch Porter						✗																		✗	✗	✗	
Madison River Brewing Company																											
Copper John Scotch Ale						✗																				✗	
Hopper Pale Ale						✗																				✗	
Irresistible E.S.B.						✗																				✗	
Salmon Fly Honey Rye						✗																				✗	
Magic Hat Brewing Company																											
Magic Hat Brewing #9						✗																		✗		✗	
Magic Hat Brewing Blind Faith						✗																					
Magic Hat Brewing Circus Boy						✗																					
Magic Hat Brewing Fat Angel						✗																					
Magic Hat Brewing H.I.P.A.						✗																					
Magic Hat Brewing Hocus Pocus						✗																					
Magic Hat Brewing Jinx						✗																				✗	
Magic Hat Brewing Mother Lager						✗																					
Magic Hat Brewing Participation Ale									✗																		
Magic Hat Brewing Ravell						✗			✗																		
Magic Hat Brewing Roxy Rolles						✗			✗																		
Maine Coast Brewing																											
Jack's Best Brown						✗																					
Maine Coast Brewing Black Irish Style Stout						✗																					
Maine Coast Brewing Eden Porter						✗																					
Maine Coast Brewing Wild Blueberry Ale						✗																					
Mammoth Brewing Company																											
Mammoth Brewing Company Amber						✗																					
Mammoth Brewing Company Double Nut Brown						✗																					
Mammoth Brewing Company Gold						✗																					
Mammoth Brewing Company India Pale Ale						✗																					

Brewery Brand Name	Contact Brewery	Cans	7 oz	8 1/2 oz	10 oz	12 oz	16 oz	20 oz	22 oz	24 oz	1/2 liter	25 oz	32 oz	64 oz	1 liter	1 1/2 liter	375 ml	500 ml	750 ml	40 oz	2 liter	Growlers/Jugs	3 liter	1/6 Keg	1/4 Keg	1/2 Keg	Keg (Non-Specified Size)
Mammoth Brewing Company Pale Ale						✗																					
Mantorville Brewing Company LLC																											
Mantorville Brewing Stagecoach Ale	✗																										
Marin Brewing Company																											
Marin Brewing "Old Dipsea" Barleywine Style Ale									✗															✗		✗	
Marin Brewing Albion Amber Ale									✗															✗		✗	
Marin Brewing Blueberry Ale									✗															✗		✗	
Marin Brewing Hefe Doppel Weizen									✗															✗		✗	
Marin Brewing Hefe Weiss									✗															✗		✗	
Marin Brewing Hoppy Holidaze Flavored Ale									✗															✗		✗	
Marin Brewing India Pale Ale									✗															✗		✗	
Marin Brewing MT. Tam Pale Ale									✗															✗		✗	
Marin Brewing Point Reyes Porter									✗															✗		✗	
Marin Brewing Raspberry Trail Ale									✗															✗		✗	
Marin Brewing San Quentin's Breakout Stout									✗															✗		✗	
Marin Brewing Star Brew									✗															✗		✗	
Marin Brewing Stinson Beach Peach									✗															✗		✗	
Marin Brewing Tripel Dipsea									✗															✗		✗	
Marin Brewing White Knuckle Ale									✗															✗		✗	
Maritime Pacific Brewing Company																											
Maritime Pacific Flag Ship Red Ale						✗																		✗		✗	
Maritime Pacific Imperial Pale						✗																		✗		✗	
Maritime Pacific Islander Pale						✗																		✗		✗	
Maritime Pacific Nightwatch Dark						✗																		✗		✗	
Mehana Brewing Company, Inc.																											
Mehana Brewing Hawaii Lager						✗																					
Mehana Brewing Humpback Blue Beer						✗																					
Mehana Brewing Mauna Kea Pale Ale						✗																					
Mehana Brewing Roy's Private Reserve						✗																					
Mehana Brewing Volcano Red Ale						✗																					
Mendocino Brewing Company																											
Mendocino Brewing Black Hawk Stout						✗																					✗

How Supplied *Continued*

Locally available bottle and keg sizes may vary.

Brewery Brand Name	Contact Brewery	Cans	7 oz	8 1/2 oz	10 oz	12 oz	16 oz	20 oz	22 oz	24 oz	1/2 liter	25 oz	32 oz	64 oz	1 liter	1 1/2 liter	375 ml	500 ml	750 ml	40 oz	2 liter	Growlers/Jugs	3 liter	1/6 Keg	1/4 Keg	1/2 Keg	Keg (Non-Specified Size)
Mendocino Brewing Blue Heron Pale Ale						✗																					✗
Mendocino Brewing Eye of the Hawk						✗																					✗
Mendocino Brewing Peregrine Golden Ale						✗																					
Mendocino Brewing Red Tail Ale						✗																					✗
Mendocino Brewing Red Tail Lager						✗																					✗
Mendocino Brewing White Hawk Select IPA						✗																					✗
Mercury Brewing Company																											
Farmington River Blonde Ale						✗																		✗		✗	
Farmington River Mahogany Ale						✗																		✗		✗	
Mercury Brewing Dog Pound Porter						✗																		✗		✗	
Mercury Brewing Eagle Brook Saloon's Blueberry Ale																						✗		✗		✗	
Mercury Brewing Ipswich Dark Ale						✗																		✗		✗	
Mercury Brewing Ipswich Harvest Ale						✗																		✗		✗	
Mercury Brewing Ipswich IPA						✗																✗		✗		✗	
Mercury Brewing Ipswich Nut Brown						✗																✗		✗		✗	
Mercury Brewing Ipswich Oatmeal Stout						✗																✗		✗		✗	
Mercury Brewing Ipswich Original Ale						✗																✗		✗		✗	
Mercury Brewing Ipswich Porter						✗																		✗		✗	
Mercury Brewing Ipswich Summer Ale						✗																		✗		✗	
Mercury Brewing Ipswich Winter Ale						✗																		✗		✗	
Mercury Brewing Stone Cat Ale						✗																		✗		✗	
Mercury Brewing Stone Cat Barley Wine						✗																		✗		✗	
Mercury Brewing Stone Cat Blonde						✗																		✗		✗	
Mercury Brewing Stone Cat Blueberry						✗																		✗		✗	
Mercury Brewing Stone Cat ESB						✗																		✗		✗	
Mercury Brewing Stone Cat IPA						✗																		✗		✗	
Mercury Brewing Stone Cat Octoberfest						✗																		✗		✗	
Mercury Brewing Stone Cat Pumpkin Porter						✗																		✗		✗	
Mercury Brewing Stone Cat Scotch Ale						✗																		✗		✗	
Mercury Brewing Stone Cat Wheat Beer						✗																		✗		✗	
Mercury Brewing Stone Cat Winter Lager						✗																		✗		✗	

397

Brewery Brand Name	Contact Brewery	Cans	7 oz	8 1/2 oz	10 oz	12 oz	16 oz	20 oz	22 oz	24 oz	1/2 liter	25 oz	32 oz	64 oz	1 liter	1 1/2 liter	375 ml	500 ml	750 ml	40 oz	2 liter	Growlers/Jugs	3 liter	1/6 Keg	1/4 Keg	1/2 Keg	Keg (Non-Specified Size)
Michigan Brewing Company, Inc.																											
Michigan Brewing Celis Grand Cru									X																		X
Michigan Brewing Celis Pale Bock									X																		X
Michigan Brewing Celis Raspberry									X																		X
Michigan Brewing Celis White									X																		X
Michigan Brewing Golden Ale									X																		X
Michigan Brewing High Seas IPA									X																		X
Michigan Brewing Mackinac Pale Ale									X																		X
Michigan Brewing Nut Brown Ale									X																		X
Michigan Brewing Peninsula Porter									X																		X
Michigan Brewing Petoskey Pilsner									X																		X
Michigan Brewing Sunset Amber Lager									X																		X
Michigan Brewing Superior Stout									X																		X
Michigan Brewing Wheatland Wheat Beer									X																		X
Middle Ages Brewing Company																											
Middle Ages Apricot Ale	X																										
Middle Ages Beast Bitter	X																										
Middle Ages Black Heart Stout	X																										
Middle Ages Dragonslayer Imperial Stout									X																		
Middle Ages Druid Fluid Barley Wine									X																		
Middle Ages Grail Ale							X																				
Middle Ages Highlander Scotch Ale	X																										
Middle Ages Impaled Ale							X																		X	X	
Middle Ages Kilt Tilter Scotch Style Ale									X																		
Middle Ages Old Marcus Ale	X																										
Middle Ages Raspberry Ale	X																										
Middle Ages Swallow Wheat	X																										
Middle Ages Syracuse Pale Ale	X																										
Middle Ages The Duke of Winship Scottish Style Ale	X																										
Middle Ages Tripel Crown							X																				
Middle Ages Wailing Wench									X																X	X	
Middle Ages Winter Wheat	X																										

398

Locally available bottle and keg sizes may vary.

Brewery Brand Name	Contact Brewery	Cans	7 oz	8 1/2 oz	10 oz	12 oz	16 oz	20 oz	22 oz	24 oz	1/2 liter	25 oz	32 oz	64 oz	1 liter	1 1/2 liter	375 ml	500 ml	750 ml	40 oz	2 liter	Growlers/Jugs	3 liter	1/6 Keg	1/4 Keg	1/2 Keg	Keg (Non-Specified Size)
Middle Ages Wizard's Winter Ale						✗																					
Midnight Sun Brewing Company																											
Midnight Sun Arctic Devil Barley Wine									✗															✗		✗	
Midnight Sun Arctic Rhino Coffee Porter									✗															✗		✗	
Midnight Sun Co Ho Ho Imperial IPA									✗															✗		✗	
Midnight Sun Epluche-Culotte Trippel									✗															✗		✗	
Midnight Sun Full Curl Scotch Ale									✗															✗		✗	
Midnight Sun Kodiak Brown Ale									✗															✗		✗	
Midnight Sun La Miatresse du Moine									✗															✗		✗	
Midnight Sun Mammoth Extra Stout									✗															✗		✗	
Midnight Sun Saison of the Sun									✗															✗		✗	
Midnight Sun Sockeye Red IPA									✗															✗		✗	
Millstream Brewing Company																											
Millstream Brewing Colony Oatmeal Stout						✗																					
Millstream Brewing German Pilsner						✗																					
Millstream Brewing John's Generations White Ale						✗																					
Millstream Brewing Manifest						✗																					
Millstream Brewing Oktoberfest						✗																					
Millstream Brewing Schild Brau Amber						✗																					
Millstream Brewing Schokolade Bock						✗																					
Millstream Brewing Warsh Pail Ale						✗																					
Millstream Brewing Wheat						✗																					
Minhas Craft Brewery																											
Extreme Rockhead Malt Liquor	✗																										
Hi Test Malt Liquor	✗																										
Huber Bock Beer						✗																					
Huber Light Beer		✗				✗																					
Huber Premium Beer		✗				✗																					
Mountain Creek Classic Lager		✗																									
Rhinelander		✗																									
Wisconsin Club						✗																					

399

Locally available bottle and keg sizes may vary.

Brewery / Brand Name	Contact Brewery	Cans	7 oz	8 1/2 oz	10 oz	12 oz	16 oz	20 oz	22 oz	24 oz	1/2 liter	25 oz	32 oz	64 oz	1 liter	1 1/2 liter	375 ml	500 ml	750 ml	40 oz	2 liter	Growlers/Jugs	3 liter	1/6 Keg	1/4 Keg	1/2 Keg	Keg (Non-Specified Size)
Mishawaka Brewing Company																											
Founders Classic Dry Stout						✗			✗																		✗
Four Horsemen Irish Ale						✗			✗																		✗
Hop Head Ale						✗			✗																		✗
INDIAna Pale Ale						✗			✗																		✗
Lake Effect Pale Ale						✗			✗																		✗
Mishawaka Kolsch						✗			✗																		✗
Raspberry Wheat Ale						✗			✗																		✗
Seven Mules Kick-Ass Ale						✗			✗																		✗
Wall Street Wheat Ale						✗			✗																		✗
Mississippi Brewing Company																											
Mississippi Mud Black & Tan							✗																				
Mississippi Mud Lager							✗																				
Moab Brewery																											
Dead Horse Amber Ale						✗																					
Scorpion Pale Ale						✗																					
Molson Coors Brewing Company																											
Blue Moon Belgian White						✗																		✗		✗	
Blue Moon Pumpkin Ale						✗																					
Coors		✗				✗																		✗	✗	✗	
Coors Extra Gold		✗				✗																		✗	✗	✗	
Coors Light		✗				✗																		✗	✗	✗	
Coors Non-Alcoholic		✗				✗																					
George Killian's Irish Red Lager						✗																					✗
Keystone		✗				✗																					✗
Keystone Ice		✗				✗																					✗
Keystone Light		✗				✗																					✗
Winterfest						✗																					
Mount Hood Brewing Company																											
Mount Hood Brewing Cascadian Pale Ale	✗																										
Mount Hood Brewing Cloudcap Amber Ale	✗																										
Mount Hood Brewing Double T Porter	✗																										

400

How Supplied *Continued* — Locally available bottle and keg sizes may vary.

Brewery / Brand Name	Contact Brewery	Cans	7 oz	8 1/2 oz	10 oz	12 oz	16 oz	20 oz	22 oz	24 oz	1/2 liter	25 oz	32 oz	64 oz	1 liter	1 1/2 liter	375 ml	500 ml	750 ml	40 oz	2 liter	Growlers/Jugs	3 liter	1/6 Keg	1/4 Keg	1/2 Keg	Keg (Non-Specified Size)
Mount Hood Brewing Highland Meadow Blonde Ale	✗																										
Mount Hood Brewing Hogsback	✗																										
Mount Hood Brewing Ice Axe IPA	✗																										
Mount Hood Brewing Imperial Ice Axxe	✗																										
Mount Hood Brewing Multorporter	✗																										
Moylan's Brewing Company																											
Moylander: Double IPA									✗															✗		✗	
Moylan's Celts Golden Ale									✗															✗		✗	
Moylan's Hopsickle Imperial Triple Hoppy Ale									✗															✗		✗	
Moylan's India Pale Ale									✗															✗		✗	
Moylan's Kilt Lifter Scotch Ale									✗															✗		✗	
Moylan's Old Blarney Barleywine Style Ale	✗								✗															✗		✗	
Moylan's Paddy's Irish Style Red Ale									✗															✗		✗	
Moylan's Ryan O'Sullivan's Imperial Stout									✗															✗		✗	
Moylan's Tipperary Pale Ale									✗															✗		✗	
Moylan's Wheat Berry Ale									✗															✗		✗	
Mt. Shasta Brewing Company																											
Abner Weed Amber Ale						✗																		✗		✗	
Brewers Creek Pale Ale						✗																		✗		✗	
Mountain High IPA						✗																		✗		✗	
Shastafarian Porter						✗																		✗		✗	
Weed Golden Ale						✗																		✗		✗	
Mudshark Brewing Company																											
Mudshark Brewery Full Moon Belgian White Ale	✗																										
Mudshark Brewery Dry Heat Hefeweizen		✗																									
Nashoba Valley Brewery																											
Nashoba Valley Brewery Barleywine Ale	✗																										
Nashoba Valley Brewery Belgian Double	✗																										
Nashoba Valley Brewery Belgian Pale Ale	✗																										
Nashoba Valley Brewery Blackberry Ale	✗																										
Nashoba Valley Brewery Bolt 117 Lager	✗																										
Nashoba Valley Brewery Dunkelweizen	✗																										

Locally available bottle and keg sizes may vary.

Brewery / Brand Name	Contact Brewery	Cans	7 oz	8 1/2 oz	10 oz	12 oz	16 oz	20 oz	22 oz	24 oz	1/2 liter	25 oz	32 oz	64 oz	1 liter	1 1/2 liter	375 ml	500 ml	750 ml	40 oz	2 liter	Growlers/ Jugs	3 liter	1/6 Keg	1/4 Keg	1/2 Keg	Keg (Non-Specified Size)
Nashoba Valley Brewery Heron Ale	✗																										
Nashoba Valley Brewery Imperial Stout	✗																										
Nashoba Valley Brewery IPA	✗																										
Nashoba Valley Brewery Oaktoberfest Lager	✗																										
Nashoba Valley Brewery Peach Lambic	✗																										
Nashoba Valley Brewery Special Reserve-Kerry's Kolsch	✗																										
Nashoba Valley Brewery Summer Stout	✗																										
Nashoba Valley Brewery Wattaquadoc Wheat	✗																										
Nectar Ales																											
Nectar Ales IPA Nectar						✗																					
Nectar Ales Pale Nectar						✗																					
Nectar Ales Red Nectar						✗																					
New Belgium Brewing Company																											
New Belgium 1554 Brussels Style Black Ale						✗																		✗	✗	✗	
New Belgium 2 Below						✗																		✗	✗	✗	
New Belgium Abbey Belgian Style Ale						✗																		✗		✗	
New Belgium Blue Paddle Pilsner						✗																		✗	✗	✗	
New Belgium Fat Tire Amber Ale						✗				✗														✗	✗	✗	
New Belgium Saison Harvest Ale						✗																		✗	✗	✗	
New Belgium Skinny Dip						✗																		✗	✗	✗	
New Belgium Springboard						✗																		✗	✗	✗	
New Belgium Sunshine Wheat						✗																		✗	✗	✗	
New Belgium Trippel Belgian Style Ale						✗																		✗		✗	
New Century Brewing Company																											
Edison The Independent Light Beer						✗																					
Moonshot						✗																					
New England Brewing Company																											
New England Brewing Atlantic Amber		✗																									
New England Brewing Elm City Lager		✗																									
New England Brewing Sea Hag IPA		✗																									
New Glarus Brewing																											
New Glarus Brewing Belgian Red																			✗						✗		

How Supplied *Continued*

Locally available bottle and keg sizes may vary.

Brewery Brand Name	Contact Brewery	Cans	7 oz	8 1/2 oz	10 oz	12 oz	16 oz	20 oz	22 oz	24 oz	1/2 liter	25 oz	32 oz	64 oz	1 liter	1 1/2 liter	375 ml	500 ml	750 ml	40 oz	2 liter	Growlers/Jugs	3 liter	1/6 Keg	1/4 Keg	1/2 Keg	Keg (Non-Specified Size)
New Glarus Brewing Copper Kettle Weiss						X																			X	X	
New Glarus Brewing Enigma						X																			X	X	
New Glarus Brewing Fat Squirrel						X																			X	X	
New Glarus Brewing Hop Hearty Ale						X																			X	X	
New Glarus Brewing Raspberry Tart																			X						X		
New Glarus Brewing Road Slush Oatmeal Stout						X																			X	X	
New Glarus Brewing Spotted Cow	X																								X	X	
New Glarus Brewing Totally Naked						X																			X	X	
New Glarus Brewing Uff-da Bock						X																			X	X	
New Glarus Brewing Yokel						X																			X	X	
New Holland Brewing Company																											
New Holland Black Tulip									X															X		X	
New Holland Blue Goat Doppelbock									X															X		X	
New Holland Dragon's Milk									X															X		X	
New Holland Ichabod						X																		X		X	
New Holland Mad Hatter						X																		X		X	
New Holland Pilgrim's Dole									X															X		X	
New Holland Red Tulip						X																		X		X	
New Holland Sundog						X																		X		X	
New Holland The Poet						X																		X		X	
New Holland Zoomer Wheat Ale						X																		X		X	
New Knoxville Brewing Company																											
New Knoxville Brewing Honey Wheat						X																					
New Knoxville Brewing India Pale Ale						X																					
New Knoxville Brewing Porter						X																					
New Knoxville Brewing Traditional Pale Ale						X																					
New Knoxville Brewing XX Pale Ale						X																					
New River Brewing Company																											
New River Pale Ale						X																					X
New South Brewing Company																											
New South India Pale Ale																										X	
New South Lager																										X	

403

Locally available bottle and keg sizes may vary.

Brewery Brand Name	Contact Brewery	Cans	7 oz	8 1/2 oz	10 oz	12 oz	16 oz	20 oz	22 oz	24 oz	1/2 liter	25 oz	32 oz	64 oz	1 liter	1 1/2 liter	375 ml	500 ml	750 ml	40 oz	2 liter	Growlers/Jugs	3 liter	1/6 Keg	1/4 Keg	1/2 Keg	Keg (Non-Specified Size)
New South Nut Brown Ale																										X	
New South Oktoberfest																										X	
New South White Ale																										X	
Nicolet Brewing																											
Nicolet Brewing Blonde						X																					X
Nicolet Brewing Classic Pilsner						X																X					X
Nicolet Brewing Dark Pilsner						X																X					X
Nicolet Brewing Oktoberfest						X																X					X
Nicolet Brewing Prostrator Doppelbock						X																X					X
Nicolet Brewing Winter Fest Beer						X																X					X
Nimbus Brewing Company																											
Nimbus "Old Monkeyhine" English Strong						X																X					X
Nimbus Blonde Ale						X																X					X
Nimbus Brown Ale						X																X					X
Nimbus Oatmeal Stout						X																X					X
Nimbus Pale Ale						X																X					X
Nimbus Red Ale						X																X					X
Nine G Brewing Company, Inc.																											
Bitchin' Betty Citrus Wheat Beer						X																					X
Blacksnake Porter						X																					X
Infidel Imperial India Pale Ale						X																					X
Wingman Amber Ale						X																					X
North Coast Brewing Company																											
North Coast ACME California Pale Ale						X																		X		X	
North Coast ACME IPA						X																		X		X	
North Coast Blue Star Wheat Beer						X																		X		X	
North Coast Brewing Brother Thelonious										X														X		X	
North Coast Old No. 38 Stout						X																		X		X	
North Coast Old Rasputin Russian Imperial Stout						X																		X		X	
North Coast Old Stock Ale						X																		X		X	
North Coast Pranqster Belgian Style Golden Ale						X																		X		X	
North Coast Ruedrich's Red Seal Ale						X																		X		X	

Brewery Brand Name	Contact Brewery	Cans	7 oz	8 1/2 oz	10 oz	12 oz	16 oz	20 oz	22 oz	24 oz	1/2 liter	25 oz	32 oz	64 oz	1 liter	1 1/2 liter	375 ml	500 ml	750 ml	40 oz	2 liter	Growlers/Jugs	3 liter	1/6 Keg	1/4 Keg	1/2 Keg	Keg (Non-Specified Size)
North Coast Scrimshaw Pils						✗																		✗		✗	
O'Fallon Brewery																											
O'Fallon 5-Day IPA (in MO only)						✗																		✗			
O'Fallon Blackberry Scottish Ale						✗																		✗			
O'Fallon Cherry Chocolate Beer						✗																		✗			
O'Fallon Gold (in MO only)						✗																		✗			
O'Fallon Light						✗																		✗			
O'Fallon Pumpkin Ale						✗																		✗			
O'Fallon Smoked Porter						✗																		✗			
O'Fallon Summer Brew (in MO only)						✗																		✗			
O'Fallon Wheach						✗																		✗			
O'Fallon Wheat						✗																		✗			
Oak Creek Brewing Company																											
Oak Creek Amber Ale						✗																					✗
Oak Creek Golden Lager						✗																					✗
Oak Creek Hefeweizen						✗																					✗
Oak Creek Nut Brown Ale						✗																					✗
Oak Creek Pale Ale						✗																					✗
Oak Pond Brewery																											
Oak Pond Brewing Dooryard Ale									✗																		✗
Oak Pond Brewing Laughing Loon Lager									✗																		✗
Oak Pond Brewing Nut Brown Ale									✗																		✗
Oak Pond Brewing Oktoberfest									✗																		✗
Oak Pond Brewing Storyteller Doppelbock									✗																		✗
Oak Pond Brewing White Fox Ale									✗																		✗
Oaken Barrel Brewing Company																											
Oaken Barrel Brewing Alabaster						✗																					
Oaken Barrel Brewing Gnaw Bone Pale Ale						✗																					
Oaken Barrel Brewing Indiana Amber Ale						✗																					
Oaken Barrel Brewing Razz-Wheat						✗																					
Oaken Barrel Brewing Snake Pit Porter	✗																										

Locally available bottle and keg sizes may vary.

Brewery / Brand Name	Contact Brewery	Cans	7 oz	8 1/2 oz	10 oz	12 oz	16 oz	20 oz	22 oz	24 oz	1/2 liter	25 oz	32 oz	64 oz	1 liter	1 1/2 liter	375 ml	500 ml	750 ml	40 oz	2 liter	Growlers/ Jugs	3 liter	1/6 Keg	1/4 Keg	1/2 Keg	Keg (Non-Specified Size)
Oceanside Ale Works																											
Oceanside Ale Works Pier View Pale Ale	X																										X
Oceanside Ale Works San Luis Rey Red	X																										X
Odell Brewing Company																											
Odell Brewing 5 Barrel Pale Ale						X																					X
Odell Brewing 90 Shilling						X																					X
Odell Brewing Curmudgeons NIP						X																					X
Odell Brewing Cutthroat Porter						X																					X
Odell Brewing Double Pilsner						X																					X
Odell Brewing Easy Street Wheat						X																					X
Odell Brewing Isolation Ale						X																					X
Odell Brewing Levity Amber						X																					X
Old Dominion Brewing Company																											
Dominion Ale						X																					X
Dominion Lager						X																					X
Dominion Millennium						X																					X
Dominion Oak Barrel Stout						X																					X
Dominion Octoberfest						X																					X
Dominion Pale Ale						X																					X
Dominion Spring Brew						X																					X
Dominion Summer Wheat						X																					X
Dominion Winter Brew						X																					X
New River Pale Ale						X																					X
Tuppers' Hop Pocket Ale						X																					X
Tuppers' Hop Pocket Pils						X																					X
Olde Saratoga Brewing Company																											
Olde Saratoga Brewing Saratoga Lager						X																		X	X	X	
Olde Towne Brewing																											
Olde Towne Amber						X																					X
Olde Towne Pale Ale						X																					X
Oregon Trail Beaver Tail									X																		
Oregon Trail Brown Ale									X																		

Locally available bottle and keg sizes may vary.

Brewery / Brand Name	Contact Brewery	Cans	7 oz	8 1/2 oz	10 oz	12 oz	16 oz	20 oz	22 oz	24 oz	1/2 liter	25 oz	32 oz	64 oz	1 liter	1 1/2 liter	375 ml	500 ml	750 ml	40 oz	2 liter	Growlers/ Jugs	3 liter	1/6 Keg	1/4 Keg	1/2 Keg	Keg (Non-Specified Size)
Oregon Trail Ginseng Porter									✗																		
Oregon Trail IPA									✗																		
Oregon Trail Wit									✗																		
Orlando Brewing Partners, Inc.																											
Orlando Brewing Blackwater Ale	✗																										
Orlando Brewing Blonde Ale						✗																		✗		✗	
Orlando Brewing Mild Ale	✗																										
Orlando Brewing Olde Pelican Ale	✗																										
Orlando Brewing Pale Ale						✗																		✗		✗	
Oskar Blues Grill & Brew																											
Oskar Blues Grill & Brew Dale's Pale Ale		✗																						✗	✗		
Oskar Blues Grill & Brew Gordon		✗																						✗	✗		
Oskar Blues Grill & Brew Leroy		✗																						✗	✗		
Oskar Blues Grill & Brew Old Chub		✗																						✗	✗		
Otter Creek Brewing Company																											
Otter Creek Brewing Alpine Ale						✗																		✗	✗		
Otter Creek Brewing Anniversary IPA										✗														✗	✗		
Otter Creek Brewing Copper Ale						✗																		✗	✗		
Otter Creek Brewing ESB						✗																		✗	✗		
Otter Creek Brewing Oktoberfest						✗																		✗	✗		
Otter Creek Brewing Otter Summer Ale						✗																		✗	✗		
Otter Creek Brewing Pale Ale						✗																		✗	✗		
Otter Creek Brewing Stovepipe Porter						✗																		✗	✗		
Otter Creek Brewing Vermont Lager						✗																		✗	✗		
Wolaver's Organic Brown Ale						✗																		✗	✗		
Wolaver's Organic India Pale Ale						✗																		✗	✗		
Wolaver's Organic Oatmeal Stout						✗																		✗	✗		
Wolaver's Organic Pale Ale						✗																		✗	✗		
Wolaver's Organic Wit Bier						✗																		✗	✗		
Pabst Brewing Company																											
Ballantine Ale		✗				✗																					
Blatz		✗																									

407

Locally available bottle and keg sizes may vary.

Brewery / Brand Name	Contact Brewery	Cans	7 oz	8 1/2 oz	10 oz	12 oz	16 oz	20 oz	22 oz	24 oz	1/2 liter	25 oz	32 oz	64 oz	1 liter	1 1/2 liter	375 ml	500 ml	750 ml	40 oz	2 liter	Growlers/Jugs	3 liter	1/6 Keg	1/4 Keg	1/2 Keg	Keg (Non-Specified Size)
Carling Black Label		X				X																					
Colt 45		X				X														X							
Country Club Malt Liquor		X																									
Haffenreffer's Private Stock		X				X																					
Lone Star		X				X																					
Lone Star Light		X				X																					
McSorley's Black & Tan						X																					
McSorley's Irish Ale						X																					
National Bohemian		X																									
Old Milwaukee		X				X																					
Old Milwaukee Ice		X																		X							
Old Milwaukee Light		X				X																					
Old Milwaukee Non-Alcoholic		X				X																					
Old Style		X				X																					
Old Style Light		X				X																					
Olympia		X																									
Pabst Blue Ribbon		X				X																					
Pabst Blue Ribbon Light		X				X																					
Pabst Blue Ribbon Non-Alcoholic		X				X																					
Pearl		X				X																					
Piels		X																									
Piels Light		X																									
Rainer		X				X																					
Rainer Ale		X				X																					
Rainer Light		X				X																					
Schaefer		X				X																					
Schlitz		X																									
Schlitz Bull Ice		X				X																					
Schlitz Malt Liquor		X																									
Schlitz Red Bull		X				X																					
Schmidt's		X																									
Schmidt's Ice		X				X																					

Locally available bottle and keg sizes may vary.

Brewery / Brand Name	Contact Brewery	Cans	7 oz	8 1/2 oz	10 oz	12 oz	16 oz	20 oz	22 oz	24 oz	1/2 liter	25 oz	32 oz	64 oz	1 liter	1 1/2 liter	375 ml	500 ml	750 ml	40 oz	2 liter	Growlers/Jugs	3 liter	1/6 Keg	1/4 Keg	1/2 Keg	Keg (Non-Specified Size)
Schmidt's Light		X				X																					
Special Export		X				X																					
Special Export Light		X				X																					
St.Ides		X																		X							
Stag		X				X																					
Stroh's		X				X																					
Stroh's Light		X				X																					
Palmetto Brewing Company, Inc.																											
Palmetto Brewing Amber Lager	X																										
Palmetto Brewing Lager	X																										
Palmetto Brewing Pale Ale	X																										
Palmetto Brewing Porter	X																										
Paper City Brewery Company																											
Paper City Brewing 1 Eared Monkey						X																					
Paper City Brewing Banchee Extra Pale Ale						X																					
Paper City Brewing Blonde Hop Monster						X																					
Paper City Brewing Cabot Street Summer Wheat						X			X					X													
Paper City Brewing Denogginator						X																					
Paper City Brewing Dorado						X																					
Paper City Brewing Goats Peak Bock						X			X					X													
Paper City Brewing Golden Lager						X																					
Paper City Brewing Holyoke Dam Ale						X			X					X													
Paper City Brewing India's Pale Ale						X			X					X													
Paper City Brewing Ireland Parish Golden Ale						X			X					X													
Paper City Brewing Nut Brown						X																					
Paper City Brewing P.C. Blue						X																					
Paper City Brewing Red Hat Razzberry						X																					
Paper City Brewing Riley's Stout						X			X					X													
Paper City Brewing Summer Brew						X																					
Paper City Brewing Summer Time Pale Ale						X																					
Paper City Brewing Summit House Oktoberfest						X																					
Paper City Brewing Winter Lager						X																					

409

How Supplied *Continued*

Locally available bottle and keg sizes may vary.

Brewery / Brand Name	Contact Brewery	Cans	7 oz	8 1/2 oz	10 oz	12 oz	16 oz	20 oz	22 oz	24 oz	1/2 liter	25 oz	32 oz	64 oz	1 liter	1 1/2 liter	375 ml	500 ml	750 ml	40 oz	2 liter	Growlers/Jugs	3 liter	1/6 Keg	1/4 Keg	1/2 Keg	Keg (Non-Specified Size)
Paper City Brewing Winter Palace Wee Heavy						X			X					X													
Peak Organic Brewing Company																											
Peak Organic Amber Ale						X																					
Peak Organic Nut Brown Ale						X																					
Peak Organic Pale Ale						X																					
Pelican Pub & Brewery																											
India Pelican Ale									X																		
Penn Brewery (Pennsylvania Brewing)																											
Kaiser Pils						X																		X	X	X	
Penn Crew Lager						X																		X	X	X	
Penn Dark Lager						X																		X	X	X	
Penn Gold						X																		X	X	X	
Penn Maibock						X																		X	X	X	
Penn Marzen						X																		X	X	X	
Penn Oktoberfest						X																		X	X	X	
Penn Pilsner						X																		X	X	X	
Penn Weizen						X																		X	X	X	
St. Nikolaus Bock Bier						X																		X	X	X	
Pennichuck Brewing Company																											
2-6-0 Mogul						X																				X	
Engine Number 5						X																				X	
Pozharnik Espresso Russian Imperial Stout																					X					X	
The Big O						X																				X	
Pete's Brewing																											
Pete's Wicked Ale						X																					
Pete's Wicked Rally Cap Ale						X																					
Pete's Wicked Strawberry Blonde						X																					
Pete's Wicked Wanderlust Cream Ale						X																					
Pig's Eye Brewing Company																											
Pig's Eye Lean		X																									
Pig's Eye Pilsner		X				X																				X	
Pig's Eye Pitt Bull		X																									

410

Locally available bottle and keg sizes may vary.

Brewery / Brand Name	Contact Brewery	Cans	7 oz	8 1/2 oz	10 oz	12 oz	16 oz	20 oz	22 oz	24 oz	1/2 liter	25 oz	32 oz	64 oz	1 liter	1 1/2 liter	375 ml	500 ml	750 ml	40 oz	2 liter	Growlers/ Jugs	3 liter	1/6 Keg	1/4 Keg	1/2 Keg	Keg (Non-Specified Size)
Pike Brewing Company																											
Pike Brewing Company India Pale Ale						✗																		✗	✗	✗	
Pike Brewing Company Kilt Lifter Scotch Ale						✗																		✗	✗	✗	
Pike Brewing Company Monk's Uncle	✗																										
Pike Brewing Company Naughty Nellie's Ale						✗																		✗	✗	✗	
Pike Brewing Company Old Bawdy Barley Wine	✗																										
Pike Brewing Company Pale Ale						✗																		✗	✗	✗	
Pike Brewing Company Tandem									✗															✗	✗	✗	
Pike Brewing Company XXXXX Stout									✗															✗	✗	✗	
Pisgah Brewing Company																											
Pisgah Equinox																						✗					
Pisgah Pale Ale																						✗					
Pisgah Porter																						✗					
Pisgah Solstice																						✗					
Pisgah Stout																						✗					
Vortex I																						✗					
Pittsburgh Brewing Company																											
American		✗																									
American Ice		✗																									
American Light		✗																									
Augustiner Amber Lager		✗				✗																					
Augustiner Dark		✗				✗																					
IC Light						✗																					
Iron City Beer Premium Lager		✗																									
Old German		✗																									
Pony Express Brewing Company																											
Pony Express Gold Beer						✗																					
Pony Express Original Wheat						✗																					
Pony Express Rattlesnake Pale Ale						✗																					
Pony Express Tornado Red Ale																											✗
Port Brewing Company																											
Sharkbite Red Ale						✗																		✗		✗	

411

Locally available bottle and keg sizes may vary.

Brewery / Brand Name	Contact Brewery	Cans	7 oz	8 1/2 oz	10 oz	12 oz	16 oz	20 oz	22 oz	24 oz	1/2 liter	25 oz	32 oz	64 oz	1 liter	1 1/2 liter	375 ml	500 ml	750 ml	40 oz	2 liter	Growlers/Jugs	3 liter	1/6 Keg	1/4 Keg	1/2 Keg	Keg (Non-Specified Size)
High Tide Fresh Hop IPA									X															X		X	
Old Viscosity Ale									X															X		X	
Santa's Little Helper Imperial Stout									X															X		X	
The Lost Abbey Avant Garde																			X					X		X	
The Lost Abbey Cuvee de Tomme																	X										
The Lost Abbey Judgment Day																			X					X		X	
The Lost Abbey Lost & Found Abbey Ale																			X								
The Lost Abbey Red Barn Ale																			X					X		X	
The Lost Abbey The Angel's Share																	X	X									
Wipeout IPA									X															X		X	
Port Townsend Brewing Company																											
Port Townsend Dry-Hopped IPA									X																		
Port Townsend Reel Amber									X																		
Pyramid Brewery																											
Pyramid Brewery Amber Weizen						X																		X		X	
Pyramid Brewery Apricot Weizen						X																				X	
Pyramid Brewery Curve Ball Kolsch						X																		X		X	
Pyramid Brewery Hefeweizen						X			X															X	X	X	
Pyramid Brewery Snow Cap Ale						X																		X		X	
Pyramid Brewery ThunderHead IPA						X			X															X		X	
R.J. Rockers Brewing Company																											
R.J. Rockers Bald Eagle Brown						X																		X		X	
R.J. Rockers Buck Wheat																								X		X	
R.J. Rockers First Snow Ale																								X		X	
R.J. Rockers Liberty Light																								X		X	
R.J. Rockers Patriot Pale Ale						X																		X		X	
R.J. Rockers Star Spangled Stout																								X		X	
Rahr & Sons Brewing Company																											
Rahr Brewing Blonde Lager						X																					
Rahr Brewing Bucking Bock - Miabock						X																					
Rahr Brewing Buffalo Butt Beer						X																					
Rahr Brewing Pecker Wrecker Imperial Pilsner																											X

Locally available bottle and keg sizes may vary.

Brewery / Brand Name	Contact Brewery	Cans	7 oz	8 1/2 oz	10 oz	12 oz	16 oz	20 oz	22 oz	24 oz	1/2 liter	25 oz	32 oz	64 oz	1 liter	1 1/2 liter	375 ml	500 ml	750 ml	40 oz	2 liter	Growlers/ Jugs	3 liter	1/6 Keg	1/4 Keg	1/2 Keg	Keg (Non-Specified Size)
Rahr Brewing Rahr's Red						✗																					
Rahr Brewing Summer Time Wheat						✗																					
Rahr Brewing Ugly Pug						✗																					
Ramapo Valley Brewery																											
Ramapo Valley Brewery Copper Ale	✗																										
Ramapo Valley Brewery Honey Lager						✗																					
Ramapo Valley Brewery India Pale Ale	✗																										
Ramapo Valley Brewery Octoberfest	✗																										
Ramapo Valley Brewery Ramapo Razz Ale	✗																										
Ramapo Valley Brewery Skull Crusher						✗																					
Ramapo Valley Brewery Suffern Station Porter	✗																										
Ramapo Valley Brewery Christmas Ale	✗																										
Real Ale Brewing Company																											
Real Ale Brewing Brewhouse Brown Ale						✗																			✗	✗	
Real Ale Brewing Fireman's #4 Blonde Ale						✗																			✗	✗	
Real Ale Brewing Full Moon Pale Rye Ale						✗																			✗	✗	
Real Ale Brewing Rio Blanco Pale Ale						✗																			✗	✗	
Real Ale Brewing Shade Grown Coffee Porter									✗																✗	✗	
Real Ale Brewing Sisyphus Barleywine Ale						✗																			✗	✗	
ReaperAle, Inc.																											
Reaper Ale Deathly Pale Ale									✗																		
Reaper Ale Inevitable Ale									✗																		
Reaper Ale Mortality Stout									✗																		
Reaper Ale Redemption Red Ale									✗																		
Reaper Ale Ritual Dark Ale									✗																		
Reaper Ale Sleighor Double IPA									✗																		
Red Bell Brewery & Pub																											
Red Bell Brewing Philadelphia Original Light Lager						✗																		✗		✗	
Red Lodge Ales Brewing Company																											
Red Lodge Ales Glacier Ale						✗																		✗		✗	
Red Lodge Ales Hefeweizen						✗																		✗		✗	

413

How Supplied *Continued*

Locally available bottle and keg sizes may vary.

Brewery / Brand Name	Contact Brewery	Cans	7 oz	8 1/2 oz	10 oz	12 oz	16 oz	20 oz	22 oz	24 oz	1/2 liter	25 oz	32 oz	64 oz	1 liter	1 1/2 liter	375 ml	500 ml	750 ml	40 oz	2 liter	Growlers/Jugs	3 liter	1/6 Keg	1/4 Keg	1/2 Keg	Keg (Non-Specified Size)
Redhook Ale Brewery, Inc.																											
Redhook Ale Brewery Blackhook Porter						✗																		✗	✗	✗	
Redhook Ale Brewery Blonde Ale						✗																		✗	✗	✗	
Redhook Ale Brewery Copperhook						✗																		✗	✗	✗	
Redhook Ale Brewery ESB						✗				✗														✗	✗	✗	
Redhook Ale Brewery IPA						✗																		✗	✗	✗	
Redhook Ale Brewery Late Harvest Autumn Ale						✗																		✗	✗	✗	
Redhook Ale Brewery Sunrye						✗																		✗	✗	✗	
Redhook Ale Brewery Winter Hook						✗																		✗	✗	✗	
Rheingold Brewing Company																											
Rheingold Beer						✗																					
Rio Grande Brewing Company																											
Rio Grande Brewing Bock Holiday	✗																										
Rio Grande Brewing Desert Pils						✗																					
Rio Grande Brewing Elfego Bock						✗																					
Rio Grande Brewing IPA	✗																										
Rio Grande Brewing Outlaw Lager						✗																					
Rio Grande Brewing Pancho Verde Chile Cerveza	✗																										
Rio Grande Brewing Stout	✗																										
Rio Grande Brewing Sunchaser Ale	✗																										
River Horse Brewing Company																											
River Horse Belgian Frostbite Winter Ale						✗																		✗		✗	
River Horse Hop Hazard Pale Ale						✗																		✗		✗	
River Horse Lager						✗																		✗		✗	
River Horse Special Ale						✗																		✗		✗	
River Horse Summer Blonde						✗																		✗		✗	
River Horse Tripel Horse						✗																		✗		✗	
Rock Art Brewery, LLC																											
Rock Art Brewery American Red Ale						✗																		✗		✗	
Rock Art Brewery Brown Bear Ale									✗															✗		✗	
Rock Art Brewery Hell's Bock						✗			✗															✗		✗	
Rock Art Brewery India Pale Ale						✗			✗															✗		✗	

Locally available bottle and keg sizes may vary.

Brewery Brand Name	Contact Brewery	Cans	7 oz	8 1/2 oz	10 oz	12 oz	16 oz	20 oz	22 oz	24 oz	1/2 liter	25 oz	32 oz	64 oz	1 liter	1 1/2 liter	375 ml	500 ml	750 ml	40 oz	2 liter	Growlers/Jugs	3 liter	1/6 Keg	1/4 Keg	1/2 Keg	Keg (Non-Specified Size)
Rock Art Brewery Infusco									✗															✗		✗	
Rock Art Brewery Magnumus ete Tomahawkus						✗			✗															✗		✗	
Rock Art Brewery Midnight Madness Smoked Porter						✗																		✗		✗	
Rock Art Brewery Ridge Runner Mild Barleywine						✗			✗															✗		✗	
Rock Art Brewery River Runner Summer Ale									✗															✗		✗	
Rock Art Brewery Stock Ale									✗															✗		✗	
Rock Art Brewery Stump Jumper Stout									✗															✗		✗	
Rock Art Brewery Sunny and 75									✗															✗		✗	
Rock Art Brewery The Riddler									✗															✗		✗	
Rock Art Brewery The Vermonster									✗															✗		✗	
Rock Art Brewery Trail Cutter Dark Lager									✗															✗		✗	
Rock Art Brewery Vermont Maple Wheat									✗															✗		✗	
Rock Art Brewery Whitetail Ale						✗																		✗		✗	
Rocky Bay Brewing Company																											
Rocky Bay Black Castle Ale	✗																										✗
Rocky Bay Brewing Foghorn Ale	✗																										✗
Rocky Bay Brewing Katie's Celtic Red Ale	✗																										✗
Rocky Bay Brewing Nor' Easter Stout	✗																										✗
Rocky Bay Brewing Schooner Point Lager	✗																										✗
Rocky Bay Brewing Seasider Oktoberfest	✗																										✗
Rocky Bay Brewing Whitecap Ale	✗																										✗
Rocky Coulee Brewing Company																											
Fireweed Honey Blonde						✗																		✗		✗	
Rogue Ales																											
Morimoto Black Obi Soba									✗																✗		
Rogue American Amber Ale						✗			✗																✗		
Rogue Brutal Bitter						✗			✗																✗		
Rogue Chamomellow Ale									✗																✗		
Rogue Chipotle Ale									✗																✗		
Rogue Chocolate Stout									✗																✗		
Rogue Dad's Little Helper Malt Liquor									✗																✗		
Rogue Dead Guy Ale						✗			✗					✗											✗		

415

How Supplied *Continued*

Locally available bottle and keg sizes may vary.

Brewery / Brand Name	Contact Brewery	Cans	7 oz	8 1/2 oz	10 oz	12 oz	16 oz	20 oz	22 oz	24 oz	1/2 liter	25 oz	32 oz	64 oz	1 liter	1 1/2 liter	375 ml	500 ml	750 ml	40 oz	2 liter	Growlers/ Jugs	3 liter	1/6 Keg	1/4 Keg	1/2 Keg	Keg (Non-Specified Size)
Rogue Half-E-Weizen									✗																	✗	
Rogue Hazelnut Brown Nectar									✗																	✗	
Rogue I2PA Imperial India Pale Ale						✗						✗														✗	
Rogue Imperial Stout						✗						✗							✗							✗	
Rogue Juniper Pale Ale									✗																	✗	
Rogue Kells Irish Lager									✗																	✗	
Rogue Mocha Porter						✗			✗																	✗	
Rogue Monk Madness Ale									✗																	✗	
Rogue Morimoto Imperial Pilsner										✗																✗	
Rogue Morimoto Soba Ale									✗																	✗	
Rogue Old Crustacean Barleywine																			✗							✗	
Rogue Oregon Golden Ale									✗																	✗	
Rogue Santa's Private Reserve						✗			✗																	✗	
Rogue Shakespeare Stout									✗																	✗	
Rogue Smoke Ale									✗																	✗	
Rogue St.Rogue Red						✗			✗																	✗	
Rogue Uberfest Pilsner									✗																	✗	
Rogue Younger's Special Bitter									✗																	✗	
Roslyn Brewing Company																											
Roslyn Brewing Brookside Pale Lager							✗																				
Roslyn Brewing Roslyn Dark Lager Beer							✗																				
Ruby Mountain Brewing Company																											
Ruby Mountain Brewing Angel Creek Amber Ale									✗																		
Ruby Mountain Brewing Bristlecone Brown Porter									✗																		
Ruby Mountain Brewing Vienna Style Lager									✗																		
Ruby Mountain Brewing Wild West Hefeweizen									✗																		
Rush River Brewing																											
Rush River Brewing BubbleJack IPA																								✗		✗	
Rush River Brewing Lost Arrow Porter																								✗		✗	
Rush River Brewing Small Axe Golden Ale																								✗		✗	
Rush River Brewing The Unforgiven Amber Ale																								✗		✗	

How Supplied *Continued*

Locally available bottle and keg sizes may vary.

Brewery / Brand Name	Contact Brewery	Cans	7 oz	8 1/2 oz	10 oz	12 oz	16 oz	20 oz	22 oz	24 oz	1/2 liter	25 oz	32 oz	64 oz	1 liter	1 1/2 liter	375 ml	500 ml	750 ml	40 oz	2 liter	Growlers/Jugs	3 liter	1/6 Keg	1/4 Keg	1/2 Keg	Keg (Non-Specified Size)
Russian River Brewing Company																											
Russian River Brewing Beatification																	X										
Russian River Brewing Damnation																			X								
Russian River Brewing Depuration																	X										
Russian River Brewing Redemption																			X								
Russian River Brewing Salvation																			X								
Russian River Brewing Sanctification																			X								
Russian River Brewing Supplication																	X										
Russian River Brewing Temptation																	X										
SAB Miller Corporation																											
Hamm's		X																		X						X	
Hamm's Special Light						X																					
Henry Weinhard's Blue Boar Pale Ale						X																					
Henry Weinhard's Classic Dark																											
Henry Weinhard's Hefeweizen						X																					
Henry Weinhard's Northwest Trail Blonde Lager						X																					
Henry Weinhard's Private Reserve						X																					
Henry Weinhard's Summer Wheat						X																					
Icehouse		X	X			X			X				X							X					X	X	
Icehouse 5.0		X	X			X			X				X							X					X	X	
Icehouse Light																											
Magnum Malt Liquor		X											X							X							
Mickey's Ice						X																					
Mickey's Malt Liquor		X				X	X		X				X							X							
Miller Geniune Draft		X	X			X							X							X					X	X	
Miller Geniune Draft Light		X				X																				X	
Miller High Life		X	X			X	X			X			X							X					X	X	
Miller High Life Light		X				X																				X	
Miller Lite		X	X			X	X	X		X			X							X					X	X	
Milwaukee's Best		X				X							X							X						X	
Milwaukee's Best Ice		X				X							X							X							
Milwaukee's Best Light		X				X																				X	

417

Locally available bottle and keg sizes may vary.

Brewery Brand Name	Contact Brewery	Cans	7 oz	8 1/2 oz	10 oz	12 oz	16 oz	20 oz	22 oz	24 oz	1/2 liter	25 oz	32 oz	64 oz	1 liter	1 1/2 liter	375 ml	500 ml	750 ml	40 oz	2 liter	Growlers/ Jugs	3 liter	1/6 Keg	1/4 Keg	1/2 Keg	Keg (Non-Specified Size)
Old English 800 Malt Liquor						X																					
Olde English HG800		X							X				X							X							
Olde English HG800 7.5		X							X				X							X							
Peroni Nastro Azzurro						X																					
Pilsner Urquell						X			X																	X	
Red Dog		X				X			X				X							X						X	
Sharp's		X				X																					X
Southpaw Light		X				X																			X	X	
Sparks		X																									
Sparks Light		X																									
Sparks Plus 6%		X																									
Sparks Plus 7%		X																									
Steel Reserve High Gravity		X							X	X																	
Steel Reserve Triple		X							X	X																	
Sacramento Brewing Company, Inc.																											
Sacramento Brewing Hefeweizen						X			X															X		X	
Sacramento Brewing India Pale Ale						X																		X		X	
Sacramento Brewing Red Horse Ale						X			X															X		X	
Sacramento Brewing River Otter Ale						X																		X		X	
Sacramento Brewing Russian Imperial Stout									X															X		X	
Sacramento Brewing Sacsquatch Ale						X			X															X		X	
Saint Arnold Brewing Company																											
Saint Arnold Brewing Abbey American Quadruppel						X																		X		X	
Saint Arnold Brewing Amber Ale						X																		X		X	
Saint Arnold Brewing Barleywine						X																		X		X	
Saint Arnold Brewing Brown Ale						X																		X		X	
Saint Arnold Brewing Christmas Ale						X																		X		X	
Saint Arnold Brewing Double IPA						X																		X		X	
Saint Arnold Brewing Elissa IPA						X																		X		X	
Saint Arnold Brewing Fancy Lawnmower Beer						X																		X		X	
Saint Arnold Brewing Oktoberfest						X																		X		X	
Saint Arnold Brewing Spring Bock						X																		X		X	

Locally available bottle and keg sizes may vary.

Brewery / Brand Name	Contact Brewery	Cans	7 oz	8 1/2 oz	10 oz	12 oz	16 oz	20 oz	22 oz	24 oz	1/2 liter	25 oz	32 oz	64 oz	1 liter	1 1/2 liter	375 ml	500 ml	750 ml	40 oz	2 liter	Growlers/ Jugs	3 liter	1/6 Keg	1/4 Keg	1/2 Keg	Keg (Non-Specified Size)
Saint Arnold Brewing Summer Pils						X																		X		X	
Saint Arnold Brewing Texas Wheat						X																		X		X	
Saint Arnold Brewing Winter Stout						X																		X		X	
Sand Creek Brewing Company, LLC																											
Badger Porter						X																		X		X	
Cranberry Special Ale						X																		X		X	
Pioneer Black River Red						X																		X		X	
Pioneer Lager						X																		X		X	
Pioneer Oderbolz Bock						X																		X		X	
Sand Creek Brewing English Style Special Ale						X																		X		X	
Sand Creek Brewing Golden Ale						X																		X		X	
Sand Creek Brewing Groovy Brew						X																		X		X	
Sand Creek Brewing Oscar's Chocolate Oatmeal Stout						X																		X		X	
Sand Creek Brewing Wild Ride IPA						X																		X		X	
Sand Creek Brewing Woody's Wheat						X																		X		X	
Santa Cruz Mountain Brewing																											
Santa Cruz Mountain Brewing Amber Ale									X															X		X	
Santa Cruz Mountain Brewing India Pale Ale									X															X		X	
Santa Cruz Mountain Brewing Nicky 666									X															X		X	
Santa Cruz Mountain Brewing Organic Devout Stout									X															X		X	
Santa Cruz Mountain Brewing Organic Dread Brown Ale									X															X		X	
Santa Cruz Mountain Brewing Pale Ale									X															X		X	
Santa Cruz Mountain Brewing Wilder Wheat									X															X		X	
Santa Fe Brewing Company																											
Santa Fe Brewing Santa Fe Chicken Killer Barley Wine									X																		
Santa Fe Brewing Santa Fe Nut Brown Ale						X																					
Santa Fe Brewing Santa Fe Pale Ale						X																					
Santa Fe Brewing Santa Fe State Pen Porter						X																					
Santa Fe Brewing Santa Fe Wheat						X																					
Scuttlebutt Brewing Company																											
Scuttlebutt 10 Below									X																		
Scuttlebutt Amber Ale						X			X																		

419

Locally available bottle and keg sizes may vary.

Brewery / Brand Name	Contact Brewery	Cans	7 oz	8 1/2 oz	10 oz	12 oz	16 oz	20 oz	22 oz	24 oz	1/2 liter	25 oz	32 oz	64 oz	1 liter	1 1/2 liter	375 ml	500 ml	750 ml	40 oz	2 liter	Growlers/Jugs	3 liter	1/6 Keg	1/4 Keg	1/2 Keg	Keg (Non-Specified Size)
Scuttlebutt Gale Force IPA						✗			✗																		
Scuttlebutt Homeport Blonde						✗			✗																		
Scuttlebutt Porter						✗			✗																		
Scuttlebutt Weizenbock									✗																		
Seabright Brewery																											
Seabright Brewery Blur IPA									✗																		✗
Seabright Brewery Oatmeal Stout									✗																		✗
Seabright Brewery Resolution Red									✗																		✗
Sebago Brewing Company																											
Sebago Brewing Bass Ackwards Berryblue Ale						✗																		✗		✗	
Sebago Brewing Boathouse Brown Ale						✗																		✗		✗	
Sebago Brewing Frye's Leap India Pale Ale						✗																		✗		✗	
Sebago Brewing Hefe-Weizen						✗																		✗		✗	
Sebago Brewing Lake Trout Stout						✗																		✗		✗	
Sebago Brewing Midnight Porter						✗																		✗		✗	
Sebago Brewing Northern Light Ale						✗																		✗		✗	
Sebago Brewing Runabout Red Ale						✗																		✗		✗	
Sebago Brewing Slick Nick Winter Ale						✗																		✗		✗	
Schlafly Beer																											
Schlafly American Pale Ale						✗																		✗		✗	
Schlafly Christmas Ale						✗																		✗		✗	
Schlafly Coffee Stout						✗																		✗		✗	
Schlafly Hefeweizen						✗																		✗		✗	
Schlafly IPA						✗																		✗		✗	
Schlafly Irish Extra Stout						✗																		✗		✗	
Schlafly No. 15						✗																		✗		✗	
Schlafly Oatmeal Stout						✗																		✗		✗	
Schlafly Oktoberfest						✗																		✗		✗	
Schlafly Pale Ale						✗																		✗		✗	
Schlafly Pilsner						✗																		✗		✗	
Schlafly Pumpkin Ale						✗																		✗		✗	
Schlafly Raspberry Hefeweizen						✗																		✗		✗	

420

Locally available bottle and keg sizes may vary.

Brewery / Brand Name	Contact Brewery	Cans	7 oz	8 1/2 oz	10 oz	12 oz	16 oz	20 oz	22 oz	24 oz	1/2 liter	25 oz	32 oz	64 oz	1 liter	1 1/2 liter	375 ml	500 ml	750 ml	40 oz	2 liter	Growlers/ Jugs	3 liter	1/6 Keg	1/4 Keg	1/2 Keg	Keg (Non-Specified Size)
Schlafly Saison						✗																		✗		✗	
Schlafly Scotch Ale						✗																		✗		✗	
Schlafly Summer Kölsch						✗																		✗		✗	
Schlafly Winter ESB						✗																		✗		✗	
Sheepscot Valley Brewing Company																											
Sheepscot Valley Brewing Boothbay Special Bitter																						✗		✗		✗	
Sheepscot Valley Brewing Damariscotta Double Brown																						✗		✗		✗	
Sheepscot Valley Brewing Monhegan Wheat																						✗		✗		✗	
Sheepscot Valley Brewing Pemaquid Ale																						✗		✗		✗	
Shenandoah Brewing Company																											
Shenandoah Brewing Big Meadow Pale Ale						✗																✗				✗	
Shenandoah Brewing Black and Tan Beer						✗																✗				✗	
Shenandoah Brewing Old Rag Mountain Ale						✗																✗				✗	
Shenandoah Brewing Skyland Red Ale						✗																✗				✗	
Shenandoah Brewing Stony Man Stout						✗																✗				✗	
Shenandoah Brewing White Water Wheat						✗																✗				✗	
Sherwood Forest Brewers																											
Sherwood Forest Archer's Ale	✗																										
Shipyard Brewing Company																											
Shipyard Brewing Battleground Ale						✗																		✗		✗	
Shipyard Brewing Bluefin Stout						✗																		✗		✗	
Shipyard Brewing Brown						✗																		✗		✗	
Shipyard Brewing Chamberland Pale Ale						✗																		✗		✗	
Shipyard Brewing Export Ale						✗																		✗		✗	
Shipyard Brewing IPA						✗																		✗		✗	
Shipyard Brewing Light						✗																		✗		✗	
Shipyard Brewing Longfellow						✗																		✗		✗	
Shipyard Brewing Old Thumper Extra Special Ale						✗																		✗		✗	
Shipyard Brewing Prelude Special Ale						✗																		✗		✗	
Shipyard Brewing Pumpkinhead Ale						✗																		✗		✗	
Shipyard Brewing Summer						✗																		✗		✗	
Shipyard Brewing Winter Ale						✗																		✗		✗	

Locally available bottle and keg sizes may vary.

Brewery / Brand Name	Contact Brewery	Cans	7 oz	8 1/2 oz	10 oz	12 oz	16 oz	20 oz	22 oz	24 oz	1/2 liter	25 oz	32 oz	64 oz	1 liter	1 1/2 liter	375 ml	500 ml	750 ml	40 oz	2 liter	Growlers/Jugs	3 liter	1/6 Keg	1/4 Keg	1/2 Keg	Keg (Non-Specified Size)
Shmaltz Brewing Company																											
Shmaltz Brewing Bittersweet Lenny's R.IPA									✗																		✗
Shmaltz Brewing Genesis 10:10									✗																		✗
Shmaltz Brewing Genesis Ale						✗																					✗
Shmaltz Brewing Jewbelation									✗																		✗
Shmaltz Brewing Messiah Bold						✗																					✗
Short's Brewing Company																											
Short's Brew Mystery Stout						✗													✗								✗
Short's Brew The Curl (50 IBU)						✗													✗								✗
Sierra Blanca Brewing Company																											
Sierra Blanca Brewing Alien Amber Ale						✗																					
Sierra Blanca Brewing Nut Brown						✗																					
Sierra Blanca Brewing Pale Ale						✗																					
Sierra Blanca Brewing Pilsner						✗																					
Sierra Nevada Brewing Company																											
Sierra Nevada Bigfoot Ale						✗																				✗	
Sierra Nevada Celebration Ale						✗																			✗	✗	
Sierra Nevada Pale Ale						✗				✗															✗	✗	
Sierra Nevada Porter						✗																				✗	
Sierra Nevada Stout						✗																				✗	
Sierra Nevada Summerfest						✗																			✗	✗	
Sierra Nevada Wheat Beer						✗																				✗	
Siletz Brewing Company, Inc.																											
Siletz Brewing Company Amber Ale									✗																		
Siletz Brewing Company Black Diamond Imperial Porter									✗																		
Siletz Brewing Company Chocolate Porter									✗																		
Siletz Brewing Company Lovin Lager									✗																		
Siletz Brewing Company Noggin Knocker									✗																		
Siletz Brewing Company Oatmeal Cream Stout									✗																		
Siletz Brewing Company Paddle Me IPA									✗																		
Siletz Brewing Company Red Ale									✗																		
Siletz Brewing Company Spruce Ale									✗																		

422

Locally available bottle and keg sizes may vary.

Brewery / Brand Name	Contact Brewery	Cans	7 oz	8 1/2 oz	10 oz	12 oz	16 oz	20 oz	22 oz	24 oz	1/2 liter	25 oz	32 oz	64 oz	1 liter	1 1/2 liter	375 ml	500 ml	750 ml	40 oz	2 liter	Growlers/ Jugs	3 liter	1/6 Keg	1/4 Keg	1/2 Keg	Keg (Non-Specified Size)
Siletz Brewing Company Winter Warmer									✗																		
Siletz Brewing Company Wooly Bully									✗																		
Silver Gulch Brewing & Bottling																											
Silver Gulch Coldfoot Pilsner Lager						✗																					✗
Silver Gulch Copper Creek Amber Ale						✗																					✗
Silver Gulch Fairbanks Lager						✗																					✗
Silver Gulch Old 55 Pale Ale						✗																					✗
Silver Gulch Pick Axe Porter						✗																					✗
Ska Brewing Company																											
Ska Brewing Buster Nut Brown Ale									✗															✗		✗	
Ska Brewing Decadent Imperial IPA									✗															✗		✗	
Ska Brewing Mexican Logger						✗																		✗		✗	
Ska Brewing Nefarious Ten Pin Imperial Porter									✗															✗		✗	
Ska Brewing Pinstripe Red Ale						✗																		✗		✗	
Ska Brewing Special ESB		✗																									
Ska Brewing Steel Toe Stout						✗																		✗		✗	
Ska Brewing Ten Pin Porter						✗																					
Ska Brewing 7 Blonde Ale						✗																					
Ska Brewing 7 Blonde Dubbel									✗																		
Skagit River Brewing																											
Skagit River Brewing Sculler's IPA									✗																		
Skagit River Yellow Jacket Pale Ale									✗																		
Slab City Brewing																											
Slab City Brewing Esker Alt	✗																					✗					
Slab City Brewing Milkhouse Stout	✗																					✗					
Slab City Brewing Old 47 Pale Ale	✗																					✗					
Slab City Brewing Shawano Gold	✗																					✗					
Slab City Brewing W.C. Bitter	✗																					✗					
Slab City Brewing Xenabock	✗																					✗					
Sly Fox Brewing Company																											
Sly Fox Black Raspberry Reserve																		✗						✗			
Sly Fox Christmas Ale	✗																										

423

Locally available bottle and keg sizes may vary.

Brewery / Brand Name	Contact Brewery	Cans	7 oz	8 1/2 oz	10 oz	12 oz	16 oz	20 oz	22 oz	24 oz	1/2 liter	25 oz	32 oz	64 oz	1 liter	1 1/2 liter	375 ml	500 ml	750 ml	40 oz	2 liter	Growlers/Jugs	3 liter	1/6 Keg	1/4 Keg	1/2 Keg	Keg (Non-Specified Size)
Sly Fox Dunkel Lager		X																									
Sly Fox Gang Aft Angley	X																										
Sly Fox Ichor																			X								
Sly Fox Incubus																			X								
Sly Fox Instigator Doppelbock									X															X			
Sly Fox Odyssey	X																										
Sly Fox Oktoberfest									X															X			
Sly Fox Phoenix Pale Ale		X																						X			
Sly Fox Pikeland Pils		X																						X			
Sly Fox Route 113 India Pale Ale									X															X			
Sly Fox Royal Weisse		X																	X					X			
Sly Fox Saison VOS																											
Smuttynose Brewing Company																											
Smuttynose Brewing Baltic Porter									X																		
Smuttynose Brewing Barleywine Style Ale									X																		
Smuttynose Brewing Big A IPA									X																		
Smuttynose Brewing Farmhouse Ale									X																		
Smuttynose Brewing Imerial Stout									X																		
Smuttynose Brewing Imperial IPA									X																		
Smuttynose Brewing IPA (65 IBU)						X																					
Smuttynose Brewing Maibock									X																		
Smuttynose Brewing Octoberfest									X																		
Smuttynose Brewing Old Brown Dog Ale						X																					
Smuttynose Brewing Portsmouth Lager						X																					
Smuttynose Brewing Pumpkin Ale						X																		X			
Smuttynose Brewing Really Old Brown Dog Old Ale									X																		
Smuttynose Brewing Robust Porter						X																					
Smuttynose Brewing Scotch Style Ale									X																		
Smuttynose Brewing Shoals Pale Ale						X																		X			
Smuttynose Brewing S'muttonator Doppelbock									X																		
Smuttynose Brewing Summer Weizen						X																					
Smuttynose Brewing Weizenheimer						X																					

Locally available bottle and keg sizes may vary.

Brewery / Brand Name	Contact Brewery	Cans	7 oz	8 1/2 oz	10 oz	12 oz	16 oz	20 oz	22 oz	24 oz	1/2 liter	25 oz	32 oz	64 oz	1 liter	1 1/2 liter	375 ml	500 ml	750 ml	40 oz	2 liter	Growlers/Jugs	3 liter	1/6 Keg	1/4 Keg	1/2 Keg	Keg (Non-Specified Size)
Smuttynose Brewing Wheat Wine Ale									✗																		
Smuttynose Brewing Winter Ale						✗																					
Snake River Brewing Company																											
Snake River Lager						✗																		✗		✗	
Snake River OB-1 Organic Ale						✗																		✗		✗	
Snake River Pale Ale						✗																		✗		✗	
Snake River Zonker Stout						✗																		✗		✗	
Snipes Mountain Brewing Company																											
Snipes Mountain Brewing Coyote Moon						✗																		✗		✗	
Snipes Mountain Brewing Crazy Ivan's Imperial Stout	✗																										
Snipes Mountain Brewing Extra Blonde Ale						✗																					✗
Snipes Mountain Brewing Harvest Ale																											✗
Snipes Mountain Brewing Hefeweizen																											✗
Snipes Mountain Brewing India Pale Ale									✗															✗		✗	
Snipes Mountain Brewing Porter						✗																		✗		✗	
Snipes Mountain Brewing Red Sky Ale									✗																		✗
Snipes Mountain Brewing Roza Reserve									✗															✗		✗	
Snipes Mountain Brewing Sunnyside Pale Ale						✗																		✗		✗	
Snoqualmie Falls Brewing Company																											
Avalanche Winter Ale									✗																		
Copperhead Pale Ale									✗																		
Harvest Moon Festbier									✗																		
PGA (Perfectly Great Amber)									✗																		
Spring Fever									✗																		
Steam Train Porter									✗																		
Summer Beer									✗																		
Wildcat IPA									✗																		
Snowshoe Brewing Company																											
Snowshoe Brewing Grizzly Brown Ale						✗																		✗	✗	✗	
Snowshoe Brewing Snoweizen Wheat Ale						✗																		✗	✗	✗	
Snowshoe Brewing Thompson Pale Ale						✗																		✗	✗	✗	

Locally available bottle and keg sizes may vary.

Brewery / Brand Name	Contact Brewery	Cans	7 oz	8 1/2 oz	10 oz	12 oz	16 oz	20 oz	22 oz	24 oz	1/2 liter	25 oz	32 oz	64 oz	1 liter	1 1/2 liter	375 ml	500 ml	750 ml	40 oz	2 liter	Growlers/Jugs	3 liter	1/6 Keg	1/4 Keg	1/2 Keg	Keg (Non-Specified Size)
Sonoran Brewing Company																											
Sonora Brewing Burning Bird Pale Ale																								X		X	
Sonora Brewing C.I.A. — Citrus Infused Ale																								X		X	
Sonora Brewing Desert Amber																								X		X	
Sonora Brewing India Pale Ale																								X		X	
Sonora Brewing Mandarin Orange Hefeweizen																								X		X	
Sonora Brewing Old Saguaro Barley Wine																								X		X	
Sonora Brewing Top Down Red Ale																								X		X	
South Shore Brewery																											
South Shore Brewery Herbal Cream Ale						X																		X		X	
South Shore Brewery Honey Pils						X																		X		X	
South Shore Brewery Nut Brown Ale						X																		X		X	
South Shore Brewery Rhodes' Scholar Stout						X																		X		X	
Southampton Publick House																											
Southampton 10th Anniversary Old Ale																			X								
Southampton Abbot 12																			X								
Southampton Biere de Garde									X										X								X
Southampton Double White Ale						X																					X
Southampton Grand Cru																			X								
Southampton Imperial Porter									X																		X
Southampton IPA						X																					
Southampton May Bock									X																		X
Southampton Pumpkin Ale									X																		X
Southampton Saison									X										X								X
Southampton Secret Ale						X			X																		X
Southampton Triple																			X								
Southern Tier Brewing Company																											
Southern Tier Brewing Belgian Triple Ale						X																					
Southern Tier Brewing Big Red Imperial Red									X																		
Southern Tier Brewing Black Water Series Imperial Stout						X																					
Southern Tier Brewing Harvest Ale						X																					
Southern Tier Brewing Heavy Weizen									X																		

426

Locally available bottle and keg sizes may vary.

Brewery Brand Name	Contact Brewery	Cans	7 oz	8 1/2 oz	10 oz	12 oz	16 oz	20 oz	22 oz	24 oz	1/2 liter	25 oz	32 oz	64 oz	1 liter	1 1/2 liter	375 ml	500 ml	750 ml	40 oz	2 liter	Growlers/Jugs	3 liter	1/6 Keg	1/4 Keg	1/2 Keg	Keg (Non-Specified Size)
Southern Tier Brewing Hop Sun Summer Ale						✗																					
Southern Tier Brewing IPA						✗																					
Southern Tier Brewing Old Man Winter Warmer						✗																					
Southern Tier Brewing Phin & Matt's						✗																					
Southern Tier Brewing Porter						✗																					
Spanish Peaks Brewing Company/ United States Beverage																											
Black Dog Ale						✗																					
Black Dog American Pale Ale						✗																					
Black Dog Honey Raspberry Ale						✗																					
Black Dog Summer White Ale						✗																					
Speakeasy Ales & Lagers, Inc.																											
Speakeasy Big Daddy IPA						✗																					
Speakeasy Double Daddy Imperial IPA						✗																					
Speakeasy Prohibition Ale						✗																					
Speakeasy Untouchable Pale Ale						✗																					
Spilker Ales																											
Spilker Ales Hopluia Ale		✗																						✗		✗	
Sprecher Brewing																											
Sprecher Brewing Abbey Triple							✗								✗										✗	✗	
Sprecher Brewing Barley Wine							✗								✗												
Sprecher Brewing Black Bavarian							✗																		✗	✗	
Sprecher Brewing Dopple Bock							✗																		✗	✗	
Sprecher Brewing Generation Porter															✗						✗				✗	✗	
Sprecher Brewing Hefe' Weiss							✗																		✗	✗	
Sprecher Brewing Imperial Stout							✗																		✗	✗	
Sprecher Brewing India Pale Ale							✗																		✗	✗	
Sprecher Brewing Irish Stout							✗																		✗	✗	
Sprecher Brewing Mai Bock							✗																		✗	✗	
Sprecher Brewing Micro-Light Ale							✗																		✗	✗	
Sprecher Brewing Oktoberfest							✗																		✗	✗	
Sprecher Brewing Piper's Scotch Ale							✗																		✗		
Sprecher Brewing Pub Ale							✗																		✗	✗	

Locally available bottle and keg sizes may vary.

Brewery / Brand Name	Contact Brewery	Cans	7 oz	8 1/2 oz	10 oz	12 oz	16 oz	20 oz	22 oz	24 oz	1/2 liter	25 oz	32 oz	64 oz	1 liter	1 1/2 liter	375 ml	500 ml	750 ml	40 oz	2 liter	Growlers/Jugs	3 liter	1/6 Keg	1/4 Keg	1/2 Keg	Keg (Non-Specified Size)
Sprecher Brewing Special Amber							X																		X	X	
Sprecher Brewing Winter Brew							X																		X	X	
Springfield Brewing Company																											
Springfield Brewing Munich Lager						X																		X		X	
Springfield Brewing Pale Ale						X																		X		X	
Springfield Brewing Porter						X																		X		X	
Springfield Brewing Unfiltered Wheat						X																		X		X	
St. Croix Beer Company																											
St.Croix Maple Ale						X																					X
St.Croix Serrano Pepper Ale						X																					X
St. George Brewing Company																											
St. George Brewing Company Golden Ale						X																		X		X	
St. George Brewing Company IPA						X																		X		X	
St. George Brewing Company Pale Ale						X																		X		X	
St. George Brewing Company Porter						X																		X		X	
St. George Brewing Company Vienna Lager						X																		X		X	
St. George Brewing Fall Bock						X																		X		X	
Stampede Brewing Company																											
Stampede Light						X																					
Starr Hill Brewery																											
Starr Hill Amber Ale						X																					
Starr Hill Dark Starr Stout						X																					
Starr Hill Jomo Lager						X																					
Starr Hill Pale Ale						X																					
Steamworks Brewing Company																											
Backside Stout									X															X	X	X	
Colorado Kolsch									X															X	X	X	
Conductor									X															X	X	X	
Engineer Light Lager						X																		X	X	X	
Lizard Head Red									X															X	X	X	
Spruce Goose									X															X	X	X	
Steam Engine Lager		X				X																		X	X	X	

428

Locally available bottle and keg sizes may vary.

Brewery Brand Name	Contact Brewery	Cans	7 oz	8 1/2 oz	10 oz	12 oz	16 oz	20 oz	22 oz	24 oz	1/2 liter	25 oz	32 oz	64 oz	1 liter	1 1/2 liter	375 ml	500 ml	750 ml	40 oz	2 liter	Growlers/Jugs	3 liter	1/6 Keg	1/4 Keg	1/2 Keg	Keg (Non-Specified Size)
Third Eye Pale Ale						X																		X	X	X	
Stevens Point Brewery																											
Point Cascade Pale Ale						X																					
Point Classic Amber						X																					
Point Honey Light						X																					
Point Premier Light						X																					
Point Special Lager						X																					
Point Spring Bock						X																					
Point White Bière						X																					
Stone Brewing Company																											
Arrogant Bastard Ale									X															X	X	X	
Double Bastard Ale									X																	X	
Stone Anniversary Ale																							X			X	
Stone Imperial Russian Stout									X																	X	
Stone IPA						X			X															X	X	X	
Stone Levitation Ale									X																		
Stone Old Guardian Barley Wine									X																	X	
Stone Pale Ale						X			X															X	X	X	
Stone Ruination IPA						X			X																	X	
Stone Smoked Porter									X															X	X	X	
Stone Vertical Epic Ale									X																	X	
Stone Coast Brewing Company																											
Black Bear Porter	X																										
Jackson's Winter Ale	X																										
Knuckleball Bock	X																										
Stone Coast 420 India Pale Ale	X																										
Sunday River Alt	X																										
Sunday River Lager	X																										
Sunday River Sunsplash Golden Ale	X																										
Stoudt's Brewing Company																											
Stoudt's Abbey Triple						X																		X		X	
Stoudt's American Pale Ale						X																		X		X	

Locally available bottle and keg sizes may vary.

Brewery / Brand Name	Contact Brewery	Cans	7 oz	8 1/2 oz	10 oz	12 oz	16 oz	20 oz	22 oz	24 oz	1/2 liter	25 oz	32 oz	64 oz	1 liter	1 1/2 liter	375 ml	500 ml	750 ml	40 oz	2 liter	Growlers/Jugs	3 liter	1/6 Keg	1/4 Keg	1/2 Keg	Keg (Non-Specified Size)
Stoudt's Blonde Double Maibock						X																				X	
Stoudt's Double India Pale Ale						X																		X			
Stoudt's Fat Dog Stout						X																		X		X	
Stoudt's Gold Lager						X																		X		X	
Stoudt's Oktoberfest						X																		X		X	
Stoudt's Pils						X																					
Stoudt's Scarlet Lady Ale						X																		X		X	
Stoudt's Weizen						X																		X		X	
Stoudt's Winter Ale						X																		X		X	
Straub Brewing																											
Straub						X																			X	X	
Straub Light						X																			X	X	
Streich's Brewing Company, LLC																											
Streich's Brewing Naughty Fish Pale Ale	X																										
Sudwerk																											
Sudwerk Doppelbock						X																		X	X	X	
Sudwerk Hefe-Weizen						X																		X	X	X	
Sudwerk Lager						X																		X	X	X	
Sudwerk Leatherneck						X																				X	
Sudwerk Marzen						X																		X	X	X	
Sudwerk Pilsner						X																		X	X	X	
Summit Brewing Company																											
Summit ESB						X																		X	X	X	
Summit Extra Pale Ale						X				X														X	X	X	
Summit Grand Pilsner						X																		X	X	X	
Summit Great Northern Porter						X																		X	X	X	
Summit Hefe Weizen						X																		X	X	X	
Summit India Pale Ale						X																		X	X	X	
Summit Maibock						X																		X	X	X	
Summit Oktoberfest						X																		X	X	X	
Summit Scandia Ale						X																		X	X	X	
Summit Winter Ale						X																		X	X	X	

Locally available bottle and keg sizes may vary.

Brewery / Brand Name	Contact Brewery	Cans	7 oz	8 1/2 oz	10 oz	12 oz	16 oz	20 oz	22 oz	24 oz	1/2 liter	25 oz	32 oz	64 oz	1 liter	1 1/2 liter	375 ml	500 ml	750 ml	40 oz	2 liter	Growlers/Jugs	3 liter	1/6 Keg	1/4 Keg	1/2 Keg	Keg (Non-Specified Size)
Surly Brewing Company																											
Surly Brewing Bender		X																									
Surly Brewing Furious		X																									
Sweetwater Brewing																											
Sweetwater Brewing 420 Extra Pale Ale						X																		X	X	X	
Sweetwater Brewing IPA						X																		X	X	X	
Sweetwater Brewing Sweet Georgia Brown						X																		X	X	X	
Sweetwater Brewing Sweetwater Blue						X																		X	X	X	
Sweetwater Brewing Sweetwater Festive Ale						X																		X	X	X	
Telegraph Brewing Company																											
Telegraph Brewing California Ale																						X					
Telegraph Brewing Golden Wheat Ale																						X					
Telegraph Brewing Stock Porter																						X					
Terrapin Beer Company																											
Terrapin All American Imperial Pilsner						X																		X		X	
Terrapin Big Hoppy Monster						X																		X		X	
Terrapin Golden Ale						X																		X		X	
Terrapin Rye Pale Ale						X																		X		X	
Terrapin Rye Squared						X																		X		X	
Terrapin Wake-N-Bake Coffee Oatmeal Imperial Stout						X																		X		X	
Terre Haute Brewing Company																											
Terre Haute Brewing Champagne Velvet Amber						X																					
Terre Haute Brewing Champagne Velvet Bock						X																					
Terre Haute Brewing Champagne Velvet Pilsner						X																		X		X	
The Academy of Fine Beers, LLC																											
Josef Bierbitzch Golden Pilsner						X																					
The Bethlehem Brew Works																											
Bethlehem Brew Works Pumpkin Ale						X																					
Bethlehem Brew Works Rude Elf's Reserve						X																					
The Black Mountain/Chili Beer Company																											
Black Mountain Cave Creek Chili Beer						X																					
Black Mountain Frog Light						X																					

Brewery / Brand Name	Contact Brewery	Cans	7 oz	8 1/2 oz	10 oz	12 oz	16 oz	20 oz	22 oz	24 oz	1/2 liter	25 oz	32 oz	64 oz	1 liter	1 1/2 liter	375 ml	500 ml	750 ml	40 oz	2 liter	Growlers/Jugs	3 liter	1/6 Keg	1/4 Keg	1/2 Keg	Keg (Non-Specified Size)
Black Mountain Gold						X																					
Black Mountain Juanderful Wheat						X																					
Black Mountain Ocotillo Amber						X																					
Black Mountain South of the Border Porter						X																					
The Boston Beer Company																											
Sam Adams 1790 Root Beer Brew						X																					
Sam Adams George Washington Porter						X																					
Sam Adams James Madison Dark Wheat Ale						X																					
Sam Adams Light						X				X																	
Sam Adams Traditional Ginger Honey Ale						X																					
Samuel Adams 375 Colonial Ale						X																					
Samuel Adams Black Lager						X																					
Samuel Adams Boston Ale						X																				X	
Samuel Adams Boston Lager						X				X														X	X	X	
Samuel Adams Brown Ale						X																					
Samuel Adams Cherry Wheat						X																				X	
Samuel Adams Chocolate Bock																			X								
Samuel Adams Cranberry Lambic						X																					
Samuel Adams Cream Stout						X																					
Samuel Adams Double Bock																			X								
Samuel Adams Hefeweizen						X																					
Samuel Adams Holiday Porter						X																					
Samuel Adams Honey Porter						X																					
Samuel Adams Imperial Pilsner										X																	
Samuel Adams Millennium																			X								
Samuel Adams Octoberfest						X				X														X	X	X	
Samuel Adams Old Fezziwig Ale						X																					
Samuel Adams Pale Ale						X																					
Samuel Adams Scotch Ale						X																					
Samuel Adams Summer Ale						X				X														X	X	X	
Samuel Adams Triple Bock				X																							
Samuel Adams Utopias										X																	

Locally available bottle and keg sizes may vary.

Brewery / Brand Name	Contact Brewery	Cans	7 oz	8 1/2 oz	10 oz	12 oz	16 oz	20 oz	22 oz	24 oz	1/2 liter	25 oz	32 oz	64 oz	1 liter	1 1/2 liter	375 ml	500 ml	750 ml	40 oz	2 liter	Growlers/Jugs	3 liter	1/6 Keg	1/4 Keg	1/2 Keg	Keg (Non-Specified Size)
Samuel Adams White Ale						✗																		✗		✗	
Samuel Adams Winter Lager						✗				✗														✗	✗	✗	
The Church Brew Works																											
Church Brew Works Blast Furnace Stout									✗																		
Church Brew Works Celestial Gold						✗																					
Church Brew Works Millenium Trippel Ale																			✗								
Church Brew Works Pious Monk Dunkel		✗				✗																					
Church Brew Works Pipe Organ Pale Ale						✗																					
Church Brew Works Quadzilla																			✗								
The Defiant Brewing Company																											
Defiant Brewing 3	✗																										
Defiant Brewing Big Thumper Ale	✗																										
Defiant Brewing Christmas Ale	✗																										
Defiant Brewing ESB	✗																										
Defiant Brewing Inspiration Ale	✗																										
Defiant Brewing Little Thumper Ale	✗																										
Defiant Brewing Pearl River Lager	✗																										
Defiant Brewing Pilsner	✗																										
Defiant Brewing Porter	✗																										
Defiant Brewing Stephano's Stout	✗																										
Defiant Brewing The Horseman's Ale	✗																										
The Dock Street Brewery Company																											
Dock Street Amber						✗																				✗	
Illuminator Dock Street Bock						✗																				✗	
The Fort Collins Brewery																											
Fort Collins Chocolate Stout						✗																		✗		✗	
Fort Collins Edgar Lager						✗																		✗		✗	
Fort Collins Major Tom's Pomegranate Wheat						✗																		✗		✗	
Fort Collins Retro Red						✗																		✗		✗	
Fort Collins The Kidd Lager						✗																		✗		✗	
Fort Collins Z Lager						✗																		✗		✗	

Locally available bottle and keg sizes may vary.

Brewery Brand Name	Contact Brewery	Cans	7 oz	8 1/2 oz	10 oz	12 oz	16 oz	20 oz	22 oz	24 oz	1/2 liter	25 oz	32 oz	64 oz	1 liter	1 1/2 liter	375 ml	500 ml	750 ml	40 oz	2 liter	Growlers/Jugs	3 liter	1/6 Keg	1/4 Keg	1/2 Keg	Keg (Non-Specified Size)
The Matt Brewing																											
Saranac 12 Beers of Summer						✗																					
Saranac 12 Beers of Winter						✗																					
Saranac Adirondack Lager						✗																		✗		✗	
Saranac Black & Tan						✗																					
Saranac Black Forest						✗																		✗		✗	
Saranac Caramel Porter						✗																		✗		✗	
Saranac India Pale Ale						✗																		✗		✗	
Saranac Lager						✗																		✗		✗	
Saranac Octoberfest						✗																		✗		✗	
Saranac Pale Ale						✗																		✗		✗	
Saranac Season's Best						✗																		✗		✗	
Saranac Trail Mix						✗																					
The Narragansett Brewing Company																											
Narragansett Beer		✗							✗																		
The Northern Lights Brewing Company																											
Northern Lights Blueberry Creme Ale	✗																										
Northern Lights Chocolate Dunkel	✗																										
Northern Lights Creme Ale	✗																										
Northern Lights Crystal Bitter	✗																										
Northern Lights Pale Ale	✗																										
Northern Lights Winter Ale	✗																										
The Palisade Brewery																											
The Palisade Brewery Farmer's Friend						✗																✗					✗
The Palisade Brewery Orchard Amber Ale						✗																✗					✗
The Palisade Brewery PAL Beer						✗																✗					✗
The Palisade Brewery Red Truck IPA						✗																✗					✗
The Sea Dog Brewing Company																											
Sea Dog Apricot Wheat Beer						✗																		✗		✗	
Sea Dog Blue Paw Wheat						✗																		✗		✗	
Sea Dog Old East India Pale Ale						✗																		✗		✗	
Sea Dog Old Gollywobbler Brown Ale						✗																		✗		✗	

Locally available bottle and keg sizes may vary.

Brewery Brand Name	Contact Brewery	Cans	7 oz	8 1/2 oz	10 oz	12 oz	16 oz	20 oz	22 oz	24 oz	1/2 liter	25 oz	32 oz	64 oz	1 liter	1 1/2 liter	375 ml	500 ml	750 ml	40 oz	2 liter	Growlers/Jugs	3 liter	1/6 Keg	1/4 Keg	1/2 Keg	Keg (Non-Specified Size)
Sea Dog Owls Head Light Ale						X																		X		X	
Sea Dog Riverdriver Hazelnut Porter						X																		X		X	
Sea Dog Topsham Pale Ale						X																		X		X	
Sea Dog Windjammer Blonde Ale						X																		X		X	
The Spoetzl Brewing																											
Shiner 96 Marzen Style Ale						X																					
Shiner Blonde						X																					
Shiner Bock						X																					
Shiner Dunkelweizen						X																					
Shiner Hefeweizen						X																					
Shiner Kolsch						X																					
Shiner Light						X																					
The Weeping Radish Brewery																											
Weeping Radish Altbier						X					X				X									X		X	
Weeping Radish Black Radish						X					X				X									X		X	
Weeping Radish Christmas Bier						X					X				X									X		X	
Weeping Radish Corolla Gold						X					X				X									X		X	
Weeping Radish Corolla Light						X					X				X									X		X	
Weeping Radish Fest						X					X				X									X		X	
Weeping Radish Kolsch						X					X				X									X		X	
Weeping Radish Maibock						X					X				X									X		X	
Weeping Radish Marzen						X					X				X									X		X	
Weeping Radish Weizen						X					X				X									X		X	
Thirsty Dog Brewing Company																											
Thirsty Dog Balto Heroic Lager						X																		X		X	
Thirsty Dog Hoppus Maximus						X																		X		X	
Thirsty Dog Old Leghumper						X																		X		X	
Thirsty Dog Siberian Night						X																		X		X	
Thomas Creek Brewery																											
Thomas Creek Amber Ale						X																		X		X	
Thomas Creek Dopplebock						X																		X		X	
Thomas Creek IPA						X																		X		X	

435

Locally available bottle and keg sizes may vary.

Brewery Brand Name	Contact Brewery	Cans	7 oz	8 1/2 oz	10 oz	12 oz	16 oz	20 oz	22 oz	24 oz	1/2 liter	25 oz	32 oz	64 oz	1 liter	1 1/2 liter	375 ml	500 ml	750 ml	40 oz	2 liter	Growlers/Jugs	3 liter	1/6 Keg	1/4 Keg	1/2 Keg	Keg (Non-Specified Size)
Thomas Creek Jingle Bell Bock																								✗		✗	
Thomas Creek Multi Grain Ale						✗																		✗		✗	
Thomas Creek Octoberfest																								✗		✗	
Thomas Creek Pilsner						✗																		✗		✗	
Thomas Creek Porter																								✗		✗	
Thomas Creek Red Ale						✗																		✗		✗	
Thomas Creek Vanilla Cream Ale						✗																		✗		✗	
Thomas Hooker Brewing Company																											
Thomas Hooker American Pale Ale						✗																		✗		✗	
Thomas Hooker Blonde Ale						✗																		✗		✗	
Thomas Hooker Hop Meadow IPA						✗																		✗		✗	
Thomas Hooker Imperial Porter																		✗						✗		✗	
Thomas Hooker Irish Red						✗																		✗		✗	
Thomas Hooker Liberator Doppelbock																		✗						✗		✗	
Thomas Hooker Munich Golden Lager																		✗						✗		✗	
Thomas Hooker Octoberfest						✗																		✗		✗	
Thomas Hooker Old Marley Barley Wine																		✗						✗		✗	
Three Floyds Brewing Company																											
Three Floyds Brewing Alpha King						✗																					
Three Floyds Brewing Behemoth Barleywine									✗																		
Three Floyds Brewing Black Sun Stout									✗																		
Three Floyds Brewing Brian Boru									✗																		✗
Three Floyds Brewing Christmas Porter									✗																		
Three Floyds Brewing Dreadnaught IPA									✗																		
Three Floyds Brewing Gumballhead									✗																		
Three Floyds Brewing Pride & Joy Mild Ale						✗																					
Three Floyds Brewing Rabbid Rabbit Saison									✗																	✗	
Three Floyds Brewing Robert the Bruce Scottish Ale						✗																				✗	
Tommyknocker Brewery																											
Tommyknocker Alpine Glacier Lager						✗																✗		✗	✗	✗	
Tommyknocker Butt Head Bock						✗																✗		✗	✗	✗	
Tommyknocker Imperial Nut Brown Ale						✗																✗		✗	✗	✗	

How Supplied *Continued*

Locally available bottle and keg sizes may vary.

Brewery Brand Name	Contact Brewery	Cans	7 oz	8 1/2 oz	10 oz	12 oz	16 oz	20 oz	22 oz	24 oz	1/2 liter	25 oz	32 oz	64 oz	1 liter	1 1/2 liter	375 ml	500 ml	750 ml	40 oz	2 liter	Growlers/Jugs	3 liter	1/6 Keg	1/4 Keg	1/2 Keg	Keg (Non-Specified Size)
Tommyknocker Jack Whacker Wheat Ale						✗																✗		✗	✗	✗	
Tommyknocker Maple Nut Brown Ale						✗																✗		✗	✗	✗	
Tommyknocker Ornery Amber Lager		✗																				✗		✗	✗	✗	
Tommyknocker Pick Axe Pale Ale						✗																✗		✗	✗	✗	
Tommyknocker Tundrabeary Ale						✗																✗		✗	✗	✗	
Tractor Brewing Company																											
Tractor Brewing Double Plow Oatmeal Stout						✗																		✗	✗	✗	
Tractor Brewing Farmer's Tan - Red Ale						✗																		✗	✗	✗	
Tractor Brewing Haymaker - Honey Wheat Ale						✗																		✗	✗	✗	
Tractor Brewing Sod Buster Pale Ale						✗																		✗	✗	✗	
Trailhead Brewing Company																											
Missouri Brown Dark Ale						✗																✗					
Old Courthouse Stout						✗																✗					
Riverboat Raspberry Fruit Beer						✗																✗					
Trailblazer Blonde Ale						✗																✗					
Trailhead Red Amber Ale						✗																✗					
Trailhead Spiced Pumpkin Ale						✗																✗					
Traverse Brewing Company																											
Traverse Brewing Batch 500 IPA	✗																										
Traverse Brewing Manitou Amber Ale	✗																										
Traverse Brewing Old Mission Lighthouse Ale	✗																										
Traverse Brewing Power Island Porter	✗																										
Traverse Brewing Sleeping Bear Brown Ale	✗																										
Traverse Brewing Stout	✗																										
Traverse Brewing Torch Lake Light Ale	✗																										
Traverse Brewing Voss Wend Wheat	✗																										
Tremont Brewery/Atlantic Coast Brewing Company																											
Tremont Brewing Old Scratch Barley Wine						✗																		✗		✗	
Tremont Brewing Tremont Ale						✗																		✗		✗	
Tremont Brewing Tremont IPA						✗																		✗		✗	
Tremont Brewing Tremont Summer						✗																		✗		✗	
Tremont Brewing Winter						✗																		✗		✗	

Locally available bottle and keg sizes may vary.

Brewery / Brand Name	Contact Brewery	Cans	7 oz	8 1/2 oz	10 oz	12 oz	16 oz	20 oz	22 oz	24 oz	1/2 liter	25 oz	32 oz	64 oz	1 liter	1 1/2 liter	375 ml	500 ml	750 ml	40 oz	2 liter	Growlers/Jugs	3 liter	1/6 Keg	1/4 Keg	1/2 Keg	Keg (Non-Specified Size)
Tröegs Brewing Company																											
Tröegs Brewing Dreamweaver Wheat						X																		X		X	
Tröegs Brewing Hopback Amber						X																		X		X	
Tröegs Brewing Mad Elf						X																		X		X	
Tröegs Brewing Nugget Nectar						X																		X		X	
Tröegs Brewing Oatmeal Stout						X																		X		X	
Tröegs Brewing Pale Ale						X																		X		X	
Tröegs Brewing Rugged Trail Ale						X																		X		X	
Tröegs Brewing Sunshine Pils						X																		X		X	
Tröegs Brewing Troegenater Double Bock						X																		X		X	
Trout River Brewing Company																											
Trout River Brewing Hoppin' Mad Trout						X																		X		X	
Trout River Brewing Rainbow Red Ale						X																		X		X	
Trout River Brewing Scottish Ale						X																		X		X	
Tuckerman Brewing																											
Tuckerman Brewing Headwall Alt						X																					
Tuckerman Brewing Pale Ale						X																					
Tuscan Brewing Company																											
Tuscan Paradise Pale Ale						X																					
Tuscan SunDown Brown Ale						X																					
Twisted Pine Brewing Company																											
Big Daddy Espresso Stout									X																		X
Billy's Chilies Beer									X																		X
Twisted Pine American Amber Ale						X																					X
Twisted Pine Blond Ale						X																					X
Twisted Pine Honey Brown Ale						X																					X
Twisted Pine Hoppy Boy						X																					X
Twisted Pine Raspberry Wheat Ale						X																					X
Twisted Pine Red Mountain Ale						X																					X
Twisted Pine Twisted Stout						X																					X
Two Brothers Brewing Company																											
Two Brothers Bare Tree Weiss Wine																			X								

How Supplied *Continued*

Locally available bottle and keg sizes may vary.

Brewery / Brand Name	Contact Brewery	Cans	7 oz	8 1/2 oz	10 oz	12 oz	16 oz	20 oz	22 oz	24 oz	1/2 liter	25 oz	32 oz	64 oz	1 liter	1 1/2 liter	375 ml	500 ml	750 ml	40 oz	2 liter	Growlers/Jugs	3 liter	1/6 Keg	1/4 Keg	1/2 Keg	Keg (Non-Specified Size)
Two Brothers Project Opus																	X										
Two Brothers Cane and Ebel									X																		
Two Brothers Dog Days Dortmunder Style Lager						X																		X		X	
Two Brothers Domaine Dupage French Country Ale						X																		X		X	
Two Brothers Ebel's Weiss Beer						X																		X		X	
Two Brothers Heavy Handed India Pale Ale						X																		X		X	
Two Brothers Hop Juice Double India Pale Ale									X																		
Two Brothers Monarch White						X																					
Two Brothers Northwind Imperial Stout									X															X		X	
Two Brothers Prairie Path Golden Ale						X																		X		X	
Two Brothers The Bitter End Pale Ale						X																		X		X	
Tyranena Brewing Company																											
Bitter Women IPA						X																					
Brewers Gone Wild! Bitter Women From Hell Extra IPA						X																					
Brewers Gone Wild! Hop Whore Imperial IPA						X																					
Brewers Gone Wild! Spank Me Baby Barley Wine						X																					
Brewers Gone Wild! Who's Your Daddy? Imperial Porter						X																					
Chief Black Hawk Porter						X																					
Fargo Brothers Hefeweizen	X																										
Fighting Finches Mai Bock	X																										
Gemuetlichkeit Oktoberfest	X																										
Headless Man Amber Alt						X																					
Rocky's Revenge						X																					
Shantytown Doppelbock	X																										
Stone Tepee Pale Ale						X																					
Three Beaches Honey Blonde	X																										
Uinta Brewing Company																											
Uinta Brewing Anglers Pale Ale						X																		X		X	
Uinta Brewing Anniversary Barley Wine						X																		X		X	
Uinta Brewing Bristlecone Brown Ale						X																		X		X	
Uinta Brewing Club Pils Pilsner						X																		X		X	
Uinta Brewing Cutthroat Pale Ale						X																		X		X	

Locally available bottle and keg sizes may vary.

Brewery Brand Name	Contact Brewery	Cans	7 oz	8 1/2 oz	10 oz	12 oz	16 oz	20 oz	22 oz	24 oz	1/2 liter	25 oz	32 oz	64 oz	1 liter	1 1/2 liter	375 ml	500 ml	750 ml	40 oz	2 liter	Growlers/Jugs	3 liter	1/6 Keg	1/4 Keg	1/2 Keg	Keg (Non-Specified Size)
Uinta Brewing Gelande Amber Lager						X																		X		X	
Uinta Brewing Golden Spike Hefeweizen						X																		X		X	
Uinta Brewing King's Peak Porter						X																		X		X	
Uinta Brewing Solstice Kölsch						X																		X		X	
Uinta Brewing Trader IPA						X																		X		X	
Upland Brewing Company																											
Upland Brewing Company Amber						X																					
Upland Brewing Company Bad Elmer's Porter						X																					
Upland Brewing Company Dragonfly India Pale Ale						X																					
Upland Brewing Company Maibock	X																										
Upland Brewing Company Pale Ale						X																					
Upland Brewing Company Valley Weizen						X																					
Upland Brewing Company Wheat Ale						X																					
Utah Brewers Cooperative/Wasatch																											
Chasing Tail Golden Ale						X																					
Squatters Captain Bastard's Oatmeal Stout						X																					
Squatters Full Suspension Pale Ale						X																					
Squatters Hefeweizen						X																					
Squatters India Pale Ale						X																					
Squatters Provo Girl Pilsner						X																					
Wasatch 1st Amendment Lager						X																					
Wasatch Apricot Hefe-Weizen						X																					
Wasatch Bobsled Brown Ale						X																					
Wasatch Evolution Amber Ale						X																					
Wasatch Polygamy Porter						X																					
Wasatch Pumpkin Ale						X																					
Wasatch Raspberry Wheat Beer						X																					
Wasatch Special Reserve Pale Ale						X																					
Victory Brewing Company																											
Victory Festbier						X																				X	
Victory Golden Monkey						X													X					X		X	
Victory 'Hop' Wallop						X																					X

Locally available bottle and keg sizes may vary.

Brewery / Brand Name	Contact Brewery	Cans	7 oz	8 1/2 oz	10 oz	12 oz	16 oz	20 oz	22 oz	24 oz	1/2 liter	25 oz	32 oz	64 oz	1 liter	1 1/2 liter	375 ml	500 ml	750 ml	40 oz	2 liter	Growlers/Jugs	3 liter	1/6 Keg	1/4 Keg	1/2 Keg	Keg (Non-Specified Size)
Victory HopDevil Ale						✗																		✗		✗	
Victory Lager						✗																		✗		✗	
Victory Moonglow Weizenbock						✗																		✗		✗	
Victory Old Horizontal Ale						✗																				✗	
Victory Prima Pils						✗				✗															✗		
Victory St. Boisterous						✗																					✗
Victory St. Victorious						✗																		✗		✗	
Victory Storm King						✗																					✗
Victory Sunrise Weissbier						✗																		✗		✗	
Victory Throwback Lager																											✗
Victory V Saison						✗													✗							✗	
Victory V Twelve						✗													✗								
Victory Victorious Doppelbock						✗																					✗
Victory Whirlwind Witbier						✗																		✗		✗	
Viking Brewing																											
Viking Brewing Whole Stein						✗																					
Viking Brewing Abby Normal						✗																					
Viking Brewing Berserk						✗																					
Viking Brewing Big Swede						✗																					
Viking Brewing Blonde						✗																					
Viking Brewing Copperhead						✗																					
Viking Brewing Dim Whit						✗																					
Viking Brewing Honey Pale Ale						✗																					
Viking Brewing HoneyMoon						✗																					
Viking Brewing Hot Chocolate						✗																					
Viking Brewing Invader						✗																					
Viking Brewing J.S. Bock						✗																					
Viking Brewing JuleOL						✗																					
Viking Brewing Lime Twist						✗																					
Viking Brewing MjOd						✗																					
Viking Brewing Morketid						✗																					
Viking Brewing Queen Victoria's Secret						✗																					

Locally available bottle and keg sizes may vary.

Brewery / Brand Name	Contact Brewery	Cans	7 oz	8 1/2 oz	10 oz	12 oz	16 oz	20 oz	22 oz	24 oz	1/2 liter	25 oz	32 oz	64 oz	1 liter	1 1/2 liter	375 ml	500 ml	750 ml	40 oz	2 liter	Growlers/Jugs	3 liter	1/6 Keg	1/4 Keg	1/2 Keg	Keg (Non-Specified Size)
Viking Brewing Rauch						X																					
Viking Brewing Sylvan Springs						X																					
Viking Brewing Vienna Woods						X																					
Viking Brewing Weathertop Wheat						X																					
Wachusett Brewing Company																											
Wachusett Black Shack Porter						X																					
Wachusett Blueberry						X																					
Wachusett Country Ale						X																					
Wachusett Green Monsta						X																					
Wachusett IPA						X																					
Wachusett Nut Brown Ale						X																					
Wachusett Octoberfest						X																					
Wachusett Quinn's Amber Ale						X																					
Wachusett Summer Breeze						X																					
Wachusett Winter Ale						X																					
Wagner Valley Brewing Company																											
Wagner Valley Brewing Caywood Oatmeal Stout						X																					X
Wagner Valley Brewing Dockside Amber Lager						X																					X
Wagner Valley Brewing Grace House Wheat						X																					X
Wagner Valley Brewing Indian Pale Ale						X																		X		X	X
Wagner Valley Brewing Mill Street Pilsner						X																					X
Wagner Valley Brewing Sled Dog Dopplebock						X													X					X		X	X
Wagner Valley Brewing Tripellbock Reserve																			X								X
Waimea Brewing Company																											
Waimea Brewing Captain Cook's Original IPA						X																					
Waimea Brewing Luau Lager						X																					
Waimea Brewing Na Pali Pale Ale						X																					
Waimea Brewing Pakala Porter						X																					
Waimea Brewing Wai'ale'ale Ale						X																					
Waimea Brewing Waimea Bay Pale Ale						X																					
Warbird Brewing Company																											
Warbird Brewing P47 Warbird Wheat		X																									

How Supplied *Continued*

Locally available bottle and keg sizes may vary.

Brewery / Brand Name	Contact Brewery	Cans	7 oz	8 1/2 oz	10 oz	12 oz	16 oz	20 oz	22 oz	24 oz	1/2 liter	25 oz	32 oz	64 oz	1 liter	1 1/2 liter	375 ml	500 ml	750 ml	40 oz	2 liter	Growlers/Jugs	3 liter	1/6 Keg	1/4 Keg	1/2 Keg	Keg (Non-Specified Size)
Warbird Brewing T-6 Red Ale		✗																									
Weyerbacher Brewing Company																											
Weyerbacher Brewing Autumn Fest						✗																		✗	✗		
Weyerbacher Brewing Black Hole						✗																		✗	✗		
Weyerbacher Brewing Blanche						✗																		✗	✗		
Weyerbacher Brewing Blithering Idiot						✗																		✗	✗		
Weyerbacher Brewing Decadence						✗			✗															✗	✗		
Weyerbacher Brewing Double Simcoe IPA						✗			✗															✗	✗		
Weyerbacher Brewing Eleven						✗																		✗	✗		
Weyerbacher Brewing ESB Ale						✗																		✗	✗		
Weyerbacher Brewing HefeWeizen						✗																		✗	✗		
Weyerbacher Brewing Heresy Imperial Stout						✗																		✗	✗		
Weyerbacher Brewing Hops Infusion India Pale Ale						✗																		✗	✗		
Weyerbacher Brewing Imperial Pumpkin Ale						✗			✗															✗	✗		
Weyerbacher Brewing Insanity						✗																		✗	✗		
Weyerbacher Brewing Merry Monk's Ale						✗																		✗	✗		
Weyerbacher Brewing Old Heathen						✗																		✗	✗		
Weyerbacher Brewing Prophecy						✗			✗															✗	✗		
Weyerbacher Brewing QUAD						✗																		✗	✗		
Weyerbacher Brewing Raspberry Imperial Stout						✗																		✗	✗		
Weyerbacher Brewing Scotch Ale						✗																		✗	✗		
Weyerbacher Brewing Winter Ale						✗																		✗	✗		
Whitstran Brewing Company																											
11th Hour Pale Ale	✗																										
Friar Lawrence Belgium-Style Ale	✗																										
Decadence Chocolate Chocolate Imperial Stout	✗																										
Friar's Penance Barley Wine	✗																										
Highlander Scottish Style Ale	✗																										
Horse Heaven Hefe Bavarian Style Hefeweizen	✗																										
O20 Heavy Water Stout	✗																										
Over-The-Edge Dry-Hopped Pale Ale	✗																										
Steamy Cream California Common Ale	✗																										

Locally available bottle and keg sizes may vary.

Brewery / Brand Name	Contact Brewery	Cans	7 oz	8 1/2 oz	10 oz	12 oz	16 oz	20 oz	22 oz	24 oz	1/2 liter	25 oz	32 oz	64 oz	1 liter	1 1/2 liter	375 ml	500 ml	750 ml	40 oz	2 liter	Growlers/ Jugs	3 liter	1/6 Keg	1/4 Keg	1/2 Keg	Keg (Non-Specified Size)
Widmer Brothers Brewing Company																											
Widmer Brothers Brewing Company Broken Halo IPA						✗																		✗	✗	✗	
Widmer Brothers Brewing Company Drop Top Amber Ale						✗																		✗	✗	✗	
Widmer Brothers Brewing Company OKTO						✗																		✗	✗	✗	
Widmer Brothers Brewing Company Snowplow Milk Stout						✗																		✗	✗	✗	
Widmer Brothers Brewing Company Summit Pale Ale						✗																		✗	✗	✗	
Widmer Brothers Brewing Company W '06 N.W. Red Ale						✗																		✗	✗	✗	
Widmer Brothers Brewing Company Widmer Hefeweizen						✗				✗														✗	✗	✗	
Wiedenmayer Brewing Company																											
Wiedenmayer Jersey Lager						✗																					
Wild Goose Brewery, LLC																											
Blue Ridge Amber Lager						✗																				✗	
Blue Ridge ESB Red Ale						✗																					
Blue Ridge Golden Ale						✗																					
Blue Ridge HopFest						✗																					
Blue Ridge Porter						✗																					
Blue Ridge Snowball's Chance						✗																					
Blue Ridge Steeple Stout						✗																					
Blue Ridge Subliminator Dopplebock						✗																					
Crooked River ESB						✗																					
Crooked River Irish Red Ale						✗																					
Crooked River Kolsch Ale						✗																					
Crooked River Pumpkin Harvest Ale						✗																					
Crooked River Robust Porter						✗																					
Crooked River Select Lager						✗																					
Crooked River Yuletide						✗																					
Hudepohl 14 – K						✗																					
Little Kings Cream Ale						✗																					
Wild Goose Amber						✗																		✗		✗	
Wild Goose India Pale Ale						✗																		✗		✗	
Wild Goose Nut Brown Ale						✗																		✗		✗	
Wild Goose Oatmeal Stout						✗																		✗		✗	

Locally available bottle and keg sizes may vary.

Brewery Brand Name	Contact Brewery	Cans	7 oz	8 1/2 oz	10 oz	12 oz	16 oz	20 oz	22 oz	24 oz	1/2 liter	25 oz	32 oz	64 oz	1 liter	1 1/2 liter	375 ml	500 ml	750 ml	40 oz	2 liter	Growlers/Jugs	3 liter	1/6 Keg	1/4 Keg	1/2 Keg	Keg (Non-Specified Size)
Wild Goose Porter						X																		X		X	
Wild Goose Pumpkin Patch						X																		X		X	
Wild Goose Snow Goose						X																		X		X	
Williamsburg AleWerks																											
Williamsburg AleWerks Brown Ale						X																					
Williamsburg AleWerks Chesapeake Pale Ale						X																					
Williamsburg AleWerks Colonial Wheat Ale						X																					
Williamsburg AleWerks Drake Tail India Pale Ale						X																					
Williamsburg AleWerks Washington's Porter						X																					
Williamsburg AleWerks Winter Barleywine						X																					
Woodstock Beer																											
Woodstock India Pale Ale	X																										
Woodstock Pilsner	X																										
Woodstock Inn Brewery																											
Woodstock Inn Brewery Pig's Ear Brown Ale						X																					
Woodstock Inn Brewery Red Rack Ale						X																					
Yards Brewing																											
Yards Brewing Extra Special Ale						X																		X		X	
Yards Brewing General Washington Tavern Porter						X																		X		X	
Yards Brewing India Pale Ale						X																		X		X	
Yards Brewing Love Stout						X																		X		X	
Yards Brewing Philadelphia Pale Ale						X				X														X		X	
Yards Brewing Poor Richard's Tavern Spruce						X																		X		X	
Yards Brewing Saison						X																		X		X	
Yards Brewing Thomas Jefferson Tavern Ale						X																		X		X	
Yazoo Brewing																											
Yazoo Brewing Amarillo Pale Ale						X																					
Yazoo Brewing Dos Perros						X																					
Yazoo Brewing Hefeweizen						X																					
Yazoo Brewing Onward Stout						X																					
Yazoo Brewing Sly Rye Porter						X																					
Yazoo Brewing Yazoo ESB						X																					

445

Locally available bottle and keg sizes may vary.

Brewery / Brand Name	Contact Brewery	Cans	7 oz	8 1/2 oz	10 oz	12 oz	16 oz	20 oz	22 oz	24 oz	1/2 liter	25 oz	32 oz	64 oz	1 liter	1 1/2 liter	375 ml	500 ml	750 ml	40 oz	2 liter	Growlers/Jugs	3 liter	1/6 Keg	1/4 Keg	1/2 Keg	Keg (Non-Specified Size)
Yellowstone Valley Brewing																											
Yellowstone Valley Black Widow Oatmeal Stout						✗																					
Yellowstone Valley Grizzly Wulff Wheat						✗																					
Yellowstone Valley Renegade Red ESB						✗																					
Yellowstone Valley Wild Fly Ale						✗																					
Zuma Brewing Company																											
Cancun						✗																					
Morena	✗																										

 VII BREWERY PORTFOLIOS

This section lists alphabetically the breweries participating in *The Essential Reference of Domestic Brewers and Their Bottled Brands (DBBB)*.

Each brewery portfolio lists the brewery's name, address, phone number, and if provided, company web site, additional contact and tour information, and detailed listings of the brewer's brands. Each brewery has provided the labels for the brands listed as well as a brewery written description of each.

Alaskan Brewing Company

5429 Shaune Drive
Juneau, AK 99801
907-780-5866
www.alaskanbeer.com

At the turn of the 20th century hardy gold miners enjoyed a particularly fine brew created by a brewery near Juneau, Alaska. Nearly 100 years later, Alaskan Brewing Co. started a small gold rush of its own with Alaskan Amber, which is based on that historic recipe.

Since opening in 1986, we have learned the hard way that brewing beer in the Last Frontier isn't easy. In the coastal community of Juneau, without road connections to the lower 48 states, everything arrives and leaves by water or air, and the weather always has the last word. But the same environment that makes production and distribution a challenge also gives us the ingredients and inspiration to make exceptional beer. The water for our Alaskan beers comes from glacier melt and over 90 inches of rainfall that Juneau receives each year.

From our very modest start, we have grown to become the most award-winning craft brewery in the history of the Great American Beer Festival and the nation's eighth-largest domestic craft brewery. Alaskan Brewing offers eight great tastes of Alaska: Alaskan Amber, Alaskan Pale, Alaskan ESB, Alaskan Stout, Alaskan IPA, Alaskan Smoked Porter, Alaskan Winter Ale and Alaskan Summer Ale. Our beers are available in Alaska, Arizona, California, Idaho, Montana, Nevada, Oregon, Washington and Wyoming.

Alaskan Amber

Our flagship brew is Alaskan Amber, which is based on a recipe from a turn-of-the-century brewery in the Juneau area. The name of this beer style comes from the German word "alt" meaning "old." This refers to the aging that alts undergo since they ferment more slowly and at colder temperatures than most ales. Slow fermentation helps condition the flavors in Alaskan Amber, contributing to its overall balance and smoothness. The result is a brew that is richly malty and long on the palate, with just enough hop backing to balance this beautiful amber-colored beer.

Alaskan Amber pairs well with a variety of foods. Serve with king or silver salmon, flavorful meats, hearty Italian dishes and pizza. This is the perfect beer for first-time craft beer drinkers as well as seasoned connoisseurs.

Available: Year Round,
6-pack, 12-pack, loose 24, draft (1/2 keg, 1/6 keg).

PORTFOLIO INDEX (Alphabetical)

Alpine Beer Company

2351 Alpine Blvd.
Alpine, CA 91901
415-863-8350
www.alpinebeerco.com

Alpine Beer Company is family owned and operated by Patrick and Valerie McIlhenney. Patrick is a full time Fire Captain and the Brewmaster. Valerie is the bookkeeper and greets customers who visit our 550 barrel a year microbrewery. Their son, Shawn, fills many rolls working in the brewery. The brewery has a small tasting room that's open from noon until 6 Tuesday through Saturday. There is a full range of ales on the lineup: Alpine Ale, McIlhenney's Irish Red, Mandarin Nectar,Captain Stout, Willy and Pure Hoppiness. Occasional specialties are brewed with some barrel aging and Belgian Styles in their repetioure. Demand often exceeds capacity and temporary outages occur. Some prestigious World Beer Cup and GABF medals have fallen their way. The future holds an expansion on the horizon. So, Drink Alpine Ale or Go To Bed!

Pure Hoppiness

A West Coast Double IPA. Several different techniques are used to give this big beer a mega-hoppy flavor and intense aroma. Multiple hop additions to the kettle and a large "hop back" give the bitterness and aroma a start. An unprecedented amount of dry hops with a big hop punch intensify the floral bouquet. 1.074 O.G. – 1.012 F.G. Classified IBU 8% ABV

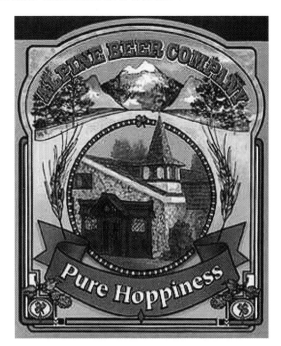

Available: Year Round
22 oz Bomber, Growler fills,
5 gallon kegs, 15.5 gallon kegs.

449

Anchor Brewing Company

1705 Mariposa Street
San Francisco, CA 94107-2334
415-863-8350
www.anchorbrewing.com

Anchor Brewing has played a significant role in San Francisco's rich history. Anchor's eight unique beers – including Anchor Steam® – are all produced in one of the most traditional and handsome breweries in the world. Each brew is virtually handmade from an all-malt mash in a handcrafted copper brewhouse, a veritable museum of the simple, traditional breweries of old.

The rich history of Anchor Brewing can be traced all the way back to the Gold Rush, when German brewer Gottlieb Brekle arrived in San Francisco with his wife Marie and infant son Frederick. Brekle applied for citizenship in 1854, and his brewing and business acumen would soon lead to his ownership of a little San Francisco brewery on Pacific, between Larkin and Hyde, which would one day become known as Anchor.

Anchor Brewery inherited a long tradition of brewing what had come to be known as steam beer, one of the quaint old nicknames for beer brewed along the West Coast under primitive conditions and without ice. Today "steam" is a trademark of Anchor Brewing.

Anchor Brewing remains one of the smallest and most traditional breweries in America. Though its beers – especially Anchor Steam Beer – are known throughout the world, they are all still handmade in its handsome copper brewhouse in San Francisco.

Steam

San Francisco's famous Anchor Steam®, the classic of American brewing tradition since 1896, is virtually handmade, with an exceptional respect for the ancient art of brewing. The deep amber color, thick creamy head, and rich flavor all testify to our traditional brewing methods. Anchor Steam is unique, for our brewing process has evolved over many decades and is like no other in the world.

The Anchor Brewing Company has been making beer in San Francisco since 1896. Uniquely San Franciscan, Anchor has played a significant, though small, role in California's majestic history.

4.9% ABV
Available: Year Round

450

Anderson Valley Brewing Company

17700 Highway 253
Boonville, CA 95415
707-895-2337
www.avbc.com

Located in Boonville, California, in scenic Mendocino County, Anderson Valley Brewing Company, is one of California's oldest craft breweries and home to the Legendary Boonville Beers. The quality and popularity of their products has allowed the brewery to expand from a small brewpub to an internationally recognized regional brewery. Each beer blend is hand-crafted using only the purest natural ingredients. Pristine water, rich in bicarbonates and chemical-free, is drawn from deep wells on the brewery grounds. Neither artificial preservatives nor flavor-destroying pasteurization processes are used when producing these exceptional brews. Now a destination brewery, visitors can sample award-winning world-class beer at the Visitor Center, sit under the oaks in the beer garden, arrange a game of disc golf on the 18-hole course, browse the gift store, tour the brewery, take a ride in the carriage drawn by Shire horses and frolic in pastures with pygmy goats. Along with producing extraordinary beer, Anderson Valley Brewing Company gives back to the community by hosting its annual Boonville Beer Festival with all proceeds donated to local nonprofit organizations. The festival is a favorite among participating breweries and the public. Interested in the environment, the solar-powered brewery has been a six-time recipient of California's Waste Reduction Awards Program (WRAP) for the methods of daily operation it implements that reduces waste and protects the environment. Check out an AVBC brew and their web site to see what Bahl Hornin' is really all about: www.avbc.com.

Boont Amber Ale

Our flagship ale is a medium-bodied pale ale with a beautiful copper color, a robust head and the perfect balance of malt sweetness and mild hop aroma. Described as "an essay in balance," Boont is the classic American-style Amber Ale. This very smooth and exceptionally drinkable beer is excellent with steaks, chicken, pasta or all by itself.

5.8% ABV
Available: Year Round
12 oz. bottles, 22 oz. bottles, 6-packs,
1/2 barrels, 1/6 barrels.

Hop Ottin' India Pale Ale

HopHeads take note – Hop Ottin' India Pale Ale is as Hoppy as they come. The name means "hard working hops" in Boontling, a lingo created by Anderson Valley residents in the late 1800s. Generous additions of high-alpha Pacific Northwest hops added during a vigorous boil, plus traditional dry hopping, give this ale a delicious citrus aroma and an intense hoppy bite. This is a hop lover's dream.

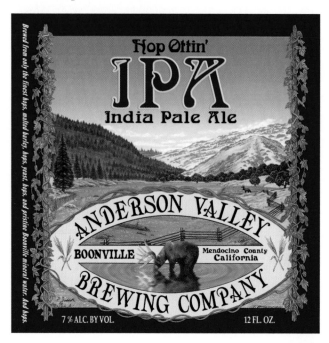

7.0% ABV
Available: Year Round,
12 oz. bottles, 22 oz. bottles, 6-packs,
1/2 barrels, 1/6 barrels.

Barney Flats Oatmeal Stout

Barney Flats Oatmeal Stout is a full-bodied creamy stout, lovingly handcrafted from the finest pale, caramel and chocolate malted barleys, blended with oats then balanced with generous additions of our special blend of hops. Deep, dark brown-black and velvety-smooth – an intesely rich and complex experience with a mocha character and gratifyingly bitter-sweet finish.

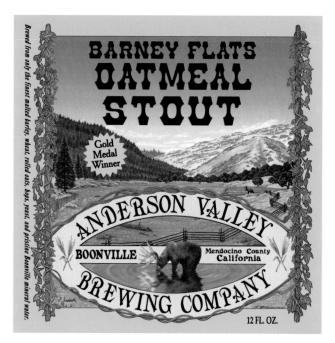

5.7% ABV
Available: Year Round
12 oz. bottles, 22 oz. bottles, 6-packs,
1/2 barrels, 1/6 barrels.

Boont Extra Special Beer

One of our most sought-after ales, this GABF gold medal winner is full-bodied with arousing aromatics and a bitter bite. This brew stands as a perfectly balanced ESB. WARNING: This beer is not for light beer drinkers or for those desiring no aftertaste.

6.8% ABV
Available: Year Round
12 oz. bottles, 22 oz. bottles, 6-packs,
1/2 barrels, 1/6 barrels.

Angel City Brewing

833 W. Torrance Blvd. STE #105
Torrance, CA 90502
310-329-8881
angelcitybrewing.com

Angel City Brewing is "The Best Little Craftbrewery in Southern California." Featuring the award-winning recipes of two-time "California Homebrewer of the Year," Michael Bowe, Angel City Brewing continues to brew handcrafted ales and lagers for an expanding market.

Located in Historic Alpine Village in Torrance, CA, and brewed in the oldest microbrewery in Southern California, Angel City brews and bottles nine different styles, including five lagers, many of which are decoction brewed and lagered up to eight weeks resulting in crisp, well balanced beers. Visit our website: angelcitybrewing.com

Angel City Ale

Angel City Ale is our flagship brew, an amber ale. Our brewmaster describes it as an American styled ESB. It is medium gravity with a malty middle, beautiful amber color and sparkling clear. Angel City Ale utilizes Northern Brewer and Yakima Golding hops in three kettle additions giving it subdued yet complex bittering and providing a thirst quenching dry finish.

Available: Year Round
12 oz 6-packs, 22 oz bottles
and in 5.3 & 13.2 gallon kegs.

PORTFOLIO INDEX (Alphabetical)

Anheuser-Busch, Inc.

One Busch Place
St. Louis, MO 63118
314-577-2000
www.anheuser-busch.com

When Eberhard Anheuser (1805-1880), a prosperous soap manufacturer, acquired a failing Bavarian Brewery in 1860 it ranked only 29th of 40 breweries in St. Louis. A short time later, Adolphus Busch (1839-1913), his son-in-law, joined him as a salesman and manager, becoming a full partner in 1869. Following Eberhard's death in 1880, Adolphus became company president.

Busch built the brewery into the industry leader through the application of modern technology and marketing. He was the first brewer in the United States to use pasteurization and bottled beer extensively. His successful use of artificial refrigeration, refrigerated rail cars and other technological innovations allowed him to produce a higher-quality beer more efficiently and market it throughout the country in an era when most brewers were strictly local.

August A. Busch Sr. (1865-1934) and Adolphus Busch III (1891-1946), the son and grandson, respectively, of Adolphus, led the brewery through the difficult times of World War I, Prohibition, the Great Depression and World War II. Within a year of repeal, August Sr. died and his eldest son, Adolphus Busch III, succeeded him. In 1946, August A. Busch Jr. (1899-1989) succeeded his brother as president of the company.

August A. Busch III became the fourth generation of his family to lead the company when he was named president in 1974 and CEO in 1975. In 2002, Patrick T. Stokes succeeded August A. Busch III as president and CEO of Anheuser-Busch Companies, and August A. Busch IV was named president of the domestic brewing company, Anheuser-Busch, Inc.

In 2006, August A. Busch IV was named president and CEO, Patrick T. Stokes became chairman of the board and August A. Busch III remains on the board of directors.

Today, Anheuser-Busch operates 12 breweries in the United States and several others overseas.

Redbridge

Redbridge is a rich, hearty, full-bodied lager with a well-balanced, moderately hopped taste. It also is the first nationally-available beer made with sorghum – a safe grain for those allergic to wheat or gluten. Sorghum is grown in the United States, Africa, Southern Europe, Central America and Southern Asia. Sorghum beers have been available internationally for years and are popular in many African countries. Other ingredients in Redbridge include water, yeast, imported Hallertau and domestic Cascade hops, and corn.

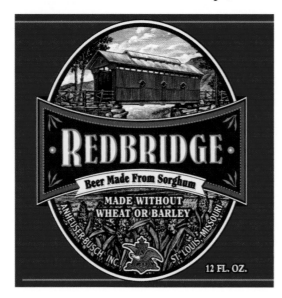

4.8% ABV
Available: Year Round
12 oz. 6-pack.

Stone Mill Pale Ale

Stone Mill Pale Ale is a classic pale ale with a fruity aroma and a perfect balance of maltiness and hop bouquet. It is brewed with Cascade and Hallertau hops and 100 percent organic Metcalf and Harrington barley malts, certified by the United States Department of Agriculture and the independent organic organization, Quality Assurance International (QAI). The barley malt is supplied by small, family-owned organic farms. Stone Mill Pale Ale is brewed by an organically certified brewery and its packaging is made from 100 percent recycled materials.

5.5% ABV
Available: Year Round
12 oz. 6-pack, draught (1/6 keg).

Wild Hop Lager

Wild Hop Lager has a signature body with Cascade hop aroma and hints of caramel sweetness. It is brewed with Cascade, Willamette and Saaz hops and 100 percent organic Metcalf and Harrington barley malts certified by the United States Department of Agriculture and the independent organic organization, Quality Assurance International (QAI). The barley malt is supplied by small, family-owned organic farms. Wild Hop Lager is brewed by an organically certified brewery and its packaging is made from 100 percent recycled materials.

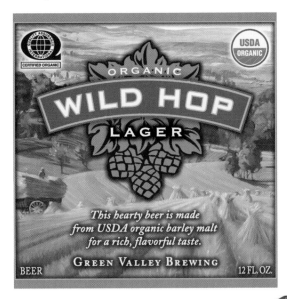

5% ABV
Available: Year Round
12 oz. 6-pack, draught (1/6 keg).

Jack's Pumpkin Spice Ale

Jack's Pumpkin Spice Ale is an all-malt seasonal brew with a deep copper color imparted from two-row, caramel and carapils barley malts. This beer is brewed with a blend of classically aromatic Saaz and imported Hallertau hops, Golden Delicious pumpkins and select seasonal spices, including nutmeg, ginger, cinnamon and clove.

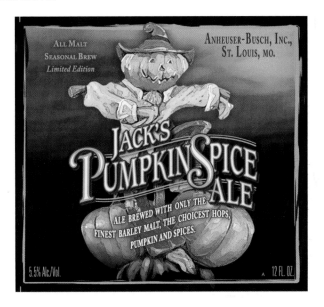

5.5% ABV
Available: Fall Seasonal
12 oz. 6- and 18-packs,
draught (1/2 keg, 1/6 keg).

Winter's Bourbon Cask Ale

Winter's Bourbon Cask Ale is an auburn-colored beer with a smooth, robust taste, full of rich aromas, hints of vanilla and flavorful hops. This beer is brewed with dark roasted carapils, caramel and two-row barley malts and imported Hallertau and Alsace hops, and is then aged on bourbon oak casks and whole Madagascar vanilla beans.

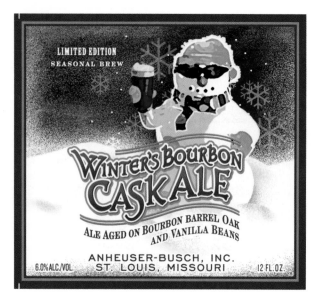

6% ABV
Available: Winter Seasonal
12 oz. 6-pack,
draught (1/2 keg, 1/6 keg).

Spring Heat Spiced Wheat

Spring Heat Spiced Wheat is a naturally cloudy, unfiltered Belgian-style wheat ale brewed with orange, lemon and lime peels and coriander; two-row barley and wheat malts; and classically aromatic Cascade and Willamette hops and imported Hallertau hops. Spring Heat Spiced Wheat won a gold medal at the 2006 North American Beer Awards in the Belgian Wit (White) category.

5.2% ABV
Available: Spring Seasonal
12 and 22 oz. bottles,
draught (1/2 keg, 1/6 keg).

Beach Bum Blonde Ale

Beach Bum Blonde Ale is an all-malt, American blonde ale with a golden color, pleasant hop aroma and slightly spicy and malty taste. Brewed with the finest pale and caramel roasted barley malts, Beach Bum Blonde Ale is dry-hopped with imported Alsace and Hallertau hops and Cascade hops from the Pacific Northwest. At the 2006 North American Beer Awards, Beach Bum Blonde Ale won a bronze medal in the blonde ale category.

5.4% ABV
Available: Summer Seasonal
12 oz. 6-pack,
draught (1/2 keg, 1/6 keg).

Michelob

Michelob is a malty and full-bodied lager with an elegant European hop profile. Full, distinctive and classic, Michelob is brewed with 100 percent malt and a blend of two-row and caramel malts and balanced with European noble aroma hop varieties from the Hallertau and Tettnang regions.

5% ABV
Available: Year Round
7 oz., 12 oz. and 24 oz. bottles,
12 oz. aluminum cans,
16 oz. aluminum bottles,
draught (1/2 keg, 1/4 keg, 1/6 keg).

459

Michelob AmberBock

Michelob AmberBock is rich, full-bodied and smooth with a deep, dark color and a roasted, malty taste that finishes clean. Brewed using 100 percent dark-roasted and caramel malts, and all imported hops, Michelob AmberBock complements grilled, barbecued and German-style foods.

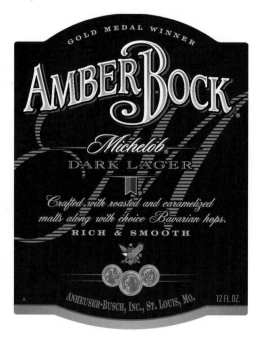

6% ABV
Available: Year Round
12 oz. bottle, 16 oz. aluminum can,
draught (1/2 keg, 1/4 keg, 1/6 keg).

Michelob Honey Lager

Michelob Honey Lager is a full-bodied, naturally sweet and uniquely soft beer with a balanced, floral character. Brewed using the finest two-row and caramel barley malts, a blend of aromatic European imported hops, and a touch of natural wildflower honey to enhance the naturally round, malty and slightly sweet flavor of the beer. Michelob Honey Lager complements soups and sandwiches.

4.9% ABV
Available: Year Round
12 oz. 6-pack.

Budweiser Brew Masters' Private Reserve

Budweiser Brew Masters' Private Reserve is a smooth, all-malt lager with a distinguishable honey color and rich, robust taste. Steeped with history, Brew Masters' Private Reserve is based on a time-honored Budweiser brewmaster holiday tradition of collecting the richest part of the brew as it is tapped to the brew kettles to toast the holiday season. This richer, more flavorful reserve – prized for its unusual smoothness despite its robust alcohol content – was always a favorite and something Anheuser-Busch brewers and friends looked forward to year-after-year. This beer can be enjoyed in a traditional pilsner-style or wide mouthed glass and paired with full-flavored meats such as a rib eye or grilled veal tenderloin.

8.5% ABV
Available: Winter Seasonal
32 oz. bottle and 45.6 oz.
magnum bottle with swing top closures.

Michelob Celebrate Chocolate

Michelob Celebrate Chocolate is brewed with caramel malts, roasted malts and matured on real cocoa beans. The beer has a deep, dark chocolate color and aroma, and is best enjoyed in a snifter, opening its bouquet and pushing the scents toward the nose. This beer complements a variety of desserts, including raspberry crème brulee.

Michelob Celebrate will also be available in chocolate cherry for 2007.

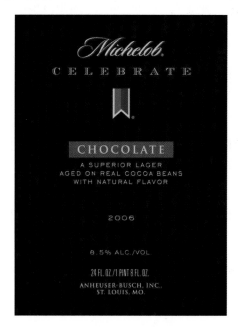

8.5% ABV
Available: Winter Seasonal
24 oz. bottle.

PORTFOLIO INDEX (Alphabetical)

Arcadia Brewing Company

103 West Michigan Avenue
Battle Creek, MI 49017
269-963-9690
www.arcadiabrewingcompany.com

Arcadia Brewing Company was established in 1996 as a micro-brewery specializing in handcrafted British-style ales. All of our beers are produced in small batches, and our 25 Barrel Peter Austin Brewery and methods originated in England, which allows this style of beer to reflect over 250 years of world class brewing heritage.

In addition to brewing on authentic British equipment, Arcadia uses only the finest malted barley from England, and when combined with the freshest hops from the Pacific Northwest of our United States, and our legendary Ringwood yeast, the result is some of the best and freshest handcrafted ales available, on any continent.

In fact, several of our beers have received international recognition with medals and awards. The Traditional Beer Festival in Edinburgh, Scotland honored Arcadia ESB as the first American, and one of the finest cask ales served in their 1997 festival. The World Beer Championships of 1998 awarded a Bronze Medal to our Angler's Ale, a Silver Medal to Arcadia Whitsun, and a Gold Medal and the highest score ever for an American made India Pale Ale to Arcadia IPA. Arcadia has received the distinction of "Best of the Great Lakes Brewery Award," (Tap into the Great Lakes, by John Bice – Thunder Bay Press, 1999). Arcadia Ales are distributed throughout Michigan, Illinois, Indiana, Ohio and Wisconsin.

Tours of the brewery and packaging hall are given on Saturday afternoons or by appointment.

India Pale Ale

The first in our Brew Crew Big Beer Series, Arcadia HopMouth Double IPA is a tasty fix for your hop jones. Huge Maris Otter Malt and a more than generous amount of fresh hops make this beer memorable.

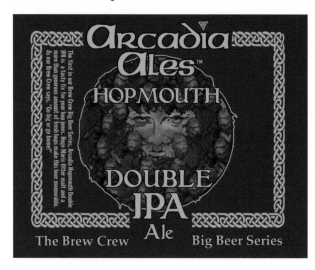

Available: Year Round
6-pack & draft 1/2 bbl. 1/6 bbl.

PORTFOLIO INDEX (Alphabetical)

Atlanta Brewing Company

2323 Defoor Hills Rd. NW
Atlanta, GA 30318
(404) 881-0300
www.atlantabrewing.com

Founded in 1993, the award-winning Atlanta Brewing Company (ABC), is the oldest operational brewery in the state of Georgia. Red Brick Ale was the first beer brewed by ABC and remains its flagship brand; it is available year round, as are Peachtree Pale Ale and Red Brick Blonde. In 2006, Numbers Ale and Reverend Mudbone Ale were developed to compliment the menus of Concentrics Hospitality Group and Jim N' Nick's BBQ, respectively. ABC currently offers a traditional, German-style Hefe Weizen in the summer months, and a Double-Chocolate, Oatmeal Porter in the winter with more seasonal brews slated to join the line-up in 2007.

Atlanta Brewing Company produced approximately four thousand barrels of beer in 2006 and will produce upwards of 8,000 in 2007. ABC is moving its entire facility in the spring of 2007. The new location will allow for the expansion of our capacity by approximately 4 times. We will have some new brewing equipment, including a custom manufactured, stainless steel, steam-generated brew kettle and three 100 barrel fermentors.

Atlanta Brewing Company hosts a tour and tasting every Wednesday, Friday and Sunday from 5pm to 7pm. We feature live, local music on Wednesdays and Fridays. Usually four to six beers, including seasonals, are offered on tap at the tasting. The brewery tour, which is led by our knowledgeable staff, is highly informative and educational. Our new tasting room is built for comfort, with a state of the art pouring system and plenty of seating.

Red Brick Ale

Red Brick Ale is a full-bodied brown ale with big malt flavors and subtle notes of chocolate and coffee. Made with seven roasted malts, Red Brick Ale pours a deep garnet color with a rich, creamy head. It's our highest gravity beer at just under 7% ABV and was a Gold Medal winner at the World Beer Cup in 1998.

Available: Year Round
6-pack, 1/2 keg, 1/6 keg.

PORTFOLIO INDEX (Alphabetical)

Avery Brewing Company

Arapahoe Avenue, Unit E
Boulder, CO 80303
303-440-4324
www.averybrewing.com

Established in 1993, Avery Brewing Co. is a family owned and operated micro-brewery dedicated to brewing the finest quality English and Belgian style ales.

From humble beginnings, brewing 800 barrels of three different beers in 1994, we have progressed to brewing over 10,000 barrels and nineteen different styles beers in 2007. We attribute this success to beer drinkers gravitating to beers with more interesting flavor profiles.

Avery is on the for-front of the "Big Beer" or "Extreme Beer" movement with style-stretching and huge flavor profile beers such as Hog heaven Barley Wine-style Ale, Maharaja Imperial IPA and Mephistopheles' Belgian Imperial Stout.

Avery beers are available, currently, in 26 states and select parts of Europe.

India Pale Ale

In the 1700's one crafty brewer discovered that a healthy dose of hops and an increased alcohol content preserved his ales during the long voyage to India (as depicted in our label) to quench the thirst of British troops. Today, we tip our hat to that historic innovation by brewing Colorado's hoppiest pale ale. Avery IPA demands to be poured into your favorite glass to truly appreciate the citrusy, floral bouquet and the rich, malty finish. Brewed by hopheads for hopheads! Avery IPA was awarded the Great American Beer Festival Gold Medal in 2004 in the Strong American Pale Catagory

Available: Year Round
6-pack & draft - 1/2 bbl. 1/6 bbl.

464

PORTFOLIO INDEX (Alphabetical)

Ballast Point Brewing Company

10051 Old Grove Road Suite B
San Diego, Ca 92131
858-695-2739
www.ballastpoint.com

IN THE BEGINNING:

The brewery was only a dream to the owners of Home Brew Mart when their home brew supply store opened in 1992. Finally, in 1996 the brewery was installed by New World Brewing Systems in the space behind the retail store, and production began in September. In 2003 we opened our second San Diego brewery. Our goal of brewing world class beer fresh in San Diego is reflected in the numerous Gold Medals our beers have won, including the Great American Beer Festival and the World Beer Cup.

BALLAST POINT?

The name for the brewery comes from the point where Spanish explorers first set foot in California. Located on the Point Loma peninsula, Ballast Point is considered the gateway to San Diego harbor and the Plymouth Rock of the West Coast. Stones from this area were used as ballast in the cargo holds of sailing ships returning to the eastern seaboard. Many New England streets are still lined with the ballast brought back from San Diego.

Come to our brewery and we will gladly give you a tour and allow you to sample our newest selection of beers.

Ballast Point
Yellowtail Pale Ale

Yellowtail Pale Ale is styled after the crisp golden Kölsch ales of Cologne, Germany.

Traditional German hops and malts, combined with a long cold aging process, create a uniquely refreshing and full flavored ale.

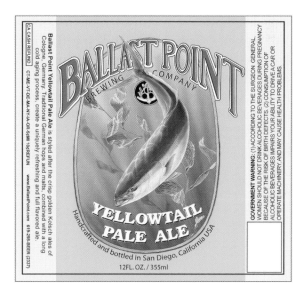

Available: Year Round,
6-pack, loose 24, 1/2 barrel keg.

PORTFOLIO INDEX (Alphabetical)

Bard's Tale Beer Company

211 NW Ward Road
Lee's Summit, MO 64063
203-831-8899
www.bardsbeer.com

The Bard's Tale Beer Company, LLC was founded in order to develop a line of craft brewed commercial beers using gluten free brewing grains. We have spent considerable resources in finding the optimum brewing techniques and specific ingredients in order to brew the highest quality beers. We pride ourselves on our innovative nature, our dedication to quality and the importance of building upon the rich history of the brewing industry. At Bard's Tale Beer we are extremely confident that you will find our products competitive with the best microbrews and imports in respect to taste, aroma, texture and enjoyment.

Dragon's Gold

Dragon's Gold brewed with 100% sorghum malt and naturally gluten free. This beer is for the American Lager drinker that is looking for more taste than the traditional mass produced beers. We do not short cut the traditions of craft brewing by using syrups, raw grains, industrial enzymes, rice or honey to produce beer. The process is all natural and the result is a beer that is rich and satisfying.

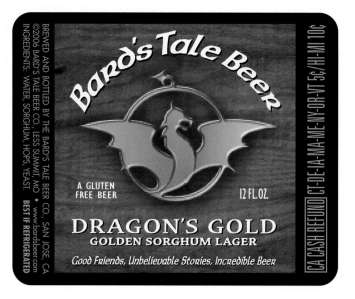

Available: Year Round,
6-pack

PORTFOLIO INDEX (Alphabetical)

Berkshire Brewing Company

P.O. Box 251 12 Railroad Street
South Deerfield, MA 01373
413-665-6600
www.berkshirebrewingcompany.com

Berkshire Brewing Company Inc., is a Micro brewery located in South Deerfield, MA., established in 1994 by Christopher T. Lalli and Gary A. Bogoff. Our goal is to produce clean, fresh, well-balanced ales & lagers in small batches (620 gallons). At the present time we are capable of producing 420 barrels (13020 gallons) of fresh beer each week. All of our beer is unfiltered, unpasteurized and contains no chemical additives or preservatives. As craft brewers, we are now producing fifteen styles of beer, nine year round and a number of seasonals. We self distribute our products in all of Massachusetts and Connecticut. We also have distributors in Vermont and Rhode Island. If you have any questions about the Berkshire Brewing Co., Inc. or its fine selection of Ales please call 413-665-6600. Brewery Tours are every Saturday at 1:00 p.m. CHEERS, THINGS ARE LOOKING UP!!!!

Steel Rail Extra Pale Ale

Steel Rail Extra Pale Ale is a light colored, medium bodied, full flavored American style Ale. Steel Rail E.P.A. is our flagship product that has a full malt flavor and is balanced with a pronounced hop flavor and bitterness. 5.3% v/v.

Available: Year Round,
6-pack, loose 24, 1/2 barrel keg

Big Sky Brewing Company

5417 Trumpeter Way
Missoula, MT 59808-7170
406-549-2777
www.bigskybrew.com

Where To Find Our Beers

Big Sky Brewing Company is currently selling its tasty brews across the entire Northwest and Northern Plains of the USA. We have begun tittilating tastebuds in the Midwest as well. Our beers are distributed in Alaska, Washington, Oregon, Idaho, Montana, Wyoming, North Dakota, South Dakota, Minnesota, and parts of Wisconsin. Big Sky Brewing's fine ales are on tap in over 1500 restaurants and taverns throughout the region. If you are having a tough time finding our beers in any of these states just e-mail us and we will give you a helping hand!

Crystal Ale

Crystal Ale has a delicate hop aroma and flavor resulting from combinations of Hallertau, Liberty and Crystal hops.

Balanced by malty undertones, Big Sky's Crystal Ale is a perfect year 'round choice. Seasons change, your taste for Crystal Ale will not.

BIG SKY BREWING CO.
MISSOULA, MONTANA

3.8% alcohol by weight
4.7% ABV
Available: Year Round

PORTFOLIO INDEX (Alphabetical)

The Black Mountain/Chili Beer Brewing Company

6245 E. Cave Creek Road
Cave Creek, AZ 85331-9046
602-488-4742
www.chilibeer.com

Black Mountain Brewing Company was established in 1989 next to the Satisfied Frog Restaurant, in Cave Creek, Az. Black Mountain started with a small Micro Brewery and now has expanded to contract brew their Cave Creek Chili Beer at several larger brewerys in the USA and Mexico.

Black Mountain currently ships Cave Creek Chili Beer to 20 states in the USA, the UK, Australia, New Zealand, Japan and Viet Nam.

Cave Creek Chili Beer

Cave Creek Chili beer is the only beer in the world with a chili pepper inserted, by hand, in every bottle. This beer was invented by Ed Chilleen the owner of Black Mountain Brewing Company, in 1991.

Available: Year Round,
6-pack.

469

BluCreek Brewing

2310 Daniels Street, Suite 148
Madison, WI 53718
608-204-0868
www.blucreek.com

BluCreek Brewing was founded with a simple guiding principal – to provide our customers with high quality microbrewed beers that they will truly appreciate and enjoy. We listen to consumers and always ask: what kind of American microbrewed beer would they like to drink now?

BluCreek Brewing specializes in producing unique, hand-crafted beers that stand out from the other beers crowding today's shelves. We challenge ourselves to excite, intrigue and satisfy our customers discerning tastes with innovative new-age styles and creative ale flavors.

The result has been a consistently growing appreciation and demand for our unique hand-crafted ales. BluCreek beers have created a reputation with our loyal customers who truly enjoy the quality and highly drinkable nature of the beers we produce.

We hope you enjoy our beers as much as we do!!

BluCreek Zen IPA

India Pale Ale brewed with Natural Green Tea! An intense infusion of fresh Chinook, Cascade, and Centennial hops combined with natural green tea imparts this traditional English-style Pale Ale (English IPA) with something a little beyond the ordinary … A little extraordinary! A beer that transcends beyond anything you have ever experienced before, the smooth and subtle green tea aroma and taste perfectly compliment the refreshing crispness of an English IPA. The result will satisfy those who are looking for something more mystical … magical … wonderful. Created for the IPA lover interested in more than just substantial hops character.

Available: Year Round,
6-pack, draft 1/2 keg (special order).

PORTFOLIO INDEX (Alphabetical)

Blue Point Brewing Company

161 River Avenue
Patchogue, NY 11772
631-475-6944
www.bluepointbrewing.com

Blue Point Brewing Company is long island's only microbrewery. It was founded in 1998 by two long-time friends Mark Burford and Peter Cotter.

The brewery was inspired by their life-long dream and built from a rare assemblage of equipment collected from Breweries from around the United States. Storage tanks, fermentation vessels and other brewing equipment were gathered from breweries like Frederick, LaJolla, Red Hook, Pilgrim and others.

The brewery's unique direct-fire, brick brew kettle, dismantled brick by brick from a brewery in Maryland and rebuilt in Patchogue, imparts a lightly toasted, complex taste to produce a line of ultra premium microbrews.

Located in the 1970's Penguin ice factory on River Avenue in Patchogue, Blue Point Brewing Company's 5000 square foot facility gives them ample space for brewing over 10,000 kegs of beer a year. Kegs from the brewery are unpasteurized and delivered cold to ensure they are as fresh tasting as possible.

Tours and tastings:
Thursday and Friday 3pm - 7pm and on Saturday 12 noon - 7pm.

Blue Point Toasted Lager

Blue Point Brewing's award-winning Toasted Lager is our flagship product. It won the gold medal at the 2006 World Beer Cup and the silver medal at the 2006 Great American Beer Festival. Copper in color this brew is made from six different malts including: English Pale, Crystal, Munich, Carapils, Wheat and Belgian Caravienna. Toasted Lager displays a balanced flavor of malt and hop which makes for easy drinking. Special lager yeast is used to produce that long lasting, smooth finish. The "toasted" part of the name refers to our direct-fire brew kettle's hot flames that impart a toasted flavor to our most popular microbrew.

Available: Year Round,
6-pack, 12-pack, 24-pack, 1/2 keg,
1/6 keg, and Growlers.

471

Bluegrass Brewing Company

636 East Main Street
Louisville, Kentucky 40202
502-584-BREW (2739
www.bluegrassbrew.com

The Bluegrass Brewing Co. was established in 1993 and is proud to be Kentucky's largest brewery. The city of Louisville has a rich and complex brewing history that reaches back over 100 years. This heritage has provided the BBC with a strong foundation on which to build and offers a challenge that we enthusiastically embrace everyday. To truly enjoy life you have to love what you do and we love brewing.

Brewmaster David Pierce has been producing award-winning, handcrafted BBC beer for fourteen years. His bold style and uncompromising commitment to quality allows us to work with an extensive palette of malts and hops to produce the finest beer available. Every beer we brew at Bluegrass Brewing Company are carefully crafted with diligence and discipline to ensure consistency and distinction in every batch. Our sole focus is making great beer. We hope that you will appreciate the artistic flair and creative style that has inspired every BBC beer that you drink.

The BBC brewery is located on the corner of Clay and Main Streets in Downtown Louisville, Kentucky. The Taproom is open Tuesday through Friday from 4:00 p.m. until 10:00 p.m. and includes a Kentucky Brewing History Museum with local beer memorabilia dating back to the 1800's. Tours are available during Taproom hours or by appointment.

BBC American Pale Ale

Bluegrass Brewing Co. Brewmaster David Pierce spent two years perfecting this American Pale Ale to satisfy his own selfish appetite for beer. The resulting BBC American Pale Ale is a rich, copper colored ale with fresh, citrus-like hop aromas and a full-bodied hoppy flavor supported by generous amounts of malted barley. We use only the highest-quality Centennial and Willamette hops and hand-selected Special Pale, Caramunich, Flaked Barley, and Special B barley malted to our specifications. Our award-winning BBC American Pale Ale has won the hearts of beer lovers and tasting judges far and wide. It quickly became our flagship beer and set the benchmark for quality and commitment in everything we brew. We hope you enjoy it as much as we do.

5.5% ABV, 55 IBU
Available: Year Round,
6-pack (12 oz. bottle),
4/6-pack 24 case (12 oz. bottle),
draft (15.5 gallon keg, 5 gallon keg).

PORTFOLIO INDEX (Alphabetical)

The Boston Beer Company

30 Germania Street
Boston, MA 02130
617-368-5000
www.samueladams.com

The Boston Beer Company is America's leading brewer of hand-crafted, full-flavored beer. Founder and Brewer, Jim Koch, brews Samuel Adams® using the time honored, traditional four-vessel brewing process and the world's finest all-natural ingredients. Beer lovers can enjoy 18 styles of Samuel Adams® beers that range from light-bodied to bold, traditional to extreme. The brewery has won more awards in international beer-tasting competitions in the last 20 years than any other brewery in the world. Samuel Adams Boston Lager®, the Company's flagship brand, is brewed using the same recipe and processes that Jim Koch's great great grandfather used in the mid 1800s. The result is a beer renowned by drinkers for its full flavor, balance, complexity and consistent quality. For more information, visit www.samueladams.com.

Samuel Adams Boston Lager®

Complex and balanced with a beautiful hop aroma.

Award winning Samuel Adams® beers have led a return to flavorful American beer. Using only the four classic ingredients and traditional brewing methods, Samuel Adams Boston Lager® is carefully crafted for a symphonic complexity and a rich balance. This unique beer is internationally recognized as "The Best Beer in America."

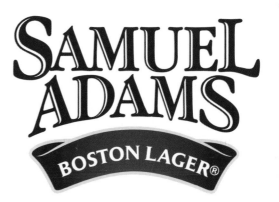

Available: Year-round
Packages: 6-pack, 12-pack, loose 24,
draft (1/2 keg, 1/4 keg, 1/6 keg).

Sam Adams Light®

In January 2005, Sam Adams Light® became the first American light beer to ever win a medal at a German beer tasting competition.

There was no light beer category.

Sam Adams Light® is not just a lighter version of our Samuel Adams Boston Lager® but rather the culmination of over two years of experimentation and brewing trials. It proved to be worth the wait. Brewed using only the finest two-row malt and Bavarian Noble hops it has a smooth, complex roasted malt character that is superbly balanced with the subtle citrus fruit notes of the Noble hops. Sam Adams Light® finishes crisp and smooth without any lingering bitterness, leaving you yearning for more.

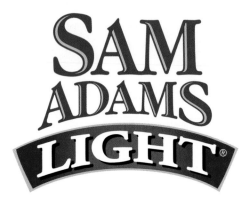

Available: Year-round
Packages: 6-pack, 12-pack, loose 24.

Samuel Adams® OctoberFest

Hearty and smooth, brewed with select Moravian malt.

We brew Samuel Adams® OctoberFest to celebrate the arrival of autumn. This hearty lager is rich with a blend of four malts, carefully balanced with hand-selected Noble Bavarian hops. The rich, deep golden amber hue of Samuel Adams® OctoberFest is reflective of the season.

Available: Late August through October
Packages: 6-pack, 12-pack, loose 24,
draft (1/2 keg, 1/4 keg, 1/6 keg).

Samuel Adams® Summer Ale

Bright and citrusy, brewed with mysterious Grains of Paradise.

Samuel Adams® Summer Ale – Refreshing, crisp, and tangy, Summer Ale is brewed with wheat malt, lemon zest and Grains of Paradise, a long-forgotten and mysterious brewing spice used by medieval brewers centuries ago. This mix of spices creates a crisp and spicy flavor and body. Enjoy this beer's clean finish, perfect for warm summer days.

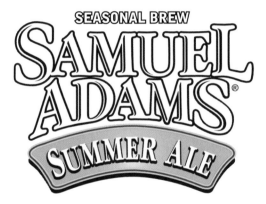

Available: April through August
Packages: 6-pack, 12-pack, loose 24,
draft (1/2 keg, 1/4 keg, 1/6 keg).

Samuel Adams® White Ale

Spicy yet smooth. Brewed with 10 exotic spices.

This unfiltered wheat ale is a fresh American version of a classic Belgian white ale. An intricate blend of 10 different spices creates its distinctive and refreshing taste. White Ale is unfiltered, resulting in a beautiful cloudy haze from the malt proteins, with a fine sediment at the bottom of the bottle.

Available: Late January through March
Packages: 6-pack, 12-pack, loose 24,
draft (1/2 keg, 1/4 keg, 1/6 keg).

Samuel Adams® Winter Lager

Bold and rich, with a touch of holiday spice.

For centuries, brewers have crafted special beers to celebrate winter. In this tradition, we brew Samuel Adams Winter Lager to share with friends. Brewed with winter spices such as orange zest, cinnamon, and fresh ginger to add a note of spicy complexity, this rich and hearty dark brew is one of the finer pleasures of a winter evening.

Available: November through January
Packages: 6-pack, 12-pack, loose 24, draft (1/2 keg, 1/4 keg, 1/6 keg).

Portfolio Index (Alphabetical)

Boulder Beer Company

2880 Wilderness Place
Boulder, CO 80301-2258
303-444-8448
www.boulderbeer.com

In 1979 two CU professors applied for and received the 43rd brewing license issued in the United States, creating Boulder Beer Company, Colorado's 1st Microbrewery. The original site of the brewery was a small farm northeast of Boulder, the brewhouse sharing space with a few goats. Early on, the brewery won industry and consumer accolades for its line of Boulder Beers: Boulder Porter, Stout and Extra Pale Ale. Five years later, the brewery moved to its current site in Boulder and has since expanded from an original one-barrel brewing system to a 50-barrel brew house with top-of-the-line packaging equipment. The facility has a capacity to produce 43,000 barrels of award-winning beer annually.

Since 1990, Brewmaster David Zuckerman has overseen brewing and production of all brands, some of which include Hazed & Infused Dry-Hopped Ale, MoJo India Pale Ale and Singletrack Copper Ale. Since 1992 Boulder Beer Company has received more than 40 awards and citations for excellence in brewing, packaging and business.

By the spring of 2003, the complete family of Boulder Beers had been reintroduced and repackaged, followed by the successful launch of Hazed & Infused Dry-Hopped Ale. "Hazed" has since spawned a new line of innovative specialty brews called the Looking Glass Series, which also includes MoJo IPA, MoJo Risin' Double IPA, Sweaty Betty Blonde wheat beer, Never Summer Ale, Cold Hop British-Style Ale and Killer Penguin Barleywine.

Hazed & Infused Dry-Hopped Ale

Hazed & Infused is "hazed" in its natural unfiltered state, and "infused" with a massive dry-hop addition during fermentation. This secondary hop infusion creates big hop flavor and aroma without added bitterness. Hazed is truly a unique, unforgettably different beer.

Available: Year-round,
6-pack, 12-pack, 22 oz. bottles,
1/2 bbl, 1/6 bbl.

PORTFOLIO INDEX (Alphabetical)

Boulevard Brewing Company

2501 Southwest Boulevard
Kansas City, MO 64108
816-474-7095
www.boulevard.com

Established in 1989, Boulevard Brewing Company has grown to become the largest specialty brewer in the Midwest. Our mission is simple: to produce fresh, flavorful beers using the finest traditional ingredients and the best of both old and new brewing techniques. We offer five beers year-round: Pale Ale, Unfiltered Wheat Beer, Lunar Ale, Bully! Porter, and Dry Stout. Watch for our seasonal beers: Irish Ale in the spring, ZÔN in summer, Bob's '47 in the fall, and our winter holiday treat, Nutcracker Ale. Throughout our territory, Boulevard beers have become favorites, known for their full flavor, distinctive character, and unsurpassed quality.

The Boulevard story begins in 1988, when founder John McDonald started construction of the brewery in a turn-of-the-century brick building on Kansas City's historic Southwest Boulevard. A vintage Bavarian brewhouse was installed, and the first batches of beer were produced in the fall of 1989. That November, the first keg of Boulevard Pale Ale was delivered — in the back of John's pickup truck — to a restaurant just a few blocks away.

The popularity of our beers has since spread to eleven Midwestern states, necessitating a brewery expansion project completed in the Fall of 2006. The new 70,000 square foot facility includes a state-of-the-art, 150-barrel brewhouse, business offices, and a unique hospitality suite open to guests and visitors.

For information on brewery tours and other topics, visit us online at www.boulevard.com.

Boulevard Lunar Ale

Everything about Boulevard Lunar Ale is distinctive, from its cloudy, rich mahogany color and spicy aroma to its rounded, mellow flavor and crisp dry finish. Stylistically, Lunar Ale is neither a brown ale nor a dunkel weiss, but a little of both – offering its own unique harmony of malt, hops and yeast. Lunar Ale is Boulevard's first new year-round beer in more than a decade.

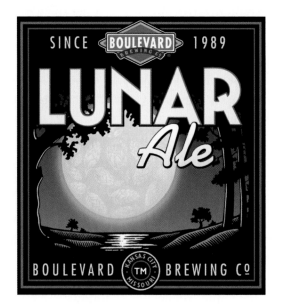

Available: Year-round,
6-pack, 1/2-bbl keg, 1/6-bbl keg.

Boulevard Pale Ale

Boulevard Pale Ale is a smooth, fruity, well-balanced beer with year-round appeal. A variety of caramel malts imparts a rich flavor and amber color, while liberal use of whole hops adds zest and aroma. Pale Ale is the first beer we brewed, and continues to be a perennial favorite.

Available: Year-round,
6-pack, 12-pack, 20-packs,
1/2-bbl keg, 1/6-bbl keg.

Boulevard Unfiltered Wheat Beer

Boulevard Unfiltered Wheat Beer is a lively, refreshing ale with a natural citrusy flavor and distinctive cloudy appearance. This easy-drinking American-style wheat beer has become our most popular offering, and the best-selling craft beer in the Midwest.

Available: Year-round,
6-pack, 12-pack, 20-packs,
1/2-bbl keg, 1/6-bbl keg.

Brewery Ommegang

656County Highway 33
Cooperstown, NY 13326
607-544-1800
www.ommegang.com

Nestled into the rolling hills near Cooperstown, New York, Brewery Ommegang is the premier brewery in North America, dedicated to producing all bottle-conditioned Belgian-style ales. Founded in 1997, Ommegang is now run under the auspices of Duvel Moortgat, of Puurs Belgium, the leader in Belgian specialty beers. Now in its ninth year, and boasting a portfolio of five Belgian-style ales and distribution in over 30 states, Brewery Ommegang, along with Duvel, is dedicated to bringing the passion and expertise of Belgian brewing to a thirsty and appreciative North American audience.

Ommegang beers are brewed using our own water, the best of Belgian and American ingredients, proprietary yeast strains, and are bottle-conditioned and warm-cellared on the premises. The beers are packaged in 12 ounce bottles, 750 mL cork-finished bottles, 3 Liter Jeroboams, and in a range of keg sizes. Ommegang also brews batches of limited edition beers for special events and occasions.

The brewery itself is built in the traditional Belgian farm-house style, on a 136 acre former hop farm in the Susquehanna River valley. The brewery offers free tours and tastings 7 days a week, sponsors six annual festivals between May and December, and presents a series of beer and food tasting events from mid-January to mid-April. The best-known event at the brewery is the annual "Belgium Comes to Cooperstown" Belgian beer festival. Over 150 authentic Belgian imports and Belgian-style beers, from Belgium and all across North America, are sampled at the mid-July festival.

Three Philosophers
Quadrupel Ale

Three Philosophers is a dark Belgian-style quadrupel ale, blended with authentic Kriek, a cherry-lambic from Belgium. It has complex flavors of chocolate, dark cherries, caramel malt, and toffee. Serve at a cool temperature. Pair with roasted meats, rich cheeses, and desserts. Excellent to cellar. Belgian Pils, Amber, and Caramel malts, Styrian Golding and Czech Saaz hops.

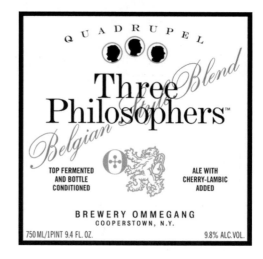

9.8% ABV
Available: Year Round,
12 oz 4-pack; 25.4 oz cork-finished bottle;
3 Liter Jeroboam, draft (1/6 bbl, 1/2 bbl).

PORTFOLIO INDEX (Alphabetical)

Butternuts Beer & Ale

4021 State Hwy 51
Garrattsville, NY 13342
(607) 263-5070
www.butternutsbeerandale.com

Butternuts Beer & Ale is located on a retired dairy farm in Otsego County, New York. The farm property is maintained by local farmers, bailing hay and grazing cattle. The brewery will begin growing its own hops and some grains for use in our farmhouse beers. Butternuts Beer & Ale belives in producing fresh, minimaly processed beer. As a farmhouse Micro-Brewery we produce and package our beer on-premis, choosing to can our products rather than bottle. We currently produce four brands, one is a weissbier using traditional Weinstephaner yeast and the other three are English inspired American ales. For more information please visit www.butternutsbeerandale.com

PORKSLAP Pale Ale

PORKSLAP Pale Ale is an american session beer. With an alcohol content of 4.1% abv it is designed to have a malty flavor and still be refreshing. Proper balance of malt and hops make PORKSLAP a crisp, clean ale, leaving your pallet ready for another sip.

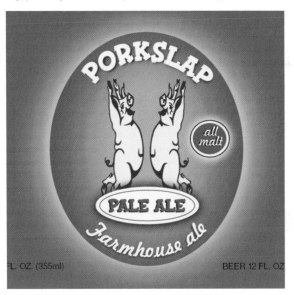

Available: Year Round,
6-packs, draft, Cask.

Caldera Brewing Company

540 Clover Lane
Ashland, Oregon 97520
541-482-4677
www.calderabrewing.com

Caldera Brewing Company is an award winng microbrewery dedicated to brewing uncompromised quality craft ales and lagers. Located in beautiful Ashland, Oregon, Caldera Brewing was founded by Proprietor/Head Brewer, Jim Mills in 1997. Caldera uses only the finest ingredients available, including premium domestic as well as imported malted barley, fresh whole flower hops, and soft mountain water. Caldera is the first craft brewery in Oregon to brew and can its own beer.

Caldera Pale Ale

Caldera Pale Ale is a fresh microbrew in a can. The bold flavors of Caldera Pale Ale come from using premium malted barley, whole flower Cascade hops, and soft mountain water. Deep golden in color, this ale has an explosion of whole flower Cascade hops which coats the tongue and then finishes crisp and clean.

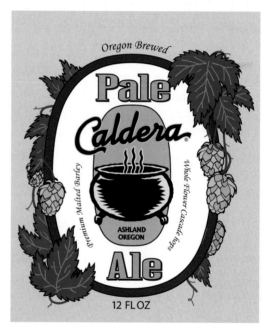

Available: Year Round,
6-pack 12 oz. can.

Capital Brewery Company, Inc.

7734 Terrace Ave.
Middleton, WI 53562
608-836-7100
www.capital-brewery.com

Capital Brewery, brewers of traditional world class beer, is located in Middleton, WI. Open to the public Wednesdays, Thursdays, and Fridays from 4-9pm, Saturdays from 1-5 in the winter and 1-9 in the summer, the Brewery is a great place to enjoy an afternoon. In the summer, enjoy live music and other entertainment, including one of the only outdoor, surround sound theaters in the country, in the Bier Garten. During the winter months, warm up in our cozy Bier Stube. Space is available for private parties. Please contact the Brewery for more information.

Tours are offered on Fridays at 3:30pm and Saturdays at 1:30 & 3:30. Private group tours are available, please contact the Brewery for more information.

Capital Brewery produces 8 annuals, 4 seasonals, and up to 4 limited release brews through out the year. Kirby Nelson, the Brewmaster, has gained world wide recognition for his award-winning brews.

Island Wheat Ale

An American Style Wheat Ale produced using wheat grown on Wisconsin's Washington Island off the tip of Door County. A refreshingly different brew that brings a special part of Wisconsin to any event.

Available: Year Round,
6-pack nr's, 12-pack nr's,
12-pack cans, 4/6pk case,
draught (1/2 keg, 1/4 keg).

483

Carolina Beer & Beverage, LLC

110 Barley Park Lane
Mooresville, NC 28115
704-799-BEER
www.carolinablonde.com

Carolina Beer & Beverage, LLC was founded in 1997 by CEO J. Michael Smith and President John Stritch. The company is the creator and maker of nearly a dozen, high-quality, craft beers sold under the Carolina Blonde and Cottonwood Ales brands.

The company produces about 12,000 barrels annually including the company's flagship brand, Carolina Blonde made from 100% barley. The company's other beers include a lighter version of its signature Blonde called Carolina Lighthouse and introduced its Strawberry Ale in 2006. In addition, under the Cottonwood Ale label, varieties include the Endo IPA, Low Country Pale, Low Down Brown, and award-winning seasonal beers including Pumpkin Ale, Irish Red, Great American Wheat, Scottish Ale and Frostbite.

Carolina Beer Company's goal is to establish itself as the premiere regional brewery of the Southeast and to produce high-quality beers with world-class taste. The company's brews are distributed in North Carolina and in parts of South Carolina, southern Virginia, Georgia and Tennessee.

The company's brewhouse and state-of-the-art packaging facility are located in Mooresville, NC, approximately 20 miles north of Charlotte. Tours and tastings are available every Saturday from noon-2pm. Please visit www.CarolinaBlonde.com for more information.

Carolina Blonde

Carolina Blonde is a lighter ale brewed with select pale malts and perfected with a blend of special hops. Made with 100% barley, this beer is exceptionally smooth, crisp and very drinkable with a rich gold color.

ABV 5.0, Calories 120
Available: Year Round,
6-pack bottles,
24-12 oz. cans or bottle cases;
1/2 keg, 1/6 keg.

Climax Brewing Company

112 Valley Road
Roselle Park, New Jersey 07204
908-620-9585
www.climaxbrewing.com

Dave Hoffman developed a love of flavorful beer from his father Kurt, who came to the United States from Germany in 1958. "Over there, beer is considered food," Kurt Hoffman said. Dave started as a homebrewer nearly two decades ago. He brewed his first batch of beer from a kit ordered from Popular Science.

Climax now produces on their much larger system, as many as twenty different brews including regulars: ESB, Cream Ale, IPA, Nut Brown Ale & Roselle Park Centennial. They also produce many specialty and seasonal beers such as: Bavarian Black, Oktoberfest, 10th Anniversary Barleywine and their widely popular line of Hoffmann Lagers. Climax has an annual capacity of 4,000 barrels and currently produces 60 barrels a month.

Climax is available on tap in many popular New York/New Jersey/Pennsylvania locations as well as in their recognizable brown-glass half-gallon growlers, "Each of these is a walking advertisement," Hoffman said. "They are so big, they stand out like a sore thumb in a liquor store." Michael Jackson described Climax's IPA as "smooth with a layered malt background; very long, late soft development of hop character. A hoppier beer but remarkably well balanced."

Hoffmann Doppel Bock

Dark brown in color with a very large malty body this luscious lager beer has a very pronounced chocolaty flavor backed by a nice spicy hop finish. This beer is made from only the finest german malt noble hops fermented with our special strain of lager yeast from Bavaria. Availability is from Christmas till Easter. This beer pairs well with any game meats or any rich chocolate desserts.

Call brewery for availability,
Keg, Growlers.

485

Clipper City Brewing Company, LP

4615 Hollins Ferry Rd, Suite B
Baltimore, MD 21227
410-247-7822
www.cccbeer.com

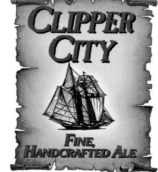

Founded by Baltimore brewing pioneer Hugh Sisson, Clipper City is named for the famed Clipper ship – first developed and built in the port of Baltimore. The Clipper ship is a symbol for much that is good about our region – a strong nautical heritage with a committment to craftmanship of the highest caliber.

Clipper City brews 14 distinctive beers that fall into 3 different brands. The "Clipper City" brand, comprising a lager, marzen, pale and gold ales, are currently only available in the DC, MD, and VA markets.

Our "Oxford" brand is comprised exclusively of wheat beers and currently features a Bavarian style hefeweizen and a raspberry weizen. These beers are available to all of our current markets.

Our "Heavy Seas" brand represents our highest expression of the brewer's art. Each beer is bottle conditioned and represents a very robust style – usually in excess of 7% ABV. Currently there are 3 year round beers and 5 seasonals in the "Heavy Seas" line, and these beers are available to all of our current markets. Loose Cannon Hop3 Ale is the flagship beer in the portfolio.

Loose Cannon Hop3 Ale

An interpretation of American IPA, this beer uses approximately 3 pounds of hops per barrel and is triple hopped – in the kettle, in the hop back, and dry hopped. The focus is on hop aroma and flavor, not the "strip the enamel off your teeth" bitterness so common with many strong IPAs. The result is an ale that is burnished gold, with rich hop aroma and flavor, yet enormous drinkability! Approximately 7.25% Alc. by Vol. Winner for 2 years straight (2005 & 2006) of the Maryland Governor's Cup as the best beer brewed in Maryland.

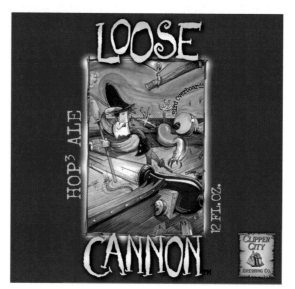

Available: Year Round,
6-pack, 50L keg, 1/6 keg.

486

PORTFOLIO INDEX (Alphabetical)

Cooper's Cave Ale Company, LTD.

2 Sagamore Street
Glens Falls, NY 12801
518-792-0007
www.cooperscaveale.com

Cooper's Cave Ale Company, Ltd. is the realized goal of three ale lovers, Ed, Pat and Adrian Bethel. Established on St. Patrick's Day, 1999 we are a 7 BBL micro-brewrery, producing ales and lagers, gourmet sodas and ice cream for both retail and wholesale consumption. We use only the finest ingredients available and believe that ales and lagers flourish with minimal intervention. Our tasting room is open daily and brewery tours are offered at the discretion of the brewers. The creation of The Warren County Bike Trail in 2000 has enhanced our business and our ice cream take-out window is open year round. Lew Bryson, author of 'New York Breweries' calls us "one of the most successfully integrated community brewing businesses I've ever seen."

Radeau Red Ale

Radeau Red Ale is our flapship ale. It is a traditional Irish Red Ale. Full bodied and packed with flavor it has turned the heads of many "dyed in the wool" American lager drinkers. Our Radeau Red is named after the 18th century seven-sided gunboat that is still on the bottom of Lake George, NY. It is the oldest, intact warship in North America.

OSG 1.054 IBU 35
Available: Year Round,
22 oz. bottles, 1/2 keg, 1/4 keg, 1/6 keg.

PORTFOLIO INDEX (Alphabetical)

Cricket Hill Brewing Company Inc.

24 Kulick Road
Fairfield, NJ 07004
973-276-9415
www.crickethillbrewery.com

Cricket Hill Brewery produced its first beers in January of 2002. Our philosophy is to produce very drinkable "session beers" that are as gentle in syle as possible. Our goal is to provide the general public with all malt microbrews as an alternative to the every day boring American lagers. We believe that curious beer drinkers are stepping out from under the mind-numbing barrage of large brewery advertising and deciding for themselves what beers they enjoy. Our beers are designed for these selective, independent beer enthusiasts.

Brewing is an old world craft. Great beers have always been made with 100% barley and Cricket Hill continues that tradition today. You will not find rice, corn or any other impurities in our world-class lagers and ales.

I encourage you to take the time to taste different craft-brewed beers. Embrace and enjoy the craftsmanship and dedication that goes into these exquisite beers I am certain that our beers will start you on a wonderful adventure into the world of Microbrews!

Cricket Hill East Coast Lager

A wonderful balance of crisp malt flavor and a flowery hops finish highlight this easy-drinking golden lager. Brewed specifically to offer a gentle and delicate finish, our East Coast Lager shows well with light fare but stands alone magnificently.

6-pack, 12-pack, loose 24,
draft (1/2 keg, 1/4 keg, 1/6 keg).

D.G. Yuengling & Son, Inc.

5th & Mahantongo Streets
Pottsville, PA 17901
570-622-4141
www.yuengling.com

Since opening its doors in Pottsville, PA in 1829, the Yuengling Brewery has endured and prospered through a civil war, prohibition, the great depression, and most significantly, through five generations of continuous family ownership. The importance of tradition has not only helped shape the company's image, but has earned D.G. Yuengling & Son the honor of being recognized as America's Oldest Brewery.

Under the leadership of 5th generation owner, Richard Yuengling, Jr., D.G. Yuengling & Son has grown to be the 5th largest brewery in the United States. Since purchasing the brewery from his father in 1985, Dick not only increased annual sales by 400%, but also added two new production facilities to the business. He purchased a former Stroh's brewery in Tampa, FL and built a new facility right outside of Pottsville in an effort to meet their growing product demand. Yuengling is currently distributed in over ten states along the East Coast.

The Yuengling Brewery produces a complete line of products to satisfy the most discerning tastes. This hometown brewer has the distinction of being a regional brewery without sacrificing flavor to appeal to the masses. Yuengling currently brews seven unique beers including its flagship brand, Yuengling Traditional Lager. Other fine flavors are Light Lager, Original Black & Tan, Dark Brewed Porter, Lord Chesterfield Ale, Premium and Light beer.

For information about America's Oldest Brewery and tour times, visit our website at www.yuengling.com.

Yuengling Traditional Lager

Yuengling Traditional Lager is a classic beer that combines a deep amber color with a mild hop flavor to create a refreshing taste and aroma. Characterized as an American-style premium Lager, it is brewed with caramel roasted malts for a toasty sweetness that finishes smooth.

Introduced in 1987, the beer quickly grew to be Yuengling's flagship brand recognized by consumers coast-to-coast. Yuengling Traditional Lager has become so well known in its core market that patrons in local Pennsylvania bars ask for it simply by the name Lager. Its mass appeal has earned it various honors including the (2001-04) Hot Brand Award, (2004) IRI #1 Ranked "Power Brand," (2005) Cheers Growth Brand Award, and (2006) Impact Blue Chip Brand Recipient.

Available: Year Round,
6-pack NR, 12-pack NR, 24-loose NR,
6-pack can, 12-pack can,
24-loose suitcase can, 16 oz can,
22 oz NR, 32 oz NR, slim 1/4 keg, 1/2 keg.

Deschutes Brewery, Inc.

901 SW Simpson Avenue
Bend, OR 97702
541-385-8606
www.deschutesbrewery.com

Overlooking the wild & scenic Deschutes River in Central Oregon, Deschutes Brewery has brewed exceptional handcrafted ales since 1988. Deschutes Brewery opened as a small brew pub serving locals their favorite beers in downtown Bend and then in 1993, moved into its current brewing facility and has continued expanding and improving the facilities. With a 50-barrel traditional gravity brew house and a new state-of-the-art 131-barrel Huppmann brew system from Germany, Deschutes now creates and experiments with specialty batches of limited beers like The Abyss, while brewing year-round favorites like Black Butte Porter. Consistently producing the highest quality beers is always Deschutes' number one priority and commitment.

Year-Round Beers: Black Butte Porter, Mirror Pond Pale Ale, Inversion IPA and Obsidian Stout. **Seasonal Beers:** Cinder Cone Red (Winter), Buzzsaw Brown (Spring), Twilight Ale (Summer) and Jubelale (Holiday). **Bond Street Series (22 oz limited batch beers):** Hop Trip, Hop Henge, and other eclectic ales.

The Deschutes Brewery & Public House continues brewing unique beers at its original location while serving the finest Northwest pub cuisine. So when you find yourself in Bend, stop in and have a pint of Bachelor Bitter, the locals' favorite, or any of the other distinctive ales brewed on-site.

Gift Shop & Tasting Room Open Tuesday through Saturday from 12 to 5 PM. Guided Brewery Tours offered Tuesday through Saturday at 1, 2:30 and 4 PM.

Black Butte Porter

Deschutes Brewery's flagship beer, Black Butte Porter has built a dedicated following since its first pint. Rich in flavor yet easy to drink with its creamy, smooth mouth feel, Black Butte Porter dispels the myths about dark beer. The slight hop bitterness up front enhances the distinctive chocolate and roasted finish.

ABV 5.2% IBUs 30
Available: Year Round,
6-pack, 12-pack, loose 24,
draft (1/2 keg, 1/4 keg, 1/6 keg).

PORTFOLIO INDEX (Alphabetical)

Dick's Brewing Company

5945 Prather Road
Centralla, WA 98531
800-586-7760
www.dicksbeer.com

As a young boy Dick recalls watching his father farming the fields as he was growing up in the 50s. The farm produced a variety of grains, including barley. Years later Dick's Brewery combines barley & hops to create a variety of distinctive brews that recall the simplicity of an earlier age; an age when folks took pride in the pleasures of work and the joys of craftmanship.

Dick's Brewery opened in 1994 after two years of planning and applying for permits. What a process! The brewery is housed in a 2100 square foot building located next door to NW Sausage & Deli. The brewery features a 15-barrel brew house with the capacity to brew over 2,000 barrells of beer annually.

NW Sausage & Deli is Dick's other business. It opened in 1982, and here Dick produces Old World style sausages that are all smoked on premise in modern electric forced air smokehouses. Dick's Beer is available on draft and in bottles at NW Sausage & Deli. We are open Monday through Thursday 9:30-5:00, Friday 9:30-9:00 and Saturday 9:30-5:00. Lunch is served daily and dinner is served Friday night. Enjoy a Dick's Beer with lunch, dinner or Dick's sausages at our retail deli!

A wide variety of ales are made on premise in a true microbrewery. Ours is one of only a few dozen Craft Breweries in Washington State. Dick's Beer has a distinctive full-bodied taste and continues to appeal to an ever-growing audience throughout the Northwest and beyond.

Enjoy your visit to our Deli and Brewery and remember to keep your glass full of Dick's Beer!

Dick Danger Ale

Dick Danger Ale 5.5% ABV OG=1.052 TG=1.010 Our flagship beer. A large percentage of black malt give this distinctive ale its dark brown/black color and that slightly roasted flavor. Magnum hops provide a backbone of bitterness and large additions of Mt. Hood hops later in the boil come right through the in the finish. The result is a highly drinkable dark ale which bridges the gap between pale and porter.

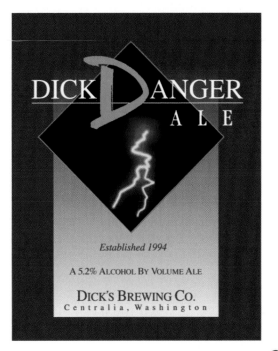

6-pack, case (24),
draft (1/2, 1/4 & 1/6 barrell).

491

PORTFOLIO INDEX (Alphabetical)

Dogfish Head Craft Brewery

6 Cannery Village Center
Milton, DE 19968
888-836-4347
www.dogfish.com

Brewery Tours available Monday, Wednesday & Friday at 3:00pm (year-round)

Saturdays at 3:00pm (Memorial Day – Labor Day)

Beer and Merchandise purchases M - F, 9am to 5pm

Our Rehoboth Beach brewpub/distillery is located just a short drive away!

Check us out online for lots of beer/spirits/restaurant info and merchandise purchases.

Dogfish Head began in 1995 as Delaware's first brewpub, and two years later began distribution. Dogfish now brews more than 18 styles of beer throughout the year and distributes to more than 20 states. A small distillery is housed in the brewpub and Dogfish now makes Blue Hen Vodka, a few styles of rum, and gin. In the fall of 2005, the first Dogfish Head Alehouse opened in Gaithersburg, Maryland.

Dogfish Head is known for producing "off-centered ales, for off-centered people," with strange ingredients (such as dates, figs, chicory, pumpkin, juniper and raisins), and high alcohol contents (some clock in at more than 18%!). Come visit and find out why beer writer Michael Jackson calls Dogfish Head, "America's most interesting and adventurous small brewery!"

Dogfish Head 60 Minute IPA

Our flagship beer, a session India Pale Ale brewed with Warrior, Amarillo & 'Mystery Hop X.' A powerful East Coast IPA with a lot of citrusy hop character. This is THE session beer for beer geeks like us!

Make sure and try the stronger versions of this beer too – 90 Minute IPA (9% ABV and 120 Minute Imperial IPA (20% ABV).

6% ABV, IBU 60
Available: Year Round,
6 pack, draft (1/2 keg, 1/6 keg)
Tasting notes: Citrus, cedar, pine & candied-orange flavors, floral.
Food pairing recommendations:
Spicy foods, pesto, grilled salmon,
soy-based dished, pizza.
Glassware recommendation: Pint
Wine comparable: Busty Chardonnay.

Dunedin Brewery

937 Douglas Avenue
Dunedin, FL 34698
727-736-0606
www.dunedinbrewery.com

Dunedin Brewery is a craft brewery, located in the Gulf Coast town of Dunedin, Florida. Nestled in the quaint downtown area, just blocks from the Gulf of Mexico. We started as a family business in 1996, and still hand craft & bottle each 40 keg batch of beer. Our localized brand of award winning fresh ales are enjoyed across the state of Florida, and our snug brew pub is a venue for local & international music, art & entertainment.

Beach Tale Brown Ale

Beach Tale Brown Ale, a beach town beer with a tan. Its chocolate and roasted malts give this beer something to talk about. The hoppy finish is delivered in our typical craft-brewed way.

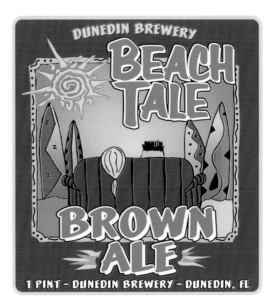

Available: Year Round,
4-pack, draft, keg.

493

Ellicottville Brewing Company

28A Monroe Street
Ellicottville, New York 14731
716-699-2537
www.ellicottvillebrewing.com

Located in the village of Ellicottville, a ski hamlet in the rolling hills of Western New York, we are a brew pub unlike any other. The Ellicottville Brewing Company is considered a local marvel for its architecture, menu, and craft beers. Managed by a fairly young group of talented people, the brewery has placed first in most local beer festivals and has won the Buffalo People's Choice Award twice, for its first two years of operation. Founded by co-owners Allen and Walter Yahn and Peter Kreinheder, the Ellicottville Brewing Company is the culmination of a combined effort inspired by the desire to open a family business. Its location in Ellicottville was inspired by a skiing trip to Vail, and the realization that the Aspen of the East, as Ellicottville is referred to, could be an exciting location for a craft Brewery and Grill. In the summer months, come in and enjoy our authentic German Beer Garden. The only open air dining in Ellicottville, the Beer Garden with its beautiful European flowers, climbing hops vines and brick patio is the place to be on hot summer nights. NOW Open EBC West, Downtown Fredonia. Our all new operation in the Fun filled College town, home to SUNY Fredonia. Bringing Great Beers to a Great Lake!

Blueberry Wheat

Our unique contribution to the fruit category, this beer features a nutty quench of wheat ale combined with the delightful aroma and subtle flavors of Oregon blueberries. Filtered to a golden clarity. 4.2% ALC • 18 IBU • 2.5°L

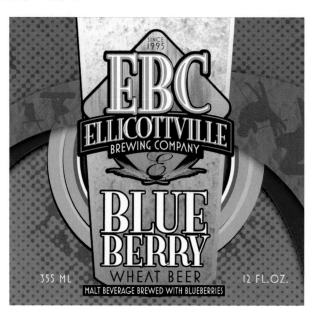

Available: Year Round,
6-pack, 24 bottle case, 1/6 keg, 1/2 keg.

PORTFOLIO INDEX (Alphabetical)

Empyrean Brewing Company

729 Q Street
Lincoln, NE 68508
402-434-5959
www.empyreanbrewingco.com

Our brewery began with a dream that we could brew full-flavored beers for the good people of Nebraska. In 1991 that dream became our state's first brewpub, Lazlo's Brewery & Grill. By 1998 the demand for excellent beer was such that we expanded our pub, and Empyrean Brewing Company was born. Today we still dream big even while we continue to hand craft our beers in small, flavor–filled batches using traditional methods and quality ingredients.

Our fine ales and lagers are only available in Nebraska. Please visit us in Lincoln or look for the nearest Lazlo's Brewery & Grill or FireWorks Restaurant when you travel to our fair state. Drink Empyrean beers, the taste of dreams come true!

LunaSea ESB

Brewed in the English tradition, LunaSea is our brewer's pride and joy, that's why we call it "Extra Special" Bitter. Big, sweet, caramel and biscuit flavors are delicately balanced with crisp, cedary, American hops. Brewed with English grown Marris Otter, Crystal and Aromatic malts and American grown Galena and Cluster hops.

5.7% ABV, IBU 31,
Original Gravity 14.5, SRM 17
Available: Year Round,
6-pack case, 1/2 keg, 1/6 keg.

495

Fish Brewing Company

515 Jefferson St SE
Olympia WA 98501
360-943-6480
www.fishbrewing.com

Nestled in the lush bosom of the Republic of Cascadia, Fish Brewing Company has been locally-owned and proudly hand crafting exceptional beers since the latter half of the 20th Century. Working from their steam-fired 40-barrel brewhouse the Mighty Fish Brewers create Fish Tale Organic Ales and German-style Leavenworth Beers. Their celebrated brewery is also the home of specialty Reel Ales, as well as Spire Mountain Ciders, the nation's oldest brand of commercial craft cider.

Charter members of the Cascadian Craft Brewers' Guild, the Mighty Fish Brewers produce Fish Tale Organic Ales purely from Certified Organic malted barley and the finest hops available. The result is robustly delightful ales that salute organic agriculture and all the benefits it holds for wild salmon habitat and our environment in whole.

At Fish Brewing we believe that fresh beer, fine food and hearty friendships are what the Cascadian life is all about. We are honored to be a part of this happy tradition and look forward to sharing it with all who visit our fair Republic.

Fish Tale Organic India Pale Ale

Incredible brewery freshness.... A gloriously fresh and clean beer; criminally appetizing."

– Michael Jackson, author of *Ultimate Beer*

Here is a hearty thirst quencher of Northwestern proportions. Medium bodied and richly golden, Fish Tale Organic IPA sports crisp bright flavor that's hard to resist. The Mighty Fish Brewers chose three organic malts to lay down Organic IPA's firm body. This provides the backbone for an assertively zesty hop profile featuring organic Pacific Gems. The result: A Cascadian treasure and Gold Medal winner at the 2004 Brewing Industry International Awards in London.

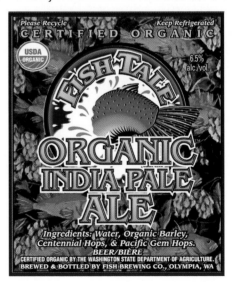

Available: Year 'round
6-pack, draft, cask.

PORTFOLIO INDEX (Alphabetical)

Florida Beer Company

2500 South Harbour City Blvd
Melbourne, FL 32901
321-728-3412
www.FloridaBeer.com

The Florida Beer Company, located in Melbourne, Florida, is the largest brewer of premium, handcrafted beers in Florida. Its many styles of beer are sold by a network of distributors, not only in the state of Florida, but also in Georgia, Alabama, Virginia, Illinois and New York. Florida Beer Company also conducts business in the Bahamas and Virgin Islands.

The Florida Beer Company portfolio of Florida lifestyle beers includes Key West, Hurricane Reef, Ybor Gold, Beachside, La Tropical and Kelly's Hard Cider.

Along with production of these equity brands, Florida Beer Company's production also includes contract beers.

For more information regarding The Florida Beer Company, please go to www.FloridaBeer.com.

Our Tasting Room is opened Monday-Friday 12-5pm. We serve all of our beers that are in current production.

Key West Sunset Ale

Key West Sunset Ale is an American medium-bodied Amber Ale with a tropical twist. It is brewed with pale and caramel malt, blended with hops to create a crisp, satisfying taste.

- Original Gravity - 12.00
- Apparent Extract/Final Gravity - 2.60
- Alcohol by Weight - 3.91
- ABV% - 5.06
- Bitterness (IBU) - 16.0
- Color SRM (EBC) - 10.6

Available: Year Round,
6-pack, case, draft (1/2, 1/6 bbls.)

497

Portfolio Index (Alphabetical)

Flying Dog Brewery

2401 Blake Street
Denver, CO 80205
303-292-5027
www.flyingdogales.com

Flying Dog is Denver's largest brewery and the second largest craft brewery in the state of Colorado. Their award-winning "litter of ales" are available in 45 states. The Brewery is located at 2401 Blake Street, just 2 blocks north of the baseball stadium. Tours are given weekdays at 4pm and Saturdays at 1pm and 3pm. Hunter S. Thompson, the infamous gonzo journalist, had a hand in the brewery's development, and the beers are easily spotted thanks to Gonzo artist Ralph Steadman, the packaging designer. For information on brewery tours or events, call 303.292.5027 or visit www.FlyingDogAles.com.

Flying Dog Pale Ale

Meet the Alpha of the pack...Flying Dog Classic Pale Ale is brilliant amber in color and dry hopped with buckets full of Cascades for an unrivaled hop flavor and aroma. This is a true representation of an American-style pale ale, using the finest ingredients. Flying Dog Classic Pale Ale is a multi-award winning product and is consistently ranked as one of the best pale ales in the U.S. This is what craft beer is all about.

Available: Year Round

Portfolio Index (Alphabetical)

Flying Fish Brewing Company

1940 Olney Avenue
Cherry Hill, NJ 08003
856-489-0061
www.flyingfish.com

In 1996, Flying Fish Brewing Company, located in Cherry Hill, New Jersey, approximately seven miles east of Philadelphia, opened. In a state that once boasted 50 breweries, it is the first brewery in Southern New Jersey and the first new brewery built in that part of the state in more than half a century. From its opening in late 1996, Flying Fish has quadrupled its capacity and become the largest of the approximately 20 craft breweries in the state.

Flying Fish now produces four full-time styles, as well as a variety of seasonal beers.

The key word to describe all Flying Fish beers is "balance." The beers are full-flavored, yet highly drinkable. Flavors harmonize, not fight for individual attention. Seeing beer as equal to, if not superior to, wine, Flying Fish beers are designed to complement food.

Free brewery tours/tastings are conducted every Saturday between 1-4pm.

Flying Fish Abbey Dubbel

While Belgian-style beers are quite common now, Flying Fish was an early producer of such styles among American breweries. An exceptionally complex beer with many interwoven flavors, this classic-style Abbey beer features an immense head with a fruity nose and a generous body. Malty in the middle, with a clean, almondy dry finish and a slight alcohol warmth. This Dubbel uses a traditional Belgian fermentation process to impart its unique flavors.

Alcohol by volume: 7.1% Bittering: 20 IBU; Original Gravity: 1.060

Says Michael Jackson about Flying Fish Dubbel: "A wonderful example of the style."

Available: Year Round,
6-pack, 4/6/12, 24/12, 1/6 keg. 1/2 keg.

499

PORTFOLIO INDEX (Alphabetical)

The Fort Collins Brewery

1900 E. Lincoln Ave. #B
Ft. Collins, CO 80524
970-472-1499
fortcollinsbrewery.com

The Fort Collins Brewery is the newest micro brewery on the Front Range of Colorado's Napa Valley for Beer. Specialty brews like Major Tom's Pomegranate Wheat, Chocolate Stout and Retro Red are the most popular sellers in Colorado and many of the other states. Brewing both ales, lagers and seasonal beers gives the consumer a wide variety of beers to choose from. Kidd lager and Z lager are available year round, but the Seasonal GABF winner Dopplebock and Spring Bock are brewed in limited quantities.

Please check our website for additional information and to contact the brewery.

Major Tom's Pomegranate Wheat

Not a fruite beer, but a nice, sweet-tart Wheat Ale brewed with pomegranates. Unlike anything else you've every tried.

Available: Year Round,
6-pack, 1/2 keg, 1/6 keg.

PORTFOLIO INDEX (Alphabetical)

Four Peaks Brewing Company

1340 E. 8th St. #104
Tempe, Az. 85281
480-303-9967; fax:480-303-9964
www.fourpeaks.com

We at Four Peaks Brewing Company, like many fine small breweries across the country, are proud to offer only the highest quality, hand-crafted ales. Our brewery distributes fresh kegged and bottled beer to supermarkets, grocery stores, restaurants, bars, resorts, and liquor stores around the state. Our brewpub offers up to 10 different styles of beer on tap, including a cask conditioned ale drawn with an authentic beer engine.

Our 20 barrel brewhouse has a yearly production capacity of 20,000 barrels of beer (that's 40,000 kegs). Four Peaks uses reverse-osmosis to strip its water free of contaminants. Naturally occurring salts and chemicals are then added back into the water to emulate the great brewing waters of Europe. For Example, we use a Burton water for our 8th St. Ale and our Hop Knot Ale. This is a very hard water from the middle of England where Bass and Double Diamond brew their famous pale ales.

The brewery building is located on 8th Street in Tempe at the Old Bordens Creamery building. It is a beautiful turn of the century brick warehouse with significant historical value. Pacific Creamery and later Bordens Creamery pasteurized and bottled milk and produced ice for the local citizens of Tempe. The building was originally constructed in 1892, and has had a number of additions over the years through 1927. Since then the building has not changed and its Mission Revival style still sets the mood for the building's design and the surrounding neighborhood. The building is constructed almost entirely of red brick, with wooden ceilings and a glass parapet reaching as high as 35 feet supported by steel suspension. Truly an inspiration!

Kiltlifter Scottish Style Ale

You have the combination of pure water, North American malt, fresh Kent Golding hops and clean, strong yeast. An ale, artfully crafted in Tempe, Arizona and eagerly shared by Four Peaks Brewing Company. Kilt Lifter is brewed in the long tradition of smooth, full bodied Scottish ales. It is marked by a warm balance of hop and malt, with the slightest hint of peat-smoked barley. A traditional touch for a fine ale whose merits are many.

Available: Year Round,
6-pack, 24 pack, 1/2 barrel, 1/4 barrel, 5 gallon.

501

Full Sail Brewing Company

506 Columbia Street
Hood River, OR 97031
541-385-8606
www.fullsailbrewing.com

Look down. Candy-colored sails skim the Columbia like swarms of graffittied dragonflies. Look out. Snow-topped volcanic peaks descend into wildflower meadows, merge into evergreen forests, then abruptly stop at vertical basalt cliffs punctuated by pencil-thin waterfalls. Look up. Dry blue skies deliver the scent of ponderosas baking in the summer sun.

Sitting on the deck of the brewery here in Hood River on a brilliant August day never ceases to make us eternally grateful for every moment we get to spend in this amazing place. A little town full of blossoming fruit orchards and postcard-quality roadside stands, where every summer a landlocked surf town magically emerges from its winter ski-village cocoon.

It is here that we at Full Sail Brewing Company make our award winning beers in our brewhouse overlooking the most epic wind and kite surfing spot in the world. At this very moment, our specialists in the liquid refreshment arts are crafting barley and hops into your next beer. Independent and employee owned, we have been named "One of the Top 20 Breweries in the World" by ratebeer.com and are proudly celebrating our tenth gold medal for our Amber beer.

Next time you are in our neck of the woods, swing by for a pint, grab a bite, tour the brewery, or just soak up the view. Open daily from 12-9:00PM Cheers – The Full Sail Crew

Full Sail Amber

Amber – Oregon's Original Amber, this ridiculously tasty Amber Ale is a Northwest classic. Don't just take our word for it, Full Sail Amber has brought home 9 Gold Medals from the World Beer Championships and one Gold from the Great American Beer Festival.

Malty sweet, medium bodied with a reddish amber hue and a spicy floral hop finish, this is one great tasting beer.

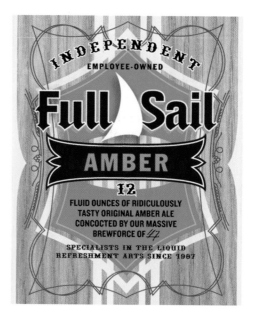

ABV 5.5%
Available: Year Round,
6-pack, 12-pack, draft 1/2, 1/6, 1/4.

Glacier Brewing Company

6 Tenth Ave. East
Polson, MT 59860
406-883-2595
www.glacierbrewing.com

The Glacier Brewing Company is a microbrewery located on the southern end of Flathead Lake, in beautiful northwest Montana. We produce six styles of beer, mostly German styles, and two craft soda; root beer and cherry crème soda. We package all our products in draft and currently offer five beer and the root beer in six packs. We are open year-round and invite everyone into our tasting room to sample our fine beers and sodas. Check our website, www.glacierbrewing.com, for current specials and events!

Glacier Select Oktoberfest

One of the first things you notice about our Glacier Select Oktoberfest is the beautiful dark copper-amber color. Next, you enjoy the subtle aroma of Noble German hops. Finally, a complicated but balanced malt and hop mouthfeel.

Truly, worthy to be poured all year!

Available: Year Round,
6-pack, draft.

503

PORTFOLIO INDEX (Alphabetical)

Gluek Brewing Company

PO Box 476, Cold Spring, MN 56320
320-685-8686
www.gluek.com

Gluek Brewing Company, the largest brewery in Minnesota, is a leader in making and selling high quality beer and non-alcoholic beverages. By combining the pure spring water of Cold Spring with its original recipes, Gluek produces hundreds of beverages for national and international companies. Gluek's head brewmaster is a top award winner in national brewing competitions.

Gluek is the #1 energy drink and specialty drink producer in the country and the #1 producer of exclusive beer and craft beer brands for major retailers in the United States and other companies throughout the world. Gluek offers its Gluek, Stite, and Northern brew products that include ambers, pilsners, bocks, ales, and lagers. The company traces its roots to a German immigrant named Gottlieb Gluek, who started the brewery in 1857. For more information, visit www.gluek.com.

Stite

A fine German style Pils brewed with a patented process since 1948. The entire Stite family of beers is rich with a full bodied taste. Stite is packaged in the new Alum-a-bottle, which keeps beer colder longer and goes where glass can't.

Available: Year Round,
six pack and 12 pack Variety pack.

Great Lakes Brewing Company

2516 Market Avenue
Cleveland, OH 44113
216-771-4404
www.greatlakesbrewing.com

Great Lakes Brewing Company is a principle-centered, environmentally respectful and socially conscious company committed to crafting fresh, flavorful, high-quality beer and food for the enjoyment of our customers. We aspire to maintain our status as the premier craft brewery in the Great Lakes region and are dedicated to uncompromising service, continuous improvement and innovative consumer education. The care that goes into our beer resonates from a commitment to our community and environment, otherwise known as the "Triple Bottom Line" – to engage in economic, social and environmental practices that achieve a sustainable, yet profitable, business. These include:

- Reducing, reusing and recycling
- Changing natural resource use from "Take, Make, Waste" to "Take, Make, Remake"
- Implementing efficient energy practices
- Investing in the community through non-profit organizations
- Supporting sustainable urban renewal projects

The three waves in our company logo not only reflect this Triple Bottom Line philosophy, they represent a concerted effort to the respectful use of beer's most valuable ingredient – water. Since beer is over 90% water, we understand that quality water translates into a great beer drinking experience, so only the freshest water from the Great Lakes region is used.

Brewery Office Hours: Monday - Friday: 8:00 AM - 4:00 PM.
Brewery Tour Hours (free): Fridays: 5:00 PM - 9:00 PM (on the hour); Saturdays: 1:00 PM - 9:00 PM (on the hour).

Dortmunder Gold Lager

Our Dortmunder Gold Lager is a smooth lager that strikes a delicate balance between sweet malt and dry hop flavors. The name of our flagship beer reflects the unprecedented accolades and recognition it has earned in major worldwide beer tasting competitions.

TYPE/STYLE:
Dortmunder: During the mid-19th century, seven breweries within the city of Dortmund, Germany, began brewing beers in the same manner, resulting in what has come to be known as the "Dortmunder" style.

FOOD COMPLEMENTS:
Because neither malt nor hops dominate this beer, it complements most foods, especially salads, fish and chicken.

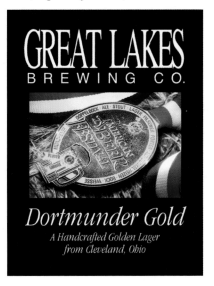

Available: Year Round,
6-pack, 12-pack,
Sampler pack, 1/2 keg, 1/6 keg.

505

Great Sex Brewing, Inc.

12763 Encanto Way
Redding, CA 96003
530-275-2705
www.greatsexbrewing.com

Great Sex Brewing (GSB) began as an idea in the early 1990's when Doug Talbot and some friends attempted to purchase an old historic building near Vail, Colorado for micro-brewing purposes. Doug's intent was to use the name as it appears now. After a number of twists, turns, bumps and grinds Jeff Talbot (the other half of the Gemütliche Brothers™) became involved and GSB was eventually incorporated in California at the turn of the century. Our main office is in Redding, CA, so you might say Redding is "The Home of Great Sex!"

Asking for Great Sex...beer...will add an exciting new experience to your life. The risqué, humorous double-meaning creates an immediate charged atmosphere of fun. And, our crisp, sweetly refreshing Adam & Eve Ale provides more bang for your buck – containing 6% alcohol by volume.

GSB invites you to learn about all our unique ideas, story, and products which include a suitable array of stylized hats and t-shirts; spaghetti-string tanks; witty bumper stickers and a lot more. Please all your senses – join the Gemütliche Brothers™. Visit us online at: www.greatSEXbrewing.com.

Adam & Eve Ale

Great Sex Brewing's Adam & Eve Ale is a light golden beer that is clean, crisp, easy to drink and pleasing to the eye. This outstanding beer's finish is slightly dry, adding encouragement for patrons to "have another." Rich malt flavor is prevalent due to Vienna malts and there is the hint of caramel sweetness brought forth by the addition of Crystal malts. The bitterness level is present only to maintain proper balance. Lower ale fermentation temperatures coupled with discerning yeast and hop selection ensures a delightfully smooth beer containing six-percent alcohol.

Available: Year Round,
6-pack, full-keg.

Gritty McDuff's Brewing Company, LLC

396 Fore Street
Portland, ME 04101
207-772-2739
www.grittys.com

Gritty McDuff's is Maine's original brewpub. The Brewpub started in 1988 in Portland's old Port and since have added two more locations in Freeport and Auburn. Like most brewpubs, they brew and sell their ales on site at all three locations. Gritty's is also sold in kegs and bottles to a wide range of retail outlets. They offer four "year around" beers: Best Bitter, Best Brown, Original Pub Style and Black Fly Stout. These beers can be purchased anytime of the year. Gritty's also offers four special seasonal ales: Halloween Ale, Scottish Ale, Christmas Ale and Vacationland Summer Ale. These beers are limited runs and only available during specific times of the year.

Original Pub Style

Original Pub Style harkens back to the very first brews Gritty's produced at our Portland Brew Pub back in 1988. "We wanted to make a beer that captures what made people fall in love with craft brewing in the first place; a fresh, classic pale ale with plenty of hop character." says Brewmaster Ed Stebbins. "This is the kind of beer that really started the whole Maine brewing revolution."

Available: Year Round,
6-pack, 12-pack, 1/2 keg, 1/4 keg, 22 ounce bottles.

Harpoon Brewery

306 Northern Avenue
Boston, MA 02210
888-HARPOON
www.harpoonbrewery.com

Rich Doyle and Dan Kenary started the Harpoon Brewery on the Boston waterfront in 1986 because – like today – they love beer and wanted more good beer choices. Over twenty years later they still revel in making great beer and sharing that joy with friends and neighbors. The Harpoon Brewery distributes its locally brewed products throughout the Northeast. Harpoon's line of craft beer features six year-round beers, including their flagship Harpoon IPA and popular UFO Hefeweizen, and four seasonal selections. In 2003 they created the Harpoon 100 Barrel Series, a limited edition line of beers created to showcase the Harpoon brewing staff's talent and passion for beer. In June 2000, the Harpoon Brewery purchased a second brewery in Windsor, Vermont to keep up with the growing demand.

Visitors are welcome for tastings at both Boston and Windsor breweries year-round. In addition, Harpoon hosts renowned festivals at both breweries annually to celebrate drinking great beer with friends.

Harpoon IPA

Harpoon IPA is our interpretation of a classic English style using hops and malt grown in the United States. The pronounced hop aroma and the deep copper color make an immediate sensory impression. Northwest Cascade hops are used generously in the recipe. The aroma is floral, distinctly different from the herbal aromas of other hop varieties. The hops are balanced by a blend of three different malts.

The lingering bitter finish of this beer is crisp and pronounced. This is created, in part, by dry hopping – a technique that involves adding fresh hops to the conditioning beer to provide a fresh hop aroma.

Harpoon IPA is floral, medium-bodied with an aggressive, clean hop finish. It is our bestselling beer.

Available: Year Round,
6-pack, 12-pack, loose case, 4/6 case,
1/2 keg, 1/6 keg, 22 oz. bottles,
fresh growlers can be purchased at the brewery.

Karl Strauss Brewing Company

5985 Santa Fe Street
San Diego, CA 92109
858-551-2739
www.karlstrauss.com

Karl Strauss Brewing Company was founded by two college roommates on a mission to revive the art of craft brewing in Southern California. With the help of an uncle – renowned Master Brewer Karl Strauss – they began drafting their business plans on the beaches of San Diego in 1989. Shortly thereafter, Karl Strauss Brewing Company was born. It was the first brewery to have opened in San Diego in more than 50 years – paving the way and providing inspiration for the many fine craft breweries that have put San Diego on the map as a city known for its exciting and innovative beer scene.

Karl Strauss Brewing Company artfully brews both lagers and ales. Their core lineup includes: Karl Strauss Amber Lager, Red Trolley Ale, Windansea Wheat Hefeweizen, Stargazer I.P.A., Woodie Gold Pilsener, Downtown After Dark Brown Ale, Endless Summer Light, and Karl Strauss Oktoberfest (seasonal). All are brewed with the same commitment, expertise, and passion as when the company first opened back in 1989. Distributed only in Southern California, Karl Strauss beer can be found in the best establishments from San Diego to Santa Barbara.

Karl Strauss Amber Lager

Karl Strauss Amber Lager is medium in body, moderate in alcohol, and has a rich copper color. We use plenty of Munich and Caramel malts to give it a distinct toasted caramel flavor and just enough Cascade hops to create a delicately spicy backdrop. This crisp, smooth lager has lots of flavor while being incredibly balanced. The first beer we brewed when we opened in 1989, Karl Strauss Amber Lager remains our most popular beer. And it was Karl's favorite.

Available: Year Round,
6-pack, 12-pack, loose 24,
draft (1/2 keg, 1/4 keg).

PORTFOLIO INDEX (Alphabetical)

Landmark Beer Company

3650 James Street, Room 105
Syracuse, NY 13206
315-720-2013
www.landmarkbrewing.com

Our Story

Founded in 2006 we are a small brewery in Syracuse, New York dedicated to brewing quality ales and lagers. Our beers are sold throughout Central and Western New York.

Our goal for 2007 is to expand our brand into the rest of New York State and select markets in surrounding states.

Our Motto

"Great Beer for Great People"

Vanilla Bean Brown Ale

A classic English brown ale brewed with the addtition of premium Madagascar vanilla bean. Available year round in draft and bottles.

Available: Year Round,
6-pack, 1/2 keg, 1/4 keg.

Lang Creek Brewery

655 Lang Creek Road
Marion, MT 59925
406-858-2200
www.langcreekbrewery.com

LANG CREEK BREWERY
MARION, MONTANA
AMERICA'S MOST REMOTE BREWERY

Lang Creek Brewery was founded in 1993 in the beautiful, remote Thompson River Valley in N.W. Montana. John Campbell, a private pilot, built the original brewhouse within the walls of his airplane hanger to open America's first Aviation Theme brewery. Our brewery is also known as America's "Most Remote Brewery." It is located 42 miles west of Kalispell, MT – off of Highway #2. Our brochure advises," For tours and tasting, call for directions before you come. For if you don't you may be too old to enjoy our tasty brews by the time you find us."

Our fine ales are brewed in small batches by craftsmen who love their work and know good beer. Lang Creek Brewery is dedicated to the abolishment of mundane, tasteless swill you've been programmed to know as "beer." We promise to brew only full-flavored, good tasting beer that will cause your taste-buds to think they've died and gone to heaven.

Tours and tasting: Monday thought Friday 10 to 4. Saturday 11 to 5 and Sunday 1 to 5.

Tri-Motor Amber

Tri-Motor Amber is a deep amber ale, broadly in the style of ESB. Tri-Motor is Lang Creek Brewery's flagship brand, winning gold, silver and bronze medals in the NABA competition in the ESB category. It is rich with malt character, well balanced for a long finish. Tri-Motor is brewed in small batches by craftsman, who love their work and have pride in what they do.

Available: Year Round,
6-pack, 1/2 keg, 1/4 keg.

PORTFOLIO INDEX (Alphabetical)

Left Hand Brewing Company

1265 Boston Avenue
Longmont, CO 80501
303-772-0258
www.lefthandbrewing.com

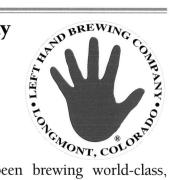

Left Hand Brewing Company has been brewing world-class, award-winning beers since its founding in 1993. We see our beers as a wonderful liquid food to complement meals and social occasions. We strive for the perfect balance and harmony between malt and hops in every beer – from our lightest to our darkest – allowing our consumers a truly unique and flavorful experience in every glass.

The name Left Hand comes from the Arapahoe Indian word "niwot" which means left hand. Niwot was a Southern Arapahoe Indian Chief who wintered with his tribe in the Boulder Valley area of Colorado. There is a town, a creek, a canyon, a mountain and now an award-winning brewery named after Chief Niwot!

Milk Stout

Strong roasted malt and coffee flavors build the foundation of this classic cream stout. The addition of milk sugar mellows the intense roastiness and gives this beer the most incredible creamy mouth feel.

COLOR	Black, 470° SRM
BODY	Full-bodied
ABV	5.2%
IBU'S	22
PLATO	15.50°
MALTS	Premium Pale 2-row, Crystal, Munich, Roast Barley, Flaked Oats, Flaked Barley and Chocolate
HOPS	Magnum and US Goldings

Available: Year Round,
6-pack, draft.

PORTFOLIO INDEX (Alphabetical)

The Long Trail Brewing Company

Jct. Route 4 & 100A, P.O. Box 168
Bridgewater Corners, VT 05035
802-672-5011
www.longtrail.com

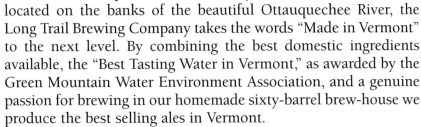

Since 1989, the Long Trail Brewing Company has been a regional brewer of high-quality, Vermont hand-crafted alternatives to imported beer. Centrally located on the banks of the beautiful Ottauquechee River, the Long Trail Brewing Company takes the words "Made in Vermont" to the next level. By combining the best domestic ingredients available, the "Best Tasting Water in Vermont," as awarded by the Green Mountain Water Environment Association, and a genuine passion for brewing in our homemade sixty-barrel brew-house we produce the best selling ales in Vermont.

The Long Trail Brewing Company not only makes great tasting beer of the highest quality, but we also hold our commitment to enviromental consciousness and the promotion of healthy active lifestyles to the highest standard. In following with these efforts, we at Long Trail Brewing remain highly involved in the activities of our local community, Vermont and beyond. By actively promoting both outdoor sport and great tasting, handcrafted beer, we encourage everyone to live well. It is our hope that by setting a leading example in not just quality of beer, but also quality of life, we are able to inspire others to do the same.

We welcome you to be our guest year round. Self guided brewery tours and our Trail Head Pub & Visitor Center are open 10 am - 6 pm seven days a week. Please sample our Family of Fine Ales, and make your journey better by taking the Long Trail!

Cheers!

Long Trail Ale

Long Trail Ale is a full-bodied amber ale modeled after the "Altbiers" of Dusseldorf, Germany. Our top fermenting yeast and cold-finishing temperature result in a complex, yet clean, full flavor. Originally introduced in 1989, Long Trail Ale quickly became, and remains, the largest selling craft beer in Vermont. It is a multiple medal winner at the Great American Beer Festival.

Available: Year Round,
12 ounce bottle, 22 ounce bottle,
6-pack, 12-pack,
draft (5 gallon "log," 50 liter keg).

Blackbeary Wheat

Our summer brew is light, crisp and refreshing. This wheat beer is brewed with a hint of blackberries adding a subtle fruit flavor to this summer quencher.

<6 grams of carbs.

Available: March through August,
12 ounce bottle, 6-pack, 12-pack,
draft (5 gallon "log," 50 liter keg).

Double Bag

This full-bodied double alt is also known as "Stickebier" – German slang for "secret brew." The secret is that this brew is so smooth you'd never believe it has an alcohol content of 7.2%!!!

Indulge in moderation…

Available: Year Round,
12 ounce bottle, 22 ounce bottle, 6-pack,
draft (5 gallon "log," 50 liter keg).

PORTFOLIO INDEX (Alphabetical)

Harvest

Our northern English style brown ale features a blend of 7 types of malted barley & wheat that yields a light brown brew with a smooth, sweet finish.

SMOOTH BROWN...SMOOTH DOWN!!!

Available: September through October,
12 ounce bottle, 6-pack, 12-pack,
draft (5 gallon "log," 50 liter keg).

Hefeweizen

Here is our "Wheat beer with Yeast," or Hefeweizen. Beers brewed with a high proportion of wheat yeild a crisp and refreshing flavor profile, while the addition of our special yeast adds a blend of complex citrus and spice flavors... forget the lemon wedge, this Bavarian style Hef' has plenty of flavor!

Available: Year Round,
12 ounce bottle, 6-pack, 12-pack,
draft (5 gallon "log," 50 liter keg).

Hibernator

A hearty and robust Scottish Ale, this full-bodied, malty brew with a smooth finish features a blend of 6 malts and a dash of honey.

A great winter warmer!

Available: November through February,
12 ounce bottle, 6-pack, 12-pack,
draft (5 gallon "log," 50 liter keg).

Traditional IPA

Real IPA, as it was first enjoyed by the British colonial troops in India, was not the carefully filtered brew that we call IPA today. Traditional IPA's were unfiltered and featured extra hops and higher strength as a preservative for the trip from England to the colony of India. As a refreshing celebration of the heritage of this great beer style Long Trail Brewing offers you a real IPA, both dry-hopped and unfiltered. Try one, and raise your glass with us in the spirit of tradition!

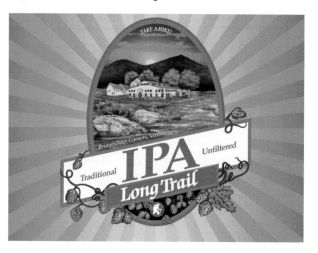

Available: Year Round,
12 ounce bottle, 6-pack, 12-pack,
draft (5 gallon "log," 50 liter keg).

Lost Coast Brewery

123 W. 3rd St.
Eureka, CA 95501
(707) 445-4484
www.lostcoast.com

The Lost Coast Brewery and Café began in 1986, when Barbara Groom, a pharmacist, and Wendy Pound, a family counselor, wondered what it would require to start their own brewpub. After years of experimental home brewing, planning and studying, which included visiting scores of pubs in England & Wales, Barbara and Wendy were ready to transform their dream into a reality.

In 1989 they purchased a historical building in Eureka, California, in which to open their brewpub. After spending the winter and spring engaged in extensive remodeling, the Lost Coast Brewery and Café became a living dream in July of 1990.

The cool maritime climate of the Humboldt Bay region has proved to be very conducive to brewing quality ales. The year round average temperature of 55° Fahrenheit is ideal for top-fermenting ale yeast. While embracing the rich tradition of English-style ales, Master Brewer Barbara Groom has added a distinctive West Coast flavor to her ales by brewing with Western Plains barley and wheat and the exceptionally clean water of Humboldt County.

Since it's humble beginning in 1990, the brewery has outgrown the original facilities and moved production to a larger site down the street. After a record breaking year in 2006, producing over 29,000 barrels, Lost Coast Brewery has expectations of breaking the 35,000-barrel mark in 2007. Lost Coast Brewery is the 46th largest brewery in the United States and distributes its fine ales in 19 states. Brewery Tours are available by appointment. The cafe is located at 617 4th St., Eureka, CA, and is open 7 days a week.

Great White Beer

An American version of the Belgian style, this unfiltered beer has a translucent golden color with white clouds. It has a full-bodied mouth feel, yet is surprisingly light to drink. Great White is topped with a hint of citrus provided by coriander and a secret blend of herbs. Original Gravity: 1.050, Alcohol Content: 4.8% ABV.

Awards:
Silver	2006 Humboldt County Fair	Gold	2004 Humboldt County Fair
Silver	2006 California State Fair	Silver	2004 Portland Spring Fest
Silver	2005 L.A. County Fair	Silver	2003 California State Fair
Silver	2005 Portland Spring Fest		

Available: Year Round,
6-pack, 12-pack, loose 24,
draft (1/2, 1/4, and 1/6 bbls).

Mad River Brewing Company

P.O. Box 767 195 Taylor Way
Blue Lake, CA 95525
707-668-4151
www.madriverbrewing.com

Mad River Brewing Company was founded in 1989 and is located in the beautiful, small town of Blue Lake, Humboldt County, California nestled among the coastal redwoods. Founder Bob Smith's dream to open a small brewery began in the late seventies and he was among a small number of innovative brewers who were laying the foundation of the craft beer movement in California.

Now in our second decade, we continue our commitment to producing fine ales using traditional brewing methods. At Mad River Brewing Company we are long on tradition and continue to handcraft our ales in the truest sense in small batches. Our award winning ales have become renowned for their unique flavor profiles and consistent quality.

Utilizing an environmentally sound approach the brewery practices nearly zero waste and has won the WRAP Award (Waste Reduction Awards Program) ten years in a row.

The brewery is open for tastings and retail shopping Monday-Friday 10 a.m. - 5 p.m. and tours are available by appointment. Contact our sales department at (707) 668-4151 or at sales@madriverbrewing.com.

Steelhead Extra Pale Ale

Our flagship brew, Steelhead Extra Pale Ale is what gave us our start back in 1989. Our unique Extra Pale Ale is a golden colored ale with a crisp freshness that comes from our special blend of five different whole hops. Our pale ale will delight your palate with its spicy, floral hop flavor, mild bitterness and bright golden hue. Extra Pale goes well with poultry or fish/sushi and is a perfect accompaniment to spicy foods or any summertime barbeque.

Available: Year Round,
6-pack, 12-pack, loose 24,
draft (13.2 gallon, 1/4 keg, 1/6 keg).

Mercury Brewing Company

23 Hayward Street
Ipswich, MA 01938
978-356-3329
www.mercurybrewing.com

Located in historic Ipswich, MA, Mercury Brewing Company emerged in 1999 when Rob Martin, then Director of Operations for Ipswich Brewing Company, purchased the brewery and renamed the company Mercury Brewing and Distribution Company. While continuing production of Ipswich Ale, Martin expanded the company with Stone Cat Ales and Lagers, Mercury Premium Sodas, and numerous contract brewing agreements.

Today Mercury is one of the fastest growing microbreweries in New England. Our current roster includes over 50 different beverages. 2006 saw upwards of 10,000 BBLs in soda and beer production. Distribution can be found in 6 states including Massachusetts, Connecticut, Rhode Island, New York City, New Jersey, and North Eastern Pennsylvania.

Additional year-round styles include Ipswich IPA, Dark Ale, Nut Brown, Porter, and our award winning Oatmeal Stout. Seasonal styles include our light-bodied, yet flavorful Ipswich Summer Ale, highly hopped Harvest Ale, and dark and rich Winter Ale.

Hand crafted from the finest barley malt, hops and yeasts North America has to offer, our superior brews are naturally conditioned, unfiltered and unpasteurized. All Ipswich Ales are brewed in historic Ipswich, MA, the birthplace of American Independence.

Contact us at 978-356-3329 or www.mercurybrewing.com for more information.

Ipswich Original Ale

Not since the merchant ships regularly sailed into Ipswich Bay has New England known a brew like this. Named one of the World's Ten Best Beers by Wine Spectator Magazine, Ipswich Ale has satisfied discerning craft beer drinkers since 1991. A New England classic, Ipswich Ale is a medium-bodied, unfiltered English style pale ale with subtle hoppiness and a smooth malty flavor.

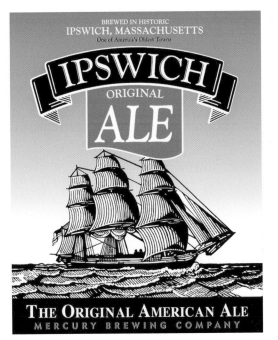

5.4% ABV, 30 IBU's
Available: Year Round,
6-pack, 12-pack, 64 oz. growlers,
draft (1/2 BBL, 1/6 BBL).

Portfolio Index (Alphabetical)

Midnight Sun Brewing Company

7329 Arctic Boulevard, Suite #A
Anchorage, AK 99518
907-344-1179
midnightsunbrewing.com

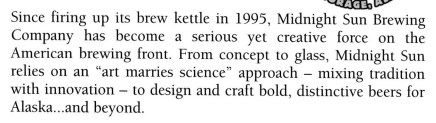

Since firing up its brew kettle in 1995, Midnight Sun Brewing Company has become a serious yet creative force on the American brewing front. From concept to glass, Midnight Sun relies on an "art marries science" approach – mixing tradition with innovation – to design and craft bold, distinctive beers for Alaska...and beyond.

Inspired by the untamed character and rugged beauty of the Last Frontier, Midnight Sun develops unique beers that pique the adventurous spirit found in Alaska. The company's true focus remains in its dedication to producing consistently high-quality beers that provide satisfying refreshment in all seasons for Alaskans and visitors alike.

From our extreme Pacific Northwest locale, we offer our wonderful beers on draft throughout Alaska and in 22-ounce bottles throughout Alaska and Oregon. We invite you to visit our hard-working, little brewery in South Anchorage every chance you get! Check out our free brewery tours (with samples) every Friday at 6 PM.

Sockeye Red IPA

Brewed in the bold spirit of Alaska, Sockeye Red IPA is a finely crafted Pacific Northwest-style India Pale Ale with a real bite. Ample pale two-row malt creates a fresh, firm body while specialty malts impart a spawning red hue. The predominant character of this fiesty catch comes from outlandish portions of Centennial, Cascade and Simcoe hops, giving this beer tremendous citrus and floral aroma and flavor. Determinedly bitter yet balanced, Sockeye Red IPA is gnarly enough to take you hook, line and sinker.

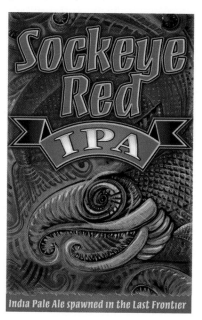

India Pale Ale spawned in the Last Frontier

5.7% ABV, 70 IBU's
Available: Year Round,
22-ounce bottles, 1/2-bbl keg, 1/6-bbl keg.

New Belgium Brewing

500 Linden Street
Fort Collins, CO 80524-2457
970-221-0524
www.newbelgium.com

New Belgium Brewing Company, makers of Fat Tire Amber Ale and a host of Belgian-inspired beers, began operations in a tiny Fort Collins basement in 1991. New Belgium produces six year-round beers; Fat Tire Amber Ale, Sunshine Wheat, Blue Paddle Pilsener, 1554 Black Ale, Abbey, and Trippel. A special release program allows for creative experimentation resulting in beers like La Folie, a sour brown ale aged up to three years in French Oak.

In addition to producing world-class beers, New Belgium takes pride in being a responsible corporate role model. Progressive programs like employee ownership, open book management and a trip to Belgium after five years employment are all part of the corporate culture. New Belgium is wind-powered and employee-owned.

Fat Tire Amber Ale

Fat Tire Amber Ale's appeal is in its sense of balance: toasty, biscuit-like malt flavors coasting in equilibrium with hoppy freshness. Named in honor of our founder's bike trip through Belgium, Fat Tire is still crafted following its original homebrew recipe.

Available: Year Round,
6-pack, 12-pack, loose 24,
draft (1/2 keg, 1/4 keg, 1/6 keg).

PORTFOLIO INDEX (Alphabetical)

New Century Brewing Company

P.O. Box 1498
Boston, MA 02117
781-963-4007
www.edisonbeer.com and www.moonshotbeer.com

New Century Brewing Company was founded in April 2001 by Rhonda Kallman, a beer industry veteran, to bring innovative American beer styles to market. The company's two products – Edison, the only beer brewed to be light, is made from scratch to be light, not a watered down version of any other, formulated by the late Dr. Joseph Owades who is the brewmaster credited with the invention of light beer in 1967. Edison's patented formula makes it full bodied and smooth. Perfect for light beer drinkers who don't want to follow the crowd.

Moonshot, the original premium beer with caffeine is an uncommonly drinkable premium beer and 69 mgs of natural caffeine with none of the sugars and/or artificial ingredients of other energy drinks on the market today. Perfect for drinkers who are looking for a pick-me-up.

Both beers are contract brewed by Matt Brewing Company in Utica, New York. Moonshot and Edison light beer can be found wherever beer is sold throughout Massachusetts and NYC as well as Trader Joe's markets nationally.

Edison

Today, corporate giants control the light beer scene. We believe light beer drinkers deserve a better choice. That's why we've introduced Edison, the independent light.

There is no 'regular' Edison. This is a freestanding light, a smooth hones beer that stands up for itself.

Just as the craft movement sparked a renaissance of long-suppressed styles, Edison brings new energy to light.

4.0% ABV
Available: Year Round,
109 calories and 6.6 carbohydrates
per 12 ounce bottle.

PORTFOLIO INDEX (Alphabetical)

Nimbus Brewing Company

3850 E. 44th Street
Tucson, AZ 85713
520-745-9175
www.nimbusbeer.com

Nimbus Brewing Company is proud to offer the Southwest's finest styled ales and stouts. The distinctive and assertive character of our products begins with natural well water drawn from a mineral enriched aquifer hundreds of feet below the Arizona desert. Add only the finest grades of the various America and European malts and hops detailed in our recipes. Then pay meticulous attention to even the smallest of details of our "old world" style brewing craftsmanship in our "new world – state of the art" three vessel brewhouse. The final product yields exceptional quality and taste found consistently in a Nimbus Beer.

Since opening in 1996, as it remains to this day; the steadfast commitment of owner, Jim Counts and head brewer, Scott Schwartz to place our emphasis on quality over quantity when it comes to any of the craft-brewed beers we produce. It is the same commitment that has won Nimbus Brewing Company the acclaim of critics and the accolades of everyday beer drinkers and awards too numerous to list. Our brewery currently distributes six different styles of beer in bottles and kegs to markets throughout Arizona and California.

The brewery also offers a taproom open for lunch, dinner and for evening enjoyment allowing sampling of our products almost anytime directly from the source. We offer a minimum of seven completely different styles of beer as well as seasonal specialties. Cask-conditioned ales drawn from beer engines are also available during certain times of the year.

Nimbus Blonde Ale

"Balance" is the key description for this smooth and refreshing Southwestern-style Blonde Ale. This beer is brewed with the finest domestic two-row pale malts and world-class Cara-Pils and Munich malts. Our use of select Perle and German Hallertau hops lends to the beer's pleasant floral nose: low in fruitiness and mild in ester production. This combination produces a light, clean and crisp balance between malts and hops. Our Blonde's subtle sweet undertones are derived from pure mesquite-flavored "killer-bee" honey that is harvested from actual killer bee hives in Bisbee, Arizona.

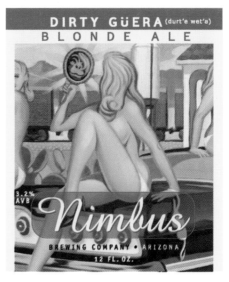

Available: Year Round,
6-pack, case, 1/2 gal. growler and keg.

Nimbus Pale Ale

Nimbus Pale Ale just happens to be our company's "flagship beer" and is a perfect representation of an aggressive Northwestern-style Pale Ale. Nimbus Pale's intense bitterness and aroma comes from being aggressively "hopped" four times during the brewing process using generous quantities of choice Chinook, Columbus and Cascade hops. We balance the flavor with just enough malt sweetness from five varieties of fine pale malts: Two-Row, Pale, Caramel, Cara-Pils and Munich malts.

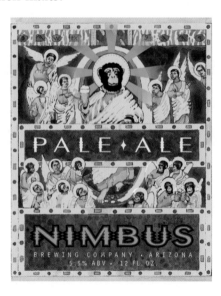

Available: Year Round,
6-pack, case, 1/2 gal. growler and keg.

Nimbus Red Ale

Nimbus Red Ale is a rich, medium-bodied American-style amber ale. Known for its sophisticated mouth feel and exceptional drinkability, our Red Ale is a true classic. Copper-hued and well-balanced, Nimbus Red Ale has a lightly sweet taste enhanced with the flavor of four different malt varieties and flaked barley. We brew this beer with a generous selection of hand-picked Chinook and Cascade hops. This combination gives our Red a mild malt sweetness and a relatively dry, aromatic finish.

Available: Year Round,
6-pack, case, 1/2 gal. growler and keg.

Nimbus Brown Ale

Nimbus Brown Ale is a rich, medium-bodied American-style brown ale known for its exceptional character and light, friendly flavor. Unlike heavier English-style brown ales, the light, smooth Nimbus Brown is sure to please even the most discriminating dark beer lovers. Nimbus Brown will even win over light beer drinkers who typically shy away from dark beers because of the alcohol content and heaviness.

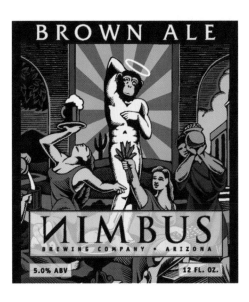

Available: Year Round,
6-pack, case, 1/2 gal. growler and keg.

Nimbus Oatmeal Stout

Nimbus Oatmeal Stout is a full-bodied beer, 5.0% alcohol by volume, with a distinct dark roasted, almost burnt flavor. Completely black in color, our Oatmeal Stout is rounded with the smooth flavor of oats and English Kent Goldings hops. The hop aroma is very subdued and the beer's slight bitterness ideally balances its malty profile. This combination produces a creamy stout with a bold, yet smooth, flavoring and a relatively dry finish.

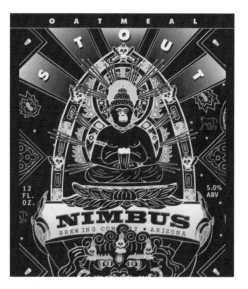

Available: Year Round,
6-pack, case, 1/2 gal. growler and keg.

"Old Monkeyshine"
English Strong

Our Old Monkeyshine Ale is an exceptional example of a true, traditional-style English Pub beer. Nimbus Old Monkeyshine Ale is medium bodied and possesses a distinct, dark roasted flavor. Its sweet malty taste is derived from liberal use of seven varieties of specialty malts and a touch of brown sugar. Our Old Monkeyshine Ale is dark in color, beginning with a slight caramel malt overtone and rounded with a relatively dry finish from its English Kent Goldings hops. The hops aroma is mildly subdued and the bitterness is just enough to balance the profile of this beer.

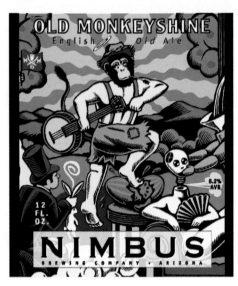

Available: Year Round,
6-pack, case, 1/2 gal. growler and keg.

PORTFOLIO INDEX (Alphabetical)

Otter Creek Brewing, Inc.

793 Exchange Street
Middlebury, VT 05753
800-473-0727
www.ottercreekbrewing.com

Located in beautiful Middlebury, Vermont, we shipped our first keg of Copper Ale in March of 1991. Four years later, after having quickly outgrown our original site, we moved into a new state-of-the-art brewery just down the street.

In 1998, we began producing Wolaver's certified organic ales – a brand with a focus on the environment and sustainable living – in partnership with Panorama Brewing Company.

In May of 2002, the Wolaver family purchased Otter Creek Brewing. Otter Creek remains a family owned Vermont company which produces all Otter Creek and Wolaver's brands for distribution throughout the country.

Now available in over 19 states, we produce over 30,000 barrels a year and distribute to states as far and wide as North Carolina and California.

Otter Creek continues to expand their distribution and Wolaver's remains the #1 selling organic beer in the country.

Otter Creek craft beers and Wolaver's organic ales enjoy a complexity of flavor, natural carbonation, and a creamy texture that is enjoyed by beer enthusiasts across the country.

Copper Ale

Copper Ale, our flagship brew, was awarded the Gold Medal at the 2003 Great American Beer Festival, in the German-style altbier category. It is a medium bodied, amber ale inspired by the Altbiers of Northern Germany. Brewed with six different malts, three hop varieties and our special house yeast, Copper Ale is characterized by a well balanced blend of malty notes and mild bitterness.

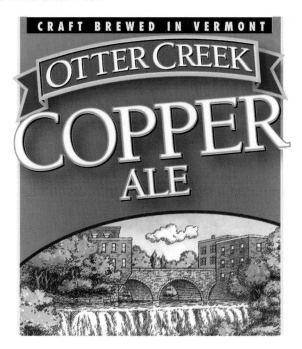

5.4% ABV
Available: Year Round,
6 pack, 12 pack, 24 pack,
draft (1/2 BBL, 1/6 BBL).

Penn Brewery (Pennsylvania Brewing)

800 Vinial Street
Pittsburgh, PA 15212-5128
412-237-9400
www.pennbrew.com

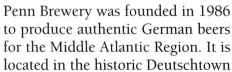

Penn Brewery was founded in 1986 to produce authentic German beers for the Middle Atlantic Region. It is located in the historic Deutschtown section of Pittsburgh in the old Eberhardt & Ober Brewery (1848). New brewing equipment was imported from Germany along with a German brewmaster (Weihenstephan graduate) and German ingredients. Penn Brewery produces 5 brands year round and 5 seasonal brands, which have won numerous medals and awards at the GABF, World Beer Cup, World Beer Championships, United States Beer Tasting Championship and many local events. The brands are available in bottles and draft. Penn Brewery operates a German theme restaurant at the Brewery where the public can see much of the brewing operation Monday thru Saturday from 11 am to midnight. There is live music Wed thru Sat night, a full bar, party room available and an out door biergarten.

Penn Pilsner

Penn Pilsner is a smooth, mellow lager, with deep golden color and elegant hope aroma from the finest noble hops imported from the Hallertau Region in Germany. The finish is smooth with a hint of malt and hop aroma. This is a very drinkable beer. Penn Pilsner was introduced in 1986 and first brewed under contract but now, as with all the brands, is brewed only in house.

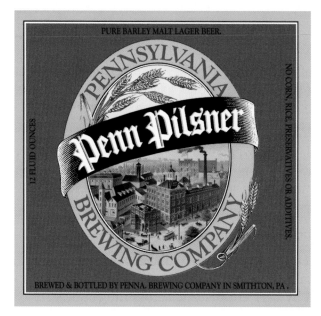

Available: Year Round,
12 oz. bottle, 6-pack, 24 pack,
1/2 bbl, 1/4 bbl, 1/6 bbl.

Pyramid Brewery

91 South Royal Brougham
Seattle, WA 98134
206-682-8322
www.PyramidBrew.com

Unfiltered, straight forward, pure and honest. What else would you expect from the only remaining independent craft brewer in the Northwest? Since 1984, our "unfiltered" approach to brewing at Pyramid has consistently produced the best wheat and craft beers in America. But don't just take it from us. Pyramid has been winning awards since its conception and to date has over 40 brewing medals to its history.

Headquartered in Seattle, WA, we brew the majority of our award-winning craft beers in Portland, OR and Berkeley, CA. These selections are featured at our four Pyramid Alehouses located in Seattle, WA, Sacramento, CA, Berkeley, CA, and Walnut Creek, CA as well as our MacTarnahan's Tap Room in Portland, OR. You can also find Pyramid at an airport Taproom location in Seattle and Sacramento, as well as at grocery stores across the Western U.S., and on tap at your favorite watering hole.

In a world where everything comes to you filtered, Pyramid keeps it real. We pride ourselves on offering consumers a wide array of distinctive, full-flavored craft beers for the whole beer experience. Our "Weizen" lineup consists of unfiltered wheat beer that's distinctly cloudy, yet smooth and refreshing. To maximize flavor and distinctiveness, Pyramid beers are made using only natural ingredients from the Pacific Northwest and are never pasteurized. It's what you would expect from a craft brewer – beer with actual beer stuff in it.

Hefe Weizen

Unfiltered for extra flavor, our gold medal winning wheat beer is exceptionally smooth and refreshing for the whole beer experience. Our Bavarian-inspired recipe calls for 60% malted wheat for maximum taste. 2004 Gold Medal Winner. American-Style Hefe Weizen, Great American Beer Festival.®

REFRESHINGLY UNFILTERED™

5.20% ABV
Available: Year Round,
6-pack, 12-pack, 22 oz. loose, 1/2, 1/4, 1/6 keg.

Apricot Weizen

The gold-medalist of fruit beers, this adventurous unfiltered wheat beer offers a pleasing aroma and flavor of fresh apricots while delivering the smooth and refreshing character for which our wheat beers are recognized. 1994 Gold Medal Winner, Fruit Beers, Great American Beer Festival®

5.20% ABV
Available: Year Round,
6-pack, 12-pack, 1/2 keg.

Amber Weizen

Rich amber in color, this full-flavored unfiltered wheat beer features three different kinds of caramel barley malts and nugget hops, delivering a smooth and malty sweet aroma and flavor.

5.10% ABV
Available: Year Round,
6-pack, 1/2 keg, 1/6 keg.

Thunderhead IPA

Nicknamed "Hophead Nectar," Pyramid's Thunderhead India Pale Ale has the distinctively hoppy flavor and aroma that craft beer enthusiasts demand. An abundant helping of Tomahawk hops help give this ale its unique flavor.

6.70% ABV
Available: Year Round,
6-pack, 12-pack, 22 oz. loose
1/2 keg, 1/6 keg.

Curve Ball

Inspired by the traditional Kölsch style beers of Cologne, Germany, Curve Ball boasts a clean, crisp slightly herbal taste and a lighter body. The perfect accompaniment to summer grilling and ballpark outings on hot summer days.

4.90% ABV
Available: March – September
6-pack, 12-pack, 1/2 keg, 1/6 keg.

Snow Cap

A rich, full-bodied winter warmer crafted in the British tradition of holiday beers. This deep mahogany colored brew balances complex flavors with a refreshingly smooth texture, making Snow Cap a highly drinkable and desirable cold weather companion.

7.0% ABV
Available: October – February
6-pack, 12-pack, 1/2 keg, 1/6 keg.

Redhook Ale Brewery, Inc.

14300 NE 145th Street
Woodinville, WA 98072
425-483-3232
www.redhook.com

The Mission

Defy Ordinary. A simple mission that began in 1982, when the first pint of Redhook forever changed the way we looked at beer. A local beer with amazingly complex flavors and aromas. A beer that was not for everyone, but certainly a beer you could believe in. A beer that stretched our thinking and defied the ordinary. A mission that continues today in every bottle of Redhook.

The Brewery

The Redhook Ale Brewery has transformed this mission into one of the leading craft breweries in America. With uncommon passion, leadership and innovation, the Redhook brand will continue to deliver unique and outstanding beers for our customers.

Redhook ESB

A rich, distinctive ale with a brilliant copper-color, remarkable aromas and unique balance of flavors. Redhook ESB is not just another amber ale, it's the original and the standard that is more flavorful and more satisfying.

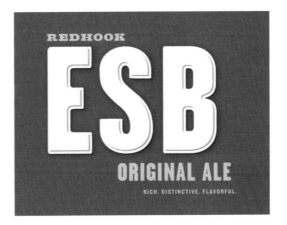

5.77% ABV
Available: Year Round,
on draught (1/2, 1/4, 1/6),
6-pack bottles, 12-pack bottles and 24 loose.

PORTFOLIO INDEX (Alphabetical)

River Horse Brewery

80 Lambert Lane
Lambertville, NJ 08530
609-397-7776
www.riverhorse.com

Our Story

While we might be new to your area, we have been brewing fine craft ales and lagers along the banks of the Delaware River since April of 1996. River Horse is an operating brewery producing both bottled and draft beer. Our award winning beers are predominantly distributed within the Mid-Atlantic Region including Pennsylvania, New Jersey, Delaware, Maryland, New York State, Ohio, Long Island, Massachusetts, New York City, and Connecticut, and we have been featured by several well-known beer-of-the-month clubs. We use choice, all-natural ingredients and local spring water to produce the best product made in our area. You will notice that all of our products are pure representations of their respective styles, very clean and very well balanced.

Our Location

If you aren't familiar with Lambertville, NJ, it is located on the banks of the Delaware River, just a "short" canoe ride south of Easton, PA and directly across the River from New Hope, PA.

Our Brewery is opened for tours and sampling 7 days per week from 12-5 pm.

Visit our gift shop and take home some fresh beer and merchandise from a wide variety of River Horse brand name items.

Summer Blonde Ale

Seasonal

Great summer memories are born out of uncomplicated times. We've made that the basis for our summer blonde recipe and kept this ale pure and simple. Relax and enjoy this all natural, light, golden beauty; a seasonal offering from the River Horse Brewing Company.

4% ABV
Available: April through August.
All natural, golden ale. Low bitterness,
light and fresh. Easy to drink
with a lower carb content.
Also Available in 1/2 and 1/6 Barrels.

Rock Art Brewery, LLC

254 Wilkins St.
Morrisville, VT 05661
802-888-9400
www.rockartbrewery.com

Rock Art Brewery was born in the mountains of Vermont, inspired by the spirit of Kokopelli and guided by the beers of the world. Our small family owned brewery is celebrating 10 years of brewing great beers! We love all that is wonderful in life, great beer, good music, tasty food, our families and friends. Stop by for a look around, pick up a beer or two, or just say Hi…. Call me to get directions and brewery hours, see you soon. Matt

If you can't make it for a visit, no worries, we now offer our beer in VT, MA, CT, NYC, NJ, PA thru select outlets!

Magnumus ete Tomahawkus

Excitement on the horizon … we have some delicious offerings in the tanks, bottles and kegs as we speak, I have always loved to cook and create in my kitchen at home and of course that spins off very well in my brewing adventures. We have cultivated some new yeasts here and added a few new ingredients in some interesting new beers…first up is an extreme series "Magnumus ete Tomahawkus" an ESB to the second. This beer features Magnum and Tomahawk variety hops as well as an appearance of Tettnanger dry hop…. I must admit that the Tomahawk has swallowed the Tettnanger and did not spit it out. This beer is 8.0000% (In Vermont we're restrained unfairly to 8.0%) and 80 IBUs. "Magnumus ete Tomahawkus" is an unfiltered beauty and is not for the faint at heart nor a soul that is fearful of hops, tomahawks and testing their taste buds….   Cheers!   Matt

Available: Year Round,
4-pack 12 oz, 22 oz Dinner Bottle
draft (1/2keg,1/6 keg).

535

PORTFOLIO INDEX (Alphabetical)

Rocky Coulee Brewing Company

17477 Rd S NE
Marlin, WA. 98832
509-345-2216
www.rockycouleebrewingco.com

Rocky Coulee Brewing Co. opened its doors June 1, 2002 and will be celebrating its 5 year anniversary this year. Located at 205 N 1st St. in Odessa WA. the brewery is open every Friday from 2:00 pm until closing, and complete with a tasting room and gift shop visitors are always welcome. Since opening we have maintained a philosophy of slow steady growth and have just recently started to bottle. Our distribution area is the Columbia Basin Region as well as East of Odessa reaching into the Spokane area. For more info about Rocky Coulee Brewing Co. and upcoming events in our area please visit our website at www.rockycouleebrewingco.com.

Fireweed Honey Blonde

Fireweed Honey Blonde is our most popular beer. Made with grains from the Pacific Northwest and hops from the Yakima Valley make this beer a homegrown favorite. We use only the freshest Fireweed Honey from Silverbow Honey Co. to give this beer the taste that makes it so unique. This is the only beer that we are currently bottling and it is available in 6-packs as well as 24 bottle cases around the Basin Area.

Available: Year Round,
6-pack, 24 case, 1/2 bbl keg, 1/6 bbl keg.

Rogue Ales

2320 SE OSU Drive
Newport, OR 97365
541-867-3660
www.rogue.com

Celebrating its second century, Rogue Ales is an Artisan Varietal Brewery founded in Oregon in 1988, making it one of America's first 50 microbreweries. Rogue has won 350+ awards for taste and quality. It is located in Newport, OR.

Dead Guy Ale

World Beer Championship: Gold

Dead Guy Ale is made in the style of a German maibock using our Pacman ale yeast. Deep honey in color with a malty aroma, a rich hearty flavor and a well balanced finish.

IBU 40, Plato 16, AA 78, 16 L
Available: Year Round,
6 pack, 22 oz. bottles, 64 oz. bottles, 1/2 keg.

Portfolio Index (Alphabetical)

Saint Arnold Brewing Company

2522 Fairway Park Drive
Houston, TX 77092-7607
713-686-9494
www.saintarnold.com

Saint Arnold Brewing Company, founded in 1994, is the oldest and largest microbrewery in Texas. The company's 18 dedicated, beer loving employees work passionately at creating world class beers. The brewery offers free tours every Saturday at 1 PM.

Saint Arnold brews five year-round beers: Saint Arnold Amber Ale, Saint Arnold Brown Ale, Saint Arnold Elissa IPA, Saint Arnold Fancy Lawnmower Beer and Saint Arnold Texas Wheat. In addition, to celebrate the different times of year, Saint Arnold brews five seasonals: Saint Arnold Christmas Ale, Saint Arnold Winter Stout, Saint Arnold Spring Bock, Saint Arnold Summer Pils and Saint Arnold Oktoberfest. The brewery also offers very limited quantities of some of its beers cask conditioned, served from traditional firkins, or casks. Periodically Saint Arnold releases a beer in its Divine Reserve series. Each batch is made with a completely different recipe. Production is very low on each of these batches.

The brewery is proud of the many awards it was won, including 10 medals at the Great American Beer Festival and 5 at the World Beer Cup. Saint Arnold's beers are available only in Texas.

Saint Arnold Amber Ale

Well balanced, full flavored, amber ale. It has a rich, malty body with a pleasant caramel character (derived from the Caravienne malt). A beautiful hop aroma, with a hint of floral and citrus comes from the combination of Cascades and Liberty hops. The light fruitiness, characteristic of ales, is derived from our special proprietary yeast. This beer is best consumed at between 50° and 55°.

None of our beers are pasteurized or have additives.

Specifications:
Original Gravity: 1.0545
Color: . . . . .Amber
Bitterness: . . . . .29 IBU
Alcohol Content By: . .6.5% ABV

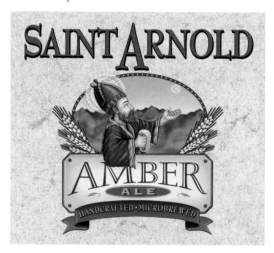

Available: Year Round,
6-pack, 12-pack, draft (1/2 bbl, 1/6 bbl).

Sand Creek Brewing Company, LLC

320 Pierce Street, PO Box 187
Black River Falls, WI 54615
715-284-7553
www.sandcreekbrewing.com

Black River Falls, Wisconsin
www.sandcreekbrewing.com

The Sand Creek Brewing Company was founded in 1999 by Jim Wiesender and Cory Schroeder and was originally built on the Schroeder farm near Downing Wisconsin. With the help of friends and family, they converted a large shed into the brew house, and turned a 32-foot refrigerator semi-trailer into the beer cooler. They scrounged brewery materials from sales around the Midwest, using pudding tanks to make the mash and brew kettles. After 4 years of operation on the farm, a decision was made to expand the fledgling operation

In March of 2004, the Sand Creek Brewing Company teamed up with Todd Krueger, the Brewmaster of the Pioneer Brewing Company of Black River Falls, and purchased the historic building and business. The building is the site where in 1856, Ulrich Oderbolz pioneered Western Wisconsin's first large scale brewery in western Wisconsin. The Oderbolz Brewing Company operated until just prior to Prohibition.

Today, the Sand Creek Brewing Company continues that proud tradition by offering great beers brewed at the same location Ulrich brewed his beer over 148 years ago. Currently the Sand Creek Brewing Company produces over 29 different products on a proprietary and contract level. They specialize in premium craft brewed lagers and ales.

Tours are encouraged to learn of the fascinating history of beer in Black River Falls. Tours are available by appointment. Please give us a call at (715) 284-7553.

Oscar's Chocolate Oatmeal Stout

Oscar's Chocolate Oatmeal Stout is a very full-bodied, yet smooth drinking beer. It has a complex nutty flavor with a hint of chocolate – not for the meek! Oscar's is the number one selling beer of the Sand Creek Brewing Company and is sold in three states.

Try some today and find out why it won a GOLD MEDAL in the 2000 World Beer Cup in the Oatmeal Stout Category!

Available: Year Round,
6-pack, draft (1/2 BBL, 1/6 BBL).

PORTFOLIO INDEX (Alphabetical)

Santa Cruz Mountain Brewing

402 Ingalls Street, Suite 27
Santa Cruz, CA 95060
831-425-4900
www.santacruzmountainbrewing.com

Santa Cruz Mountain Brewing is literally a family owned and run operation. Emily gained a deep appreciation for beer and brewing from her uncles while she attended college in Portland, Oregon. She, in turn, taught Chad who fell in love with the craft. After several years of toiling away in the garage, Chad, with the help of Emily's brother, Nick, brings their love of ales to the public. If you visit, you are likely to see parents, kids, aunts, uncles and friends, up to their elbows in the brewing business. Santa Cruz Mountain Brewing only brews organic beer. Organic beer? Stop frowning. It's not like we made a beer that's good for you. So, what is organic beer, you ask? Well, it is beer that is brewed in the traditional fashion – hard work and a lot of luck. Only this beer is made with organic malts and organic whole cone hops.

Organic Devout Stout

ORGANIC DEVOUT STOUT is a religious experience. From the first appearance of the Devout Stout there is no question about the style of this beer. It is a stout in all its depth, darkness and flavor. Imagine an aroma of the darkest Italian roasted coffee, bittersweet chocolate and a hint of anise. Despite what people think, this stout is not made with coffee just organic barley, organic hops and water. Devout Stout has a thick, creamy head that settles lightly on an almost voluptuous body. The mouthfeel is rich and warming. The flavors of the Devout Stout, ebb and flow through sweet and bitter to create an intoxicating elixir that will leave you utterly devoted.

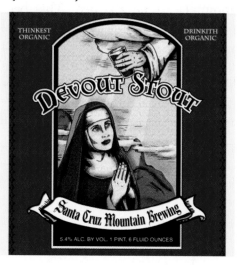

Available: Year Round,
22 ounce, 1/2 keg, 1/6 keg.

540

Organic Dread Brown Ale

ORGANIC DREAD BROWN ALE WINS GOLD MEDAL and 1st PLACE in DIVISION OF AMERICAN BROWN ALES, CALIFORNIA STATE FAIR. This is the first ale by brewster, Emily Thomas, co-owner of Santa Cruz Mountain Brewing. Thomas brewed up her first batch of brown ale in the bathtub of her college apartment almost ten years ago. Now she is brewing up thousands of gallons at the brewery with husband, Chad Brill and brother, Nick Thomas. The ebony appearance of the Dread Brown Ale gives the illusion of being a porter or stout. Don't be deceived. This is definitely brown ale. The aroma is roasted coffee intermingled with freshly baked bread, and a hint of cardamom. Don't be alarmed. This beer doesn't have any of those wacky ingredients in it, just organic barley, organic hops and water. The mouthfeel is surprisingly light and crisp but finishes with a bite. The balanced flavors of the Dread Brown Ale create a subtle fluidity of sweet, roasted, and crisp.

Available: Year Round,
22 ounce, 1/2 keg, 1/6 keg.

Organic Amber Ale

ORGANIC AMBER ALE – This is the official PARTY BEER of the brewery. The lightly sweet malted flavor has become a hands down favorite at college parties, supper clubs, and live music. The presence of organic hops is subtle but adds an aroma of blackberry. This beer pairs especially well with food.Our Amber is an all grain, close fermented, lightly hopped, handcrafted ale. Nothing in our brewery is automated, ensuring that each step in the brewing process is hand crafted. We use a hand selected blend of organic malts with a primary base of Gambrinus pale malt. The Gambrinus pale malt is known for it's high yield and full flavor. We add top-secret amounts of caramel malts to give the ale a richer flavor and colour. The results are clear.

Available: Year Round,
22 ounce, 1/2 keg, 1/6 keg.

PORTFOLIO INDEX (Alphabetical)

Sea Dog Brewing Company

26 Front Street
Bangor, ME 04401
207-947-8009
www.seadogbrewing.com

The Sea Dog Brewing Company was founded on the coast of Maine in 1993. Sea Dog's high quality ales are hand-brewed using time-honored methods and only the finest ingredients.

Sea Dog is committed to brewing the freshest, most flavorful, full-bodied beer available and currently produces 7 varieties of hand-crafted, award-winning, year-round and seasonal ales. In addition, Sea Dog also produces its own traditional, handcrafted root beer. Sea Dog is available in over 20 states across the U.S.

In Maine, you can visit the Sea Dog Brewing Company's Brew Pubs at one of our two waterfront locations – overlooking the Androscoggin River in Topsham or along the historic Penobscot River in Bangor. Serving lunch and dinner daily and offering a full line of handcrafted ales that capture the spirit of Maine's sea-faring history.

Wild Blueberry Wheat Ale

Sea Dog Wild Blueberry Wheat Ale is our unique contribution to the fruit ale category. It features the refreshing taste of wheat ale with the delightful aromatics and subtle fruit flavor contributed by Maine Wild Blueberries.

4.6% ABV
Available Year Round
6-pack, 12-pack, draft (1/2 keg, 1/6 keg).

PORTFOLIO INDEX (Alphabetical)

Sebago Brewing Company

48 Sanford Drive
Gorham, ME 04038
207-856-2537
www.sebagobrewing.com

Sebago Lake is the true spirit of Maine and its water supplies the brewery with some of the finest brewing water on the planet. The name and logo for our company invokes the image of lake life in Maine. The antique wooden boat symbolizes quality craftsmanship, art, history and design as does our beer.

Sebago Brewing Company was founded on three dreams that formed one concept, Sebago Brewing Company… "Where the food is as great as the beer!"

We realized that the synergy of our individual strengths created a concrete formula for success; Sebago Brewing Company, Maine's premier restaurant & brewery. The concept of Sebago Brewing Company and its evolution stemmed from the meeting of three energetic and ambitious individuals, Kai Adams, Tim Haines and Brad Monarch, who created a business plan focused on the Maine experience of life on Sebago Lake. The brewery and sales operations are overseen by Kai, while the restaurant operations are lead by Brad and the marketing and finance by Tim.

Frye's Leap IPA

Frye's Leap IPA is an intense experience. This hoppy medium-bodied ale is full of character. From the caramel malt which gives our IPA its golden color to the distinct fruity hoppiness, this beer is every bit as exciting as its namesake, the popular cliffs on Sebago Lake. Enjoy this refreshing beer with seafood, spicy foods and all things grilled. Take the Leap!

5.7% ABV
Available: Year Round,
6-pack, 12-pack draft (1/2 keg, 1/6 keg).

Portfolio Index (Alphabetical)

The Shipyard Brewing Company

86 Newbury Street
Portland, ME 04101
1-800-BREW-ALE
www.shipyard.com

The Shipyard Brewing Company was founded in 1994 by entrepreneur, Fred Forsley, and master brewer, Alan Pugsley. Shipyard's high quality English-inspired ales are hand-brewed using time-honored methods and only the finest ingredients.

Shipyard is committed to brewing the freshest, most flavorful, full-bodied ales available and currently produces 13 varieties of hand-crafted, award-winning, English style and seasonal ales. In addition, Shipyard also produces its own traditional, handcrafted Capt'n Eli's Soda.

Shipyard prides itself on the consistency and freshness of its products. The Shipyard Brewing Company's fine line is hand-made from recipes developed by the British-born Pugsley, who is one of the most influential people in the craft brewing movement in North America.

Shipyard Export Ale

Shipyard Export Ale, the flagship brand of Shipyard Brewing Company, is a full-bodied ale, with a hint of sweetness up-front, a subtle and distinctive hop taste, and a very clean finish.

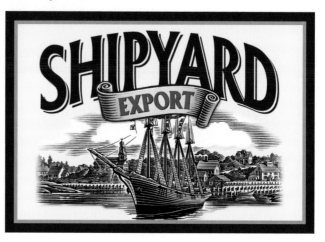

5.1% ABV
Available: Year Round
6-pack, 12-pack, draft (1/2 keg, 1/6 keg).

Portfolio Index (Alphabetical)

Shmaltz Brewing Company

912 Cole Street, #338
San Francisco, CA 94117
www.shmaltz.com

Conceived in San Francisco. Brewed in New York. Since 5757 (1996). Shmaltz Brewing Company is dedicated to hand crafting the highest quality beer and the highest quality shtick available... L'Chaim!

HE'BREW Genesis Ale

Our First Creation. Crisp, smooth and perfectly balanced between a west coast style pale and amber ale, with a supple malt sweetness and a pronounced hop flourish. Malts: 2-row, Caramel 40L, Dark Crystal, Munich. Wheat Hops: Warrior, Northern Brewer, Willamette. "4 Stars...This lovely ale deserves a wide interdenominational audience." – San Diego, Union-Tribune. "Our favorite" – The New York Times.

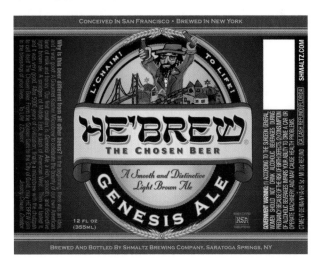

5.6% ABV
Available: Year Round,
12 ounce 6-packs and draft.

PORTFOLIO INDEX (Alphabetical)

Ska Brewing Company

545 Turner Drive
Durango, CO 81301
970-247-5792
www.skabrewing.com

Ska Brewing took shape in 1995 out of a love of brewing and drinking finely crafted beers, and listening and dancing to ska music. Located in the beautiful Southwestern Colorado town of Durango, we like to think that we're giving the famous Durango Silverton Narrow Gauge Railroad, as well as mountain biking, a run for their money as far as Durango's true allure goes, although the train might beg to differ.

Ska is the Four Corners region's most award winning brewery, hand-crafting at any given time 10 different brews, including our 12 oz. Flagship Series, the Robust Reincarnations in 22 ounce "dinner bottles," and Ska's Special ESB in cans.

Folks are always welcome and encouraged to stop by, say "hi," take a tour and try our beers. In fact we are building a new brewery two blocks up the road in order to accommodate more production and more folks stopping by. We hope to be moved in by May, 2008.

Ska beers are currently available throughout Colorado, Arizona, NM, NC, and Illinois. For more info go to www.skabrewing.com

Decadent Imperial I.P.A.

Citrus aroma prevails. Mounds of fresh hops and caramel malts explode to mask the potent 10% ABV of the Decadent. Originally produced to celebrate our tenth year in business, this Imperial IPA hides nothing of our tendency toward self-indulgent behavior.

Awards:
2006 Bronze Medal – L.A. County Fair Commercial Beer Competition, Decadent Imperial IPA, Imperial Red Category

10% ABV, 100 IBU's
Available: Year Round,
22 oz. "Dinner" Bottles, 1/6 bbl, 1/2 bbl.

Nefarious Ten Pin
Imperial Porter

King of the alley — this Imperial Porter reigns supreme with a mighty 8% Alcohol by Volume and 77 IBUs. Creamy, chocolaty sweet, with hints of coffee and bing cherry, the Nefarious is wickedly outrageous.

Awards:
2007 Silver Medal – World Beer Championships, Imperial Category

8% ABV, 77 IBU's
Available: Year Round,
22 oz. "Dinner" Bottles, 1/6 bbl, 1/2 bbl.

Pinstripe Red Ale

Our Flagship among our Flagships. Teetering toward an American Amber Ale, the Pinstripe is brewed with caramel malts and Liberty hops, culminating with a slight fruity finish and dance.

Awards:
2005 Gold Medal – Colorado State Fair National Commercial Microbrew Competition, Pinstripe Red Ale, English Bitter Category

5.15% ABV, 42 IBU's
Available: Year Round,
12 oz 6-pack, 12-pack, 1/6 bbl, 1/2 bbl.

True Blonde Ale

A crisp Blonde Ale. Golden in color, medium in body – she's brewed with the help and the honey of Durango's Honeyville bees.

Awards:

2006 Bronze Medal – Great American Beer Festival, English-Style Summer Ale Category

2006 Gold Medal – L.A. County Fair Commercial Beer Competition, English Summer Ales

2006 Bronze Medal – Colorado State Fair National Commercial Microbrew Competition, Light Ale Category

2005 Regional Champion – United States Beer Tasting Championships, Golden Ale/Kolsch

2005 Gold Medal – Colorado State Fair National Commercial Microbrew Competition, True Blonde Ale, Light Ale Category

5.3% ABV, 40 IBU's
Available: Year Round,
12 oz 6-pack, 1/6 bbl, 1/2bbl.

Buster Nut Brown Ale

This Brown Ale has a touch of nuttiness provided by our good friends Mr. and Mrs. Victory and Munich Malt. The addition of Northern Brewer, Cascade, and Willamette hops smooth this beer out to create an incredibly drinkable Brown Ale.

Awards:

2006 Silver Medal – L.A. County Fair Commercial Beer Competition, English Style Brown Ales

2006 Silver Medal – Colorado State Fair National Commercial Microbrew Competition, Buster Nut Brown, Brown Ale Category

2004 Gold Medal – Great American Beer Festival, English-style Brown Ale category

2003 Gold Medal – Great American Beer Festival, English-style Brown Ale category

2002 Bronze Medal – Great American Beer Festival, English-style Brown Ale category

5.15% ABV, 30 IBU's
Available: Year Round,
22 oz. "Dinner" Bottles, 1/6 bbl, 1/2 bbl.

Steel Toe Stout

In a nod to our working class sisters and brothers everywhere, we present you with the Steel Toe, a rich, creamy working class milk stout with all of the pull-through needed after a long day spent providing for the family, working for The Man.

This traditional English Cream Stout is jet black in color and brewed with actual milk sugar to create a sweet and fortifying brew.

Awards:

2007 Silver Medal – World Beer Championships, Sweet Stout Category

2006 Silver Medal – Great American Beer Festival, Sweet Stout Category

2006 Bronze Medal – L.A. County Fair Commercial Beer Competition, British Stout Category

2004 Bronze Medal – World Beer Cup, Sweet Stout Category

5.4% ABV, 29 IBU's
Available: Year Round,
12 oz. 6-packs, 1/6 bbl, 1/2 bbl.

Ska Special ESB

This English Special Bitter is our "Special Brew." Special because it is one of only a handful of canned microbrews in the nation. Special because the Galena hops and pale ale malts create a crisp first sip, a hoppy tongue, and a malty sweet finish. Though "bitter" is part of the name, "better" would be a more accurate term.

Fresh and lively, this canned beer suits the needs of any outdoor enthusiast. Like it says on the can: Fish, Luau, Golf, Raft, Toboggan. Ska can!

Awards:

2006 Bronze Medal – Colorado State Fair National Commercial Microbrew Competition, British Bitter Category

2003 Silver Medal – Colorado State Fair National Commercial Microbrew Competition, British Bitter category

5.7% ABV, 58 IBU's
Available: Year Round,
6-pack 12 oz. cans.

PORTFOLIO INDEX (Alphabetical)

Snake River Brewing Company

P.O. Box 3317, 265 South Millward
Jackson Hole, WY 83001
307-739-2337
www.snakeriverbrewing.com

Snake River Brewing Company is located in Jackson Hole, Wyoming nestled beneath the towering Teton Mountain Range and along the great Snake River. The brewery and restaurant opened it's doors in March of 1994 making it the oldest microbrewery and brewpub in Wyoming and has been serving the public with fresh, unique, award-winning microbrews ever since.

Snake River Brewing has four "Flagship Beers" available in 12 ounce bottles, 1/2 barrels and 1/6 barrels: Snake River Pale Ale, Snake River Lager, OB-1 Organic Ale and Snake River Zonker Stout. We also feature over 20 different seasonal brews that we create throughout the year and have on tap at various times at our brewpubs in Jackson Hole and Lander, Wyoming.

All four of our Flagship Beers have been recognized with regional, national and international awards for brewing excellence. In the 13 years of our operation, Snake River has received eight medals from the World Beer Cup and 23 medals from the Great American Beer festival, making Snake River Brewing Company the most award-winning microbrewery in the country over that period of time. We were also awarded the prestigious honor of being named the Small Brewery of the Year and Brewmaster of the Year for 2000 and 2001. No microbrewery has repeated this honor.

Presently, our products are distributed in Wyoming, Montana, Idaho, Colorado, Wisconsin and Ohio. For more information, visit www.snakeriverbrewing.com.

OB-1 Organic Ale
Federally certified organic amber ale

Snake River OB-1 Organic Ale is an English style Amber Ale, made with 100% organic US malts and 100% organic New Zealand and German hops both in the brew kettle and dry hopping. Teton mountain spring water and English ale yeast create an exceptionally drinkable, amber-hued brew with subtle, earthy hop undertones.

Snake River Brewing unveiled the OB-1 Organic Ale in the summer of 2006 and is proud to be there first and only manufacturer of certified organic beer in the state of Wyoming.

Gold Medal Winner, 2006 North American Brewers Association, Mountain Brewers Festival.

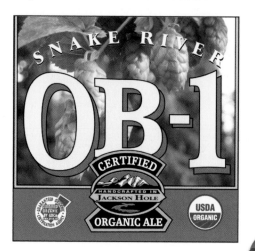

Available: Year Round,
6-pack, draft(1/2 keg, 1/6 keg).

PORTFOLIO INDEX (Alphabetical)

Southampton Publick House

40 Bowden Square
Southampton, NY 11968
631-283-2800
www.publick.com

Southampton Publick House is proud to have our Ales & Lagers poured at the finest establishments as well as available at retailers and specialty stores throughout the Northeast.

The word about the quality of our beer began to get around the metro New York region as soon as we turned on the spigots and started to serve it in our Southampton restaurant. Almost from day one, leading restaurants, pubs and taverns have requested our crafted brews for their own patrons. In 2004, we were Ranked #8 Speciality Brewery in World by RateBeer.com.

Our Brewmaster, Phil Markowski (Winner, 2003 Association of Brewers Russell Schehrer Award for Innovation in Craft Brewing) has personally directed the flow of our ales and lagers into the finest outlets. Our Mission is to offer a wide variety of specialty ales and lagers. Our small batch brews range from classic farmhouse styles to traditional session beers to be enjoyed year-round.

The Southampton Publick House, located in historic Southampton, NY, is an award-winning microbrewery restaurant offering world class beers and first class hospitality!!

Double White Ale

Southampton Double White is our "Double Gravity" version of classic Belgian-style white ale. Brewed with quality grains and hops. Lightly spiced with coriander and Curacao orange.

Available: Year Round,
6-pack.

Southern Tier Brewing Company

2051A Stoneman Circle
Lakewood, New York 14750
716-763-5479
www.southerntierbrewing.com

Behind the brewery walls a time old art is practiced. Creativity and imagination are mixed together with nature and science creating an elixir of great magnitude. It is our greatest honor to share it with you.

Brewery tours are offered to the public on Saturdays at 4 pm only. We open at 2 pm, and recommend arriving before 4 to ensure a spot on the tour because space is limited. Admission charge is $5 per person; you'll have a thorough tour of the facility from the grain room and the brew house to the fermenters and all the way through the packaging process. You'll also sample each beer we have available that day – and you can keep your glass as a souvenir! Feel free to ask your tour guide questions along the way. Expect the tour to last for 45-60 minutes.

Our bar at the brewery, The Empty Pint, is open Friday and Saturday and always features at least eight beers on draught. Hours: Friday 4-8 pm, and Saturday 2-8 pm.

Imperial India Pale Ale

Unearthly: "An uninhibited infusion of hops"

At the Southern Tier Brewing Company, vigorously hopped beer is our standard and inspiration. We continue a commitment to innovation with our most aggressive offering yet. Unearthly is a manifestation of the brewer's craft; skillfully balancing art and the forces of nature to produce a divine liquid. Delicately pour a taste into a fluted glass. Smell the enchanting aromas of the hops waft forward as your first sip divulges this beer's fervent soul. To underestimate Unearthly is to trifle with the mysteries of the universe, so please consume wisely.

11.0% ABV, 153 IBU
Available: Year Round,
22 oz bottles, 12 bottle case, 1/6 keg.

St. George Brewing Company

204 Challenger Way
Hampton, VA 23666
757-865-7781
www.stgeorgebrewingco.com

St. George started as a brew on premise in VA Beach in 1996. The beers were getting good reviews, so we started a microbrewery. When the brewhouse from DME arrived so did our Brewmaster, Andy Rathmann. Once St. George Brewing Co. opened its doors in 1999, it went for a little over a year and a fire (Christmas Eve 2000) raged through the building destroying everything except the office paperwork! After the fire came contract brewing, lots of traveling, and even the use of a locally failed brewpub…and never forget the hotdog stand. All that behind us, the new brewery was running March of 2002. Fastforward to 2005 and we have come a long way. We have seven year round beers and our four seasonals. Come 2006, we will be adding a few one runs and some other special projects…be ready!!!

The brewery itself is almost 10,000 sqft, 1200 of that is a cold box. Our brewhouse is a 30-BBL Newlands/DME System. Tours of the brewery are walk-ins during the week and on request on the weekends. There is also a retail shop.

St. George Brewing Co. I.P.A.

A traditional English style ale with a distinct hop spiciness from imported 100% UK Fuggles hops. Deep copper in color, our IPA has a full malt base resulting in lots of body as well as a rich malt character. A pronounced hop aroma is a result of dry hopping. Also in CASK!!

5.5% ABV
Available: Year Round,
on draught (1/6, 1/2),
six pack bottles, case.

553

Stone Brewing Company

1999 Citracado Parkway
Escondido, CA 92029
760-471-4999
www.stonebrew.com

Founded in 1996, the Stone Brewing Co. is one of the fastest growing breweries in the United States. Additionally, Stone Brewing is one of the highest rated breweries in the world according to both RateBeer.com and BeerAdvocate.com. Stone brews a wide variety of beers from medium-bodied IPAs to full-bodied Imperial Russian Stouts, and their beers certainly live up to the company motto of "Be Amazing." Stone Brewing Co. is currently open seven days a week for tours and tastings at ther brand new brewery located in North County San Diego. For more information go to www.stonebrew.com.

Stone Ruination IPA

Stone Ruination IPA is so named because of the "ruinous" effect on your palate! This massive hop monster has a wonderfully delicious and intensely bitter flavor on a refreshing malt base. One taste and you can easily see why we call this brew "a liquid poem to the glory of the hop!" Those who seek, crave and rejoice in beers with big, bold, bitter character will find true nirvana in Stone Ruination IPA!

Available: Year Round,
6-pack, 22oz bottles, 1/2 keg.

PORTFOLIO INDEX (Alphabetical)

Summit Brewing Company

910 Montreal Circle
St. Paul, MN 55102
651-265-7800
www.summitbrewing.com

Summit Brewing Company was founded by Mark Stutrud in 1986 with one goal: To bring back the remarkable craft beers once brewed throughout the Upper Midwest.

Summit beer quickly grew into a local favorite, placing Summit Brewing Company well ahead of a trend of craft brewing that would eventually sweep the nation. To keep up with demand, the brewery had to grow.

In 1993 alone, Summit Brewing Company tripled in size. Mark and his dedicated staff were working diligently to quench the thirst of an ever-widening fan base, leading them in 1998 to build the first new brewery Minnesota had seen in over 75 years.

Summit prides itself on introducing people to great beers. Beer that reflects Summit's own tastes and beliefs about what great beer should be. That's the thing about a craft brewery, craftsmanship. When you put love into what you make, you end up with a better beer.

Beer lovers all across the Upper Midwest and beyond have come to appreciate Summit's commitment to producing a quality beer, and it's an appreciation that grows with every glass poured. Summit Brewing has come a long way over the years.

We invite you to visit the brewery for a free tour and a cold one on us. Tours available every Tuesday, Thursday, & Saturday @ 1pm (except on holiday weekends). Reservations are required.

Summit Extra Pale Ale

More than our flagship beer, Summit Extra Pale Ale is many a beer lovers' first and most frequent encounter with Summit. Its distinctive hop flavor, light bronze color, and crisp full-body have been whetting beer appetites since 1986.

Malts Utilized: 2-row Harrington, Caramel

Hops Utilized: Horizon, Fuggle, Cascade

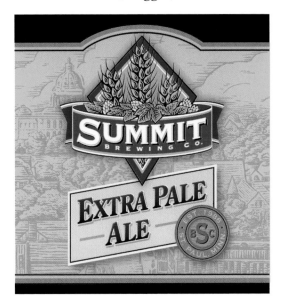

5.1% ABV
Available: Year Round,
6-pack, 12-pack, loose 24,
draft (1/2 keg, 1/4 keg, 1/6 keg).

Summit Great Northern Porter

Summit Great Northern Porter is a dark, but surprisingly lighter-bodied ale, with a robust, malty character and a delightfully sweet finish. One of our very first brews, the Porter has won numerous awards, including the gold medal at the Great American Beer Festival in Colorado.

Malts Utilized: 2-row Harrington, Caramel, Black Malt

Hops Utilized: Horizon, Fuggle, Cascade

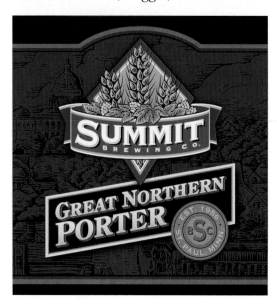

4.8% ABV
Available: Year Round,
6-pack, 12-pack,
draft (1/2 keg, 1/4 keg, 1/6 keg).

Summit India Pale Ale

In the great British tradition, Summit India Pale Ale has a distinctive, earthy hop flavor and a bright amber hue. With it's floral hop aromas and significant mouthfeel, this IPA pairs well with sharp cheeses and spicy fare.

Malts Utilized: 2-row Harrington, Caramel, Special B

Hops Utilized: Northern Brewer, East Kent Golding Dry hopped with whole flower East Kent Golding

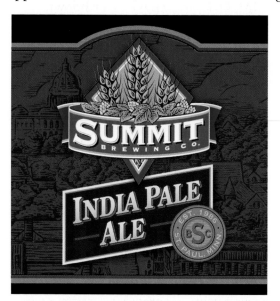

5.8% ABV
Available: Year Round,
6-pack, 12-pack,
draft (1/2 keg, 1/4 keg, 1/6 keg).

Summit Extra Special Bitter

Summit ESB is styled after the Extra Special Bitters found in pubs throughout England. This beer is rich and unique and has a balance of flavors with a dark amber color which makes for a truly rich and distinctive experience. This beer is brewed in the British tradition with all British malts and hops.

Malts Utilized: 2-row Harrington, Golden Promise, Maris Otter, Crystal Medium

Hops Utilized: Target, Fuggle, Northdown

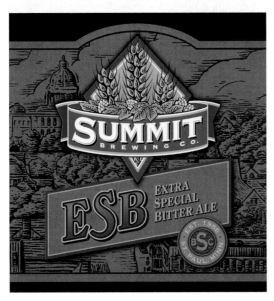

5.0% ABV
Available: Year Round,
6-pack, 12-pack,
draft (1/2 keg, 1/4 keg, 1/6 keg).

Summit Winter Ale

Summit Winter Ale is brewed in the tradition of winter warmer ales, with a robust, full-bodied flavor and a tangy hint of spice that can take the chill out of even the coldest nights.

Malts Utilized: 2-row Harrington, Caramel, Black Malt

Hops Utilized: Willamette, Fuggle, Tettnanger

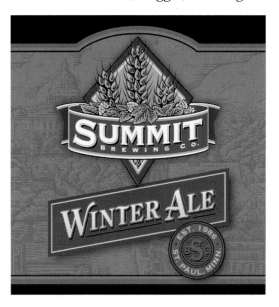

5.9% ABV
Available: November - January,
6-pack, 12-pack,
draft (1/2 keg, 1/4 keg, 1/6 keg).

557

Summit Scandia

Summit Scandia is our Scandinavian intrepretation of a Belgian wit ale with spice notes of cardamom, coriander, and bitter orange peel. Scandia pours cloudy with a light, white foamy head and refreshing flavor profile.

Malts Utilized: 2-row Harrington, Oats, Wheat, Acidulated Malt

Hops Utilized: Vanguard

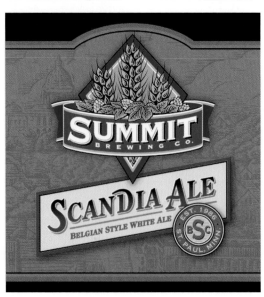

5.0% ABV
Available: May - September,
6-pack, 12-pack,
draft (1/2 keg, 1/4 keg, 1/6 keg).

Summit Pilsener

A Bohemian style pilsener with a golden color and well-balanced body that pays homage to the original pilsener the Czechs invented in 1842. Authentic Saaz hops round out this crisp, refreshing Czech-style pilsener.

Malts Utilized: Harrrington, Caramel

Hops Utilized: Horizon, Vanguard, Saaz

5.3% ABV
Available: Year Round,
6-pack, 12-pack,
draft (1/2 keg, 1/4 keg, 1/6 keg).

PORTFOLIO INDEX (Alphabetical)

SweetWater Brewing Company

195 Ottley Drive
Atlanta, GA 30324
404-691-2537
www.sweetwaterbrew.com

SweetWater was created just after the Olympics rolled through Atlanta in 1996. Partners Freddy Bensch and Kevin McNerney saw all the folks rollling into town, and took the opportunity to make the dream of owning and running their own brewery a reality. A few loans from some wonderful friends and family and a few from the Government got them on their way. The idea began back in college with attending the University of Colorado in Boulder, and it was finally here.

Sweetwater is a 40,000-barrel microbrewery that specializes in producing aggressive West Coast style beers to be enjoyed in the Southeast US. The beer is unpastuerized and meant to be drank at it's freshest, so that is why there are no plans to spread beyond our backyards (unless its for a good music festival, or other bootleg expedition).

Having had great success, (2002 Small Brewery of the Year at the GABF!) Sweetwater's taste has grown throughout Georgia and the Southeast by word of mouth. 10 years into this gig our beers can be found in most of Georgia, Asheville, NC, Chattanooga and Nashville, TN. Birmingham and Auburn, AL and the Panhandle of Florida from Tallahassee west. It's a local brew for local folks and we'd like to thank each and every one of you for enjoying the good beer as much as we do!

SweetWater 420 Extra Pale Ale

SweetWater 420 Extra Pale Ale has become our flagship brand with it being the largest volume brew and the 1st offering whenever we start selling beer in any new town. This hoppy pale ale weighs in at a modest 5.4% alc and finishes pretty clean leaving thristing for more. Like we say in the brewery "Drink em if you got em"

Available: Year Round,
6-pack, 12-pack 1/2 keg, 1/4 keg, 1/6 keg.

559

Terrapin Beer Company, LLC

196 Alps Rd #2-237
Athens, Ga 30606
706-202-4467
www.terrapinbeer.com

Terrapin Beer Company was founded by two brewers who share a commitment to creating world class beers unsurpassed in character and flavor. In a salute to their entrepreneurial spirits Spike and John struck out on their own to satisfy their passion for creating innovative and aggressive beers.

The Terrapin Rye Pale Ale was released in Athens, GA in April of 2002 at the Classic City Brew Fest. Six months later this beer was awarded the American Pale Ale Gold Medal at the 2002 Great American Beer Festival. By Terrapin's second anniversary in April 2004, The Terrapin Golden Ale was released as the Company's second year round beer. Only two weeks later the Golden Ale won a Silver Medal at the 2004 World Beer Cup.

In 2004 Spike and John turned their attention to creating a line of seasonal beers that pushed the envelope of traditional brewing. It was this desire to challenge the palates of beer drinkers everywhere that led to the creation of the Monster Beer Tour – Big Hoppy Monster, Wake-n-Bake Coffee Oatmeal Imperial Stout, Rye Squared, and All American Imperial Pilsner. This series of beers has proven to be a huge success.

From the beginning they knew that Terrapin Beer Company would be located in Athens, GA. It is a city that reflects Spike and John's socially conscious philosophy. The city and the company are committed to the environment, have a great love of music, and practice living life to the fullest. At long last, Terrapin Beer Company will have their brewery in Athens and will be open for tours by late summer 2007.

Terrapin Rye Pale Ale

By using an exact amount of rye, a grain seldom found in other micro brewed beers, the Rye Pale Ale acquires its signature taste. Made with five varieties of hops and a generous amount of specialty malts, it offers a complex flavor and aroma that is both aggressive and well balanced - a rare find among beers.

The Terrapin Rye Pale Ale was released in Athens, GA in April of 2002 at the Classic City Brew Fest. Six months later this beer which was sold only in Athens was awarded the American Pale Ale Gold Medal at the 2002 Great American Beer Festival, the most prestigious competition in North America. We hope you will agree with our peers in the brewing industry that this is truly one of the best pale ales in the country.

Available: Year Round,
6-pack, 1/2 keg, 1/6 keg.

The Lion Brewery, Inc.

700 N Pennsylvania Ave
Wilkes-Barre, PA 18705
(570) 823-8801 or
(800) 233-8327
www.lionbrewery.com

WILKES-BARRE, PENNSYLVANIA

With a proud brewing heritage of its own dating back to 1905, The Lion Brewery merges rustic architecture with state-of-the-art brewing technology, a contrast typified by the gleaming stainless steel aging tanks that sits alongside the traditional copper brew kettle. Our brewing process utilizes the traditional English method of upward infusion mashing in our combination mash/lauter tun to create lagers and ales inspired by old world values, but with modern quality and consistency.

The staff at The Lion Brewery is dedicated to producing true hand-crafted beers, made right here in our century-old brewhouse. All of our premium beers are made using only the four basic ingredients allowed by the Reinheitsgebot, or German purity law.

Under the skillful supervision of our Master Brewer, Leo Orlandini, each of our lagers and ales are brewed in small batches using only the finest hops and malts available, to guarantee the highest quality and freshness. Each product we brew is an original recipe, especially created to deliver a fuller flavor than ordinary beers, yet with an approachable style and character. As a result, our beers have garnered numerous medals from the Great American Beer Festival and the World Beer Championships in recent years.

Stegmaier Brewhouse Bock

Stegmaier Brewhouse Bock features domestic two-row pale and Munich malt to give this brew a very distinctive full-bodied malt flavor and deep copper color, in the German tradition. Stegmaier Brewhouse Bock is a bottom-fermented beer that takes extra time lagering (cold storing) to smooth the brew. In Medieval days, this type of beer was brewed during the sign of the Capricorn (thus, the goat reference) and was a symbol of better times to come-moving from Winter and welcoming Spring. "Der bockbier mit Tritt" – The Bock Beer With Kick.

Available: February thru
the beginning of April,
6-pack, loose 24, draft (1/2 keg, 1/6 keg).

561

The Matt Brewing Company

811 Edward Street
Utica, New York 13502
315-624-2400
www.saranac.com

Our family-owned Brewery was founded in 1888 by German-born immigrant Francis Xavier Matt, or F.X. as he was commonly known. In 1985, the Brewery decided to brew an all malt specialty beer – something with flavor and distinction, and the original Saranac 1888 was born. Today, our Brewery's focus is producing high-quality specialty products, like the Saranac award winning family of beers and our specialty soft drinks. The company is led by the 3rd and 4th generations of the Matt family, but we still brew to the exact standards set forth by our founder over a century ago. In every product we make, you'll find a commitment to quality and patient attention to detail that has become the signature of The Matt Brewing Company. As the second oldest Brewery in the United States, the Matt Brewery enjoys the reputation as one of the most respected breweries in America. For more information please visit www.saranac.com.

Saranac Pale Ale

Saranac Pale Ale is aggressively hopped; look for a rich, fruity hop bouquet and aroma balanced with a crisp finish. Made with Cascade, English Fuggles, English East Kent Goldings hops, and Crystal Malt, which gives it a medium body and copper/amber color.

5.5% ABV, 4.3% Alcohol by Weight
Kosher
Available: Year Round,
6-pack, 12-pack, 1/2 keg, and 1/6 keg.

Portfolio Index (Alphabetical)

Thomas Creek Brewery

2054 Piedmont Highway
Greenville, SC 29605-4840
864-605-1166
www.thomascreekbeer.com

Thomas Creek Brewery is situated in the heart of Upstate, SC creating an array of craft ales, lagers and bocks. During a 20 year career of bartending, Brewer Thomas Davis developed a serious liking for good beers. He decided to give making them a try as a homebrewer. Several years and many brews later he realized he had a knack for it. His father came on board (also a Thomas) and the love affair with creating great tasting beer for their customers began. Tom Davis' goal is to make the finest hand crafted beers and please every beer lover that tries a Thomas Creek brew. Award-winning Thomas Creek beers are made using only the finest American barley, hops and yeast. Hand Crafted beer since 1998, Thomas Creek is distributed throughout South Carolina, North Carolina, Georgia and Tennessee, winning the hearts and taste buds of beer lovers across the Southeast.

Thomas Creek Red Ale

The flagship beer of Thomas Creek Brewery, our Red Ale is a medium-bodied and extremely smooth Irish style red. Deep caramel barley varieties, strong roasted malt tones and an even texture and flavor throughout make this beer an easy Southern favorite.

Awards:

Gold Medal – 2006 Carolinas Championship of Beer

Silver Medal – 2003 World Beer Championships

Available: Year Round,
6-pack, 1/2 keg draft, 1/6 keg draft.

563

PORTFOLIO INDEX (Alphabetical)

Tractor Brewing Company

120 Nelson Lane
Los Lunas, NM 87031-8299
505-866-0477
www.getplowed.com

Tractor Brewing Company was established in 1999. Mike Campbell, New Mexico's Beer Farmer, has been creating world-class beers since 1989 and has won three medals at the Great American Beer Festival (the highest honors in American brewing) as assistant brewer for Wolf Canyon Brewing. Nick Pecastaing, the Ad Farmer, has been heading up management and marketing since 2003.

The Tractor Brewpub's farm theme is evident even from the outside, where several restored antique tractors are parked on the patio. Continuing inside, over 200 collectable tractor models are mounted on walls. There's a Ferris wheel and even a giant rotating carousal. Our tasting room is covered by a barn-like roof, and is affectionately known as "The Beer Farm."

Taking the utmost in brewery equipment care and ingredient selection, we provide our yeast with a clean, healthy environment in which to work its magic. This ensures that you get a consistently good beer people ask for again and again.

Farmer's Tan – Red Ale

We bottled this beer first for a couple of reasons. It is the most "user friendly," meaning it isn't overly bitter, overly sweet, or overly too much of anything. It's a very easy drinking mild ale. Other craft breweries that started small and are now giant, like Sam Adams and New Belgium (Fat Tire), all started out with a user friendly beer like the Farmer's Tan. It has a nice elegant red/brown glowing color with a roasty, toasty flavor and a slightly sweet caramel-like finish. You can compare it to Killian's Red and Newcastle.

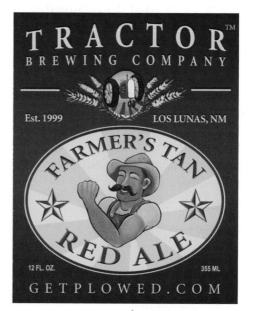

5.4% ABV
Available: Year Round,
1/2 Barrels, 1/4 Barrels, 1/6 Barrels, and 6-pack.

Tremont Brewery/Atlantic Coast Brewing Company

P.O. Box 52328
Boston, MA 02205
800-347-1150
www.tremontale.com

Tremont gets its name from the historic three hills of Boston: Mount Vernon, Beacon, and Pemberton.

Originally, just a thin bridge of land connected Boston to the mainland. The Charles River divided the peninsula from the mainland and an extension of the harbor known as "Town Cove" divided Boston into the North and South Ends. Through the center of the peninsula rose the historic Trimountain area – three hills known as Mount Vernon, Beacon Hill, and Pemberton Hill.

Earth removed from these three mountains filled in the coves and coastline to connect Boston to the mainland and create the landscape of the city we know today. In the process, Mount Vernon and Pemberton Hill were leveled and Beacon Hill, which still remains, is now just a fraction of its former height.

We named our beers Tremont – as Trimountain came to be called – to honor our connection to the very foundation of what makes Boston the great city is it today.

Founded in 1993, Tremont soon grew to become a favorite Boston brand. More than a decade later, we have established a team to bring this brand to new heights.

Tremont Ale

Tremont Ale is our flagship offering and is an English-style pale ale. Tremont Ale has a deep copper color, a malty middle, crisp hoppy flavor, and a dry refreshing finish. Tremont Ale's unique hopping combines the best of Britain with the best of America.

Style: English Pale Ale
Malt: Pale, Crystal, Torrified Wheat, Chocolate
Hops: Cascade, English Fuggles, Tettnang, East Kent Goldings
Yeast: Ringwood

4.8% ABV
Available: Year Round

565

PORTFOLIO INDEX (Alphabetical)

Tröegs Brewing Company

800 Paxton Street
Harrisburg, PA 17104
717-232-1297
www.troegs.com

The Tröegs Brothers' Biography

"We aren't concerned with making beer to a particular traditional style, as much as we want to brew a quality beer with our own vision – that's what is really important."

— *Chris and John Trogner*

Chris and John Trogner have been working hard to get Central Pennsylvania on the brewing map. Since 1997, these Pennsylvania natives have been handcrafting world-class beers that combine traditional European brewing techniques with the eclecticism of new American brewing. Today, Tröegs Brewery produces seven different beers including Hopback Amber Ale, Troegenator Doublebock, Rugged Trail Nut Brown Ale, DreamWeaver Wheat, Tröegs Pale Ale, Dead Reckoning Porter (seasonal), Sunshine Pils (seasonal), and The Mad Elf (seasonal).

Tröegs currently distributes its beers throughout the Mid-Atlantic Region; Pennsylvania, New Jersey, Maryland, Delaware and Virginia. For more information please visit www.troegs.com

Troegenator Double Bock

Troegenator Double Bock, for periods of fasting without solid foods. Monastic brewers relied on the double bock; a stronger, richer beer to fulfill their basic nutritional needs. Known to them as "liquid bread," a double bock has a strong malt aroma and chewy rich body. In the spirited tradition of naming a double bock in the suffix "ator," we give you Troegenator to provide warmth and richness through the early spring months.

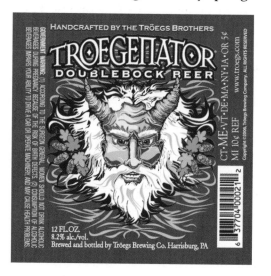

8.2% ABV
Available: Draft and Bottles Year Round.

Two Brothers Brewing Company

30W 114 Butterfield Road
Warrenville, IL 60555
630-393-4800
www.twobrosbrew.com

Brothers Jim and Jason Ebel founded Two Brotheers Brewing Co. in 1996. Two Brothers began as a draft only production brewery. The brewhouse was produced in Vancouver and based on the traditional 3-vessel brewhouse's of Germany. The balance of the brewery was mostly donated! The Ebel Brother's grandfather, a retired dairy farmer, donated his bulk milk tanks, which were quickly converted to fermenters. In 1998 Two Brothers secured an 8-head bottling line. Today, the only thing left of the original brewery is the brewhouse itself. Due to increased sales and demand, Two brothers replaced the 8-head bottle filler, in the spring of 2003, with a state of the art 20 head filler. Three 30 barrel fermenters, two 60 barrel fermenters, and two 50 barrel fermenters have replaced the 500 gallon dairy tanks once in their place. Two Brothers are now currenty planning in 2007 to build a new brewhouse and this will double their current capacity of 5,000 barrels. Two Brothers brews four year round beers and four seasonals. There are two others lines that are even smaller releases and those are their Artisan and Project Opus lines. The Artisan line are normal beer styles twisted and turned only the way they now how. Project Opus is their Lambic line of beers that rivals the Belgiums. This growth just goes to show it's good to drink the award winning, family run, down home, craft beers of Two Brothers Brewing Co. You can find Two Brothers beers in Illinois, Wisconsin, Indiana, Ohio, Massachusettes and Pennsylvania.

Domaine DuPage

Domaine PuPage is a rural northern France amber colored ale. This well balanced beer is full and sweet up front with carmel, toasty and fruity characters. The finish has a gentle floral and spicy hop balance that cleanses the palate.

5.9% ABV
Available: Year Round,
6-pack, 1/6 barrel, 1/2 barrel.

Uinta Brewing Company

1722 South Fremont Drive (2375 West)
Salt Lake City, UT 84104
801-467-0909
www.uintabrewing.com

Uinta Brewing was established in 1993 to produce fresh, full-flavored beers for distribution. Named after Utah's highest mountain range, Uinta was the first distributing craft brewed brewery in Salt Lake City.

At the time, no other brewery was concentrating on supplying the demands of Utah's many pubs and restaurants. Our brews quickly gained a strong following.

The requests for bottled beer became louder and more frequent. In 1996, Uinta began to bottle its award-winning beers and quickly grew to become the largest craft brewery in Utah. In 2002, Uinta produced over 14,000 barrels. Cutthroat Pale Ale, Uinta's flagship brand, is now the number one selling craft beer in the state.

Uinta moved into a new facility in 2000. The 26,000 square foot brewery is located in the southwest section of Salt Lake City at 1722 South Fremont Drive (2375 West) and is open for tours and tastings weekdays from 11 am to 7 pm.

Solstice Kölsch

The Solstice Kölsch style Ale is a refreshing golden beer. Named for the lighter style ales from the city of Cologne, this delicious beer is flavorful and delicately hopped.

Uinta invites you to celebrate the comings and goings of the sun (and seasons) with our thirst-quenching brew.

5% ABV
Available: Year Round on draught,
6-pack bottles.

PORTFOLIO INDEX (Alphabetical)

Victory Brewing Company

420 Acorn Lane
Downingtown, PA 19335
610-873-0881
www.victorybeer.com

"Far better it is to dare mighty things, to win glorious triumphs, even though checkered with failure, than to take rank with those poor spirits that neither enjoy much nor suffer much because they live in the grey twilight that knows not VICTORY nor defeat"

– Theodore Roosevelt

These words inspired us as we endeavored to open the doors of our brewery and restaurant in 1996. Since then, critics and consumers have said that our beers are mighty things. We feel that they are small 'victories' for those who appreciate flavorful beer.

Cheers,
Bill & Ron
Brewmasters of Victory

HopDevil Ale

Menacingly delicious, with the powerful, aromatic punch of whole flower American hops backed up by rich, German malts. HopDevil Ale offers a roller coaster ride of flavor, coasting to a smooth finish that satisfies fully.

PRAISE FROM THE PROS
Champion American Beer: Great British Beer Festival 2002
Domestic Beer of The Year: Malt Advocate Magazine 1999

6.7% ABV
Available: Year Round,
Malts: Imported, German 2 row
Hops: American whole flowers
six pack bottles and 12-pack bottles.

The Weeping Radish Farm Brewery

6810 Caratoke Highway
Jarvisburg, NC 27947
706-202-4467
www.weepingradish.com

Proudly brewed & packaged on the Outer Banks of North Carolina since 1986!

Have you ever wondered how fresh, natural beer is made – the authentic German way? All Weeping Radish beers adhere to the German Purity Law of 1516 (the Reinheitsgebot) and are hand-crafted from only the finest malt, hops, yeast, and water. We pride ourselves on the full, fresh flavor of our beers and we think you will notice the difference.

Join us at the Weeping Radish Eco Farm and Brewery in Jarvisburg for our brewery tours. You can stand right next to Uli while listening to his famous brewery tour. Of course, there are samples for everyone all around after the tour.

Brewery tours take place during the summer months on Wednesdays at 3 PM. No reservations are required in the summer, except for large groups of 10 or more. Groups may request a tour at other times. There is no charge for the tours. Brewery Tours in the shoulder seasons are by appointment, so please call ahead.

Our new brewery in Jarvisburg is open for business. You can watch the brewing process, take a self guided tour and sample the freshly brewed products right on site.

Black Radish

Black Radish (Schwarzbier) – a medium-light to medium bodied, dark German lager style beer. Clean lager character with an aftertaste that tends to dry out slowly and linger, featuring hop bitterness with a complementary but subtle roastiness in the background. A regional specialty from southern Thuringen and northern Franconia in Germany.

Listed in "50 Beers to drink before you die: the full list" from The Brew Site.com

ABV 4.6%, IBU's 27, SRM 22.6
Available: Year Round,
12-pack 1/2 liters, liters, 1/6 keg, 1/2 keg.

PORTFOLIO INDEX (Alphabetical)

Widmer Brothers Brewing Company

929 N Russell
Portland, OR 97227
503-281-2437
www.widmer.com

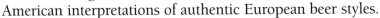

The legend goes like this: After living in Germany and enjoying fine European beers in the 1970s, Kurt Widmer returned to Portland, Oregon, with a mission to create American interpretations of authentic European beer styles.

Kurt's search for an original beer experience led him back to a brewery in Düsseldorf, where he studied the recipes of the famous brewing center. He brought back a special brewing yeast obtained from the world-renowned Brewing Research Institute in Weihenstephan, Bavaria, and this special yeast has been maintained at the brewery since the beginning, and is an important part of the Widmer Brothers' brewing process.

Together, the Brothers pioneered American Style Hefeweizen beer in 1986, and Widmer Hefeweizen – America's Original Hefeweizen®, has grown in popularity over the past decade. This golden, cloudy Widmer beer is kegged and bottled directly from the lagering tank and is not filtered, leaving Widmer's special yeast suspended in the beer. Widmer's Hefeweizen has been Oregon's top-selling draught craft brew for nearly 20 years. Its tempting appearance and aroma combined with its robust taste and texture have distinguished Widmer Hefeweizen® as a Widmer Brothers classic.

Widmer Hefeweizen

Our Flagship – America's Original Hefeweizen

A golden unfiltered wheat beer that is truly cloudy and clearly superb. Ever since Widmer introduced Hefeweizen to America in 1986, ours has been the standard by which all other Hefeweizens are judged.

1998 and 2006 GABF Gold Medal Award Winner 2004 Gold Medal Beer Cup.

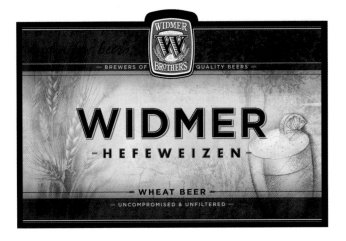

Available: Year Round,
6-pack, 12-pack, loose 24,
draft (1/2 keg, 1/4 keg, 1/6 keg).

Wild Goose Brewery, LLC

4607 Wedgewood Boulevard
Frederick, MD 21703-7120
301-694-7899
www.wildgoosebrewery.com

Wild Goose brands are available in five different styles that can be found year round, including IPA, Amber, Oatmeal Stout, Porter and Nutbrown as well as two popular seasonals, Pumpkin Patch and Snowgoose. Wild Goose brands are distributed in five states across the Mid-Atlantic region. For more information about Wild Goose, log on to www.wildgoosebrewery.com.

Wild Goose IPA

Wild Goose India Pale Ale (IPA) – And English style ale with roots dating back to the British Empire. IPAs were traditionally brewed to mature during shipment from Britain to India and were heavily hopped to keep the ale fresh. In that spirit, Wild Goose IPA is a crisp, clean ale with a long, hoppy finish.

ABV: 5.5%
Available: Year Round

Wolaver's Organic Ales

793 Exchange St.
Middlebury, VT 05753
800-473-0727
www.wolavers.com

Wolaver's
certified organic ales

Robert and Morgan Wolaver have combined their passion for exceptional beers with their belief in the benefits of organic farming to create Wolaver's: a superb handcrafted ale brewed with only the finest organic barley and hops, grown by small independent farms.

Back in 1997, the Wolavers formed Panorama Brewing Co. Under this name, they formed partnerships with five breweries to brew their delicious organic beers for distribution throughout the country. Otter Creek Brewing was one of those five breweries.

With the huge growth of the organic market, the Wolavers knew they needed their own brewery. In 2002, they purchased Otter Creek Brewing in Middlebury, Vermont. Otter Creek Brewing continues to brew both the Otter Creek line of beers, and Wolaver's organic ales. The small company was the perfect match for the Wolavers, sharing their philosophy of caring for community and the environment – while brewing great beers!

For those who simply love great beer, Wolaver's is a delicious choice – and know that every purchase supports a healthier environment for us all.

India Pale Ale

A generous amount of hops has been used to produce this classic India pale ale. Crisp and clean, with a delicious hop spiciness and subtle malt balance. A strong beer, great with spicy foods and for those who enjoy a good, full flavored, well hopped beer.

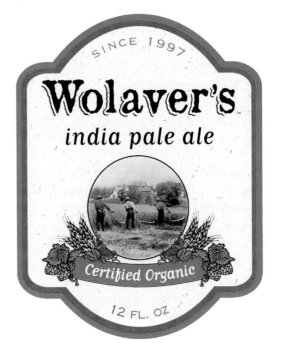

SINCE 1997

Wolaver's
india pale ale

Certified Organic

12 FL. OZ

5.9% ABV
Available: Year Round,
6-pack, 24-pack, draft (1/2 BBL, 1/6 BBL).

Yards Brewing Company

2439 Amber Street
Philadelphia, PA 19125
215-634-2600
www.yardsbrewing.com

YARDS BREWING COMPANY was founded by two college friends (Tom Kehoe and Jon Bovit) in Philadelphia in 1994 and began brewing in early 1995. From the beginning the goal has been to craft the best tasting, freshest Ales in the region.

The original brewery was located in the city's Manayunk section and cost a modest $24,000 to construct. The facility was only 900 square feet and most of the equipment was engineered and built by brewery personnel, along with help from some very dedicated friends.

YARDS debuted its flagship beer, Extra Special Ale, at the Philadelphia Craft Brewers Festival in April, 1995. In November of 1996, construction began at the second brewery in the Roxborough section of Philadelphia. Just as the first brewery, the company self-designed the new facility and had local tradesmen fabricate the equipment. A bottling line was added and tank capacity was increased to 3,500 barrels per year. This expansion enabled YARDS to produce more beer and also expand its product line. With its growing demand, YARDS needed to expand again. In April of 2002 Yards began producing in the Kensington section of Philadelphia. This building is the former home of the Weisbrod & Hess Oriental Brewing Company, which closed its doors in 1939. Tours are given on Saturday between noon and 3 pm.

Extra Special Ale

Enjoy a Philadelphia legend – Yards Extra Special Ale. The finest ingredients deliver a perfectly rounded amber colored ale of full malt body and aromatic hop finish.

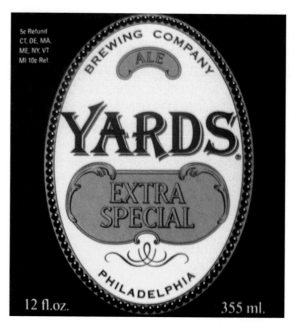

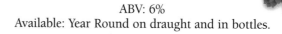

ABV: 6%
Available: Year Round on draught and in bottles.